...h, through the Centre of Wardour House, Wilts.

GEORGIAN BUILDINGS

A Palladian staircase hall in North Audley Street, Mayfair, designed *c*1730 (the balustrade is of 1921).

A Guide to the
GEORGIAN BUILDINGS
of Britain & Ireland

Dan Cruickshank

RIZZOLI, NEW YORK
THE NATIONAL TRUST
THE IRISH GEORGIAN SOCIETY

AUTHOR'S PREFACE

The structure of this book needs some explanation, as do the criteria by which buildings have been selected for inclusion.

The structure is simple. The main text is divided into chapters on building types, so that through a comparison of like with like a picture can emerge of how architecture developed between 1714 and 1830: two dates which encompass a relatively coherent architectural epoch. These chapters refer, whenever possible, to existing buildings. The selection of buildings for inclusion in both the text and the gazetteer is an attempt to perform a balancing act between the essential and obvious buildings (St Martin-in-the-Fields, Houghton Hall) and the more ordinary and representative provincial buildings which reveal how the majority of buildings were designed during the period, for without these a guide becomes merely a list of the unusual and atypical. The gazetteer is divided into three distinct sections. London is listed in detail, with general descriptions of streets followed by individual house numbers. The rest of Britain is less fully covered but with more description for individual buildings. Ireland is treated differently, and I hope contains enough of curious and particular interest to save it from the danger of recording only the obvious.

Last, if any readers feel outraged by errors or omissions I hope they will contact me so that their information can be incorporated in any revised edition of this book.
Dan Cruickshank, Spitalfields, London

First published in the United States of America in 1986 by
RIZZOLI INTERNATIONAL PUBLICATIONS, INC.
597 Fifth Avenue, New York, NY 10017

Copyright © 1985 Dan Cruickshank

First published in Great Britain in 1985 by
George Weidenfeld and Nicolson Ltd

All rights reserved. No part of this publication may be reproduced, stored in a retrieval system, or transmitted, in any form or by any means, electronic, mechanical, photocopying, recording or otherwise, without the prior permission of the publisher.

Library of Congress Cataloging in Publication Data

Cruickshank, Dan.
 The National Trust/Irish Georgian Society guide to the Georgian buildings of Britain and Ireland.

 Includes index.
  1. Architecture, Georgian—Great Britain—Guide-books.
  2. Architecture, Georgian—Ireland—Guide-books.
  3. Buildings—Great Britain—Guide-books. 4 Buildings—Ireland—Guide-books. I. National Trust (Great Britain) II. Irish Georgian Society. III. Title.
 NA966.C78   1986   720'.941   85-43049
 ISBN 0-8478-0669-3

Typeset and printed by Butler & Tanner Ltd,
Frome and London

Previous page: The Piece Hall, Halifax, probably by Thomas Bradley, 1775: a magnificent cloth market of Roman gravity.

Endpapers: Section through Wardour Castle, Wiltshire, designed by James Paine and built 1770-76.

CONTENTS

Introduction 6

Buildings in Towns 20

Buildings in the Country 51

Churches 104

Commercial and Engineering Buildings 127

Government and Institutional Buildings 143

Places of Public Resort 170

Gazetteer 180

Great Britain 180   London 260   Ireland 284

BIBLIOGRAPHY 300
ACKNOWLEDGMENTS 301
GLOSSARY 302
INDEX OF BUILDINGS AND PLACES 304
INDEX OF ARCHITECTS AND DESIGNERS 315

INTRODUCTION

The years between 1710 and 1715 were among the most dramatic and eventful of the eighteenth century. A new dynasty was established on the British throne, the foundation was laid for nearly fifty years of Whig political supremacy, and a rebellion was suppressed. And, significantly for this story, architecture was in the very forefront of these events. It not only reflected moments of confidence and moments of uncertainty but, more importantly, was regarded by both Whigs and Tories as an important political tool, as a means of propaganda and of making power visible.

In 1710 the Tories gained power in England and in 1713 they signed the Treaty of Utrecht, which put an end to a long European war and established a period of confidence that encouraged a long-suppressed building boom in both town and country. In 1711 they had managed to have an act passed which allowed money raised in London by a coal tax to be used to build fifty new churches in and around London (p104). These churches, of which only twelve were eventually built, were intended to be monumental, inspiring awe and respect for the Tory High Church Establishment in the rapidly expanding – and potentially disorderly – areas of London which they served.

This overt use by the Tories of architecture as political propaganda provoked a Whig response. In 1712 Lord Shaftesbury, in a letter 'Concerning Art, or the science of design', attacked the then triumphant baroque school for its rejection of rational principles of design, for its subservience to foreign (particularly French) influence and for its inability to provide 'more serious and noble' monuments: 'Through several reigns we have patiently seen the noblest public buildings perish (if I may say so) under the hand of a single court-architect,' said Lord Shaftesbury in a lightly veiled attack on Wren. But the state, thought Shaftesbury, 'may prove perhaps more fortunate than our Church [another dig at Wren and St Paul's] in having wayted until a National Taste was formed.'

By the year this letter was published, 1714, the wait was nearly over. Queen Anne, the last Stuart, died that year and the Whigs succeeded in establishing the Hanoverians on the throne and themselves in power. In the following year an ill-conceived Jacobite rebellion was quashed and a Scottish one-time advocate and baroque designer, Colen Campbell, gave Shaftesbury's plea for a 'National Taste' a physical form.

In 1715, the first volume of Campbell's *Vitruvius Britannicus*, or *The British Architect*, was published under the patronage of that prominent Whig, the second Duke of Argyll. On one level it functioned as a display of the most influential buildings erected in England from the early seventeenth century to the current day and, in its one hundred plates, included many baroque buildings as well as Campbell's own revolutionary design for Wanstead House, Essex (p52). This broad approach was well calculated to give the book a wide appeal. But on another and far more significant level it represents the first shot in the campaign that was to lead to the overthrow of the baroque and the establishment of the school of classical design that was to become known as Palladian.

Andrea Palladio was a sixteenth-century Paduan who had developed a rational form of classical design where function and design were related, simplicity was a virtue, the details and proportions of the classical orders were respected, and a system of proportion – as immutable as the harmonies of music – governed the relationship between elements in an elevation and between the elevation and the plan. Nothing, of course, could be more different from baroque classicism, where the architect was at liberty to transform or invent within the classical idiom and even to use its detail irrationally.

Sir Christopher Wren (1632–1723) devised a theory to allow a co-existence between these two approaches to classicism. To him there was 'natural' beauty which, being geometrically or mathematically based, was akin to the perfect harmonic beauty sought by the early eighteenth-century Palladians. Then there was his 'customary' beauty, where things not in themselves naturally beautiful could be regarded as beautiful by association or familiarity. The key point is that by not acknowledging the dominance of absolute objective beauty, the baroque architect permitted himself the freedom to choose, to invent, and to justify all by the laws of custom.

But how was Campbell to link Palladio, a

Inigo Jones's Piazza at Covent Garden, 1631: the first British example of a uniform, palace-fronted terrace.

distant Italian, with the Whigs' desire for a 'National Taste' free from French influence and worthy of the new age of Whig power? The answer to his problem was Inigo Jones who, though deferred to even by leading baroque architects (p67), had not been a major influence on architecture since before the Civil War. A masque designer at the Stuart court of James I, he travelled to Italy in c1567–1603 and selected Palladio's rational style (Palladio could be far from rational in some of his designs) as the medium in which to build for both the court and aristocratic clients. Notable examples are the Queen's House, Greenwich, 1616–35; the Prince's Lodging at Newmarket, 1619 (long demolished), which derived from Palladio's town house for the Capra family in Vicenza; the Banqueting House, Whitehall, 1619–32, a vast double-cube aisleless basilica with giant order columns rising from the floor and supporting a gallery; and the austere St Paul's Church and the uniform arcaded terrace (the first time in Britain that individual houses had been composed as a long 'palace' façade) in Covent Garden, 1631–5 (p20).

Being an Englishman, this early master of Palladian classicism was just what Campbell needed. In the preface to the 1715 volume of *Vitruvius Britannicus* (other volumes were to appear in 1717 and 1725) Campbell picked up Shaftesbury's line and condemned the prevailing preference for things foreign, attacking especially the seventeenth-century Italians of the baroque school, singling out the 'affected and licentious' work of Bernini, Fontana and particularly Borromini. Against this Campbell set Palladio and, the essential ingredient, he then named Jones 'this great master' who had 'outdone all that went before' and who proved that 'in most we equal, and in some things, surpass, our neighbours'.

To increase the influence of this emerging school, the Italian Giacomo Leoni issued the first complete English translation of Palladio's *Quattro Libri dell'Architettura* (*Four Books of Architecture*) of 1570 between 1715 and 1720; and in 1714 Alessandro Galilei was brought to England from Florence by 'the new Junta for architecture' as part of the campaign to introduce a more classical style into British architecture. The 'Junta' – pre-dating the Burlington-led Palladian revival – was formed by members of the Whig aristocracy including John Molesworth and Sir Thomas Hewett. Hewett managed to get himself made Surveyor of the Royal Works in 1719, succeeding William Benson, a Whig and amateur architect who, with Colen Campbell as his deputy, had supplanted Wren in 1718. This Palladian pair were hustled out of office after attempting to persuade the House of Lords that their chamber was in a state of collapse and should be replaced: unfortunately they overlooked the fact that the chamber was demonstrably sound. Hewett, on the other hand, held the post until his death in 1726, and, through his influence especially, the Palladians secured key public offices in the 1720s and '30s and were in a good position to promote Palladian architecture so that it became the unofficial house style of the Whig aristocracy. But special credit must go to Campbell: with consummate skill and great subtlety he codified the works of Palladio, Inigo Jones and John Webb, and through attractive illustrations provided models, easily copied or adapted by provincial builders and fashion-conscious aristocrats. This persuasive presentation, coupled with an appeal to nationalism, was propaganda of the highest order.

Palladian dictatorship

Palladianism quickly became something more than just an architectural style: it became almost a religion with immutable laws, the rejection of which was condemned as either arrogance or sad ignorance. The ancients, by trial and error, had devised the true and universal laws of architecture which they enshrined in their three orders – Doric, Ionic and Corinthian – and which had been revived by Palladio and passed to England by Inigo Jones. It was an architect's duty, therefore, to build according to the true rules.

The man responsible for this curious elevation of Palladianism to the rank of a quasi-religion was the influential Whig, Richard Boyle, third Earl of Burlington, who commissioned Colen Campbell in 1716 or 1717 to remodel his London home, Burlington House in Piccadilly, along the lines of a Palladian palazzo (completed in 1719, and partly surviving in a very altered state). At about the same time Burlington began to develop the small estate behind his house. Although never a display of co-ordinated town planning, it did become a showcase of Palladian design containing many eighteenth-century Palladian 'firsts', such as the first uniform astylar terrace, 31–34 Old Burlington Street by Colen Campbell (1718–23, p31); the first astylar Palladian town mansion, Mountrath House, 30 Old Burlington Street (1721, demolished 1935), by Burlington himself; and the first temple-fronted Palladian town mansion in a terrace, Queensberry House, 7 Burlington Gardens, by Giacomo Leoni (1721–3).

Burlington quickly became a leading and particularly scholarly Palladian, designing a Pantheon-inspired garden building at Chiswick in 1717, Tottenham Park, Wiltshire, in 1721 (p69), the remarkably chaste Westminster School dormitory in 1722 (p163), and a dramatic house for General Wade on the Burlington estate in 1723 (demolished 1935). This building, based on a Palladio drawing in Burlington's possession, had immense influence: it introduced Palladio's mannerist style – heavy rustication and multi-layered façade – to an eager English audience and so heralded the 'decorated' form of English Palladianism as represented by Kent's Treasury of 1733 (closely modelled on Wade's house) and the Horse Guards of 1748. The house also introduced a Palladio detail – the Venetian window set within a relieving arch – that was afterwards to become a favourite design element throughout the eighteenth century. Burlington's archaeological approach to design became typical of the Palladian movement, which sought to develop its architecture through the imitation and the refinement of acknowledged models. Palladio, Inigo Jones and Jones's pupil John Webb were regarded as legitimate quarries for ideas and entire buildings, and the copies were, without compunction, copied again.

Of seventeenth-century buildings that were imitated, a good example is the Queen's Gallery at Somerset House, Strand, London, which was almost certainly designed by John Webb and was built in 1662 as a rare Jonesian-style building emerging in the middle of the then burgeoning French-influenced baroque school. It was based on Palladio's Palazzo Iseppo Porto at Vicenza (c1550) with a touch of Donato Bramante's Palazzo Caprini, Rome (1513). Not demolished until 1776 during Chambers' reconstruction of Somerset House (p146), the gallery became a model for urban town houses; indeed Campbell's house for Burlington was modelled on it, as was Leoni's Queensberry House. It remained a model for country houses right through the eighteenth century, such as Sir Robert Taylor's Heveningham Hall, Suffolk (1778, p85), and for government and institutional buildings such as the Mansion House, York (1726), by William Etty (p151) and the Strand elevation of Sir William Chambers' Somerset House (1776–1801, p146).

But the rise of Palladianism was not due just to the influence of built examples on aristocratic west London estates. Burlington created a circle which included not only practising architects such as Campbell, William Kent, Roger Morris and later Henry Flitcroft and Isaac Ware (who were all dependent on Burlington's patronage and influential contacts), but also architectural theorists such as Robert Morris (cousin of Roger) and Robert Castell who published, with Burlington's encouragement, his *Villas of the Ancients* in 1728 (including a part reconstruction of Pliny the Younger's villa at Laurentium); poets and writers such as Alexander Pope; and leading provincial figures such as the Scottish Whig and anglophile Sir John Clerk. A friend to both Burlington and another Palladian peer, Lord Pembroke, Clerk founded his own Palladian circle in Scotland in the 1720s with William Adam as its leading architect and Allan Ramsay as its leading poet. It was this combination of skills and talents, coupled with a fervent belief in the rightness of their cause, that kept the Palladians in power until the 1750s. In 1728 Robert Morris wrote an *Essay in Defence of Architecture*, a vocally violent, almost rabid, attack on the baroque in which examples of baroque design 'lately erected' were picked to pieces and compared with correct Palladian compositions.

In his *Lectures on Architecture*, published in 1734 and 1735, Morris attempted to explain Palladian aesthetic theory, and produced a series of proportions derived from Palladio's seven ideal room proportions and published in his *Quattro Libri*. Morris explained that it

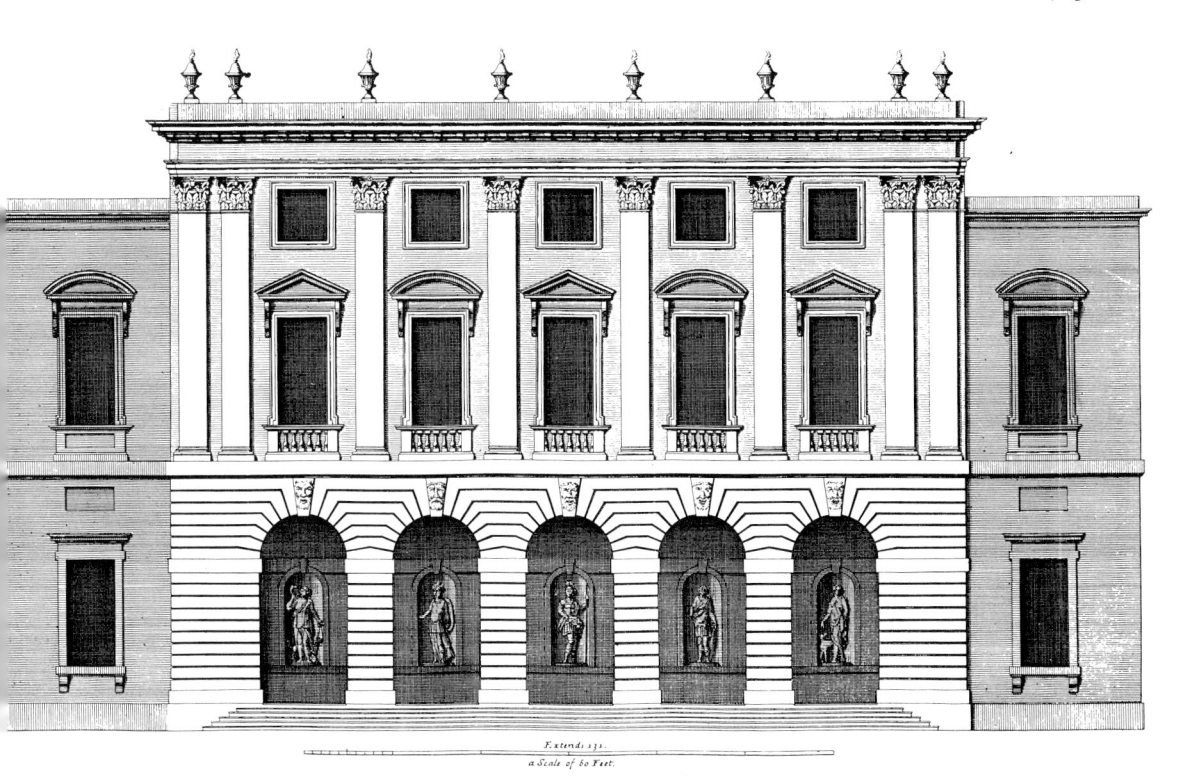

Above: Elevation published in *Vitruvius Britannicus* of the Queen's Gallery on the river front of old Somerset House. Demolished in 1776, the elevation, designed by John Webb in 1662, had a great influence on early eighteenth-century urban design.

Below: The street front of Andrea Palladio's Palazzo Iseppo Porto, Vicenza, c1549. This elevation, shown here as published in Isaac Ware's 1738 translation of Palladio's *Quattro Libri*, was the original influence on designs such as Webb's Queen's Gallery and many eighteenth-century façades.

Below: Elevation published in *Vitruvius Britannicus* of the house that Lord Burlington designed in 1723 for General Wade at 29 Old Burlington Street. Demolished in 1935, this influential design was based closely on a Palladio drawing in Burlington's possession.

The quintessence of the battle between the Palladian and the baroque. These comparative designs appear in Robert Morris's *Essay in Defence of Ancient Architecture*, 1728. The one on the left is described as 'a monstrous lump of deformity'; the other is designed according to the precepts of the ancients.

was necessary to 'divide the external and internal parts of a building by harmonick proportions not using feet and inches for the divisions, but by the analogous principle', in other words, ratios. 'In musick are only seven distinct notes, in architecture likewise are only seven distinct proportions, which produce all the different buildings in the universe, viz. the cube; the cube and half; the double cube; the duplicate [or ratios] of 3:2:1; 4:3:2; 5:4:3 and of 6:4:3 produce all the harmonick proportions of rooms.'

It must be said that Morris, in basing these proportions on Palladio, believed that he was reflecting ancient, indeed divine, principles of proportion. In his *Defence of Ancient Architecture*, Morris expressed the belief that 'The Grecians were the first happy inventors [of architecture], they extracted the beauteous ideas of it from rude and unshapen trees, the products of nature, and embellished it, by degrees of perfection, with those necessary ornaments which have been since practised by those of the most sublime genius [and] collected by the indefatigable care and industry of Palladio.'

The philosopher Francis Hutcheson, in his *Inquiry into [the] Original of our ideas of beauty and virtue* (1726), put the objective view of beauty thus: 'What we call beautiful in objects, to speak in the mathematical style, seems to be in a compound ratio of uniformity and variety, so that where the uniformity of a body is equal, the beauty is the variety, and where the variety is equal, the beauty is in the uniformity.' This notion – that the beauty in a largely uniform structure lies in its elements of variety and that the beauty in a largely varied structure lies in its elements of uniformity – is fascinating when applied to Palladian design, especially street architecture, in which the uniformity of the broad composition and the variety of its detailed embellishments are often so skilfully balanced.

The Palladians' self-righteous message and shameless pushing and manipulation, though successful in spreading the doctrine, made many enemies, among them William Hogarth. With his belief in a fluent, serpentine, rococo 'line of beauty' promoted in his *Analysis of Beauty* (1753), Hogarth represented the new thinking that was to lead to the overthrow of the Palladians (p14). The renewed belief in the individual, subjective beauty (not unrelated to Wren's 'customary beauty') was summed up by Lord Kames in his *Elements of Criticism* (1761). 'By many critics it is taken for granted that in buildings there are certain proportions that please the eye, as in sound there are certain proportions that please the ear, and that in both equally the slightest deviation from the precise proportions is disagreeable.' This was Burlington's opinion; but, as Kames went on to point out, as we move around a room the proportions of length to breadth and height vary constantly, and if the eye were an absolute judge of proportion we 'should not be happy but in one precise spot, when the proportions appear agreeable'; and so we should think ourselves

Right: Robert Morris's seven ideal proportions – C to I – as published in his *Lectures on Architecture*, 1734. C, D and E correspond to Palladio's seven ideal proportions, while F to I are developed out of Palladio as commensurate extensions of the double cube.

Below: Palladio's seven ideal room proportions as illustrated by Isaac Ware in his 1738 edition of the *Quattro Libri*. Top right to left: circle; square; square and a third; $\sqrt{2}$; bottom right to left: square and a half; square and two thirds; double square. Since room plans, house plans and elevation were to be designed in proportional relationships, these seven 'room' proportions provided the key to the designs of entire palazzos and villas.

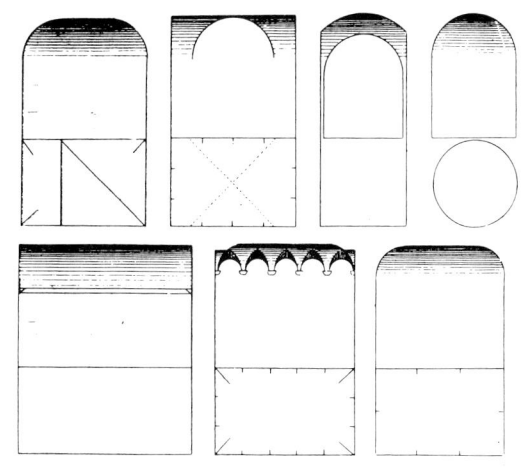

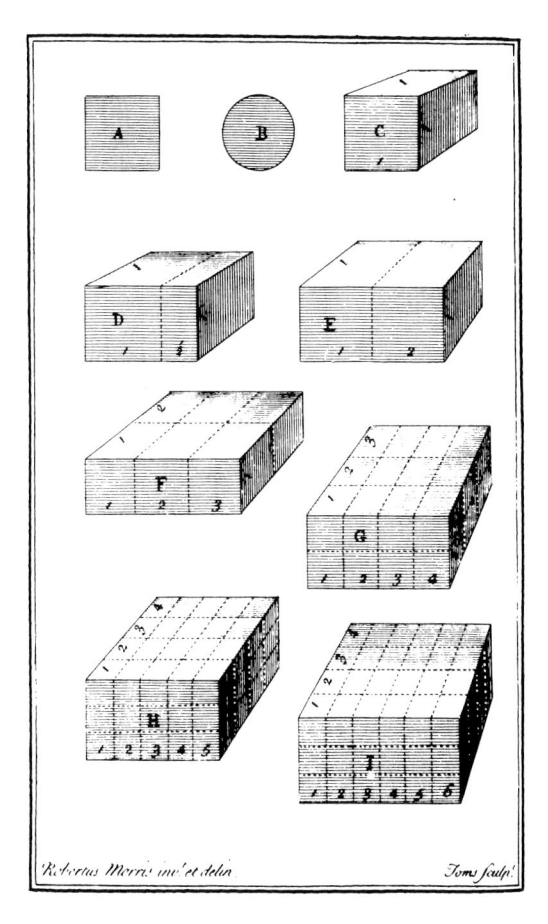

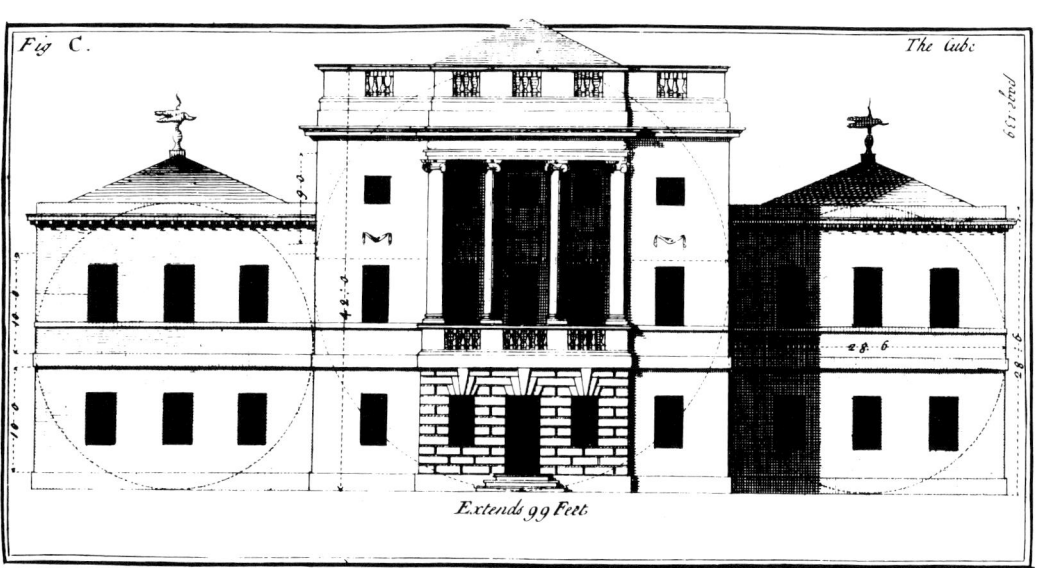

An elevation, published by Robert Morris in his *Lectures on Architecture*, showing a house designed in accordance with one of his seven ideal proportions. The house is composed of three cubes whose dimensions are in the ratio of 2:3 – Morris's cube and a half.

lucky that the eye is not 'as delicate with respect to proportion as the ear with respect to concord' for it would be 'the source of continuous pain and uneasiness'.

Interestingly, Sir William Chambers, who promoted many of the early Palladian doctrines, had, by the time he published his mighty *Treatise on Civil Architecture* in 1759 (revised edition 1791), moved away from the Renaissance music/architecture proportions analogy cited by those such as Robert Morris, and now took an extremely empirical view of proportion and beauty. In place of an argument for objective beauty Chambers suggested, in his 1791 edition, that beauty perceived in architecture was derived from a design's convenience (or fitness to purpose), custom, prejudice or association of ideas. He also asserted, like Kames, that the effects of proportion vary according to the position of the spectator, and even argued that the double-cube room – a proportion beloved by early eighteenth-century Palladians – looked too high when viewed from the ends and too low when seen from the sides.

Before we continue with the examination of the means by which the Palladian dictatorship of taste was dismantled after c1750, we need to see how architecture had progressed in Ireland and the provinces in the first half of the eighteenth century.

Building in Ireland and in the English provinces

The Palladian movement in Ireland emerged and indeed developed largely independently of England. The initial stimulus may have been the English Whig 'new Junta for architecture' (among them John Molesworth and his father Viscount Molesworth, who had estates in and around Dublin and who introduced Alessandro Galilei into Ireland in 1718), but the real moving force behind Irish Palladianism was Sir Edward Lovett Pearce. He gave the movement in Ireland an independent direction by galvanizing Burlingtonian Palladianism with the English baroque school of Vanbrugh, to whom he was related. The fresh and dynamic architecture that was the result of this fusion – in which Palladian classical purity of formal detail is combined with baroque movement of plan and decoration – is examined on pages 57 and 144 as part of the discussion of Pearce's buildings, notably his Parliament House, Dublin (1729), and of the development of the Irish Palladian country house.

In the English provinces the preference on the part of merchants for showy baroque designs, coupled perhaps with a rural Tory reluctance to embrace Whiggish town architecture, slowed down the advance of Palladianism and, in the process, produced some curious backwaters of taste. In manufacturing and commercial centres, such as the Cotswolds, Gloucestershire, parts of Lincolnshire, especially Stamford (p244), and Bristol (p191), major buildings were still being embellished with baroque details in the 1740s and '50s. Indeed, in parts of the Cotswolds, not even the baroque had arrived, with eighteenth-century cottages in Chipping Campden (such as Malt House, High Street) and Bisley being built with steep pitched roofs, mullioned windows and seventeenth-century-style drip moulds and string courses (as were cottages in Frome, Somerset, p210).

This provincial conservatism coupled with Tory aloofness could produce a curious effect even in country house building in the early eighteenth century. Lord Bathurst, rebuilding his house at Cirencester Park, Gloucestershire, in 1714-18, and using the services of a provincial architect still working in the established baroque manner, asked his friend Alexander Pope, 'How comes it to look so oddly bad?' The answer was that Bathurst, despite a certain reluctance, had begun to develop the Palladian taste.

Apart from these national issues there were other more parochial influences on the development of local styles. The presence of a country house designed by an influential architect could generate a local style for years to come. For example, details cribbed by local builders from Vanbrugh's Blenheim Palace, Oxfordshire (p257), crop up in Hope House, Woodstock, Oxfordshire (c1720), and a terrace house in St Michael's Street, Oxford (c1720), is plainly inspired by the spirit of Blenheim and Hawksmoor's Easton Neston, Northamptonshire (1702).

On another level, craftsmen who worked on great houses carried the influence into their own jobs. William Etty worked for Colen Campbell supervising the erection of Baldersby Park, North Yorkshire (p54), while also working for Sir John Vanbrugh as Clerk of Works at Seaton Delaval Hall, Northumberland, from 1718 onwards and at Castle Howard, Yorkshire, from 1721 onwards. But when he came to design for himself, notably the Mansion House, York, of 1726-33 (p151) and, probably, Holy Trinity Church, Leeds, of 1722-7 (p113), Etty used what he had learned from Campbell to raise his design above the usual works of provincial builder/architects.

On the other hand, Nathaniel Ireson, who built Stourhead, Wiltshire, to the designs of Colen Campbell in c1720, reverted to his provincial baroque upbringing (he had been apprenticed to Francis Smith of Warwick) when, as late as 1734, he designed Crowcombe Court, Somerset, in a baroque style incorporating Borrominiesque Ionic capitals.

Another important factor in the formation of regional differences was the availability of building materials. Until the growth of the canal system in the 1770s only major country houses and public buildings were regularly constructed of materials from outside the region; for example many of London's churches and public buildings were faced with Portland stone from Dorset. Occasionally, however, this prestigious use of alien materials can be found in more humble works, such as Longstone Hall, Great Longstone; Parwich Hall; and Sycamore Farmhouse, Hopton. All of these were built in Derbyshire in 1747 of a conspicuously fashionable brick in a thoroughly stone-built region.

By 1750 the most striking regional design differences had been ironed out, mostly as a result of architectural pattern books. These were either humble affairs, produced by craftsmen for craftsmen and offering advice on construction and design with plates of the latest London fashions (invariably Palladian), or more learned tomes by leading architects, like Campbell's *Vitruvius Britannicus* and Kent's *Designs of Inigo Jones* (1727), which were intended to champion a style and promote the author. But even this type made themselves humble servants to 'gentlemen who might be concerned in buildings, especially in remote parts of the country, where little or no assistance for design can be procured', as James Gibbs wrote in the preface to his *Book of Architecture* (1728, reissued 1739). This book, partly provoked by the fact that Gibbs had been entirely excluded from Campbell's books, proved to be perhaps the most influential of all the eighteenth-century pattern books. It influenced the doorcase and interior design of speculative terrace houses (a house in White's Row, Spitalfields, London, of c1730 has a doorcase based exactly on a Gibbs pattern), church design, and many a building erected in the English colonies during the eighteenth century and into the nineteenth century.

Remarkably few architectural books were

A built example of a Gibbs design c1730 in White's Row, Spitalfields, London.

produced in Ireland in the eighteenth century. The first, *A General Treatise on Architecture* (1754) written by John Aheron, is, unfortunately, a book of little importance;[1] the most interesting is the Rev. John Payne's *Twelve Designs for Country Houses* (1757) which recommends designs sporting familiar Irish Palladian features like Venetian doors and Gibbs surrounds.

But just when the Palladian style had established itself, when regular designs from a myriad of pattern books were loitering in vast numbers in virtually every high street in

Doorcase designs by James Gibbs published in his *Book of Architecture* of 1728, possibly the most influential of all the eighteenth-century pattern books.

the land, and country houses were being plucked from the pages of publications and placed upon the ground in brick and stone, there came a revolution in taste.

The romantic revolution
The seeds of this revolution, which overthrew the Palladian bondage of the orders in favour of a richer, more varied classicism mixed with exotic styles, had been sown early in the eighteenth century. Indeed, the most common exotic styles – Chinese and Gothic – ran parallel to the Palladian and had been used, in suitably relaxed circumstances, as alternatives to classicism by leading Palladians (p97).

Pope created a notable Gothic folly called Alfred's Hall at Cirencester Park in 1721-32, and William Kent designed a Gothic gateway in Clock Court, Hampton Court Palace, in 1732, embellished Wolsey's Tower, Esher, Surrey, in 1733 and built Gothic garden ornaments (now demolished) in Richmond Gardens, Surrey, between 1730 and 1735. A little later James Gibbs built his Gothic garden house at Stowe, Buckinghamshire (1741), and chinoiserie was so well established – having been popular for internal decoration from the late seventeenth century – that the 1744 edition of the guide to Stowe does not bother even to give a full description of the Chinese Bridge (c1738) because it was in a style thought too familiar to need detailed amplification. But after 1750 the pace of development and place of use of exotic styles changed dramatically. Designers such as Batty Langley, who published *Ancient Architecture Restored and Improved* (1741), established Gothic as a sort of indigenous version of rococo with romantic associations, to be used as an alternative to classicism. Although initially it was used only for interiors, by the mid-1750s entire houses, such as Arbury Hall, Warwickshire (p77), were designed in this romantic manner.

Quite suddenly Palladianism was robbed of the moral superiority with which Lord Burlington had imbued it and became just one of the options in the spectrum of architectural styles. For example, one of the pioneering rococo Goths, Sanderson Miller, who designed a picturesque thatched cottage at Edgehill, Warwickshire, in 1743 in Gothic style (p97) and built a series of mock castle/follies, including one at Hagley Hall, Hereford and Worcester, in 1747-8 (p97), used the Palladian style when designing the Shire Hall in Warwick in 1754 (p150) and Hagley Hall itself in 1754. Another exponent of this mixed approach was Henry Keene, who designed the Guildhall, High Wycombe, Buckinghamshire, in Palladian style in 1757, and Hartwell Church, Buckinghamshire, in Gothic style in 1753-5. Horace Walpole explained this curious schism: Palladianism was, indeed, the antithesis of the emerging romantic movement, but was still suitable for public buildings in which gravity, not Gothic-

A plate from Batty Langley's *Ancient Architecture restored and improved* ... of 1741, showing his attempt to order Gothic details in the manner of classical architecture.

A Greek Doric portico published in *The Antiquities of Athens*, 1762, by James Stuart and Nicholas Revett, who explain that this reconstruction was based on what was 'generally supposed to be the remains of a temple dedicated to Rome and Augustus'.

inspired 'charming irregularity', was required.

The next decade, 1760–70, saw the revolution expand its domain. The classicism of Palladio – based on Renaissance interpretations of Roman buildings and ancient writings (notably Vitruvius's *Ten Books of Architecture* dating from *c*50 BC) – received a profound challenge in 1762 when James Stuart and Nicholas Revett's *Antiquities of Athens* was published. This book, full of drawings and reconstructions of Greek buildings, revealed that the ancient world was far richer and more varied in building types and decoration, and less bound by rules, than Palladio and the Renaissance had ever suggested. With earlier publications, notably J.D. Le Roy's *Ruines des Plus Beaux Monuments de la Grèce* (1758) and Robert Wood's *Ruins of Palmyra* (1753) and *Ruins of Baalbec* (1757), this book fuelled the neo-classical revolution. This, as with Gothic, first manifested itself in the design of garden buildings, such as Stuart's Greek Doric temple fronts at Hagley Hall in 1758 and Shugborough, Staffordshire, in 1764 (p99). Robert Adam, who returned from Italy in 1758 (p82) and in 1764 published his own contribution to the new age of archaeological classicism, *The Ruins of the Palace of the Emperor Diocletian at Spalatro*, was the first architect to synthesize these new ideas with English classical traditions to form an original and inspired style (p82), while Stephen Riou, in his *Grecian Order of Architecture Delineated and Explained* (1768), attempted to give wider currency to the discoveries of Stuart and Revett and to demonstrate how Grecian features could be accommodated within conventional Palladian design.

But this new movement was not to develop unopposed. James Paine, a free-thinking and original mid-eighteenth-century architect, could only view Greek architecture as 'despicable ruins' (p81) and Sir William Chambers, the stalwart of the late Palladian school who, in certain circumstances, approved both Chinese buildings (he designed a pagoda at Kew Gardens in 1761) and Gothic buildings (Milton Abbey House, Dorset, 1771–6, p78) would have nothing to do with Greek. In the preface to the 1791 edition of his *Treatise on Civil Architecture* he insisted that 'our knowledge ought ... to be collected from [the] purer, more abundant force' of Roman classicism, as opposed to the Greek with 'their gouty columns, their narrow intercolumniations, their disproportionate architraves, their temples, which they knew not how to cover'. But Chambers was addressing a dwindling audience.

Archaeologically influenced buildings had appeared under the supervision of Robert Adam at Kedleston, Derbyshire, 1760–70 (p82); of James Stuart at Nuneham Courtenay, Oxfordshire, 1764 (p116); and of Nicholas Revett at Ayot St Lawrence, Hertfordshire, in 1778 (p116). But this first flowering of archaeologically based neo-classicism was not to hold the centre of the architectural stage for long. The 'remarkable improvement in the form, convenience, arrangement, and relief of apartments ... an almost total change' in architecture, for which Adam gave himself credit when he wrote these words in the preface of his *Works in Architecture* of 1773 (or what Chambers called in 1791 'boyish conceits and trifling complicated ornaments ... ransacked [from] barbarous times'), became itself a source of reaction. In the mid-1770s architects such as Robert Mylne and Henry Holland tired of the polychromatic, complex and idiosyncratic decoration of Robert Adam and turned to austere French-derived neo-classicism, which had the authority of Palladianism and the boldness of the Greek. As Horace Walpole said in the mid-1780s, after witnessing the 'taste and propriety' and 'august simplicity' of Holland's Carlton House, London (begun in 1783 and demolished in 1827), 'How sick one shall be after this chaste palace of Mr Adam's gingerbread and snippets of embroidery.'

But this Graeco-Palladian style of Holland's and Mylne's was also overtaken by events. On the one hand there were George Dance the Younger and his pupil John Soane's attempts to develop 'a modern architecture based on classical forms, but freed from the inhibitions of the Vitruvian and Palladian past',[2] which led to a very individual, almost mannered, interpretation of neo-classicism, with the abandonment of the classical column and entablature and their ornaments, and the use of shallow domes, segmental arches and antique motifs such as paterae and acroteria. The architectural products of this quest were brilliant and represent an important aspect of late eighteenth-century classicism, especially Soane's rustic and neo-classical rural buildings, such as the dairy at Hamels, Hertfordshire (1781, remodelled 1830), and the austere lodges to Tyringham House, Buckinghamshire (1793); houses such as Saxlingham Rectory, Norfolk, 1784–7 (p87) and Shotesham Park, Norfolk, *c*1785 (p85), and the Bank of England, built after 1788 and largely demolished in the 1930s. However, though admired, Soane's classicism was too personal and difficult to copy to form the basis of a school (p122), so he had little direct influence on his contemporaries; his style died with him in 1837.

On the other and more influential hand

there was also, in the late 1770s, the emergence of the asymmetrical picturesque style. This can be traced back to Vanbrugh's 'castle air' in the very early eighteenth century, indeed to his own castle of 1717 in Greenwich (p76) and to Pope's Grotto (c1718) at Twickenham (surviving in a subway beneath a road called Cross Deep) and his asymmetrical Gothic detached and castellated folly, Alfred's Hall (1721-32), in Cirencester Park, Gloucestershire (p97). Downton Castle, Hereford and Worcester, begun in 1772 by picturesque pioneer Richard Payne Knight, was castellated and asymmetrical but still a little forced and artificial (p78).

It was not till picturesque theories were combined with a fully absorbed Greek, or with a Gothic that was more than just superficial decoration, that the picturesque was to find its own architectural form (p91) in such Italianate villas as Nash's Cronkhill, Shropshire (1802), and L.W. Wyatt's Cuerden Hall, Lancashire (1815). With its classical detailing, corner towers and a central belvedere forming a clerestory, the latter attempts a picturesque skyline reflecting the theories of Sir Uvedale Price, who codified the principles of the picturesque movement in his *Essay on the Picturesque as Compared with the Sublime and the Beautiful* (1794, enlarged edition 1810). For Price the essential quality of the picturesque, as opposed to 'The Sublime and the Beautiful', were variety, movement, irregularity, intricacy and roughness.[3] These qualities were pursued through all styles of architecture, including those derived from the relatively recent native past, as in J. A. Repton's neo-Elizabethan Bourn Hall, Cambridgeshire, 1817 (p96), as well as the Norman style, often referred to in contemporary accounts as 'Saxon', and in even more ancient and alien styles such as Egyptian, which enjoyed a brief vogue after 1807. Eclecticism now flourished. The Greek revival established an early superiority both in country house design – for example George Dance the Younger's Stratton Park, Hampshire, 1803 (p91) and William Wilkins' The Grange, Hampshire, begun in 1804 (p91) – and in the design of public buildings, such as Dance's Royal College of Surgeons, Lincoln's Inn Fields, London, 1806-13 (p155) and Wilkins' Downing College, Cambridge, 1807-21 (p166). In Ireland James and George Richard Pain, like Nash and Repton in England, felt able to offer their clients a series of stylistic options when commissioned to design a country house. For Dromoland, Co. Clare (1826), they proffered Palladian and Italian as well as the baronial design that was chosen. In Ker Street, Devonport, John Foulston designed in 1821-4 an astonishing collection of buildings – a 'Hindoo' chapel (destroyed), an Egyptian library, a Greek town hall and a palace-fronted Roman Corinthian terrace (destroyed) because, as he later wrote, it occurred to him that 'if a series of edifices, exhibiting the various features of the architectural world, were erected in conjunction, and skilfully grouped, a happy result might be obtained [and] a picturesque effect' achieved.[4]

During the 1820s the moral tone which was to become strident in the writings of post-1830 commentators such as A.W.N. Pugin and John Ruskin began to creep into architectural debate. In 1823 Soane's classical design for a law court at the Palace of Westminster was approved, begun on site, stopped, then partially demolished and rebuilt in a Gothic style following objections from MPs who thought that the ancient Palace of Westminster would be best served by a sympathetic Gothic, rather than classical, addition (p154). At about the same time C.R. Cockerell began to see the absurd side of the Greek revival, which produced gentlemen's country houses fitted up internally for modern and comfortable living and dressed up outside as ancient temples. Of The Grange, Hampshire, Cockerell confided to his diary: 'I am sure that the grave and solemn architecture of Temples [was] never adapted to houses, but a much lighter style, as we may judge by the vases.'[5]

As well as the development of new aesthetic theories of design and the instant waxing and waning of architectural fashions, the early nineteenth century saw the emergence of an architectural attitude that was quite as revolutionary. There was no attempt in the eighteenth century to display structure or make an ornament of it: rather it was either concealed or actually contradicted by the stylish exterior skin. In eighteenth-century Gothic – which can be defined as a decorative as opposed to a constructional revival of Gothic – vaults, like stage sets, are made of timber and plaster, and arches, like that over the chancel at St John Evangelist's, Shobdon, Hereford and Worcester (c1753), are formed in a way that defies structural logic.[6]

This failure to realize the possibilities offered by structural expression is made more curious when one realizes that, from the middle of the century a popular debate had centred around the proposition that the origins of classical architecture lay in a simple, primitive structure. In 1753 the French Abbé Laugier, in his *Essai sur l'Architecture*, popularized a theory (at least as old as Vitruvius)

Early nineteenth-century rendering of the primitive hut derived from the thinking of Abbé Laugier and Sir William Chambers.

that the Greek temple evolved out of a primitive post and lintel construction in which tree trunk columns supported timber beams, decorative motifs such as triglyphs and guttae were derived from fixing pegs and carved joist ends, and all was covered with a thatched pitched roof creating a pediment/gable façade. This theory, which demonstrated that classical architecture evolved out of a rational structural system, was pursued by Sir William Chambers, who published a Laugier-like drawing of a primitive hut in his *Treatise on Civil Architecture* (1759), and by Humphry Repton in *Designs for the Pavilion at Brighton* (1808).[7] The only eighteenth-century buildings in which the structure was regularly exposed – though hardly expressed – were utilitarian buildings such as farms (some of which made direct references to the primitive hut, p101), mills and warehouses. But in these buildings the structure was left exposed for reasons of economics and function rather than as a result of an architectural theory (p127).

After 1800 there were signs of interest in the use of structure for architectural effect. This new interest seems to have been stimulated by the emerging post-Industrial Revolution building technology and new materials, which suggests that eighteenth-century apathy towards structure may have been due largely to the moribund nature of eighteenth-century building technology, which forced original and inventive architects to devote their energies to stylistic rather than structural developments. The first manifestations are slight, for example S.P. Cockerell's staircase of 1805 at Sezincote, Gloucestershire, where the cast-iron structural girders are exposed and embellished.[8] Most tentative moves towards structural expressionism were related to the Gothic revival which, as Gothic began to be studied more seriously, stimulated architects to imitate its structural qualities as well as its appearance. In 1811 George Saunders gave an important lecture on the structural nature of the Gothic vault (published in 1814) and between 1820 and 1824 James Savage roofed St Luke's, Chelsea, with a properly constructed masonry vault (p122) – a move soon followed by John Sempel in Ireland (p122).

An important consequence of the stylistic pluracy that characterizes Regency architecture was the growing tendency for designers to choose a style that suited the function or the site of the building: an obvious point, but one that was very rarely considered in the eighteenth century when it was virtually unknown for the brief – rather than the currently fashionable architectural style – to

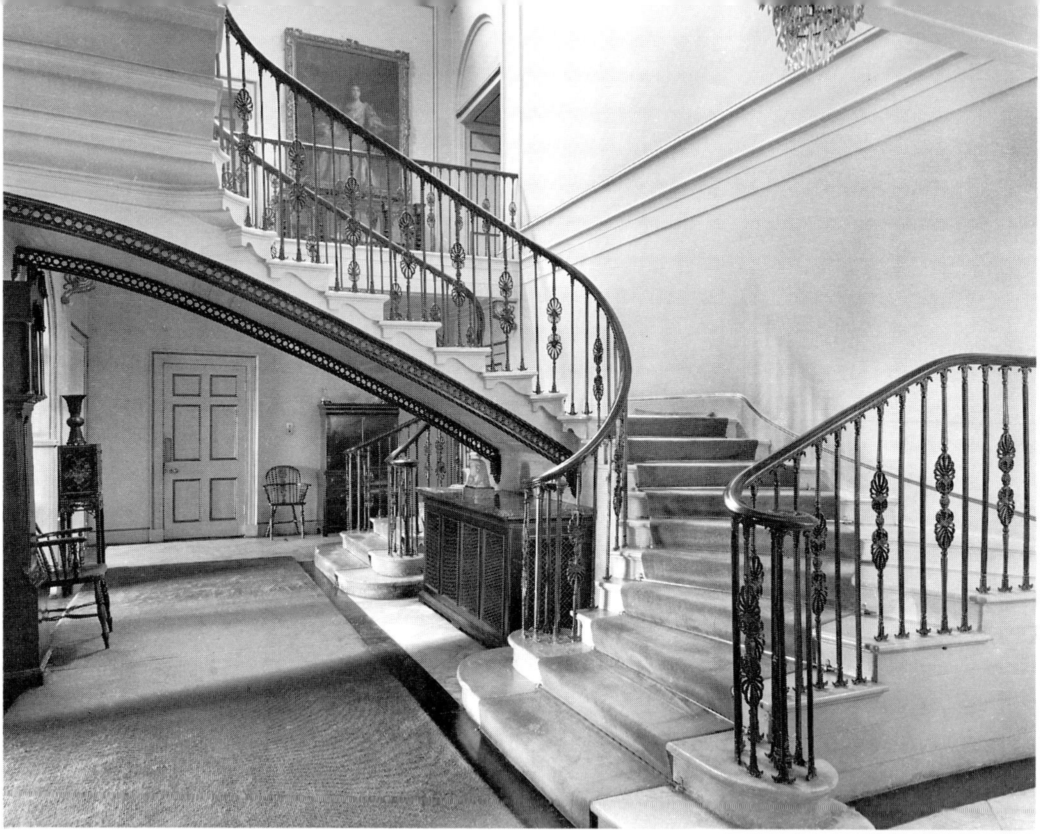

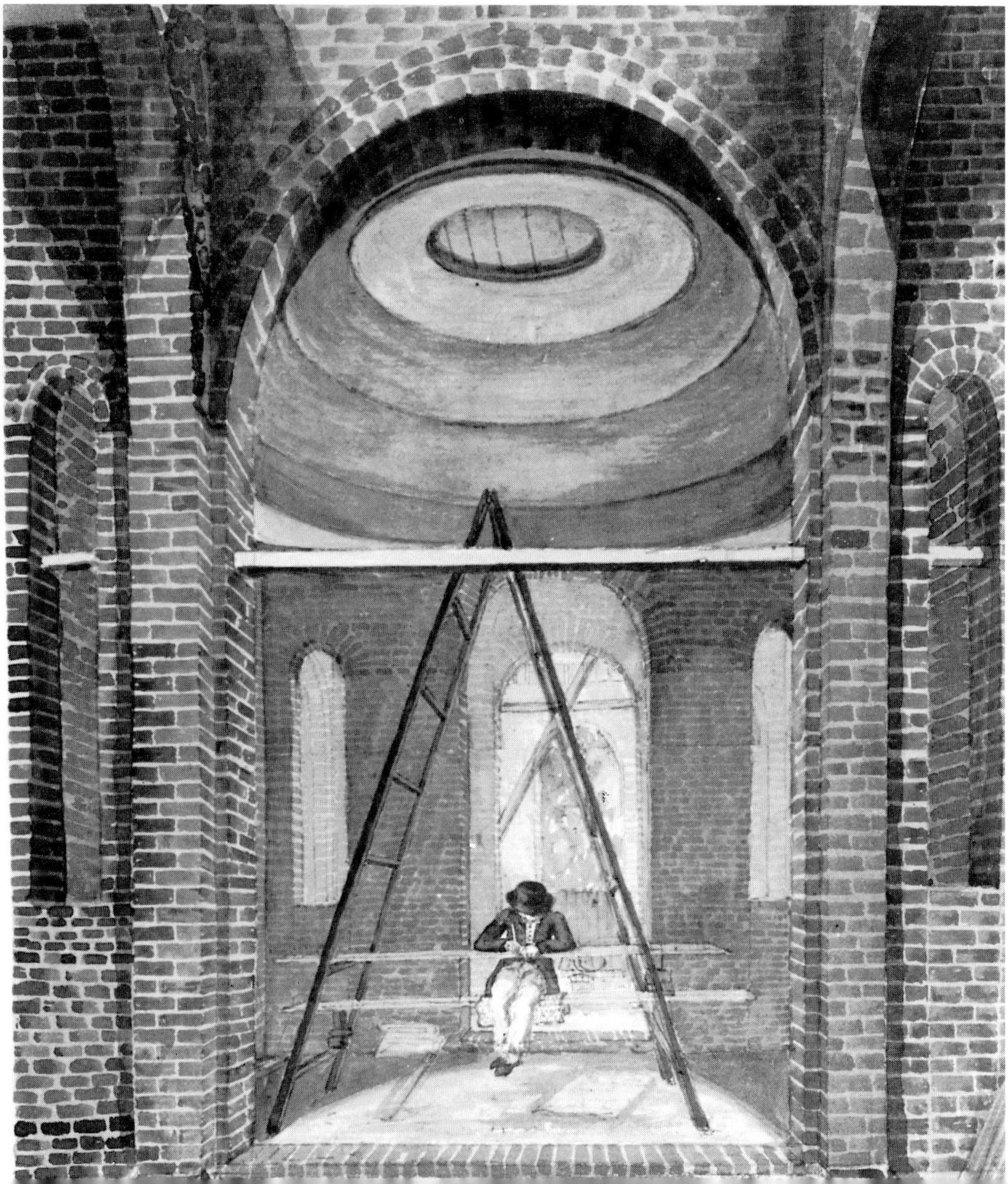

Opposite above: The staircase at Sezincote House, Gloucestershire, of *c*1805 by S. P. Cockerell. An early example of the expression and decoration of structure – in this case the cast iron girder carrying the stairtreads.

Opposite below: A drawing by a pupil of Sir John Soane showing the mausoleum attached to the Dulwich Picture Gallery during construction, *c*1811. The dome is of brick, rendered ready for applied plaster decoration.

generate the design. It is for this reason, of course, that town halls, market halls, country houses and town mansions can all look disarmingly alike, and why the Assize Court, York (1773–7), and the Female Prison, York (1780–3), both by John Carr, despite their difference of use and interior planning, are virtually identical externally.

The architects

Something should be said of the life of those who designed and built in eighteenth- and early nineteenth-century Britain. It was clearly not an easy task and the potential pitfalls were numerous, ranging from the temptation to indulge in a little fraud over materials to the problem of being an honest man in charge of a team of crooked builders. The pressures were great and seem to have proved too much for some members of the profession. James Peacock, Assistant Clerk of Works to the City of London from 1771 to 1814, took refuge in writing. John Carter threw himself into measuring, drawing and fighting for the preservation of Gothic cathedrals and in publishing lurid accounts of his unhappy love-life under the pseudonym of John Ramble.

Ruin and disgrace could come with dramatic finality. Francis Sandys – one of the very few Irish-born architects who worked in England – was commissioned in 1809 to design and build a court house and gaol in Durham. Unfortunately he failed to stop the builder behaving in a fraudulent manner and eventually had the colossal sum of £20,000 damages awarded against him, which instantly terminated his promising career. No more is heard of him after 1814. The fate that befell David Laing was equally devastating. Surveyor to the Board of Customs, President of the Surveyors' Club, and Master of the Tylers' and Bricklayers' Company, Laing rebuilt the Custom House in the City of London between 1813 and 1817. All was well until 1825 when part of the façade suddenly collapsed, owing, as subsequent investigations revealed, to unusually inadequate foundations. Laing, it was decided, had been either grossly incompetent, negligent or in collusion with the builder to commit a fraud over materials. Dismissed from office, he spent the rest of his long life living on charity disbursed by benevolent societies founded for the relief of distressed artists and architects.

Both these actions involved public buildings, whose clients were powerful enough to have recourse to the law, and one wonders how many smaller, private buildings were constructed, unpenalized, in the same spirit. But if the works we are about to examine in detail were frequently designed and built by rogues, incompetents and hucksters of all descriptions, we must marvel at the fact that somehow so many works of real and lasting quality, indeed of genius, were produced.

Notes

1 'A very bad book', says Maurice Craig in his authoritative *The Architecture of Ireland*, 1982, page 191.
2 Howard Colvin, from the Sir John Soane entry in his *Dictionary of British Architecture 1600–1840*, 1978 edition.
3 David Watkin, *The Buildings of Regency Britain*, 1982, page 14.
4 John Foulston, *The Public Buildings erected in the West of England as designed by John Foulston FRIBA*, 1838. See David Watkin, *The English Vision*, 1982, pages 191–2.
5 J. Mordaunt Crook's *The Greek Revival*, 1972 edition, page 134.
6 Some domes, vaults and arches, such as those raised by Sir John Soane at the Bank of England, City of London (1788–1833) and at the Dulwich Picture Gallery (1811–13), were structural – that is constructed with brick and stone, rather than being merely lath and plaster affairs suspended from a concealed and differently formed primary structure. But these examples reflect a coincidence between decorative intent and structural expediency rather than being genuine examples of structural expression for its own sake.
7 There were significant differences between Laugier's and Chambers' interpretation of the primitive hut. Broadly, Chambers saw it as merely the first stage in the evolution of classical architecture, whereas Laugier saw it as a basic model of perfection; a view comparable with Rousseau and his Noble Savage. See John Harris's *Sir William Chambers*, 1970, page 134.
8 For the corridor, Brighton Pavilion (1815–21) John Nash designed a pair of staircases of decorated cast iron, including pierced risers and bamboo pattern handrails. He also used cast-iron shafts, topped with bamboo fronds, to support the kitchen ceiling. This is one of the earliest structural uses of cast iron in a domestic setting.

BUILDINGS IN TOWNS

The eighteenth century was an age obsessed by town planning. In the seventeenth century small attempts had been made to tame the free-ranging, intensely individual building system in order to create coherently planned, socially balanced and architecturally related urban developments. The most notable example was Inigo Jones's development of the Piazza in Covent Garden, London (1631), for the Duke of Bedford, where rows of individual houses were given a unified, pilastered palace front. Containing a church and the Duke's own house, it was an attempt at combining various uses and social classes in a distinct architectural composition. Jones's inspiration came from Palladio's designs for urban palazzi; the Piazza d'Armée at Leghorn (Livorno), c1590, which John Evelyn said 'gave the first hint to the building both of the church and piazza in Covent Garden', and which Jones could have seen on his first Italian visit; and the Place Royale (now Place des Vosges), Paris (begun 1605), which Jones must have seen under construction in 1609. Less architecturally coherent than Covent Garden, though even more socially engineered, were two London squares: Bloomsbury Square, developed in 1660 by the Duke of Bedford with several classes of house, a market and, finally, in 1716, a church (St George's, by Hawksmoor, p106), and St James's Square, where a year later Lord St Albans created his 'small town' of regular and reticent courtiers' brick houses, with a church at the north end of the square (St James's, Piccadilly, by Wren 1676–84), a market, and adjacent streets of more modest houses.

This was the ideal of estate development that was carried into the eighteenth century, and which was to play such a key role in the formation of ideas about larger-scale town planning and urban development. But, as recorded by numerous eighteenth-century critics, when related to the pragmatic realities of large-scale development, these ideals proved incredibly hard to realize. John Gwynn, for example, writing in 1766 in *London and Westminster Improved*, observed that even the aristocratic and architect-ridden west London estates such as the Grosvenor and the Cavendish-Harley were 'too loosely controlled', and argued for a 'general plan' for London. The problem can be traced back to Sir Christopher Wren's ambitious plan for rebuilding the City of London in 1666. He recognized that there were aesthetic and practical advantages in an overall rebuilding plan but was unable, like later planners, to reconcile this ambition with the vested interests of individual site owners, who were more interested in quick rebuilding on old sites than in participating in the time-consuming creation of a classical city. Individual self-interest, coupled with royal or corporate reluctance to force through unpopular planning legislation, compromised all eighteenth-century attempts at town planning. Indeed, it was not until John Nash engineered the building of Regent Street in the 1820s, which involved the development of the Crown estates at Regent's Park and St James's Park, that Britain saw its first real piece of publicly supported large-scale and architecturally coherent urban reconstruction.

As well as the entrenched freeholder jealously guarding his rights, there was another element in the urban building system which made this ideal so hard to realize. Virtually all the urban domestic building of Georgian Britain was undertaken on a speculative basis, and all estate developments were carried out by owners who, despite their best intentions, were often unable to put the generally admired principles of town planning into practice. Even the Regent Street development, despite its royal associations and support, was still carried out as a private venture, with individual speculators undertaking to build sections of the new thoroughfare under the architectural guidance of Nash. The affluence, ability, profession or trade of these speculators varied from place to place and throughout the period, but typically they were modest master builders (though often not involved in the building world) with enough taste and business sense to design attractive façades in the local fashion, but not enough money to build more than a couple, or perhaps a small group of houses at a time. Later in the century the undertakings of these men grew, and it became common for speculators to control (though not necessarily to finance) the building of entire streets, as the Woods did in Bath, for instance, where they built the Royal Crescent in 1767, and as James Burton did in

Colen Campbell's unbuilt design of 1725 for part of the east side of Grosvenor Square: an early example of eighteenth-century uniform terrace design, which, had the estate been willing to finance it, would have been the first palace-fronted terrace built in Britain since the 1630s.

Bloomsbury in the first decade of the nineteenth century. Generally in the early eighteenth century even the grandest parts of the grandest West End estates were built by these men who, by their necessarily pragmatic approach to building, managed to compromise any particularly ambitious scheme and, indeed, invoked criticism from such as Gwynn.

On the Grosvenor estate, for example, for which a development act was passed in 1710 and on which building began in c1720, a massive square was created as the central feature of a development including a chapel – in South Audley Street – within its grid of streets (but strangely not a market). For the east side of the square the pioneering Palladian designer Colen Campbell (p6) in 1725 designed a uniform terrace which would have been the first palace-fronted terrace built in Britain since the 1630s. Typically, the estate was unwilling to finance or subsidize the buildings, nor were speculators prepared to spend money on expensive and commercially unnecessary items such as giant columns and stone, and so a compromise was reached. Between 1725 and 1753 a speculating builder called John Simmons erected a standard astylar terrace, but with the addition of a pediment on the centre building and an extra attic storey on the end-of-terrace houses to form a terminating feature. Though not quite the palace façade envisaged by Campbell, even this modestly uniform composition was an advance on what was erected elsewhere. Another attempt to give the square some uniformity was undertaken on the north side by Edward Shepherd, but this merely resulted in the creation of a long range with a pompous, but off-centre, five-bay pediment, which Ralph, in 1734, called 'a wretched attempt at something extraordinary'.[1] Interestingly, Gwynn implies that some early picturesque notion may have been at work, for he recorded in 1766 that the reason then given for the square's irregularity was that, if uniform, 'it would have resembled an hospital'. Gwynn scorns this excuse and seems to regard it as the rather lame piece of post-rationalization that it most probably was.

In smaller streets, in which houses were usually built as small lots by separate developers, sustained uniformity was not generally even attempted in the early to middle eighteenth century. Visual harmony was created only if each speculating builder followed roughly the same architectural fashion, was subjected to the same technological and financial constraints and building regulations, and had to comply with the rudimentary development control enforced by some of the grander estates. On the Cavendish-Harley estate, for example (begun after 1717 and laid out by John Prince), James Gibbs was appointed estate architect with the job of approving the design of all elevations. He seems to have had little influence in the design of street architecture, however (though he did design the estate church, St Peter, Vere Street, and market, the Oxford Market, long demolished), and was irrelevant to the development of the estate's main ornament – Cavendish Square – for the plots here were developed very slowly (it was not completed until the 1770s), and consequently were built in the most irregular way.

The Bedford estate, when developing its Bloomsbury land in the late eighteenth century, managed to instil increasing regularity into its operations, and created London's first uniform square – Bedford Square (1776-86). But even here Soane could detect the 'spirit of speculation' at work.[2] The Bedford estate development controls were mainly concerned with financial and structural matters rather than aesthetic, so that Bedford Square, although conceived in a noble manner, is blemished in its execution by some strangely clumsy details. The elevations, possibly designed by Thomas Leverton,[3] are a neo-classically detailed rendering of the Grosvenor Square type, plus a pedimented centre and end pavilions, emphasized in this case by the end house breaking forward slightly and being topped by a taller balustraded parapet. From the start this palace front was a little compromised by a determination to emphasize each door.

These designs were accepted by William Scott and Robert Grew (the main undertakers for the development of the square) in their building agreement with the Bedford estate, but in execution the centre of the north side gained a four-bay pediment, leading to the unfortunate classical solecism of a pilaster, not a space, beneath the apex of the pediment.

The main problem for the speculative builder was, of course, how to fit the maximum number of standard lettable houses behind the sophisticated palace front, and sometimes, clearly, the two demands just could not

The palace-fronted north side of Bedford Square. Begun 1776 by William Scott and Robert Grew, it shows how the proportions of the astylar Georgian terrace façade are derived from the proportions of the columned temple front.

be reconciled. Another of the conflicts between the interests of the estate owner and the interests of the speculating builder is well illustrated by the development of the Bedford estate. The estate owner tended to look to long-term profit and the maximum increase in the value of his land, and so tended to encourage the construction of larger, more expensive (and thus more solidly constructed) houses which would attract tenants of stature and secure means to his estate. The speculating builder, on the other hand, tended to look for short-term profit achieved with minimal risk, and so preferred to construct smaller houses more cheaply and more quickly. The Bedford estate possesses some fascinating correspondence illustrating this conflict between the builder, Thomas Lewis, and the estate steward, about the construction of houses in Keppel Street in 1807. In one of his letters Lewis attempts to justify his non-compliance with a building agreement by saying that he had advised other builders in the street 'to make [the houses] smaller than they had intended, knowing that in these times many genteel families will give more for a small house on a good situation than for a large one'.[4]

The speculative building system

The speculative building system, upon which the construction of Georgian towns and cities in Britain and Ireland depended, seems to have evolved during the reconstruction of the City after 1666 and to have been refined by one of the leading speculators of the seventeenth century, Nicholas Barbon. The method was for the builder to acquire a site from the ground landlord on a building lease. Interestingly, building leases grew progressively longer: if this is seen as a concession on the part of the estate owner, it can only mean that the supply of building land being offered by estates was greater than the supply of responsible speculative builders. In the 1630s the building leases in Covent Garden had been thirty-one years. The Bedford estate was offering leases of sixty-one years on its Bloomsbury land in the 1720s (as was usual elsewhere), then of eighty years and ninety-nine years after c1780. In Bath ninety-nine-year leases were usual in the later eighteenth century, being granted, for example, for the development of the Paragon in 1767 and Great Pulteney Street in 1788.

The object of the builder, after acquiring his building lease, was to erect the shell of a building, roofed and floored and usually with the bare internal walls roughly plastered out, and sell it on before ground rent became payable; invariably, as part of the building agreement, the speculator only paid a peppercorn rent on the site for the first few months so that all his capital could go into construction. The first occupier would then complete the shell to suit his own taste and pocket. The end result, if all went well, was that the estate got itself developed for minimal investment, with a modest income from ground rents and eventual possession of the structures when the leases finally expired. The builder made a profit on the sale of the shell, and the occupier, who bought the remainder of the lease, got a home finished to his own taste. But often all did not go well. Property speculation was sensitive to all manner of external problems as well as those created by the speculator getting his sums wrong or building the wrong sort of houses in the wrong sort of place. Political unrest, by slowing up investment in property, could leave a builder with an incomplete or unsold shell and a massive debt. For example, Bedford Square took ten years to complete because, as Grew wrote to the Bedford estate agent Robert Palmer in February 1784, 'The great scarcity of money, occasioned by the unhappy American war, so severely affected many of the persons concerned under us [Grew and Scott had sublet the construction of part of the square], that some were compelled to stop.' R. Campbell, in his *London Tradesmen* of 1747, could not resist observing that many speculating builders only managed to 'build themselves into debtors' gaol'.

As the century wore on and as speculators undertook larger-scale developments, the risks (and the potential profits) became enormous. Even such eminent and rich members of the building trade as the Adam brothers only just escaped complete ruin in a speculation that went wrong. In 1768 they took a ninety-nine-year lease from the Duke of St Albans on a muddy Thames-side site, covered with wharfs, just south of Covent Garden. Here they had erected by 1772 a massive vaulted substructure supporting a long, tall riverside terrace – with a uniform front emphasized by pilasters – behind which ran two other terraces overlooking a new street. This centre block of two parallel terraces was flanked by shorter terraces running at right angles to the river (part of these, with a fragment of one of the terraces overlooking the new street, are all that now remains – in Robert Street, Adam Street and John Adam Street). As was increasingly the practice in the late eighteenth century, the houses were also finished out internally, in a fairly uniform manner, by the speculator.

Unfortunately, despite its imposing appearance, the brothers found the Adelphi – as they appropriately called the development – almost impossible to let. The brothers were only saved from bankruptcy by being given permission by Parliament to hold a lottery in which the individual houses would be offered as prizes; luckily there was a great run on the tickets.

The system of speculative building also had a very direct influence on how buildings were constructed. Builders, under the constant threat of bankruptcy, built as cheaply and quickly as possible. In London cheap, badly made or under-fired 'place' bricks were used for concealed work, even if it was structurally important, with only façades being wrought in good quality face bricks laid, apparently, in Flemish bond. But even here economy struck. The well-wrought and fashionably detailed façades are invariably only one brick (four inches) thick, the header being broken in half and butted up against the concealed piers of place brick, with only an occasional header bonding through when the courses of the face work and the concealed work happen to align. This lack of structural stability was increased by the use of softwood timber in brickwork, and lime mortar mixed with street dirt. A professional contemporary comment can be found in Isaac Ware's *A Complete Body of Architecture* (1756):

> ... the nature of the tenure of London has introduced the art of building slightly. The ground landlord is to come into possession at the end of a short term and the builder, unless his grace tyes him down in articles, does not choose to employ his money to his advantage. ... It is for this reason we see houses built for 60, 70 or the stoutest kind for 99 years. They care they shall not stand longer than their time occasions, many fall before it expires; nay some carried the art of slight building so far, that their houses have fallen before they were tenanted.

Irish town development

In Dublin estate owners followed the London pattern and teamed up with speculators. Lord Fitzwilliam of Merrion released land he owned on the south side of the city for building, and in 1762 Merrion Square was laid out. This was the first of Dublin's consciously planned squares: St Stephen's Green, earlier in origin, had grown organically rather than as a planned urban unit. Architecturally, the moving force behind Merrion Square may have been John Ensor; certainly he was building here in 1766, and earlier had undertaken to build the entire northern side of Rutland (now Parnell) Square. But if he was in charge of the appearance of Merrion

24 / *Georgian Buildings*

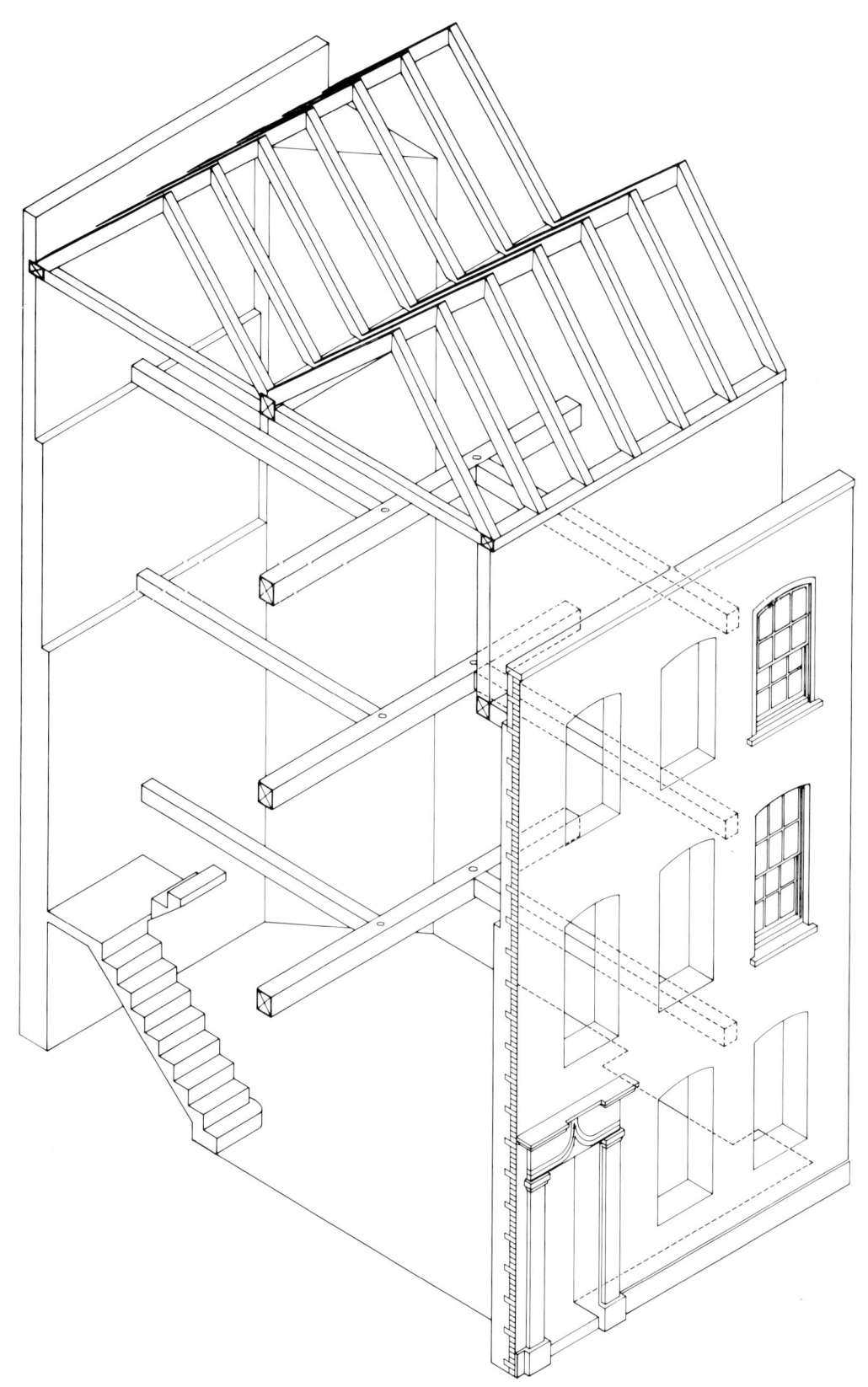

Axonometric of a typical early Georgian London house (31 Fournier Street, Spitalfields), showing the timber structure within the brick shell and the construction of the façade. The Flemish 'bond' of the facing bricks is in fact four inches thick, with headers snapped in half and only occasionally bonded into the weaker, often ill-wrought and under-fired, but structurally important 'place' bricks behind. In the top window the box sash is set flush with the façade, while the lower window has the sash set back four inches as required by the 1709 Building Act.

Square Ensor made no attempt to enforce a uniform palace front upon the individual speculators. The empathy of the different builders, however, was such that the square achieved (and retains) an extraordinary monumental, if not slavishly repetitive, quality. The vitality and variety of the different detailing (even the colour of the brickwork varies slightly) is contained within a broadly uniform composition: all the buildings are the same height, façades are proportioned in the same manner, and the doors are nearly all treated as wide, round-arched openings, filled with a huge fanlight over a tripartite composition in which the door is flanked by narrow side lights, often with intricate geometric glazing. By 1770–75 this type of four-storey, three-bay elevation had become standard for better quality Dublin developments.

In part this standardization was due to the work of the Wide Streets Commission which was established by act of Parliament in 1757 to push through a new street to connect the new Exchange (p131) with the river. In 1783 the Commission censored the windows of a house for being 'too high by four inches and a half' and got them changed,[5] and by 1799 it was ensuring that the newly created Westmorland and D'Olier Streets were given uniform frontages (designed by H.A. Baker) and even uniform shop-fronts (p130). After 1802, when it was chastised by the Treasury in London for overspending, the Commission's influence waned, and in 1826 its annual grant was cut.

Building Acts
Legislation in England, originating in London and far more formalized than the terms of the Dublin Commissioners, had a profound influence on eighteenth-century and early nineteenth-century urban design. The Buildings Act of 1667, which was intended to govern the rebuilding of London after the Great Fire, influenced both the design and construction of terrace houses and town planning generally throughout the country. Indeed, by the late eighteenth century legislation had united with the new technology emerging from the Industrial Revolution to transform the embellishment of the terrace house.

The 1667 act was concerned primarily with ensuring that new buildings should be as soundly constructed and fire-proof as possible, so it specified that all new houses be constructed in their external and party walls with brick. The act also related the size of the house not only to its structure but also to its position in the city. Small houses were to be in by-streets and lanes, with only the largest houses on the principal thoroughfares: an interesting point, for this provision gave statutory power to the principles that became the cornerstone of eighteenth-century town planning, namely that the size of a building should relate to the width of the street or square on which it stood, and that houses in the same street should be of more or less regular height.

These principles were, of course, followed in the great London West End estates, like the Grosvenor estate, where the grand houses were in the square and smaller houses on secondary streets, but their most powerful manifestation is the New Town of Edinburgh, laid out for the city corporation by James Craig in 1766. Here three main broad, parallel streets – Princes, George and Queen Streets – were crossed by three evenly spaced shorter streets to form an oblong grid, creating eight large oblong plots for building. These plots were further divided by two small streets running parallel to the three main streets. At each end of the grid were broad squares – Charlotte Square and St Andrew's Square. Thus a hierarchy of building plots was created. The best, biggest houses were in the squares; the second best in the three long streets, with slightly more modest houses in the three cross streets; and the most modest, artisan dwellings in the two long narrow streets which also gave access to mews behind the main street houses. The extraordinary thing about Edinburgh New Town is not only that this rigid grid was adhered to, but also that the elevations that lined it were markedly uniform. The squares were a little different. In 1791 the city commissioned Robert Adam to produce an elevation for Charlotte Square in a style 'not much ornamented but with elegant simplicity'.[6] The result was one of the most spectacular urban compositions in Britain. Adam indulged his prefer-

The north side of Charlotte Square, Edinburgh, 1791 by Robert Adam. The hierarchical principles of town planning dictated that the squares should contain the grandest houses.

ence for late Palladian austerity, but mixed it with bold, simple, neo-classical motifs. The ground-floor elevation is conceived as a rustic base, and centres and ends of terraces are emphasized with pediments and pavilions. The intention was to site public buildings to terminate the central long axis between the two squares. This happened in Charlotte Square where Adam's church, modified by R. Reid, closes the vista down George Street, but in St Andrews Square the site on axis with George Street was finally acquired by Lord Dundas for his town house (p51), and the church intended for the site found a far less dominating site in George Street (p118).

The other city in which the architectural hierarchy outlined by the 1667 act determined the character of urban development is

Plan of Bath in 1790. The rectilinear layout of the Queen Square area, c1729, is in the centre with, to the north, the picturesque sequence of the Circus and the Royal Crescent.

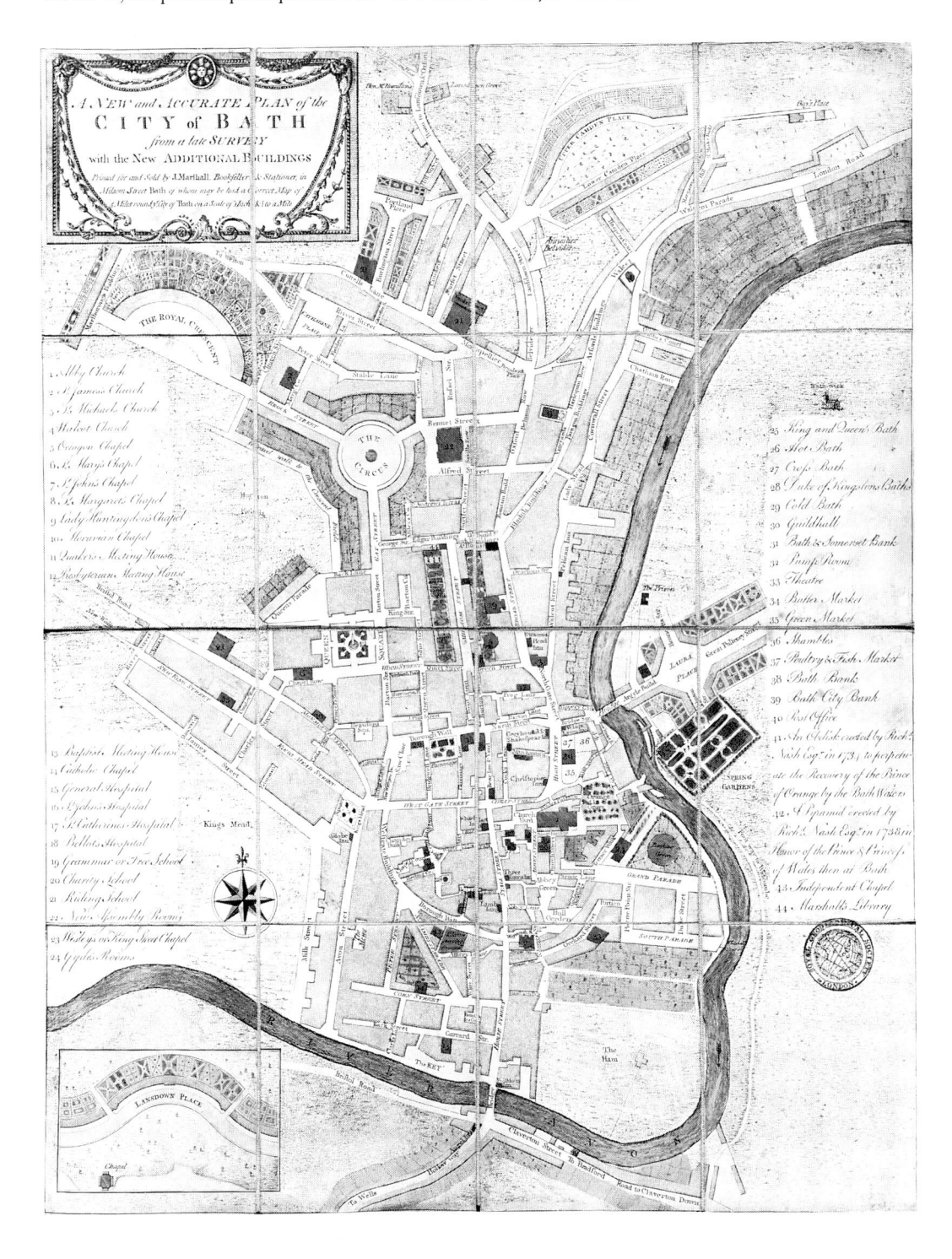

Bath. Unlike Edinburgh New Town, the dominant planning device at Bath was not the right-angular grid but more sinuous, picturesque forms. True, John Wood the Elder had undertaken to build the right-angular Queen Square in the late 1720s, and in so doing realized Colen Campbell's vision for Grosvenor Square, building the north side as a Palladian palace elevation of twenty-three bays, with a five-bay central pediment with columns beneath and three-bay end pavilions embellished with giant pilasters. The square was connected by Gay Street (built 1735-55 under Wood's control) to the Circus (1754-66), designed by Wood in a particularly idiosyncratic and monumental manner. This in turn was connected by the relatively modest Brock Street (1763-7) to the large and splendid Royal Crescent, begun under the younger Wood's control in 1767.

For the influence of buildings acts on façade design and construction we have to look to the act of 1707, which explained itself as 'an act for the better preventing of mischiefs that may happen by fire'. Its main importance was that, with a supplementary act passed in 1709, it dramatically affected the appearance of early Georgian houses, initially in the Cities of London and Westminster (where the acts first applied), and gradually throughout the country. The 1667 act had enforced brick construction and façades on London buildings. The 1707 act barred decorative wooden eaves cornices because of the ease with which fire would spread from house to house along large and exposed wooden cornices. For better protection still, the act suggested that the façade of the house should be continued above the eaves and party wall by at least eighteen inches to form a parapet to protect the roof timbers from sparks.

The 1709 act was almost as dramatic. Since the last decade of the seventeenth century most urban houses in all but the most backward areas of the country (p12) had been lit

Royal Crescent, Bath, designed in 1767 by John Wood the Younger. The centre is emphasized by the subtlest of means . .

by movable window frames which ran in timber boxes; in 1742, for example, John Wood observed in his essay on Bath that sash windows had been introduced into Bath 'a year or two' after 1694 'by one Philip Taylor, a chairman'.[7] This sash system seems to have been developed in the 1670s and replaced with extraordinary speed the traditional system, in which leaded lights hung on hinges from stone or wooden mullions which, in larger windows, were braced with horizontal transoms. But, despite the apparently compulsive charms of the sash window's classically proportioned grid, mullions did linger on in certain areas, such as the Cotswolds, dedicated to archaic vernacular designs.

From the first the sash box, of commodious size to accommodate sturdy frames with stout sashes, was fixed into the window void to be flush with the façades. So much exposed wood was thought to be a fire risk, however, and after 1709 the sash box was commanded to be set back at least four inches into the façade of houses built in the Cities of London and Westminster.

While discussing the influence of legislation on windows and façade design it is essential to mention the window tax, which is now popularly held to be responsible for every blank window on Georgian façades, be they in town or country. Often it was, but not always, for blank windows were also used as a design device to keep the rhythm of a façade going when an opening was not required. The window tax was introduced in 1696, and its scope was gradually extended throughout the eighteenth century, with irksome consequences for the occupants of even humble houses. Houses with seven windows or more, for example, became eligible for taxation in 1766, and in 1784 the tax was extended to houses with only six windows. That occupiers did react by stopping up lights is shown by the fact that, despite the increase of buildings, the number of taxable houses was smaller in 1800 than in 1750.[8]

In the long term the influence of these three London building acts was profound, though sometimes a little uncertain at first; even in the Cities of London and Westminster box sashes continued to be used until the early 1730s, simply because it was the established practice and there seems to have been no effective means of enforcing the act. Towns devastated by fire or undertaking major reconstructions obtained acts closely modelled on the London legislation, in Northampton, for example, in 1675, Warwick in 1694, Blandford Forum, Dorset, in 1731, Tiverton, Devon, in 1731 and Wincanton, Somerset, in 1747. By this means the elevational designs and details that evolved in London passed, gradually and with adaptations, into the vernacular of the provincial builder. In Ireland the principles of classical urban design were spread not through the reconstruction of devastated towns but by the creation of new ones – a form of property investment by landowners not generally undertaken in England since the Middle Ages and paralleled only to a small degree in eighteenth-century Scotland, and even less in Wales. Good examples of these 'planted' towns, which have their origins in the seventeenth century, are Tullamore, Co. Offaly, erected by the Earl of Tullamore, which has a long, wide central square lined with plain two-storey houses; Mitchelstown, Co. Cork, where the magnificent Kingston College (p162) takes the form of a large urban square; Portarlington, Co. Laois, which, although laid out in 1667 for the Earl of Galway to house Huguenot refugees, was largely built up in the eighteenth century; and Westport, Co. Mayo, laid out in 1780 for the Marquess of Sligo and composed around a canalized river, an octagonal square and the Marquess's own Westport House.

Eighteenth-century Scottish planned towns included Inveraray, Strathclyde, begun c1743 for the Duke of Argyll, for which plain three-storey tenements were designed first by Robert Mylne (1774-6) and by John Adam (c1780); Charlestown, Fife, founded by the Earl of Elgin in 1770, taking the plan of the letter E, and Eaglesham, Strathclyde (1765), created by the Earl of Renfrew as a cotton-spinning community, taking the plan of the letter A; Fochabers, Grampian, which was planted beside Gordon Castle and laid out by John Baxter in 1775-90; and Ardrossan, Strathclyde, which Peter Nicholson laid out for the Earl of Eglinton in 1806. A Welsh example, halfway between planted town and model village, is Tremadog, Gwynedd, which was founded by W. Madock in 1805 as a model coaching town, with market hall, square and church.

The final eighteenth-century London Building Act – drafted by Sir Robert Taylor and George Dance the Younger and passed in 1774 – had none of the ambiguity that characterized the earlier acts. Indeed, its purpose was to consolidate, enforce and strengthen the provisions for sound construction enshrined in the previous acts, and apart from anything else it was very explicit about non-

Plan, sections and elevation of a 1774 Building Act 'Third rate house' from Peter Nicholson's *The New and Improved Practical Builder* of 1823.

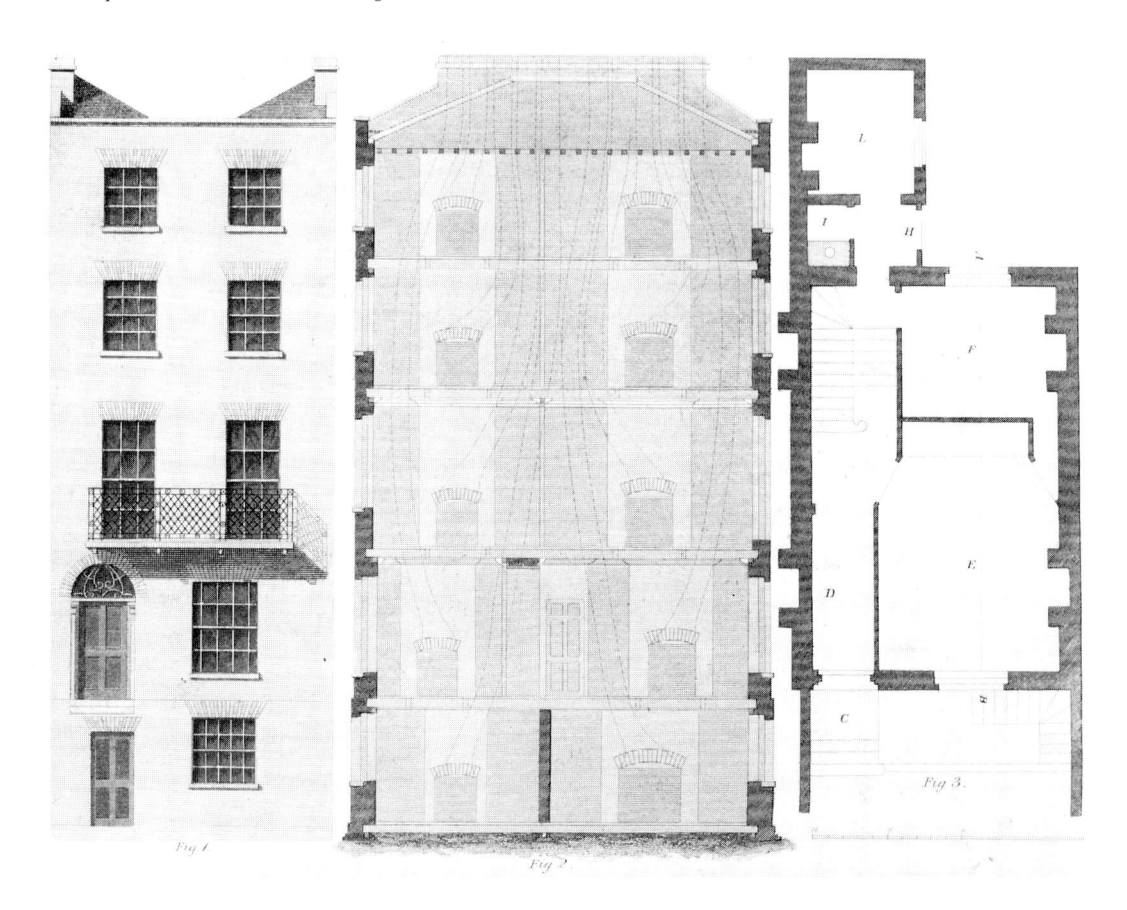

compliance. Work not executed in accordance with the act could be demolished or amended, and the workmen were liable to a fine of fifty shillings and to be 'committed to the house of correction'. This act's main effects on building design were that it took fire prevention a step further and banned all wooden decoration from façades (sash boxes were now not only to be set back four inches but also concealed behind the brick window jambs), and that it divided buildings into seven different classes or rates according to their volume, expense of construction, use and location. The influence of this piece of legislation was immense. It virtually dictated the form that late Georgian domestic building should take, first in London and then in other cities, for it provided, and indeed enforced, a set of standard models. Of the seven rates the fifth and sixth referred to buildings in isolated positions, and the seventh dealt with such special structures as windmills and crane houses. All three of these categories were permitted a fair freedom of design and construction under the act. It was rates one to four that were strictly controlled.

For example, large dwelling houses worth at least £850 and exceeding nine 'squares of building' (a 'square' was 100 square feet) had to comply with the constructional standards imposed on first-rate buildings. These, as with the following three rates, insisted on certain wall thicknesses for façades and party walls related to their height, and controlled the use of materials and means of construction. At the other end of the scale, houses of only one storey above ground and worth not more than £150 had to comply with the scale of standards for fourth-rate buildings. As well as providing models for house builders – and many late Georgian pattern books and builders' manuals, such as Peter Nicholson's *Practical Builder* (1823), published house designs based on the rating specifications – the act, albeit unintentionally, set speculators a minimum standard to which to work.

Standardization was further helped by the products of the Industrial Revolution, which were beginning to appear in the early 1770s. Coade of Lambeth, founded in 1769 to produce terracotta items that looked like Portland stone but weathered better, manufactured mouldings and neo-classical details right into the 1830s. Of a standard to please the most scrupulous of designers, these details also had the advantage of identical repetition, which in the late eighteenth century was seen as the great advantage (not the disadvantage it has now become) of mass-production.

Coade cornered the market in artificial stone, while Carron iron works in Falkirk and the Coalbrookdale company, Ironbridge, supplied vast amounts of decorative external ironwork. The products of these companies are found all over England and Ireland. The doors of Bedford Square, London (1776–86), are all embellished with Coade rustic blocks and river god keystones, as are the doors of terraces in Southernhay, Exeter, and of a house of *c*1800 in the Great North Road, Hatfield. The ground-floor windows of the houses in the Crescent, Shrewsbury (*c*1790), are embellished with semicircular Coade bat's wing decoration, as is 34 Colebrook Street, Winchester (*c*1790); and Belmont, Pound Street, Lyme Regis, Dorset, has a main façade (1785) loaded with Coade details, including an enriched string course, quoins, window surrounds, keystones and impost blocks, some moulded with masks and dolphins. If the house looks like an advertisement for Coade that is exactly what it was, for Eleanor Coade lived there after 1784.

Terrace design

There are two types of terrace house: those which reflect the seventeenth-century Palladian ideal first realized in Covent Garden, and which form part of a uniform street composition, and those which were conceived and built as individual units within a street. Those town houses which are both architecturally self-contained and physically free-standing are dealt with elsewhere (p36), while those that are built within a terrace, without being part of it either physically or visually, are examined here to discover what sort of architectural language was used, how it changed with fashion, and how it related to the design of country houses.

Of the two types of terrace composition – the one made up of houses of individual design and size and the other conceived as a uniform design – it was, of course, the uniform terrace that was striven for during the eighteenth century. On balance, it represents the Georgian period's most important contribution to the development of urban design. I say on balance because the eighteenth-century ideal of imposing uniformity on diversity – an ideal represented by John Gwynn in 1766 when he wrote, 'it is essential for the architectural effect to receive a similar appearance of all buildings belonging to the same scheme'[9] – was already being challenged in the very early years of the nineteenth century by the picturesque notion of diversity in uniformity. Sir John Soane, in his Royal Academy lectures given between 1809 and 1836, said of eighteenth-century uniform urban design, 'by this very regularity we have exchanged the grand effects of architecture for disgusting insipidity and tiresome monotony'. He even went so far as to observe that 'the old town of Edinburgh by the variety and breaks in the outline of its buildings is more beautiful, and possibly not less convenient, than the New Town, with all its polish'. Significantly, when building much of the early nineteenth-century second New Town at Edinburgh – for example Royal Circus, Circus Gardens, and Circus Place (1821-3) – W.H. Playfair explained that he paid 'the strictest attention to the nature of the ground, and none whatever to the neatness of the plan, as it appears on paper';[10] a criticism, of course, of the earlier right-angular, grid-obsessed town planning of the Craig variety.

This thinking found physical expression in some of the urban works of John Nash, such as the asymmetrical and picturesquely grouped Italianate and neo-Tudor villas and cottages of Park Village, Regent's Park (1824-8), and Decimus Burton's equally suburban, picturesquely sited and Italianate Calverley Park estate, Tunbridge Wells (1828). But generally even the most picturesque of early nineteenth-century designers, including Nash himself, tended towards the ideal of the palace front when undertaking major urban designs, as is shown by Nash's Regent's Park compositions, York Terrace (1822) and Cumberland Terrace (1826, designed with James Thomson), the last word in grandiose palace-fronted terrace design. Impressive provincial evidence of the abiding fascination among early nineteenth-century speculative builders for the uniform palace-fronted terrace can be seen in Carlton Place, Glasgow (1802), by Peter Nicholson, and Brunswick Terrace, Hove (1825-7), by Charles Busby.

The uniform terrace
Uniform terrace composition falls into two categories. There are those uniform terraces composed with emphasis – usually a centrally placed pediment and end pavilions – to create a true palace front, such as Simmons' modest success at Grosvenor Square (1725) and John Wood's triumph at Queen Square, Bath (1729). Then there are those uniform terraces that are merely regimented façades without emphasis. This is the sort of elevational design, combined with vigorous gridiron planning, that in 1766 provoked John Gwynn to comment on the 'new building' in Marylebone as giving 'no better idea to the spectator than that of a plain brick wall of prodigious length'.[11]

To discover the British origins of both these types of uniform terrace we need only look at the designs of Inigo Jones. His Covent Garden piazza terraces (1631), though lacking central or terminal emphasis in the form of pediments or pavilions, were dressed with pilasters and a cornice, and had a rusticated arcaded base that gave the blocks a palatial grandeur. This was soon followed in London by similarly pilastered houses in Great Queen Street, Covent Garden, and Lincoln's Inn Fields, Holborn (c1640), and, in a far more rustic form, in Newington Green, Hackney (c1650), of which one group survives. A few years after Covent Garden, in c1638, Jones designed a block of buildings for Lord Maltravers, to be built in Lothbury, in the City of London, which was the first example of a classical uniform astylar urban terrace.

The astylar terrace
The Lothbury astylar appearance was the first to be imitated in the eighteenth century. A curious and early example of a semi-uniform terrace survives in Albury Street, Deptford: built between 1706 and 1717, it contains two-storey terrace houses constructed behind a façade designed by master builder Thomas Lucas (who had worked in the nearby St Paul's Church, designed by Thomas Archer and begun in 1713). The width of the individual houses ranges from two and a half bays to four, but the variety is accommodated within the elevation design, which is articulated with recessed vertical

31-32 Old Burlington Street, Mayfair, London, 1718-23: the first example of eighteenth-century Inigo Jones-inspired uniform astylar terrace design. The third floor is a later addition.

window bays set between full-height pilaster strips. The 'pilasters' have no capitals, and the regular rhythm of the bays disguises the fact that the houses, and even some of the windows, are of different widths.

The first major eighteenth-century example of the uniform astylar terrace was Colen Campbell's 31-34 Old Burlington Street, Westminster, London, built between 1718 and 1723. Based on Jones's Lothbury designs, the elevation was austere and proportioned according to the Palladian canon: in the London street scene of the day, it must have appeared almost as revolutionary as Jones's design had been eighty years earlier.

The façades of these houses are of a consistent cool colour – yellow/brown brick – with recessed window sashes and straight window arches (in contrast to segment-headed windows, popularized by Wren and inspired by the Louvre, Paris, which were common in London from 1720 to 1730), and have reticent stone doorcases, moulded stone surrounds to first- and second-floor windows, a stone string course at first-floor level and a stone block cornice at parapet level. It must be remembered that between the arrival of Jones's Palladian street architecture and Campbell's revival there had been the baroque dominance of Wren, Hawksmoor and Vanbrugh, and the common London terrace of the 1720s still displayed many of the characteristics of the domestic classicism of Wren: red dressings to windows and segmental red-brick arches, red-brick moulded string courses, and façades generally of brown/purple bricks. Box sashes were flush and doorcases, even by the late 1720s, still demonstrated the skill of individualistic and baroque-influenced carvers and joiners.

The proportions of Campbell's façade were as controlled as its detailing. The ideal town house, such as those Campbell designed for Grosvenor Square in 1725, was embellished with the full regalia of the Roman temple front: entablature, columns or pilasters, and a rusticated ground floor basement. At Old Burlington Street Campbell had stripped this away, but proportioned the façades, particularly the vertical spacing of the window openings, as if they were embellished with a correctly proportioned invisible order. To reinforce this impression he embedded reminders of the theoretical temple front on crucial parts of the façade; a cornice marks the top of the temple entablature, while a deep string course marks the base of the columns and the start of basement level. The windows were also proportioned to reinforce the hierarchy of the temple. In the baroque-inspired town houses of the day the main rooms, as in contemporary baroque country houses (p54), could be on the ground floor – though because of the noise and dirt in town they were often on the first floor. Campbell abolished this choice. As with Palladian country houses, the ground floor was to be treated as the basement of a temple and given squarer windows and lower floor height (and, later in the century, embellished with rustication, even on astylar terraces); the first floor was to be the true *piano nobile* containing the main entertaining rooms, as in Palladian country houses (p54), and had the highest ceilings, tallest windows and richest decorations; and the floors above diminished, perhaps ending in square attic windows, as Campbell proposed in an astylar design for Grosvenor Square. The continuation of an elevation above the cornice line was unthinkable for a pure Palladian of Campbell's stamp. Not only did it spoil the classical temple look of the house but it was also a characteristic device of the ousted baroque school of designers, who gave their town houses extra accommodation, and verticality, by the use of attic storeys (for example, 9 Lendal, York c1718; Couper House, c1734, at Blandford Forum, Dorset, and 68 The Close, Salisbury, c1718).

Campbell's elevational treatment – though initially imitated only by fellow Burlingtonian Palladians, such as Roger Morris at 61 Green Street, Westminster (1730), and Henry Flitcroft at 36 Sackville Street, Westminster (1732), and 9 and 10 St James's Square, Westminster (1735-6), and copied in a slightly misunderstood fashion by speculative builders on the edge of the Palladian camp such as Edward Shepherd at 4 St James's Square (1726) – after 1740 became the standard form for advanced astylar urban terraces in London and leading provincial towns. Examples are Southampton Place, Bloomsbury, London (perhaps designed under the supervision of Flitcroft, c1745), and Grand Parade, Bath (1740), by John Wood the Elder, which had the additional Palladian touch of pedimented first-floor windows with architraves to the windows above, a design slightly modified but still acceptable nearly thirty years later, in 1768-71, when T.W. Atwood built the long, curving Paragon in Bath.

In the majority of the provincial towns, however, the Palladian influence on terrace design was not so marked on the composition of the elevation as it was on the details. 12-16 Market Place, Yarm, Cleveland (c1760), is a regular brick terrace, but it still displays the segmental windows popular with London builders in the 1720s and an eaves cornice with no parapet above, and 55-63 North Bar, Beverley, Humberside, is another mid-eighteenth-century uniform terrace in which the only Palladian influences are the simple regular pedimented doors and square attic windows.

By the last decades of the eighteenth century, however, the austere astylar uniform terrace, pioneered by Jones and revived by Campbell, had entered thoroughly into builders' vernacular, as can be seen at Abbey Square, Chester (completed 1780); Parliament Street, Kingston-upon-Hull, Humberside (1796-1800); Lemon Street, Truro, Cornwall (begun in 1794), and, most dramatically, the post-1800 development of the Bedford estate, Bloomsbury, London, which was undertaken mainly by James Burton. Here entire streets, such as Bedford Place and Montague Street (both c1800-1), have extremely austere brick façades with equally spaced windows, stucco ground floors and third-floor cill courses to imply a cornice level. Despite this repetition and austerity, however, the bold and generous proportions of the façades – which have a well emphasized *piano nobile* – save these houses from any feeling of meannesss.

Although this sort of severity was becoming the rule for astylar terrace design there are exceptions to the general pattern, and it is the exceptions that make the study of eighteenth-century architecture so rewarding. 124-136 High Street, Boston, Lincolnshire, is a truly remarkable composition. Its appearance defies dating on stylistic grounds. It is probably mid-eighteenth-century, but could be much earlier. The doors are round-headed (a detail generally fashionable in the late eighteenth century), the windows are segmental with keystones (a design fashionable in the 1720s-30s) and the elevation is articulated with thin pilaster strips breaking forward and dividing the façade into vertical bays containing flush box sashes (as in Albury Street, Deptford, of c1706-17). Interestingly the façade has no parapet, the pilaster strips are linked by shallow arches, and the second floor windows are no taller than the first floor. This group represents a form of sophisticated, stripped-down classicism worthy of some of the works of Vanbrugh and the aspirations of neo-classical designers such as Sir John Soane and reflected in early nineteenth-century compositions like Downing Terrace, Lensfield Road, Cambridge (c1815), and the stuccoed terrace (1824) in Cowley Road, Camberwell, London, attributed to J. M. Gandy.

The palace-fronted terrace

The development of the palace-fronted terrace – with central feature and end pavilions – did not make its first eighteenth-century appearance in Simmons' design for Grosvenor Square. Five years earlier, in 1720, John Price had produced a design for a site at Headley, near Epsom, Surrey, which envisaged a central porticoed building flanked by two identical ranges of nine houses. The scheme, never completed, was demolished in the nineteenth century. It was in Bath where the palace front was first realized – by John Wood in 1729 – and it was also in Bath that this particular urban composition was to be developed during the eighteenth century. John Wood the Elder's Circus, begun in 1754, is a rather unconventional member of the family, having no central emphasis as such but instead an elevation (inspired by the exterior of the Colosseum in Rome) with three tiers of attached columns, each with its own appropriate entablature. But the Royal Crescent, Bath, begun in 1767 by Wood the Younger, is a supreme example of the palace front. Its front is embellished with 114 giant Ionic columns rising from

North side of Queen Square, Bath, built 1729 to the designs of John Wood the Elder: the first fully-fledged eighteenth-century palace-fronted Palladian domestic terrace with pedimented centre and emphasized ends. The drawing is from Wood's 1765 edition of his *Essay towards a description of Bath*.

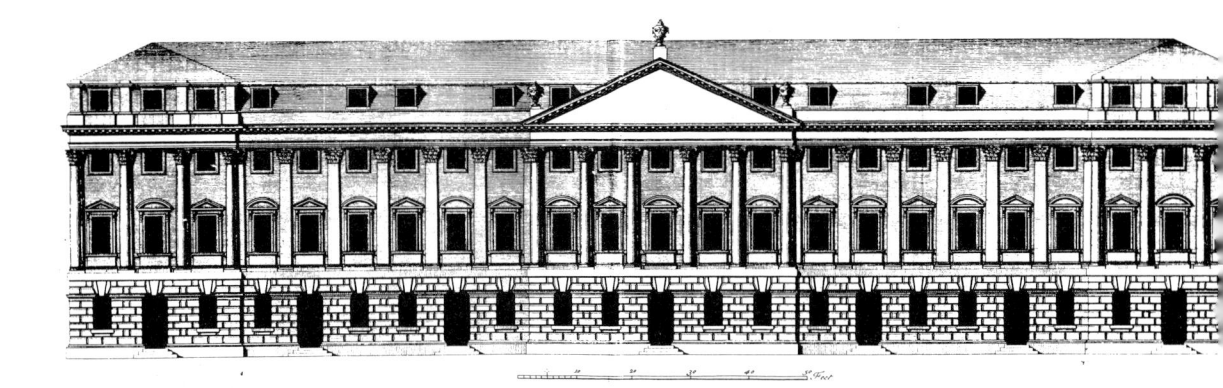

first-floor level, with central emphasis created by simply doubling up the columns each side of the centre bay (in which the first-floor window is round-headed). This subtlety was not appreciated by at least one contemporary observer, who complained in *The Stranger's Assistant and Guide to Bath* for 1773 that 'the wretched attempt to make a centre to the Crescent where none is necessary is absurd and preposterous, in a high degree'.

Thomas Baldwin's Somersetshire Buildings, Milsom Street, Bath (1781-3), is a seventeen-bay composition of three storeys, with three-bay Corinthian pediments acting as unconventional terminal features, and a three-bay and three-storey curved bow in the centre which is dressed with engaged Corinthian columns. The ground floor is treated as a rusticated arcade. This theme was carried out in reverse by John Palmer at Lansdown Crescent (1789-93), where the four-bay central pediment, supported on Ionic pilasters rising from a rusticated ground floor, is balanced by a pair of terminal bow-fronted houses, and by Thomas Baldwin in Great Pulteney Street (begun in 1789), where long terraces have terminal, intermediate and central pedimented and pilastered features.

Such monumental architecture, outside Bath and Edinburgh, was largely beyond the pockets or ambitions of most developers. Those which were built were usually on the initiative of rich aristocratic landlords, such as the pilaster-clad Crescent at Buxton, Derbyshire, designed by John Carr and begun in 1780 for the Duke of Devonshire.

The more humble developers did, nevertheless, find ways of achieving some monumentality of design with the most modest of means. Sometimes this merely took the form of placing a pediment in the centre of a standard terrace, as at 233-291 Kennington Road, London (c1788), 51-75 Rodney Street, Liverpool (c1790), and 32-37 Castle Square, Caernarvon (c1800). More inventive was the approach of architect/builder Michael Searles who in 1795 designed Surrey Square, Southwark, of which a long brick terrace with centrally placed five-bay pediment survives. He broke up the long elevations flanking the pedimented centre into separate compositions by the simple means of giving appropriate houses arcaded, as opposed to square, ground-floor doors and windows.

Searles' subtle use of rhythm and alternating features can best be seen at Gloucester Circus, Greenwich (1790), composed of semi-detached houses, some pedimented and linked by lower entrance blocks, and the Paragon, Blackheath (1793, p265), a crescent of large semi-detached houses linked by colonnades. This means of articulating a uniform terrace by breaking it down into linked pavilions, rather than using columns or pilasters, became a characteristic early nineteenth-century device – and was no doubt partly a reflection of the picturesque ideal described by Soane (p29). A good example is Lansdown Place, Cheltenham (1825-9), by J.B. Papworth, where pairs of tall houses are linked by lower, slightly set-back entrance blocks.

More significant than notions of the picturesque in the early nineteenth century was the arrival of the vogue for Greek as opposed to Roman classicism (p15). This deference to Greek fashions usually took the form of simply substituting Greek details for Roman, as in Nash and Thomson's Cumberland

A late eighteenth-century design drawing by Michael Searles (c1790) showing alternative compositions for a section of Gloucester Circus, Greenwich. The recessed link buildings are on flaps of paper that can be folded back to create varied compositional effects.

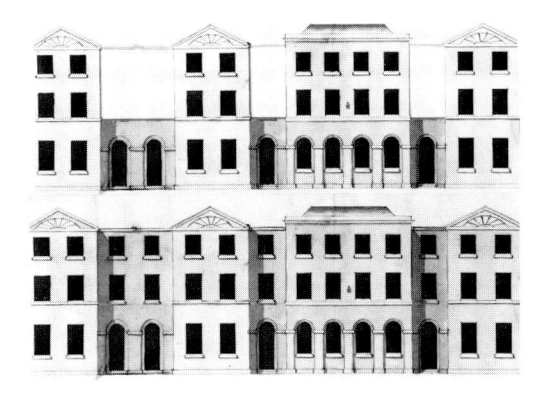

Gloucester Circus, c1790-1807, now with later nineteenth-century alterations.

Terrace, Regent's Park (1826-7). In Edinburgh, however, there were some more thorough-going attempts at Greek revival terrace compositions, as at St Bernard's Crescent by James Milne (1824, p206), where the centre is emphasized by massive two-storey Greek Doric columns rising from the ground and supporting a deep entablature. But, as was typical of the period, elsewhere in the development of the second New Town this Greek revival design was accompanied by late Palladian Adamesque compositions such as J.G. Graham's Moray Place (1822-30). The centre blocks of this faceted circus are emphasized by Roman Tuscan columns supporting a pediment and rising, in the Palladian manner, from a rusticated arcaded ground floor.

The palace-fronted street
The change of scale of urban development after about 1800, when it became common for a single speculator to be responsible for the development of whole streets or entire quarters, meant that the palace-front principle was extended from the design of terraces, circuses, crescents or squares, and applied to the design of continuous and often curvaceous streets. Palace-fronted street architecture was not new in the early nineteenth century; it had been carried out in Bath (at Somersetshire Buildings, Milsom Street 1781-3, and Great Pulteney Street, 1789 onwards, both by Thomas Baldwin) and in London (by the Adam brothers at Portland Place from 1776), but it was Nash, with his Regent Street development of 1811-30, who was to develop and establish the idea. Here he organized things so that three and a half miles of largely individual buildings – between Park Crescent in the north, with its pedimented end bays (1812), and the magnificent palace-fronted Carlton House Terrace (1827-33) to the south – were given monumental and architecturally emphasized elevations, usually related to the street block.

The influence of Regent Street was immense and immediate. In Brighton, Charles Busby laid out Kemp Town which, with its mix of house types and flamboyant architecture, owed much to Nash. At its core is a series of interrelated compositions fanning out from Sussex Square (the only part not stuccoed), which is dressed with pilasters and terminates in a pair of monumental terraces facing the sea. The connecting element, Lewes Crescent, is a particularly interesting example of how to apply the grand urban manner to a potentially unpromising location. As it was a crescent in plan and located on a slight hill, it would have been extremely unsatisfactory visually to embellish the entire façade with pilasters: because of the fall of the land, this would have resulted in the palace front going up the hill in fits and starts. Equally, it was unthinkable for such a key element in a development of Kemp Town's pretensions to be astylar. What Busby did was to construct the houses in units of three, with slightly different floor levels in every group to accommodate the changing ground level, and then to emphasize every third house by breaking forward its façade and dressing it with giant pilasters. Monumentality is achieved and an awkward problem solved.

In 1828 James Burton, who had been involved with the construction of several of Nash's Regent's Park terraces and who had developed part of Regent Street under Nash's control, transported some of this metropolitan splendour to Hastings, where he developed the resort of St Leonard's-on-Sea. But the most splendid provincial reflection of Regent Street is John Dobson's work for Richard Grainger in Newcastle upon Tyne. Here, between 1825 and 1840, they redesigned the city centre in the manner of Nash, creating, initially, the wonderfully austere ashlar-faced Eldon Square in 1825 (only one side survives) followed by Leazes Terrace in 1829 (built by Thomas Oliver and incorporating smaller houses behind in the manner of Nash's Regent's Park) and culminating in Grey Street (1835-40), in which the individual and monumental blocks (which also descend a hill, and, like Lewes Crescent, are cunningly stepped) are composed with central emphasis and terminating features.

Uniform groups
As well as being conceived as part of a large urban unit – whether a long plain terrace as in Bloomsbury or a palace-fronted composition – the terrace house was also built in small uniform groups in which symmetry was achieved by subtle means appropriate to the modest size of the composition. 16-22 Upper Brook Street, Oswestry, Shropshire, is a group of four houses of c1790, with an extremely sophisticated elevation. Adjoining houses have mirror plans and are entered through a shared pedimented doorcase. Each group of four houses of c1790 with an extremely sophisticated elevation. Adjoining floors are tripartite, and the second floor has square windows. Between these paired houses is a single bay with an arched door leading to the rear. A gesture towards contemporary fashion is made by the ground- and first-floor windows, which are all set beneath blank arches, in the manner of Wyatt, containing a bat's wing decorative panel probably made of Coade stone. (A similar decorative – and

A provincial baroque house in the Market Place, Blandford Forum, Dorset of c1734 by John Bastard.

3-5 Downham Road, Ely: an interesting provincial example of two houses as one composition.

visually unifying – motif is used in the Crescent, Town Walls, Shrewsbury, c1790.) The pediment – that symbol of unified terrace design – was particularly popular for centralizing slightly larger urban groups. In the Market Place, Blandford Forum, Dorset, a small group (c1734) by John Bastard is given focus by the use of a central one-bay open pediment supported on a pair of curiously detailed pilasters. A group of three houses on the west side of Queen Square, Bath, designed by John Wood the Elder in c1730, unites to form a seven-bay Palladian country house composition with a three-bay pediment. This same illusion was practised in 1746 in the design of Caius House, Middleton Street, Wymondham, Norfolk – only this time in the language of baroque classicism. This seven-bay building with a three-bay pediment is embellished at the corners of the building and below the ends of the pediment with four giant Doric pilasters, rising from ground level to the eaves and placed without regard to correct intercolumniation. Most characteristically the small urban composition was achieved by the grouping of just two houses – a unit size which made sense to modest speculators because two houses could be constructed more economically than one.

These attempts at miniature monumentality reveal the fertile imagination of the speculative builder, for many ingenious solutions were found to the problem of unifying pairs of terrace houses. The most common device was the simplest: paired door surrounds, as in Oswestry and Cork, where this became something of a local speciality. 5-7 Queen Street, Lancaster (c1750), a pair of plain three-storey houses, share a large swan-necked pediment; 23-24 Lawrence Street, Chelsea (c1720), share a triangular pedimented surround, as do 127-129 Long Westgate, Scarborough (c1760), and 23-24 High Street, Kingston upon Hull, Humberside (1751). Other, more individual, examples of paired compositions are 66-67 High Street St Martin's, Stamford, Lincolnshire (c1735), where a simple unity of composition is achieved by giving all the ground-floor windows matching Gibbs surrounds; and 3-5 Downham Road, Ely, Cambridgeshire: a remarkable two-storey pair, probably dating from before 1750, and united by the use of Venetian windows and round blank windows.

119-120 St Stephen's Green, Dublin (c1740-50), is two houses united by the familiar Richard Castle country house motif of a blank-centred Venetian window (p59). Here, at first-floor level, a large round-headed blank window placed over the party wall is linked by a cornice to the adjoining window of each house to form a tripartite composition; above it, at second-floor level, is a round niche. (A similar device decorates houses in St John's Square, Limerick, c1751, perhaps by Francis Bindon.)

The pediment was also used even in these diminutive groups. A pair of houses of c1750 in South Brink, Wisbech, Cambridgeshire, are linked by a four-bay pediment; 59-60 West Stockwell Street, Colchester, Essex (c1750), share a three-bay pediment which contains the pedimented front doors to both houses, separated by a Venetian window; a pair of houses in the High Street, Halstead, Essex (c1770), share a pediment containing a massive tracery-filled second-floor fanlight, with a Venetian window lighting the first floor and a pair of off-centre porticoed doors below; and in Nelson Street, Stroud, Gloucestershire, a two-storey ashlar-faced pair of

59-60 West Stockwell Street, Colchester, Essex, c1750. Two terrace houses united within a striking pedimented composition.

houses (c1815) have adjoining front doors set below a round blank arch. The whole is crowned with a pediment at eaves level which embraces the flanking first-floor windows as well as the doors.

The single terrace house
The last major type of terrace house is that which contradicts the economic logic and visual benefits of building in groups, and is part of a terrace as if by accident. This apparently reluctant participant in the urban scene makes a fascinating study. On one level such houses can be modest affairs merely following the current architectural fashions, but there are also those terrace houses which make obsessive use of the whole gamut of compositional devices – single-bay pediments, paired columns, one-bay frontispieces, Gibbs surrounds, Venetian windows and curved or faceted bays – to proclaim their individuality.

Some houses make an effect by the lavishness of their stonework, like 3 South Bailey, Durham (c1730), and others by the rich decorative quality of their brickwork, such as the Museum, West Street, Farnham, Surrey (dated 1718), 211 High Street, Lewes, East Sussex (c1720), and Sherman's House, High Street, Dedham, Essex (c1730).

Then there are those early eighteenth-century houses that have recourse to baroque design devices: the most common of these – which entered the builder's vernacular to create a curious sub-style in the West Country – is the embellishing of the façade with columns or pilasters arranged to emphasize the centre windows and door. Hawksmoor used a variation of this device at Easton Neston, Northamptonshire (1702), when he framed the centre windows of each main façade with a pair of giant columns; a device used on a more modest scale on Vanbrugh House at 20 St Michael's Street, Oxford, of c1720, on houses of c1728 at 70 Prince Street and 12 St James's Barton, Bristol, on a pair of houses in the Market Place, Blandford Forum, Dorset (c1734), and on 11-12 and 13-14 High Ousegate, York, which look c1710 but are dated on (probably later) hopper heads 1758 and 1763 respectively. Tiers of columns of different orders were also used to emphasize the centre bay, a compositional device taken to extremes by English West Country baroque designers: Druce's Hill House, Church Street, Bradford-on-Avon, Wiltshire (c1720), has a three-storey frontispiece composed of tiers of columns of different orders flanking the centre windows, as does the side elevation of Westbury House, Bradford-on-Avon (1720). Other examples are 5 Trim Street, Bath (c1725), the Midland Bank, Fore Street, Trowbridge, Wiltshire (c1730), which has a first floor window flanked by Corinthian columns set above a door embellished with Tuscan columns, and Portway House, Portway, Warminster, Wiltshire (c1740), which has tiers of pilasters each side of the centre bay.

These exotic baroque compositions are the exception, however. Individuality was more usually asserted through such devices as the Gibbs surround to windows or doors, a motif which proclaimed solidarity with the London-based fashion of Gibbs (p109) and reveals the dependence of most speculators on pattern books for ideas (p13). 35 High Street St Martin's, Stamford, Lincolnshire – a town dedicated to the Gibbs surround – is a five-bay two-storey house (c1735) which is given presence by having every aperture embellished with Gibbs block architraves.

Another architectural device beloved by the builder seeking to give his house some extra grandeur was the giant pilaster, usually Doric or Tuscan, a motif used by Serlio[12] which became a seventeenth-century English building tradition, for example Dulwich College, London (1613), and Peacock's School, Rye, East Sussex (1636). The baroque builder would use this merely as a decoration, usually at the end of the main elevation or to emphasize any break in the plane of the main façade: for example, Abbotsford House in the Market Place, Warwick (1714, probably by Francis Smith), St Edward's House (c1720) in the Market Place, Stow-on-the-Wold, Gloucestershire, and 4-6 Fournier Street, Spitalfields, London (1726, by the speculating builder Marmaduke Smith for himself). A rare example of the use of carved brick

Ionic capitals survives at 14-15 Tooks Court, City of London (c1725).

The more academically-minded baroque architects, such as the designers of what is now the Wesleyan Chapel, High Street, Burford, Oxfordshire (c1720), of General Wade's House, Abbey Churchyard, Bath (c1720), and of 21 High Street, Stamford, Lincolnshire (1732), realized that there was more to classical pilasters than mere decoration. In these buildings a screen of pilasters (rising from ground level at Burford and first-floor level at Bath and Stamford) is placed to create a miniature palace front reminiscent of Inigo Jones's larger-scale designs at Covent Garden. It was, of course, this Jonesian device that was picked up by Palladian designers of palace-fronted terrace houses. Giacomo Leoni's Queensberry House, Burlington Gardens, Westminster, London (1721-3), dressed with giant Corinthian pilasters, was inspired by Webb's Jonesian Queen's Gallery at Somerset House (p8), and 57-58 Lincoln's Inn Fields, Holborn, London (designed by Henry Joynes in c1730), was based on the adjoining palace-fronted Lindsey House (1640-45) which, though probably designed by Nicholas Stone or Peter Mills, was thought in the eighteenth century to have been the work of Inigo Jones. But in the design of individual terrace houses as well as in the composition of large-scale uniform terraces, the Palladian designer tended to drop the use of applied orders in favour of the more subtle approach of merely implying the presence of an architectural hierarchy.

A Palladio-designed precedent for the pedimented town house from the 1738 edition of his *Quattro Libri*.

41 Friar Gate, Derby, 1768, probably by Joseph Pickford: Palladian and neo-classical details (the doorcase) set in a complex layered façade reminiscent of the early eighteenth-century baroque school.

The most common method used to draw attention to an astylar Palladian terrace house was the crowning pediment, a composition that had the excellent pedigree of being included amongst the designs for town houses in Palladio's *Quattro Libri*. In large houses they could be three bays wide or occasionally five, as in 20 St Andrewgate, York (c1780), by T. Atkinson, and in smaller houses only one, as at 28 West Street, Farnham (c1718), and 60 North Hill, Colchester (c1760). Good examples of three-bay-pedimented terrace houses are a house now called the Granville Club in Belmont, Shrewsbury (c1740); 88-90 Micklegate, York (1753), by John Carr; 52-54 Micklegate, York (1757), which has the unusual embellishment for an astylar façade of a full Doric entablature; Haggersgate House, Whitby, North Yorkshire (c1760); 20 High Street, Boston, Lincolnshire (c1760); Fairfax House, York (completed by Carr in 1762); the Museum, Park Street, Cirencester, Gloucestershire (1765-70); 41 Friar Gate, Derby (1768), by Joseph Pickford for himself – an extraordinarily complex composition with a layered façade and a giant three-storey arch beneath the pediment framing the centre bay of the house; 42 Miller Street, Glasgow (c1775), by John Craig and 40 Holywell Hill, St Albans, Hertfordshire (1783), which was possibly designed by Sir Robert Taylor. Three-bay-pedimented houses were occasionally built in groups to create a most striking terrace: fragments of this arrangement survive in Duke Street, Liverpool (c1765), and one five-bay two-storey house with a three-bay pediment survives of the Adam brothers' late eighteenth-century development of Charlotte Street, Glasgow.

Even with no crowning pediment an

astylar terrace house could still be given individuality and central emphasis by the embellishment of the centre bay. This could take the form of loading the centre window with architraves or a pediment, as at Argyll House, King's Road, London, by Giacomo Leoni (c1723) and 18 St James Street, Monmouth (c1780), or of making the centre window a different shape: a round-arched first-floor window set amongst flat-arched windows was a favourite Palladian device, as at 9 Henrietta Street, Dublin, designed in 1729 by Pearce (a copy of Lord Burlington's 30 Old Burlington Street, Mayfair, of 1721), and 110 High Street, Huntingdon (1727).

Last, and perhaps most engaging, are the terrace houses with centre bays given up to the display of a variety of flamboyant window forms. The house designed by the Bastard brothers for Sir Peter Thompson in Market Street, Poole, Dorset, has a stucco centre containing the conventional Palladian hierarchy of first-floor Venetian window, with a Diocletian window above it at second-floor level. Variations on this theme are the Mansion, Church Street, Ashbourne, Derbyshire (1764), and East Hill House, High Street, Tenterden, Kent (c1780), the latter with a round, not a Diocletian, window on the second floor. An early example is the garden front of Peckover House, Wisbech, Cambridgeshire (1727). A house in Standard Road, Wells-next-the-sea, Norfolk, has a large first-floor central Venetian window rising into the second floor; and a two-storey house (c1750-60) in Portarlington, Co. Laois, has a grand tripartite pedimented door topped by a massive Diocletian window in the manner of Newberry Hall, Co. Kildare, and Colganstown, Co. Dublin (p75).

A completely different solution to the problem of giving a single house individuality was to abandon altogether the idea of central emphasis – really rather a baroque concern – and to go for the all-over exquisite Palladian uniform (worn by many a country house) in which the various horizontal levels received the treatment appropriate to their function: ground floor rusticated, first-floor *piano nobile* emphasized with pedimented window surrounds, top floor treated as an attic with square windows. Such houses can be seen at 15 St George's Street, Westminster, London (c1720); the Museum, King Street, King's Lynn, Norfolk (c1730-40); 45 Berkeley Square, Westminster, London (c1745), probably by Isaac Ware; 85 St Stephen's Green, Dublin (c1745), by Richard Castle; and 26 St Andrew's Square, Edinburgh (c1770), probably by Sir William Chambers, where neo-classical detail replaced Palladian.

A particularly interesting example is 61 Green Street, Mayfair, designed in 1730 by the arch-Palladian Roger Morris for himself. It is a large composition consisting of a centre block of three widely spaced bays flanked by two slightly recessed two-bay, three-storey wings. The exterior is perfectly plain except for a first-floor string course: the original impact of the exterior lay in the fact that here Morris attempted to 'express the idiom of the Palladian villa in the language of London street architecture'.[13] The centre block of the house was originally only two storeys, while the flanking wings were, as now, three storeys, and so Morris created a town version of the Palladian tower house, such as his own Combe Bank, near Sandridge, Kent, of c1725 (p61) and Kent's Holkham Hall, Norfolk, of 1731 (p68).

The interiors of these houses sometimes belie the austerity of the exterior. 61 Green Street (where the plan is related harmonically to the façade, for both are based on commensurate proportions (p10), is richly decorated inside, and the same is true of 11 North Audley Street, Mayfair, London. Here a plain brick face of c1725-30 by Edward Shepherd (now covered with Regency stucco) conceals a remarkable interior possibly designed by Sir Edward Lovett Pearce: it includes, on the ground floor, a top-lit octagonal room beside an oval staircase, and a fifteen-foot domed cube room on the garden front flanked by a pair of ten-foot cube vaulted rooms, a tripartite composition very similar to an apartment (now demolished) created by Pearce at Summerhill, Enfield, Co. Meath (c1732).

The possible connection between Pearce and this house is interesting, for the combination of austere exterior and rich interior became something of an Irish speciality. There are of course good English examples of this contrast – so often cited as a wonderful example of the reticent English character in built form, as Inigo Jones himself observed (p7), such as 1 Greek Street, Soho, London (c1746), which has a spectacular rococo interior; 44 Berkeley Square, Westminster, London (1742), which contains possibly the richest eighteenth-century town house interior in the country by William Kent, who repeated the treatment – though not quite so dramatically – at 22 Arlington Street, Westminster, London (c1741, completed by Stephen Wright in 1750); and Maisters House, 160 High Street, Kingston upon Hull, Humberside (by Joseph Page, 1744), which contains excellent rococo plasterwork.

The most extreme examples of this contrast are to be found in Dublin, however – and the

44 Berkeley Square, Mayfair: 1742-4: an exquisite Palladian composition relying for its effect on contrasting window proportions and the powerful door design.

The staircase of 44 Berkeley Square – a richly detailed and ingeniously planned construction hardly hinted at by the relatively restrained façade.

Irish character is very different to the English: the common link, of course, is the love of Palladio, whose work provides the precedent for this approach (p6). The best early eighteenth-century examples in Dublin are in Henrietta Street, built between c1725 and 1750; one of the most satisfying Georgian streets in the British Isles. The dozen or so houses that form its two sides face each other across a wide street (with Gandon's King's Inns at one end, p154) and are all huge – four tall storeys with four or five widely spaced bays, the windows being mere holes (though exquisitely proportioned, see p292) punched in a vast area of brick. The only external embellishments are the doorcases, which are mostly of fine, pedimented form and constructed of stone (as are all Dublin eighteenth-century doorcases) not wood (as are virtually all London eighteenth-century doorcases). In their noble proportions and austerity these houses parallel the most sophisticated contemporary London houses (p31) and anticipate by a decade at least the work of most London or English provincial builders. Inside, they have a most generous

9 Henrietta Street, Dublin, c1729 by Sir Edward Lovett Pearce. The round-headed first-floor window became a standard Palladian device for emphasizing the centre of a composition.

The entrance hall of 9 Henrietta Street: a fine Palladian design.

This rich rococo interior of 1758 by Robert West cavorts behind the tall, austere brick façade of 20 Dominick Street, Dublin.

plan (conceived along country house lines) and are richly decorated, the best – numbers 9 and 10, designed by Pearce, and number 13 – being in a rich Palladian architectural manner (p64). Number 9 has an excellent Palladian plaster compartment ceiling to its generous colonnaded staircase hall.

The most dramatic contrast between inside and outside in Dublin is 20 Dominick Street (1758), which has a large, imposing, but unpromising brick exterior, and inside contains the best of Robert West's extraordinarily rich and inventive three-dimensional rococo plasterwork. Later examples are Ely House, Ely Place, Dublin (1771), by Michael Stapleton, which has a seven-bay, four-storey brick exterior (undivided by string courses, like all Dublin houses) and a richly plastered interior in the Adam manner. The stair is particularly remarkable: the balustrade is decorated with animals representing the labours of Hercules, who stands, life-size, at the foot of the stairs. A last, and slightly later example of the manner is Belvedere House, Great Denmark Street, Dublin (1786), which Michael Stapleton decorated in an even more lavish Adam manner than Ely House, but with a more conventionally decorated iron staircase.

By way of contrast Dublin also contains an excellent example of the other approach to building a big and expensive house in town. Powerscourt House (by Robert Mack, 1771) is the sort of demonstrative, ungainly building one would expect to find in an unsophisticated provincial city and, Dublin being neither of those things in the eighteenth century, its appearance when spied down narrow South William Street can still come as something of a shock. A stone-clad three-storey house, nine bays wide over a tall basement, it is loaded with Palladian and baroque decoration: pedimented first-floor windows with rusticated pilaster strips emphasizing the corners, and the centre three bays breaking forward, carrying a pediment, and containing a massive Venetian window at first-floor level. Above the pediment, over the centre three bays, rises a tall, windowless attic, embellished with scrolls and topped by a cornice reminscent of the other Powerscourt, Co. Wicklow (c1731-40, p61). This mighty block is linked to the modest terrace houses that flank it by short quadrant walls attached to pavilions on the same building line as the rest of the street – a form of composition popular in Dublin for integrating larger houses into the street (for example Charlemont House, Parnell Square, 1763, by Sir William Chambers, and Aldborough House, Portland Row, 1798). Needless to say, the interior of Powerscourt House can only be an anti-climax after the exterior, but it is still interesting, for the staircase hall is decorated in the lingering Dublin rococo manner by James McCullagh, while the reception rooms, by Michael Stapleton, are Adamesque.

The Venetian window

As well as experimenting with various compositions the early and mid-Palladian designers of terrace elevations cultivated the use of certain distinctive features. The Venetian window – promoted by the Palladians, though often used by baroque designers – remained a popular device throughout the century, as speculating builders attempted to give their houses some individuality.

71 South Audley Street, Westminster, London, designed by Edward Shepherd 1736-7, is provided with a hierarchy of Venetian windows, the first-floor one being embellished with columns loaded with rustic blocks; 18 Low Pavement, Nottingham (c1745-50), is a magnificent affair with a three-bay three-storey façade containing six Venetian windows (the door is pushed to one side), those on the ground floor having portions of pediments over the side lights and a keystone in the arch of the centre window.[14] James Essex managed to do almost as well with a house of 1768 at 74 Trumpington Street, Cambridge, where he squeezed four Venetian windows into a three-bay, four-storey composition; 61 Broad Street, Worcester, also of c1760, is a four-storey, one-bay house which contains three Venetian windows, all with keystones bearing a humorous eighteenth-century face peering to one side or the other; while 39 Broad Street, Ludlow, Shropshire (c1765), and the house on the corner of Vicarage Street, Leominster, Hereford and Worcester (c1770), manage, like the house on Low

6 East Street, New Alresford, Hampshire, c1780.

Guildhall, Mill Street, Ludlow, Shropshire, 1774–6 by T. F. Pritchard.

Above left: Venetian door of c1750 in Duke Street, Whitehaven, Cumbria; *above right:* Door of c1810 in High Street, Witney, Oxfordshire; *below:* Pair of fanlight doorcases, Merrion Square, Dublin, c1762.

39 Broad Street, Ludlow, Shropshire: a house of *c*1765 dedicated single-mindedly to the Venetian window.

Pavement, to be virtually all Venetian windows and nothing else. A little more sophisticated is Perrott House, Bridge Street, Pershore, Hereford and Worcester (*c*1775), where the door and most of the windows are based on the Venetian window motif.

The bay
Another feature commonly used to give the individual façade distinction was the bay. It came in many forms – semicircular, half-hexagonal (called canted), occasionally half-octagonal, segmental or elliptical. These various shapes enjoyed vogues (hexagonal *c*1750-70; semicircular *c*1770-1820; elliptical *c*1790-1830) but were used only gradually and sparingly on town houses (though they were more common on rear elevations), in contrast with the success they enjoyed in country house design, where they became very popular in Ireland after *c*1730 and in England after *c*1750 (p60). There are interesting early examples in England, however, such as the extraordinary Parnella House, 23 Market Place, Devizes, Wiltshire (*c*1740-45). The way in which bays were used – be they single-storey or the full height of the elevation – was fairly consistent. The most common composition was for them to rise full height each side of a central single door and, very often, a first-floor Venetian window, such as at Grey Friars House, High Street, Colchester (1755); 87 High Pavement, Chesterfield, Derbyshire (*c*1765); and Clavering House, Clavering Place, Newcastle upon Tyne (1784). Later eighteenth-century/early nineteenth-century

Above: Rear elevation of 15 Belmont, Shrewsbury: an excellent example of the use of full-height canted bays as compositional devices.

Below: 12 West Street, Builth Wells, Powys, *c*1815, showing the Regency use of full-height curved bays.

versions of this composition, with rounded, not canted, bays, are 2 Highweek Street, Newton Abbot, Devon (*c*1790–1800), and 12 West Street, Builth Wells, Powys (*c*1815).

Bays and Venetian windows could be combined, for example at 41 Gay Street, Bath, designed in 1740 by John Wood the Elder: occupying the corner of this building, which faces into Queen Square, is a three-storey round bay, with Venetian and tripartite windows decorated with rustic blocks.

As the Palladian grip on architectural fashion loosened in the 1740s and '50s (p14) terrace house façades became extraordinarily inventive. Not only did the rococo Gothic emerge, either in the design of details – such as the Batty Langley Gothic door on the Guildhall, Mill Street, Ludlow, Shropshire (*c*1774), and the classical/Gothic door on 54 Head Street, Colchester, Essex (1767) – or as the inspiration for entire houses, such as the extraordinarily ornate Speedwell Castle, Market Place, Brewood, Staffordshire (*c*1750), but also after *c*1765 a new, fresh spirit of classicism (p14) began to make itself felt in urban design.

In country house design it had expressed itself in the revolutionary villas of Sir Robert Taylor, Sir William Chambers, James Paine and John Carr (p71). In urban building these same men had introduced elements into elevational design that foreshadowed the coming neo-classical revolution, and which make Palladianism look as tame, not to say as dull, as most people in the 1760s thought it to be. Taylor is particularly interesting, for as late as 1771 he was able to design 3, 4, 5 and 6 Grafton Street, Westminster, London, in a truly monumental, austere and Palladian fashion, while at the same time, both at Ely House, 37 Dover Street, 1772–6 (a continuation of Grafton Street), and at 3 The Terrace, Richmond Hill, Richmond-upon-Thames, he was creating extraordinary terrace houses in which standard Palladian details such as the arcaded, rusticated ground floor, and architrave-clad second-floor attic windows, were combined with pedimented and columned aedicules to the first-floor window.

The same inventive spirit of the villa can be found at Castlegate House, 26 Castlegate, York (by John Carr, 1762), which has a blind arcade on the first-floor front (an early use of a device that became a cliché in the 1820s) and, on the rear elevation, a pair of full-height canted bays flanking a central door and a first-floor Venetian window. Equally original is 37 King Street, Covent Garden, London (*c*1775), which on stylistic grounds has been attributed to James Paine. Here three first-floor windows sit in a blind arcade, while the top floor is formed by a huge brick arch within an open pediment.

The neo-classical revolution

The neo-classical designers of the last quarter of the eighteenth century continued this spirit of diversity and innovation. The approach was established as early as 1764 by James Stuart with Lichfield House, 15 St James's Square, Westminster (p280), where he attempted to apply what he had learnt in Athens of Greek classicism to a London terrace site. The three-bay house he built was conventionally Palladian in its proportions, but the detail was revolutionary, for the capitals of the Ionic columns supporting the three-bay pediment are exact replicas of those on the Erechtheion in Athens. Adam's neo-classically inspired elevation design can now be understood only by looking at the remains of his Adelphi (1768–72) and particularly at the Royal Society of Arts building in John Adam Street (1772), a standard London late Palladian terrace house, but pilastered and embellished with his own slick brand of neo-classical decoration. A more ornate work by Adam is 20 St James's Square, Westminster, London (1771–4), which, faced with a screen of pilasters sitting on a rusticated basement, is a Palladian design in everything but its details (and not dissimilar to James Wyatt's early stuccoed house at 9 Conduit Street,

Speedwell Castle, Brewood, Staffordshire, *c*1750: a rare and early example of the application of rococo Gothic embellishments to a town house elevation.

Above: The top-lit oval staircase at Robert Adam's 20 Portman Square of 1773-6: the form is that of the contemporary country villa.

Below: 12, 13, 14 Lincoln's Inn Fields, Holborn, London, built to the designs of Sir John Soane in stages between 1792 and 1824. The design of 13 – with its projecting stone screen – represented a revolutionary break with the traditions of terrace house design.

Westminster, London, 1779). By an unknown designer is the striking neo-classical 14-16 Castle Street, Cirencester, Gloucestershire (*c*1780), which has a main three-bay, two-storey ashlar façade focused by a one-bay pediment and containing six Venetian windows set within blank arches – in the Palladian/Adam manner – and all linked horizontally by continuous imposts and cill courses. More conventionally Palladian is Adam's Home House, 20 Portman Square, Westminster, London (1773-6), which, perhaps like Taylor's nearly contemporary Grafton Street terrace, shows that the conventional astylar Palladian terrace façade pioneered by Campbell in 1718 (p31) was still considered the acceptable non-committal form to assume when all the attention and money was going – as at Home House – on interior fittings and arrangements.

Although the discipline of classical design and the conventional attitudes of eighteenth- and early nineteenth-century designers make it possible – just – to discuss the design of terrace houses as a continuing, interrelated process, there are also those buildings produced during the early years of the nineteenth century, when classical dogmas were being rethought or overthrown, that are so individual that they have to be considered independently or ignored altogether. The latter course would be unfair, for they are too entertaining or too important to be dismissed, and in following the former course, unfortunately space permits consideration of only a few examples.

Most notable is Sir John Soane's group of three houses at 12, 13 and 14 Lincoln's Inn Fields, London. He built number 12 for his own use in 1792-4 and gave it an extremely modest façade. It is three bays wide and was three storeys high (a fourth was added in the 1820s), of pale brick with a rendered ground floor. It has some unusual details (such as the scroll-patterned iron first-floor balcony) and is well built, but it is very much in the simple urban tradition of the time. In 1812, however, when he rebuilt number 13 as his home, Soane attempted something very different, indeed unique. Abandoning the conventions of elevational design, he constructed a three-storey, three-bay house fronted by a three-storey stone loggia which, breaking forward some feet in front of the building line of the neighbouring houses (a feat achieved only after successfully contesting a court action brought by the outraged district surveyor), has three arched bays on the ground floor, three arched bays on the first floor and only one, centrally placed, bay on the second floor to create a stepped effect. The flanking second-floor bays are set back on the same plane as the neighbouring houses, which makes the loggia read very much as a stone screen placed in front of a conventional terrace house – an impression strengthened when a fourth floor was added in 1825-6, on the same plane as the neighbouring house, and when the loggia openings were glazed in 1834.

The extraordinary loggia-cum-screen – embellished with characteristic Soanian motifs, such as pilaster strips incised with Greek fret pattern decoration, Coade stone caryatids modelled on those at the Erechtheion and bold acroteria – was made the centrepiece of a tripartite composition when in 1823-4 Soane acquired and rebuilt number 14 to match number 12.

Contemporary with this later phase of Soane's embellishment of Lincoln's Inn Fields is 363 Kennington Lane, London, built in 1825 by Soane's long-term employee J.M. Gandy, which has a two-storey tripartite bow window set within a three-storey arch. This is not so unusual in itself, but with its array of sub-Soanian neo-Greek detail the house is a remarkable departure from the standard terrace house of its date, and makes an interesting comparison with Gandy's essay in country house design, Storr's Hall, Windermere, Cumbria, 1808-11.

Also Greek and also unusual is Pelham Crescent, Hastings (by J. Kay, 1824-8), where each house is one tripartite window wide, all are uniformly and extraordinarily embellished with verandas to first- and second-floor windows, and the skyline is studded with acroteria. To a degree this crescent evokes the spirit of some of Nash's more remarkable – and long lost – Regent Street terraces, such as numbers 224-40 (built by Samuel Baxter in 1822), which had gigantic crowning acroteria, incised Grecian ornament, and long narrow attic windows enclosing Grecian urns set *in antis*. Parallel to the fashion for the Greek was a short-lived vogue for things Egyptian. The first full-blooded architectural manifestation of this was P.F. Robinson's long-demolished Egyptian Hall, Piccadilly, London (1812), with perhaps the last expression being the Egyptian House (*c*1830) in distant Penzance, Cornwall, which, if a little behind the times, is a truly flamboyant essay in the Egyptian. It has tapering apertures, and indeed the whole façade is made to taper within a decorative frame topped by a mighty coved cornice. The first-floor window is a tripartite affair with Egyptian-faced terms serving as columns, and truly excellent Egyptian columns flank the door.

Plans

A little must be said about the plans of terrace houses. Those of large-scale houses display a variety impossible to catalogue. Roughly, the disposal of the main elements – such as the staircase, hall and saloon – reflects the fashions followed in country houses of the time: for example, the early eighteenth-century 14 St Nicholas Street, Scarborough, has a pair of identical staircases each side of a central passage, in the manner of Palladian country houses and villas. The main difference is, of course, that the plans of terrace houses – even very large ones – were compromised by the restrictions and character of each urban site: shape and size, orientation to view and sunlight and street noise. In large early eighteenth-century town houses, for instance, staircases tended to be in compartments at the rear or side of the house, but if the best views were to be had from the garden front the stair could be located on the street side. Interestingly, in Colen Campbell's 31 Old Burlington Street, Westminster, London (1718), the staircase rises in the front, taking up a window on the street façade. On the other hand, Sir Robert Taylor's 33 Upper Brook Street, Westminster (1767), and Adam's Home House, Westminster, London (1773-6), reflect exactly the country house fashion of the day, with a top-lit round staircase and a bay-fronted octagonal room.

The plan of the smaller terrace house, however, was quickly standardized, and provides clues to the way in which modest urban houses were occupied. The terrace in Albury Street, Deptford, London, of 1706-17 (p30) is like a testing ground for compact urban plans, and contains types which range from miniature open-well stairs, as in contemporary country houses, to modest newel staircases and dog-leg stairs, in which floors are reached by two flights, running parallel, and joined by a half-landing or a half-turn of winding stairs.

It was this dog-leg type, placed at the rear of the house against the party wall, that became standard after *c*1720, for as well as being compact, if designed properly it offered the opportunity for a little architectural show, with turned balusters and newels and carved tread-ends. The plan of the house itself also reached a standard form in *c*1720, with a room at the front and a room at the back and, very often, the addition of a third small room per floor, in the form of a narrow closet reached off the back room. By this device the early eighteenth-century builder managed to create, in vertical form, the sort of apartments found in contemporary country houses such as Houghton Hall, Norfolk (p62). In the front of the house was a drawing room, behind it a bedroom/withdrawing room, and beyond that a closet which, in a larger terrace house, could be reached (as in a country house) by a small secondary staircase which allowed the removal of night soil out of sight of the rest of the house. Presumably, as in a country house, each apartment belonged to a different member of the family, who would gather in one or more of the front drawing rooms and dine in that nearest the basement kitchen. Later in the century, again as in country houses, the use of rooms became more formalized, with the creation of rooms furnished and used solely for the purpose of dining, entertaining and withdrawing.

Curiously, as in some country houses (p94) the dining rooms in the more ambitious town houses could be a little archaic in decoration. 29 Percy Street, London, part of an early (for London) uniform street (1764-70), has a ground-floor front room panelled in the manner of c1735-45, with alternate wide and thin panels, flush panelling below dado level, and a pair of Ionic columns at the end of the room opposite the windows. The first-floor drawing room, on the other hand, is spot on for the date, with plaster wall and cornice, and no doubt would have been given a light and pretty air as the feminine counterpart to the dining room.

In Dublin a similar plan form evolved. After c1760 the semicircular rear elevation became common – as it did in London a decade or so later – with closet wings being reached from the stair half-landing. In larger Dublin houses by 1775 the entrance hall had been replaced by a narrow passage leading to the stairs, which were set towards the rear of the house and very often rose only to first-floor level, with a secondary stair serving the bedrooms above.

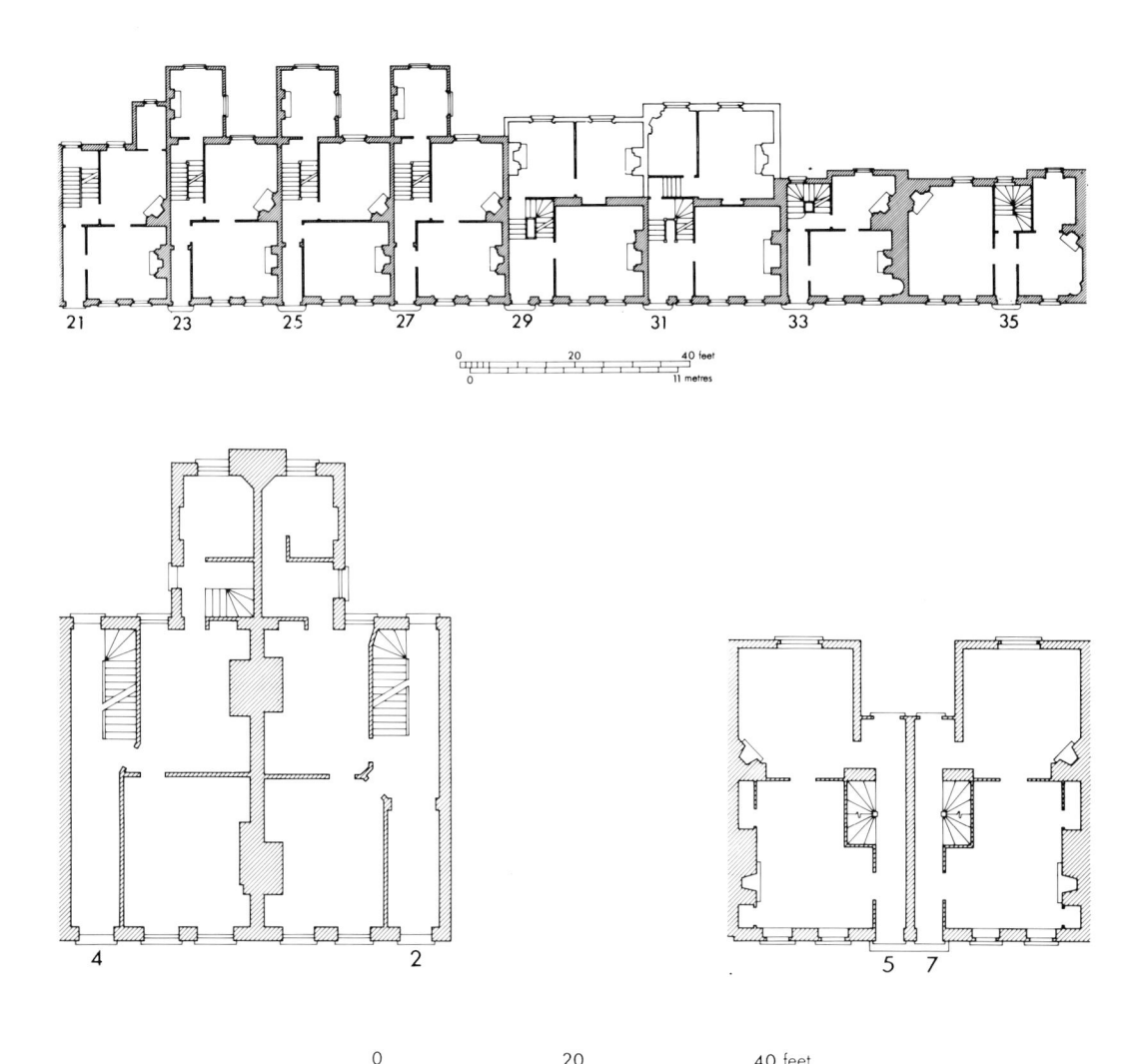

Buildings in Towns / 47

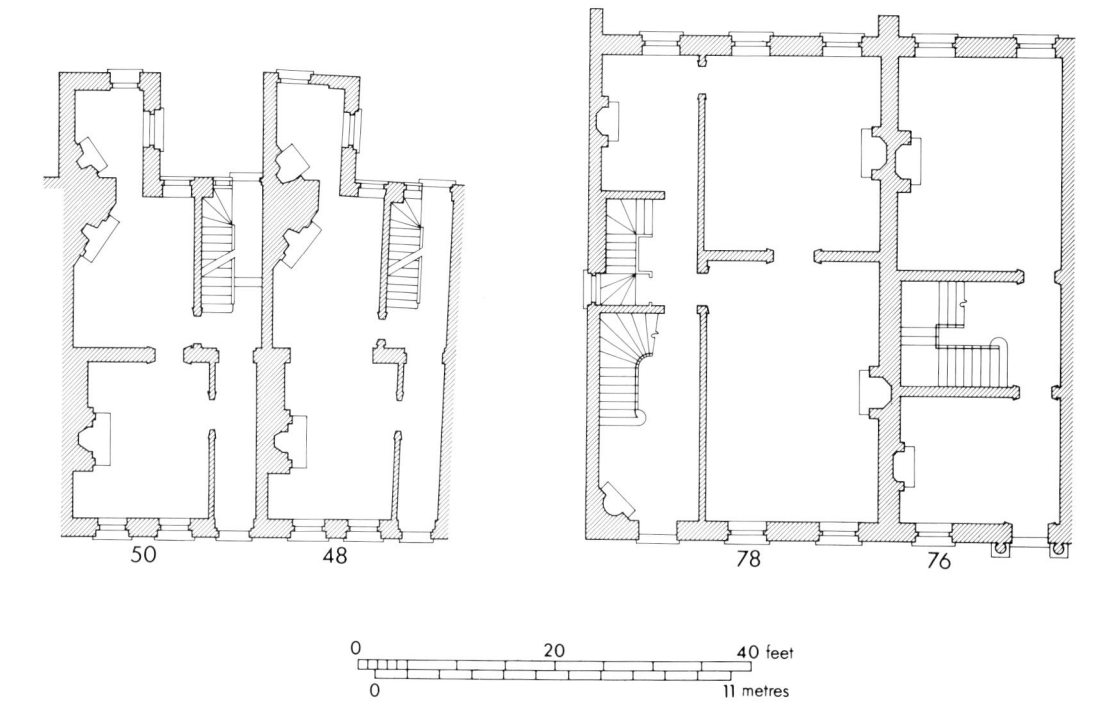

```
     50        48              78        76
```

0   20   40 feet
0   11 metres

Opposite above: Ground floor plan of 21–35 Albury Street, Deptford, c1706–1717, showing variety of staircase types – dog-leg (21–27), newel (35), open well (29–31) – chimney stack placing, and plan forms. The plan of No. 21, with a closet off the back room and dog-leg stair, was to become the standard London type. Walls in outline only are later additions.

Opposite below: Two early eighteenth-century London terrace house ground plans; left, a now demolished pair, 2 and 4 Millman Street, Bloomsbury, c1721, with dog-leg stair, chimney stacks placed centrally on party walls and closet wings – one of which contained a small secondary or service staircase running full height of house. Right, 5 and 7 Elder Street, Spitalfields, 1725, with seventeenth-century type central newel staircases and angle flues in the rear rooms.

Above: Early eighteenth-century London terrace house ground plans. On the left is the builders' standard speculative type, 48 and 50 Broadwick Street, Soho, 1722–3, with dog-leg stair, and closet off rear room. Above right, 76 and 78 Brook Street, Mayfair, of similar date (1726), but of more regular design. The architect for both these houses was Colen Campbell. Fireplaces are centrally placed, staircases arranged to allow full-width back and front rooms, and the plan of 76 – Campbell's own house – is based on Palladio's 'ideal' room proportion of $\sqrt{2}$. No. 78 has now been demolished. (Plans from *Survey of London*, Vol XL.)

Overleaf above: Ground floor plans of three mid-eighteenth-century terrace houses. Left: 8 and 9 the Circus, Bath, c1755 by John Wood the Elder. The façades are uniform but the plans differ to reflect the tastes and pockets of the first tenants.

The spacious staircase landing at 8 is a Bath characteristic (from Walter Ison's *Buildings of Bath*). Centre: 33 Upper Brook Street, Mayfair, London, 1767–8. Designed by Sir Robert Taylor, it reveals how some of the principal planning characteristics of the contemporary villa notably the octagonal room – could be fitted within the standard London terrace plan. Right: 63 Merrion Square, Dublin, c1762. Typical of mid-eighteenth-century speculative houses in both Dublin and London, this plan has all the basic ingredients, of late seventeenth-century origin seen at 21 Albury Street of c1706. The bowed back is an innovation, and the closet has been extended into a rear wing. This was the standard technique for increasing the accommodation of large terrace houses with wide plots.

Overleaf below: Ground floors of four substantial houses erected in London between 1772 and c1780, showing the scale and variety of accommodation created on terrace plots. Far left: 18 Queen Anne's Gate, 1772–4 with a very deep plan and a centrally placed top-lit stair; centre left: a typical house in Bedford Square, Bloomsbury, c1780 – strikingly similar to 63 Merrion Square; centre right: 11 Queen Anne's Gate, 1772–4, with a standard alternative plan to the dog-leg stair/closet type. The top-lit, centrally placed stair allows full width back and front rooms, connected by a passage which can be used either for communication (if the house was divided into chambers or separate apartments per floor) or as a closet/wardrobe. Right: 20 St James's Square, Westminster, built in 1772 to the design of Robert Adam. A is dining room, B music room, C library, D dressing room, E powdering room. The closet, seen modestly extended at 63 Merrion Square, is here a fully developed rear wing.

48 / *Georgian Buildings*

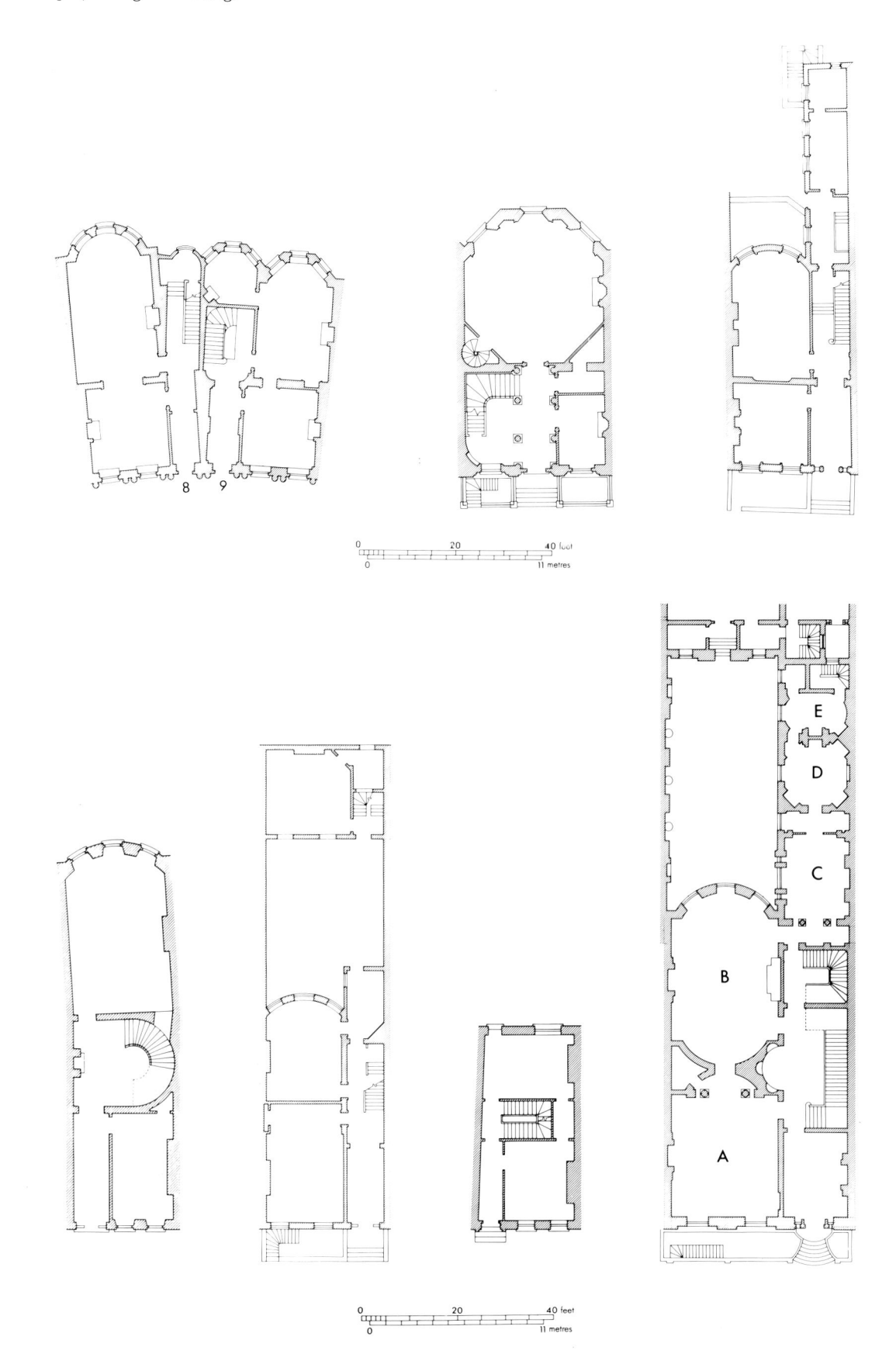

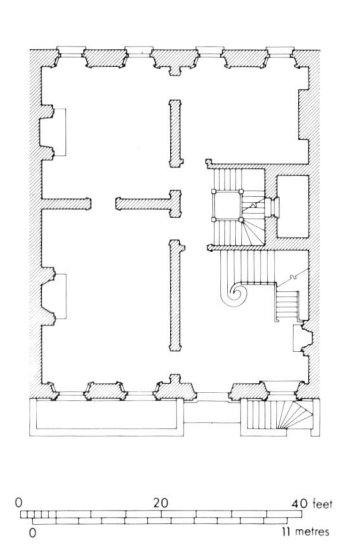

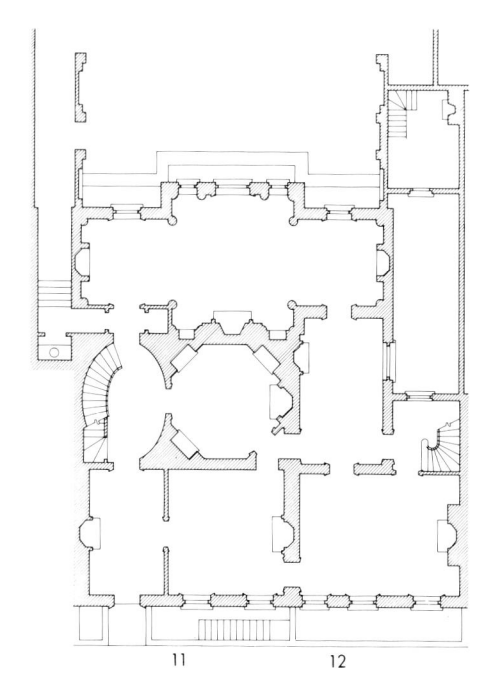

Buildings in Towns / 49

Ground floor plans of four urban houses occupying sites that are either larger than the average terrace plot or of unusual shape or proportions. Three of these are first-generation Palladian, to demonstrate the variety possible within one architectural style.

Above left: 31 Old Burlington Street, 1718–23 by Colen Campbell, with rooms proportioned according to the Palladian theory explained by Robert Morris in his *Lectures on Architecture*. The rear right hand room, for example, is a cube and a half. *Above right:* 11, 12 North Audley Street, built c1725–30 and shown here as they were in c1800. The garden rooms (top) comprise a 15ft domed cube flanked by 10ft cube rooms. *Below left:* 61 Green Street, Mayfair, built 1730 to the design of Roger Morris, is a sophisticated composition with the various elements of the plan and decoration being proportionately related. The large rear room (top) is 3:2:1 (Robert Morris's ideal room proportion F) while the room to its right is of the 2:3:3 – a permutation of Morris's cube and a half ideal proportion. The main staircase originally rose behind the pair of columns. *Below right:* Home House, 20 Portman Square, built 1774–8 to the designs of Robert Adam. A front parlour; B back parlour; C library. The plan is most striking for the introduction of fashionable country house features – especially the oval top-lit stair – into a terrace house.

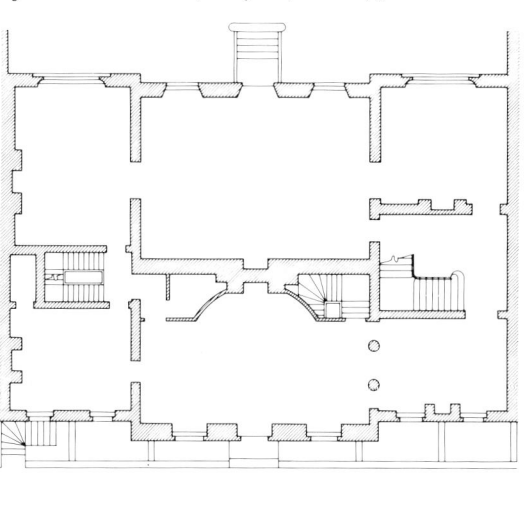

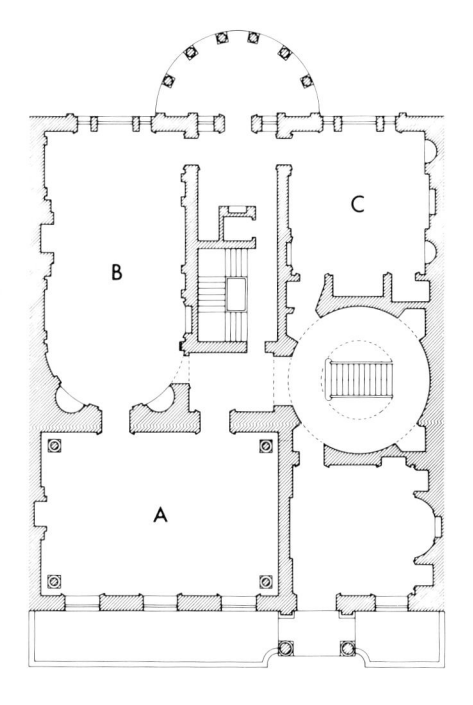

12 Merrion Square, Dublin, c1762, illustrating a typical Dublin terrace house arrangement, where the main staircase stops at first-floor level.

Notes

1 James Ralph's 'A Critical Review of the Publick Buildings ... In, and about, London', 1734, page 108. Also *Survey of London*, vol XL, 'The Grosvenor Estate in Mayfair', Part II, page 134. A French precedent for a square formed by uniform, palace-fronted and pedimented terraces was J.-H. Mansart's Place Vendôme, Paris, of 1690.
2 Sir John Soane's *Lectures on Architecture*, 1809-1836, edited by A. T. Bolton, 1929, page 179. Also Sir John Summerson's *Georgian London*, 1969 edition, page 165.
3 The attribution of the design of Bedford Square is discussed in detail by Donald J. Olsen in *Town Planning in London: the Eighteenth and Nineteenth Centuries*, 2nd edition 1982, pages 45-6.
4 Donald J. Olsen, op. cit., Appendix II, pages 224-7.
5 Maurice Craig, *The Architecture of Ireland*, 1982, page 242.
6 Letter to Robert Adam of 23 March 1791, quoted in A. J. Youngson's *The Making of Classical Edinburgh*, 1968 editions, page 96.
7 John Wood, *An essay towards a description of Bath* (1742), page 220 of 1765 edition.
8 M. Dorothy George, *London Life in the 18th Century* (1925), page 86 of 1976 edition.
9 John Gwynn, *London and Westminster Improved*, 1766.
10 In this approach Playfair was inspired by William Stark who had written a Report in 1814 on 'Laying out the Grounds for building between Edinburgh and Leith', in which he argued that the architect has to appreciate and then exploit the merits of his site and not impose upon it. See A. J. Youngson's *Making of Classical Edinburgh*, 1968 edition, pages 149-52.
11 John Gwynn, *London and Westminster Improved*, 1766.
12 Sebastiano Serlio's *Tutte l'opere d'architettura*, published 1537-47, was first published in English in 1611.
13 *Survey of London*, vol XL, 'The Grosvenor Estate in Mayfair', Part II, page 190.
14 Design derived from Plate 51 of Batty Langley's *The City and Country Builder's Treasury of Designs*, 1745.

BUILDINGS IN THE COUNTRY

Before discussing the various forms of country building – houses, garden buildings, follies, model farms, estate buildings and cottages – it is essential to understand two things. First, that country houses, though hardly representative of popular taste, ambitions or architectural achievement in the eighteenth century (to discover these we must look to the more modest architecture of towns), are the best building type to examine to discover the architectural movements of the period 1714-1830. Free of the constraints of regulations that increasingly governed the design of buildings in towns, and indulged with extraordinary amounts of money,[1] country house building provided the field in which architectural styles competed, played themselves out, or evolved.

Second, what is a country house? This question is not as easy to answer as it might seem. There are the obvious candidates, the great piles standing in the heart of, and supported by, large estates, and then there are the monuments to one man's fortune and ambition, erected and maintained by money raised elsewhere. But also there is that smaller variety of country house found throughout the eighteenth century that is striking because it appears to be a town house that has wandered abroad.

This singular quality is the result not only of the fact that these urban refugees were conceived in two dimensions, the only consciously designed areas tending to be the front and back elevations (indeed many of the great country houses suffer from this problem), nor because of their modest scale (again many important country houses are not large), nor, indeed, because of their simplicity of decoration (which is one of the most striking things about many of the grandest country houses) but, rather, because they are all these three things at once. Good examples of this type are Gateley Hall, Norfolk, a five-bay, two-storey brick box (1726); Boyles Court, Great Warley, Essex (1776), by Thomas Leverton; and Moccas Court, Hereford and Worcester (1775-81), by Anthony Keck. All look as if they have been transplanted from a Bloomsbury square.

In Ireland the two-dimensional country house was a refugee not so much from the city as from the seventeenth century, with gable end walls usually incorporating wide chimney stacks, such as at Milltown, Shinrone, Co. Offaly (c1750). These houses are relatively rare in a country where, from the early eighteenth century, even modest country houses were generally designed in the round.

One of the major reasons for this '*urbs in rure*' was that certain town houses, well known because of their locations or associations with rank or genius, were taken as models by provincial designers and thus bred slightly ungainly country cousins. For example, Buckingham House (1705), designed by William Winde and sitting grandly on the main axis of St James's Park, spawned many imitations, including Wotton House, Buckinghamshire (1720), and Castletown Cox, Piltown, Co. Kilkenny (1767), by Davis Ducart; Lindsey House, Lincoln's Inn Fields (c1640), believed in the eighteenth century to be the work of Inigo Jones (it was probably by Peter Mills or Nicholas Stone), was reproduced by Daniel Garrett in c1735 at Forcett Park, North Yorkshire; Lord Burlington's London house for General Wade of 1723 (based on a drawing by Palladio) inspired copies in England and Ireland (p8) including the centre block of the extraordinary Hovingham Hall, North Yorkshire (c1750), by Sir Thomas Worsley, where the ground floor is given over to a riding school; and Sir William Chambers' major building in the Scottish capital inspired an imitation. Dundas House, St Andrew's Square, Edinburgh (1771), was copied by William Elliot in 1796 when designing Ladykirk House, Berwickshire (demolished).

Discussion of the urban-looking country house leads naturally to consideration of its near relative, the country house that has strayed into town, in the form of the nobleman's free-standing town residence. Good examples are Spencer House, St James's, designed in 1756 by John Vardy; Leinster House, Dublin (1745), by Richard Castle; the provincial town house of the local magnate or rich merchant such as Marlow Place, Marlow, Buckinghamshire (c1720) – a seven-bay by six-bay three-dimensionally designed country house; the little baroque palace of Ivy House, Chippenham, Wiltshire (1730); Fydel House, Boston, Lincolnshire (1726),

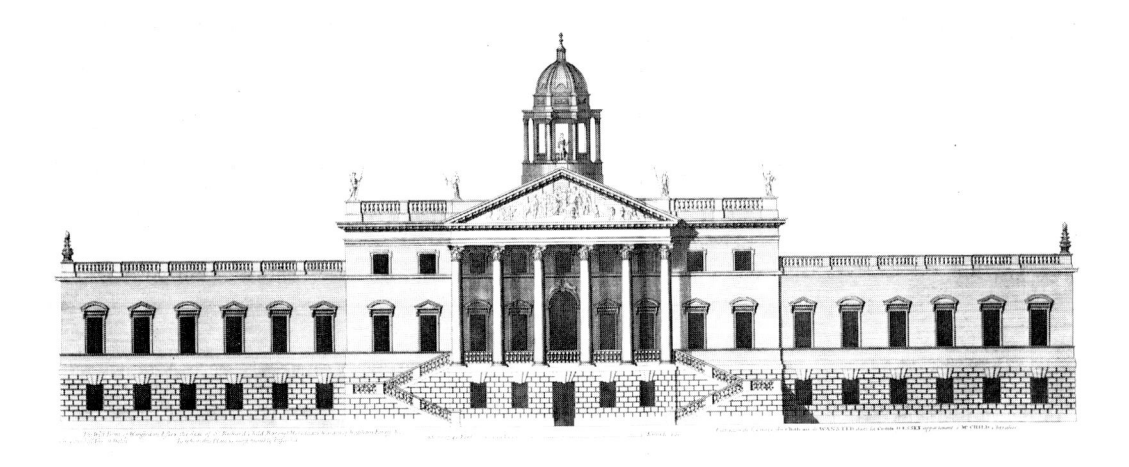

The entrance front of Colen Campbell's Wanstead House, as built in 1713–20 (demolished 1824). Engraving from *Vitruvius Britannicus*, Volume 1, 1715.

and Swan Hill Court, Shrewsbury (1764), by T.F. Pritchard. Since the same spirit moves through these buildings as through more conventional country houses (significantly most urban building acts did not apply strictly to houses of the 'first kind'), they have been included.

The country house

In 1713 something quite extraordinary took place. On the eastern edge of London, at Wanstead (now in Redbridge), a house began to rise which was to have the most profound effect both on the design of country houses and on architecture generally in the eighteenth century.

Wanstead House, built from 1713 to 1720 to the design of Colen Campbell (demolished 1824), was the first fully developed expression of that version of classicism which was to be called Palladian and which dominated British architecture for the next three decades of the eighteenth century (p7). Not since Inigo Jones's and John Webb's buildings before the

Section through Wanstead showing saloon/hall axis on the *piano nobile* over the ground floor 'rustic'. Engraving from *Vitruvius Britannicus*, Volume 1, 1715.

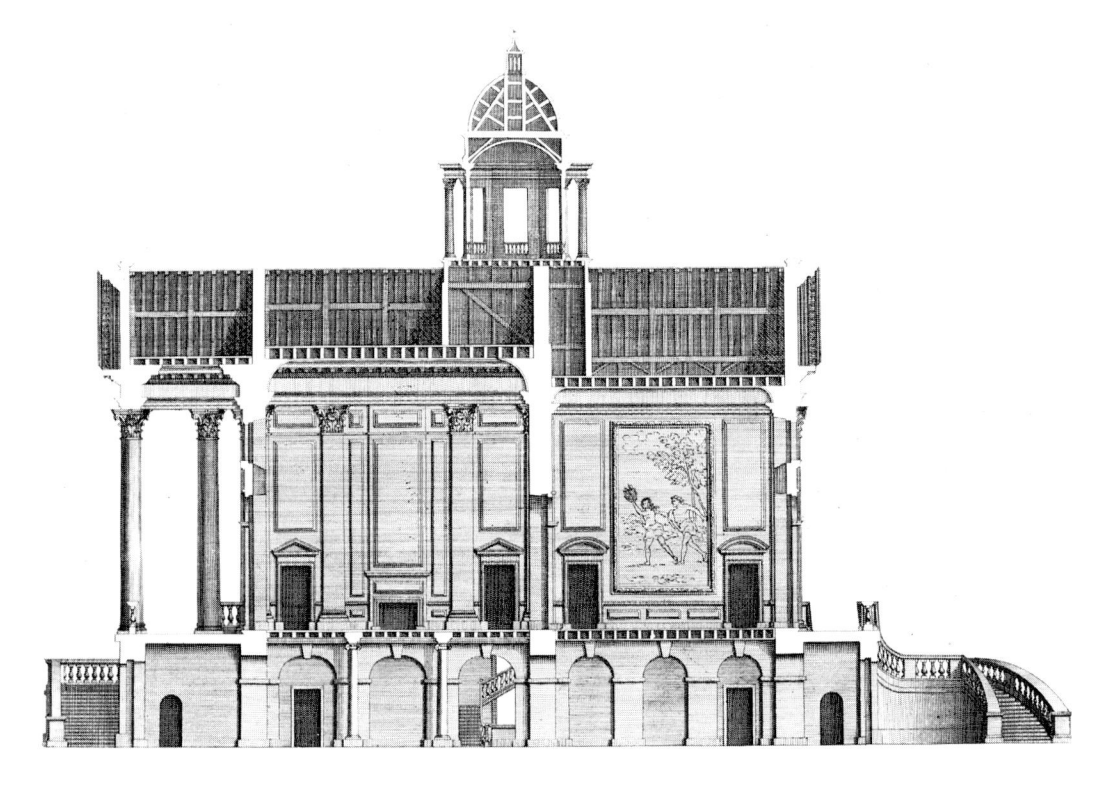

English Civil War, and Roger Pratt's immediately after, had the dominant influence of Continental baroque been challenged in such a convincing manner. Here was a house, in contrast to contemporary baroque mansions such as Vanbrugh's Blenheim (1705-16) or Thomas Archer's Roehampton House (1710-12), where the doctrines of Palladio were obeyed rather than loosely interpreted or ignored; where the architect was at pains to create a chaste simplicity and serenity, and where the orders of ancient Rome were invoked for the benefit of an early eighteenth-century financier. The components of the elevation were limited in number and disposed with great horizontal emphasis – as opposed to the verticality of baroque composition – and the portico, which Campbell called 'a just Hexastyle, the first yet produced in this manner in the Kingdom',[2] had a ridge that continued visibly over the hall and saloon behind it, so that it looked as if a Roman temple had been set into the house.

Inigo Jones's Queen's House at Greenwich (1616-19 and 1630-35); Sir Roger Townsend's Raynham Hall, Norfolk (1621-35); John Webb's Amesbury, Wiltshire (1640 and 1660); Wilton House, Wiltshire, by Isaac De Caux with the assistance of Jones and Webb (1635-49); Sir Roger Pratt's Coleshill (begun 1649 and destroyed by fire in 1952) which boasted a ceiling copied from the Queen's House; and Hugh May's houses such as Eltham Lodge, Greenwich (1663), are among the ancestors of the eighteenth-century Palladian country house – but there is a nearer link. In *c*1708 William Benson began to build himself a house in Wiltshire, naming it Wilbury after the neighbouring Wilton and Amesbury, then thought to be exclusively the work of Inigo Jones. Indeed Benson's homage went further: for his little house was merely a version of the principal floor of Amesbury and, although the finished result (now much altered) had something of the Dutch baroque about it, this villa marks the beginning of the rehabilitation of Jones which was to lead Campbell, in 1715, to call him 'this great master' who had 'outdone all that went before'. Jones's return to favour was helped, no doubt, by the fact that Benson had strong political contacts and was one of the leading figures of the Whig promotion of Palladianism after 1715 (p7).

The other significant point about Benson's villa is that he raised it on a Palladio villa plan with the main elements based on the Villa Pogliana. There is an oblong hall, with its long side to the front elevation leading to an oblong saloon, and its short side to the rear elevation. Placed symmetrically each side of the saloon are matching stairs, then two pairs of rooms, two of which are square, complete the ground floor plan. This, broadly, was to become the model for countless eighteenth-century houses and Palladian villas, but it was not quite as revolutionary as this pioneering role may imply, for by 1708 Palladio was nothing new. When Wanstead rose in 1713 its appearance was startlingly new, but its plan was not. Indeed, the plan of the principal floor of the main block would have been as familiar as the exterior was strange. The plans of Palladio and that other Renaissance rationalist Serlio were generally known after 1600 (Serlio was published in English in 1611), were experimented with by Elizabethan draughtsmen such as John Thorpe, and became one of the major elements of seventeenth-century building

William Benson's proto-Palladian Wilbury House, Wiltshire, of *c*1708, inspired by Wilton and Amesbury (as its name reveals) and Palladio's Villa Pogliana plan.

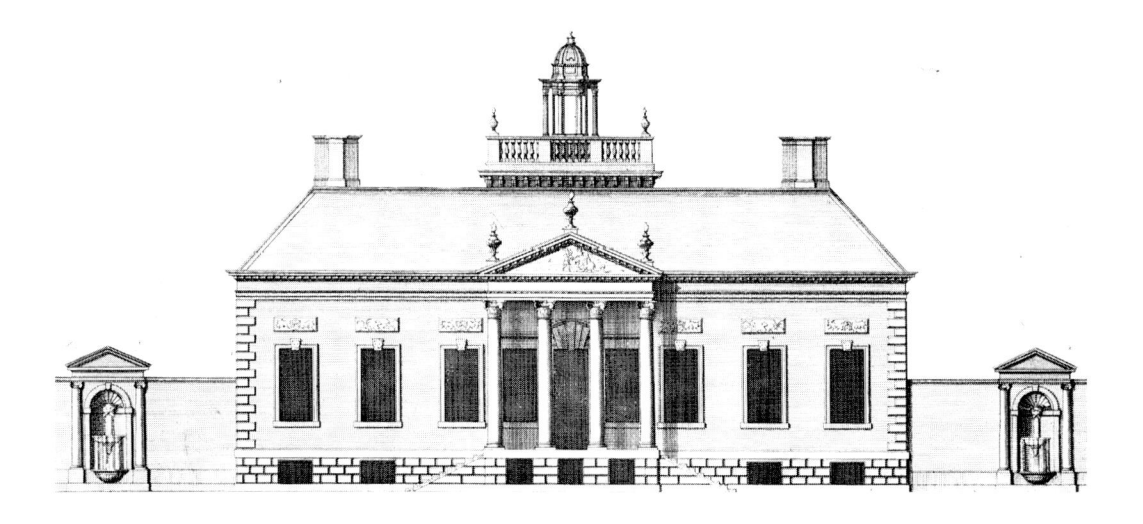

design (the T-plan relationship of the hall and saloon of the Villa Pogliana is found at Raynham Hall, 1621); indeed, the mighty baroque houses that Campbell sought to put to shame were, in many cases, based on versions of Palladio's symmetrical villa plans. Like Campbell's Wanstead they had on their principal floors a central hall and saloon occupying the main axis of the house (at Wanstead Campbell used the Villa Pogliana relationship of hall and saloon) with a stair, or stairs, on the narrower cross axis – a device, for example, favoured by the baroque architect William Talman. What Wanstead did not have, and what had been thought essential by any baroque architect was an architecturally emphasized and formal axis of honour. Vanbrugh at Blenheim (1705–16) and William Talman at Chatsworth (1687–96) arranged the plan so as to provide a series of apartments, each consisting of three to four rooms, which led off in enfilade from a central hall, one connecting with the other in a straight line, becoming increasingly small and private – antechamber, withdrawing chamber, bedchamber, closet. This device was intimately linked with the formal social manners of the seventeenth century, where life was lived mainly in one's own or another's private apartments – where one's rank would be acknowledged by the depth of penetration from antechamber to closet – and only occasionally in the formal hall or saloon. The fact that this enfilade arrangement of apartments is suppressed at Wanstead (the only concession is the alignment of the doors of the main rooms) was more because it was out of fashion than because it was classically impure. Another thing which Wanstead did not have in common with its contemporaries was the level at which activities took place. In the large baroque houses of the early eighteenth century the main rooms were on the ground floor and decorative external giant columns rose either from mere plinths, as at Vanbrugh's Seaton Delaval, Northumberland (1717–29), and Francis Smith's Buntingsdale, Shropshire (1721); from squat podiums containing basement windows, as at Stoneleigh Abbey, Warwickshire, by Francis Smith (1714–26); or simply from ground level, as at Barnsley Park, Gloucestershire (1720–21), perhaps by John Price, and Sutton Scarsdale, Derbyshire (1724), by Smith. Indeed the ground-floor columned Corinthian portico which Sir James Thornhill gave Moor Park, Hertfordshire, in 1725 was placed firmly on the ground, as an overt statement of baroque principle, and as a challenge to Campbell's Corinthian 'just Hexastyle' at Wanstead.

At Wanstead the principal floor was raised onto first floor level – the Renaissance *piano nobile* – with a rusticated basement level (called the rustic in the eighteenth century) on ground level. From this low rugged storey sprang the columns of the portico. An interesting earlier example of this composition is Burley House, Burley-on-the-Hill, Leicestershire (1694–c1705). Here the two-storey pilasters of the pedimented frontispiece rise from a rusticated ground floor as at Wanstead but, unlike Wanstead, this ground floor contains important rooms in the baroque manner, and is robbed of its true classical basement quality by being undermined by lower basement windows.

The Palladian villa
After Wanstead, Campbell was to score another first in the evolution of the eighteenth-century Palladian country house. In the relative security that followed the Peace of Utrecht in 1713 and the removal of the immediate Stuart threat in 1715, there was a building boom in the countryside which reached a climax in 1720–24, when twice as many country houses were begun as in any other quinquennium in the eighteenth century.[3] The building form favoured was that of the villa, and the builders were generally members of the newly rich merchant class who were looking for small compact country establishments independent of, and unsupported by, large estates. For such a brief the Palladian villa proved an irresistible model, as Campbell was only too ready to show.

In about 1718 he designed Baldersby (originally Newby) Park, North Yorkshire, perhaps the first true eighteenth-century Palladian villa; but, being of only two storeys, it has no rustic, so the giant columns of its pedimented frontispiece sit on the ground in the baroque manner. The interior was damaged by fire in 1900, but there was originally a double-height entrance hall, square in plan,

Colen Campbell's Mereworth Castle, Kent, 1722; the most faithful eighteenth-century rendering of Palladio's Villa Rotonda.

Stourhead, Wiltshire, c1720 by Colen Campbell, the first fully developed eighteenth-century British neo-Palladian villa. The wings were added in 1792-1804.

separated from a slightly shallower saloon by a pair of stairs flanking a central passage. Each side of the hall/saloon axis were apartments of three rooms, set in enfilade, and comprising two rectangular rooms separated by a small closet. This general arrangement was repeated on the first floor. In c1720 Campbell designed Stourhead, Wiltshire, which has a free-standing portico (built only in 1841 but to Campbell's original designs) on a rustic which, though somewhat squat, was at least present. The solecism of Baldersby was not to be repeated. And in 1722 Campbell designed Mereworth Castle, Kent, the first and most correct of four eighteenth-century renderings of Palladio's Villa Rotonda. The design for this revolutionary house, which was quickly followed the next year by Lord Burlington's rendering of the Villa Rotonda at Chiswick, reveals something about Campbell's origins as the first eighteenth-century Palladian architect.

As discussed on p104, in 1712 Campbell was producing baroque church designs in the manner of Sir Christopher Wren and then, in 1713, came Wanstead. The catalyst for this quick transition may have been the Scottish architect James Smith, who had perhaps travelled in Italy in the 1660s[4] and who led a peculiar architectural double life in Scotland. He practised in the conventional baroque style but indulged in Palladian fantasies in private. Presumably his conservative Scottish clients were not ready for the purity of Palladio. However, when Smith built a house for himself in c1690 he pursued his Palladian principles. Whitehall, as his house was called, has been identified as the centre block of Newhailes House near Musselburgh.[5] It is a remarkable proto-Palladian tripartite design, being of seven bays and two storeys over a basement, with the centre three bays breaking forward beneath a pediment and centrally placed on both front and rear elevations. The plan is a little less well organized, and rather less conscientiously Palladian. A drawing by Smith of what appears to be Whitehall before alteration survives in the RIBA[6] and shows the house to have had at ground-floor level an off-centre square hall, flanked by an oval staircase leading to a slightly larger square hall. To one side of this central axis was a large full-depth saloon with, on the other side, a bedroom with two small closets, rather in the manner of Coleshill. It seems that Campbell was influenced directly both by this house (his now demolished Shawfield, Glasgow, 1711, was derived from Whitehall) and by other Smith designs. In 1705 Smith was drawing variations on the plan of Palladio's Villa Rotonda and others of his palazzi. Campbell obtained these in about 1707 and, in the second edition (1717) of *Vitruvius Britannicus*, called Smith 'the most experienced architect' in Scotland. By this Campbell meant, presumably, not that Smith had built a great deal but that he had great 'experience' of the true classical building of Palladio.[7]

But it was not Smith, who died in 1731, who was to establish Palladianism in Scotland. This was achieved by William Adam, father of Robert, who began after 1720 to develop his own Palladian style. Initially baroque in detail, it was increasingly influenced by the southern Palladian movement. In 1721 William Adam designed the centre of the east front at Hopetoun House, Lothian, as a spirited baroque composition; but a villa at Mavisbank, Lothian, which he designed two years later, is an elegant mix of Palladian forms and baroque detail. This was for Sir John Clerk, friend of Burlington, who was to set himself up as a Palladian pundit, publishing a poem in 1727 called, *The Country Seat*, which set out the rules for designing and siting various types of country house. After Mavisbank, Adam produced a series of austere Palladian boxes, occasionally embellished with baroque flourishes, such as Lawers House, Tayside (1724-6); Dalmahoy, Lothian (1725); The Drum, Liberton, Lothian (1726-30); and Arniston, Lothian (1726-32). The last is a direct reflection of the theories of Sir John Clerk, being a house designed for 'convenience and use'. This Scottish Palladian school continued through the following decades, notable buildings being Haddo House, Grampian, by Adam (1732-5) with much debt to Clerk, and Galloway House, (1740), by Clerk's protégé John Baxter. But it was not until 1761 that the first major and pure Palladian house, untainted by Scottish baroque mannerisms, was built. Penicuik House, Lothian, designed by Sir John's son, James, with John Baxter, was an essay on Wanstead – but even by Scottish standards it was more a monument to a past style than a model to copy, for the next year the young William Chambers was building his revolutionary Duddingston nearby (p73).

Irish Palladian houses
Meanwhile in Ireland a parallel Palladian revival, in many ways independent of that taking place in England and Scotland, had got under way. In 1709 Thomas Burgh had designed a proto-Palladian house called Oldtown at Naas, Co Kildare (mostly demolished in 1950), and in 1719 the Florentine architect Alessandro Galilei produced an elevation for Castletown, Co. Kildare, which not only led to the construction of an astonishing Italian town palazzo in the Irish countryside, but also launched Irish Palladianism and, in the most dramatic way, put an end to Ireland's long period of architectural provincialism.

Though recognizably Palladian, Castletown is very different from the Palladian designs being built across the water – but then Galilei was a very different architect from Campbell and Burlington. He had been carried to London in 1714 by John Molesworth and other members of 'the new junta for architecture' (p7) but, although he dabbled in church design, failed to find any commissions, with the exception of the massive portico on the east front of Vanbrugh's Kimbolton, Cambridgeshire (c1718). He had presumably seen the English Palladian movement emerging and had examined – in the flesh or in design – Campbell's Wanstead and perhaps Burlington House; but Burlingtonian Palladianism was not what Galilei brought to Ireland. He had experienced the full power and richness of Florentine Renaissance architecture, and one can only imagine that he found the aspiring English followers of Palladio (who was, after all, of the Veneto not of Tuscany), obsessed as they were with the problems of transforming the Roman temple into houses for affluent English merchants and noblemen, faintly gauche and not a little ridiculous. For him it was far preferable to

Castletown, Celbridge, Co. Kildare, begun c1719-22 to the design of Alessandro Galilei and completed after 1726 by Sir Edward Lovett Pearce. This house introduced sophisticated Continental neo-Palladianism to Ireland.

build in the manner of his native country, where classical design had been refined over centuries. And this is what he did at Castletown. Galilei had been chosen by the 'junta' because it thought him 'the best architect in Europe', able to give British architecture more classical correctness. Castletown proves them right in the latter point if not, perhaps, in the former. Its regimented entrance façade with correctly emphasized *piano nobile* (more emphasized before the ground-floor windows were lowered in the later eighteenth century) and a handsome attic below a suitable cornice, is Palladian in the English sense, as is his use of colonnaded links to lower pavilions to provide wings in the manner of Palladio's villas in the Veneto. But what is not strictly Palladian – as Campbell understood it – is the absence of a proper rustic, which leaves the main rooms on the ground floor, and the presence of baroque detail, such as the scrolls beneath the window cills and the somewhat over-articulated architrave window surrounds. The plan is also different from the form being developed by the English Palladians, but this was probably not devised by Galilei, who returned to Italy in late 1719. It was perhaps the work of Sir Edward Lovett Pearce who in 1724 returned to Ireland from Italy, where he had studied the buildings of Palladio and thoroughly annotated his copy of Palladio's *Quattro Libri*.

What is almost certainly Pearce's is the double-height entrance hall with a screen of columns carrying a balustraded gallery; but whether Pearce inserted this into a plan that had already been resolved or simply made it the centrepiece of a plan initially devised by him is still unclear. During the four years between Galilei's departure and Pearce's arrival, a local architect, John Rothery, may have been in charge of executing the façade and may, indeed, have drawn up a plan. This was not beyond Rothery's powers for he and his family were the architects of the enigmatic Mount Ievers, Sixmilebridge, Co. Clare (c1736), which is a tall provincial Palladian house of great quality that seems inspired by illustrations of Chevening, Kent, as published in *Vitruvius Britannicus*.[8]

Castletown's plan is a strange mix of cosmopolitan grandeur and provincialism. Along the ground floor garden front the rooms are arranged in enfilade in the seventeeth-century baroque tradition, meeting in a central saloon and terminating in closets. The saloon connects to the entrance hall in the manner established in the seventeenth-century houses of advanced design, such as Robert Hooke's Ragley Hall, Warwickshire (1679-83), and Roger Pratt's Coleshill, Oxfordshire (c1650), now demolished. Also as at Coleshill, the hall is crossed by a spine corridor which creates a cross axis through the length of the house and gives the plan a double-pile form. Above the ground-floor corridor is a second corridor, at first-floor level, which crosses the hall on the balustraded gallery supported on the pairs of columns. This device – of a columnar screen placed against the inside wall of the entrance hall – is one of the elements introduced into Ireland at Castletown (although already familiar in England and used, for example, at Ragley), and which became part of the Irish eighteenth-century classical vocabulary, with versions at Bessborough, Piltown, Co. Kilkenny, by Francis Bindon (1744); Castle Ward, Co. Down (1760-73); and Castletown Cox, Piltown, Co. Kilkenny (1767-71) by Davis Ducart. Another feature of the Castletown plan that entered the Irish vocabulary is the staircase, or rather its relationship to the hall. The stairs are not paired as in contemporary English Palladian country houses, and put beside the saloon (as at Wilbury and Wanstead) or within a cross axis corridor; instead the staircase is placed in a generous hall beside the entrance hall.

Castle Ward and Castletown Cox, as might be expected, followed this staircase form, as do later houses such as Lucan House, Lucan, Co. Dublin (c1775), and Rokeby, Co. Louth (1785), by Cooley and Johnston (p86). However, there are some interesting attempts in Ireland at the Palladian reflecting stair, such as at Ledwithstown, Ballymahon, Co. Longford (dated 1746 on a hopper head), by Richard Castle; Cashel Palace, Cashel, Co. Tipperary (1730-32) by Pearce; and Ballyhaise, Co. Cavan (c1733), where stairs of different sizes face each other rather informally across the entrance hall.

The first generation of Irish Palladian houses did not follow immediately on the heels of Castletown, for in Ireland, unlike England, the early eighteenth-century country house building boom did not begin until the mid-1730s.[9] And when building began it was not Galilei's work at Castletown that provided the direct model and inspiration – it was too large and, perhaps, too foreign for that – but rather the genius of Sir Edward Lovett Pearce, who, as we have seen, was responsible for those details of Castletown that were to be much imitated. Pearce, who was related to Vanbrugh, and no doubt partly educated in architecture by him, quickly developed a remarkable style. Combining the baroque inventiveness, movement and boldness of Vanbrugh with the English Palladians' grammar and gravity, it

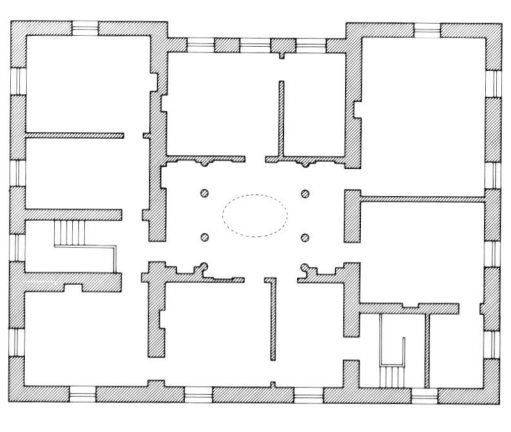

Above: Bellamont Forest, Co. Cavan, *c*1730 by Sir Edward Lovett Pearce; Ireland's first fully-formed Palladian villa.

Top: The first-floor columnar lobby at Bellamont Forest, the first use of a feature that was to become common in Irish eighteenth-century country house design.

Right: Ground and first-floor plan of Bellamont Forest. Unlike English Palladian mansions and villas, where the stairs tended to be paired and placed on a cross axis, the stair at Bellamont is in a compartment off the entrance hall, as at Castletown.

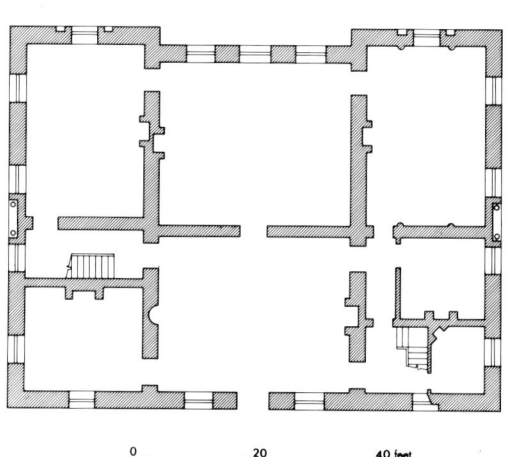

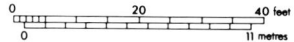

did much to establish the individuality of Irish Palladian architecture.

The other formative influence in Irish eighteenth-century classical architecture was Richard Castle, who worked closely with Pearce and who, like Galilei, was Continental (in fact from Hesse Kassel) bringing mainstream Franco-Dutch Palladian/baroque influences into the Irish building world. The importance of this pair is underlined by the fact that the country houses they designed in $c1730$–40 were not only to be major influences on the development of Irish classical architecture, but were also of international significance, for they pioneered certain details and plan forms.

Bellamont Forest, Co. Cavan, designed in $c1730$ by Pearce, introduced the thoroughly designed, four-square Palladian villa to Ireland. With a plan loosely inspired by Palladio's Villa Pisani at Montagnana, Bellamont has an oblong entrance hall leading into a slightly squarer saloon (the long sides of the two rooms run parallel with each other and with the front and back façades). The stairs, as at Castletown, are in an apartment (here a very modest apartment) off the hall. Also, as at Castletown (and, for that matter, as at Campbell's earlier Baldersby), there is no rustic but merely a squat rusticated basement, which forms a somewhat inadequate base for that necessary stamp of antique authority, the portico. The small scale of the portico at Bellamont Forest leads to the design's only serious solecism when considered by the criteria of English Palladianism. The cornice of the portico runs round the house and so sits between the handsome *piano nobile* and the first-floor windows, which consequently are rendered as square attic windows. This decorative use of the cornice breaks a fundamental Palladian tenet, for it denies its functional/structural origin as part of the roof and also ruins the illusion of the house as temple. This was a compositional freedom not often repeated by eighteenth-century Irish Palladians, notable exceptions being two Castle houses: Russborough, Blessington, Co. Wicklow (1741), and Tyrone House, Marlborough Street, Dublin (1740).

Two of the details that Pearce seems to have introduced into Irish architecture are found at Bellamont. First there is a generous columnar first-floor staircase landing – a planning device which almost immediately entered Irish country house design vocabulary – and in the side elevations there is a variation on the Venetian window theme, where blank niches are closely flanked and architecturally united with windows. This motif was used a little earlier ($c1725$–30) by Pearce for the centre piece of the south front of Drumcondra House, Co. Dublin, where it is contained within an aedicule (i.e. flanked by columns supporting an entablature and pediment), and is also found at Bellinter, Co. Meath ($c1750$), by Richard Castle, and Dysart, Delvin, Co. Westmeath (1757), by George Pentland.

Before the decade was out two other villas were built – one probably and one possibly by Pearce – that provide interesting variations on the Bellamont Forest theme. Woodlands, Santry, Co. Dublin, built $c1730$–35 on a 42-foot square plan, is designed in the round, with elevations that are a skilful essay upon the side elevations of Coleshill – even to the presence of tall chimney stacks on front and rear elevations and a crowning lantern. This reference to Coleshill is particularly interesting, and helps to substantiate the attribution to Pearce of the Castletown plan, also derived from Coleshill. (Coleshill was a particular favourite with the Irish Palladians, for Castle used the plan via Castletown as the basis for his organization of Leinster House, Dublin, 1745–7.) The plan of Woodlands, based on tripartite divisions, is simplicity and boldness combined. Down the centre of the house, from the front door at one end to the staircase at the other, runs a hall which, with rooms on each side, creates a tripartite plan. The hall itself is divided, architecturally, into three cubical compartments, each groin-vaulted. The accommodation each side of the hall is divided equally so that the back rooms are approximately square in plan and roughly one third the size of the longer, larger front rooms.

The other villa is Seafield, Donabate, Co. Dublin ($c1735$–40), which is certainly influenced by Pearce, although there are so many curiosities – not least the fact that while the front elevation is consciously designed and Palladian the other elevations are surprisingly rustic – that he could not have been very closely involved with the design of the house before his death in 1733. The front, with its two-storey, four-columned Tuscan Doric portico, is obviously derived from Bellamont Forest, but here a squat attic has been squeezed in with horizontal windows placed between cornice and string course in the manner of Palladio's Villa Sarraceno at Finale. The plan is tripartite with, in the centre, a breathtaking double-height hall, with a gallery at one end connecting the first-floor rooms, and the staircase in a compartment off. This lofty hall, running the full length of the house, together with the part-recession of the portico vestibule into the body of the house, is curiously reminiscent of James Gibbs's Sudbrook Park, Richmond, London ($c1717$–20).

60 / *Georgian Buildings*

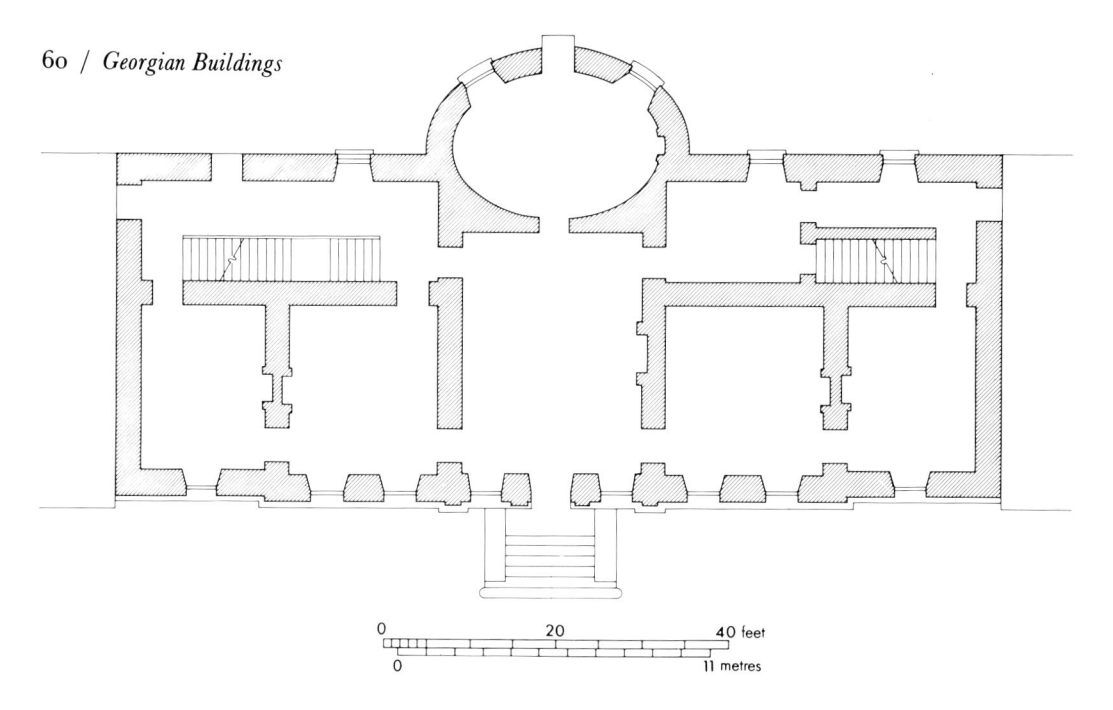

Ground plan of Ballyhaise House, Co. Cavan, *c*1733 by Richard Castle: this design introduced the centrally placed bow on the garden front expressing a round or oval saloon on axis with the hall. This became a common eighteenth-century Irish planning device, which later became popular in England.

The second major Irish prototype was built in *c*1733 to the designs of Richard Castle. Externally, Ballyhaise, Co. Cavan, is in the European baroque tradition rather than the English Palladian, and reflects some of the confusion (as did Leoni's work in England) of a baroque designer turning Palladian. Indeed Ballyhaise even shares some elevation devices with Leoni's Clandon Park, such as single storey pilasters emphasizing a central feature. But inside Ballyhaise has a conventional Palladian plan (even with rudimentary reflecting stairs on a cross axis) with the remarkable addition of a saloon on the axis of the hall, which is oval and expressed in the centre of the garden front as an elliptical bay rising the full height of the elevation.

This room is not without precedent – in Europe there were the Palazzo Barberini, Vaux-le-Vicomte and the Château de Tourney, and in England, Talman's north front at Chatsworth (*c*1687) with a huge five-bay, three-storey segmental bay with quadrant corners, and his Panton Hall, Lincolnshire (*c*1719), now demolished, with a central bay containing the apse of an elongated oval saloon. But it was startlingly new in Ireland, where it immediately entered the vocabulary

Ground plan of Belvedere, Co. Westmeath, *c*1740 by Richard Castle. This house is important for the early use of bows. Here they are two storeys high.

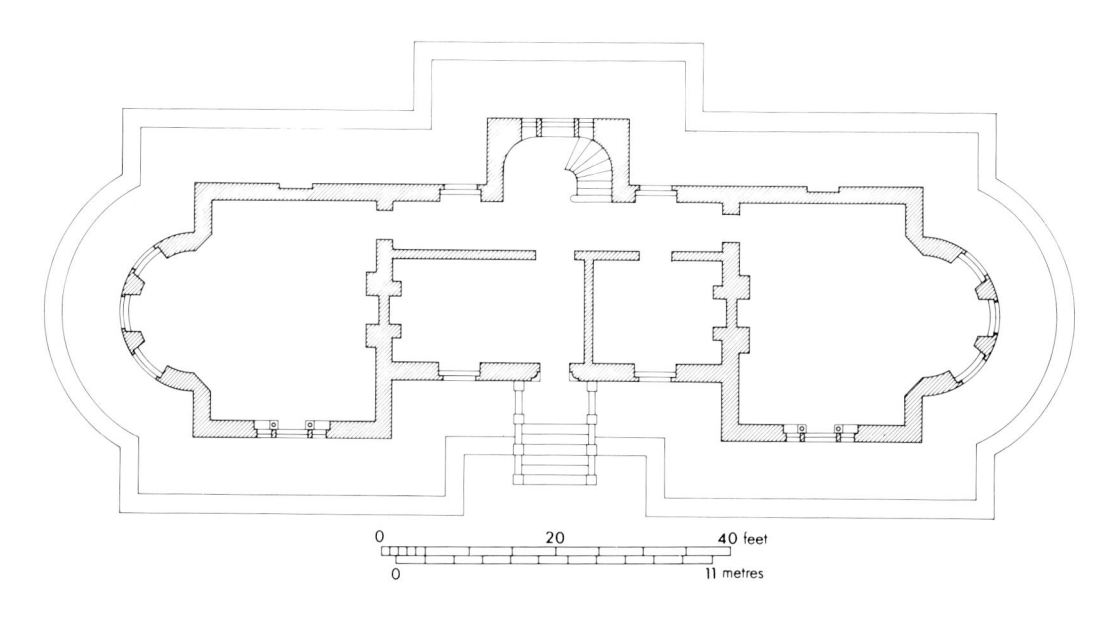

of house design, and anticipated the English fashion for oval bays in saloons by forty years.

An alternative arrangement of curved bays was also pioneered by Castle. Belvedere, Lough Ennell, Co. Westmeath, was designed *c*1740, by which time he had developed a fairly conventional Palladian manner for his elevations, even if the plan – with the end bays of the elevation breaking forward – is still baroque. But it is the side elevations, not the front, of Belvedere that are important, for they contain full-height semicircular bays lighting oblong drawing rooms.

The use of such bays was a baroque conceit favoured by Vanbrugh (at Blenheim, 1705-16, Castle Howard, *c*1700-26, and the Old Board of Ordnance, Woolwich *c*1717), but eschewed by the English Palladians, who loved only straight-line geometry. In Ireland, however, the curved bay flourished, and this particular arrangement of bays in the side elevation was quickly imitated at Drewstown, Athboy, Co. Meath, of *c*1745, probably by Francis Bindon (which has a bay on only one side), and Dysart, Delvin, Co. Westmeath (1757), by George Pentland.

The stairs at Belvedere are arranged in a staircase tower placed in the centre of the rear elevation; this may seem somewhat awkward, but a similar solution had been used by Roger Morris at the seminal English Palladian villa, Combe Bank, Kent, in *c*1725. Also Palladian are the balustrades, whose profile is inspired by those used over a century earlier by Inigo Jones at the Queen's House, Greenwich.

It was also Castle who pioneered the canted bay in Ireland. At Anneville, Mullingar, Co. Westmeath (*c*1740-45), he designed a five-bay, two-storey entrance front with a full-height centrally placed canted bay containing the front door and serving a square staircase hall. This arrangement was soon imitated and combined with side bays of the Belvedere type. Dromard, Rathkeale, Co. Limerick (*c*1750), has a full-height central bay to the entrance front and single-storey bays on the side. New Hall, Ennis, Co. Clare (*c*1760), probably by Francis Bindon, has a canted-front full-height bay with an octagonal entrance hall and full-height curved end bays. More direct essays on Anneville are Belline, Piltown, Co. Kilkenny (*c*1790), which has only a full-height central entrance bay with octagonal hall, and Lisdonagh, Headford, Co. Galway, also of *c*1790, which has a curved full-height entrance bay.

As well as these Palladio-inspired villas there were in the 1730s a few larger country houses built in Ireland which, like the villa, had design details that both correspond and conflict with contemporary English practice. Summerhill, Co. Meath, begun in 1731, showed Sir Edward Lovett Pearce at his most Vanbrughian. Massive in scale, with a central block dominated by a frontispiece of four inset giant Corinthian columns and flanked by long, tall, two-storey quadrant wings terminating in octagonal domed towers, the house really had nothing of the English Palladian school about it except for the reflecting stairs and the hall/saloon axis. Indeed, among its most notable features were its arcaded chimney stacks, inspired by Vanbrugh's work at King's Weston, near Bristol (1712-14), and Eastbury, Dorset (*c*1718). Summerhill was burnt down in 1922 and the ruin was demolished in *c*1960, to Ireland's great loss.

Almost contemporary with Summerhill was the remodelling by Richard Castle of Powerscourt, Enniskerry, Co. Wicklow, completed in 1740, which became one of the major monuments of Irish Palladianism. The entrance front has a mighty five-bay pediment supported by two-storey Ionic pilasters rising above a rusticated ground floor containing a low entrance hall. As in contemporary English Palladian mansions, the main rooms were on the first floor, including, until destroyed by fire in 1974, a splendid double-height colonnaded Egyptian hall, comparable with Burlington's at York (p174) and Dance the Elder's in the Mansion House, City of London (p151). The rear elevation is entirely rusticated and, unlike any English Palladian house of that date, is flanked by full-height curved bays that almost read as corner towers – as do the corner bays, interestingly, at the now ruined Wardtown, Ballyshannon, Co. Donegal (1740). Also un-English, but very Irish, are the complexity and extent of the wings at Powerscourt. One year after completing Powerscourt, Castle began Russborough which, with a 700-foot-long frontage, is the last word in the use of wings. Here a central block, closely modelled on Pearce's Bellamont Forest (but with the portico compressed into a pedimented pilastered frontispiece), is extended via colonnaded quadrant wings to seven-bay, two-storey pavilions, which are linked to a single-storey barn and stables by a long wall embracing a centrally placed rusticated and pedimented arch.

Bellinter, Navan, Co. Meath (1750), is one of Castle's last country houses. Like Powerscourt and Russborough, the wings are extensive and complex; but even more characteristic are the details in the elevation, which reveal the Irish Palladians' debt to English baroque. The door is devised from a pedimented tripartite type used by Vanbrugh at King's Weston; and the blind niche above

Bellinter's front door, which we noticed on the side elevation of Pearce's Bellamont Forest, was a favourite device of the Pearce/Castle school, resolving the problem of the blank centre created when an elevation was an equal number of bays wide. English baroque architects had employed this device, for instance at Finchcocks, Kent (1725), Sherman's, Dedham, Essex (c1730), and Combe Hay Manor, Avon (c1730), perhaps by John Strahan, where the niche is part of a tripartite Venetian window composition. Other Irish examples of the use of the blank, centrally placed niche are found at Castle Blunden, Kilkenny, Co. Kilkenny (c1750), and at Bessborough, Piltown, Co. Kilkenny (1744), by Francis Bindon. At Mantua House, Castlerea, Co. Roscommon, these elements are combined: a tripartite door is topped by a round-headed blank niche flanked by half windows, with above it a blank oculus, also flanked by half windows.

We must now rejoin the Palladian mainstream in England to see how its great houses evolved and how they differed from their Irish contemporaries.

English 'power houses'
Between designing Stourhead in 1720 and starting on Mereworth in 1722, Colen Campbell began work on one of the major Palladian houses of the eighteenth century, Houghton Hall, Norfolk. Houghton was a prime example of a type of house that became increasingly common during the eighteenth century – a house that was like a villa, not merely a natural extension of the estate on which it stood and for which it might serve as an administrative centre, but a symbol of power that was not just built but also maintained by a fortune made elesewhere. In the case of Houghton the fortune came from 'public service', for its builder, Sir Robert Walpole, had made a fortune out of politics. Like other great houses of the eighteenth century, Houghton, though perhaps partly maintained by local rents, had little to do with the local economy; it was a statement of individual power on the part of the builder. As Mark Girouard has explained in his *Life in the English Country House*, Houghton was a 'power house' whose purpose was to put Walpole on the social as well as the political map.

The plan that Campbell provided for Walpole expresses the social aspirations of the new age. As at Wanstead, the principal storey is placed upon a rustic which, as well as changing the external appearance of the country house, also revolutionized its use, adding another, more informal, dimension to country house life and entertaining.

At Wanstead the rustic contained, in 1722,

The west front of Houghton Hall, Norfolk, built 1721–5 to the design of Colen Campbell. The domes to the 'towers' were added by James Gibbs.

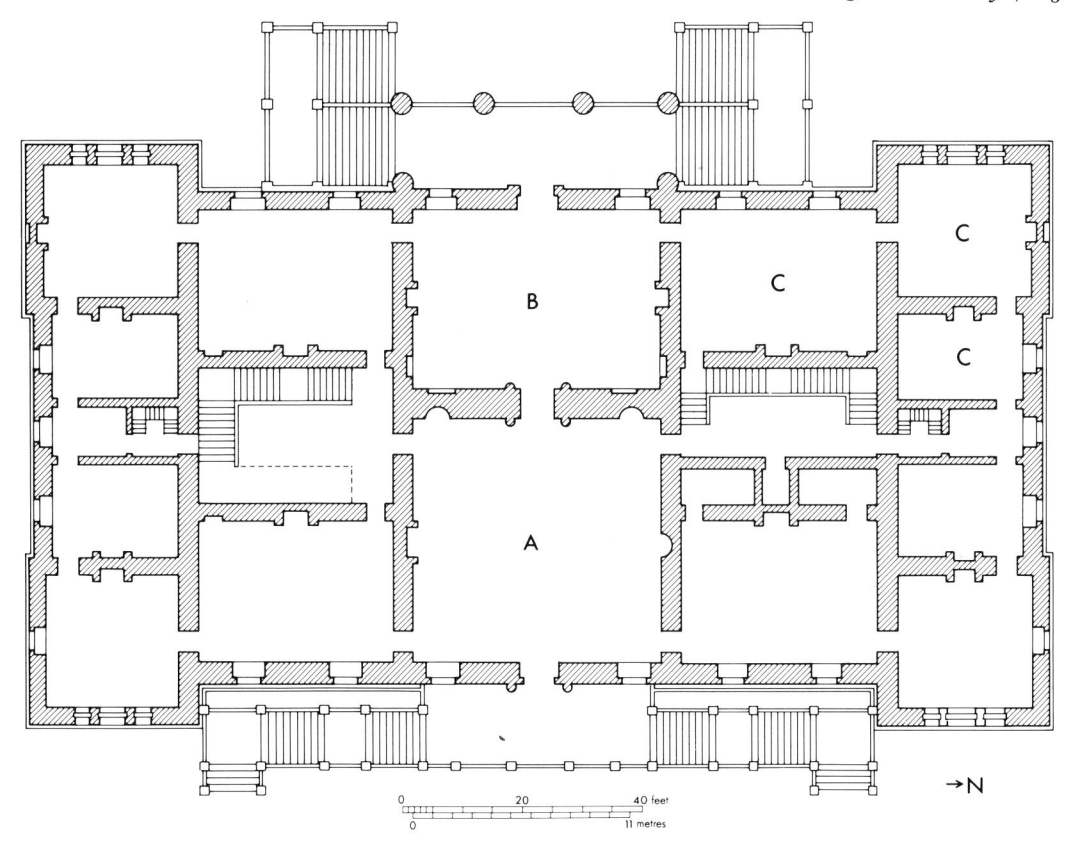

Plan of Houghton Hall, Norfolk, at *piano nobile* level. The external stair and portico as originally envisaged by Campbell are shown. A is the stone hall, B the saloon, C an apartment. The apartment in the north-east corner was altered by William Kent between 1728 and 1731 to form the marble dining parlour and picture cabinet.

family rooms and an apartment 'designed for the entertainment of their friends', which presumably included the informal dining room below the great hall. The Houghton rustic was described by Lord Hervey as the storey dedicated to hunters, hospitality, noise, dirt and business.[10] Not surprisingly, it was in the rustic that Walpole held twice-annual 'congresses', when he invited government colleagues and local gentry to spend a week at Houghton plotting, drinking and hunting. The entry into this strangely subterranean and usually vaulted world (the centre of the rustic at Houghton is called the Colonnades) might, extraordinarily enough, be the main entrance into the house. On the principal front at Holkham in Norfolk, begun in 1734 (and of which more later), a grand external stair was intended to reach up to the portico (but was never executed) in the conventional way, emphasizing the saloon/hall axis on the *piano nobile*, but on the other side of this oblong house the only entry is via the small door in the rustic. At the Palladian Marble Hill, a villa erected at Twickenham by Roger Morris and Lord Pembroke at roughly the same time as Houghton (*c*1724), the *sole* entry is the squat door in the rustic.

Above the rustic at Houghton was a very different house, designed for a different life, which Lord Hervey described as being dedicated to 'taste, expense, state and parade'. Round the formal central axis of hall and saloon was a series of four symmetrically designed three-room apartments, each made up of drawing room, bedroom and closet (although William Kent altered one apartment to form the marble dining parlour and picture cabinet between 1728 and 1731). Though not arranged in enfilade as in great baroque houses, these self-contained apartments, leading off the central formal hall and saloon, similar in arrangement to such houses as Ragley Hall (1674) by Robert Hooke, proclaimed that life in the country house had not, above the rustic, changed that much. Polite entertaining and eating were still performed in either one's own or another's private apartments, with an occasional formal gathering in the hall and saloon.

Walpole's gamble paid off: he had the money, got the house, and increased his power. But this was not always the case. One of the most extraordinary of country houses, Claydon House, Buckinghamshire, is a sad monument to a gamble that failed. In the

1760s the owner, the second Earl Verney, made a bid to unseat the Grenvilles, lodged in the splendour of Stowe House, Buckinghamshire, as the social and political leaders of the county. An essential part of this campaign was the enlargement and embellishment of his house which, with the help of the gentleman amateur architect Sir Thomas Robinson, Verney turned into a massive austere Palladian shell, decorated internally with the most sumptuous of rococo plasterwork, designed and executed by Luke Lightfoot. This included Chinese and Gothic rococo rooms, a serpentine stair with inlaid treads too good to walk on, and a 70 by 50 by 40 foot ballroom which was demolished in 1791, along with two-thirds of the house (much of which had never been completed), when Verney died a bankrupt – broken by his attempt to build himself into national prominence.

What remains of the house is interesting on another level: it reveals the fate that befell the pioneering English Palladians, such as Campbell, Burlington and, indeed, Robinson, who was a friend of Burlington and designed Claydon in the simplest, purest Palladian manner. There was a double-cube hall which, along with the cube room (as Inigo Jones had proportioned the hall at the Queen's House), became the trade-mark of the early Palladians. However, the dramatic qualities of the tall entrance hall (even if not exactly based on the ratio of 1:1:1 or 1:1:2) had not been lost on the contemporary baroque architects (p53). Vanbrugh had created a cube hall at Blenheim; Hawksmoor at Easton Neston, Northamptonshire, in 1702; and James Gibbs, who ploughed an individual furrow between Palladianism and baroque, at Sudbrook Park, Richmond, London (c1717–20), where the entire centre of a relatively modest brick house is occupied by a sumptuous cube hall with apartments off each side. These can be compared with other Palladian cubes such as the stone hall at Houghton, the cubic entrance halls at Althorp, Northamptonshire, and Trafalgar House, Wiltshire, both of 1733 by Roger Morris; the Queen's House/Houghton-derived hall at Wentworth Woodhouse, South Yorkshire (c1750), by Henry Flitcroft and the hall at Northwick Park, Avon (1732), by Lord Burlington, where even the ceiling is based on that of the Queen's House at Greenwich.

But at Claydon, in addition to this volumetric display of solidarity with the Palladian movement, we can detect something else. The key to this revelation is the degree to which Robinson hated Lightfoot. He regarded him, or rather his work, as 'absurd' and claimed to discern 'no small trace of madness in his compositions'. Lightfoot's work, with all its convoluted rococo complexity and eclectic mix of dramatically different historical and geographical sources, may look mad, but – more to the point – it was of its time; and that is what Robinson did not like.

Robinson, three years older than Burlington, was a Palladian of the first generation and, though only an amateur, had built one of the most earnest of Palladian houses in 1725–30 at Rokeby Hall, North Yorkshire. Here he embodied the Palladian precepts to be expressed in 1734 by Robert Morris in his *Lectures on Architecture*,[11] concerning the beauty of buildings composed with proportions commensurate with the cube (p10).

Understandably for a man wedded to the benefits of the cube, Robinson did not like the way things were unfolding at Claydon. His generation had managed to create rational and harmonic architecture out of baroque chaos, but already, before they were even dead, he saw in the works of Lightfoot the old ungovernable whimsy of the baroque creeping back. But what would Robinson have preferred? The answer is perhaps a little dull – more of the same on the inside as on the outside.

Palladian interiors
The early English Palladians were appalled by the licentious decorative excesses of the baroque interiors, a lingering version of which can be seen at Mawley Hall, Shropshire (1730), where Francis Smith designed a stair with the curves and head of a snake and a bedroom decorated with pilasters topped with capitals sporting cherubs kissing. Smith also produced a baroque variant on the idea of decorating the interior like an exterior, notably at Davenport House, Shropshire (1726), where the hall is painted to resemble ashlar. At Parbold, Lancashire (1730, not by Smith), the staircase hall is covered with wooden blocks, rusticated to look like masonry. Indeed, Vanbrugh had produced a good line in architectural interiors at Blenheim, and Hawksmoor followed this trend

Rococo Chinese decoration of c1765 by Luke Lightfoot at Claydon House, Buckinghamshire.

The stone hall, Houghton Hall, Norfolk, 1721-35. A 40-foot cube created by Colen Campbell and largely decorated by William Kent.

with the long gallery, which he decorated in 1722 in full Doric dress, columns, entablature, attic storey and all. It was this trend that the early Palladians developed.

In the hands of a decorative genius like William Kent, this style became every bit as successful and moving as the best baroque interiors. Kent decorated the great 40 by 40 by 40 foot stone hall at Houghton (exactly the same size as the hall at the Queen's House) with full entablature surmounting the gallery, and pedimented consoled doorcases draped with lolling putti, the whole being topped with a somewhat baroque coved ceiling, with the legs of disporting putti hanging down over the supporting architecture. In *c*1730 he gave the entrance hall at Ditchley Park, Oxfordshire (designed by James Gibbs in 1720), a Roman gravity by the careful use of self-contained architectural elements such as pedimented doors and fireplaces; and in 1738-41 he used the same elements at Rousham, Oxfordshire, but to very different effect, lending a little parlour an extraordinary dignity with an exquisitely scaled pedimented overmantel and ceiling.

A slightly different tack was pursued at Burlington's Chiswick House, which Kent decorated from 1723 to 1729. Here he accentuated the curiously small scale of this perfect little building by using internally details scaled for external use. Exactly the same pattern was used for pedimented internal doorcases as was used for the pedimented windows of the *piano nobile*. A similar over-scaling of interior detailing can be seen at Fox Hall, West Sussex (1730), by Roger Morris and Lord Burlington, and at Kent's Worcester Lodge, Badminton House, Avon (1746).

Handled with a little less skill and flair, the Palladian architectural interior could be unspeakably dull. Thomas Ripley entered the architectural scene as a carpenter and coffee house keeper in about 1705, and became a creature of Walpole; he was charged with rebuilding the Admiralty in Whitehall in 1723 (p143) – a job from which his reputation never recovered – and also took over responsibility for building Campbell's designs for Houghton. Here he learned to become a Palladian, and when, in 1727, Walpole's brother required a house at Wolterton in Norfolk, Ripley was set the task of designing it. Externally, the house he built was impeccably sober. It was in the brick astylar Palladian mode evolved by Campbell in his urban developments of *c*1718 (p31), and also practised by Burlington's protégé, Henry Flitcroft, at Bower House, Havering-atte-Bower, and Boreham House in Essex, both under construc-

At Rousham Kent created in 1738-41 this exquisitely detailed parlour, filling it with bold, large-scale architectural decoration.

The staircase at Wolterton Hall, 1727-41, where Thomas Ripley designed an architectural interior incorporating external elements.

tion in 1729. Wolterton is three storeys high, has a three-bay pediment and stands on a rustic base which an account of 1754 confirms was put to the same sort of family and informal uses as at Wanstead and Houghton. Above this rustic was the *piano nobile* with the hall, saloon, drawing room, dining room, parlour and 'two apartments consisting of a bedchamber and dressing room', on the second floor were nothing but 'lodging rooms', and all were connected by a generous staircase rising up a vestibule embellished as if it were an external courtyard or, indeed, an atrium. Floor levels are marked by windows, complete with architraves and glazing bars, doors on landings are embellished with architraves and cornices, and surmounting it all is a full entablature and glazed, squat, attic windows, not dissimilar in design to those decorating the exterior of the house.

In Ireland things had been very different. Although this sort of architectural exterior/interior had been attempted – for instance at Florence Court, Enniskillen, Co. Fermanagh (c1770), where the hall has architectural decoration reflecting the exterior; and in the double-height hall at Gloster, Brosna, Co. Offaly (c1730) – the first generation of Palladians found no problem in accepting baroque interior decorations. Indeed, designers like Pearce and Castle, more than half baroque themselves, encouraged the use not of the reformed classical decorations of the English Palladians but of the flowing lines of the Italian baroque, preferably executed by Italians. Russborough, Blessington, Co. Wicklow (1741–50), by Richard Castle is an excellent example of the Irish Palladian school, filled with the most exquisite baroque plasterwork, some of which was executed by the Italian Francini brothers.

Palladian and baroque
In England the bleakness of the architectural interior proved too much for the second generation of Palladian architects, such as Isaac Ware, John Vardy and John Sanderson. Like Lightfoot at Claydon, they chose to combine rococo interiors with warmed up Palladian exteriors, and so revived the latent baroque spirit in England which the first generation of Palladians had tried so hard to destroy. Indeed, in some quarters this spirit was far from latent. From the dates of the baroque houses already mentioned it is clear that the school penetrated deep into the eighteenth century. Two of the quintessential houses of the English baroque movement, Chicheley, Buckinghamshire, and Stoneleigh Abbey, Warwickshire (both sporting mannered Michelangeloesque details and both by Francis Smith), were not completed until 1725 and 1726 respectively. The fully blown Vanbrughian Clarendon Park, Wiltshire dates from 1737, and Swinfen Hall, Staffordshire, though in the style current in c1710, was designed by Benjamin Wyatt as late as 1759 – the year before Robert Adam began the revolutionary neo-classical remodelling of nearby Kedleston.

To make things more complicated, there was a school of sophisticated baroque/Palladian architects who, from the very earliest days of the Palladian movement, borrowed or echoed its forms and combined them with a baroque sense of movement in order to create a style calculated to appeal to the traditional baroque tastes of the generality of clients. Indeed the Earl of Malton, when remodelling Wentworth Woodhouse, South Yorkshire, was in such confusion that while still building a baroque west front, begun in c1725, he commissioned Henry Flitcroft to design a Palladian east front based on Wanstead, which was under way by 1734.

The most capable of these baroque-inclined Palladians was James Gibbs, who designed Ditchley Park, Oxfordshire, in 1720–31, made a spectacular octagonal addition to Orleans House, Twickenham, in 1720, and remodelled Wimpole Hall in Cambridgeshire c1719–21. His influence (particularly in the use of certain details like block surround windows, which he used to such dramatic effect at Ditchley) can be seen throughout the country, including Stockten Hall, Leicestershire (c1735), and in the court of Gilling Castle, North Yorkshire, remodelled c1725 by William Wakefield. It can be seen in innumerable houses in Ireland, such as Cashel Palace, Co. Tipperary (1730), by Sir Edward Lovett Pearce, Florence Court, Co. Fermanagh (c1770), and Dromana, Cappoquin, Co. Waterford (c1740), where there is an excellent pedimented Gibbs door.

A more ambiguous member of this baroque Palladian school was Giacomo Leoni who, being the first translator of Palladio's *Quattro Libri* into English (published 1716–20), ought to have merged firmly into the ranks of the first-generation Palladians. However, he did not. Perhaps, being an Italian, he knew that Palladio's works were far richer and more varied than Burlington's and Campbell's narrow definition of Palladianism implied. Clandon Park, Surrey (1730–33), and Alkrington Hall, Lancashire (1735), both by Leoni, have plans not dissimilar to Wanstead, with a pair of stairs on the cross axis and a saloon and hall (double-height in the case of Clandon) on the main axes. But externally they are tainted with too many un-

Burlingtonian details to be allowed into the Palladian camp. At Clandon and Lyme Park, Cheshire (1725), attics rise prominently above the cornice (a detail studiously avoided by Palladians, p59) and on the east front of Clandon the centre of the *piano nobile* is emphasized by small one-storey pilasters which are used too superficially and decoratively to be acceptable to Burlingtonian Palladians.

Apart from the synthesizers of baroque and Palladian ideas, like Leoni, Pearce and Castle, there was also, in England, a school of country house design that continued as a peculiar but true offshoot of the English baroque tradition right up to the mid century. But this was a baroque not of overblown or irrationally used classical motifs, as seen at Swinfen Hall; it was, rather, a development of the picturesque ideas pioneered by Vanbrugh, combined with a simple and freely interpreted classicism. Encombe House, Dorset, constructed in about 1735, though a rational building, conforms to rules dictated by its lakeside valley setting rather than to a theory of proportion and decoration. It is a long, low house, symmetrical, stripped of all unnecessary decoration, and relying on its forms and proportions to proclaim its roots in classicism. It has the flavour of Vanbrugh in his most simple mood, but the designer is not known. (It may perhaps have been amateur architect John Pitt, who inherited the estate in 1734.)

An earlier and perhaps key example of this simple, inventive, free baroque style is Warbrook House, Hampshire, designed in 1724 by John James for himself. It has a plain and original elevation, built of brick embellished with a white painted frame which implies pilasters and entablature beneath a pediment. In 1711 James had written that the 'beautys of architecture may consist of the greatest plainness of structure', which he declared, like any Palladian, 'has scarce been hit by the Tramontani [those north of the Alps] unless by our own famous Mr Inigo Jones'. Perhaps their mutual admiration for Jones is what allowed this free baroque school to co-exist with the Palladians. But the influence seems to have gone both ways. For example, William Kent's last country house, Wakefield Lodge, Potterspury, Northamptonshire, undertaken in 1748, had a curiously rugged and cyclopean quality reminiscent of Vanbrugh, with massive Diocletian windows. Inside, however, Jones is invoked, with a saloon and spiral 'mathematical' stair modelled on those in the Queen's House.

Second-generation Palladians

How, given such creative and influential opposition, coupled with a certain failing of enthusiasm amongst the younger generation for Palladianism in its purest, most austere, form, did the Palladian influence on country

Encombe House, Dorset, *c*1735, possibly by John Pitt: a late expression of stripped-down English baroque of the Vanbrugh utilitarian type.

house building survive beyond the first generation and, even stranger, how did it become part of the provincial building vernacular?

Perhaps the two-word answer to this is Holkham Hall, which was built in Norfolk from 1734 to 1761 to the design of William Kent and Lord Burlington. More than nearby Houghton, the exterior design of Holkham provided, if not exactly a model, a good starting point for architects undertaking more modest works.

It was in the undecorated Palladian style and more important, was of brick. It displayed a selection of preferred Palladian details – notably the Venetian windows on the *piano nobile* – which were all ripe for copying, and its plan was decidely more relevant to the second quarter of the eighteenth century than was Houghton's. Much of the accommodation within the rustic was sacrificed to provide space for the magnificent double-height marble hall, which was entered at ground level through the usual modest door, and which included a stately flight of steps up to the *piano nobile*. This hall, incidentally, provides another clue to the influence of Holkham: more than any other interior before, this space, with its alabaster columns, bold patterned string course, coffered apse and niches, invoked an authentic antique feel. Indeed, the hall was based on a Roman basilica plan described by Vitruvius, and reconstructed in plan by Palladio in his *Quattro Libri*. Kent's adherence to this prototype, no doubt under Burlington's influence, went as far as placing water closets in the voids behind the apse, which Palladio had marked on his plan as 'places for filth'.

This sort of accuracy, coupled with Kent's inventive flair for adapting unlikely ancient models for modern use, was important to later eighteenth-century country house architects, increasingly obsessed with the archaeologically based reconstruction and adaptation of antique buildings.

When reached, the *piano nobile* at Holkham also had something new to offer. Beyond the stairs from the hall was, indeed, still the saloon, with the giant portico beyond, and nearly half of the remainder of the *piano nobile* was given over to two bedchambers, with their related withdrawing rooms, dressing

The south front of Holkham Hall, Norfolk, the pre-eminent Palladian tower house which inspired a generation of country house designers.

A plan of Holkham at *piano nobile* level from Woolfe and Gandon's 1771 volume of *Vitruvius Britannicus*: formal apartments give way to rooms for communal relaxation and entertainment, which were neither part of someone's apartment nor lofty and formal.

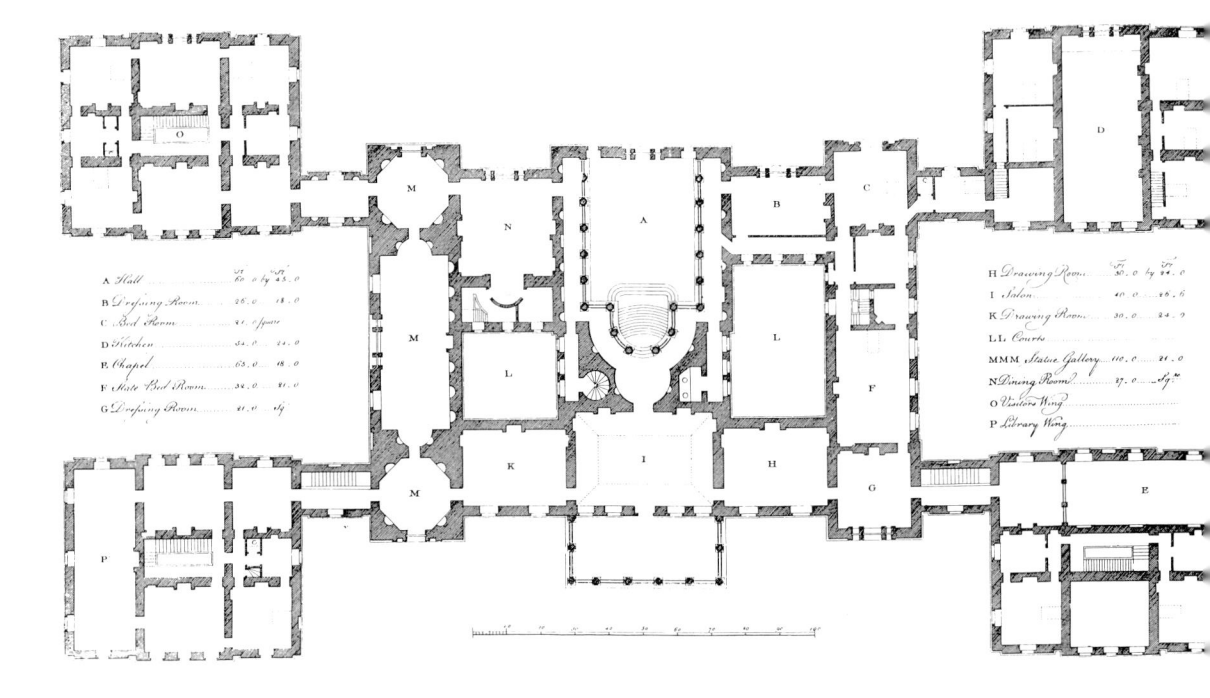

The marble hall at Holkham, Kent's major triumph of inventive archaeological reconstruction, uniting the influences of Vitruvius and Palladio.

rooms and closets. But the rest of the main floor was for communal use, where company could meet in rooms that were not part of someone's personal apartments, nor lofty and coldly formal like the saloon or hall. In one sense this was bringing the rooms, and life, of the rustic to the respectable first floor. Such a rearrangement involved not just the inclusion of a dining room on the first floor, but also a pair of drawing rooms, and a long gallery for the display of sculpture – no doubt a suitable place to dally.

To compensate for the traditional accommodation lost by this redisposition, four wings were built; one contained family rooms, including the library, a second the chapel, a third, kitchens, and the fourth, bedchambers. This was a pattern of use that continued through the eighteenth century and into the nineteenth. Libraries, which became essential country house ornaments after about 1740, often acquired a wing to themselves, as at James Wyatt's Heaton Hall, Manchester (1772), and John Wood the Younger's Buckland House, Oxfordshire (1755).

Although the surrounding countryside is scattered with bits of Holkham – such as at Hilborough Hall, Norfolk, built in 1779 for the then agent at Holkham, which sports the older house's first-floor windows over balusters – it was not just the details that were copied. The forms were also followed, most conspicuously the pyramid-roofed corner towers which do so much to stop Holkham actually looking like a Roman temple.

This element was not invented at Holkham: the immediate precedent had been set in about 1650 at Wilton, Wiltshire, where the truncated scheme for the house was rounded off by a couple of terminating pedimented towers, inspired in their details, no doubt, by Serlio's *Five Books of Architecture* (1537–47) and Scamozzi's *Dell'idea dell'Architettura* (1615), both of which were generally available in seventeenth-century England (though neither of them actually shows terminating towers with pediments).

Because the name of Inigo Jones was strongly associated in the early eighteenth century with the somewhat pragmatic design of Wilton, corner towers became a favourite device in the Palladian repertoire. But the first post-Wilton essays on their use seem to be pre-Palladian. Robert Hooke's Ragley Hall, Warwickshire (1679), has four corner towers in plan, even if they are not expressed as such in elevation, and Talman's Blyth Hall, Nottinghamshire (1683), now demolished, had square corner towers, the upper portions of which were rebuilt or extended in the eighteenth century to become conventional Palladian pyramid-roofed towers.

Campbell produced a theoretical design for adding corner towers to Wanstead in 1720 and had intended them for Houghton, but Gibbs managed to get the job of adding curious domes instead. Burlington had succeeded in adding four towers to Tottenham Park, Wiltshire (c1721), now altered out of recognition; Roger Morris copied him at Combe Bank, Kent (1725), and Sir Thomas Robinson had included a pair at Rokeby, North Yorkshire, by 1730. Even Vanbrugh was not in this respect immune to Palladian influence, and by 1722 had built a pair of towers, complete with Venetian windows as at Houghton, at Grimsthorpe, Lincolnshire. Indeed the unbuilt south front was to be an essay on Houghton, and the great hall is a double cube.

This unselfconscious imitation may seem extraordinary now, when art and individuality are held to be synonymous. But to the Palladians, who copied obsessively, it was a way of refining their style; everything, even the work of Palladio and Jones, could be improved or at least creatively adapted. Hence in one year (1735) Wanstead was followed by three other houses: James Paine's Nostell Priory, West Yorkshire (itself 'improved' at

Kirtlington Park, Oxfordshire, in 1742); Prior Park, Bath, by John Wood the Elder, who copied an early unbuilt version of Wanstead; and Wentworth Woodhouse, South Yorkshire, by Flitcroft. Of the other pure Palladian models, Marble Hill, Twickenham (c1723), by Roger Morris, was copied perhaps (but certainly not improved) by Francis Cartwright in 1740 at Kingsnympton Park, Devon; and the design of Stourhead, Wiltshire (by Campbell, 1720), was livened up with a bit of baroque movement probably by John Strahan or William Halfpenny and reproduced in 1731 at Frampton Court, Gloucestershire.

There were other forms of imitation: Ponsonby Hall, Cumbria (1780), was copied from the published design of James Paine for the now demolished St Ives, West Yorkshire, and certain architects simply reproduced their own designs. Hatton Grange, Shropshire (1764), and Brockhampton, Hereford and Worcester (1750), both by T.F. Pritchard, are plainly based on the same drawings; the elevation of Sir John Soane's Piercefield Park, Gwent (completed 1793), is a variation on his slightly earlier Shotesham Park, Norfolk; and at Berrington Hall, Hereford and Worcester (1778), Holland used the same designs for the library ceiling as he had used seven years earlier at Claremont, Surrey. But the tower house was the most imitated of all country house forms, and it was the Holkham/Wilton formula – of towers placed on virtually the same plane as a long, low, single-storey main façade with a feature centrally placed – that spawned the most direct copies.

Lydiard Tregoze, Wiltshire (1743-9), perhaps by Roger Morris, imitates the relationship; and Langley Park, Norfolk, remodelled by Matthew Brettingham the Elder (the architect who had supervised the erection of Holkham), was furnished in 1745 with four towers spaced between long and short elevations. However, the trim here is provincial baroque, with no rustic, rusticated pilasters on the entrance front, and even a tall attic above cornice level. This all, presumably, reflects an older house. In 1754 Sanderson Miller, better known for his pioneering rococo Gothic work (p14) gave Hagley Hall, Hereford and Worcester, four pyramidal corner towers and pedimented windows to the *piano nobile*, with those in the towers furnished with stone balustrades as at Holkham, and set the whole on a rustic base. At about the same time, Miller was involved, with Lancelot Brown, in the design of Croome Court, Hereford and Worcester, which is modelled on Hagley; and in about 1755 Kimberley Hall, Norfolk, was given four neat pyramidal towers by amateur architect Thomas Prowse.

The interiors of these houses that followed Holkham were very different. The plan of Hagley is a curious cross between Houghton and Holkham, having a fine internal staircase (indeed a pair) like the former and, like the latter, a long gallery and dining and drawing rooms on the *piano nobile*, along with the hall, saloon and three two-bedroom apartments. Langley has fine rococo plasterwork of c1745, especially in the hall where allegorical figures abound, and a Monkey Room by the French room-painter J.F. Clermont, who was in England from 1745 to 1755 and created similar rooms full of cavorting monkeys at Narford Hall, Norfolk, and Kirtlington Park, Oxfordshire. Hagley has much light rococo plasterwork and, in the hall, a fireplace formed by a pair of writhing Hercules supporting a cornice; and Croome Court, completed internally after 1760, contains early neo-classical work by Robert Adam.

The leap is complete – from the Palladian architectural interior through rococo to the dawn of neo-classicism – and all within the form of the Palladian tower house.

But this is a deceptive view for, as we have seen, by 1760 a fundamental change had taken place in the plan, more particularly in the size, position and role of staircases – a topic of some importance, for the renaissance of the staircase after 1750 is one of the most extraordinary aspects of country house development.

The staircase

To the pure English Palladian, the internal stair in a country house was of little importance. The state rooms were all on one level and so the means of communication between levels did not have to match the state apartments in grandeur. Relatively functional pairs of stairs were arranged symmetrically on a minor cross axis not only at Wanstead, but also before at Wilbury, and later at Inveraray Castle, Strathclyde (a Palladian house in castellated guise by Roger Morris in 1745); Stowe, Buckinghamshire; Kirtlington Park, Oxfordshire (1742), by W. Smith and John Sanderson; Bank Hall (now the Town Hall), Warrington, Cheshire, by James Gibbs (1750) and Hagley Hall (1754-60).

There was little precedent in Palladio's villas for large internal stairs and, perhaps more to the point, they were difficult to accommodate in formal early Palladian houses. Obviously, if a grand stair were to be included then it would have to be in either the hall or saloon – a fact faced by Sir Roger Pratt who when designing Coleshill, Oxfordshire, in the late 1640s placed the stair in the great hall and had, in the Elizabethan way, a great dining hall or chamber on the first floor. Vanbrugh found another solution at King's Weston, Avon, of 1712, where the grand staircase rises through the hall.

For the designers of the largest Palladian houses the choice was not quite so dramatic: the grandest of staircases, as at Houghton, could be inserted without compromising the apartment plan. But what happened within the smaller Palladian house? We have seen that Ripley made a fetish of the staircase at Wolterton, trapping it within a top-lit architectural box; at Marble Hill, Twickenham, a stockily detailed open-well stair rises in a stair compartment on one side of the plan, and at Stourhead, where the plan (with a 30 by 30 by 30 foot central hall leading to a saloon) is a smaller version of a great Palladian house, the stairs are between hall and saloon. At Roger Morris's Combe Bank the stairs are virtually chucked out of doors, being placed originally in a little protruding tower, as at Richard Castle's Belvedere (p61), with an even smaller secondary stair creeping up in the corner of one of the Palladian front towers.

Wolterton provides the key to the future. If the levels were to be linked in a style comparable with the pretensions of the grand rooms, indeed if the stairs were to be included in the formal circuit of the house, then a centrally placed top-lit arrangement was the answer. Indeed in the 1720s Burlington had hit upon this solution when designing Richmond House, Whitehall. Being in London, the house was limited in size, so Burlington inserted a compact circular staircase with the aim of gaining in geometrical appeal what it lost in volume. When the second generation of villa builders got under way in about 1750 this was precisely the formula that was followed. As with the post-1715 villa boom in England, the clients in the 1750s were men who had made their money in the colonies or the cities, and who wanted compact country seats in manageable little parks.

Villas in the 1750s

What external form should this new breed of villa take? The 'great plainness' preferred by John James, and mentioned earlier, and the rigidity of the Palladians, who followed Inigo Jones's doctrine that architecture should mimic the outward behaviour of 'every wyse man' who 'carrieth a graviti in Publicke Places' while 'inwardly hath his immaginarcy set on fire and sumtimes licenciously flying out', had produced memorable architecture full of surprises. Who would guess from the chaste exterior of Chiswick or Mereworth the richness of gilt paint and plaster within, or divine the rich rococo interiors hidden within the plain shells of Claydon, Buckinghamshire, Gately Hall, Norfolk (1726), and Catton Hall, Derbyshire (1741)?

But for the villa campaign of the 1750s the stately Palladian façade concealing interior riches, be they of the formal Palladian kind or wild rococo, was not the answer. A new informal plan was evolved with, to complement it, a new form of external composition reflecting the volumes of the new interior. Both the interior and the exterior were based on a single key element: inside, the centrally placed, top-lit staircase; outside, the bay.

It was at this point that the country house architecture of England and Ireland left its parallel paths and began to merge. The compositional device of the curved or canted, full-height or one-storey bay, which had been developed in Ireland since Castle's Ballyhaise (1733) and Belvedere (c1740), was also embraced by English architects. Another reason for this convergence of English and Irish architectural intent must be the fact that in about 1760, for the first time in the century, leading English and Scottish architects – Chambers, and later Gandon and James Wyatt – were given the opportunity to design major buildings in Ireland.

The bow

The bow is worth pursuing at a little more length, for its arrival in English country house architecture in the middle of the century had such dramatic results – or rather its revival, for the curved or faceted bay had been a major element in country house design during the sixteenth century, and full-height curved bays had been used by Vanbrugh at Blenheim (1705-23), Castle Howard (c1700-26) and the Old Board of Ordnance, Woolwich (1718), and by Talman at Panton Hall, Lincolnshire (1719). At Chettle House, Dorset (c1720, probably by Thomas Archer), the entrance hall has been given more architectural interest and chamfered corners by being extended outwards to create a shallow bow, rather in the manner of much later Irish houses like Longfield, Goold's Cross, Co. Tipperary. In the 1720s this was all stopped in England by the first-generation Palladians, but by the 1740s even Burlington had to acknowledge the possibilities of the bay – albeit canted rather than curved – by using them at Kirby Hall, North Yorkshire. This new acceptance was confirmed in 1750, when that arch-Palladian theorist and champion of the cube, Robert Morris, published in his book *Rural Architecture* a design for 'a structure overlooking a valley', which consisted of a

Above: Rear elevation of Sir Robert Taylor's Harleyford Manor, Buckinghamshire, 1755, the first expression of the English mid-eighteenth-century villa boom.

Right: Plan of the principal floor of Harleyford. The rooms, of different shapes, revolve around a centrally placed top-lit stair. Rooms interconnect to form a circuit round the house for evenings of entertainment. A is the library, B the drawing room, C the dining room.

square containing four octagonal rooms, each expressing itself in the form of a three-sided canted bay. The second-generation rococo Palladians such as Isaac Ware were quick to follow. In 1754 Ware produced Wrotham Park, Hertfordshire, a Palladian country house full of movement, including not only the essential detached portico fronting the entrance hall, but also flanking bays containing Venetian windows and octagonal domed pavilions. A similar composition was followed by David Hiorne in 1759 for Foremark Hall, Derbyshire (which in many ways is an abbreviated copy of Wrotham), and in 1755 Sir Robert Taylor designed Harleyford Manor, Buckinghamshire, which used a variety of bays in combination and also reflected some of the major changes that were taking place in the way country villas were used – indeed in the way country houses and the country were perceived.

By the mid-eighteenth century the idea of being perched above ground level in order to enjoy distant prospects had lost its appeal. The informality of landscape garden design pioneered by William Kent at Carlton House, London, in 1734 and developed at Stowe and Rousham, and an increasing awareness and appreciation of the country in its 'natural' state (or rather in a state of nature as formed by those such as Lancelot Brown and later Humphry Repton) meant that as the century progressed, more and more houses had their main floors at ground level. Thus nature could flow more easily into the drawing room, or at least the garden could be reached without a tiresome trek through the rustic.

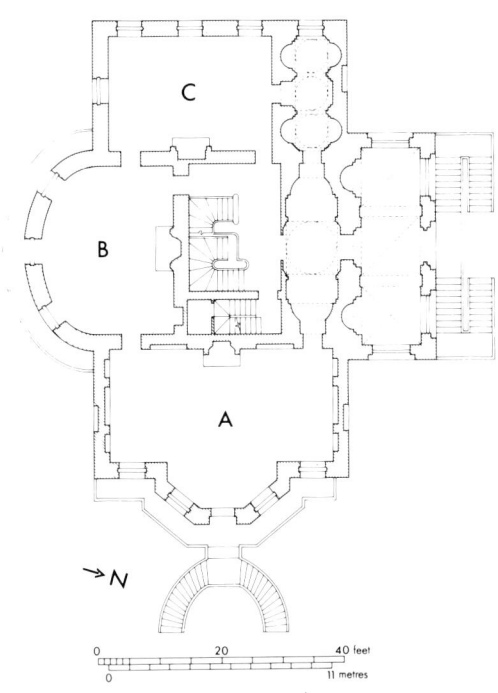

The villas of Sir Robert Taylor, James Paine and Sir William Chambers were the first expression of this new taste for close contact with the garden; but this was not all they pioneered. Gone, also was the formal hierarchy of axially related saloon and hall. In its place was a circuit of rooms for communal use and informal entertaining, of equal size and importance, though often of different shape and colour, and revolving round and generally connecting with the central top-lit staircase. At Harleyford the ground floor was still not quite in touch with the garden – it was placed on an *unrusticated* semi-basement – but it did contain the main rooms. The entrance front was emphasized in the Palladian way, with a three-bay pediment breaking forward in a five-bay façade, and the exterior, too, was still treated in austere Palladian fashion. But behind the pediment was a vestibule leading to a central top-lit stair, round which revolved three rooms of equal importance. In the daytime these rooms were called the drawing room (with a curved bay), the library (with a canted bay) and the dining room, which was rectangular; but on nights when the house was opened up for entertaining, with guests following a circuit from room to room rather than standing or sitting formally in a circle in the saloon or hall, they became card room, ballroom and supper room. The floors above were used as bedrooms (with a pair of oval rooms fitted behind the curved bay) and the main kitchen was in a detached building connected to the villa by a tunnel – one of the tricks (learned from Palladio) that allowed the designers to make their villas so compact.

A similar villa to Harleyford was built at Barlaston, Staffordshire, in 1756, almost certainly to the design of Taylor, and is peculiar not only for its display of two- and four-storey bays, but also for the eclectic mix of its decorations. The exterior is in the austere brick astylar Palladian style, with bold cill and string courses and a strong block cornice, as favoured by Taylor; and the five-bay entrance front still reflects the conventional Palladian villa's arrangement of windows, with a three-bay centre flanked by recessed single bays. But the main door speaks in a different language – the baroque. It has a segmental pediment and a rusticated frame, and on the ground floor Taylor revived Gibbs's baroque block window surrounds, combining them with mannered triple keystones and segmental pediments.

Palladian and rococo
What all this reflects is the spirit of freedom that followed in the wake of the collapse of Palladian authority. Gradually the rococo spirit of invention, which had been indulged inside houses since the early 1740s, was beginning to creep outside. Taylor was to produce other villas of this type: Asgill House, Richmond upon Thames (1760–65); Danson Park, Bexley (1760–65), completed internally by Sir William Chambers c1770); Chute Lodge, Wiltshire (1760), with a beautiful winding top-lit stair; and Purbrook, Hampshire (1770, demolished 1829), which had an unprecedented and Pompeii-inspired colonnaded atrium instead of a central staircase. At Sharpham, Devon (1770), Taylor made another leap that landed him firmly in the vanguard of the picturesque movement. Here he perched the villa high above the river Dart – in what can only be called a sublime position – with all its main windows positioned to provide the best possible vistas. As Taylor pioneered the villa form, John Carr quickly threw off his somewhat dull provincial Palladian mantle (Huthwaite, North Yorkshire, 1748) to explore and expand the possibilities of the type with Constable Burton, North Yorkshire (1762), inspired by Palladio's Villa Emo; Denton, North Yorkshire (1770), and Norton Place, Lincolnshire (1776). But it was left to Chambers to put the villa back firmly in its historical context, and to launch it in the direction it was to follow for the remainder of the eighteenth century, and, indeed, into the nineteenth century.

In 1760 Chambers designed at Roehampton, London, a building now called Manresa House, a somewhat predictable, if elegant, essay on Campbell's Palladian Stourhead. Two years later, at Duddingston, just outside Edinburgh, he created a villa which was – externally at least – the neo-classical riposte to Stourhead. Gone was the Palladian baroque form adhered to by Taylor. Here was a chastely detailed two-storey villa, with a five-bay entrance front supporting a free-standing Corinthian portico which, like a classical temple (and like temple-fronted baroque houses such as Moor Park, p54) had columns that sat firmly on the ground. For the first time in the eighteenth century a Scottish building was not only in the mainstream of country house development in Britain but actually in the vanguard. Moreover the service block is set asymmetrically to the main block, foreshadowing a picturesque grouping that was to become common after about 1780. But in his evocation of the temple front Chambers was not alone; in Buckinghamshire at virtually the same time Chambers' great future rival, Robert Adam, was raising a strangely similar portico at Shardeloes. Three years later, in 1765, Chambers designed Peper Harow, Surrey. Now much altered, the house was an astylar version of Duddingston externally, though with more decoration on its wall surfaces; but it displayed the same grave interiors where, as with the first-generation Palladian houses, architectural elements rather than rococo patterns were used for embellishment.

Villa design was not a world in itself, however; the ingenuity of plan and movement of façade pioneered by the architects of those compact buildings influenced the design not only of small country houses, such as the extraordinary geometrical Moor Park, near Crickhowell, Powys (c1770), but also of larger ones. The man who best represents this leap is James Paine. Early in his career Paine revealed a strong tendency towards the fast disappearing romantic baroque school. Wadworth Hall, South Yorkshire, designed in c1750, has a cyclopean scale to certain of its

Duddingston House, Lothian, 1762–7 by Sir William Chambers in a chaste, neo-classical style anticipating later eighteenth-century villa design.

parts that is pure Vanbrugh with a dash of Piranesi. Ormsby Hall, Lincolnshire (1752), and Stockeld Park, North Yorkshire (1758), hover between baroque and Paine's own unique Palladian style, but Brocket Hall, Hertfordshire, of 1760 put Paine firmly in the avant-garde of villa architects. Yet Brocket is no villa; its garden front – four storeys high over a basement and five bays wide – is flanked by a pair of three-window-wide four-storey-high canted bays, clearly positioned not only to give the façade a sense of movement but also to afford vistas and to catch the sun. Bywell Hall, Northumberland, also *c*1760, is interesting as a play on the conventional Palladian house. Here is a rusticated ground floor which is no longer a rustic, for it is high and contains the main rooms of the house. Upon this base sits the pedimented and columned frontispiece, which rises through the first and second floors but fronts nothing other than the first-floor breakfast room. The portions of the façade flanking it – as if to challenge the now spurious superiority of the central giant pediment – sprout more modest pediments of their own. As well as pointing out the conflict between old ideas of hierarchically composed exteriors (where pediments or porticoes were meant to front main rooms) and the new egalitarian plan, this design also gives the house a picturesque gabled silhouette which is very much in the spirit of the time, and very different from the Palladian idea of temple-like horizontality.

Sandbeck Park, South Yorkshire (1763), with a projecting Corinthian portico on irregularly spaced columns, all sitting on a rustic arcade, is one of Paine's most dramatic houses and also one of the most interesting. The saloon, which stretches the length of the house, has a ceiling designed in 1775 and, like Encombe and Warbrook, represents one of the tributaries of eighteenth-century taste that ultimately led nowhere. The ceiling is in Paine's neo-classical style which he evolved out of his earlier rococo manner (Wadworth Hall) as an alternative to the neo-classicism of Adam. Adam, of course, won; and not only in general but also in particular, for Paine had the mortification of seeing Adam supersede him in the design and decoration of three major country houses, including Kedleston, Derbyshire. The last Paine house to examine is Wardour Castle, Wiltshire, which, more than Bywell even, can be seen as a parody of and epitaph for the Palladian movement.

Wardour is externally almost perfect Palladian, and appears comparable with Paine's Thorndon Hall, Essex, which was completed in the year Wardour was begun (1770). There is a properly proportioned rustic containing a main door so small that one almost has to crawl through it (a grand external stair to the first floor had been planned). Above the rustic rise, on the garden front, two-storey giant Corinthian columns supporting a three-bay pediment. Here things start to go astray. The columns are irregularly spaced, with a pair serving to emphasize each end of the pediment, while coupled pilasters make a sudden appearance to emphasize the corners of the main façade. But never mind, the *piano nobile* is truly noble with pedimented windows and lots of wall above, and the second-floor windows are so attic-like that they are not just square, which would have been good enough, but are actually squeezed into horizontally stressed oblongs. On the entrance front, as on the eastern short elevation, is the traditional mark of the Palladian – the Venetian window.

Inside, however, Paine drops the Palladian pun and applies with great force the design principles of the mid-century villa, sweeping the rustic storey up to the *piano nobile* with a magnificent, curving, top-lit central staircase which, placed in a colonnaded circular compartment 60 feet high, is one of the most spectacular staircases to be built in eighteenth-century England.

This play upon Palladian themes was paralleled in some contemporary Irish country house architecture, but with very different results. This was partly due to the difference in the emphasis placed upon Palladian elements by English and Irish architects: the latter, for example, remained obsessed with the use of wings which, as shown by Lodge Park, Straffan, Co. Kildare (1775), and Colganstown, Newcastle, Co. Dublin (*c*1765), both probably by Nathaniel Clements, became more extensive and geometrically

Ceiling detail from Sandbeck Park, showing Paine's blending of neo-classical, rococo and Palladian elements.

South front of Wardour Castle, Wiltshire, 1770-76 by James Paine: a Palladian design that verges on the ironic, with an extra-small rustic entrance door and visibly 'squashed' attic windows.

complex as the century wore on. The difference was also partly the result of conflicting and in some cases incompatible traditions in English and Irish country house design. For example, the large and architecturally embellished first-floor staircase lobby, which Pearce had introduced at Bellamont Forest in 1730 (p59) remained in favour during the 1760s and, indeed, through the following decades, so preventing the development of the imposing centrally placed top-lit stair that characterized contemporary English country houses and villas. The difference is well illustrated by Vernon Mount, Douglas, Co. Cork (c1785), where a fine stone and wrought iron cantilevered stair curves up to, but not within, a handsome first-floor colonnaded oval lobby, and this lobby is given priority as an architectural space over the staircase hall. Such was the strength of this Irish tradition that even Castle Coole, Enniskillen, Co. Fermanagh, despite being largely the design of James Wyatt, contains a grand first-floor staircase lobby.

Another of the major differences between English and Irish late Palladian essays is more difficult to pin down, but has to do with a boldness of thinking and daring disregard for the conventions of scale and composition: qualities that characterize such Irish houses as Newberry Hall, Carbury, Co. Kildare. Built in about 1765, perhaps to the design of Nathaniel Clements, Newberry is of three bays and two storeys; the centre bay in the entrance front is pedimented and breaks forward, and contains a tripartite door with a massively scaled Diocletian window above. The other second-floor windows have to be square, like attic windows, to correspond with the depth of the Diocletian; and a Venetian window, topped with a small Diocletian window, is placed on the side elevation to light the stairs. On the back elevation, following the tradition established by Castle at Ballyhaise in 1733, is a full-height curved bay lighting the saloon.

This original and logical combination of familiar classical motifs and traditional plan arrangement makes for a visually powerful building of real distinction. Colganstown, Newcastle, Co. Dublin, of roughly the same date and probably by the same designer, presents the same main elevation (though without the pediment and rendered rather than brick-fronted) but has the stair rising in the full-height, centrally placed rear bay. Other examples of bold mid-eighteenth century Irish design are Castlecor, Ballymahon, Co. Longford (c1760-80), which has a large, open, octagonal core (complete with a centrally placed, four-faced chimney stack), to which are attached four projecting arms of equal size and shape, two of which link to form an entrance block; and Millmount, Maddockstown, Co. Kilkenny (c1765), by William Colles, which has a cruciform plan with full-height curved bays in the ends of two opposite arms, and pediments over the other arms.

The Irish baroque revival

The differences between the Palladian essays of Paine in England and Irish Palladian survivals and adaptations pale to nothing when the other Irish architectural trend of the 1760s is considered – the baroque revival. It was the work of one architect, Daviso de

Newberry Hall, Co. Kildare, a powerful design using large-scale Palladian motifs.

Arcourt, or Davis Ducart as he became known in Ireland. He arrived in about 1765, seems to have left in 1771, and he came directly from northern Italy[12] to Cork or Limerick without spending time in England. Consequently his Franco-Italian baroque manner arrived in Ireland undiluted by contemporary English architectural theories or fashions, as is only too apparent in his designs. These, from the mid-eighteenth-century English point of view, are quite astonishingly unprincipled and shameless in their baroque references. Kilshannig, Co. Cork (c1765), has a plan, albeit reduced and simplified, derived from Vanbrugh's Castle Howard, North Yorkshire: in it are incorporated a circular stair inspired by Jones's model in the Queen's House, Greenwich, and an entrance front that is an extraordinary essay in Continental baroque. There is a single-storey three-bay frontispiece in which the ground-floor openings – topped by round niches – are embraced by stocky Doric pilasters supporting a full entablature. The rest of the front is three storeys, for a square mezzanine window is slipped between ground and first floor – a device virtually unknown in main elevations in both England and Ireland since the beginning of the eighteenth century. By contrast, Lota, Glanmire, Co. Cork (1765), is surprisingly Palladian, with the conventional emphasis of a three-bay pedimented centre breaking slightly forward. But the porch in the centre of this façade is so baroque, with its banded columns, block pilasters and curving entablature, that it has been described by Maurice Craig as looking like a Victorian addition by a member of the Barry School.[13]

Castletown Cox, Piltown, Co. Kilkenny, is Ducart's last Irish country house, built 1767–71, and although it has an entrance/stair hall relationship inspired by the older Castletown, the front elevation is a return to the baroque. It has stout two-storey Corinthian pilasters embracing the three centre bays and supporting a full entablature, above which rises an attic storey. All this is evidently derived from that influential model for early eighteenth-century English country house designers, William Winde's Buckingham House, London, which was built in 1705.

The Gothic country house

While the Palladian precepts of the early eighteenth century were being adapted and enlivened with bows, bays and ingeniously scaled details by the new generation of mid-eighteenth-century villa architects, another more revolutionary development had taken place. The Gothic country house appeared; or rather, reappeared. In c1717, before the

Vanbrugh Castle, Maze Hill, Greenwich, London, c1717 by Sir John Vanbrugh in his symmetrical castle style, with classical openings. The wing was added in 1723 to make the composition asymmetrical.

Palladian movement had even established itself, Vanbrugh had built himself Vanbrugh Castle in Greenwich. The castle was a strong evocation of the past and, by being almost theatrically military in appearance, managed simultaneously to express Vanbrugh's interests in war, architecture and theatre. And although it was intensely personal it was not without progeny, for from it followed a long line of castellated houses, half follies and half homes, that stretched right through the eighteenth century and into the nineteenth century. Significantly, Vanbrugh's castle did not contain Gothic detail. The windows were round-headed, the details spare classical and the plan symmetrical (until he extended it in c1723 and made it asymmetrical), which gave the structure the air of a Roman bastion rather than a medieval castle. The 'castle air' which Vanbrugh had discussed in 1707 in relation to Kimbolton Castle, Hampshire (1707–19), made, as he said, 'a very noble and masculine shew'.

The same cannot, perhaps, be said of the other brand of Gothic medievalism, which made itself felt in country house design in the 1740s and was part of the rococo fashion. This type of Gothic, closely akin to the decorated buildings that both Kent and Gibbs had been designing as garden ornaments in the 1730s (p97) was really just a variety of rococo where English traditional motifs were substituted for Italian classical (or, indeed, Chinese). One of the major promoters of this style was entrepreneur, publisher and designer Batty Langley, who published his *Ancient Architecture Improved* in 1741, gauging the oncoming rococo Gothic fashion, and offering decorative rococo Gothic designs within a framework of orders based on the classical model (see p14). Langley's influence can be found in numerous country houses, such as the fireplaces at Stout's Hill, Gloucestershire (1743, perhaps by William Halfpenny), Alscot, Warwickshire (*c*1750, by John Phillips), and Tissington Hall, Derbyshire, where the hall fireplace is closely based on a design in Langley's book.

Although initially popular primarily as a form of interior decoration, rococo Gothic also developed for a while as an alternative to classicism for the exterior embellishment of country houses, when Gothic of a pretty and domestic scale, as opposed to a castle style, was required. One of the earliest Gothic exteriors is Radway Grange, Worcestershire, an Elizabethan house transformed in 1744 by the pioneering rococo Gothicist Sanderson Miller, who in 1755 gave the great hall at Lacock Abbey, Wiltshire, the 'monastic' rococo Gothic treatment. But the most influential, if not the earliest, of rococo Gothic houses was Strawberry Hill, Twickenham, which from 1751 Horace Walpole turned into a mock medieval asymmetrical fantasy. It contained not only inventive and original designs, such as the staircase and hall by Richard Bentley (1751–61) and ceiling and chimneypiece by Robert Adam (1760), but also spurious attempts at historical authenticity, with fireplaces and bookcases based on the designs of medieval tombs, and ceilings copied from medieval window tracery. Of particular interest are the Gothic gateway and Beauclerk Tower of 1776, designed by James Essex, who was possibly the first architect in the eighteenth century to have a real antiquarian knowledge of both Gothic construction and decoration. In the decade 1752–62 three other notable rococo Gothic country houses were built: Arbury Hall, Warwickshire (*c*1755), which had its own little Committee of Taste to design it (as Walpole had at Strawberry Hill), including Sanderson Miller, Henry Keene and Richard Bentley, and which contains arguably the best rococo Gothic interiors in the country, especially the lavish fan-vaulted plasterwork of the saloon; Ecton Hall, Warwickshire (1756), attributed to Sanderson Miller; and Donnington Grove, Berkshire (*c*1762), designed by John Chute, who was on Walpole's Committee of Taste.

In Ireland rococo Gothic arrived late but with style. In 1760 Castle Ward, Strangford, Co. Down, was designed for Lord and Lady Bangor, a husband and wife with different architectural tastes. The husband's entrance elevation is copybook Palladian – rusticated ground floor, three-bay pediment with engaged columns – while the wife's garden elevation is Strawberry Hill Gothic, with seven bays and three storeys of ogee- and two-centre pointed windows, and a battlemented parapet. The split is followed internally, with spectacular plaster fan vaulting in the drawing room and a classical entrance hall with a column and stair relationship as at Castletown. The only other major example of mid-eighteenth-century country house rococo Gothic is Moore Abbey, Monasterevin, Co.

Above: The Gothic elevation of Castle Ward, Co. Down. The other elevation is text book Palladian.

Below: The interior of Castle Ward is both Gothic and classical: the drawing room is particularly dramatic, with udder-like pendentives.

Kildare (1767), which has a rather plain three-storey, seven-bay main block with two-storey attached wings, all containing pointed windows. Inside there is modest Gothic plasterwork in the drawing and dining rooms, which, like Batty Langley's Gothic, follows the classical canon and its conventions of proportions and composition.

After the decade 1752–62 the rococo Gothic began to founder, being superseded by castellated Gothic for exteriors, and by a more refined Gothic – in keeping with the delicacy of the fashionable neo-classicism of Robert Adam – for interiors. At Sheffield Place, East Sussex for example, James Wyatt designed in c1780 an elegant Gothic staircase landing, with quatrefoil-section columns supporting a dome decorated with light Gothic tracery.

After castellated and rococo came a third strand of Gothic, which might more properly be called eighteenth-century good manners. Throughout the century it was not unusual for a house to be enlarged or altered in keeping with the dominant style of the original building. For example, when in 1760 Timothy Lightoler altered the entrance hall, long gallery and staircase hall of Burton Constable Hall, Humberside, built in the sixteenth century, he worked in a kind of Jacobean revival style, as did the architect who designed the mid-eighteenth-century Jacobean-style fireplaces at Baggrave Hall, Leicestershire. And when Temple Newsam, Leeds, had a south wing added by local architect Thomas Johnson in 1796 it was in the Jacobean/Carolean style of the main house, as was some of the work by Wyatville in 1806–11 at Longleat Wiltshire. Consequently there are a number of major Gothic houses which are Gothic merely out of sympathy, or by association with an existing structure. A notable example is Milton Abbey, Dorset, which the unlikely figure of Sir William Chambers enlarged between 1769–75, in a Gothic style intended to invoke a memory of the old building and to blend with what remained of it.

After the collapse of the rococo Gothic came the full-blooded revival of Vanbrugh's 'castle style'. His picturesque, romantic castellated folly house at Greenwich had not been imitated immediately – although there is at Somersby, Lincolnshire, a funny little house, dated 1722 and previously attributed to Vanbrugh, though it is more likely to be by Robert Alfrey, which, while pedimented, has machicolations on its emphasized end bays.

A more startling early castellated house is Clearwell in Gloucestershire, built 1725–30 to the designs of Roger Morris who, despite his sound Burlingtonian Palladian credentials, went on in 1745 to design the first major castellated country house since Vanbrugh. At Inveraray, Strathclyde, the Palladian and Gothic were mixed with delightful relish. The plan is Palladian – pairs of stairs of equal size with the hall, vestibule and gallery on axis in the *piano nobile*, above a basement which looks into a dry moat. The window openings are pointed, and the symmetrical, oblong house, with four round corner towers, is topped with a Doric block cornice. After 1760 these delightful mock castles appeared with increasing speed. Stoke Park, Stoke Gifford, Avon, was castellated c1760 by Thomas Wright; in 1764 Robert Adam created a toy fort at Ugbrooke Park, Devon, and a few years later he castellated Mellerstain, Borders, while at the same time providing it with an exquisite neo-classical interior. In 1775 John Carter, who was to become a pioneer in the antiquarian approach to the Gothic revival (p19) designed the playful triangular Midford Castle, Avon, while in 1777 Robert Adam designed one of the finest of his romantic castellated houses, Culzean, Strathclyde.

The castle movement
To understand the twin prongs of the castle movement as it developed after 1770 we must compare Culzean with Downton Castle, Hereford and Worcester, designed in 1772 by the pioneer of the late eighteenth-century picturesque movement, Richard Payne Knight. Downton, like Culzean, is stone, castellated and – like all Adam's castles – had its walls pierced with classical windows (Gothicized in the nineteenth century). Downton's interior is fitted out in highly coloured neo-classical and neo-antique style: the keep, for example, contains a domed dining room inspired by the Pantheon in Rome.

But significantly Downton, unlike Culzean, is forcefully asymmetrical. So although both castles are in a sense picturesque, Culzean is looking back to the picturesque of Vanbrugh; indeed Adam had great admiration for Vanbrugh and wrote in his *Works on Architecture* (1773) that 'Sir John Vanbrugh's genius was of the first class – and in point of movement, novelty, ingenuity, his works have not been exceeded by anything in modern times.' Downton, on the other hand, looks forward into the dawning age of the picturesque movement, which influenced architecture, landscape design, painting and literature at the end of the eighteenth century. But what of the contradictory mix of medieval asymmetrical exterior and neo-antique symmetrical interior that Knight pursued at Downton? The 1805 edition of his *Analytical Inquiry into the Principles of Taste* contains the clue. 'The

Culzean Castle, Strathclyde, 1777-92 by Robert Adam, one of the most important examples of his symmetrically planned, classically detailed castle manner. The irregularly disposed service buildings give the castle a picturesque appearance.

best style of architecture for irregular and picturesque houses', said Knight, 'is that mixed style which characterises the buildings of Claude and the Poussins [which are] distinguished by no particular manner of execution, or class of ornament, but admit of all promiscuously, from a plain wall or buttress, of the roughest masonry, to the most highly wrought Corinthian capital.'

Both these visions of the castellated country house thrived simultaneously, and it was not until the early years of the nineteenth century that the asymmetrically planned and massed house finally surpassed the symmetrical. The romantic symmetrical Vanbrugh type remained particularly popular in Scotland, where it was turned out in large numbers, as at Melville Castle, Lothian (1786-91), by James Playfair. Robert Adam was the chief exponent, however, with Dalquharran Castle, Strathclyde (1790), Stobs Castle, Borders (1793), and particularly Seton Castle, Lothian (1790-91), which is even more symmetrical and Vanbrughian than Culzean.

This symmetrical manner also became popular in Ireland, where it was introduced by Robert Adam in 1783 at his remodelling of Castle Upton, Templepatrick, Co. Antrim, and by James Wyatt in 1785 at Slane, Co. Meath (which even has a magnificent Gothic saloon incorporated in its classically planned and decorated interior). It was soon developed by Irish architects such as Thomas Wogan Browne, who built the symmetrical Castle Browne, Clane, Co. Kildare (1788). Having started later in Ireland, the symmetrical castellated house also survived a little later, for example at Gormanston Castle, Gormanston, Co. Meath (c1810); in the remodelling of Luttrellstown Castle, Clonsilla, Co. Dublin; and at Shelton Abbey, Arklow, Co. Wicklow (c1819), to which Sir Richard Morrison gave a spiky 'abbey style' elevation and a mixture of Gothic rooms, such as the drawing room with plaster fan-vaulted ceiling with pendants, and restrained classical rooms.

The other prong of the castle movement, the largely asymmetrical picturesque type, first took root in Wales and the English southwest: for example James Wyatt's Lasborough

Above: Downton Castle, Hereford and Worcester, 1772, by Richard Payne Knight. An important, pioneering example of the picturesque, asymmetrical country house.

Below: Plan of Downton Castle (walls in outline are post-1780). A, ballroom; B, library; C, drawing room; D, morning room; E, dining room; F, kitchen; G, servants' hall.

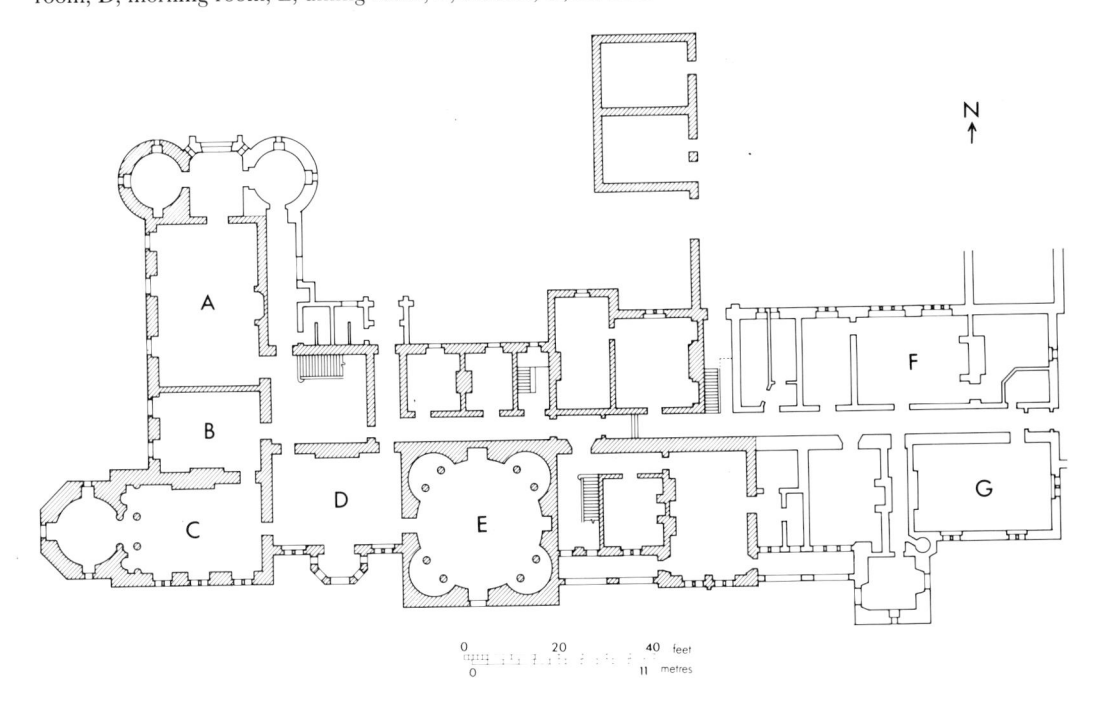

Park, Gloucestershire (1794); Pennsylvania Castle, Dorset (1799); the massive Ashridge Park, Hertfordshire (begun 1806), and Norris Castle, Isle of Wight (1799), where Wyatt initiated neo-Norman detailing in country house design. Meanwhile, in the same asymmetrical castellated manner, John Nash had designed Clytha Park, Gwent (c1795), Luscombe Castle, Devon (1799-1804), and Caerhayes Castle, Cornwall (c1808). Interestingly, the process by which Luscombe was designed by Nash with Humphry Repton reflects very accurately both the architectural variety and the tastes of the time. They produced two designs for the house – one a standard, freestanding mid-Palladian house placed boldly in the landscape, and the other an irregular house, with a broken outline, merging into the landscape. This second design, with its irregular plan, rooms of different shapes framing different views and Gothic details, was clearly the house that Nash wanted to build – and, given the prevailing taste for the picturesque, was also the one the client wanted, or was gently persuaded to want. A little earlier, in 1802, at Nonsuch Park, Surrey, Wyatville had created an asymmetrically planned house with a neo-Tudor elevation – a Gothic variation used earlier by William Wilkins senior at Stanfield Hall, Wymondham, Norfolk (1792), and soon (1805) used by Nash at Longner Hall, Shropshire. Both these Gothic variations – the neo-Norman and the Tudor Gothic – soon became the avant-garde style in country house design (p16).

In Scotland and the north the creation of asymmetrically planned, castellated houses generally began later, although Joseph Bonomi's Lambton Castle, Co. Durham, is an exception, being a particularly early example (c1796). The first Scottish country house to be Gothic inside as well as out is Scone Palace, Tayside, by William Atkinson (1803-12), and Taymouth Castle, Tayside, begun in 1806 to the designs of Archibald and James Elliot, which has a castle keep reminiscent of Inveraray containing a magnificent Gothic staircase hall, and is grouped asymmetrically with lower wings added in 1818. J.G. Grahame's earlier Drumtochty Castle, Grampian (c1815), was rather advanced, with a picturesque grouping of towers inspired by Warwick Castle, and Kinfauns Castle, Tayside (1820), shows Sir Robert Smirke's stripped Graeco-cubic manner (p151) in castellated dress. Meanwhile in 1816 William Atkinson had designed Abbotsford, Borders, for Walter Scott, so promoting the baronial style which became the dominant expression in Scotland of the Gothic revival, and which produced such remarkable pinnacled piles as William Burn's Tyninghame House, Lothian (1829).

In Ireland the first deliberately asymmetrical castle-style country house was Charleville Forest, Tullamore, Co. Offaly, designed c1800 by Francis Johnston. Inside is a Gothic entrance hall (still related to the staircase hall in the manner of Castletown) with plaster groin vaulting, and on the first floor (which, interestingly, contains the major rooms) are a vast saloon with a vaulted ceiling with gigantic pendants, and a dining room with a fireplace modelled on the west door of Magdalen College Chapel, Oxford. Slightly later are Ballyheigue Castle, Tralee, Co. Kerry, which was remodelled by Sir Richard and William Vitruvius Morrison in c1809 to look like a Gothic building dating from different periods, and Castle Howard, Avoca, Co. Wicklow (1811), where Sir Richard Morrison combined monastic with castle Gothic.

Neo-classicism

While Gothic developed from the decorative rococo, and in the process became increasingly thorough and archaeologically based, classicism also underwent a dramatic change. The 1760s saw not only the demise of rococo Gothic but the beginning of the end of the rococo movement generally. The reason was that a new classicism reinvigorated by fresh ideas, theories and information about Greek and Roman antiquity had arrived (p15). Books were now published which revealed for the first time what Grecian as well as Renaissance/Roman classicism looked like. Chief amongst these works were James 'Athenian' Stuart and Nicholas Revett's *Antiquities of Athens* (1762) and Robert Wood's *Ruins of Palmyra* (1753) and *Ruins of Baalbec* (1757). An archaeological interest in classical design was in the air, and this new vision had a quick and profound influence on country house design. One of the first effects of the new information was to drive a wedge between the different persuasions of classical architects; and it was not merely a question of the generation gap. The free-thinking James Paine (not to be confused with James Pain), four years *younger* than 'Athenian' Stuart, wrote in 1767 that Wood's books were 'curious' rather than 'useful' works which furnished no new light on the great part of architecture, and which were 'only valuable for the ornaments'; and the Greek of Stuart and Revett was dismissed as 'despicable ruins' – a view also held by Sir William Chambers who was ten years younger than Stuart.

Despite opposition, from c1760 Greek-based neo-classicism ran parallel with the gradually disappearing late Palladian or

French-inspired neo-classicism of Chambers, Paine and the other architects who continued to believe in the superiority of the Roman Renaissance interpretation of classicism over the Greek. The earliest manifestations of the emerging neo-classical style were merely interior decorative schemes. Stuart's Painted Room (executed in 1759) at Spencer House, St James's, Westminster, London (designed in 1756 by John Vardy), is the earliest complete neo-classical room in Europe; and ceilings at Woburn Abbey, Bedfordshire, Osterley Park, Hounslow, and Stratfield Saye, Hampshire, were copied from patterns in Wood's book on Palmyra. But despite Stuart's favourable position as the prophet of this new movement, it fell to the ambitious Robert Adam to design the first major country house in the neo-classical style – Kedleston, Derbyshire. Having produced mediocre provincial Palladian/rococo designs in Scotland with his father William and brother John, such as the pavilions at Hopetoun House, Lothian (1752) and Dumfries House, Strathclyde (1754) – Adam left England for Italy in 1754, not to return until 1758.

He was a changed man, but the change had a little difficulty in expressing itself – partly because of the problem of synthesizing his old habits and new memories to form a coherent, original style, and partly, as he complained during his first post-Italy job, because of the difficulty of finding 'English workmen who will leave their angly stiff sharp manner'.[14] This first job, landed in 1758, was the remodelling of the interior of Hatchlands, Surrey (which had been designed c1750, probably by Thomas Ripley). An examination of the ceilings at Hatchlands is revealing in the light of our knowledge of Adam's development, for they show the agony of a man wrestling to suppress his rococo/Palladian training and allow the newly acquired neo-classical motifs – rams' heads, urns, griffins, anthemions – to coalesce into a coherent whole. The following year Adam was brought in to liven up a house at Shardeloes, Buckinghamshire, which the provincial Palladian Stiff Leadbetter had been reconstructing. Here Adam created, in 1759-61, a tall Roman Corinthian portico rising from the ground, and identical in all essentials to the portico that his future rival, Sir William Chambers, was raising at Duddingston, Lothian (p73).

The next year brought Adam's great – in some ways greatest – triumph; he succeeded in poaching the most important country house commission of the decade. Nathaniel Curzon had been rebuilding Kedleston, Derbyshire, since the late 1750s. Matthew

Robert Adam's south front to Kedleston, Derbyshire, 1760-65, displaying his flair for the imaginative use and adaptation of antique prototypes – in this case the Arch of Constantine, Rome.

Brettingham the Elder provided the basic plan for the new house, which was to have a central block linked to four wings by quadrant colonnades, as in Palladio's Villa Mocenigo. The north-east wing was indeed begun by Brettingham while the existing early eighteenth-century house was gradually demolished. In 1759 the north-west wing was built by James Paine, who obviously had designs on the whole commission because he produced elevations for the two principal fronts of the main house. But in the same year Adam came on the scene, and was put in charge of all design work for the central block. What happened next says a lot about Adam's character. He not only managed to take over a job from entrenched, established country house architects, but he also managed to produce a masterpiece which is a dazzling display of his original and creative talent – he had come a long way since Hatchlands.

Perhaps as a concession to the pair of ousted older architects, he built a modified version of the Brettingham/Paine north front, a monumental and not very imaginative essay on Wanstead. But for the south front Adam contrived to display all the advantages he had over his rivals. He used his first-hand archaeological knowledge to evoke the spirit of Rome and on a Palladian rustic basement built a four-columned frontispiece based on the Arch of Constantine. The attic of the arch rises above the parapet of the flanking elevation, which also breaks back from the arch, and the columns and entablature thrust forward within the arch and make this south front an early working example of Adam's commitment to 'movement' in architecture. Clearly under the influence of Vanbrugh,

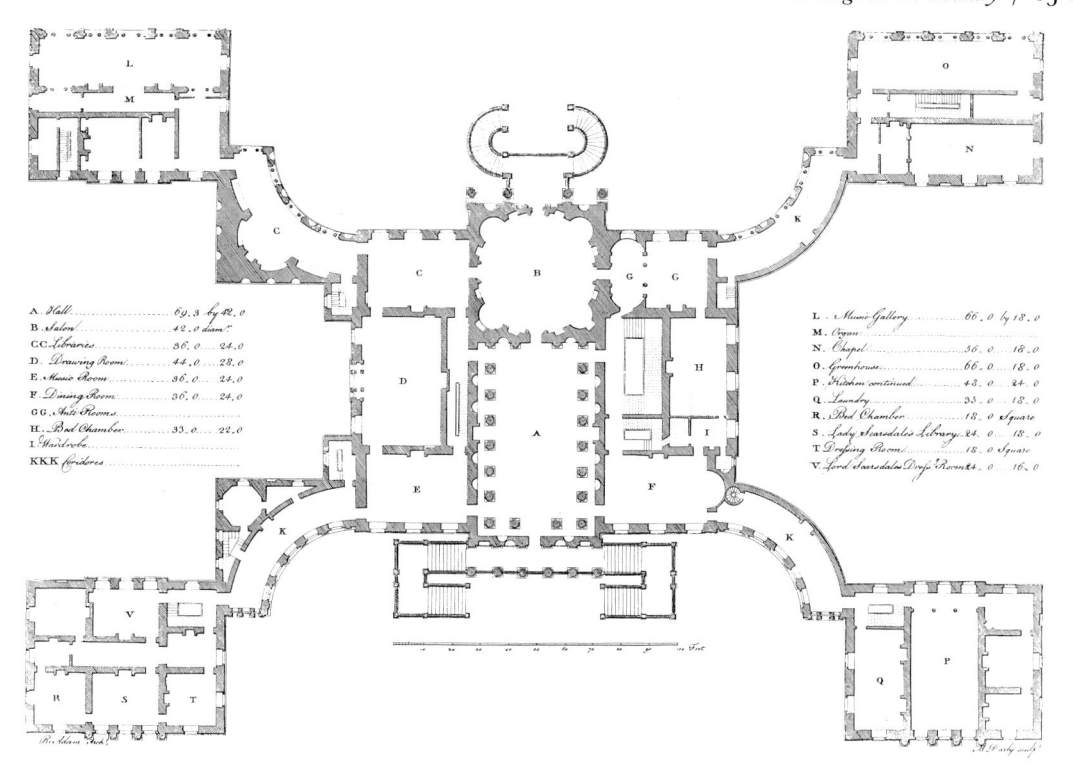

Plan of Kedleston at *piano nobile* level from Woolfe and Gandon's 1767 volume of *Vitruvius Britannicus*. The upper pair of wings were not built.

Adam explained his views in the preface to his *Works of Architecture* (1773):

> Movement is meant to express the rise and fall, the advance and recession, with other diversity of form in the different parts of the building, so as to add greatly to the picturesque of the composition. For the rising and falling, advancing and receding, with the convexity or concavity, and other forms of the great parts, have the same effect in architecture, that hill and dale, foreground and distance, swelling and sinking have in Landscape: this is, they serve to produce an agreeable and diversified contour.

Eager archaeology also characterizes the interior of the building. The hall, placed on the same axis as the saloon in the old Palladian way, is entered through the Wanstead-like north front and is treated as a Roman atrium. It is lined with alabaster columns in a way not dissimilar to the hall at Holkham on which Brettingham had worked, and the composition perhaps owes something to his earlier scheme. However, though a Palladian Egyptian hall basilica in general form, it is enriched with casts of antique busts and sarcophagus benches, a type of associative decoration that soon became a cliché (for example the entrance hall at West Wycombe Park, Buckinghamshire, *c*1765, stood on a hypocaust based on a Roman model discovered at Lincoln, thereby gaining the extra antique touch). The saloon at Kedleston is a domed rotunda, obviously derived from the Pantheon at Rome. Indeed, the relationship between the form of the hall and the saloon closely resembles the relationship of the Roman vestibule to the atrium, which Adam described in his book on the *Ruins of Spalatro* (1764). The use of the rooms on the rest of the *piano nobile* makes an interesting comparison with Houghton and Holkham. There was only one private bedroom apartment, most of the family bedrooms being on the floor above or in one of the wings (the kitchen being in the other), with the rest of the floor being given over to communal rooms such as the library, music room, dining room and drawing room.

During the rest of the decade 1760–70, when Adam enjoyed an almost unchallenged position as the country's most fashionable architect, he developed his decorative style in a series of magnificent country houses, remodelling Syon House, Brentford (1761–9); Osterley Park, Hounslow (1762–8); Harewood House, West Yorkshire (*c*1765); Nostell Priory, West Yorkshire (1766); Newby Hall, North Yorkshire (1767–72), and Saltram, Devon (1768–79). But the exteriors that he executed reveal that there was still something of the austere Palladian about him. Indeed the exterior of Kenwood, Highgate, which he built from scratch in 1767 (adding the portico in 1769) could not be in greater contrast with the richness of some of the apartments inside – notwithstanding the external pilasters carrying Adam's own brand of neo-classical decoration. Similarly, the house at Mersham le Hatch, Kent, which Adam designed in 1762 is a conventional Palladian box, while the wings he added to Compton Verney, Warwickshire, in 1765 display externally a modest deference to the baroque style of the main house.

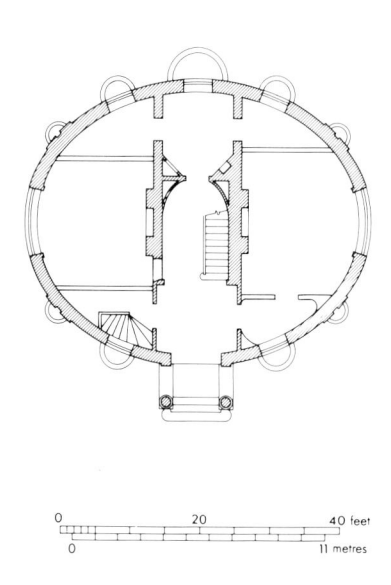

Adam did not have the next decade all his own way; the spirit of archaeology was taken up, and taken further, by others more interested in following full-blooded Greek rather than Roman precedents. For example Revett added an Ionic portico based on the Temple of Bacchus at Teos to West Wycombe Park, Buckinghamshire, in 1771, and one based on the Temple of Apollo at Delos to Trafalgar House, Wiltshire, in 1766; Giovanni Borra, who had been at Palmyra and Baalbec with Wood, created in c1775 an oval domed hall at Stowe, furnished with pink scagliola columns and a deep frieze (by Valdré) peopled with hundreds of small classical figures; and at the same time John Plaw designed Belle Isle, Cumbria, which is round and porticoed and based on the Pantheon in Rome. There were more significant developments than these tinkerings with antiquity, however. First there was the arrival on the scene of James Wyatt who, with his brother Samuel, developed a refined neo-classical style for interiors in the mode of Adam, and complemented it with his own strong exterior style. He quickly established himself with Heaton Hall, Manchester, designed in 1772 when he was twenty-six. Secondly, there was the beginning of a quick reaction against the richness, even

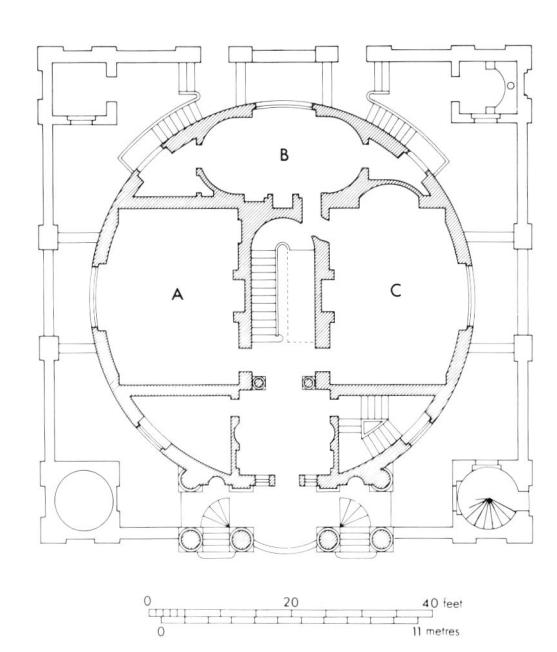

The ground floor plan of Belle Isle, c1775, *right*, and the Round House, Havering-atte-Bower, Havering, London of 1793, perhaps also by Plaw, but distinctly clumsier. A, withdrawing room; B, library: C, eating parlour.

Belle Isle, Cumbria, by John Plaw, an impressive design based on the Pantheon, Rome.

the excesses, of Adam's decorative style. But initially this revolution did not take perhaps the most obvious course, of embracing the chaste and austere Greek architecture that was becoming generally known in the 1770s. Rather, it combined some of the austerity of the Greek with the authority of the Palladian. This Graeco-Palladian style is first found in the work of Robert Mylne and Henry Holland. At Woodhouse, Shropshire (1773), Mylne raised a startlingly original portico owing very little to Adam's influence and indeed anticipating the austere neo-classicism of the 1790s. With Lancelot Brown, his future father-in-law and a former colleague of Adam, Henry Holland had already, in 1771, built the neo-Palladian Claremont at Esher, Surrey, and in 1774 the same pair designed Benham Place, Berkshire. Benham is a neo-Palladian house designed not in the semi-ironical mode of Paine's near-contemporary Wardour Castle, but as an attempt to establish an architectural and decorative alternative to Adam and Wyatt. Unlike Wardour, it reflects the current practice of positioning main rooms on the ground floor and, unlike earlier Palladian houses, it has a central, top-lit oval staircase.

In 1778, Holland, again perhaps with Brown, pursued this theme at Berrington Hall, Hereford and Worcester, where the seven-bay front is faced with a giant four-columned Ionic portico emphasizing the entrance, which leads to ground-floor main rooms and a bold, centrally lit staircase. At about the same time, *c*1775-80, the young George Dance designed a ballroom at Cranbury Park, Hampshire, which is entirely free of Adam's influence and foreshadows – particularly in the form of the pendentive ceiling over apses – the architecture of Sir John Soane.

This new, chaste neo-classicism was picked up and reflected in the work of many architects. In 1777 Thomas Leverton created, at Woodhall Park, Hertfordshire, an exquisite neo-antique staircase hall, also very different from Adam; and in 1776 that veteran country house architect John Carr designed Basildon Park, Berkshire, where he pursued a neo-Palladian line, with a porticoed entrance front (where a stair rises ingeniously from the rustic entrance door straight to an external landing, behind the portico columns, on the *piano nobile*), a grand central top-lit staircase, and a large octagonal drawing room in the centre of the garden front. Two years later that other veteran, Sir Robert Taylor, designed Heveningham Hall, Suffolk, giving it a seven-bay centre, with a deep arcaded rustic supporting a Corinthian colonnade and tall attic, the whole being linked by lower five-bay blank arcaded wings to three-bay pedimented pavilions. In this case the neo-Palladian revival met an abrupt check, for in 1780 James Wyatt replaced Taylor as architect, and promptly decorated the interior with one of his best neo-classical schemes.

In 1783 George Steuart added another dimension to this movement with Attingham Hall, Shropshire, which, boasting a gawky, attenuated giant portico, anticipates the solecisms that characterize so many early nineteenth-century classical country houses; and in 1795 Holland had the last word on the subject with Southill Park, Bedfordshire, where he designed a magnificently austere Graeco-Palladian house, and set in it a saloon in the new red and gold Empire style that was to become known as Regency.

While the austere Graeco-Palladian rose, the polychromatic neo-classicism of Adam and the Wyatts retreated into a protective shell of Greek revival gravity. Samuel Wyatt's Doddington Hall, Cheshire (1777), still displays Palladian elements, such as a rustic below the first-floor main rooms; but his Belmont Park, Kent (1782), and his villa, Coton House, Warwickshire (1785), display characteristic Wyatt family elements, such as full-height bows, round corner towers looking like tea-caddies, and tripartite windows in blank arches, all set in façades of great gravity. Likewise James Wyatt's Bowden House, Wiltshire (1796), is a compact two-storey villa, whose garden front is dominated by a massive bow and decorated by four sturdy free-standing Greek Ionic columns, behind which is an oval saloon. This powerful neo-classical composition of French origin had been used as early as 1788 by S.P. Cockerell at Daylesford House, Gloucestershire, and in *c*1792 by Sir John Soane at Tyringham, Buckinghamshire. Here Soane faced a two-storey bow, also expressing an oval room, with detached giant Ionic columns set against horizontally channelled, French neo-classical-inspired rustication. In 1803 Thomas Leverton created a similar colonnaded bow at Scampston, Humberside, at about the same time as Soane was combining the French colonnaded bow with the round Temple of Vesta at Tivoli to make the Tivoli Corner at the Bank of England (p128). And, for his houses in the south at least, Adam picked up the Wyatts' cue and, in 1784, clad his two-storey, three-bay villa at Brasted Place, Kent, in stone and embellished it with a mighty portico of Grecian Doric-derivation.

Soane at this time reflects a wide spectrum of approaches to country house design. In 1785 he made neo-Palladian additions to Chillington Hall, Staffordshire. The same year he designed the extraordinary and original Shotesham Park, Norfolk, where he superimposed a screen of Ionic pilasters and an entablature on a taller and wider brick façade which, at attic level above the applied entablature, rises to form a three-bay pediment. And in 1788 he fitted out Bentley Priory, Stanmore, in a neo-Greek fashion, the culmination of which, ten years later, was an entrance hall with a pendentive ceiling on

The entrance hall of Soane's Bentley Priory, Stanmore, 1798: an important example of early Greek revival.

sturdy Greek Doric columns supporting blocks of entablature.

Ireland

Most of these late eighteenth-century English themes are present in contemporary Irish country house design – particularly in the family of houses (which includes James Hoban's White House, Washington D.C., 1792) that began with Lucan House, Lucan, Co. Dublin, and which all reflect the same synthesis between traditional Irish eighteenth-century planning and Anglo-French neo-classicism. Conceived as a boldly planned Palladian villa, Lucan was designed *c*1775 by Agmondisham Vesey for himself but with advice from Sir William Chambers, James Wyatt and Michael Stapleton. Externally, Lucan has something of the feel of Paine's Bywell Hall, *c*1760 (p74); the pedimented three-bay centre, embellished with engaged Ionic columns rising from an arcaded, rusticated ground floor, is a storey higher than the flanking blocks, which do not have their own pediments as at Bywell. The plan follows the prototype established as far back as Ballyhaise (Richard Castle, *c*1733) and followed by Newberry (*c*1765, probably by Nathaniel Clements), with the hall leading to an oval saloon expressed externally by a full-height bow in the centre of the garden front. The saloon contains delicate neo-classical decoration in the Wyatt manner, but probably designed by Michael Stapleton. The entrance hall has a screen of columns in the manner of Castletown.

Lucan was copied directly by Whitmore Davis when he designed Charleville, Enniskerry, Co. Wicklow, in 1797, but the next house in this family is, externally, very different from Lucan. Caledon, Co. Tyrone, was begun in 1779 to the design of Thomas Cooley. As at Lucan, the entrance front is seven bays wide with a three-bay pediment – but here there are no engaged columns or pilasters, and the entrance elevation was originally of two storeys (enlarged to three in *c*1835). Inside there is a large entrance hall with a screen of columns at the further end, beyond

Above: The entrance front of Lucan House, Co. Dublin, *c*1775: a striking example of originally composed Irish late Palladianism.

Below: Ground floor plan of Lucan House. The bowed garden room on axis with a columnar entrance hall became a standard planning feature in a sequence of late Georgian Irish houses.

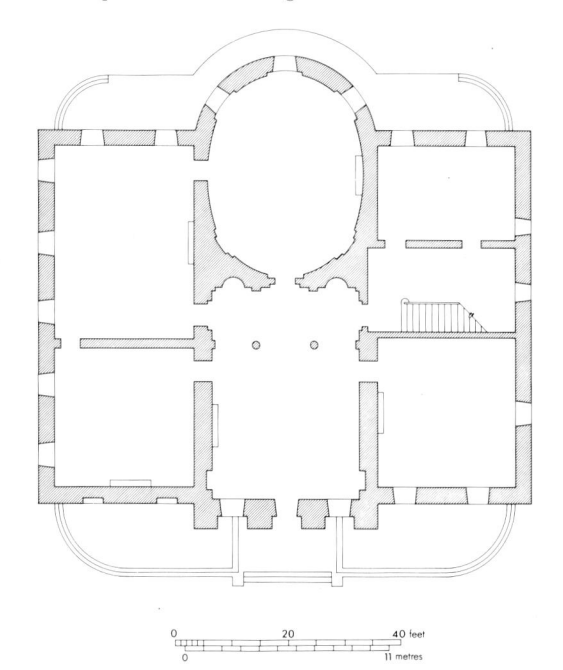

which is an oval drawing room which is expressed through the garden front as a full-height oval bay. The ground-floor windows in the bay are pedimented – emphasizing the fact that the main rooms are on the ground floor – while those flanking it are tripartite and set within a blank arch in the Wyatt manner. In 1808-10 John Nash added domed wings (one of which contains a library) and a long single-storey colonnade to the front of the house, and remodelled the oval drawing room to make it one of the most spectacular Regency rooms in Ireland.

Mount Kennedy, Co. Wicklow, pursued the type but in its front elevation, which contains a tripartite pedimented door topped by a large Diocletian window, made reference to earlier eighteenth-century Irish traditions and to Newberry (p75) in particular. Designed in 1782 by Thomas Cooley, Mount Kennedy has the familiar Castletown columnar entrance hall, with a staircase off to one side leading, again as at Castletown, to an oval drawing room expressed in the garden front as a full-height oval bay. On the first floor is an octagonal hall in the Bellamont Forest tradition, lit by a circular domed lantern. Intriguingly, James Wyatt had supplied the owners of Mount Kennedy with plans in 1772 – which Cooley presumably inherited and used or adapted at about the same time as Chambers was discussing plans with the designer of Lucan, Agmondisham Vesey.

Quite how, and if, Wyatt and Chambers both produced a similar synthesized English/Irish plan form is uncertain, but Wyatt's next Irish country house, Slane Castle, Co. Meath, certainly confirms the possibility that Wyatt – together with a group of Wyatt-directed Irish architects such as Thomas Cooley and Francis Johnston – was behind the use and development of such a plan form.[15] Externally Slane, begun in 1785 and completed by Francis Johnston, is very different from the other houses discussed so far: castellated Gothic, it has a full-height bow placed conventionally on axis with the entrance, but treated as a round tower, rising slightly higher than the symmetrically arranged main body of the house. Inside, the decoration is largely classical – with the magnificent exception of the Gothic double-storey circular ballroom set within the round tower. The entrance hall has two pairs of Greek Doric columns forming screens. Johnston was working simultaneously on Rokeby, Dunleer, Co. Louth (1785-94), where he was executing the designs of Thomas Cooley. Rokeby's seven-bay front elevation refers back to Lucan, where the three centre bays are pedimented and dressed with an order, but here pilasters not columns are used and the entire elevation is of a uniform two storeys. Inside is a Castletown-type entrance hall, but there is no bay on the garden front.

In 1789 Richard Johnston produced a plan for a house which turned out to be not only the ultimate and quintessential expression of this group of houses, but also the closest to a perfect neo-classical house in the British Isles. Castle Coole, Enniskillen, Co. Fermanagh, despite Johnston's early involvement, is largely the work of James Wyatt, who adapted Johnston's plan and improved his elevation in 1790, and worked on the house until 1798. As well as being the most thoroughly designed of the group – with all angles and details considered, all views satisfactorily terminated and definitely no loose ends left untied – it is also the largest. It has a frontage of 112 feet, consisting of a nine-bay, two-storey main block connected by straight colonnaded wings to single-storey pavilions, whose front elevations – with *in antis* columns – seem inspired by Gandon's Custom House, Dublin (p291). The centre of the entrance block is embellished with a three-bay pediment supported on giant Roman Ionic columns which rise, as was the fashion, from the ground, thus both giving the building a temple-like appearance and emphasizing the fact that the main rooms are on the ground floor. Inside is a deep single-storey hall of dramatic neo-classical simplicity, complete with the Castletown screen, which here supports a full Doric entablature running round the hall. Beyond the hall is an oval saloon which is pilastered internally, and expressed externally as a full-height oval bay embellished, like Wyatt's contemporary Bowden House, Wiltshire (p85), with full-height fluted Ionic columns. The extra width of Castle Coole allows for the development of the standard plan type: flanking the oval saloon are a handsome dining room and drawing room which all interconnect to form a magnified enfilade, or cross axis, behind the garden front. The stair rising in a hall off the entrance hall leads to a columnar landing with – in the Irish fashion that is perhaps a legacy of Johnston's initial plan – a first-floor lobby rising into a top-lit attic storey. It is embellished with a colonnade, probably inspired by the interior of the Parthenon and the Temple of Poseidon at Paestum.

As well as this strongly linked family of country houses – which relate to such English designs as Soane's Saxlingham Rectory, Norfolk, of 1784 – there are others, by different architects or by the same architects developing different ideas – that demand attention. Two of these are largely, like Castle Coole,

88 / *Georgian Buildings*

Above: Castle Coole, Co. Fermanagh. Built 1790–98, this house is the apotheosis of both Irish country house design and of James Wyatt as a country house architect.

Left: The colonnaded bow on the centre of the garden elevation of Castle Coole.

Below: Ground floor plan of Castle Coole. The general form of the plan was sketched out by Richard Johnston in 1789 and adopted by Wyatt in 1790: A, hall; B, saloon; C, dining room; D, drawing room; E, library.

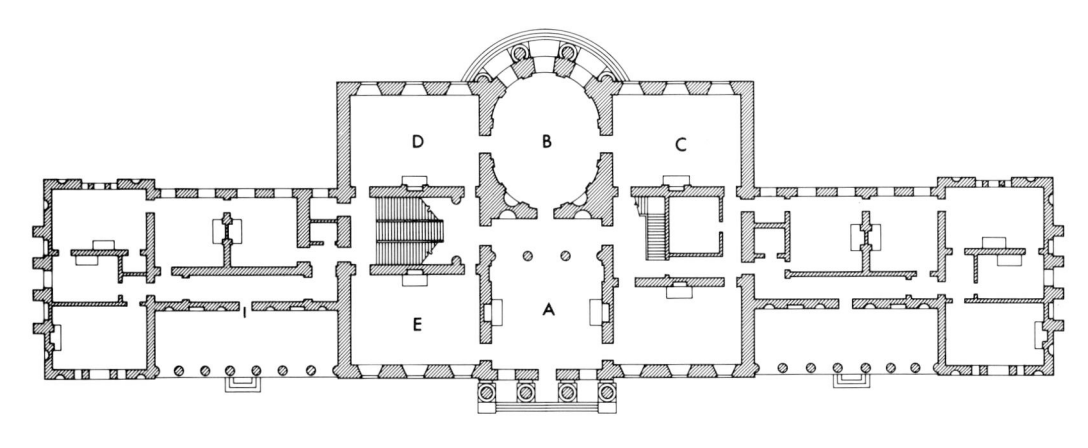

the work of English architects, and one of them, Emo Park, Portarlington, Co. Laois, can be seen as a challenge to the Lucan/Castle Coole family. Emo Park, begun in 1791 to the design of James Gandon (who had been apprenticed to Chambers), represents a more monumental, archaeological and Greek-inspired branch of neo-classicism, which anticipated some of the developments of the early nineteenth century. But for all its ambition the house is somewhat clumsy and disjointed, possibly because it took so long to build: the garden front was not completed until 1834 (by Lewis Vulliamy) and the dome was not added until 1860. But the two-storey entrance front is Gandon's work, and is clearly an essay on the Palladian tower house. In the centre is a grand two-storey pedimented portico set only slightly forward. Gone is the rustic with, instead, the main rooms on ground level, and the end bays break forward and are taller than the centre block. Inside is a single-storey entrance hall, with Gandon's characteristic segmental-apsed end, which opens into a pilastered rotunda, beneath the coffered dome of c1860. This is placed behind the garden portico in a manner reminiscent of Adam's Kedleston Hall, Derbyshire, 1760 (p82). The saloon/library is a great departure from the Lucan/Castle Coole school: set in the wing with the curved centre bay, it runs the full depth of the house from front to back, and has a screen of Ionic columns to emphasize the central portion, which is lit by the bay. The whole composition is strangely reminiscent of the long bow-windowed library in the wing of Blenheim, but is evidently derived from the North Room of Leinster House, Dublin (by Castle, 1745), which also has screens and a projecting curved bay.

The rotunda, Emo's most striking internal element, recurs at Baronscourt, Newtownstewart, Co. Tyrone, which was designed in about 1780 by the English architect George Steuart and greatly altered internally by Soane in 1791-2 and later by William Vitruvius Morrison. Here the coffered dome, pierced by an oculus, is supported by Greek Ionic columns. At Townley Hall, Drogheda, Co. Louth (1794), Francis Johnston broke entirely with the Lucan/Castle Coole tradition and experimented in the Soane/Greek revival style. There is an entrance hall, with a coffered ceiling and arched recess, and a centrally placed rotunda, also with a coffered ceiling and lit by a glazed dome. Within it curves – in the English manner – a wonderfully graceful cantilevered staircase. Externally there is a single-storey Greek Doric porch – an early example – with columns

The rotunda containing the staircase at Townley Hall, Co. Louth, 1794 by Francis Johnston: a sophisticated design with exquisite neo-classical detailing.

standing on abacus-like tablets. Sir Richard Morrison's Castlegar, Ahascragh, Co. Galway (1803), also has a top-lit, centrally placed stair, but here the stair hall is oblong, with a pendentive ceiling pierced by a round dome.

As well as reflecting current English practice, Castlegar reflects the Irish eighteenth-century obsession with bows, bays and exotically shaped rooms: the entrance door, in a shallow curved bow in the tradition of Anneville, c1740 (p61), leads to an oval entrance hall with, beyond the top-lit stair hall, a long, thin back hall with a dome supported on Doric columns. Another contemporary example of the continuing Irish delight in bows and bays is Vernon Mount, Douglas, Co. Cork (c1785), which has quadrant corners to its main elevation and full-height curved round bows in its side elevation.

After 1800
We have followed the castellated country house into the early nineteenth century (p81), and have seen how other styles that flourished

in the eighteenth century trailed into the early nineteenth century, only to become part of the extraordinary whirl of styles that characterized country house building in Britain from 1790 to 1815. It was during this period that the dogmas that had dominated country house design all through the eighteenth century – symmetry (or the reaction to it), and a classically derived vocabulary of design – were finally and effectively challenged and replaced by that 'stylistic pluralism which the Regency period raised to such a pitch [and which] allowed the adoption of totally different styles according to the functions and situations of different buildings.'[16]

Daylesford House, Gloucestershire (S.P. Cockerell, 1788-93), has a dome derived from Muslim architecture and touches of 'Hindoo' design inside; a theme he pursued in 1805 at Sezincote House, Gloucestershire, which has not only a Mogul dome but also an Indian cornice. Beaumont Lodge, Berkshire, was 'improved' by Henry Emlyn in 1789 to display his clumsy 'British Order'; Castle Goring, West Sussex, was designed in c1790 by Biagio Rebecca with a Gothic castellated entrance front and a Graeco-Palladian garden front; the same mix is also found internally and at The Gleanings, Rochester, Kent (c1800). In c1795 Francis Sandys executed a design by Marco Asprucci for Ickworth, Suffolk, which, with its vast drum of a central block, is a display of excessive neo-antique enthusiasm for the house as temple of the arts; and in the same year James Gandon designed Emsworth, a villa at Malahide, Co. Dublin, which, with its ground-floor windows in blank arches, segmental-ended apsed hall and dining room and tripartite windows, anticipated domestic fashions of the 1820s and early 1830s. In 1800 Soane designed the extraordinary and very individual Pitzhanger Manor, Ealing (then on the outskirts of London), in which he mixed Roman elements – such as the triumphal arch that embellished the entrance front – and his own brand of neo-classical detailing with Gothic; there was a Gothic 'ruin' attached to the end of the house serving as a sort of romantic open-air room. In 1802 John Nash initiated the asymmetrical, towered and deep-eaved Italianate look – seemingly inspired by the vernacular buildings in Claude's landscapes – at Cronkhill, near Shrewsbury, Shropshire (and soon repeated by him at Sandridge Park, Stoke Gabriel, Devon, c1805, and imitated by Robert Lugar in 1806 at Dunstall Priory near Shoreham, Kent). Nash took the 'Hindoo' Mogul crossed with Gothic to new extravagant and exotic extremes at the Royal Pavilion, Brighton (1815-21). Tudor Gothic was not forgotten either: in 1814 William Wilkins promoted it at Dalmeny House, Lothian.

There were even revivals of relatively recent architectural styles. In 1806 Samuel and Lewis Wyatt designed a Grinling Gibbons revival ceiling for Hackwood Park, Hampshire (Gibbons details had been reproduced, more

Cronkhill, Shropshire, 1802 by John Nash, and the first of a series of picturesquely formed, asymmetrically planned Italianate villas.

modestly and slightly earlier, at Petworth, West Sussex), while at about the same time James Wyatt was reviving the French rococo manner for a saloon at Belvoir Castle, Leicestershire; and in 1814 L.W. Wyatt added a neo-Wren dining room to Leoni's Lyme Park, Cheshire. And to this mix must be added the castellated Gothic (p78), the extraordinary and personal neo-classicism of Soane, well illustrated by the canted, pilastered façade of Butterton Farmhouse, Staffordshire, of 1815.

In the last decade of the eighteenth century country houses began to sport, like West Wycombe twenty years earlier, finely proportioned but not yet fully absorbed Greek details. For example, in 1790 Benjamin Latrobe gave the wings of Hammerwood House, East Sussex, perfect Greek Doric porches based on a mix of the Delos and Paestum orders; in the same year Samuel Wyatt used the Delos order in his circular entrance hall at Shugborough, Staffordshire; in 1791 James Playfair embellished Cairness House, Grampian, with primitive Doric columns and channelled rustication inspired by Ledoux (and also with an Egyptian billiard room); and in 1794 Latrobe fitted Ashdown House, East Sussex, with a porch of Ionic columns based on the Erechtheion.

The Greek revival
The full possibilities of the Greek revival were not to be realized until its proponents had acquired the ability both to fuse pure Greek details into a convincing whole and to accommodate early nineteenth-century country house habits and usages within the new Greek temple. Moreover they had also to reconcile the Greek revival house with contemporary notions of the picturesque, which demanded a romance and asymmetry not immediately associated with massive neo-Greek piles – unless the very incongruity of a comfortable country house posing as a Greek temple in the English countryside can be called romantic.

The first intimations of this dramatic fusion can be detected in the eighteenth century. At Longford Hall, Shropshire, designed by Joseph Bonomi in 1789, there is a hint of what was to come. A bold two-storey, four-columned Tuscan portico, sitting firmly on the ground, leads to an entrance hall bedecked with a Grecian frieze; and beside the compact two-storey villa stands a well displayed asymmetrical wing containing the office and kitchen: a composition pioneered nearly thirty years earlier by Chambers at Duddingston and which was soon followed by James Wyatt's Dodington Park, Avon, of 1798–1813 which has an asymmetrical layout and a noble giant Corinthian portico.

It was not until 1803, however, that the Greek revival became more than just one of the many exotic alternatives available for the design of country houses. In that year George Dance designed Stratton Park, Hampshire, creating a massive and austere two-storey Greek Doric portico, inspired by the temples at Paestum. Inside there was (only the portico now survives) a magnificent staircase rising to a first-floor Greek Ionic colonnade standing on a basement of channelled rustication – all inspired by L.-A. Dubut's *Maisons de Ville et de Campagne* (1803).

In the years up to 1810 the Greek revival became established and 'no longer merely a fashionable conceit [but] the very criterion of architectural distinction'.[17] In 1804 William Wilkins the Younger began remodelling The Grange, Hampshire, to create the first and also the best rendering of the country house as Greek Doric temple. The almost absurdly powerful portico (of brick and plaster, not stone) was inspired by the Theseion (which had been illustrated in Stuart and Revett's *Antiquities of Athens*)[18] and the side elevations are dominated by centrepieces with massive and deep antae supporting parapets, based on the Choragic monument of Thrasyllus (also illustrated in *Antiquities of Athens*).[19] The influence of The Grange was great but not immediate, for the transformation was not complete until 1809. Interestingly the house was made strikingly asymmetrical in 1823 when S.P. and C.R. Cockerell added guest apartments and a delightful four-columned Ionic portico, set back and much smaller but

The Grange, Hampshire, remodelled 1804–9 by William Wilkins to form the most influential of early Greek revival houses. This photograph was taken before the recent restoration.

Above: Belsay Hall, Northumberland, 1806, by Sir Charles Monck; the most austere and stunning of early Greek revival houses. *Below:* The ground floor plan. A, entrance hall; B, pillar hall; C, drawing room; D, library; E, dining room; F, servants' hall.

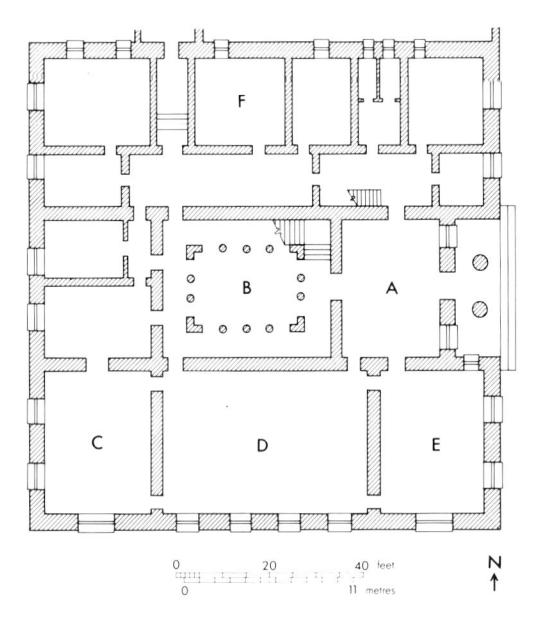

looking in the same direction as the portico.

While working here Wilkins also designed a giant Grecian Doric portico for Osberton Hall, Nottinghamshire, in 1806, the year Sir Charles Monck (with later help from John Dobson) designed the astonishingly severe Belsay Hall, Northumberland. Belsay, square in plan and inspired by Graeco-Roman peristyle plans (square plans are shared by several early Greek-inspired houses, such as Francis Johnston's Townley Hall, Drogheda, Co. Louth, of 1794 and Thomas Lee's Arlington Court, Devon, of 1820), is of two storeys with a lowering Greek Doric entablature running all round. The elevations are distinguished from each other merely by different groupings of windows – which reflect the use of the rooms within – and by pilaster strips emphasizing the corners and slight changes of plane, while the entrance is marked by a pair of massive Greek Doric columns, modelled on the Theseion and set *in antis*. Beyond the entrance hall is the centrally placed two-storey oblong Pillar Hall, where colonnades of Greek Ionic columns support a first-floor colonnade of smaller Doric columns (a minor solecism, for conventionally the more masculine orders support the more feminine). In the corner of the hall is hidden the staircase. Towards the end of this decade of Greek revival entrenchment, in 1808, J.M. Gandy designed Storrs Hall, Bowness-in-Windermere, Cumbria, and gave its entrance front a single-storey Greek Doric colonnade supporting an entablature with prominent antefixae.

The Greek revival after 1810

Once established, the Greek revival developed along those varied lines hinted at during its formative decades. Some houses followed the direction of James Playfair's Cairness House, Grampian (1791), where the Greek revival elements of eighteenth-century French neo-classicism were taken up and emphasized. In 1812, for example, at Laxton Hall, Northamptonshire, George Dance built, within a dull Greek revival house of 1805 by J.A. Repton, a powerful French-influenced double-height entrance hall. Perhaps inspired by Ledoux, Dance created a hall which had at first-floor level a screen of four Ionic columns carried on a semicircular arch that was cut boldly into a horizontally channelled rusticated wall. Nunnykirk, Northumberland, by John Dobson still, in 1825, reflected French neo-classical influence. Externally, again, there is horizontal rustication which rises the three storeys of the centre block; and inside is an oblong hall, double-height and galleried, and covered by a pendentive ceiling with a coffered segmental side vault and a central dome. At Longhirst House, near Morpeth, Northumberland, the same architect created in 1828 a double-height entrance and staircase hall of a gloom worthy of Jacques Gondoin. The whole is lit by a coffered saucer dome pierced by an oculus. The stairs, reached via a pair of Greek Ionic columns, rise within a compartment roofed with a shallow coffered segmental vault. Off the landing are coffered, segmental apses, and in the centre of it is a well, fenced off with particularly spiky railings. All the surfaces are dressed sandstone. The exterior is no less odd, being endowed with a two-storey pedimented porch with a pair of giant Corinthian columns, set *in antis*, and supporting a plain Greek Doric entablature.

An equally personal Greek revival manner was pursued by Sir Robert Smirke, who

The vaulted, stone-clad first-floor landing at John Dobson's Longhirst House, Northumberland, 1824-8. The academic gloom is reminiscent of late eighteenth-century French neo-classicism.

sought to evolve a modern architecture by stripping Greek of its embellishments and reducing all to primary forms – thus creating a sort of 'Graeco-cubic' style. An early example of this manner is Kinmount, Dumfries and Galloway (1812). Later, and more successful, is Normanby Park, Humberside (1825-30). The portico and orders are dispensed with, and all emphasis and movement are created by the articulation of planes and the addition and subtraction of storeys. Despite these deviations, the most popular path followed by the post-1810 Greek revivalists was that blazed by Stratton Park and The Grange: the house as Grecian temple, the main ingredient in the illusion being the giant portico.

Willey Hall, Shropshire, by Lewis Wyatt (1812), is an example of this type, and indeed of much else that is impressive about the Greek revival country house. Its mighty four-columned composite portico is set against a long nine-bay elevation and rises the full two storeys of the house. It also has, centrally placed on one of its shorter side elevations, a full-height semicircular bay embellished, in the manner of Soane's Tyringham (p85), with four detached Corinthian columns – equal in size to those of the portico – supporting a full entablature. To the other short elevation is attached a service wing which gives the building an asymmetrical plan. This is typical of the period. From the late eighteenth century country houses tended to become lower – a trend encouraged by the Greek revival, for a two-storey house is easier to disguise as a Greek temple – with kitchens and guest bedrooms thrown out of sub-basements and attic floors into meandering wings. (Interestingly a similar course of action had been pursued at Holkham, but, of course, with great formality.) The interior of Willey is a masterpiece of pompous Regency planning. Within the bow on ground level is a library with an apsidal end to match the curve of the bow. The library, which by 1812 was used as a sitting room and a place in which to pursue informal conversation (a separate 'lounging room' is recorded at Downhill Castle, Co. Derry, as early as 1776), leads to the slightly more formal drawing room. From here the procession to dinner – the social high point of a country house day – would begin. At Willey this involved the guests traversing the magnificent colonnaded, galleried and barrel-vaulted central hall. After dinner the ladies would retrace their steps to the drawing room where they would be joined later in the evening by the men, who had enjoyed their own company, and wines, in the dining room. At Belsay the dinner guests could step into the dining room from the library, or parade from the drawing room into the ante-room, across the full width of the Pillar Hall into the entrance hall, and then into the dining room.

The gender of the dining room and the drawing room (the former masculine, the latter feminine) was a matter of well established tradition by the early nineteenth century. It is no mere chance that, at Castle Ward, Co. Down ($c1760$), the dining room is classical, to reflect the taste of the man who built the house, while the drawing room is Gothic, reflecting his wife's taste (p77). This physical expression of the sexual divisions of the house is, of course, crucial to understanding the logic behind the differing decoration of its various parts. At Syon House, Brentford, between 1761 and 1765, Robert Adam decorated the long gallery, intended for the use of the ladies, in an almost overpoweringly effeminate manner, with pastel mauves, green and dove grey, and delicate mouldings which reached an extreme in the exquisite miniature circular bird-cage room, decorated with sugary pink and white. Meanwhile for the dining room, ante-room and hall he produced schemes of masculine Roman gravity.

This difference of decorative approach could have remarkable results if the dining room was not only masculine in its decoration but also conservative – not to say archaic. A downright disregard for fashion – which was a flighty female concern anyway – and a preference for good old values implied, presumably, both solid character and a pedigree rooted in history. The dining room and the hall (the other male preserves) were, of course, where ancestral portraits and silver went on display. This affected disregard for fashion became something of a fashion itself, leading to some of the earliest examples of self-conscious, architectural revivalism (p46): Petworth, West Sussex, for instance, has a dining room of 1794 made in the manner of $c1690$; in 1814 Lewis Wyatt added a neo-Wren dining room to Lyme Park, Cheshire; and Tatton Park, Cheshire, designed by Samuel Wyatt in $c1788$ and completed by his brother Lewis, contains a rococo dining room in the manner of 1740–50.

Strangely similar to Willey Park is Ballyfin, Co. Laois. It was begun in about 1821 by Dominick Madden, who created a colonnaded curved bay and a splendid rotunda with a coffered dome supported on Grecian Ionic columns, and completed by Sir Richard Morrison and his son William Vitruvius, who extended the main elevation, enriched the interior, and added a giant four-column Greek Ionic portico. This was one of the earliest uses of such a portico on a country house in Ireland, although Mount Stewart, Newtownards, Co. Down, was to be given one almost simultaneously (in about 1825) by the younger Morrison, and Lewis Wyatt had designed a very similar one at Mount Shannon, Castleconnell, Co. Limerick, in $c1815$.

Perhaps the most impressive of the post-Grange country house temples is Camperdown House, near Dundee, Tayside, which is in fact a rather refined but still very obvious essay on The Grange. Designed in 1824 by William Burn, the house has an Ionic rather than Doric portico, a less boldly articulated side elevation, and altogether lacks the gusto of the original. In plan it is interesting, however, for it is an early example of Burn's theory (which became standard in the later nineteenth century) in which family, guest, and state rooms are segregated.

Lastly, there are those country houses of the Greek revival that defy categorization but which display a use of Greek reference which is both archaeologically correct and artistically original. This quality is typified by Belsay (p92), where Monck strove, largely successfully, to fuse the doctrines of the Greek revival with the romantic notions of the English picturesque in order to produce an original and convincing building, placed powerfully in its landscape.

An early example of this somewhat enigmatic branch of the Greek revival is J.M. Gandy's Doric House ($c1810$). Although not exactly a country house, for it is in Sion Hill, Bath, it is also most certainly not an average terrace house. It has something of the feeling of a Grecian treasury of the sort found at Delphi. The street frontage (behind which lies a picture gallery) rises off a substantial plinth, and has a blank lower storey divided into five bays by an order of unfluted Doric columns with concave capitals and no bases.

These support an entablature, upon which sits a smaller order of Doric columns. The corners are emphasized by antae, the shorter end elevations have pediments embellished with large-scale acroteria. More overtly archaeological is C.R. Cockerell's Oakley Park, Shropshire (1819). Cockerell, in the role of intrepid archaeologist, had in 1811 helped to discover important elements of the Temple of Apollo Epicurus at Bassae. Consequently Oakley's double-height, centrally placed and saucer-domed entrance hall is endowed with a first-floor colonnade, topped with capitals copied from the Tower of the Winds in Athens, and supporting a copy of the Bassae frieze, which Cockerell had unearthed. On the ground floor are Ionic columns sporting the peculiar Bassae Ionic volutes and flared, fluted bases. In the same theme, but less strident, is Clytha Park, Gwent. Designed in 1830 by Edward Haycock, Clytha is rich in both Greek and geometrical forms. There is a curved bay with the familiar decoration of columns, here Greek Doric, and inside is a circular entrance hall leading to a staircase hall with an octagonal lantern and a screen of Greek Doric columns. Externally the hexastyle portico is embellished with exquisitely carved capitals based directly on the Erechtheion, Athens.

Other revivals

Though dominant, the Greek revival did not hold absolute sway in early nineteenth-century house design. Other styles did emerge from the melting pot of the beginning of the century, and some flourished. Disparate as they were, they had in common the fact that, more than most products of the Greek revival, they reflected the themes of the picturesque – asymmetry, romantic antiquity and rusticity – and also reflected a desire on the part of an aristocracy shaken by the French Revolution for a country house design which invoked the authority of the ruling class and at least looked impregnable. Perhaps it was this sudden desire for security that provoked a lively interest in the Norman castle style. Neo-Norman began to emerge in 1799 at Wyatt's asymmetrical Norris Castle, Isle of Wight, and in 1811 Sir Robert Smirke designed Eastnor Castle, Hereford and Worcester, in a symmetrical neo-Norman castellated manner. But the great country houses of the Norman revival were not built until the second decade of the nineteenth century, and both were by Thomas Hopper. In 1819 he designed Gosford Castle, Markethill, Co. Armagh, and in 1825 Penrhyn Castle, Bangor, Gwynedd. Both are huge, and both are asymmetrically grouped to create a sublime pic-

The hall at Thomas Hopper's Penrhyn Castle, Gwynedd, 1825-44: an early and important example of the Norman revival.

turesque effect. Gosford has a romantic assemblage of round, square and rectangular towers, all pierced with many derivations of round arches and arcaded Norman windows. Inside is Norman too, with white plaster Norman decorations in the dining room and moulded Norman bookcases in the library. Penrhyn, with its massive square keep inspired by Rochester Castle and its great hall derived from Durham, is more stupendous still. Inside there is much exotic carving and a magnificent staircase hall. The plan is a wonderful example of dynamic picturesque arrangement, calculated to enliven the procession through the house, with contrived but splendid spatial surprises: the narrow corridor from the keep leads into one corner of the tall, vaulted hall, which connects in turn with the long, asymmetrically planned library, the lower dining hall, and the magnificent staircase hall.

Alongside the neo-Norman flourished the neo-Tudor/neo-Elizabethan revival, which we observed getting under way at Wyatville's Nonsuch Park, Surrey (1802), and Wilkins' Dalmeny House, 1814 (p90). In 1816 Wilkins continued the revival with Tregothnan, near Truro, Cornwall, where he created an elaborate asymmetrical neo-Tudor mansion, inspired partly perhaps by the old house on the site. In 1817 J.A. Repton investigated the Elizabethan style when designing Bourn Hall, Cambridgeshire, and during the 1820s the style flourished as a very popular alternative to Grecian and Gothic. Particularly good examples are Carstairs House, Strathclyde, by William Burn (1822), very clearly modelled on Dalmeny; and Lilleshall Hall, Shropshire, by Wyatville (1826), which in its excess is ahead of its time and looks distinctly Victorian.

A variation of this fashion for 'old' English architecture was the Jacobean revival, of which an early example is J.B. Papworth's St Julian's Underriver, Kent (1818), and slightly later examples – all of which anticipate the mid-Victorian 'Jacobethan' revival – are Underley Hall, Kirkby Lonsdale, Cumbria, by G. Webster (1825), and Babraham Hall, Cambridgeshire, by Philip Hardwick (1829-32).

The cottage orné
Finally, a word must be said about the style of country house that was the epitome of the picturesque and the most extreme manifestations of the self-conscious vogue for rural life – the *cottage orné*. Characterized by Gothic detailing, overtly rustic construction (pioneered by Soane's dairy at Hamels Park, 1781, now lost) and asymmetrical planning, the *cottage orné* might really be cottage-sized, or it might be a medium-sized house. A-la-Ronde, Exmouth, Devon, built for the Misses Parmenter in *c*1795, is sixteen-sided, and has a 60-foot-high central hall decorated with shells and birds modelled from feathers. Derrymore House, Bessbrook, Co. Armagh (*c*1790-1800), is symmetrically Palladian in layout, with a diminutive single-storey centre block flanked by two forward-projecting wings, joined to the centre block by little quadrant walls. In the centre of the rear elevation of the main block is a full-height canted bay (again in the Irish Palladan tradition), fully glazed with mullions and transoms and flanked by quatrefoil windows under hood moulds. But to make quite clear its rustic intent both centre and wings are thatched. Houghton Lodge, Hampshire (1800), is equally ambitious, with Gothic windows, twisted chimneys, a steep (originally thatched) roof and a bow on the east front containing a circular drawing room and a sky-painted ceiling. Endsleigh, near Milton Abbot, Devon (1810), by Wyatville, is particularly important for, as well as being lavishly rustic, it has asymmetrical diagonal planning, which was revolutionary at the time and did not become fashionable until exploited by Thomas Hope in *c*1818 at his now demolished Deepdene House, Surrey. Perhaps more characteristic examples of the type are the Lodge of Gaunt's House, near Hinton Martell, Dorset (*c*1810), which has an umbrella-like thatched roof, Gothic windows and a rustic tree-trunk-

'Swiss Cottage', Cahir, Co. Tipperary, 1814, perhaps by John Nash, and an excellent and characteristic *cottage orné*.

columned thatched porch; the 'Swiss cottage', Cahir, Co. Tipperary (1814) – perhaps by John Nash – with a thatched roof and elaborate Gothic rustic veranda; Glengarriff Lodge, Glengarriff, Co. Cork (c1820), which is asymmetrical and thatched, but two storeys high with a two-storey Gothic veranda and Gothic window tracery; and Sarsgrove House, Sarsden, Oxfordshire (c1825), by G.S. Repton, with ornamental bargeboards, twisted chimney stacks and an altogether Victorian air.

Garden buildings, follies, monuments, model farms and dwellings

Garden buildings, follies, monuments and agricultural buildings represented the great escape for the architects of the eighteenth and early nineteenth centuries: in the design of these buildings they could indulge their fantasy for archaeological reconstruction of ancient buildings, experiment with unconventional forms or merely display their wit.

Garden buildings and follies

This tendency towards archaeological invention and originality of design was already apparent in the very early eighteenth century, as can clearly be seen, for example, in John Vanbrugh's austere castellated Belvedere (c1715) at Claremont, Surrey, and his four-porticoed and domed Temple of the Four Winds of 1725 at Castle Howard, North Yorkshire, inspired by Palladio's Villa Rotonda, and also in William Adam's extraordinarily lavish baroque kennels at Chatelherault, Strathclyde (1731). The first-generation Palladians continued this free approach, for they regarded garden buildings as romantic counterpoints to the formal setting and controlled elevation of the classical house, and as picturesque elements in the composed landscape garden – a view which found its full expression at Stowe, Buckinghamshire, under the direction of William Kent in the 1730s. On a more practical level this freedom represented a release from the Palladians' self-imposed bondage to classical propriety and to the orders (p8) and allowed them not only to indulge in academic recreation of wayward antique buildings, but also to dabble in baroque, Gothic, and even oriental styles. The position was well described later in the eighteenth century by Sir William Chambers – an architect who retained his Palladian principles long after they had become unfashionable in the wake of the neo-classical picturesque revolution. In his *Designs of Chinese Buildings* (1757) he approved of playful garden buildings as 'toys in architecture' which 'may be sometimes be allowed a place among compositions of a nobler [that is classical] kind'. This attitude appeared as soon as the Palladian movement emerged.

In 1718 Colen Campbell, at Ebberston Hall summer house, near Scarborough, North Yorkshire, used rustication in a baroque manner to embellish the main façade of the single-storey building and its entrance porch. William Kent continued this bold rusticated classicism with garden buildings at Stowe, notably the Temple of British Worthies (1733), and his garden buildings at Rousham House, Oxfordshire (c1738-41), where great play is made of heavy rustication and repeating pediments. Kent was perhaps also responsible for a remarkably bold Palladian temple at Euston, Suffolk (1746), and for the best example of a decorated and inventive Burlingtonian Palladian garden building: Worcester Lodge, in the grounds of Badminton House, Great Badminton, Avon, of 1746 (p65). At the same time as designing these Kent was also responsible, it must be remembered, for the most chaste of classical garden temples, such as the domed Temple of Ancient Virtue (c1735) at Stowe. Even more diverse in his taste was James Gibbs, who created full-blown essays in the style of Vanbrugh at Stowe (the Boycott Pavilions of c1726, modified c1760) and one of the earliest large-scale buildings in the Gothic revival in Britain.

The Palladian poet Alexander Pope had created Alfred's Hall, a picturesque Gothic ruin-cum-cottage in Cirencester Park, Gloucestershire, as early as 1721 (p14), but most of the Gothic revival undertakings before Gibbs's Gothic temple at Stowe (c1741) had been created either in association with existing ancient buildings (p123) or as minor additions, such as fireplaces, within buildings, or as fairly functionless follies, such as the Gothic Folly Arch (c1730) at Gobions, Brookmans Park, Hertfordshire, possibly also by Gibbs. The Gothic temple at Stowe, decidedly non-antiquarian in form, with an Elizabethan triangular plan and curious Early English decoration, set a pattern, as did the work of amateur architect Sanderson Miller. In 1745 he built an octagonal castellated Gothic tower (based on Guy's Tower at Warwick Castle) at Edge Hill, Warwickshire (he had earlier, in 1743, built a picturesque thatched cottage with Gothic windows at Edge Hill), and in 1747 he designed an even more inspired Gothic castle at Hagley, Hereford and Worcester (his Gothic castle for Wimpole, Cambridgeshire, designed in 1749, was not built until 1772).

Amongst the earliest examples of rococo Gothic garden buildings are the bizarre

The Gothic temple at Stowe, Buckinghamshire, designed c1741 by James Gibbs and an early example of eighteenth-century Gothic design.

Gothic temple with pendant tracery and ogee openings at Painshill Park, Cobham, Surrey (1742-5), the richly decorated temple at Aske Hall, North Yorkshire, possibly by Daniel Garrett (and possibly even slightly earlier than Gibbs's work at Stowe), and the Gothic orangery (c1750) at Frampton Court, Frampton, Gloucestershire (p209). With a plan based on octagons and with ogee-arched windows this delightful building is similar to a design published by William and John Halfpenny in their *Chinese and Gothick Architecture Properly Ornamented* (1752).

The other exotic style enjoyed by the Palladians, the Chinese, had a long but now less visible life in the eighteenth century. The typically flimsy timber Chinese pavilion at Stowe, built in 1738 and mentioned in the

The Casino at Marino, Dublin, 1758-76 by Chambers; an exquisite design which introduced sophisticated French-inspired neo-classicism to Ireland.

guide of 1744 (p14) is long gone, but a similar structure, dating from 1747, survives at Shugborough, Staffordshire. Of later eighteenth-century Chinese buildings three by Sir William Chambers survive: the pagoda at Kew, Richmond upon Thames (1761), the earliest and most important; a Chinese pavilion at Wrest Park, Bedfordshire (c1770); and the now greatly decayed Chinese temple at Amesbury Abbey, Wiltshire (1772); and at Woburn Abbey, Bedfordshire, there survives Henry Holland's large and remarkable Chinese dairy (1791).

While the Gothic and Chinese styles were being used to create diverting and playful garden structures, there was also a parallel development in the mid-eighteenth century in sophisticated and inventive classically based garden buildings. The epitome of this is perhaps Sir William Chambers' Casino at Marino, Clontarf, Co. Dublin (1758-76), which introduced his exquisite French-influenced neo-classical detailing to Ireland and provided an inspiration for succeeding generations of architects building in Ireland.

The mainstream of classically designed garden buildings cannot, of course, be properly represented by virtuoso displays like Kent's Worcester Lodge or Chambers' Casino. But a consistent development can be traced through the enduring eighteenth- and early nineteenth-century love for more or less accurate archaeological reconstructions of more or less ancient prototypes. The first-generation Palladians achieved some remarkable and learned reconstructions, with Palladio's designs predictably providing a popular source. Ornamental bridges based on a Palladio design, for example, were built by first-generation Palladians such as Roger Morris and Lord Pembroke at Wilton, Wiltshire, in 1737; John Wood the Elder at Prior Park, Bath, Avon, in c1755; and probably James Gibbs between 1738 and 1742 at Stowe, Buckinghamshire.[20] Later in the century, almost as an act of Palladian revivalism, further versions were constructed: by Thomas Pitt at Hagley, Worcestershire (1764), and by Robert Adam at Audley End, Essex (1782).

Reconstructions of Roman prototypes were also attempted, a typical example being William Kent's arch at Holkham Hall, Norfolk (c1740), which is an essay upon a Roman triumphal arch rendered in Palladian detail rather than a learned reconstruction. The same can be said of Thomas Pitt's Corinthian arch at Stowe (1766). In the same vein are the mid-eighteenth-century evocations of the Pantheon in Rome (Burlington had pioneered Pantheon-inspired garden buildings at Chiswick in c1717, now demolished): Henry

The Palladian bridge at Stowe, Buckinghamshire, 1738-42, one of several eighteenth-century reconstructions of a Palladio design.

The Temple of Theseus, Hagley Hall, Hereford and Worcester, 1758, by James Stuart: the first Greek Doric temple front built since antiquity.

Flitcroft's Temple of Hercules, Stourhead, Wiltshire (1754-6), Sir William Chambers' Temple of Bellona at Kew (c1760), and Garrick's Temple at Hampton Court, Middlesex (c1758). All of these reflect the original only in being domed, circular, square or octagonal buildings embellished with porticoes. Of the same casual archaeological type are such garden buildings as the Mussenden Temple at Downhill, Co. Derry, which was built in c1780-85 to the design of Michael Shanahan for the Earl-Bishop of Derry, and is loosely based on round and colonnaded Roman prototypes such as the Temples of Vesta at Tivoli and Rome. However, there were more serious attempts at reconstruction, such as Ambrose Phillips's renderings of the Roman Temple of Vesta and the Arch of Titus on his estates at Garendon Hall, Leicestershire (c1735), and the Temple of Concord at Stowe of (c1748-62). With its peristyle and portico the latter reflected Roman temples such as that at Nîmes in France (and as published by Palladio) and was designed initially (perhaps) by William Kent and Richard Grenville and finished by Giovanni Battista Borra.

This serious approach to archaeological reconstruction properly belongs, however, to the second half of the eighteenth century and the early nineteenth century, particularly to the years after the neo-classical revolution of the early 1760s (p15). Significantly, the first full-blooded example of the Greek revival was a garden building – James Stuart's Temple of Theseus at Hagley, Worcestershire (1758), which was based on a drawing Stuart had made in Athens, and was the first Grecian Doric temple front erected anywhere since antiquity. Six years later Stuart repeated the composition in the grounds of Shugborough, Staffordshire, which became to the archaeological neo-classicism of the 1760s what Stowe and Stourhead had been to the development of the landscape garden in the 1730s-50s.

At Shugborough, probably in the same year as Stuart's Hagley temple was built or a little earlier, was erected the Shepherd's Monument, which seems to proclaim the aspirations of the forthcoming neo-classical enterprise at Shugborough. Within a rustic arch, carved in stone and closely based on designs in Thomas Wright's *Six Original Designs of Grottos* of 1758, is a relief carved by Peter Scheemakers after Poussin's *Et in Arcadia Ego*. Around this rustic arch and relief is a screen of two primitive Doric columns, made up of drums which are deliberately rough-hewn and incomplete, with flutes appearing only at the bottom of each section. Stuart had drawn just such an incomplete carved antique column and is no doubt responsible for at least the screen in front of this remarkable monument to romantic neo-classicism. The other structures Stuart erected at Shugborough were less ambiguous about their ancestry. In 1761 he designed a triumphal arch based on the Arch of Hadrian at Athens, but laden with naval monuments to commemorate the career of Admiral Lord Anson, brother of the owner of Shugborough. In 1764 he designed the Lanthorn of Demosthenes, based on the Choragic monument of

Lysicrates in Athens and, at about the same time, the Tower of the Winds which was based on the octagonal tower in Athens which Stuart, with Nicholas Revett, had illustrated in Volume I of *Antiquities of Athens* (1762). These two antique prototypes enjoyed a particularly large following during the late eighteenth and early nineteenth centuries. turies. Lysicrates' monuments were erected by William Cole at Tatton Park, Cheshire, in c1820, at Alton Towers, Staffordshire (as a memorial to the fifteenth Earl of Shrewsbury), by J.B. Papworth and R. Abraham in c1825, and on Calton Hill, Edinburgh, in c1830 (as a monument to Professor Dugald Stewart) by W.H. Playfair. James Stuart erected a copy of the Tower of the Winds at Mount Stewart, Co. Down, Ireland, in 1780; Nicholas Revett designed a peculiar version with a rusticated, arcaded base at West Wycombe Park, Buckinghamshire, in c1770-75; in c1776 John Carr designed a pair of octagonal gate lodges at Basildon Park, Berkshire, based on the Athenian tower; and in 1780 James Wyatt built a Tower of the Winds pigeon house at Badger Hall, Shropshire. In this same archaeological spirit is Wyatville's Tower of Wynnstay, Powys (1810), modelled on the Tomb of Cecilia Metella in the Appian Way, Rome.

By the turn of the eighteenth century the vocabulary of garden building design was rich indeed, reflecting the astonishing plurality of architectural taste that characterized late eighteenth-century and early nineteenth-century design (p90). Greek- and Roman-inspired archaeological reconstruction, which produced such small but memorable buildings as C.R. Cockerell's lodges at Nant-y-Belan, Wynnstay, Clwyd (1827), and at Loughcrew, Co. Meath (1821-9), co-existed with exotic oriental and Gothic designs, such as the Gothic fishing lodge at Rockingham, Co. Roscommon, by Nash (c1810) and the Gothic lodges at Glin Castle, Co. Limerick (c1790-1812), and with the newly emerging austere, stripped-down neo-classicism represented by Sir John Soane's lodge at Tyringham, Buckinghamshire (1793), and James Wyatt's lodges to Dodington Park, Avon (c1802), which show the influence of Ledoux and of revolutionary French neo-classicism.

As well as being the focus of fashionable stylistic developments, garden building design also, in the 1820s, became the testing ground for new building technology. In the eighteenth and early nineteenth centuries conservatories had been roofed by constructions of wood and glass, such as Chambers' Orangery at Kew (1761). But in the second decade of the nineteenth century conservatories pioneered the use of cast-iron and glass roof construction in Britain. As early as 1798 Nash had designed a cast-iron conservatory roof – on the principle of timber roof construction – with iron trusses supporting a glass pitched roof.[21] In 1807 Thomas Hopper designed a conservatory at Carlton House, London (now demolished), which had a Gothic fan vault with the ribs of cast iron and panels of glass. Sir G.S. Mackenzie in 1815 and Loudon in 1817 realized the potential of cast-iron structures (p137) and designed glass- and iron-domed conservatories, and in 1823 Messrs Jones and Clark constructed a Camellia House in the grounds of Wollaton Hall, Nottinghamshire, as an irregular octagon in plan with corridors barrel-vaulted with curved iron plates. In 1827 W. and D. Bailey constructed a conservatory with a diameter of 100 feet at Bretton Hall, West Yorkshire,[22] and in the same year Charles Fowler began building his magnificent conservatory at Syon House, Brentford, which has a centre dome supported on tall, slender cast-iron columns, and wings with cast-iron trussed roofs sweeping forward to end in pedimented pavilions.

Model farms and estate buildings
The earliest surviving English design for a complete farmstead is by John Webb of c1650. With a regular quadrangle surrounded by a stable, barn and single-storey cowsheds, and a substantial farmhouse as the dominant feature of a symmetrical classical arrangement, this Webb design displays all the elements found in the late eighteenth century when model farmsteads began to be built in large numbers. It also reflects the salient elements of Palladio's planned farms and villas of the Venetian hinterland. These were primarily working farms, like Villa Trissino and Villa Pisani, and were at the root of eighteenth-century model farmsteads, whose designers were understandably intrigued by the challenge of working with a building type which was both hallowed by Palladio's attention and, later in the eighteenth century, seen as particularly suitable for experiments in 'primitive' classical and picturesque design.

Significantly, Palladio himself thought he was building on precedents and was merely reflecting, if slightly idealizing, the ideas of the ancients. Indeed Palladio's pupil Scamozzi published a book of ground plans for farmsteads in 1615 which he claimed were based on the villas of the ancients. The potency of this association was strong. We find Isaac Ware, in mid-eighteenth-century England, falling in line and recommending villas of ancient Romans as models for grand farms.

Ware's views accurately reflect the ideas current at his time. Despite Webb's impressive and prophetic composition, the design of model farmsteads is generally a post-1750 phenomenon, one of the earliest fully developed examples being Henry Flitcroft's work at Wentworth Woodhouse, South Yorkshire, where he designed a uniform farmyard (only the barn now survives) in 1742–4.

The model farmstead was not, however, dependent entirely for its form and details on the Palladio/Webb precedent. Admittedly there was a tradition of quadrangular, classical arcaded farms right through the late eighteenth century: Thomas Ivory's faultlessly organized and subtly detailed farmstead at Kilcarty, Kilmessan, Co. Meath (c1770–80), for example, R. Salmon's Woburn Park Farm, Bedfordshire (1795), and George Steuart's Blairuachder, Blair Atholl, Tayside (1797). There was also a liking for massive primitive Palladian barns, such as that at Home Farm, Weston Park, Staffordshire (1768), by J. Paine, and the Great Barn (c1790) at Holkham, Norfolk, by Samuel Wyatt. But the influence of the English picturesque landscape movement made itself felt early in agricultural design, with such creations as William Kent's castellated cowshed (c1738) at Rousham, Oxfordshire, which serves both its mundane function and the role of garden ornament.

This picturesque castle approach was followed by Thomas Wright with his towered and battlemented Castle Barn, Badminton, Avon (c1750); by James Paine with his Park Farm, Raby Castle, Co. Durham (c1755); by the Duchess of Norfolk with the massive Castle Farm, Worksop, Nottinghamshire (c1760), which has a court sixty yards square formed by a range of castellated cowsheds and barns; and by John Carr with his Castle Farm, Sledmere, Humberside (1778), which is a magnificent eye-catcher with a mighty twin-towered gatehouse.

With the growth of the romantic movement in the late eighteenth century the castellated farm was joined by farms detailed in other exotic styles, or in which were expressed some of the more extreme ideas of late eighteenth-century neo-classicism, for example Sir John Soane's Park Farm, Wimpole, Cambridgeshire (1794), which is constructed of timber, clapboard-clad and thatched, and S.P. Cockerell's extraordinary and asymmetrically composed Moorish farm at Sezincote, Gloucestershire (c1808). In Scotland a fairly common romantic permutation was the towered or spired farm, which could come in classical guise – such as Home Farm, Doune Park, Central Region (c1807), perhaps by William Stirling, which has a tall octagonal tower supporting a squat spire set over a large pedimented arch – or Gothic, as at the Steading (c1800) at Rosebery House, Lothian.

The effect of the revolutionary neo-classical movement on agricultural design is particularly interesting. Architects like Sir John Soane and James Playfair, freed from the constraints imposed by the design of conventional buildings, allowed their imagination to run wild and, indeed, to be stimulated by the association between the primitive nature of the building type – cattleshed or barn – and the primitive origins of classicism. For example in 1773 Robert Adam designed a primitive hut based on Abbé Laugier's influential design (p16) published in 1753[23] (earlier Robert's brother James had designed a rustic, primitive farm with thatched roof and tree-trunk-column porch). In 1781–3 Soane designed a similarly rustic dairy at Hamels near Buntingford, Hertfordshire, in 1783 a neo-classical cow-house at Burn Hall, Co. Durham, and in 1798 a 'barn à la Paestum', as Soane put it, at 936 Warwick Road, Solihull, West Midlands.

One of the most sophisticated neo-classical farmstead designs is at Carrigglas, Co. Longford, of c1795 by James Gandon. Here two courts are formed by simply-detailed one- and two-storey ranges, which are entirely without mouldings. These courts connect via an arch in a taller block (formerly with a cupola), which is on axis with the main entrance to the farmstead. This is through an astonishingly urbane entrance block that rises above, and is set at an angle to, the modest flanking ranges. Externally this block is faced with channelled rustication and contains an arch set within a larger arch – all very much in the spirit of contemporary French neo-classicism.

Model villages
The buildings erected for estate works were generally more utilitarian than utopian, although architects such as Joseph F. Gandy and John Plaw did publish designs for cottages and lodges of a studied geometrical design. The reasons behind the creation of model villages were diverse: the most common in the first half of the eighteenth century was the desire of landowners to remove unsightly groups of their tenants' dwellings from within their newly enlarged and landscaped parks. As early as 1702 Lord Oxford removed the ancient village from his park at Chippenham, Cambridgeshire, and outside the gates created a model village of rows of identical, simple, single-storey, semi-detached cottages linked by outbuildings. He also provided the

village with a handsome baroque brick school in 1712. The same policy was pursued in the early 1720s at Stowe, Buckinghamshire, where Gibbs's Boycott Pavilions mark the site of the village of that name, at Castle Howard, North Yorkshire, where Vanbrugh's temple of 1724 stands on the site of the village High Street, and at Houghton Hall, Norfolk, where in 1724 Sir Robert Walpole created New Houghton outside the gates. Here simple two-storey, detached brick houses were laid out in a straight line along the approach road to the park.

A similar lack of imaginative planning or architectural ambition was displayed in the second half of the century. In the 1760s Lord Harcourt removed the village from within his grounds at Nuneham Courtenay, Oxfordshire, and so prompted Oliver Goldsmith to reflect upon *The Deserted Village*. The village was re-sited as a parallel row of single-storey, semi-detached dwellings along the main Oxford Road just outside his park. He kept the village church within his park, but rebuilt it more as a garden ornament than a convenient place of worship (page 116). The same austerity was displayed at Milton Abbas, Dorset, a village designed initially by Sir William Chambers in c1773 and completed and modified by Lancelot Brown in c1786. Here identical blocks of three-bay, two-storey thatched cottages, with very little external detail, curve gracefully and repetitively down a gentle hillside.

More imaginative was Lowther village, Cumbria, designed for the demented Viscount Lonsdale by the Adam brothers in 1766 (built 1770–75) with the intention of removing all housing from the environs of the castle. The village was planned as a central circus of thirty-two dwellings flanked by two squares of equal size, each of which had wide roads and small residential courts off the centre of each of its sides. Only half of this ambitious scheme, perhaps inspired in its layout by Bath, was built, and that in modified form, but there is enough to show that architectural elements such as bays and string courses could be used to create harmony and break the monotony of so many model villages. A later example is East Stratton, Hampshire, which was designed by George Dance the Younger in 1806 as an avenue of picturesque brick-built thatched cottages outside the entrance gate of Stratton Park. A Scottish example of the 1780s is Scone, Tayside.

The other type of model village, that created for an economic purpose as well as a piece of estate-planning, is exemplified by Harewood village, West Yorkshire, built as a triumphal avenue on the approach to Harewood House by John Carr in the 1760s. Here houses – some almost urban, of three storeys and embellished with two-storey arcading on

The main street of the model village of Milton Abbas, Dorset, which was designed initially by Sir William Chambers c1773, with thatched cottages built c1786 under the direction of Lancelot Brown.

their elevations – mingle with plainer cottages conceived as pavilions with gable end pediments, which were intended originally as homes and workplaces for ribbon makers. Of similar origin is the village of Mistley in Essex, developed as a spa in the 1770s, with an ambitious layout including a central square, inns and lodging houses in the best Essex provincial architectural style.

The picturesquely planned – as well as detailed – estate village is best represented, perhaps, by John Nash's romantically disposed thatched cottages at Blaise Hamlet, near Bristol, of 1811 (p162), and by Tyrrellspass, Co. Westmeath, Ireland; created around a semicircular green. The early nineteenth-century taste for Gothic oddity is illustrated by cottages at Marford, Clwyd: built along the main road between 1806 and 1816 by George Boscawen, they display every possible shape and type of Gothic window and variety of Gothic decoration. The contemporary fashion for Greek-inspired neo-classicism is reflected in the two lines of stark arcaded cottages, built between 1807 and 1817, that stand on the approach to the magnificent and austere Greek revival Belsay Hall, Northumberland. The cottages, like the design of the house, were probably the inspiration of the owner, Sir Charles Monck, perhaps working with John Dobson.

Notes

1 Castle Howard, North Yorkshire, c1700–26, with its grounds and outworks, cost £59,000 – and was still incomplete. At the time a bricklayer's labourer earned 1s 6d a day. See *English Baroque Architecture* by Kerry Downes, 1966 edition, page 12.
2 *Vitruvius Britannicus*, vol I, 1715.
3 Sir John Summerson in the *Journal of the Royal Society of Arts*, CVII, 1959.
4 See John Harris's *The Palladians*, pages 58–60 of the 1981 edition, and Howard Colvin's 'A Scottish origin for English Palladianism?', *Architectural History* XVII, 1974.
5 Paul Duncan, unpublished thesis for Edinburgh University on James Smith at Whitehall, 1983.
6 435/95(a) reference at RIBA drawings collection.
7 Colvin's essay on 'A Scottish origin for English Palladianism?' (see note 4 above) records that a James Smith of Morayshire was admitted to the Scots College in Rome in May 1671 (and left in 1675). If this was the architect James Smith it suggests that he could have gained first-hand knowledge of the works of Palladio.
8 *Vitruvius Britannicus*, vol II, 1717.
9 Maurice Craig, *The Architecture of Ireland*, page 180 of 1982 edition.
10 *Lord Hervey and his Friends, 1726–38*, ed. Earl of Ilchester, 1950. See also Mark Girouard's *Life in the English Country House*, pages 160–2 of 1980 edition, and *English Decoration in the 18th Century* by John Fowler and John Cornforth, pages 60–4 of 1974 edition.
11 Published in 1734 and the only written description of Palladian aesthetic theory.
12 Ducart was described as a 'Sardinian', suggesting he was from Savoy or Piedmont. For a profile of Ducart see articles by the Knight of Glin in *Country Life*, 28 September and 5 October 1967, and Maurice Craig's *The Architecture of Ireland*, pages 192–6 of the 1982 edition.
13 Maurice Craig, op. cit., page 195.
14 Robert Adam in a letter of 1758 to his brother James, when discussing work at Hatchlands. Quoted in Geoffrey Beard's *The Work of Robert Adam*, page 8 of 1978 edition.
15 Maurice Craig, op. cit., page 244.
16 David Watkin, in the conclusion to his *The Buildings of Britain: Regency*, 1982.
17 J. Mordaunt Crook, *The Greek Revival*, page 97 of 1972 edition.
18 *Antiquities of Athens*, vol III, 1794.
19 *Antiquities of Athens*, vol II, 1787.
20 The Palladian bridge at Stowe was attributed to Gibbs by Terry Friedman in his *James Gibbs*, 1984.
21 'Conservatory for Prince of Wales': drawings now in Royal Library, Windsor, and illustrated (7c) in Sir John Summerson's *The Life and Work of John Nash, Architect*, 1980.
22 Information from Nikolaus Pevsner's *A History of Building Types*, pages 240–1 of 1976 edition.
23 Abbé Laugier's *Essai sur l'Architecture*, 1753.

2 Wren explained the thinking that lay behind the spatial organization and fittings of eighteenth-century churches when advising the 50 New Churches Commissioners of 1711: 'It is enough if they [the Roman Catholics] hear the murmur of the Mass and see the elevation of the Host, but ours are to be fitted for Auditories.'

CHURCHES

Wren's influence on church design remained unbroken in the first decades of the eighteenth century despite the eclipse of the baroque and the rise of the Palladians after 1715. This was due largely to the fact that he evolved a language of design and produced so many permutations of plan form, ceiling and vault design during his reconstruction of the City churches after 1666, that later eighteenth-century architects when designing a classical church could not help following a recipe set by Wren. But it was not the power of Wren alone that kept the baroque alive in church design long after it had faltered elsewhere. In 1711 the Tory government passed an act for building fifty churches in London. Funded by a tax on coal (the same revenue that had built St Paul's) these churches were an expression of Tory High Church ambition: placed among the expanding population of the suburbs of London, they were to be both places to worship in and symbols of state power and control.

The west front of Christ Church, Spitalfields, London, 1714-29, by Nicholas Hawksmoor. An inspired example of the English baroque school, built under the 1711 church building act.

The architectural specifications were certainly intended to create monuments. The commissioners, who included Wren, Vanbrugh and Archer, wanted free-standing churches on 'insular' sites, furnished with 'handsome porticoes' on 'such fronts as shall happen to be most open to view'. As Vanbrugh put it, the churches 'should not only serve for the Accommodation of the inhabitants ... but at the same time remain monuments to Posterity.'

Only twelve churches were built, with a further four being partly subsidized by the 1711 Church Building Commission. Significantly, eight of these were in the East End or riverside suburbs: areas of rapid expansion and little state control. But, more importantly for the story in hand, the architects chosen to build these monuments to Tory power were mostly pupils of Wren, and baroque men to the core. In 1711, it is true, any other type of architect was virtually non-existent. An interesting exception was George Clarke of Oxford, an early Palladian sympathizer who was also one of the commissioners appointed in 1712. If he sought expression of the new style he had seen evolving at Oxford (p165), however, he must have been disappointed, for even Colen Campbell, who with Wanstead House (p52) was to become the pioneer of Palladianism in 1713, in 1712 could only submit a distinctly baroque design to the commissioners (for what we can only imagine was their disapproval since Campbell received no commissions). So the significant point about the 1711 church building campaign was not that baroque architects were chosen initially (or even that they remained in favour until the last two churches built under the act – St Luke's, Old Street, and St John's, Horsleydown – were completed in 1733, to the designs of Nicholas Hawksmoor and John James), but that it provided a set of models that, together with Wren's City churches, inspired provincial church designers for many years to come. With its external pilasters and nave pediments, for example, the church at Aynho, Northamptonshire, begun in 1723, possibly to the design of local mason Edward Wing, is clearly a local attempt to capture some of the architectural quality of the London churches of 1711. So are the churches at Gayhurst, Buckinghamshire (1728), also by Wing, and

Honiley, Warwickshire (1723), which is sprinkled with a delightful mixture of Archer and Hawksmoor motifs.

Architects in Ireland, meanwhile, were pursuing another direction, taking Roman baroque churches as direct models for Irish Protestant churches. St Anne's, Dublin, begun in 1720, probably to the designs of Isaac Wills, and demolished in 1868, was an essay upon S. Giacomo degli Incurabili, Rome, by da Volterra and Maderno, while St Werburgh's, Dublin, begun in 1715 to the designs of Thomas Burgh, has a main façade (possibly designed by the Florentine Alessandro Galilei, who was to design the main front of S. Giovanni in Laterano, Rome, in 1734) derived from da Volterra's S. Chiara, Rome.

The basilica plan

Although the 1711 act was formative for eighteenth-century church design, it was not responsible for the single most influential church of the Georgian period. St Martin-in-the-Fields, which replaced a medieval church, was built between 1722 and 1726 to the designs of James Gibbs. Gibbs had built St Mary-le-Strand, Westminster, for the commissioners in 1714-17, when he was sacked for being a Scot and a Roman Catholic. At St Mary's he demonstrated his Italian baroque style to great effect but by 1722 he had modified it to suit the emerging Palladian taste of the new decade. But he had by no means surrendered entirely to the domi-

The west portico of James Gibbs's St Martin-in-the-Fields, Westminster, London, 1722-6. The design evoked the powerful image of the pedimented temple of the ancients.

nance of Lord Burlington and his followers. In its detail and its combination of parts, St Martin's is essentially a baroque building of a very personal kind (Gibbs had trained under Carlo Fontana). The mix of motifs is individual and not at all constricted by the rules of architectural propriety that obsessed the Palladians. The tower of St Martin's has the same free individuality as the body. Like Wren's towers, it renders a Gothic form in classical language but, unlike them, with the partial exception of Christ Church, Newgate

The interior of St Martin-in-the-Fields looking east. The nave colonnade carries blocks of entablature from which rise the ceiling vaults.

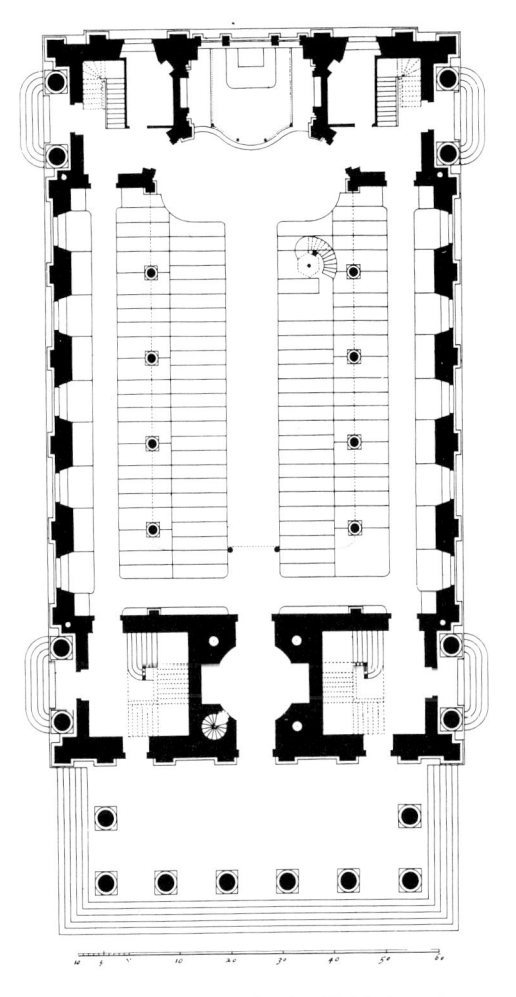

Above: Plan of St Martin-in-the-Fields from James Gibbs's *Book of Architecture* of 1728.

Below: St Martin-in-the-Fields from the south-east.

Street (1704), and St Bride's, Fleet Street, of (1701-3), the ascent from square base to pierced concave obelisk top is done in a series of well-defined stages of Palladian design.

The general design of the exterior of the church – the dominant portico and tall steeple – conforms to the criteria of the 1711 commissioners, but in his attempt to recreate the basilica of the ancients (for a generation of Church of England worshippers obsessed with the benefits of Roman classicism), Gibbs went beyond anything achieved by Hawksmoor and the other commissioners' architects. True, the basilica form – promoted by Palladio in the *Quattro Libri* – had been used earlier in England, by Wren of course at St James's, Piccadilly (1676-84), but also in the eighteenth century by John Platt for St Paul's, Sheffield (1720, now demolished), and in the same year by William Etty for Holy Trinity, Leeds. Indeed, in 1721 Gibbs himself had used a basilica plan at St Peter's, Vere Street, Westminster, which can be regarded as a smaller-scale and exquisitely detailed trial run for St Martin's.

But no architect had combined a basilica with a giant portico which not merely embellished the show front of the church, as at Hawksmoor's St George's, Bloomsbury Way (1716-31), or at John James's St George's, Hanover Square (1720-25), but with its gravity, grandeur and scale made the church into a Roman temple; an effect somewhat marred, as succeeding generations of critics have pointed out, by the tower and steeple, which conflict with the temple front by sitting in an ungainly fashion on the roof just behind it. The attempt to combine correct classicism with steeple on tower (for which classical antiquity could unfortunately offer no precedent) became one of the running battles of the Georgian church designer. The other approach, which Wren had used at St Mary-le-Bow and St Bride's, Fleet Street, and which can also be seen at Honiley Church, Warwickshire (1723), Patshull Church, Staffordshire (1742, partly reconstructed 1874), by James Gibbs, the Church of Ireland cathedral at Cashel, Co. Tipperary (1763-83), and Ballycastle Church, Co. Antrim (*c*1755), was visually to bring the tower down to the ground rather than have it rise out of the roof of the building.

Internally, St Martin's continues the principles of the Roman basilica which, with its nave and aisles (but no transept) provides a plan form not dissimilar to traditional medieval churches. There is one axis, from the west front along the centre of the nave to the altar, which is placed in a chancel created within the body of the church by the ingenious use of flanking vestries. The nave is separated by Corinthian columns on plinths from the aisles, where the vaults are slightly lower than in the nave. Within these aisles are galleries which, as in most eighteenth-century churches were provided for functional necessity rather than aesthetic benefit. In St Martin's they are placed above plinth-level halfway up the aisle columns, which they embrace with as much style as such an unlikely event as a wainscot gallery in a classical temple will permit. Indeed Gibbs himself, when discussing his rebuilding of All Saints, Derby, completed in 1725 along the same general lines as St Martin's, wrote: 'It is the more beautiful for having no galleries, which, as well as pews, clog up and spoil the inside of churches and take away from that right proportion which they otherwise would have, and are only justifiable as they are necessary.'[1]

But necessary they were. Religion in eighteenth-century Protestant England was not to be experienced but rather to be heard, seen and reasoned upon. Hence, in the 'auditory' church the congregation must all be able to see and hear the preacher, which was possible only if they were suspended among the columns of the church as well as pewed along the nave.[2]

Gibbs also regretted the pews but these, too, were necessary. The architectural implications of high box pews are interesting. The witty designer could place the block of pews in his basilican church in such a way as to create either a fake transept or a subtle baroque cross-axis, as Hawksmoor did at Christ Church, Spitalfields (1714–29),[3] where the long north and south nave walls were pierced in the centre with doors connected by a passage between the blocks of box pews. But more importantly box pews made it impossible for designers to furnish the interior with giant columns reaching from ceiling entablature or vault to the floor. Instead they had to be placed on pedestals of the same height as the top of the box pews, for if a column ran down to the ground its base moulding would obviously be lost amongst the pews. This arrangement did not worry the early eighteenth-century baroque designers, who liked the extra height and vertical thrust given by the use of pedestals and piers. But later Palladian designers, entranced by the image of the Egyptian hall as described by Vitruvius and illustrated by Palladio, in which an arcade of giant columns sat directly on floor level, must have been even more vexed than Gibbs by fitted church furniture. Mereworth Church in Kent, which we shall examine in more detail later, does have a giant order standing at floor level, along the lines of Burlington's York Assembly Room (1731) and George Dance's Egyptian Hall in the Mansion House, City of London (1739–42) (p175), but this was made possible only because it was never fitted with box pews.

To return to St Martin-in-the-Fields, Gibbs's eclectic inventiveness did not stop at modifying the Roman basilica for Anglican worship. The arcade itself is also a little unexpected. His Corinthian columns, supported on pedestals, in turn support mere square blocks of entablature from which the vault of the nave springs. These blocks of entablature (mannerist in their bizarre denial of the structural value of the classical entablature) are found in Wren's St Bride's, Fleet Street, and St Andrew's, Holborn, but were not favoured by the masculine and architectonic baroque architects of the Hawksmoor breed. To make the mix of the interior even richer, Gibbs ceiled the aisles with a series of little saucer domes.

How, and why indeed, did such a specimen of architecture become the great model for church building, not only in Britain but throughout the whole of the eighteenth- and early nineteenth-century English-speaking world? First, there was the versatility of the plan, in which the requirements of the orthodox church were so logically and cleverly combined with a correct basilica form which itself could, with minimal adaptation, be altered subtly to please different tastes. Then there was the appeal of Gibbs's architecture which, though individual, was light in character, even playful, and more amenable to copying than the grave and personal baroque manner of Hawksmoor. Also – a point not to be overlooked – St Martin's stands in a good part of town, accessible to all and, moreover, not without aristocratic connections; snobbery must not be discounted in the history of architecture. But most important of all were Gibbs's own efforts. In 1728 he published his *Book of Architecture* which, as Gibbs bluntly put it in his preface, was intended 'to be of use to such gentlemen as might be concerned in building, especially in remote parts of the country, where little effort or no assistance for designers can be procured', and which contained not just the designs for St Martin's as built, but also alternatives, especially for the tower.

The first to copy St Martin's was the Palladian acolyte of Lord Burlington, Henry Flitcroft. In 1731 he rebuilt St Giles-in-the-Fields (a work subsidized by the 1711 commission) half a mile north of St Martin's. The exterior, as is to be expected, has a little more Palladian sobriety about it, but the west door has a Gibbs surround; the interior is based on St Martin's with the addition of Kentian detail; and the tower is pure St Martin's with only a few Palladian 'improvements'.

In Glasgow in 1739 Allan Dreghorn, a local merchant and builder, began St Andrew's Church, a fully fledged and spirited copy of St Martin's with a steeple based on another of the designs published in Gibbs's book, and in 1744 Mereworth Church, Kent, was given a slender version of St Martin's tower. In 1752 David Hiorne designed Holy Cross, Daventry, Northamptonshire, on the Gibbs model, with a Doric arcade and vaulting derived from All Saints, Derby, a tower based on Flitcroft's St Giles copy of St Martin's,

North Leith Church, Leith, Edinburgh, 1814–16, by William Burn (*above*) and St George's Church, Hardwicke Place, Dublin, 1802–13, by Francis Johnston (*below*): Greek-detailed versions of St Martin-in-the-Fields.

St Andrew's Church, Glasgow, 1739–56, by Allan Dreghorn; an early, fully developed essay on St Martin-in-the-Fields.

and a steeple based on a version published by Gibbs but without the octagonal stage. Three years later St John's, Wolverhampton, was designed by William Baker with Gibbs windows and tower but – like Holy Cross – without a portico. In 1768 Anthony Keck designed St Martin's, Worcester, with a St Martin-in-the-Fields-type nave arcade and Gibbs windows. And such was the power of precedent that even well into the age of Adam and neo-classicism, and on into the 1820s, the progeny of St Martin's was still being built.

The Church of Ireland Cathedral in Waterford, by John Roberts, 1773-9, has a nave formed by Corinthian columns on high pedestals supporting blocks of entablature, and is clearly an essay on St Martin's. St Paul's, Birmingham, completed in 1777 to the design of Roger Eykyn, is Gibbs down to the blocks of entablature in the nave arcade, and the interior of St Michael's, in the grounds of Badminton House, Avon, designed by Charles Evans and completed in 1785, although embellished with neo-classical detail, even has St Martin's saucer domes in the aisles. Thomas Hardwick's St Mary's, Wanstead, London (1787-90), has an interior still inspired by St Martin's, as does the partly Gothic Christ Church, Bristol, designed by William Paty (1792). The general external composition of St Martin's – tower and spire rising immediately above and behind a great portico – was followed by Francis Johnston at St George's, Hardwicke Place, Dublin (1802-13), by William Burn at North Leith Church, Edinburgh (1814); by Francis Bedford at St John's, Waterloo Road, London (1823-4), and by Thomas Brown at St Mary's, Edinburgh (1824). In all these post-1800 churches, however, the details are now Greek rather than Roman.

In addition to these major essays in the Gibbs manner there is also many a provincial church sporting details or elevations inspired by St Martin's. All Saints, Gainsborough, built in 1736-48, owes its nave elevations to St Martin's; St Margaret's, Biddlesden, Buckinghamshire (1730), has windows with Gibbs surrounds, as do St Mary's, Conington, Cambridgeshire (1737), and St Leonard's, Over Whitacre, Warwickshire (1766). The most imitated element was the tower, either as built by Gibbs at St Martin's or as proposed and published by him in 1728. St Andrew's, Dundee, completed in 1774 to the designs of Samuel Bell, has a tower spire clearly derived from the published design of Gibbs, while John Baxter's Bellie parish kirk at Fochabers, Grampian (1795), has a four-column Doric pedimented portico behind which rises a squat and simplified but unmistakable essay on St Martin's. Perhaps the most impressive of Gibbs-derived towers is that sported by St Nicholas, Worcester, which is based almost exactly on a published unbuilt version for St Martin's. The church, built 1730-35, may have been designed and built by Humphrey Hollins. Interestingly another church in Worcester, All Saints, built in 1738-42 perhaps by Richard Squire, has a tower which still displays a distinct debt to Wren.

Although St Martin's was the model

Alternative designs for the tower of St Martin-in-the-Fields published by Gibbs in 1728 in his *Book of Architecture*. These designs, in whole or in part, provided models for many later eighteenth-century church designers.

St Nicholas's Church, Worcester, 1730–35, attributed to Thomas White or Humphrey Hollins. The tower is closely modelled on one of the published Gibbs designs.

church *par excellence*, it and its offspring together formed just one among a rich variety of solutions to church building. Taking basilica churches alone, it is intriguing to see the number of variations developed for the vaulting of the nave and aisles. As has been noted, Gibbs, both at St Martin's and at Derby parish church (now Cathedral) of 1723–5, favoured springing his vault from blocks of entablature carried by columns supported on pedestals. A popular alternative was to allow the ceiling to rise in a barrel vault from a continuous entablature running the length of the nave. In this system, which has more Roman classical authority than Gibbs's solution – and which Wren used at St Lawrence Jewry and St James Garlickhithe in London, and which was used at All Saints, Gainsborough (1736–48), and St Lawrence, Mereworth (1744) – the aisles have flat ceilings divided into compartments by entablatures or cornices. In a third version an entablature does not run the length of the nave but instead a short section of it connects the capitals of the nave arcade with the aisle wall. In this system the aisle vaults can be treated as a series of barrel vaults lit by high-level windows, as done so dramatically by Hawksmoor at Christ Church, Spitalfields, and as at St Thomas's, Stourbridge, West Midlands (1726), which closely follows the design of Wren's St James's, Piccadilly.

A further interior permutation of the basilica plan allowed the arcade or nave vault to rise, in the Renaissance manner, directly from the abacus of the capitals of the nave arcade. Wren did this at St Bartholomew's in the City (1674–9, now demolished), as did John Platt at St Paul's, Sheffield (1720–40, also demolished), and Thomas White at St Mary and St Margaret's, Castle Bromwich, West Midlands, built in 1726.

To increase the possibilities for the basilica interior yet further the nave colonnades, instead of being formed from columns on pedestals standing on the nave floor, consisted of columns on pedestals which were themselves supported on piers. The advantage of this system was that the gallery could be visually integrated into the design of the interior, because the gallery front could be combined with, and indeed echoed by, the pedestal, which was conveniently sandwiched at gallery height between column shaft above and supporting pier below. Wren used this solu-

The monumental interior of Nicholas Hawksmoor's Christ Church, Spitalfields (1714–29), with its flat ceiling and barrel-vaulted aisles, underlines the difference between the powerful English baroque school of Vanbrugh and Hawksmoor and the pretty Continental baroque, as represented by the interior of Gibbs's St Martin-in-the-Fields.

tion for the first time in 1677-87 at Christ Church, Newgate Street, St James's, Piccadilly in 1676-84 and St Bride's, Fleet Street, in 1671-8. Eighteenth-century examples are St George's, Great Yarmouth (1714-16), by John Price; St George's, Hanover Square, London (1720-25), by John James; the Grosvenor Chapel, South Audley Street, London (1730), by Benjamin Timbrell; and – a late example which has a curiously Wren-like feel – the Church of Ireland Cathedral in Waterford (1773-9) by John Roberts. The disadvantage of this system is that some visual impact is lost, for the column, the natural ornament of the basilica interior, loses much of its dignity by being reduced in scale to accommodate a plinth and pier substructure.

Other plan forms
With all these internal permutations, the basilica type tended to dominate English church building, but other plan forms were followed, nevertheless, by provincial church builders. Architects such as John and William Bastard at St Peter and St Paul's in Blandford Forum, Dorset (1735-9), and Edward Wing at St Michael's, Aynho, Northamptonshire (1723), continued to build the baroque type – with a cross-axis expressed externally on the aisle elevations, as designed by John James at Twickenham in 1715, and Thomas Archer at Deptford in 1713-30 – as a challenge to Gibbs's Palladian basilica type. There was also the occasional (and for the eighteenth century eccentric and old fashioned) cruciform plan church with transepts expressed externally, such as St George's, Reforne, Portland, Dorset. Designed in 1754 by Thomas Gilbert, this church – especially the tower – is very much in the school of Wren.

The numerous types of provincial church not directly inspired by contemporary metropolitan models must not be overlooked either. Sometimes they are distinguished by archaic features which do not seem to be the product of exotic or knowing revivalism, such as the embattled tower of St Mary's, Avington, Hampshire, which, though built in 1768, seems to be a genuine survival of late Gothic. Then there are the modest brick boxes decorated with a few Palladian or Gibbsian details plucked from pattern books, such as Knutsford Church, Cheshire (1744), or Holy Trinity, Guildford, Surrey (1749), by James Horne. Other churches, though generally modest, contain some incongruous or striking detail or element: for example, the plain little Stoke Doyle Church, Northamptonshire (1722), with its unusually fine baroque nave door or, in Ireland, St Ann's, Shandon, Cork, also of 1722, with a simple rectangular plan

The aisle pediment marking the cross axis on the baroque St Peter and St Paul's Church, Blandford Forum, Dorset, 1735-9, by John and William Bastard.

and plain nave overpowered by a massive stone tower topped, in 1749, by three square stages of diminishing size – complete with corner urns and a dome – inspired, presumably, by Wren's City churches.

The most modest type of all, the small cell-like vernacular church (often with an interior arrangement – Venetian window at the east end, gallery at the west – similar to Inigo Jones's prototype, the Queen's Chapel, 1623, at St James's Palace, Westminster), can be extraordinarily deceptive, for some of the richest church interiors in the British Isles lurk within these simple boxes. Particularly reminiscent of the Queen's Chapel is St Mary's, Glynde, East Sussex, 1763 by amateur Palladian architect Sir Thomas Robinson (who designed Rokeby, p64), which has a projecting pedimented porch, a pedimented east end with a large Venetian window and a perfect interior with a gallery at the west end. St Lawrence's, Little Stanmore, built 1714-16 by John James for the Duke of Chandos, contains a breathtakingly rich painted interior, while St Michael's, Great Witley, Hereford and Worcester, erected in 1735 perhaps under the supervision of Gibbs, was furnished in the late 1740s to make it one of the richest baroque, and certainly the most Italian ecclesiastical space in Britain. In the City of Lon-

The interior of St Michael's Chapel, Great Witley, Hereford and Worcester, 1735–c1747, perhaps by James Gibbs: it is one of the most Italianate-rococo ecclesiastical interiors in Britain. The ceiling paintings are from Cannons, in the former county of Middlesex.

don, the austere brick exterior of All Hallows, London Wall, built to the design of George Dance the Younger in 1765, contains the earliest and most impressive neo-classical Graeco-Palladian interior in the country. Tucked down an alley in Waterford, Ireland, is St Patrick's (1764) which contains a curvaceous balustraded gallery supported on fluted Doric columns and, opposite the Doric-pedimented altar, a second storey of gallery beneath the roof. The more usual astylar cell-type is represented by St Katherine's, Chislehampton, Oxfordshire (1763), where the only references to the basilica interior are paired pilasters decorating the nave wall, whose capitals are continued around the nave to form a rudimentary cornice.

It is to this brand of parish church that Nonconformist chapels naturally belong: although different in internal arrangement and orientation, these did not evolve a significantly different architectural style until the second half of the eighteenth century. In the wake of John Wesley's popularity came symmetrical and often centralized preaching halls. (Wesley himself favoured octagonally planned chapels.) Early examples of the type are the vast Octagon Chapel, Norwich, built in 1754 by Thomas Ivory for the Presbyterians, and the Octagon Chapel, Milsom Street, Bath, of 1767 by Timothy Lightoler. A later example is the Carver Street Methodist Church, Sheffield, designed by the Revd W. Jenkins in 1804, a pedimented brick oblong box which – handsome and generally unadorned – became the type for the early nineteenth-century Nonconformist chapel.

Palladian church building
Why, when it dominated every other area of the building world between 1720 and 1750, did the Palladian movement fail to make a significant impression on church design? Why was the baroque, the style of the Catholic Counter Reformation, associated with absolutist monarchy, tolerated by the Protestant establishment? Perhaps Palladian architects simply found it too difficult to reconcile the essentially anti-classical ecclesiastical requirements of steeple, pew and gallery with the classical purity of Palladian design.

As early as 1722 an attempt at a Palladian solution was made at Holy Trinity, Leeds. The designer was either William Etty, a local mason, or William Halfpenny, an associate of the leading Palladian theorist, Robert Morris (cousin of Roger). Morris produced Palladian designs for Halfpenny's *Modern Builder's Assistant*, published in 1747, and Halfpenny's *The Art of Sound Building*, of 1725, contains an illustration of a church like Holy Trinity, described as a design by Halfpenny for a church in Leeds. Like St Martin-in-the-Fields, Holy Trinity has a Roman basilica plan, with, internally, monumental Corinthian columns (whose bases were dropped two feet in the nineteenth century) supporting a straight entablature running the length of the nave. With its apsidal east end this has a strong feeling of Burlingtonian Palladianism, manifested externally in the treatment of the nave windows, which are embellished alternately with segmental and triangular pediments. This treatment invokes something of the Renaissance palace rather than the Roman basilica and is very different in feel from Gibbs's boldly decorative nave at St Martin's. Unfortunately Holy Trinity did not have a fully developed tower in the eighteenth

Holy Trinity Church, Leeds, built 1722-7, probably to the designs of William Etty, is a rare attempt at the creation of a Palladian rather than a baroque-inspired church. The tower was added in 1839. The interior (*below*) looking to the east end, where the segmental apse contains a Venetian window and other Burlington-inspired Palladian details.

Above: The west front of St Lawrence's Church, Mereworth, Kent, 1744-6, the most interesting eighteenth-century attempt at the design of a full-blooded Palladian church. The tower, however, is derived from a Gibbs design.

Below: The interior of St Lawrence is inspired by an Egyptian hall as drawn by Palladio. The *trompe l'oeil* barrel-vaulted coffered ceiling, marbled columns and Diocletian window create the atmosphere of an archaeological reconstruction of imperial Rome.

century; the present structure, in the Wren/Gibbs style, dates from 1839. Halfpenny's design shows a tower with an obelisk spire, a device that appealed to several eighteenth-century designers, who saw the obelisk as a convenient substitute for a Gothic spire (St Luke's, Old Street, London, for example, built in 1727-33 by John James and Nicholas Hawksmoor, bears a fluted obelisk of gigantic proportions). Holy Trinity had its imitators in the north (though on nothing like the scale of St Martin's), notably St Peter's, Sowerby, West Yorkshire, designed in 1761 by master mason John Wilson.

The next serious attempt at a Palladian church was St Lawrence, Mereworth, Kent, which stands near the arch-Palladian Mereworth Castle, designed in 1722 by Colen Campbell (p55). Built in 1744-6 for the Earl of Westmorland, who built the castle, the church makes reference externally to several London churches, including St Martin's (from which, as already mentioned, the tower is derived) and St Paul's, Covent Garden (1632), Inigo Jones's prototype Palladian church, to which St Lawrence's owes its Tuscan portal and columns supporting a deep eaved cornice. There is also, in the curved plan of the portico, a hint of Thomas Archer's St Paul's, Deptford (1713-30). Though distinctive, the exterior is decidedly odd and lacks coherence: it would be strange if its designer were Roger Morris, as is sometimes suggested because of his links with the Earl of Westmorland. But, as with Chichester town hall (p149) - which is also somewhat oddly put together and also attributed to Morris - it is possible that Morris supplied sketch ideas that were executed by a local builder, which would help to explain the awkwardly compiled exterior.

The interior, however, is a different matter. Although here too the designer has mixed his inspirations - Palladio and Roman archaeology - he has produced a vigorous and convincing neo-classical essay which, except for some of Lord Burlington's projects, was unprecedented in the British Isles. Palladio's Egyptian Hall is invoked by the giant Tuscan colonnade which sits firmly on the floor of the nave (or would if the moulded bases of the columns had not been omitted because the lower third of the shafts was panelled), and which is matched by a colonnade along the aisle wall, and by the relative widths of the nave and aisles (3:1). The nave colonnade supports a deep Doric entablature from which springs a barrel vault over the nave, while the aisle ceilings are flat. To complete this scene of Roman grandeur the east end is dominated by a giant Diocletian window, the columns are marbled, the nave vault is painted with coffering and the entablature embellished with *trompe-l'oeil* painting. To the later eighteenth-century eye of Horace Walpole, the church was the 'most abominable piece of tawdriness', but now it looks like an early attempt at the archaeological reconstruction of a Roman interior.

Other first- and second-generation Palladian architects also attempted church design: Richard Castle with his cruciform-planned Knockbreda Church (1737) near Belfast; John Smyth with St Catherine's, Dublin (1769), which has an admirably monumental side elevation with pediment and engaged columns, though the interior has standard aisles and galleries with a superimposed order of columns supporting a central barrel vault; and John Wood the Younger at St Nicholas, Hardenhuish, Wiltshire. This is an interesting attempt to embellish a stone box with appropriate Palladian motifs, including Venetian windows in both nave walls – but by now it was 1779, and Palladianism had long since been overtaken by other movements and fashions in architecture.

Neo-classical churches

The Gothic taste had begun to emerge as a real alternative to rococo decoration and baroque and Palladian designs as early as the mid-1740s. Very soon afterwards new forms of classicism were permeating the British architectural world. In the 1750s and 1760s books were published which revealed just what a limited view Palladio, and consequently his disciples, had had of ancient classical architecture (p15). The most influential of these new classicists were James Stuart and Nicholas Revett.

Initially the new architectural ideas affected only the design of details or elements, such as west fronts and towers; then internal spaces changed, with greater emphasis on centrally planned, even round churches, some of which were so secular (not to say theatrical) in their planning and decoration that voices of protest were raised. As early as the 1750s James Cawthorn (who died in 1761) complained in his poem *Of Taste* that:

> One might expect a scarcity of style
> August and manly in an holy pile
> And think an architect extremely odd
> To build a playhouse for the church of God.

Stuart and Revett both built churches in which, as in their other buildings, they showed a greater interest in reproducing Greek details than in promoting unconventional plan forms. This course was pursued

St Catherine's Church, Dublin, begun 1769 to the design of John Smyth. The north elevation is a fine Irish Palladian composition.

by the unknown designer of St Mary's, Stratfield Saye, Hampshire, who as early as 1754 created a church with a symmetrical Greek cross plan and a central dome on a drum pierced with round windows, and also by James Paine at his remarkable chapel, severe and centralized, at Gibside, Co. Durham (1760).

James Stuart's ecclesiastical offering was designed, with Lord Harcourt in 1764, as a garden temple-cum-parish church in the park of Harcourt's Oxfordshire mansion at Nuneham Courtenay. Envisaged as part of Capability Brown's landscape, the church was provided with a fine Greek Ionic hexastyle portico based on the fifth-century Ionic of the Temple on the Ilissus, which shades nothing but a brick wall but which looks very well in the landscape. The form of the building, on the other hand, is far from Greek, being based on Palladio's Villa Rotonda. The 'nave' is lit by Roman Diocletian windows and capped by a central dome, on a drum also pierced with Diocletian windows, reminiscent of Burlington's dome at Chiswick House (p55).

All Saints' Church, Nuneham Courtenay, Oxfordshire. Designed 1764 by the Earl of Harcourt and James Stuart, the church is an important early example of an archaeologically inspired neoclassical church with Greek revival details.

Nicholas Revett's contribution to church design came fourteen years later in 1778, with his new St Lawrence's at Ayot St Lawrence, Hertfordshire. Like Stuart's church, Revett's is more of a garden ornament than a serious attempt to realize the exciting potential for revolutionary classical design that lay in his and Stuart's book, *Antiquities of Athens* (p15). True, the columns to the portico are modelled on the Temple of Apollo at Delos and so are fluted only at the very top and very bottom. But the disposition of the church –

the stucco and entablature that stop a few feet round the corner from the main front, and the aedicules linked to the main body of the church by short colonnades – makes the building very much a conventional Palladian eye-catcher. Internally, with its arched recesses, coffered apsidal east end and Diocletian window lighting an astylar interior, Revett's church had much more in common with a Roman bath than with a Greek temple. The long axis on the altar, however, ensures that it is still very much an ecclesiastical space. To find the origins of the secular church, the church in which all the efforts of the designer seem to be directed towards the replacement of ecclesiastical associations with those of the contemporary secular interior, we have to go back to a date before either Stuart or Revett had built anything.

Anti-ecclesiastical tendencies
St Laurence's, West Wycombe, Buckinghamshire, was created from a medieval church in 1763 for Sir Francis Dashwood – the notorious founder of the Hell-Fire Club. Beneath a tower topped with a hollow gilt ball (containing seats) is a 'nave', 40 feet by 60 feet, and lined with sixteen great Corinthian columns. These are engaged with the nave wall and with bases resting almost on the nave floor, achieving an overall effect which in 1775 put a visitor in mind of a 'very superb Egyptian Hall'. The ceiling is flat, an unusual feature for a church of the 1760s, but only to be expected in a room of such dimensions and with much more of the ballroom than the church about it. The ceiling is also painted, as at Mereworth, to imitate coffering, and the church was not pewed but fitted instead with

The interior of St Laurence's Church, West Wycombe, Buckinghamshire, 1763. Built for Sir Francis Dashwood, the oblong 'nave' looks more like a ballroom than a church.

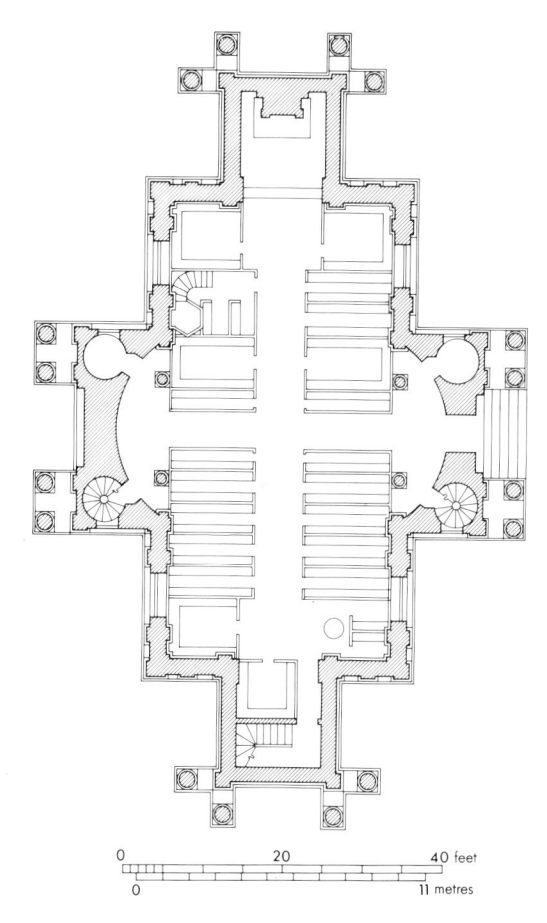

The plan of St Mary's Church, Mistley, Essex, 1776, by Robert Adam. The plan contains devices familiar from Adam's domestic interiors – especially the apses – and reintroduces the baroque cross axis. The break with the early eighteenth-century basilica plan is complete. Only the towers of this church survive.

delicate seats covered in green cloth. These, combined with the rich cornice, carved swags and round-headed windows, not to speak of the font – a slender pole around which a snake twines itself in pursuit of four doves – must have confused any but the most open-minded of eighteenth-century church-goers.

Another church which shows anti-ecclesiastical tendencies is St Bartholomew's, Binley, near Coventry. Designed in 1771, perhaps by Robert Adam (who two years earlier had designed a chaste little temple to serve as a chapel at Gunton Park, Norfolk), it has a movement and delicacy that reflect the late eighteenth-century problem of reconciling both neo-classical design, particularly the principles of 'space planning', and the picturesque theories of 'movement', which Adam described in his book of his works (p83), with the traditional orientation of the Anglican church. St Mary's, Mistley, Essex, designed by Robert Adam in 1776, reflected the same problem. Following the principles of neo-classical bi-axial planning, Adam created an interior with a long nave stretching between a pair of towers, the eastern one of which contained the chancel. Across this axis was a shorter axis connecting a pair of porches, one of which was the main entrance and the other blind. This shorter axis, as in an Adam dining room, was terminated internally by a pair of shallow apses, each screened by a pair of columns. Perhaps the demolition in the 1870s of all but the towers of the church reflects the displeasure that this sort of comfortable secular church aroused in the breasts of conventional churchmen.

A little later, in 1785, James Gandon produced a simpler but equally secular neo-classical church interior at Coolbanagher, Co. Laois: the church is simply a rectangular room into which a bow-fronted gallery protrudes from an opening above the door. The walls – impressive with their Diocletian windows and swags above niches containing large urns – supported (until it was removed in the nineteenth century) a shallow barrel vault. The box pews, as revealed in an early watercolour, appeared embarrassingly out of place in this elegant room – which not only looks like a specially fine dining room, but was in fact developed by Gandon from his designs for the Benchers' Dining Hall at the King's Inns in Dublin.

Perhaps John Carr's St Peter and St Leonard's at Horbury, West Yorkshire, of 1791, is the most extreme example of the secular church. The nave, measuring 60 feet by 30 feet, is topped with a delicately moulded segmental ceiling, and is extended at both east and west ends by full-width shallow apses embellished with Corinthian pilasters and coved ceilings. The north and south walls, as befits a bi-axial church, contain a pair of recesses each screened by a pair of Corinthian columns and containing seats, from which members of the congregation can peer down into the nave as if they were in boxes at a theatre. Another church that comes into this domestic category, though perhaps for different reasons, is St Mary's, East Lulworth, Dorset. Completed in 1786 to the design of John Tusher, it is a Roman Catholic church for which special permission to build was given on the strict condition that the completed building did not look like a church. Consequently St Mary's appears to be a cross between a garden temple and a house. There is, of course, no tower and only a modest entrance door. Inside, the plan is centralized, with four apses off a round domed area. Three of the apses contain galleries and the fourth an altar, and the interior of the dome is painted like the sky.

Above: St Chad's Church, Shrewsbury, built 1790-92 to the designs of George Steuart, and one of the most successful of the round-bodied churches built during the decade after 1780, when this form was in vogue.

Below: The interior of St Chad's, showing Steuart's characteristic attenuated columns.

Although unique in some ways, this little building, with its round, domed central space, is typical of ecclesiastical buildings appearing all over Britain at about the same time. The 1780s was the decade of the round or oval church, which no doubt reflected the excitement produced in the younger generation of French-influenced neo-classical architects by primary geometrical forms. In 1785 an oval church, St Andrew's, was erected in George Street, Edinburgh, and at about the same time the oval Presbyterian church in Rosemary Street, Belfast, was completed. In 1786 David Stephenson designed his spectacular elliptical All Saints, Newcastle; in 1790 George Steuart began his round St Chad's, Shrewsbury, which, like All Saints, Newcastle, includes an elegant curved entrance vestibule beneath a tower and is embellished in the Adam neo-classical manner; and in about 1790 a modest but also oval-planned church was built at Randalstown, Co. Antrim; and then the fashion passed. But although the vogue for round or oval churches did not last beyond about 1790 – perhaps because of the wane of French influence owing to strained relations in the wake of the French Revolution, or because round churches were acoustically disastrous – it did revive the idea of the centrally planned church, a plan form that had previously been eclipsed by the tyranny of the basilica.

Centrally planned churches

Interestingly, Gibbs himself had produced (and published in 1728) a centrally planned scheme for St Martin-in-the-Fields. He envisaged a circular auditorium, with a chancel at one end and a portico on the other. Almost certainly it was this plan that influenced William Adam when he designed his parish kirk at Hamilton, Strathclyde, in 1732, combining a circle with a cross to create four arms instead of Gibbs's two. Significantly, the exterior is furnished with Gibbs surrounds to the windows.

The centrally planned church continued, if it did not actually flourish, in Scotland, where it was one amongst several alternatives to the basilica plan which for reasons of religious practice and custom was the least popular. Of centralized plans the octagonal form was by far the most popular for Scottish churches, both established and dissenting. One circular church – Kilarrow Kirk, Bowmore, Islay, of 1769 – pre-empts the octagonal type, which did not gain favour until the 1770s. Among the earliest are Kelso, Borders, of 1773 (by John Laidlaw, James Nisbet and Robert Purves), which has a fine columned and galleried interior, and the Glassite Chapel, Dundee, of 1777. The octagonal kirk at Dreghorn, Strathclyde, dates from 1780, and the elegant Gothic revival St George's Episcopalian Chapel, Edinburgh, was built by John Adam in 1794. After 1800 the octagonal church in Scotland tended to

St James's Church, Great Packington, Warwickshire, 1790, by Joseph Bonomi and the Earl of Aylesford – a powerful and original antiquarian design influenced by the ruins of the Baths of Diocletian, Rome, and Piranesi. *Right*, the cross-vaulted nave. The Greek Doric columns are derived from the Doric temple of Neptune at Paestum.

remain in Gothic dress, as at St John's, Lockwinnoch, Strathclyde (1806); St Paul's, Perth (1807), by John Paterson, and Glen Orchy, Strathclyde (1811), by James Elliot.

In England the octagonal plan had been used (by Thomas Telford for his huge St Michael's, Madeley, Shropshire, 1794–6, and by George Dance the Younger at St Mary's, Micheldever, Hampshire, 1805) but it was never very popular, and had no influence on two of the most remarkable English centralized churches. In 1788 John Plaw used a Greek cross plan for his pleasant St Mary's, Paddington; two years later Joseph Bonomi with the Earl of Aylesford used the same plan to produce a *tour de force*. St James's, Great Packington, Warwickshire, is a romantic attempt to combine the spirit of Piranesi and Roman architecture (which Aylesford had sketched in Rome, including the Baths of Diocletian which clearly influenced the church) with the ideas and architectural elements of the emerging Greek revival. The body of the church is symmetrical, with four red-brick corner turrets, and is embellished with massive Diocletian windows. Internally four tunnel vaults spread from a square nave, where the cross-vaulting springs from four Greek Doric columns derived from those at the Temple of Neptune at Paestum. To give the right look of massive Roman construction, the plaster walls and vaults are painted in imitation of ashlar.

Two years later, in 1792, S.P. Cockerell produced the other remarkable centralized church, St Mary's, Banbury, Oxfordshire, basing his design on the theme of a circle within a square. It has a square nave in which, as at Wren's St Stephen's, Walbrook, eight of the twelve free-standing composite columns are linked by arches and support a round dome-like roof.

Two of the most interesting Scottish centralized churches – from the point of view of scale and location – came some years later.

Robert Reid's St George's, Charlotte Square, Edinburgh (1811–14), had a Greek cross plan set below a colonnaded dome, and unrelated to it, and behind a powerful portico which, with its Greek Ionic columns set *in antis*, was designed more for its contribution to the townscape than for its relation to what went on behind. More successful is St Stephen's, St Vincent Street, Edinburgh, which was designed in 1828 by William Henry Playfair and has a massive Roman, or even Vanbrughian, quality. Set on an awkward site, it is square in plan with at one corner a square tower. Within this is a flight of stairs leading diagonally into the building, which turns out to contain an octagonal nave, with stairs on the other three corners of the square.

The interior of St Mary's Church, Banbury, Oxfordshire, 1792–7 by S. P. Cockerell, a remarkable design revealing that Wren's hundred-year-old City churches were still a strong influence.

The Church Building Act 1818

In England by this time the building of such an ambitious centrally planned church had become a virtual impossibility. The Napoleonic Wars had seen a decline in church construction, followed soon after the peace of 1815 by legislation which effectively hampered the development of, or experiment with, all unconventional plan forms. The Church Building Act of 1818 granted its commissioners one million pounds to build new churches, mainly in the growing suburbs of the major cities or in rapidly expanding industrial towns. Like the act of 1711, its concerns were political and social as much as spiritual: the presence in force of the Established Church in the new and largely working class areas was considered essential if order and the *status quo* were to be maintained, with the result that about 600 new churches were built between 1818 and 1856, at an average cost of about £15,000 each. The demand for such quantity coupled with economy of construction ensured that in the quality of the architecture it generated the church building campaign of 1818 fell far below the standards of the 1711 campaign.

Under pressure from the commissioners, who wanted cheap, uniform and liturgically unadventurous preaching houses, the preferred and generally produced architecture was an oblong brick box of basilica plan, with cast-iron galleries inside and thin Grecian or Gothic details on its show facade. Despite these severe limitations, however, it must be admitted that the siting of these preaching boxes, and their contribution to the townscape, does generally compare well with the best of the 1711 churches. Several of the commissioners' architects – who included the most able of early nineteenth-century designers, such as Soane, Nash and Smirke – made fascinating experiments in solving the familiar problems of rendering the Gothic form of the tower in Greek dress, and in so doing created memorable townscape features. Many west fronts, moreover, were embellished with impressive and visually commanding Grecian porticoes. Nash's most striking and original tower was built outside London and not for the commissioners. Raised in 1816, it is attached to West Cowes Church, Isle of Wight, and takes the form of a tall square tower topped by acroteria set on a bold moulded parapet below which are long horizontal windows, one on each face, and each containing a pair of dwarf Grecian Doric columns set *in antis*. In London, Nash's most successful commissioners' church is All Souls, Langham Place (1822), which, with its round portico and tall spire, skilfully turns the corner from Regent Street to Portland Place. Equally accomplished designs are Francis Bedford's St John's, Waterloo Road (1823), which has a powerful Greek Doric portico and Grecian tower placed above and behind, like St Martin-in-the-Fields; and St Matthew's, Brixton, by Charles Porden (1822), where the spell of St Martin's has been broken, so that the mighty Greek Doric portico with four columns set *in antis* can be appreciated without the interference of the tower (which has been moved to the east end).

St Pancras new parish church, begun in 1819 but generously paid for by the parish and not the commissioners, shows what a Greek revival architect was capable of if given his head and the necessary funds. Designed by H.W. and W. Inwood, the church is decorated with a remarkable catalogue of Grecian motifs: the doors within the portico (of giant Greek Ionic columns) are reproductions of casts sent specially from Athens; two vestibules flanking the east end are reproductions of the Caryatid Porch of the Erechtheion in Athens; while the tower, though set above the portico in the Gibbsian manner, is a splendid attempt to fuse two prototypes for classical towers, the Choragic monument of Lysicrates and the Tower of the Winds in Athens. It is all in slightly 'bad taste', as C.R. Cockerell observed in his diary in July 1821, but if so no matter, for the expense alone (£70,000) prevented St Pancras new church from becoming a model for the commissioners' architects. Some of the Greek revival churches built a little later in Scotland, however, show a clear affinity with St Pancras. John Smith's North Kirk, Aberdeen (1826), has a four-columned Ionic porch and a tall square tower topped by an essay on the Choragic monument; similarly St Giles, Elgin, Grampian, built in 1827 by Archibald Simpson, has a mighty hexastyle Greek Doric portico and at its east end a square tower also carrying a version of the Choragic monument; and St John's, Montrose, by William Smith (1829) has a four-columned Ionic portico and a squat tower.

It may seem strange, given the quality of the commission's architects, that more buildings of ingenuity and invention were not produced. But the fact that even Sir John Soane was defeated by the financial and liturgical constraints of the commission reveals the depth of the problem. His three commissioners' churches, all in London (St Peter, Walworth, 1823–4; Holy Trinity, Marylebone, 1826–7; St John's, Bethnal Green, 1826–8), fail to reach the standard one would expect of a Soane work, although they are rich in

St Pancras Parish Church, Camden, London, 1819-22, by H. W. and W. Inwood: a remarkable Greek revival church. The caryatid porch is based on the Erechtheion, Athens.

curious detail – especially St John's – and have good and original towers. This is one of the minor tragedies of Georgian building, for it is fascinating to speculate as to what Soane would have done with church design, given the same sort of financial freedom that Hawksmoor enjoyed initially under the 1711 legislation. All we have are the more financially liberated works of his associates and admirers, an intriguing design made by Soane and drawn by J.M. Gandy, for a more visionary but financially unbuildable commissioners' church, and earlier church designs (also unbuilt) such as that for a sepulchral church at Tyringham, Buckinghamshire (1800). Most notable of his contemporaries' work is James Spiller's St John's, Hackney (1792–7): Spiller, a friend and collaborator of Soane, designed a Greek cross plan church with, inside, a shallow vault resting on segmental arches. The austere brick facade has squat, segmental-headed ground-floor windows and tall round-headed first-floor windows, all set within a giant two-storey blind arcade with Doric abaci as imposts. At the east end is a three-bay pediment and at the west, over the entrance, a truly extraordinary tower, added in 1812, with characteristic Soane elements supported by the somewhat baroque device of giant flying scrolls.

George Basevi, another of Soane's pupils, was one of the few architects to build a thoroughly original church for the commission. His St Thomas's, Stockport, Manchester (1822–5), has a handsome Ionic portico containing an open double stone-built staircase leading to the galleries. It is approached through the portico from the east, so the altar lies beside the main door.

By contrast St John's, Egham, Surrey, begun in 1817 to the designs of Henry Rhodes, illustrates what could happen when Soane's abstracted classicism and ideas on proportion were followed without real understanding or intuition. Far more interesting are the churches of John Semple, architect for the eastern province when working for the Irish Board of the First Fruits. Established in 1711, the Board had the power to use surplus revenue generated by income from annates (that is the first yearly revenue of a benefice, bishopric or other dignity) to build and repair churches. The surplus was minimal until 1777, when the Irish government inaugurated an annual grant to the Board. But even then the architectural results were even more depressing, on the whole, than the results of the 1818 act in England. After 1800 the Board granted £500 per church, which had to do unless more money could be raised by the parish. So all over Ireland there sprang up standard, often thinly Gothic, stunted little rectangular churches, for example Crossmolina, Co. Mayo (1810). Semple, however, managed to overcome this imposed simplicity by developing theories of decoration comparable, though not parallel, with Soane's, and theories of construction which in the circumstances were somewhat foolhardy. For decoration he rejected all conventional mouldings and substituted an abstract system of his own devising based on related planes. His constructional theories, meanwhile, entailed building three stone-vaulted churches (only a few years after the revival of the same thing in England, see p17), two of which failed. The Black Church, Mary Street, Dublin (1830), survives as a squat, pinnacled Gothic structure with a tall spire and one gigantic parabolic arch inside.

Although the commission in England did not encourage the development of an impressive body of ecclesiastical architecture, occasionally individual churches in the early nineteenth century (a very few of them for the commissioners) did nevertheless reflect some of the interesting technological and stylistic developments that were taking place in architecture generally. In 1813 Thomas Rickman and John Cragg the iron-founder designed St George's, Everton, Liverpool, filling the interior with a remarkable if archaeologically incorrect Gothic interior in which both structure and decoration, including delicate tracery, are of cast iron. Externally the building is of stone in a conventional neo-Perpendicular design. Incidentally it was Rickman who devised the categories of Gothic – Early English, Decorated and Perpendicular – in his book *An Attempt to Discriminate the Styles of English Architecture from the Conquest to the Reformation* (1817), which remained a standard text throughout the nineteenth century and one of the cornerstones of the movement towards archaeologically correct Gothic construction. But more significant than this virtuoso display of technology married to art was J. Savage's St Luke's, Chelsea (1820–24). Here, for the first time in the Gothic revival and moreover in a particularly thinly detailed commissioners' church, Savage constructed a vault that was made of stone, and structural in function, rather than being of wood and plaster and merely decorative. Significantly, seven years later he designed St James, Bermondsey, one of the more successfully detailed and composed of the commissioners' Greek revival churches. Like his eighteenth-century Gothic predecessors, Savage saw no more in Gothic than style: its moral and spiritual implications were not to be pondered until the coming of Pugin.

As well as Savage's experiment in Gothic structure there were also some curious experiments in Gothic reconstruction, most notably a massive Presbyterian church (1824–7) by William Tite in Regent Square, Holborn, London, which had a main front based on York Minster. This has been demolished, but Edward W. Corbett's Holy Trinity, Theale, Berkshire (1820), survives as an accurate essay in an Early English style derived from

Salisbury Cathedral, and St George, Ramsgate (1825-7), by Henry E. Kendall has a tower derived from that of the medieval parish church at Boston, Lincolnshire. Such reconstructions were carried out partly in the same spirit of casual and selective archaeology that distinguishes such classical churches as the Inwoods' St Pancras and Thomas Hardwick's St John's, Workington (1822), which has a Tuscan porch adapted from Inigo Jones's St Paul's, Covent Garden. But they also reflect a new and growing awareness, pioneered by such as John Carter among others (p17) and promoted by Thomas Rickman, of Gothic as a coherent body of architecture, whose development can be traced, whose structural and decorative qualities are interrelated, and whose monuments are as susceptible to archaeological analysis as are the monuments of classical antiquity.

One peripheral result of this new awareness was a short-lived Norman revival. The movement first manifested itself in the last years of the eighteenth century (p16) but did not find general expression, even in church architecture (although Henry Hakewill's remarkable Holy Trinity, Wolverton, Buckinghamshire, dates from 1810), until the 1820s, for example St Clement's, Worcester (1822), by Thomas Lee and Thomas Ingleman; St Peter's, London Colney, Hertfordshire (1825), by George Smith; and St Clement's, Oxford (1827) and St Swithun's, Kennington, Oxfordshire (1828), both by Daniel Robertson.

The story of early nineteenth-century Catholic church architecture makes a modest tale on the whole, but even before the Catholic emancipation in 1829 some Catholic churches of quality had been built, and the Greek revival was firmly embraced, as for example at Joseph Ireland's St Mary's, Walsall (1825), and his T-planned St Peter and Paul, Wolverhampton (1827-8). This preference for Greek was also felt by Irish Catholics, especially in towns, the most notable result being the Pro-Cathedral in Marlborough Street, Dublin (1816-40). This remarkable French-influenced neo-Greek building with a mighty Greek Doric portico was probably designed by John Sweetman; early accounts of the church say that it was built to designs 'sent to this country by an amateur residing in Paris', and as has been pointed out the design is dependent on Chalgrin's St Philippe-du-Roule of 1774-84.[4]

Not everything was classical, however, and it seems that in both countries designers and the Catholic church faced something of a dilemma of styles. This is illustrated delightfully in Wigan where St John's (1819) is firmly classical, with an Ionic colonnade, while St Mary's (1818) has a neo-Perpendicular façade and a pretty galleried Regency Gothic interior, with slender columns and flat ribbed ceiling.

Gothic churches in the eighteenth century

As the Gothic revival moved through its various stages – from the associative picturesque Gothic of the early eighteenth century (p165) to the decorative rococo and the Adamesque Gothic of the mid- and late eighteenth century (p77) and finally to antiquarian Gothic at the end of the eighteenth century (p17) – it can be traced with splendid clarity through church building. Amongst the earliest examples of eighteenth-century associative Gothic is Hawksmoor's tower of St Mary Cornhill, City of London (1718); a purer Gothic than his later (1734) Westminster Abbey west towers. Typical provincial examples are Paisley Leigh Kirk (1738), which has long Gothic windows inspired by the nearby Abbey Kirk, and St Nicholas, Alcester, Warwickshire (1729-30), by Edward and Thomas Woodward. St Nicholas has a Gothic exterior, apparently in an attempt to associate it stylistically with the surviving medieval tower, with a strictly classical interior, which establishes a theme that recurs throughout the eighteenth century: a classical, usually Doric, interior within a Gothic shell. At St Nicholas, Warwick, for instance, Thomas Johnson's tower is an associative Gothic design in memory of the real medieval structure, replaced in 1748, and the nave, by Johnson and Job Collins (1779-80), is Gothic outside and classical within. This unlikely marriage between Gothic and classical is displayed particularly dramatically by classically detailed churches furnished with that quintessentially medieval item, the tall, tapering, pointed spire, for example the provincial baroque St Leonard's, Over Whitacre, Warwickshire (1766, spire rebuilt 1850); Francis Hiorne's Adamesque St Bartholomew's, Tardebigge, Hereford and Worcester (1777); and St Peter's, Saxby, Leicestershire (1788), by George Richardson.

Somewhat less typical of this early period is St Peter's, Galby, Leicestershire (1741), by John Wing the Elder, where the fairly correct tracery of the nave is overshadowed by the more bizarre Gothic, almost Chinese, design of the tower which, to make the mix richer, has classical windows. And more definitely less typical is St Martin's, Allerton Mauleverer, West Yorkshire (c1745), which is in the 'Saxon' style: this to the eighteenth-century mind was only another form of Gothic, divorced from any chronological or stylistic context, and interchangeable with Romanesque. Although characteristic of the first half of the eighteenth century there were, of course, modern Gothic additions to existing Gothic buildings designed all through the century: for example Sir Robert Taylor's rococo Gothic spire (1776) to St Peter's, Wallingford, Oxfordshire. These churches of the early generation of Gothic are remarkable mainly for their oddity, for they are not, it must be admitted, architectural masterpieces. And when these were achieved, in the form of the rococo and Adamesque Gothic churches of the next generation, they were masterpieces of decorative virtuosity rather than of original and inspired architecture. It must be remembered that the Gothic of the mid-eighteenth century was essentially a decorative style, and that eighteenth-century Gothic churches differ from their classical contemporaries only in their embellishment. They were of the same structure, and if their plans changed during the eighteenth century it was only in response to the same fashions and regulations that affected church planning generally. Even during the more serious antiquarian phase in the latter part of the century, when Gothic mouldings were being reproduced correctly and attempts were made to create the space of the well-lit Perpendicular interior, no effort was made to reintroduce Gothic construction. On the contrary in fact, even in the most serious-looking antiquarian churches the products of the Industrial Revolution were used unashamedly to create the appearance of medievalism. For example, the tracery on the window of John Carline's St Alkmund's, Shrewsbury, Shropshire (1794-5), was cast in iron by the Coalbrookdale company, and the Gothic nave columns of Francis Hiorne's St Mary's, Tetbury, Gloucestershire (1771-81), have cast-iron cores. But to return to the rococo Gothic period.

In 1747 Sanderson Miller, that extraordinary gentleman architect who swerved between producing correct Palladian buildings (p70) and pioneering Gothic churches, built All Saints, Wroxton, Oxfordshire. The church is notable both as an early monument to this amateur architect's interest in rococo Gothic and for the fact that the ambitiously conceived tower and steeple promptly collapsed. Strangely, this did not lead to a corresponding collapse in Miller's reputation.

In 1753 three notable monuments to the playful decorative style were built. St John's, Shobdon, Hereford and Worcester, by an unknown hand, contains all the flights of fancy of rococo Gothic. Some of the details, like the fireplace in the squire's pew, are influenced by patterns in Batty Langley's book of 1741 (pp14 and 77), and others, like the ogee tracery in the windows and a non-structural ogee chancel arch (a strange contradiction of Gothic structural precepts) are rather like details at Strawberry Hill, Twickenham (1750s). Strawberry Hill's designer was Richard Bentley (p77) who had connections with Shobdon and might well have designed this rococo Gothic fantasy painted throughout in wedding cake white and pale blue. In Buckinghamshire Henry Keene – like Miller also a sometime Palladian – designed Hartwell Church, now a ruin, which was fitted out with the most delightful and delicate rococo Gothic plaster ceilings; and at Preston on Stour, Warwickshire, Edward Woodward remodelled St Mary's for the antiquary James West. This is a remarkable building, for it is the first convincing Gothic revival church to be designed not by an architect or enthusiastic amateur but by a mason brought up in the tradition of classicism: Gothic was beginning to enter the vernacular vocabulary as a self-conscious revival style, as opposed to the rather well-mannered associative Gothic used by masons following sympathetically in the footsteps of their forebears.

St Mary's Church, Tetbury, Gloucestershire, 1771-81 by Francis Hiorne: an early example of relatively correct antiquarian Gothic.

Interior of St John's Church, Shobdon, Hereford and Worcester, 1753, a wonderful example of the rococo Gothic style.

The years each side of 1760 saw other important developments in the Gothic style: 1760 was the year in which the self-conscious Gothic revival arrived in Ireland, with the design of the church at Hillsborough, Co. Down (perhaps by Sanderson Miller), and in Scotland with Kenmore, Tayside, by the English architect William Baker. In 1758 Thomas Prowse, at St John the Evangelist, Wicken, Northamptonshire, made a fairly serious attempt at antiquarian Gothic with no rococo flourishes, and in 1761 John Wood the Younger designed All Saints, Woolley, near Bath, Avon, which displays an idiosyncratic mix of styles, with classical cupola and Gothic windows. But most important is St Mary Magdalene, Croome d'Abitot, Hereford and Worcester. Also designed in 1761, it is the work of Robert Adam with Lancelot Brown perhaps offering advice on the exterior, for the building stands in a park of his design. The exterior, the tower especially, is an extremely serious attempt at correct Gothic, but internally all is in the elegant light decorative style typical of Adam's contemporary classical work – except that all the motifs are Gothic; the plaster frieze is formed of interlaced arches and the nave colonnade of clustered columns. This interior has nothing of the abandon of the rococo Gothic, but neither does it have any of the correctness of antiquarian Gothic. At about the same time John Wing the Younger was building the remarkable church of St John the Baptist, King's Norton, Leicestershire (c1760-75). This was Gothic of some structural boldness (indeed the tower fell soon after completion) with large Perpendicular windows (the preferred genuine Gothic style of the later eighteenth-century antiquarian Gothic designers) and an attempt to reproduce correctly profiled Gothic mouldings. Despite all this serious work, however, the fittings, with the exception of the altar rail, are classical in design.

A few years after the King's Norton church was completed Francis Hiorne began his milestone in the Gothic movement – St Mary's, Tetbury, Gloucestershire (1777-81). It contains much of the atmosphere of a genuine Perpendicular church (though with a touch of the light Georgian Gothic in its decoration). Another example of the antiquarian style is St Mary Magdalen, Stapleford, Leicestershire (1783), where there is an attempt at medievalism externally (though not as convincing as Croome d'Abitot or King's Norton) but with Adamesque Gothic detail internally. Interestingly, the romantic past and the atmosphere of medieval Christianity are evoked here by the unusual device of a collegiate seating plan (also used at Holy Trinity, Teigh, Leicestershire, in 1782).

The development of the eighteenth-century Gothic style towards ever increasing antiquarian correctness was by no means constant; there were throwbacks. Charles Beazley embellished the tower of St Mary of Charity, Faversham, Kent, with a steeple (1799) that is an elegant essay upon Wren's flying buttress design for St Dunstan-in-the-East; St Paul's, Bristol (1789), by Daniel Hague still displays the drama of the early eighteenth-century picturesque romantic Gothic of Hawksmoor's All Souls, Oxford (p165), with the style merely being seen as an excuse to abandon the constraints of classicism and invent bizarre decorative details.

But John Carline's St Alkmund's, Shrewsbury, provides a better and perhaps more representative note on which to end an examination of eighteenth-century ecclesiastical Gothic, combining as it does an interest in antiquarianism (for example the intricate nave tracery) with the belief in modern technology (for, as we have seen, the same tracery was cast in iron by the Coalbrookdale Company). An interest in genuine medieval building technology as opposed to decoration, the hallmark of thoroughgoing antiquarianism, was not to blossom until the early nineteenth century.

Notes

1 See Marcus Whiffen in *Stuart and Georgian Churches outside London, 1603-1837*, page 32 of 1947 edition. Also James Gibbs's *Book of Architecture*.

2 Wren explained the thinking that lay behind the spatial organization and fittings of eighteenth-century churches when advising the 50 New Churches Commissioners of 1711: 'It is enough if they [the Roman Catholics] hear the murmur of the Mass and see the elevation of the Host, but ours are to be fitted for Auditories.'

3 The themes of cross axis, Greek cross and basilica could even be amalgamated by the more subtle of baroque designers. The interior of Nicholas Hawksmoor's Christ Church, Spitalfields (1714-29) reads as a basilica with longitudinal emphasis when viewed from the west door, had a cross axis (virtually obliterated by the removal of the box pews and the blocking of the north and south aisle doors in the mid-nineteenth century), and could also be read as a Greek cross. This was achieved by emphasizing the second and fourth arcade columns by attaching them to piers to create the sense of a Greek cross within a square (a favourite device of Wren's) or of an oblong cube within a larger cube.

4 Maurice Craig, *The Architecture of Ireland*, page 257, and E. McFarland, 'Who was "P"?', *Architectural Review*, CLVII, 1975, pages 71-3.

COMMERCIAL AND ENGINEERING BUILDINGS

The architecture of commerce produced – in mills and warehouses – the only eighteenth- and early nineteenth-century building type in which the structure was expressed, rather than being obsessively obscured or denied (p16). The interior structure (for that is what we are talking about) was exposed largely for reasons of economy, for these were functional buildings and even style-obsessed eighteenth-century designers felt that a camouflage of decoration would be an inappropriate extra expense. It must be said, even so, that warehouse floors given over to public displays of wares were occasionally embellished, as in the New Street range of the Cutler Street Warehouses, City of London (c1792 and now gutted, p139), where the structural posts of the first floor were decorated as a Doric colonnade (while posts on other levels remained unembellished). Another reason for this unprecedented display of structure was that, after c1790, it became increasingly common for warehouses and mills to be designed, theoretically at least, as fireproof structures. This design approach led to the abandoning of any unnecessary and potentially inflammable embellishment.

Clearly the study of commercial architecture merges with the study of eighteenth- and early nineteenth-century building and engineering technology, a link that became particularly strong after the Industrial Revolution of the 1770s. But before examining these major buildings we must look at some of the other types of eighteenth-century commercial building.

Banks

Although purpose-built from the relatively early eighteenth century, banks were almost invariably housed in buildings of domestic appearance. The only notable exception was

The Consols Office, Bank of England, City of London, by Sir John Soane, 1797, demolished c1925. This and the other rooms within the Bank mark an important phase in the development of Soane's architecture and are the most romantic, if not the most representative, of eighteenth-century commercial interiors.

Soane's Bank of England (1788–1833) in the City of London: it eventually attained an external appearance appropriate to its function as the repository of the national wealth. Rather like a prison, it was surrounded by a high and largely windowless rusticated wall, pierced by various pedimented doors and decorated with exquisite neo-classical detail – notably the Corinthian-columned Tivoli corner of c1805, inspired by the Temple of Vesta at Tivoli. Enclosed within this wall were the buildings that Sir Robert Taylor had erected for the Bank between 1765 and 1774. These had Palladian exteriors of the country house type, and inside were dominated by a massive rotunda, with a coffered dome and columned wall elevation derived from the Pantheon in Rome. Off this central space radiated vaulted halls. These interiors, which already gave the Bank of England an elevated status far beyond contemporary exchanges and town halls, and which were matched in public building only by Pearce's Parliament House, Dublin, of 1729 (p144), were greatly increased in size and number by Soane. He added a series of spectacular apartments, spacious, top-lit, of Roman grandeur and sporting the full gambit of his extraordinary, original and effective neo-classical detailing. The names reveal the function to which Soane's rooms were put – the $3\frac{1}{2}$% Consols Transfer Office; the Five Pound Note Office; the Accounts Office – but their scale does not, perhaps, reveal quite accurately how banking was carried out in the eighteenth century. The rooms were intended to express the institution's power, and were much larger than the business conducted in them demanded – they must have swallowed up customer and clerk alike. They expressed the prestige of the bank rather than revealing the nature of office conditions or design in the eighteenth century (p147).

Unfortunately, despite the built-in room for expansion and astonishing architectural quality, all but the screen wall was demolished between 1921 and 1937 in what was probably the grossest piece of architectural vandalism Britain has ever seen.

More representative – both of eighteenth-century office design and of banks of the period – was the Bank of England that Taylor had been appointed to enlarge, that Soane had altered and that was also finally swept away in 1925. This first Bank of England (which had only been established in 1694 and became the government's banker in 1717) was built in 1732–4 to the design of the Bank's surveyor, George Sampson, and was described by Soane as being 'in a grand style of Palladian simplicity'. Reminiscent of

Newcomen's Bank, Castle Street, Dublin, c1780, by Thomas Ivory. This purpose-built bank, which was doubled in size in the nineteenth century, underlines the domestic origins of the building type.

Webb's Queen's Gallery at Old Somerset House (p8), it was in the grand domestic/town hall manner.

Of the same type is the bank that forms the centre block of John Carr's commercial development of 1766 in George Street, Halifax, West Yorkshire: now called Somerset House, it contains shops and houses as well as the bank, which is distinguished by extra tall first-floor windows, like those which light the writers' rooms within Sir Robert Taylor's Six Clerks' and Enrolment Office, Lincoln's Inn, London, 1775–7 (p154). Newcomen's Bank, Castle Street, Dublin (c1780), by Thomas Ivory is stone-clad, neo-classically detailed and, though imposing, looks like a monumental slice of terrace house – an impression that would have been even stronger before the bank was doubled in size in the late nineteenth century by an addition designed as an exact replica of the bank itself. Stevenson, Salt & Co's bank (now Lloyds) in the Market Square, Stafford (c1795), looks decidedly like a public building, which is not surprising since it was designed to match the nearby Shire Hall.

By 1826 there were 780 private banks in England, sixty of which were in London,[1] but it was not until after the 1840s that the bank began to emerge (owing mainly to the work of C.R. Cockerell) as a recognizable building type – which, incidentally, had none of the obvious prison-like defensible quality suggested by Soane's Bank of England. Before that date even the grandest of early nineteenth-century banks, such as the porticoed Royal Bank of Scotland, Glasgow (1827), by Archibald Elliot the Younger, remained domestic in plan, with the business rooms on the ground floor and the manager living above, for example Hoare's Bank, Fleet Street, City of London, by Charles Parker, 1829-32.

Offices
The development of a distinct office building type, related neither to national or local government buildings (p147) nor to legal establishments (p154) or banks, is really a post-1830 phenomenon. Pevsner, however, observes in his *History of Building Types* that 'the consecutive story [of offices] starts in London in the early nineteenth century with the County Fire Office of 1819.'[2] This building, designed by Robert Abraham as part of Nash's Regent Street development, had a façade based on Webb's Queen's Gallery at Old Somerset House (p8) and, though purpose-built, had nothing to distinguish it from grand domestic or institutional use.

The same can be said of the near-contemporary purpose-built chambers and offices for tobacco merchants in Virginia Street, Glasgow (1817), which are more modestly domestic in appearance, and the pompous Royal Insurance Office, Maidstone, Kent (1827), by John Whichcord. This impression is confirmed by the architect Edward I'Anson who, in a lecture at the RIBA in 1864, observed, 'the first building which I remember to have been erected for that special purpose [offices] was a stack of office buildings in Clement's Lane at the end nearest Lombard Street.' That was in *c*1823, and very unusual for the date, for I'Anson went on to note that in the 1830s it was usual for 'certain houses [to be] let out in separate floors and used as offices.'

Shops and arcades
Shops, although always interesting and sometimes important pieces of eighteenth-century design, can hardly be classed as a building type, neither did they change dramatically during the eighteenth and early nineteenth centuries. Their details reflected changes in fashion – from Palladian to rococo to neoclassical – with the only major structural trend being a gradual flattening-out of the characteristic bow front. Two bulbous bays with a door to the shop squeezed between, and another door on the side leading to the upper apartment was the usual mid-eighteenth-century practice, as at 34 Haymarket, Westminster, London, and 56 Artillery Lane, Spitalfields, London (1757), which is decorated with fine rococo motifs including swags and a cartouche. Another, somewhat later, rococo shop-front survives at 88 Dean Street, Soho, London. A shop-front of thirty years later, *c*1785-90, would be of the same general composition, but with bays of a more gradual segmental curve, such as the shop-fronts at 57 High Street, Winchester and 7 High Street, Stamford, Lincolnshire, and, on a smaller scale with only one bay, in a shop in South Street, Wareham, Dorset, and a row of uniform shop-fronts in Goodwin's Court,

Above: 56 Artillery Lane, Spitalfields, London: a rare, rococo-detailed shop-front of 1757.

Below: Typical early nineteenth-century bow shop-front in South Street, Wareham, Dorset.

Covent Garden, London. The reduction of the curve of the bow was largely the result of the London Building Act, 1774 (p 29), which ruled that bow windows of shops should not project more than ten inches into the street (or less in a narrow street). By the end of the century the fashion for chaste neo-classical austerity, coupled with the gradual appearance of large panes of plate glass, led to flat fronts, often with columns or pilasters dividing the doors from the windows, in which glazing bars were reduced in both size and number, as in 3 St James's Street, Westminster, London; 46 Stonegate, York; and 18-19 High Street, Stamford, Lincolnshire.

Of these changes it was the introduction of plate glass that had the most dramatic effect. Charles Dickens, in *Sketches by Boz* (1836), speaks of a sudden passion for plate glass taking place in 1825-30 – presumably as it became economic to produce and therefore cheap to buy. The other major change in the early nineteenth century – apart from the evolution of the design of the individual shopfront – was for shops to be designed as uniform groups in courts, such as Cubitt's Woburn Walk, Bloomsbury (1822), in arcades, and occasionally in streets.

An important early example of the uniform shopping street is D'Olier Street, Dublin, laid out by the Wide Streets Commissioners in c1799 (p25) with uniform elevations (designed by Baker) and uniform shop-fronts. These are (or were, since most are now badly mutilated) arcaded, with Ionic pilasters defining each unit, and, inside, mezzanines with U-shaped galleries with elegant anthemion cast-iron balconies. Westmorland Street, contemporary and on an adjacent site, also had uniform frontages. By contrast, this idea of urban commercial uniformity, pioneered in Paris, was generally resisted in England where, it seems, the right of traders to individual expression was seen as sacrosanct. Nash's Regent Street, particularly the Quadrant, was a rare and short-lived attempt to impose architectural uniformity on an English shopping street. Scotland boasts one major early nineteenth-century attempt at uniform shopping in a main street – that in Reform Street, Dundee, which was built as two uniform terraces between 1824 and 1833 by George Angus. These terraces, with pilastered ground floors as in D'Olier Street, have also, like the Dublin model, been badly mutilated by succeeding generations of shopkeepers striving to be individual.

Arcades, the most characteristic of early nineteenth-century shopping forms, had first appeared in London in the sixteenth and seventeenth centuries. Roofed streets of shops had been included in Gresham's Royal Exchange, City of London (1566), in the New Exchange, Strand (1608), and in the Exeter Change, Strand (1676). But it was in late eighteenth-century Paris that the idea was developed – in the Galeries de Bois by Victor Louis (1786, demolished 1826), for example. English early nineteenth-century examples of the type were exquisitely detailed and invariably uniform in their shop design. Two of the most important examples survive: the Royal Opera Arcade, Pall Mall (1816-18), by Nash and Repton, which has a vaulted roof with a small glass dome over each bay, and the Burlington Arcade (1818-19) by Samuel Ware, who described it as 'after the principle of ... Exeter Change'.[3] Burlington Arcade has a pitched glass roof on transverse arches. It was not until 1828 – with the construction of the Galerie d'Orléans in Paris – that arcades were first given glass and iron vaulted roofs.

Good British provincial arcades are the Upper and Lower Arcades, Bristol (1824-5), by James Foster, 'The Corridor', High Street, Bath (1825), by H.E. Goodridge, the Argyle Arcade, Argyle Street, Glasgow (1827-8), by John Baird, and the Crown Arcade, Virginia Street, also in Glasgow (c1820) which, though altered, retains its arcaded ground floor supporting an Ionic gallery with Diocletian windows in the wall above.

Exchanges and markets

Exchanges of all types – corn, coal, wool – are often indistinguishable from markets which, in turn, might look little different from modest town halls or court houses (p147). This is not surprising, of course, since traditionally these uses (and a few others) shared the same structure. For example, John Adam's thirteen-bay-wide and pedimented Royal Exchange, Edinburgh (1753-61; now the City Chambers) contained a Custom House.

The seventeenth-century pattern for large exchanges (as followed by Edward Jarman's Royal Exchange, City of London, 1667-71; destroyed 1838) had a cloister-like plan created by covered arcades surrounding an open court, and was pursued at the Corn Exchange (1750) and the Coal Exchange (c1755). These, now demolished, were both in the City of London, which probably explains why the conservative and not obviously appropriate cloister-like plan was followed. But from the mid-eighteenth century other building types were evoked as models for large-scale exchanges. John Wood used the image of the town mansion for the Exchange at Bristol; and for his Exchange (now the Town Hall) in Liverpool (1749-54) he used the model of the Palladian country house which, with its conventionally rusticated and arcaded ground-floor basement, was a particularly appropriate model for an exchange or market building, which demanded an open ground floor. This country-house-like appearance was emphasized when a portico was added in 1811. Previously, in 1802, a dome had been added (by J. Foster), an alteration of some significance, for the domed temple of commerce (to rival the temple of the arts, p167) was another of the models used for the design of exchanges.

Lecamus de Mézières had built a Corn Exchange in Paris in 1763-8 (now demolished) which was circular in plan (with a revolutionary and massive iron and glass dome added in 1808-13 by Bélanger). This circular plan was possibly the inspiration for Thomas Cooley's submission for the 1768 competition to find a design for a Royal Exchange in Dublin. Cooley, from London, was a protégé of Robert Mylne, whose own work clearly shows the influence of contemporary French neo-classicism. Cooley's design envisaged a domed neo-classical temple as the ideal setting for the conduct of Dublin business: the image obviously appealed and his design was built between 1769 and 1779. It is a magnificent building but was neither particularly practical nor relevant to its function. Indeed the interior is now divided and the building is used as the City Hall – for which its appearance is equally, if not more, appropriate. Entered through a magnificent Corinthian giant portico, the ground floor was originally one open space with the central area defined by a ring of columns coupled with piers and supporting the dome.

This temple of commerce imagery continued as a solution to the problem into the early nineteenth century. Nothing could be more imposing than David Hamilton's Royal Exchange, Glasgow (1827-9), which has a powerful Corinthian giant portico, a round colonnaded tower, and a Graeco-Roman interior with a Corinthian arcade supporting a shallow barrel-vaulted coffered ceiling. It is now Stirling's Library.

Another model for the design of exchanges had been experimented with in the eighteenth century. As early as 1699[4] Palladio's Basilica at Vicenza (commonly referred to as an exchange in the eighteenth century) with its double-height hall surrounded by loggias or colonnades, had been suggested as a prototype for exchange design. This idea eventually inspired not only Thomas de Thomon in his designs for the magnificent Leningrad Exchange (1804-16), but also James Peacock when he designed London's first Stock Exchange in 1801-2. This building (long demolished) had a trading floor divided into nave and aisles by an arcade, with the taller nave being top-lit by a clerestory.

Thomas Cooley's Royal Exchange (now City Hall), Dublin, begun in 1769: an ambitious neo-classical temple of commerce.

132 / *Georgian Buildings*

The Market Hall and Theatre, Bury St Edmund's, Suffolk, built 1774-80 to the designs of Robert Adam. The building is Palladian in proportion, neo-classical in detail and traditional in plan, with an (originally) open-arcaded ground floor derived from medieval and seventeenth-century exchanges and markets.

The development of the market building was even more complicated than that of the exchange, for during the eighteenth century markets were paired with all manner of building uses – and not just exchanges – some of which made very odd companions. Richard Castle's Market House at Dunlavin, Co. Wicklow (*c*1743), for example, contained a court (p152); that at Newtownards, Co. Down, by Ferdinando Stratford (1765) contained assembly rooms (p174); that at Bury St Edmunds, Suffolk, by Robert Adam (1774-80) a theatre (p170); and that at Uxbridge, Hillingdon, London (1789), served not only as a merchant exchange but also contained a charity school on its first floor.

The one architectural element common to all market halls, even the larger early nineteenth-century affairs like Charles Fowler's magnificent Covent Garden Market (1828-30), is the open arcade. In earlier, smaller, free-standing markets – like the Butter Cross, Ludlow, Shropshire, by William Baker (1743) and Martock market, Somerset (*c*1750) – these arcades could form an open substructure, as in the influential seventeenth-century Abingdon Town Hall (p180). This type was sometimes also constructed as part of a terrace, as in the mid-eighteenth-century market house at Midleton, Co. Cork, while the markets at Charleville, Co. Cork (*c*1740), at Tullamore, Co. Offaly (*c*1730), and the former Cheese Hall, Devizes, Wiltshire (1750), manage, with their pediments and arcaded ground floors, to look like ambitious town mansions, and are certainly interchangeable with town halls (p147). This eighteenth-century habit of papering the same architectural style over many functions (p17) is not, however, reflected in Robert Adam's curious little market hall at High Wycombe, Buckinghamshire (1761). Inspired, perhaps, by Palladio's functional farm buildings, it is squat, with an arcaded ground floor and a canted-bayed centre, with monopitched roofs suggesting half pediments over the flanking wings. All is humble and practical: the building could not be mistaken for a town hall or other building type and is suitably overpowered by the adjacent Guildhall by Henry Keene, 1757 (p148).

As suggested above, markets changed dramatically in scale, construction and design in the early nineteenth century. But the first indication of what was to come is found in the rapidly expanding manufacturing and industrial centres in the north of England, with the Piece Hall, Halifax, West Yorkshire (1775), being the most extraordinary example of the new form needed to accommodate the growth in manufacture and trade.

The massive square within the Piece Hall, Halifax, probably to the design of Thomas Bradley. The tiers of arcades suggest that the designer was attempting to reconstruct a Roman forum.

Designed, probably by Thomas Bradley, as a cloth market, it is massive in scale, and in form is an overblown exchange of the seventeenth-century pattern, with tiers of colonnades containing small shops and offices surrounding a massive parade-ground-like square, entered through a pedimented gate. The exterior façade is plain ashlar, mostly windowless, with an astonishing Roman severity. A splendid market square and quay was created at North Shields, Tyne and Wear, begun *c*1770: tall, handsome, neo-classical ranges incorporating a series of commercial uses, including a hotel (p174), to the design of David Stephenson were added in 1806-17. Of traditional scale and form but sporting Greek revival detailing is the Fish Market, Newcastle upon Tyne, by John Dobson (1823-5). Also Greek inspired – in form if not in detail – is the diminutive market, now a library, in Stamford, Lincolnshire, by William Legg (1804), which sports a tiny but imposing Tuscan portico temple front, an affectation shared by the larger Corn Exchange (1818) by H. Garling in Guildford, Surrey.

The arcade in the Covent Garden market, London, *c*1828-30, by Charles Fowler. The primitive Doric dwarf columns forming the clerestory and the exposed timber trusses of the roof are in strange contrast to the advanced cast-iron building technology that Fowler was utilizing for his contemporary conservatory at Syon House, Hounslow, London.

It was Charles Fowler, however, working in the south of England, who created a series of markets of advanced design, reflecting current international thinking. First, and most important, was his London Covent Garden fruit, flower and vegetable market (*c*1828-30) which, with its granite Tuscan arcades sheltering rows of shops and its glass-roofed central arcade, reflects contemporary French and American theories on market design, and combines the rationalism of French neo-classical planning with the delightful Greek revival detailing of Regency England. Interestingly, even advanced markets like Covent Garden were still of traditional construction and materials – brick, stone and timber – with the new technology of cast iron not being incorporated into market design until after 1830. Of Fowler's other markets – Hungerford, London (1831-3), Lower Market, Exeter (1835-7), and Higher Market, Exeter (1835-8), only parts of the latter survive.

Company halls
Merchant halls, and those of City companies, fall stylistically very much into the town mansion/country house category. The Coopers' Hall, King Street, Bristol (1743-4), by William Halfpenny has a provincial Palladian street façade of loosely domestic character, while the neo-classical façade that William Blackburn gave the Watermen's Hall, St Mary-at-Hill, City of London (1778-80), is that of an over-embellished terrace house. John Baxter the Younger's Adamesque Merchants' Hall, Hunter Square, Edinburgh (1788), Samuel Wyatt's Trinity House, Tower Hill, City of London (1792-4), and Robert Mylne's Graeco-Palladian elevation to Stationers' Hall, Ludgate Hill, City of London (1800), all have a dignity associated with institutional buildings such as town halls.

More difficult to classify is the Trinity House building in Kingston-upon-Hull, Humberside. Built in 1753-9, it presents an austere (now stuccoed) nine-bay, two-storey front, relieved by a three-bay pediment bearing in its tympanum a deeply carved coat of arms and sculpture. Within, the building presents a contrast of riches, with rococo and neo-classical work by Joseph Page (1773). Also in this rogue category is Robert Adam's Trades House, Glassford Street, Glasgow (1791-4, altered 1808, 1824 and 1887), to which he gave a complex and highly distinctive façade, an essay on his theories of picturesque 'movement' (p83) which does not reflect the purpose of the building in any way.

Slightly later, and indicative of the gran-

The Trades House, Glassford Street, Glasgow, 1791-4, to the designs of Robert Adam: a complex elevation reflecting Adam's picturesque theories about 'movement'.

The rear elevation of 5 and 7 Elder Street, Spitalfields, London, 1725: a pair of houses purpose-built for weaving as the upper storeys, with their mullioned window, reveal.

deur the Victorians were to lavish on company halls, are Philip Hardwick's magnificent neo-baroque Goldsmiths' Hall, City of London (1829-35), which is richly decorated with giant Corinthian columns (p263), and Henry Roberts' Fishmongers' Hall, also in the City (begun in 1831), which is conceived as a porticoed Greek temple with excellent interior detailing.

Mills and warehouses

In 1727 Daniel Defoe wondered whether Thomas and John Lombe's large new silk mill in Derby (1717; only some stone foundations and an altered tower survive) could 'answer the expence or not',[5] a natural enough question since its scale was something entirely new. It established an approach to the construction of mills and warehouses that was to form the basis of the development of this building type through the eighteenth and into the nineteenth century, and pioneered a scale of manufacturing that was gradually to destroy the established system, where many goods, especially fabrics, were manufactured in buildings of domestic use or domestic in scale. Lombe's mill was long (110 feet), multi-level (five storeys), and spare and functional in design (though still traditional in construction). It was shallow in depth and pierced by many windows to allow good light for the mill workers, to whom power was supplied by a 23-foot-diameter waterwheel. The contrast between the new and traditional manufacturing methods is stunning when demonstrated by a comparison of this new building type with some of the surviving nearly contemporary, domestic-scaled manufactories. In Bonsall, Derbyshire, are some two-storey framework knitting workshops with rows of windows, one of which, dated 1737, has a well-lit first floor approached by an external staircase. In Spitalfields, London, a silk-weaving district since the seventeenth century, two four-storey houses built in 1725 survive in Elder Street (numbers 5 and 7), with living quarters on the two lower floors and weaving lofts in the upper two (number 5 retains its long mullioned window containing leaded lights), and at Maidstone in Kent is a small-scale and picturesque paper mill, called Turkey Court and Mill, purpose-built in 1736.

This system of cottage industry survived on a small, regional scale throughout the eighteenth century and even into the nineteenth – for example, lace-weavers' cottages of c1765 survive in Mill Lane, Sevenoaks, Kent, as do weavers' houses in Barton Orchard, Bradford-on-Avon, Wiltshire, and in Union Street, Newtown, Powys (c1820). But of course it was the Lombes' scale of approach that was characteristic of eighteenth- and nineteenth-century mill and warehouse architecture. Although the general form of the large-scale industrial building was established so early, the structure within the shell was to undergo revolutionary changes during the latter part of the century, as new building technology emerged; indeed the mill, with the theatre (p170), pioneered the application of new, post-Industrial Revolution technology in building, as the designers of both these building types consistently sought fire-proof methods of construction.

Good examples of traditional pre-Industrial Revolution technology are the Pease Warehouses, Kingston upon Hull (1743-5). These are tall brick structures with small windows and deep plans (because their purpose was storage not production), of massive timber construction internally. The monumental Flour Mill at Slane, on the Boyne (1763-76), designed in the manner of a country house, with pediments, floors of graduated height and Gibbs surrounds to ground-floor windows, is ashlar externally and timber inside. House Mill, Three Mills Lane, Stratford, London (1776), is also entirely of timber construction within a brick shell, as are Grice's Granary, Rotherhithe Street, Southwark, London (c1780), which is constructed with massive timber posts, beams and braces, and the quarter-mile-long Ropery in the Royal Navy dockyard at Chatham which, completed in 1792, is still without a trace of cast iron in its structure.

The earliest of Richard Arkwright's mills at Cromford, Derbyshire, were constructed along these traditional lines; for example an early cotton spinning mill in Mill Road (c1772-7) has a brick shell and a timber interior with no attempt at fire-proofing. Interestingly, there are no windows in the lower floor. (Perhaps to prevent industrial espionage? Certainly Lombe had spied on Italian techniques and, it is said, was poisoned by an Italian woman in consequence.) But the next generation of Derbyshire mills was to be very different. In 1791 the Albion Mill in London, designed by Samuel Wyatt and built between 1783-6 as a conventional structure with a load-bearing brick shell and a timber-framed interior, was destroyed in a spectacular fire. This marked the turning point. Modest attempts at fire-proofing mills were made in the 1780s - for example the Quarry Bank Silk Mill at Styal, Cheshire (1784), was given a brick shell and an interior which is partly conventional timber frame and partly of 'filler joist' or jack arch construction, where small masonry arches span from joists running across the main internal beams, with cast iron being used for the first time in 1792 in a major structural capacity.

William Strutt, building in 1792 for his father Jedediah Strutt, who had been Ark-

The vista down the quarter-mile-long Ropery in Chatham Dockyard, Kent. Although completed in 1792 the building is still entirely timber-frame within a brick shell. No cast iron has been used.

The interior of Marshall, Benyon & Bage's Mill, Ditherington, Shrewsbury. Built 1796-7, it is the earliest multi-storey iron-framed interior. The floor above is supported by shallow brick arches spanning between iron beams, which in turn are supported by the slender cast-iron colonettes. The outer brick walls, however, are still built of load-bearing brick.

wright's partner until 1781, designed a 'fireproof mill' in Derby (now demolished) which used iron colonnettes instead of wooden posts and had floors supported on shallow brick arches. In 1793-5 Strutt built the West Mill, (demolished 1962) at Belper, Derbyshire; like its predecessor, it had iron colonnettes rather than wooden posts supporting brick arched floors but, also like its predecessor, it was essentially a transitional design, for the beams supported by the iron colonnettes and supporting the brick arch floors were still timber – usually fir and about twelve inches square. The change to iron beams came in 1796, when Charles Bage designed Marshall, Benyon and Bage's flour mill (now Allied Breweries) at Ditherington, Shrewsbury, Shropshire. Here slender cast-iron colonnettes support iron beams, between which span shallow brick arches supporting the floors.

Although the mill is the earliest cast-iron structure, it is not a fully developed iron-frame building, for the outer brick walls are still load-bearing. The first step to a fully skeletal structure was not made until after the 1830s (Pevsner says with warehouses in France in the 1860s).[6] After 1796 the idea of a complete inner iron frame was fairly widely adopted in Britain, for example in 1799 at Philips and Lee, Salford, by Boulton and Watt (now destroyed), which had cylindrical columns that served for central heating (gas lighting was installed in 1805), and in 1803-4 at the North Mill, Belper, Derbyshire, which has segmentally arched ceilings of hollow pot construction placed within the internal iron frame. A slightly later but excellent example is the Cloth Mill at King's Stanley, Stroud Valley, Gloucestershire (1812), which has an iron frame within and brick and stone without, and is constructed entirely without wood.

These were the pioneering buildings: for a long time after 1792 timber was still generally used, particularly in warehouse construction, with cast iron being used in only a limited capacity or to improve traditional timber construction techniques. For example, as early as c1770 George Dance the Younger had attempted to improve the performance of his massive 69-foot-long king-post trusses forming the roof of Whitbread's Porter Tun Room in Chiswell Street, City of London, by fixing the rafters together at the ridge and the king-post to the 69-foot-long tie beam with specially fabricated cast-iron 'shoes' and

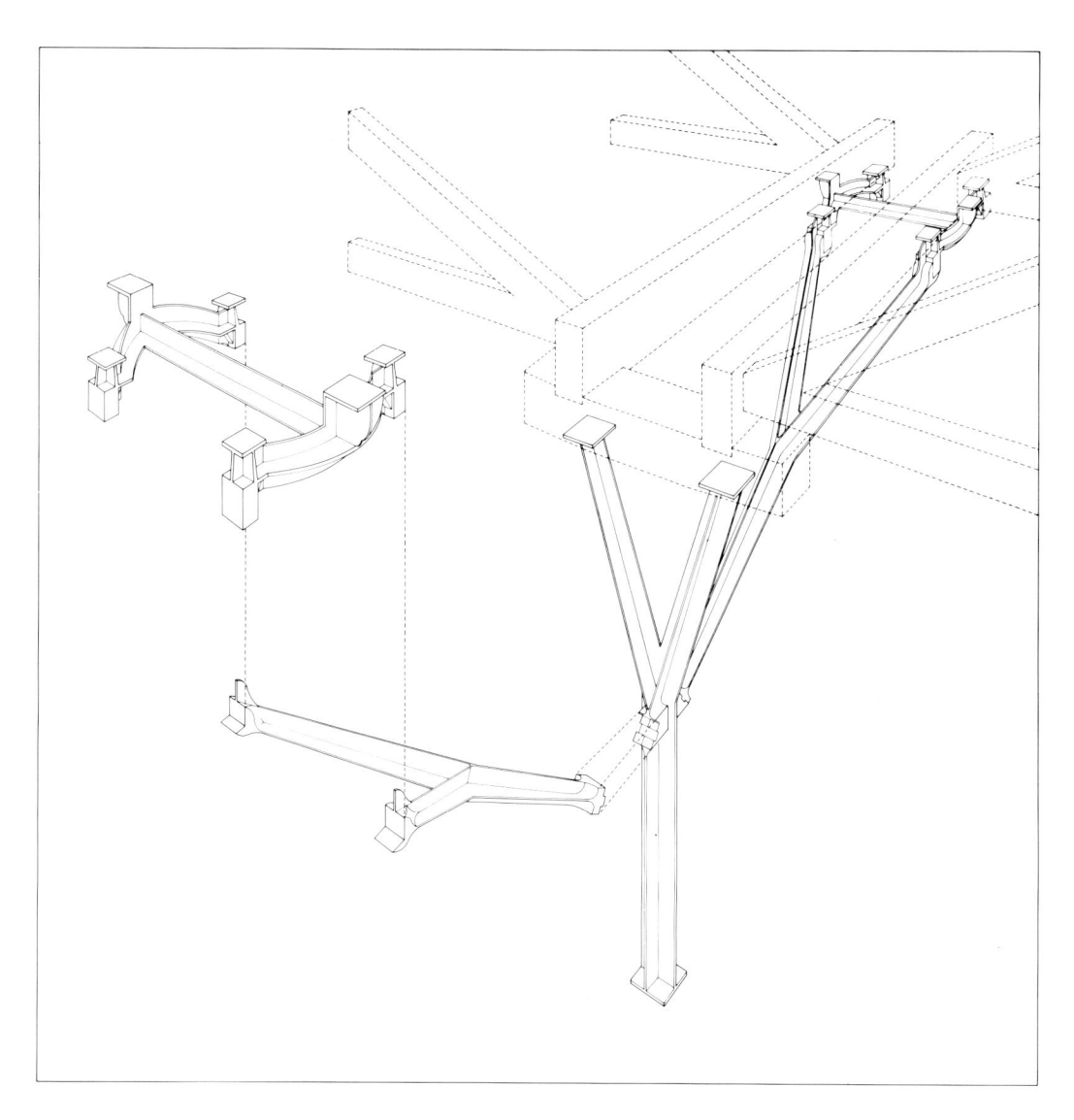

Axonometric of a cast-iron column in the Skin Floor, London Docks, Wapping, built 1811-13 to the design of D. A. Alexander. The curious design of this column – with raking struts – was to allow for the creation of a large covered space with as much open floor area as possible. Consequently this system was devised, which allows every other roof truss to be supported not on a column but by the raking struts rising from each neighbouring column.

straps. The technology was new, Dance did not fully understand the forces involved, and the 'shoes' failed – but the roof stood up and was not comprehensively repaired until the mid-1970s. The other limited use of cast iron is illustrated by warehouses in the London Docks, such as those in the West India Dock, Isle of Dogs, by George Gwilt and his son George. Despite being built between 1799 and 1802 these still contain timber floor beams with cast-iron colonnettes of various forms, sizes and sections. In the Pennington Street Stacks, London Docks (1802-5), by D.A. Alexander (now all demolished) wooden posts as well as cast-iron colonnettes were used. Indeed the warehouses-cum-barracks of 1803 at Weedon, Northampton-shire, are all constructed with wooden posts within brick shells supporting the first floors.

Cast iron had, as well as its fire-proof qualities, other characteristics that attracted the early nineteenth-century architect and engineer: members could be much thinner than wood and still be of equal strength, unsupported spans could be wider, and the individual structural members could be cast in large batches and assembled with unrivalled speed on site. A building that illustrates these points is the single-storey Skin Floor in the London Docks, Wapping, built between 1811 and 1813. The designer was D.A. Alexander, who had been appointed surveyor to the London Dock Company in 1796. The object was to create a large covered space

View within the Skin Floor, illustrating the advantages offered by cast iron. Structural members could be much thinner than wooden ones of equivalent strength, and unsupported spans could be wider.

with as much open floor area as possible. The particular reason why this clear floor space was needed is not now known, but the search for means of achieving clear spaces was an engineering challenge that many eighteenth- and early nineteenth-century architects undertook – for example George Dance the Younger with his Porter Tun Room – and certainly for roof construction (as at the Skin Floor) there were several great benefits. The wider the span the wider the pitch, which meant fewer valley gutters to maintain and, of course, the wider the span the fewer the columns, which meant a saving in cast-iron components and assembly time.

At the Skin Floor queen-post roof trusses spanning 54 feet are carried on lines of columns of 18-foot centres. However, the roof trusses covering this space occur at 9-foot centres, so only alternate trusses are supported directly by cast-iron columns, the remainder being supported on pairs of timber beams (with scarfed joints) that span between the columns. These beams in consequence needed strengthening, so a V-shaped cast-iron raking strut (one strut for each beam) extends out from halfway up the cast-iron column to reach the beams at the halfway point immediately below the truss. The result of this prodigious feat of engineering is an extraordinary tree-like cast-iron column which, seen in repetition, makes one of the most memorable vistas in British architecture.

Working conditions in the mills

A little must be said about the external appearance of the mills and warehouses, of the working conditions within them, and of the communities that were founded upon the wealth created by this early, often completely unbridled, industrialism. The construction of the huge bonded warehouse in London's docklands in the very early nineteenth century offered designers a wonderful opportunity to indulge the current fashion for austere neo-classicism while composing structures of a truly sublime Piranesian scale and mass, where the impression of strength and impregnability was a definite design requirement. This opportunity was not missed: Gwilt managed to stretch his five-storey stacks of warehouses in the West India Docks for two-thirds of a mile (only one now survives) and, like D.A. Alexander's contemporary London Dock warehouses (only fragments survive), built them of bold yellow brick, relieved only by the simplest, but always well placed, Portland stone ornamentation. Alexander's stacks in the London Docks had subtly articulated façades, windows with bold cast-iron glazing bars, and a vermiculated Portland stone base. The Cutler

The eastern courtyard, looking towards the western courtyard, Cutler Street warehouses, City of London, built c1792-7 by Richard Jupp. The right-hand building has been demolished; the rest survive as façades only. These elevations are typical of late eighteenth-century austere, monumentally scaled and detailed warehouse architecture.

Street warehouses off Bishopsgate, largely of similar date (c1769-1820, p127), survive only as façades, but here the architectural approach was the same, with tall yellow brick stacks arranged around courts, and stone decoration reserved for bold embellishment to doors, archways and the occasional plinth. In Northamptonshire the designer of the barracks/warehouses at Weedon used a little more decoration – stone Tuscan pilasters around doors and stone cornices – as befitting the depot's status as royal refuge in case of French invasion.

The architectural opportunities offered by buildings of heroic Roman scale were not missed by the mill designers in the north either. Masson Mill, Cromford, Derbyshire (1783), for Arkwright, has an extraordinary display in the centre of its façade comprising eight Venetian windows stacked up in pairs and separated by three Diocletian windows, all topped with a lantern (a favourite architectural device for enlivening the utilitarian mill façade, as for example at the mill at Styal, Cheshire, 1784, and the Silk Mill, St Albans, Hertfordshire, c1790).

This sort of architectural flourish is typical of the approach of Arkwright – and his colleagues – to mill design: give the exterior of the building a little dignity or decoration but never mind about the working conditions. Arkwright was perhaps better than most. He paid for, and Thomas Gardner designed, St Mary's Church, Mill Road, Cromford, Derbyshire, in 1792 (altered 1858) – fourteen years *after* he had built the Greyhound Inn in Cromford, and twenty years after he began building mill workers' housing. A surviving example of the latter is North Street, Cromford (1771-6), where three-storey houses have mullioned windows set in long rows to light framework knitting rooms, installed so that work could go on at home. Other examples of this type of model mill workers' housing survive at Belper, Derbyshire, an industrial town founded by Arkwright and Jedediah Strutt in 1776. Long Row, North Row and South Row are three-storey terraces of c1790 and William, George and Joseph Streets contain clusters of houses built in fours, back to back, dating from c1795. And appealing as this concern for housing conditions seems, it must be remembered that Arkwright employed mostly children, working in shifts day and night. More disturbing is Castle Mill, Linby, Nottinghamshire (1785), where James Watt set up his first steam engine for cotton spinning. The mill, garbed in all the romantic appeal of a picturesque Gothic folly, was worked mostly by poor children collected in London, 163 of whom still lie in the local churchyard, killed by the rigours and cruelty of forced labour. On such foundations was the wealth of the late eighteenth century built.

The other approach to manufacturing – where workers were treated by the mill owners with at least as much care and attention as the spinning machines – was pioneered in the late eighteenth century. New Lanark, Strathclyde, founded in the mid-1780s by Richard Arkwright and David Dale, was taken over and managed by the philanthropist and manufacturer Robert Owen from 1799 to 1824, when he left for America. At New Lanark he created a model industrial settlement which reflected his concerns for the 'living machine' as much as for the 'inanimate machine', and his belief that the 'ties between employer and employees' must not be only 'what immediate gain can each derive from the other'.[7] Consequently he reduced the working day from twelve to ten and a half hours, improved working conditions and took notice of his employees' intellectual welfare. Amongst the tall, sombre mills he constructed a school, an institute for the formation of character, housing run on a co-operative basis, an infirmary, an inn and a store, and even organized a committee to

View down the main street in New Lanark, Strathclyde, a model cotton-manufacturing village founded in c1784 and built during the following twenty-five years.

inspect each household every week – the 'committee of bughunters', as it was called by the disgruntled wives of New Lanark.[8]

The influence of New Lanark was immense but gradual, although it can already be discerned to a degree at places like Newtown, Powys, where a weaving quarter was developed in the 1820s. Here, almost in the pre-industrial pattern, workers' housing – some containing well-lit weaving lofts – is mixed with mills of modest size. Later in the nineteenth century this close mix of residential and manufacturing buildings was to be identified as a great evil – and so it was when the lowly workers' terraces were shoddily built and in the polluted shadow of the looming factory: but at Newtown a fair balance seems to have been struck. In Bryn Street (number 5) a mill and mill-owner's or manager's house form one composition (though each use has its own distinctive fenestration pattern, p231) and at 5, 6 and 7 Commercial Street a handsome red-brick building of c1820 contains a mill for twenty-four looms and rooms for six families.

Bridges

Bridge-building was a task that most architects and provincial builders felt equal to, and when contemplating the problem they seem, until late in the eighteenth century, to have devoted most of their energies to devising ways of applying the current architectural fashions to bridge elevations, rather than to rationalizing or improving construction methods. General Wade and his engineers designed an extremely stylish military bridge, complete with ramped-up sides and four obelisks, over the river Tay at Aberfeldy in 1733; James Paine designed a fashionably detailed bridge at Wallington, Northumberland, in 1755; Sir Robert Taylor one at Maidenhead, Berkshire, in 1772-7 and possibly that at Swinford, near Eynsham, Oxfordshire, in c1770.

Apart from such bridges which represent the mainstream of eighteenth-century

Pulteney Bridge, Bath, built 1764-74 to a design by Robert Adam derived from Andrea Palladio's design for the Rialto Bridge, Venice.

The Iron Bridge at Ironbridge, Shropshire, 1777-9 by T. F. Pritchard and Abraham Darby III; the first cast-iron engineered structure in the world.

development there are also those that reflect either an obsession with archaeology or, at the other extreme, with revolutionary engineering technology and new materials.

Excellent examples of the former are Robert Adam's Pulteney Bridge, Bath (1764-74), which, though an interpretation of a commonly admired design by Palladio for the Rialto Bridge, Venice, was the only attempt during the eighteenth century to render this particular ideal (p98). In place of the colonnade-covered walks of the Palladio design Adam had shops and pedimented end pavilions, with a flat road surface that connected directly to the existing street levels. In 1764 George Smith, when building Green's Bridge, Kilkenny, had cribbed directly a bridge illustrated in Palladio's *Quattro Libri*.[9]

The most important example of the latter category is the Iron Bridge at Ironbridge, Shropshire, constructed in 1777-9 to the design of T.F. Pritchard with modifications by the iron-master Abraham Darby III. It pioneered the technology of large-scale cast-iron construction. A single-arch span of 120 feet is achieved with the most slender and elegant of cast-iron structural members, a feat which made the bridge one of the wonders of the late eighteenth-century world. An interesting comparison with the Iron Bridge is the bridge over the river Taff at Pontypridd, built in 1755-6 by William Edwards, who demonstrated just how far traditional bridge construction, with traditional materials, could be pushed. It is of masonry, and has a single span which is a segment of a circle 170 feet in diameter (until this bridge no masonry structure had achieved a span of more than 100 feet since Roman times). The haunches of the bridge were lightened, without being structurally weakened, by being pierced with three cylindrical holes, a technique that was not new but which was used by Edwards to startling effect, for the bridge remains sound to this day. It was, however, his third attempt on the site, the earlier structures having collapsed, which is an indication of the difficulty of achieving such a span with traditional materials.

These were just the sort of difficulties that the designers of iron bridges claimed they could solve. Tom Paine, the political writer, not only promoted iron bridges but also in 1789 made a design for one: it was to be of cast and wrought iron, and the rib of the arch was inspired by, and looked like, a spider's web. He managed to get the components manufactured at Rotherham, and in August 1790 an iron bridge to his design was erected as an exhibition and advertisement in a field beside the Yorkshire Stingo public house in Paddington, London. It had a span of 110 feet with an arch of catenary shape. It was much visited and inspected before being dismantled in October 1791, when the metal was sent back to Rotherham rather than being used for the construction of a real bridge.

Such lack of trust in this revolutionary system of bridge construction was somewhat justified by the fate that befell some of the very early iron bridges. Rowland Burdon's bold Iron Bridge at Sunderland, Tyne and Wear (inspired by Paine's designs), begun in 1793, had a span of 236 feet, and the ironwork was erected in ten days on a scaffold rather than a centring, in order not to block navigation. But by 1805 the bridge had 'failed', owing to lateral movement – up to eighteen inches – which bent many of the joints. This was rectified, at great expense, by diagonal bracing, but in 1812 a professional visitor recorded that the arch had 'settled several inches, as well as twisted from a straight direction, and the whole vibrating and shaking in a remarkable manner'.[10] The bridge was rebuilt in 1896 and built entirely anew in 1929. An even worse fate befell John Nash's early attempt at iron bridge building when his pretty Gothic bridge – of one shallow arch and 98-foot span – at Stanford, Hereford and Worcester, suddenly collapsed soon after completion in 1795.

It was not until the early decades of the nineteenth century that iron bridge technology was fully mastered by such as Thomas Telford, with his magnificent and flamboyantly decorated cast-iron Waterloo Bridge at Betws-y-Coed, Gwynedd (1815). But by this time the technology of arch bridges – be they of solid masonry or of lattice-like iron construction – was being replaced for large spans by bridges designed on the suspension principle.

The first of these, indeed the first in the world, was the Menai Suspension Bridge, Gwynedd (1819–26), by Telford (quickly copied, in 1820, by Samuel Brown when designing a bridge near Berwick upon Tweed). Telford then produced the Conway Suspension Bridge, Gwynedd, in 1821–6, a wonderful example of early nineteenth-century revolutionary engineering combined with romanticism, for the bold iron chains of the bridge are suspended from mock-medieval towers, designed in sympathy with the neighbouring castle. A similar mixture of architectural styles and vigorous engineering is found at the most awe-inspiring of early suspension bridges: that by Isambard Kingdom Brunel at Clifton, Bristol (1829–64), where the chains are suspended from towers designed as Egyptian pylons.

Notes

1 R. D. Richard, *The Early History of Banking in England*, 1929.
2 Nikolaus Pevsner, *A History of Building Types*, page 214 of 1976 edition.
3 Quoted by Pevsner, op. cit., page 264.
4 Leonhard Christoph Sturm's edition of Nikolaus Goldman's *Vollständige Anweisung zur Civilbaukunst*, 1699.
5 Daniel Defoe, *A Tour through the Whole Island of Great Britain*, 3 vols, 1727.
6 Nikolaus Pevsner, op. cit., pages 286–8.
7 As stated by Robert Owen in his *New View of Society*, 1813–14.
8 See Colin and Rose Bell's *City Fathers*, pages 242–8 of 1972 edition, in which Owen's role as an enlightened employer is set against his obsessive attempts to indoctrinate his employees (a captive audience) with his constant and overbearing moral strictures.
9 Plate VII in volume III of Palladio's *Quattro Libri*.
10 C. Hutton, *Tracts on Mathematical and Philosophical Works*, 3 vols, London 1812.

GOVERNMENT AND INSTITUTIONAL BUILDINGS

The buildings erected by national and local government and by various institutions during the eighteenth and early nineteenth centuries fall into two main groups. There are those whose forms were largely determined by their function or by tradition and where the decoration was a direct reflection of their use: for example, the exterior design of gaols usually reflected their purpose and they were often decorated with chains and fetters. Then there were buildings which used forms developed for other purposes. Guildhalls and town halls, for example, were usually domestic in character and followed the style established for country houses or large town mansions.

National government buildings

Until the second quarter of the eighteenth century, national government had the admirable though extraordinary habit of occupying ancient and rambling premises and adapting them to its needs rather than building anew.

The grand establishments of Louis xiv's France were admired but rarely imitated in the seventeenth century, with the exception of the Hôtel des Invalides in Paris which inspired, in 1694, the transformation of Greenwich Palace into a naval hospital for old sailors, the creation of the Royal Hospital, Chelsea (1682-92), by Wren for the use of old soldiers and, slightly earlier, the construction of the Royal Hospital, Kilmainham, Dublin (1680-87), to the design of William Robinson for the use of old soldiers. When the Hanoverian dynasty was established in 1714, the royal family moved into a series of Tudor, Jacobean and Stuart apartments at St James's, Whitehall, and Kensington; Parliament still met in ancient chambers in Westminster with the various government offices clustered round Westminster Abbey and in Whitehall.

It was here, in Whitehall, that the first attempt at forming a public architecture was made. The Admiralty was begun in 1723

Parliament House (now Bank of Ireland), Dublin. Designed in 1729 by Sir Edward Lovett Pearce, this is the most important early eighteenth-century public building in the British Isles, combining the classical propriety of English Palladianism with the movement of the baroque school.

and completed in 1726 to the designs of Sir Robert Walpole's placeman Thomas Ripley (p65). This brick edifice got the new type of building off to a bad start. It was not only archaic in design, with rusticated pilaster strips and segmental windows in the convention of Wren, but positively bad. Ripley, attempting to create an imposing quadrangular building on a small site, managed to fit in all the necessary elements only at the expense of the building's proportions. The giant portico is too elongated, the court too cramped and all was eventually screened from public view by a colonnaded wall designed in 1759 by Robert Adam.

The next attempt was the Paymaster General's Office (1732-3) by John Lane: just south of the Admiralty, it is purely domestic in character with a five-bay brick front, three-bay pediment and Gibbs surrounds to the ground-floor windows. But by the time this modest building was complete, something remarkable had happened in Ireland. The Parliament House (now the Bank of Ireland) on College Green, Dublin, is of supreme importance. Designed in 1729 by Sir Edward Lovett Pearce, it is the only really major and successful public building produced by the Palladian movement in its early phase. Of course, Pearce was not a Palladian in the Burlington mould (p57) but this building, with its gravity, its powerful and classically correct external detailing and, in particular, its mighty temple-like portico, is very much in the English Palladian manner – even if the bold recession of the portico within flanking colonnaded wings is more Vanbrughian than Burlingtonian.

The interior and plan are more ambivalent still. Indeed, the centrally placed octagonal Commons' Chamber (gutted by fire in 1792) was topped by a huge stepped pantheon dome in the manner of Chiswick House, while the Lords' Chamber has a splendid neoantique coffered barrel-vaulted ceiling with an apsed end beneath a Diocletian window reminiscent of Burlington's studies of the Roman Baths. These chambers, for all their Palladian detail and form, are set within a baroque plan where, in the spirit of Vanbrugh, dramatic use is made of corridors to create long vistas, and secondary rooms are set in enfilade. But perhaps the setting of Palladian jewels within a baroque frame is not so surprising, for the baroque, with its inherent flexibility and susceptibility to inspired inventions, was more likely to offer a solution for the unique problem of accommodating a bicameral legislative (houses of commons and lords) behind a temple front than the precedent-bound Palladian movement: Palladio, after all, offers no model for a twochamber Parliament building.

Another public building – probably by Joseph Jarrett – was constructed in Dublin in c1760, with a close connection with White-

The House of Lords' Chamber in Parliament House, Dublin. By Pearce, it is a pioneering neoclassical design.

The Genealogical Office, Dublin Castle, c1760, probably by Joseph Jarrett, based on Colen Campbell's 1724 designs for Lord Pembroke's house in Whitehall. The tall cupola is derived from a design in William Kent's *Designs of Inigo Jones* (1727).

Government and Institutional Buildings / 145

The Treasury Building, Whitehall, London, 1733-6 by William Kent: a handsome essay in the decorated Palladian manner, with details derived from Lord Burlington's 1723 house for General Wade.

hall. In 1724 Colen Campbell had designed a proto-Palladian town villa in Whitehall for Lord Pembroke (rebuilt 1757). This design (published in *Vitruvius Britannicus*, Vol. III) was reproduced as the centrepiece of the north side of Upper Castle Yard, Dublin, with the addition of a tall cupola copied from William Kent's *Designs of Inigo Jones* (1727).

Meanwhile, back in Whitehall an ambitious attempt had been made to discover a Burlingtonian Palladian form for a government building. In 1732 William Kent produced a grandiose design for the British Parliament with a Pantheon-like domed elevation, and in 1733 he designed the Treasury looking on to Horse Guards Parade. Lacking the wings Kent envisaged, it is more impressive as a piece of Burlingtonian Palladian design in which reference is made to Burlington's earlier house for General Wade (p8) than as a piece of public building. The façade is fully rusticated, divided by pilasters, placed upon a rustic base and topped by a pediment; it could, indeed, be a nobleman's town house (see John Vardy's Spencer House, p280) or a provincial town hall.

Kent soon followed the Treasury with one of the major government-financed administrative buildings of the eighteenth century: the Horse Guards. Built to Kent's design by John Vardy (c1750-60) it is, like the Treasury, in the by then ageing Burlingtonian Palladian style (Kent died in 1748, Burlington in 1753). The building, as well as being embellished with Palladian details and forms such as pyramid-roofed towers (p69), also follows the theory of composition called concatenation, displayed at Holkham Hall, Norfolk, of 1731. But one of the most curious aspects of the Horse Guards is that the Palladian theory of relating exterior to interior is abandoned. Some of the attic windows are blank, while a number of Venetian windows on the *piano nobile* are partially dummy and light only small rooms. The failure to relate elevation to plan and the somewhat arbitrary form of the façade's movement were not missed by Sir William Chambers, who recorded in 1757 the 'general dislike' of the Horse Guards, and observed that 'Mr Kent ... was fond of puzzling his spectators' by an artificial complexity of design.[1]

The next major government building to be erected in London can be seen as a corrective

The Horse Guards, Whitehall, London, designed c1745-8 by William Kent and built c1750-60 by John Vardy. The Horse Guards parade ground elevation, shown here, is the supreme example of the decorated Palladian style, with fully rusticated façade.

to the Horse Guards, for it was Chambers' Somerset House. Built between 1776 and 1801, Somerset House is the apotheosis of Chambers' career. It displays with great skill the current French neo-classical fashion, and highlights both Chambers' strengths and weaknesses as an architect. He fought long and hard to get the commission – from 1774 to 1776 – visiting Paris to view the new hotels and public buildings of such as Gabriel, Gondoin and Chalgrin and writing innumerable lobbying letters. In one of these he wrote, when criticizing an initial scheme by William Robinson, 'I could easily save both [the existing Webb and Kent buildings] and many thousand pounds.'[2] In fact, when he got the job he did neither: by February 1790, long before completion, the building had cost £353,000. Robinson's 1775 estimate (the year he died) for building a new Somerset House, albeit to a simpler design than Chambers', had been £135,000.

Largely through the influence of Edmund Burke, Chambers was given the job. He designed a building which, as it rose during the late 1770s, must have looked somewhat novel – certainly bold and austere – when compared with the fashionable fripperies of Adam (p15). But it was the function of the building that was really new, and few, it seems, including Sir William Chambers, really appreciated this. For the first time the government had decided on Burke's advice to centralize various government offices, so that Chambers had to provide quarters for the Audit, Salt and Land Tax Offices, the Stamp Office, the Duchies of Cornwall and Lancaster, as well as the Navy and the Royal Academy and Society of Antiquaries in the fine rooms in the Strand block. Chambers' solution to this problem is revealing, for there is no evidence that he gave any deep thought to the development of a new building type to house a massive office complex. Rather, he used the scale of the project to embank the Thames and create subterranean warehouses as Adam had done eight years earlier at the nearby Adelphi. Then he pursued his obsession of imposing his Francophile neo-classicism upon the public – to the great discomfiture, he hoped no doubt, of his rival Robert Adam.

In this campaign Chambers was only partially successful. He produced a building that was officially acclaimed. Burke described it, in Parliament in 1781, as a building 'that did honour to the present age, and would render the Metropolis of Great Britain famous throughout Europe.' But Somerset House has never really been taken to the hearts of Londoners (perhaps because of its tax and civil

The courtyard elevation of Somerset House, London, built 1776-1801 to the designs of Sir William Chambers: purpose-built offices with exquisitely detailed domestic-looking façades.

service origins) and its architectural success lies in its detail and in some elevations. The Strand elevation is excellent: it invokes the English Palladians by being an essay upon Webb's Jonesian and highly influential Queen's Gallery of 1662 (p8) in the Old Somerset House which Chambers was obliged to demolish; and the astonishingly French ashlar elevation to the internal courtyard creates what is effectively one of the most magnificent of London squares flanked by more modest terraces. The long river elevation, no doubt inspired by Germain Soufflot's Hôtel-Dieu in Lyon, is also magnificent – a wonderful combination of Roman gravity, Palladian composition and French neo-classical detailing. Unfortunately the attempt to reconcile the scale of the inner square with the long river front led to one of the most conspicuous architectural blunders of the eighteenth century. Both the southern elevation of the square and the river elevation share the same dome, which looks well from the square but absurdly small when seen in the context of the river front. Such a failure of scale is rare in the eighteenth century but it underlines the fact that Chambers' genius lay in the creation of gem-like neo-classical compositions – the villa, the casino, the Strand front of Somerset House – rather than truly monumental compositions.

The individual building plans emphasize, in the most dramatic way, Chambers' failure to realize a new building type. With the exception of the Strand block, they are generally standard domestic terrace plans with a room front and back, and a centrally placed top-lit or dog-leg stair. Most of the buildings in the square (but not in the flanking wings) are connected by a long corridor. This type of domestic office plan had been used elsewhere, but normally in buildings of a smaller scale, such as the Royal Navy's Sick and Hurt Board Office of 1772 which survives in Trinity Square, beside the Tower of London, and is indistinguishable from an ordinary house. Even the nearby monumental late-Palladian Royal Mint (1807-12) by James Johnson and Sir Robert Smirke has separate domestic-type sets of rooms (some indeed being residential) behind its pedimented palace front. No doubt this provision of small-scale planned accommodation for office use was more a reflection of office organization in the eighteenth century than a lack of architectural vision, for offices were usually established in domestic buildings or in large clerking rooms of the type so noticeable in both Taylor's and Soane's Bank of England buildings (p128). The case for the architect as obedient servant of the client's demands is supported by the fact that another prestigious eighteenth-century public building – the Four Courts in Dublin, begun in 1786 to the design of James Gandon, a pupil of Chambers – also contained in its west wing (built by Thomas Cooley in 1777) terrace houses serving as office accommodation.

The Act of Union between England and Scotland in 1707 robbed Edinburgh architects of the opportunity to design national government buildings of the type created in Dublin (Ireland not being united politically with England until 1801) and the architectural consequences for the city were grave. As R. Chambers wrote in 1825, 'From the Union up to the middle of the century, the existence of the city seems to have been a perfect blank. No improvement of any sort marked this period. On the contrary, an air of gloom and depression pervaded the city.... In short, this may be called the Dark Age of Edinburgh.'[3] The most ambitious eighteenth-century public buildings in Edinburgh are the Royal Exchange in the High Street and the Register House in the New Town, which is set magnificently on the axis of the North Bridge.

The Exchange, designed in 1753 by John Adam and now embedded within the City Chambers, also contained a custom house and is discussed in the chapter on commercial buildings (p130). The Register House, designed (1774) by Robert Adam to house the city's records, is a sophisticated late-Palladian composition with refined neo-classical details. It is two storeys high – with the ground-floor windows set within a rusticated blank arcade – and thirteen bays wide, with the centre three set between engaged columns beneath a pediment. The end bays break forward to form pavilions containing Venetian windows and supporting handsome classical clock towers. Inside are some delightful neo-classical interiors, and the dome, which rises above the pediment, is revealed as part of a double-height rotunda with arcaded walls, gallery and excellent neo-classical plasterwork.

Local government buildings
Town halls, guildhalls and shire halls were mongrel forms closely related to markets and exchanges (p130). Their plans and disposition of space could reflect medieval origins of the type that was formalized in the seventeenth century with such buildings as Abingdon Town Hall, Oxfordshire (1678-80), by Christopher Kempster, where a first-floor council room was placed over an open ground-floor arcade which was used as a market or merchants' exchange. Eighteenth-century examples of this doubling up of local government and commerce are Monmouth

Town Hall (1724) which is based partly on Abingdon, even to the use of giant pilasters for external embellishment, and partly on contemporary local country house architecture; the Town Hall and Market House at Dursley, Gloucestershire (1738), of similar general form with an open arcade on stone columns; the Town Hall of Langport, Somerset (1733), which has a three-bay arcaded ground floor; Rye Town Hall, East Sussex (1743), by Andrews Jelfe, with brick first floor over a stone open arcade; and Whitby Town Hall, North Yorkshire (1788), with pediment, Venetian windows and stone Tuscan columns.

Slightly more ambitious are Henry Keene's Guildhall at High Wycombe, Buckinghamshire (1757), which has a three-bay pediment and an open arcade; the Guildhall at Poole, Dorset (1761), which has an arcaded ground floor and a fine double external stair leading up to the first-floor rooms; the Town Hall at Maidstone, Kent (1762), which has an arcaded ground floor, a first-floor bay and a fine, painted council chamber; the Town Hall at Woodstock, Oxfordshire, designed by Sir William Chambers (1766) in a 'simple' and 'appropriate' mid-Palladian style; the Town Hall and Assembly Rooms at Newark, Nottinghamshire (1773-6), by John Carr where a butter market occupied the rustic ground-floor storey; the Town Hall at Petworth, West Sussex (1793), designed by the estate surveyor and furnished with a stone façade, niches and a three-bay pediment; and the Guildhall and market at Newport, Isle of Wight, which was designed by John Nash (1814) and has a three-bay pedimented main front with an open arcaded ground floor which continues down the long side elevation. A particularly intriguing example is the Town Hall and Assembly Rooms at Devizes, Wiltshire, by Thomas Baldwin (1806), which has a pedimented front elevation of conventional Palladian form and with Roman Ionic capitals, and a rear elevation with a full-height bow embellished with Ionic capitals in the emerging Grecian style.

In towns large enough to support a separate market and exchange, the town hall and guildhall were conceived as independent structures and were even, in large cities, supplemented by mansion houses designed to provide official apartments and entertainment rooms for the Lord Mayor. These town halls either follow the conventions established by the combination of exchange, market and council chamber and retain rudimentary arcaded ground floors, or they are almost entirely domestic in character.

There were very few pre-nineteenth-century attempts to establish a new architecture for local government buildings, but of these the most interesting are the Town Hall at Morpeth, Northumberland, and the Guildhall at Salisbury, Wiltshire. The Morpeth building, designed in 1714 by Vanbrugh (and since rebuilt in replica), is of the usual five-bay, two-storey composition, with a three-bay pediment and arcaded ground floor, but the end bays support massive towers formed by arches supporting pediments. Certainly this building has an authority not associated with domestic architecture. The Guildhall at Salisbury was designed by Sir Robert Taylor in 1788. Unfortunately he died five days before construction began so supervision fell to William Pilkington (a pupil of Taylor), who amended Taylor's design a little. The completed building was tampered with in 1829 (when Thomas Hopper added a Tuscan portico, as was the fashion of the day) and again in 1889 and 1896. But Taylor's intentions are still discernible. He created a tall single-storey, free-standing building, with the elevational movement of his revolutionary villa designs (p72) and with bold external elements – such as Venetian windows set within tall, rusticated relieving arches – befitting a public building. The entrance was through a Doric screen running between projecting bays and via a concave flight of steps reminiscent of the compositions of contemporary French neo-classicists. The interior is dominated by the council chamber (which is balanced by a pair of court rooms), lit by a curved bay on its long side which is expressed externally as a full-height canted bay. The central rooms are top-lit, as in Taylor's Reduced Annuity Office for the Bank of England. All in all, Taylor created a building which managed to look like neither an exchange, nor a market or town house, but instead like an impressive office.

To understand Taylor's achievement it is necessary to set the building against the contemporary domestic and exchange-type town halls and guildhalls. Good examples of the domestic type are the Guildhall, Worcester (1721-3), designed by Thomas White, which is not only an extraordinary *tour de force* in provincial baroque design (White was a mason by trade and so the building is loaded with carved stonework) but is also interesting in its general plan and proportions, recalling the traditions of almshouse design. Later examples of the domestic type are the Town Hall in Stamford, Lincolnshire (1777), which has the appearance of a particularly ambitious corner terrace house, and James Wyatt's Town Hall in Ripon, North Yorkshire (1798), a simple late-Palladian five-bay-

Above: The Council House, Chichester, built 1731-3 to designs supplied by Roger Morris: an interesting essay in Anglo-Palladian design inspired by Palladio's San Giorgio Maggiore, Venice.

Left: The Town Hall, Market Place, Blandford Forum, 1734, by the Bastard Brothers in conventional Palladian style, while their church (background) 1735-9, is in the baroque manner of the London churches built under the 1711 building act.

pedimented composition slotted into a terrace overlooking the market place.

On the other hand, the Chichester Council House, West Sussex (1731-3), like Robert and James Adam's strangely plain and awkward Hertford Shire Hall (1767-9), retains the feel of the exchange-type town hall. Designed by the leading Palladian Roger Morris, it even has a rudimentary open arcade beneath part of its ground floor, more for gossiping in than for business. This feature is shared by the Town Hall erected at Blandford Forum, Dorset (1734), by the brothers John and William Bastard, which is in a sombre Palladian style despite the baroque quality of the Bastards' work generally, particularly the adjacent church which was being erected at the same time (p111). Plainly the propaganda of the Palladian movement was beginning to influence provincial architects when designing public administration buildings, if not when designing houses or places of worship.

Interestingly, the association between Palladianism and civic formality out-lasted the Palladian fashion and became the most striking manifestation of the conservative spirit that prevailed amongst provincial designers during the nineteenth century. Good examples of the civic late-Palladian style are the Guildhall, Bath (1776), by Thomas Baldwin which is in the Palladian country house manner, a general direction still being followed thirteen years later by John Johnson when he designed a shire hall at Chelmsford (1789-91), only now the conventional Palladian composition of three-bay pediment and rusticated basement was complemented by delicate neo-classical details. More exact examples of the provincial Palladian survival in public building design are the Mayoralty House, Drogheda, Co. Louth (c1760-65), by Hugh Darley; the Town Hall, Stratford-upon-Avon (1767-70), perhaps to the design of Timothy Lightoler; the Old Aberdeen Town House (1788) by George Jaffray; Glastonbury Town Hall, Somerset (1818), by J.B. Beard, and Leith Town Hall, Edinburgh (1827), by R. and R. Dickson. But on occasions the strong conventions governing official design were broken – a notable example being the façade which George Dance the Younger added to the Guildhall, City of London, in 1789. This was in the latest 'Hindoo' style, and one can only suppose that he was able to persuade the conservative aldermen that it was Gothic, which for them would have been quite daring enough.

Another curious specimen of late eighteenth-century town hall design is the Old Town Hall, Lancaster (1781-3), by Major Jarrat which, with its four-bay Doric porch and Greek revival tower, is very church-like in appearance. This ecclesiastical look for town halls and other institutional buildings was popular in the north of Britain and not unknown in Ireland. John Baxter the Younger's Town House at Peterhead, Grampian (1788), has a steeple derived from James Gibbs's designs for St Martin-in-the-Fields (p109) as does the Town House at Berwick upon Tweed (p186) which also has a pediment supported by giant rusticated columns. The design of this building, erected c1750, was strangely enough supplied by the London builders Samuel and John Worrall who had spent most of the last thirty years building terrace houses in Spitalfields in London (p276). Another notable fact about this town hall is that it contains the town gaol in its upper floor. An Irish example is the Tholsel in Kilkenny (1761) by Alderman Colles, which has a handsome five-bay Tuscan arcade over the pavement carrying the first floor, and a pitched roof crowned by a tower (reconstructed c1960) which in its form is a three-stage octagonal lantern complete with clock and concave cap.

The inclusion of a gaol within a town hall – as at Berwick – is not as odd as it may seem, for uses other than exchanges and markets were often coupled with council chambers. The new Town Hall at Nottingham (1789) by S. and W. Stretton also contained a gaol, while the Town Halls at Richmond, North Yorkshire (1756), Deal, Kent (1803), Macclesfield, Cheshire (1823), by Goodwin, and Salford, Greater Manchester (1825), contain, like Newark Town Hall, assembly rooms (p174); and shire halls, of course, contain courts. Notable examples are that at Warwick, designed by Sanderson Miller in 1754 in fine Palladian style (pp141, 251), containing a pair of octagonal domed courtrooms (p153); that at Dorchester, Dorset (1795-7), by Thomas Hardwick with a fine, original courtroom behind an austere ashlar façade still of Roman rather than Greek inspiration; and the Town Hall at Huntingdon (1745) contains a court with original fittings as well as an assembly room.

By 1800, however, a shire hall/local government complex was under construction which reveals the direction in which this building type was to develop in the early decades of the nineteenth century. Between 1788 and 1822 Chester Castle was reconstructed by Thomas Harrison to create a county court, barracks, exchequer and gaol (now demolished). This complex, approached through a Doric propylaeum (1811) inspired by the Temple of Philip at Delos and the so-called Temple of Augustus at Athens, is dominated by a severe Greek Doric hexastyle portico (in which the columns are unfluted and without moulded bases), which stands in front of the Shire Hall of 1791-1801. Chester Castle is one of the earliest Greek revival complexes in Britain and its design is one of the most inspired – not least the design of the Shire Hall itself, which is semicircular in plan and top-lit with a semicircular coffered dome supported on free-standing Greek Doric columns, all evidently derived from Gondoin's influential École de Chirurgie in Paris (1771-6). Interestingly, just after completing this hall, in 1802, Harrison designed a shire hall/court at Lancaster in which he used roughly the same semicircular plan but with Gothic details and a Gothic vault.

This Gothic experiment, though exquisite, was not to be followed for public buildings (rare exceptions are Sir Robert Smirke's Assize Courts at Carlisle, 1810, which were inspired by the castle and town walls, and at

The pure and powerful Greek Doric of the Court House, Glasgow. Built 1807-14 to the designs of William Stark, this is one of the earliest of Greek revival porticoes.

Lincoln Castle, 1823-30); it was the Greek that was to flourish and which was to become the symbol of local government authority. In 1810, John Stokoe gave the Moot Hall in Newcastle upon Tyne a massive Doric portico, and between 1807 and 1811 William Stark designed a massive Greek Doric hexastyle portico at the Glasgow Public Offices, Court House and Gaol (now much reconstructed) which is a challenge to Smirke's Covent Garden Theatre of 1808-9 (burnt 1850) as the earliest public building to be furnished with a Greek Doric portico. The Newcastle and Glasgow buildings were quickly followed by equally temple-like shire halls all designed by Sir Robert Smirke: at Gloucester (1814); Hereford (1815), where a particularly powerful Greek Doric portico modelled on the Theseion in Athens is set between massive wings; at Perth (1815) where the County Buildings have an octastyle Greek Doric portico; and at Bristol (1824) where the old Council House has a Greek Ionic façade. Other designers of this type were John Foulston with his Greek Doric Devonport Town Hall, Devon, of 1821; Goodwin with the Town Hall and Assembly Rooms of 1823 at Macclesfield; and Thomas Cooper with his massive Brighton Town Hall, East Sussex, of 1830-32.

Apart from the temple-inspired designs there are also those Greek revival government buildings that reflect more individual or inventive architectural thinking. For example, Smirke – champion of the temple shire hall – was able to pursue a more personal classicism when designing Maidstone County and Shire Hall, Kent (1824), where he created a memorable little building that is a perfect example of his astylar stripped classical and Schinkel-influenced 'Graeco-cubic' manner (p93).

Mansion houses
Mansion houses require separate consideration. Though more ambitious in scale than town halls they were often less original in design, for they were based very closely on the country house tradition both in exterior design and internal layout. The best is the Mansion House in the City of London, designed by George Dance the Elder in 1737. It has a nine-bay ashlar front with a giant six-column Corinthian portico standing on a rustic base. Above the cornice runs an attic which originally was topped by a taller attic that formed part of the building's most notable feature: the Egyptian Hall. Here Dance, following Vitruvius as interpreted by Palladio (and preceded six years before by Lord Burlington

The Mansion House, York, built 1726–33 to a design by William Etty, inspired by Palladio's Palazzo Iseppo Porto, Vicenza, via Webb's 1662 Queen's Gallery, Old Somerset House, London.

at the York Assembly Rooms, p174) created a hall of 3:1 proportion in plan, furnished with a giant colonnade and lit by a tall attic clerestory. In 1795 this was removed by Dance's son, George the Younger, and replaced by a coffered barrel-vault of Roman severity. Other notable examples of this type are the Mansion House at York, designed by William Etty (1726) in a standard Palladian country house style inspired by Webb's Queen's Gallery, Old Somerset House, London of 1662 (p8); and the Mansion House at Doncaster which was designed by James Paine in 1745–8.

Court houses
There are those courts which, externally, assume a grand domestic appearance such as the former Court House, Warwick (1725), by Francis Smith, the Middlesex Sessions House, Clerkenwell, London (1779–82), by Thomas Rogers, and the York Assize Courts (1773–7) by John Carr, which have a grand late Palladian appearance that could equally have been applied to a town mansion or any other public building. Almost identical in appearance to Carr's Assize Courts is his Female Prison which faces it across a square.

There were also those court houses that looked like town halls or exchanges, such as that at Antrim (1726) which has an open arcaded ground floor, and there are those that are actually mixed with another use – a practice not uncommon in Ireland, where courts of law and markets often found themselves housed within the same building. For example Dunlavin, Co. Wicklow (1743), probably designed by Richard Castle, is a remarkable attempt to find a dignified Palladian form for a court room-cum-market. It is cruciform in plan, heavily rusticated, with arcades in the returns of the arms of the cross, and has a centrally placed stone cupola rising from a tall round drum. Other less striking examples are the court and market at Loughgall, Co. Armagh (1746), which has an arcaded ground floor, and the Market Cross at Barnard Castle, Co. Durham, which has an arcaded ground floor (1747) supporting a first-floor court room (1814). But perhaps the most curious mix of uses is found at Castlewellan, Co. Down, which has a court house (1764) that not only looks like a church but was actually sometimes used as one.

The elevations of court houses naturally reflected changing architectural fashions through the period, culminating in an impressive group of Greek revival court houses to show that for this type of public building, as much as for the town hall, the early nineteenth-century architect favoured the authoritative stamp of the Grecian portico. They were particularly popular in the north of England, where Charles Watson designed a number of Grecian court houses which com-

The Court and Market House at Dunlavin, Co. Wicklow, 1743, perhaps by Richard Castle, and a remarkable attempt to find a Palladio-derived architectural language for the design of a minor public/commercial building.

plemented Smirke's contemporary Greek temple-like shire halls. Outstanding among Watson's designs are Beverley Sessions House, Humberside (1804-14), which has an Ionic portico and Wakefield Court House, West Yorkshire (1807-10), with a Greek Doric portico. These two edifices must compete with William Stark's Glasgow Court House and Public Offices (of which only the portico survives), 1807-14, as being the earliest public buildings in Britain to sport a Greek portico (p16).

In Ireland there are two splendid examples of early Greek revival court houses: that at Dundalk, Co. Louth, by Edward Park and John Bowden, with a fine hexastyle Doric portico modelled on the Theseion, and Carlow Court House (1830) by William Vitruvius Morrison, with an octastyle Greek Ionic porch raised on a plinth and reached via a noble flight of stairs. It is flanked by huge, full-height faceted bays which reflect the semicircular plans of the court rooms within.

Despite these external similarities with town halls and exchanges, the court house proper did develop a highly individual plan form. As has been observed by Maurice Craig there was a tradition in England for court rooms to be open-ended and placed off a public hall.[4] The spectacle of justice being seen to be done was something that demanded a theatre-like setting, it seemed. The open-ended King's Court, which survived at Westminster until 1834, was an influential precedent, and the early seventeenth-century court house at Northampton has two courts open-ended towards a common hall. James Gandon's plan for Nottingham Shire Hall, as published in *Vitruvius Britannicus*, Vol. v, 1771 (the building had just been completed in a modified form), shows a pair of courts, each separated by a screen of columns from a large public hall – a general composition which seems derived from Sanderson Miller's court room arrangement at Warwick Shire Hall of 1754-8. Gandon introduced this arrangement into Ireland with his Waterford Court House of 1784 (now destroyed) which had the plan of the Nottingham Shire Hall as published in *Vitruvius Britannicus*, and his magnificent neo-classical detailing included lighting the high-ceilinged hall with depressed lunettes set above the cornice. This plan form – a pair of courts off, and partly open to, a large public hall – was followed at Kilkenny Court House of 1794, and Derry Court House, Co. Londonderry (1813), by John Bowden which has an imposing staircase from the hall to the first floor, in common with many Irish courts: for example at Armagh (1809) by Francis Johnston; and Port Laoise (Maryborough), Co. Laois (1812), by Richard Morrison.

The reason for this ceremonial stair was that many Irish court houses had a Grand Jury room on the first floor. In Ireland the Grand Jury was not only responsible for the building of the court but also for much of local government, so, in a sense, Irish court houses equated with English town halls. At Derry, interestingly, the openings between the hall and the court, though still emphasized with a screen of columns, are reduced in size, while at Dundalk, Co. Louth (c1815-20), the courts no longer even connect with, let alone open onto, the public hall. By 1830, at Carlow Court House, there is not even a public hall adjacent to the courts. The fall from favour in the early nineteenth century of this open-ended court was, no doubt, mainly due to practical problems such as heating and sound insulation.

The fate that befell Gandon's greatest court house – the Four Courts, Dublin – reveals neatly the decline of the open-ended court room. The Four Courts, begun by Gandon in 1786 (and incorporating a building begun in 1777 by Thomas Cooley) is among the major monuments to neo-classicism in the British Isles. With a central block fronted by an imposing giant Corinthian hexastyle portico and topped by a colonnaded drum supporting a shallow saucer-dome, the building is the epitome of late eighteenth-century austere neo-classicism. Inside the central block, four courts radiate from a huge round central hall set below the dome, and were originally only separated from the hall by a double screen of columns. Almost immediately after completion, c1802, the screens were curtained (James Malton, in his description of his print of the Four Courts, mentions 'a curtain immediately at the back of

The Four Courts, Dublin, built 1786-1802 to the designs of James Gandon; the most powerful eighteenth-century neo-classical public building in the British Isles.

154 /. *Georgian Buildings*

the columns'); then they were enclosed with timber and glass screens and now (since the reconstruction following gutting by fire in 1922) are filled with masonry. To appreciate fully the quality and scale of the Four Courts and the architectural ambition and taste of the Dublin patrons and public in the late eighteenth century, we need only reflect on the fact that in Edinburgh the comparable court building of 1804-33 by, R. Reid, is redolent of dated provincialism and notable only for the magnificent Signet Library (1812-22), which Reid, with William Stark, conceived in a monumental Roman manner with a giant colonnade of Corinthian columns. And in London legal business was conducted in a collection of ancient buildings and domestic-scaled annexes until 1825, when Sir John Soane completed the new law court at the Palace of Westminster. This building, demolished in 1883, was notable not so much for its architecture as for the architectural debate that it provoked, which revealed for the first time the immense power and moral righteousness of the burgeoning Gothic revival. Soane, who had a deep admiration for the Gothic of Westminster Hall which adjoined his site, felt that a new building should be 'composed in a style totally different'. His classical design was 'highly approved' by the King and work had begun on site when it was violently attacked in Parliament by MPs who regretted that a Gothic style had not been chosen. Work was stopped and the elevation that had been erected was eventually demolished and rebuilt in the Gothic manner.

Professional institutions

Buildings to house professional institutions and their offices developed in the early nineteenth century out of a tradition which is well illustrated by the London Inns of Court. Until the early nineteenth century, the legal profession lodged itself (with members of other professions) quite happily in apartments within more or less conventionally planned terrace houses, with their dining halls and chapels, usually in ancient buildings, arranged in the collegiate manner. A more monumental approach had been attempted at Stone Buildings, Lincoln's Inn (1774-80), when Sir Robert Taylor designed a late-Palladian ashlar-clad set of chambers with pedimented columnar pavilions, which was to be of prodigious length with a lateral corridor running the full length of the buildings and linking all chambers in each storey (unlike Chambers' contemporary offices at Somerset House which were still largely conceived as a form of the conventional terrace house plan, p147). However, this ambitious scheme was not completed. More typical of eighteenth-century initiatives is Taylor's Six Clerks' and Enrolment Office (1774-80), also at Lincoln's Inn, which is modest in scale, astylar and part of a terrace, and only exceptional for its tall (almost double-height) first-floor arched windows which must have lit a writing room behind the façade. Even early nineteenth-century terraces – such as Verulam Buildings, Gray's Inn (1805-11) – follow the external pattern of contemporary domestic terrace design. Verulam Buildings' only major concession to its function as independent chambers was the robust communal stone, iron-railed stair serving the various chambers.

As with the Four Courts, which was grander than any comparable establishment in England, it was Dublin that took the lead with the construction of ambitious, purpose-designed legal quarters. The King's Inns, designed in 1795 by James Gandon and begun in 1800, is not of vast scale but is exquisitely

Six Clerks' and Enrolment Office, Lincoln's Inn Fields, 1774-80, by Sir Robert Taylor: an early example of a purpose-built office: The double-height windows suggest the beginnings of an office building type.

detailed in a refined neo-classical Greek revival manner. It has a twin-pedimented, ashlar-clad garden front (developed by Gandon from his unused Royal Exchange competition design), topped by a colonnaded cupola (of 1816 by Francis Johnston) and a wonderfully urban gateway elevation which fills the northern end of Henrietta Street. Inside are chambers, a library and a magnificent neo-classically detailed Benchers' dining hall which is related in design to Gandon's earlier Coolbanagher Church, Co. Laois (p117).

At about the same time the surgeons built colleges for themselves in Dublin, by Edward Park, and in London, by George Dance the Younger, both designed in 1806. The Dublin building is an imposing Roman Doric design with engaged columns, while the London college was fronted by a powerful unfluted Greek Ionic portico – the first of its kind in London. This set the trend, so that Sir Robert Smirke gave the Royal College of Physicians a Greek Ionic building (now part of Canada House) in Trafalgar Square in 1822, Vulliamy gave the Law Society's hall in Chancery Lane, London, a chaste Grecian exterior in 1828–32, while in Edinburgh the Greek as the expression of the professional institute reached its peak with W.H. Playfair's Royal Institution (now the Royal Scottish Academy) of 1822–6. This magnificently sited Greek Doric temple housed the Royal Society of Edinburgh, the Society of Scottish Antiquarians, the Institute for the Encouragement of the Fine Arts and the Board of Trustees for the Manufactories and Fisheries. Additions by Playfair in 1831–5 made the building even more powerfully Greek.

Military buildings

Military buildings – gates, barracks, ordnance buildings and the like – developed a distinctive style in the early eighteenth century under the influence of Sir John Vanbrugh. Vanbrugh became Comptroller of the Board of Works in 1702, which made him the deputy to Wren, who was Surveyor of the Royal Works. From then until his death in 1726 Vanbrugh's control on the board was virtually unbroken. True, he was dismissed by the Tories in 1713, but no successor was appointed and he was knighted and reinstated by the Whigs the following year. Even after 1718, when the burgeoning Palladians managed to get Wren dismissed from his Surveyorship (a post which Vanbrugh himself had refused 'out of tenderness to Wren') and Hawksmoor dismissed from his post as Secretary to the Board, Vanbrugh remained unassailable.

Detail of W. H. Playfair's Royal Institution (now Royal Scottish Academy), Edinburgh of 1822-6. The building is a powerful neo-Greek design with excellent details.

Vanbrugh's close Whig connections put him in a position to apply his masculine 'castle' style (p76) to a peculiarly appropriate subject, while the victories of Marlborough and the threat of the Old Pretender gave him the opportunity. After 1715 there was a boom in military works. The Royal Foundry had to expand and was moved from Moorfields to Woolwich, where the Board of Works was responsible for designing the Royal Brass Foundry in 1716 and the Gun-Boring Factory and Smithy in 1717. In the same year, 1717, new barracks were begun in Berwick upon Tweed which, being on the Scottish border, was of particular importance in the campaign against the Jacobites; and the great Dockyard Gate, resembling a Roman city gate, was built at Chatham. In 1718 the Board of Ordnance Model Room was built at Woolwich, with a double-height boardroom (reminiscent of Vanbrugh's Eastbury, Dorset) and a curved bay window (p71), and in 1721 the Officers' Terrace was begun at Chatham. Though unattributable directly to Vanbrugh, all these works display something – and the Chatham Gate and the Officers' Terrace a great deal – of his bold, castle-like style, where minimal classical decoration is used, windows are round and round-arched, as in Roman fortifications, battlements and

The Dockyard Gate, Chatham, *c*1717, perhaps by Sir John Vanbrugh, and certainly reflecting his predilection for a stripped classicism with which to evoke the 'castle air' appropriate for such a utilitarian and necessarily robust structure. The analogy with a Roman city gate is obvious.

cannon balls abound as motifs (as do the latter at Vanbrugh's Blenheim Palace) and all seems to be big in conception if small in actual execution.

This spirit of spare utility influenced virtually all later eighteenth-century and early nineteenth-century military building. Fort George, Highland Region, undertaken in 1746 by William Adam, and continued by his sons John and Robert after his death in 1748, under the direction of Colonel Skinner and the Board of Ordnance, displays the unmistakable influence of Vanbrugh, for whom Robert Adam admitted a great admiration (p78). This is particularly notable in the Ravelin Gate, which is pedimented and flanked by paired Tuscan pilasters embellished with rustic blocks. A much later and equally striking example of Vanbrughian influence is Fort Clarence, Rochester, Kent (1812), which is brick-built with bold round corner towers and giant-scaled stone machicolations over an entrance front pierced with round-headed windows.

Stores, administrative and residential military building of the late eighteenth and early nineteenth centuries possibly reflect Vanbrugh's spirit of spare utility, but they also reflect the current civilian fashion, which was not incompatible with Vanbrugh's austerity: architectural fashions post-1780 favoured simplicity of external detail. Excellent examples of later military administrative and residential buildings are the Royal Artillery Barracks, Woolwich (1775-1808), which is a remarkably restrained and sustained brick composition of over 100 bays with a rather weak triumphal arch in the original centre building, and the Royal Military Academy, Sandhurst, Berkshire (1807-12), by J. Sanders, which has a long austere façade embellished with a giant Greek Doric portico. Military warehouses are discussed with other buildings of this type on page 134.

Prison buildings

No building type changed so dramatically during the eighteenth century as the prison. Before 1778 little consideration was given to the nature and purpose of penal servitude and the plans of prisons were primitive. They were housed either within structures of relatively standard design, such as the Old Gaol on the High Street, Huntingdon (*c*1770), and in Sydney Court, Shrewsbury (*c*1715), or in accord with medieval

Above: The Royal Artillery Barracks, Woolwich, London, 1775–1808. Despite the prodigious length (over 1000 ft) and the pompous centrally placed triumphal arch, the architecture is essentially domestic in character.

Below: The Female Prison (now a museum), York, 1780–83, by John Carr: a prime example of the Georgian tendency to paper the same façade over diverse building types in the interests of town planning harmony. Opposite the prison, and of identical design, is Carr's Assize and Crown Court of 1773–7.

tradition, such as the gaol/clock gate (1771) which stands astride a street in Youghal, Co. Cork. When the early and mid-eighteenth-century designer did show some special consideration for the function of the building, he left the planning to tradition and spent his time thinking about the façade – whether it should look like a grand Palladian town house, as Thomas Warr Atwood contrived at Bath in 1772, or like a suave public building, as John Carr did when designing the Female Prison in York as late as 1780 (to match his earlier Assize Court, p19). Or, in the spirit of late eighteenth-century Romanticism, he might make a fetish of the symbols of oppression, such as chains and fetters, as William Tuck did at King's Lynn Gaol (1784) or as Sir John Trail did at Kilmainham Gaol, Dublin (1796). This has a door set in a rusticated wall with a tympanum embellished with chained, entwined and snarling serpents set within a frame decorated with what appear to be writhing maggots.

A more subtle variation of this symbolic approach to prison design – which has its origins in the designs of Piranesi and Ledoux – was to create elevations of an austere brooding design – a task generally achieved by the use of the innately grave Doric or Tuscan orders, heavy rustication and block window surrounds. An early, sophisticated and subtle example of this approach is Thomas Johnson's County Gaol, Warwick (1779–82, p251), which has a long two-storey façade embellished with full-height baseless Doric columns supporting a full and heavy entablature. The epitome of this type was George Dance the Younger's Newgate Gaol, City of London (1770–80), which was impressively sombre, with a blank, heavily rusticated wall and

The Gaol, King's Lynn, Norfolk, 1784, by William Tuck. The function of the building is revealed by the ominous rusticated frontispiece decorated with festoons of shackles.

menacing details that were copied by many a provincial architect: George Byfeld gave his gaol of 1803 at Bury St Edmunds, Suffolk, a bold rusticated Newgate-like arched entrance block; G. Moneypenny embellished his Sessions House and House of Correction at Knutsford, Cheshire (1817), with heavily rusticated door surrounds inspired by Newgate; Bryan Browning, at his House of Correction at Folkingham, Lincolnshire (1824-5), combined the spirit of Newgate with the influence of Vanbrugh and Ledoux. Beaumaris Gaol, Anglesey (1828-9), by Hansom and Welch is small in scale but thoroughly forbidding, with its squat proportions, rock-faced walling and rough-textured, bold window architraves.

The transformation of that ubiquitous early nineteenth-century public building embellishment, the Grecian portico, to an awe-inspiring symbol of penal servitude is best illustrated by Cork Male Prison (1818-23, p288) by James and George Pain, which is furnished with the quintessential brooding Delian Doric portico set against a blank wall with sparsely placed, heavily rusticated windows, and by Derby Gaol (1823-7), now much altered, where Francis Goodwin used a primitive Doric order, reduced to cyclopean geometrical masses, to create an effect that must have been 'almost as sublimely terrible as Newgate'.[5] Interestingly, the other symbolic and picturesque approach, perhaps more obvious — that of rendering gaols as impregnable castle keeps or dungeons — was not popular. The few examples, such as William Wilkins the Younger's castellated Norwich Gaol (1824-8) and William Parsons' baronial Leicester Gaol (1825-8), are undeniably weak when compared with their Grecian counterparts.

Gaol plans

The plans of pre-1778 prisons followed a system established before the eighteenth century, reaching its apotheosis with George Dance the Younger's Newgate Gaol which, ironically, was completed two years after the great prison reforms got under way. At Newgate, as at Bath, the blocks, arranged around central exercise courts, were in the form of wards for communal use in which prisoners of all types mucked in together. Individual cells, few in number, were reserved for special prisoners who could afford to pay for one, or perhaps those awaiting execution. All things in these prisons were for sale or had to be bought — from privacy to the foulest food.

Virtually all the eighteenth-century gaols that survive as more than façades date from the post-1778 period (Bath was rebuilt behind its façade, York was made a museum, and Newgate was demolished in 1902), a fact which reveals how advanced (for its date) thinking on penal reform was in late eighteenth-century England, for many of these post-1778 prisons remained in use into this century.

The force behind the Act of Parliament of 1778 which reformed prison design was John Howard, who had published his influential *The State of the Prisons* in 1777 (further editions 1780, 1784). He recognized that many of the evils of prisons were due to their plan form and so, to his mind, the first step to improvement was to change the architecture. Aware of St Michael's Prison in Rome, completed in 1704 to the designs of Carlo Fontana and the first prison to have tiers of private cells on each side of a central corridor, and of the Maison de Force at Ackerghem near Ghent (1773), by Jean Jacques and Philippe Villain, where the cellular system of St Michael's was coupled with an octagonal radial plan, Howard drew up a recipe for revolutionizing prison design. This included the siting of prisons by rivers, away from towns or other buildings, with cell blocks raised on arcades to leave dry exercise courts beneath as an aid to hygiene and sanitation; segregation of prisoners according to age, sex and crime; good heating and ventilation; and ease of supervision. The 1778 act reflected Howard's concern and established 'penitentiary Houses': separate confinement with useful labour, moral and religious instruction, minimum cell sizes and regular inspection. Implementation, of course, was a different matter. The first penitentiary was not built until nearly forty years after the 1778 act, so long-term prisoners, who previously would have been transported to America, were kept in hulks moored on the Thames and off Plymouth, Portsmouth and Gosport. Although this practice was reduced after transportation to Australia began in 1787, the last hulk was not destroyed until 1857.

A further act of 1782 enshrined Howard's recommendations for the segregation of prisoners. The same year a competition was held for the design of the best penitentiary. It was won by William Blackburn, who worked very closely with Howard thereafter and was commissioned to build not penitentiaries but several county gaols, such as the one at Dorchester, Dorset (1789), where only a bold rusticated portal survives. Blackburn also designed houses of correction, such as at Littledean, Gloucestershire (1787-91), and Northleach, Gloucestershire (1787-91), which with its dour, rusticated stone façade and fortress-like elevation is a good small-scale example of symbolic prison design.

Radial plans, as envisaged and promoted by Howard, were adopted for the design of county gaols after c1800 – usually with the cell blocks radiating from a taller octagonal centre block. An early example is Wyatville's Abingdon Gaol, Oxfordshire (1805), while Robert Reid designed a four-armed radial prison for Perth in 1810 (altered 1842). The first penitentiary, that at Millbank, London, begun in 1812 to the designs of Thomas Hardwick and now demolished, was an influential radial design in which the arms were linked to form a pentagon. An example of a later radial prison survives at Port Laoise, Co. Laois (c1830), probably by James and George Pain, while at Huntingdon (1828) only the octagonal block which served as a 'watching block' survives. At Nenagh, Co. Tipperary, the octagonal block is of three-storeys with excellent neo-classical decoration and served as the governor's house, as did the centre block of Montgomery County Gaol, Powys (c1830), by Thomas Penson. The octagonal block at Shrewsbury County Gaol (1787-93) by J. H. Haycock and Thomas Telford was used to house the chapel, which was an ingredient of prison design that seems greatly to have taxed late eighteenth- and early nineteenth-century prison authorities. Howard had included a chapel in a prominent place in his ideal designs for county gaols, but it seems there was concern that prisoners might use the opportunity of meeting in chapel to hatch plots or even rebel. At both Lincoln Castle Gaol (1787) by William Lumby and perhaps John Carr and at Maidstone Gaol (1811, completed by Smirke 1817-19) by D.A. Alexander (the architect of Dartmoor Prison, which contained warehouse-like blocks for French prisoners of war, 1806-9) the chapels were contrived to prevent prisoners speaking to or even seeing each other, although all were provided with a view of the preacher.

Another important gaol form was devised in the eighteenth century but did not influence prison construction until well into the nineteenth century, and then primarily in the United States. Jeremy Bentham took the idea of the radial prison to its logical conclusion with the centralized panopticon prison, in which cells were arranged symmetrically around a central point of observation. According to Bentham's proposals (published in 1787 and 1791), the building would have been fire-proof, of revolutionary cast-iron and masonry construction, with hollow iron columns carrying rainwater and acting as flues, ventilation and heating by means of floor ducts, glass roofs with remote-controlled sun-blinds, water tanks in the roof and lavatories in each cell. These proposals would not just have added to the prisoners' comfort and safety, but would also have led to more efficient supervision and prevented prisoners slacking over their work. The earliest American panopticon – or rather half panopticon, for this building was crescent-shaped – was at Richmond, Virginia. Interestingly, it was designed in 1797 by the English architect Benjamin Latrobe, based on plans supplied by the French architect Pierre Gabriel Bugniet (centralized prisons appealed, of course, to the geometrically-obsessed French neo-classicists) and brought to America by that indefatigable amateur architect and improver, Thomas Jefferson.

Infirmaries
The infirmary had no distinct architectural character in the eighteenth and early nineteenth centuries. It was domestic in appearance, occasionally being virtually no more than a regular terrace house, such as the brick-built old hospital (c1770) in the Trinity area of Frome, Somerset; or the Horton Road Hospital, Gloucester (1813-23), by W. Stark and J. Collingwood, which is treated as a stuccoed crescent. More generally, however, they looked rather like a denuded brick-built country house stranded in town with only a central pediment for aggrandizement: for example, the London Hospital, Whitechapel (1752-77), by Boulton Mainwaring and Joel Johnson; Gloucester Royal Infirmary, designed by Luke Singleton (1758-61); Worcester Royal Infirmary (1767-70) by Anthony Keck; Salisbury General Infirmary

Bootham Park Hospital (former County Lunatic Asylum), York, by John Carr 1772-7, altered 1814: an individual form had not developed in the eighteenth century for hospitals, which tended to look like country houses or town halls.

(1767-71) by John Wood the Younger; Leicester Royal Infirmary (1771) by Benjamin Wyatt; Bootham Park Hospital, York (1772-7), by John Carr; the Infirmary, Armagh (1774), by George Ensor; and the Royal Infirmary, Sheffield (1793), by John Rawsthorne. Others had a slightly grander look, such as James Gibbs's pedimented Bath stone-faced blocks at St Bartholomew's Hospital, Smithfield, London (begun 1730); John Wood the Elder's ashlar-faced and Ionic-porticoed General Infirmary, Bath (1738); Richard Castle's magnificent Rotunda Lying-in Hospital, Dublin (1751), which has strong elevational similarities to his slightly earlier Leinster House, Dublin (p51), and has a central Doric pediment crowned with a three-stage colonnaded tower topped by a dome and obelisk; Stiff Leadbetter and John Sanderson's ashlar-faced Radcliffe Infirmary, Oxford (1759-70); John Carr's Bishop's College Hospital, Lincoln (1776-7), with a central projecting pediment and lower wings with Venetian windows; and Samuel Saxon's General Infirmary, Northampton (1791-3), which is ashlar-faced and nineteen bays long, with a three-bay pediment and end pavilions.

The main blocks were either disposed parallel to the street and set back behind forecourts, such as the Bath General Infirmary and the London Hospital, or they were quadrangular, like almshouses or colleges, such as Dr Steeven's Hospital, Dublin (1721-3), by Thomas Burgh, which has a façade inspired by Pratt's Clarendon House, London, and an arcaded central court; Guy's Hospital, London (1722-5, 1738 and 1774-8), latterly by Richard Jupp, which has a quandrangle fronting a pair of large courts; and St Patrick's Hospital, Dublin (1746-8), by George Semple, which has a pedimented rusticated ashlar front block with wings running back. This type of quadrangular arrangement was developed in scale if not in architectural quality by the Navy, which built between 1746 and 1761 Haslar Royal Naval Hospital, Hampshire, to the 1745 designs (now altered) of Theodore Jacobsen with John Turner. It had paired ranges forming three sides of a huge square, with a pediment on the centre range and arcades at ground level. The quadrangle type is also to be found at the Royal Naval Hospital (now St Nicholas' Hospital), Great Yarmouth, Norfolk (1809-11), by W. Pilkington and E. Holl, which has four twenty-nine-bay blocks, the approach being through a triumphal arch. These last two establishments were financed by the government, but most infirmaries were financed by endowment and gifts from individuals (such as Guy's) or subscription (such as the London) with the Rotunda Hospital, Dublin, being subsidized, probably uniquely, by the adjacent Assembly and Card Rooms (p175).

The use to which the rooms in infirmaries were put was explained by John Wood the Elder when describing his two-storey Bath General Infirmary in 1742:[6] five wards were on the first floor, while the basement housed offices and lodging rooms for servants; on the ground floor were the apothecary, doctors' rooms, matron's parlour and bedchamber, a room for surgeons, a committee room, the secretary's office, a room for the steward and one ward for men and one for women. It was becoming clear that the proximity of rooms of such mixed occupation was unsatisfactory. John Howard, fresh from his reform of prisons (p158), took on infirmaries, and in 1789 published his *Account of the Principal Lazarettos in Europe* in which he analysed and criticized various English and foreign hospitals. Of the Radcliffe Infirmary in Oxford he said there was a 'closeness and offensiveness of four out of the five large wards', and in the London Hospital he observed that in 'a dirty room in the cellar there is a cold and hot bath which seems to be seldom used'. Howard's revelations encouraged the design of hospitals in detached pavilions, each of which could be used for a specialized function – an arrangement which he had praised at the Naval Hospital at Stonehouse, near Plymouth (1756-64), by A. Rouchead (he also praised Haslar) – but which did not become the general practice until the mid-nineteenth century.

What did change was the architectural style which, in common with other public buildings after c1810, assumed a Greek or occasionally Gothic revival skin: for example, the Royal Sea Bathing Hospital, Margate (1820), with its four-columned Grecian portico; William Burn's hospital (now St Joseph's School) at Tranent, Lothian (1822); the massive Greek Doric Royal Salop Infirmary, Shrewsbury (1828-9), by Haycock and Smirke; St George's Hospital, Hyde Park Corner, London (1827), by William Wilkins, which has a Greek-detailed stucco skin covering an internal arrangement not dramatically different from Wood's plan of ninety years earlier; William Burn's Murray Royal Asylum for the Insane (now a hospital) at Kinnoull, near Perth (1827), which, more unusually, has a Roman Doric portico; and R. Tattersall's magnificent Carlisle Infirmary, Cumbria (1830-32), where the powerful Greek Doric portico is set against a part-rusticated wall. A rare Tudor Gothic example is Gandy's Stamford and Rutland Hospital (1826), Stamford.

Almshouses and charity schools

Almshouses were closely related to infirmaries in form, function and origin; indeed, in the early eighteenth century the word hospital was used to describe any charitable institution, be it a refuge for the sick or elderly, or schoolrooms for poor children. As Bailey's Dictionary of 1733 says, 'Hospital: any house erected out of charity for the entertainment or relief of the poor, sick, impotent or aged people.' Consequently, modest specimens of charity architecture have a similarity of appearance, though commissioned from diverse sections of society, and it was common for almshouses and charity schools (known as Bluecoat schools after the uniform commonly worn by the pupils) to be contained within the same building complex: examples are at Skiddy's Almshouses, Cork (1718-19); at Dunstable, Bedfordshire (c1719); at Sevenoaks, Kent (1724-32); at the Bluecoat School, Frome, Somerset (1726), which is embellished with an impressive statue of Charity as well as the usual Bluecoat boy and girl; and the Southwell School and Almshouses, Downpatrick, Co. Down (1733). Almshouses were generally built and supported by capital sums and endowments given by companies such as the Drapers, Hosiers or Ironmongers, by one of the companies' leading members, by trades and professions such as mariners and clergymen for the lodging of their aged and impecunious brethren or their widows, or by the local gentry and nobility to keep some of the poor off the streets or out of the parish-funded, and infinitely more uncomfortable, poorhouse, such as Switsir's Asylum, Kilkenny (1803), embellished with a fine statue of Switsir himself. Charity schools were funded in similar ways (hence the physical link with almshouses) with the aim of rescuing at least a portion of the over-abundant supply of poor children of both sexes to provide honest tradesmen and neat servants. The old building of Needham's School, Ely, Cambridgeshire (1740), bears a plaque saying 'For the instruction, clothing and apprenticing of boys'.

Perhaps the most obvious architectural manifestation of this private and often arbitrarily dispensed charity was that the structures were usually overtly archaic in design: partly owing to economy in construction and partly, no doubt, as a symbolic reflection of the grateful humility of the inmates who would not dare to aspire to anything fashionable. Right through the eighteenth century the forms these buildings took were highly traditional and reflected a taste formed in the latter part of the seventeenth century: angle quoins, bold wooden cornices, richly coloured bricks and steep pitched roofs. Almshouses of

1741 in East Street, Wareham, Dorset, still display the style of brick decoration fashionable in the 1660s; the Spalden Almshouses, Ashbourne, Derbyshire (1723), still have mullioned windows, as do those in Brent Eleigh, Suffolk (1731); the Hosyers' Almshouses (1758) by Thomas Pritchard at Ludlow, Shropshire, evoke the architecture of fifty years earlier, while Sir William Harpur's School (now the Town Hall) at Bedford (1756), although a large-scale affair, is furnished with archaic mullioned and transomed windows. Indeed, this conservatism could go to extremes. The Latin House at Risley, Derbyshire, was built in 1706 in the then-fashionable brick and stone baroque style. The benefactress in her will of 1720 endowed further school buildings which duly appeared in 1724, 1758 and 1771, all identical in design and all reflecting the style of the 1706 building.

The plan form that charity buildings took was usually quadrangular, such as the Geffrye Almshouses (now a museum), Hackney, London (1715); the Bluecoat School, Liverpool (1716); Penny's Hospital, Lancaster (1720); and the Clergymen's Widows' Almshouses, Ashbourne, Derbyshire (1768). Sometimes they were designed as straight terraces, such as the Wareham Almshouses and the mid-eighteenth-century almshouses in Spain Lane, Boston, Lincolnshire, or occasionally as linked blocks, such as the Hopton Almshouses, Southwark, London (1752). These compositions invariably included a pedimented centre containing a chapel flanked by one-storey or more usually two-storey blocks, one room deep, containing modest apartments in almhouses or classrooms in schools.

Among the mass of humble almshouses and school architecture there are, however, some outstanding and ambitious monuments which either commemorate the wealth, pride and taste of some particular benefactor or, in the case of schools, emphasize the difference between charity schools with their modest architecture and schools where pupils were selected by scholarship or religious affiliation or were supported by fees. Included among the more ambitious almshouses must be the Royal Naval Hospital at Greenwich. Built from 1664 to the 1760s, after 1694 this palatial pile provided not royal apartments but government offices and accommodation for aged and decaying seamen – indeed 1,550 were housed here by 1755. But curiously, despite the scale of the hospital, the modest architectural good manners seen at Risley were followed. The west side of the Queen Anne Block, completed in 1731 under the supervision of Thomas Ripley, who succeeded Colen Campbell, matches the 1662–9 King Charles Block opposite designed by John Webb, while the Queen Mary Block, completed by Ripley in 1743, is also humbly imitative.

More conventional yet ambitious almshouses include Sevenoaks School, Kent (1724–32), designed by Lord Burlington, which combined a charity school and almshouses in an admirable Palladian villa and wing composition; Fountains Hospital, Linton, North Yorkshire (c1725), perhaps by William Wakefield, with a heroically detailed towering entrance block and a pedimented pavilion; the Clopton Asylum, Bury St Edmunds, Suffolk (c1730), which looks just like an imposing pedimented town mansion; the Southwell School and Almshouses, Downpatrick, Co. Down (1733), perhaps designed by E.L. Pearce, which has a long two-storey brick centre block with a tall pedimented centre bay supporting a bold stone tower, linked by quadrants to brick and quoined teachers' houses; and the Marlborough Almshouses, St Albans, Hertfordshire (1736), which has a seventeen-bay centre with a three-bay pediment breaking forward. Turner's Hospital, Kirkleatham, Cleveland (remodelled by Gibbs, 1741–7), has three generous ranges around a court but is distinguished by its spectacular chapel which has a centralized plan inspired by Wren's St Anne and St Agnes, City of London (1677–80), with a vaulted ceiling and rich carving; Kingston College, Mitchelstown, Co. Cork (1771–5), designed by John Morrison for the local landowning family, takes the form of a large quadrangle with pedimented accents forming one half of a large urban square; while Blaise Hamlet, Henbury, Avon (1810–11), has almshouses picturesquely grouped as individual thatched rustic *cottages ornés* designed by John Nash. A building (not quite almshouses but a municipally supported poorhouse) that must be included in this catalogue of exotic charitable buildings is Clifton House, Donegall Street, Belfast. Built in 1774, probably to the designs of Robert Joy, it looks exactly like a late Palladian country house – with a five-bay, two-storey pedimented centre block linked by lower ranges to forward-thrusting pedimented wings – with the exception of a tall spire on an octagonal base that rises behind the pediment, a device shared by Hutcheson's Hospital, Glasgow (1802), by David Hamilton.

A few charity schools were housed in buildings of some pretension, such as the former Free School, Windsor, Berkshire (1725) which has a fine and bold Vanbrughian air, and Feoffes Charity School, Rotherham, South Yorkshire (1776), by John Platt, which

Kingston College, Kingston Square, Mitchelstown, Co. Cork, a set of almshouses built 1771-5 by John Morrison for decayed gentlefolk.

could pass as a gentleman's town house. But it was the grander educational establishments that kept school architecture abreast of fashion: indeed in 1722 Lord Burlington put it in the vanguard with his austere, correct and quintessential Palladian Dormitory at Westminster School. With its noble pedimented *piano nobile* set between an (originally) open, arcaded ground floor and square-windowed second floor, this building has a functional quality and lack of architectural hierarchy that is strikingly appropriate to its use. This is a rare quality in eighteenth-century design, in which an architectural form was generally imposed upon a brief rather than the brief generating the form. King Edward's School in Bath (1752) by Thomas Jelly is also Palladian but here, more typically, the form adopted is that developed for another use – the independently designed but not free-standing town house.

More interesting Palladian essays are William Adam's provincial tower house at Robert Gordon Hospital, Aberdeen (1730–40), and Wilson's Hospital (a school for Protestant boys), Multyfarnham, Co. Westmeath (c1760), in which the architect, John Pentland, has attempted to combine the tradition of the almshouse/charity school with the Palladian villa-with-wings composition: it has a pedimented central block surmounted by a cupola and containing an arcaded court linked by curved wings to pavilions. Ireland contains another ambitious Palladian school – indeed the most ambitious in the British Isles – the Bluecoat School, Dublin (1773–80). Although a charity school it was, in fact, strictly for Protestant boys, and as an establishment promoting the minority state religion it appears to have attracted especially generous financial support – though not enough to complete the grandiose design drawn up by its architect Thomas Ivory. As at Wilson's Hospital, there is a pedimented central block topped by a cupola and attached by quadrant wings to pavilions. Without the cupola the building would be indistinguishable from a country house.

By the early nineteenth century school plans had changed so that the great teaching chambers of the eighteenth century were replaced by smaller classrooms for individual masters: the Greek revival Mill Hill School, London (originally the Protestant Dissenters' Grammar School), of 1825–7 by Sir William Tite is an early example of the new plan. Schools also changed externally as their designers attempted either to adopt and adapt the fashionable Greek revival for the classroom, as was particularly popular in Scotland, or to recognize and reproduce the architectural character of venerable and prestigious educational establishments. Examples of the former are Dollar Academy, Central Region (1818–20), by W. H. Playfair; the Greek Doric Classical and Mathematical School, Falmouth, Cornwall (1824); the somewhat dull John Watson Hospital School, Edinburgh (1825–8), by William Burn, where a powerful hexastyle Greek Doric portico is placed in front of a long low ashlar wall punctured by windows; and the Royal High School, Edinburgh (1825–9), by Thomas Hamilton, arguably the most accomplished Greek revival building in the British Isles. Financed by subscription, central government

The Royal High School, Calton Hill, Edinburgh, 1825-9 by Thomas Hamilton: perhaps the finest Greek revival composition in the British Isles, despite the un-Greek and somewhat forced symmetry of the complex.

and municipal grants and open to all boys who reached the necessary educational standard, the school sits beside Calton Hill, its magnificent hexastyle Doric portico rising from an artificial 'plateau' faced with ashlar and containing squat pedimented gates. Inside is a magnificent oval hall.

Examples of the evocation of ancient educational traditions are found first at truly venerable institutions such as Rugby School, which received irregular Tudor Gothic additions by Henry Hakewill in 1809-13, and Harrow School, which was extended in a respectful Tudor Gothic manner by C.R. Cockerell in 1818. Later, relatively new institutions aspired to venerability - for example St David's College, Lampeter, Dyfed (1822), by C.R. Cockerell is Tudor Gothic, as is John Wilson's Elizabeth College, St Peter Port, Guernsey (1826). Early examples of pointed Gothic revival are Mildenhall School, Wiltshire (1823), by R. Abraham, and the Sebright School, Wolverley, Hereford and Worcester (1829), probably by William Knight.

University buildings

The role of Oxford and Cambridge in the development of eighteenth- and early nineteenth-century architecture in Britain is significant not just because these two universities and various colleges provided leading architects with opportunities to develop their styles, but also because, in the case of Oxford particularly, they provided a breeding ground for architectural ideas.

Oxford is remarkable for its early eighteenth-century baroque buildings, Cambridge for its early nineteenth-century Greek and Gothic revival buildings. Oxford's early eighteenth-century flowering is partly to do with the proximity of Blenheim Palace, but more to do with Hawksmoor's Clarendon Building of 1711-15, erected to house the university's printing press. It brought the architectural language of Blenheim right into the heart of Oxford, associating it with a major university building. In 1714 the hall and chapel front of Queen's College was started in a style similar to that of the Clarendon Building - thick walls cut back in layers around windows, plain block architraves and heavy keystones. The authorship of the Queen's College enterprise is confused, but the influence of Hawksmoor is clear, as is that of the prominent university figure George Clarke, Fellow of All Souls and Provost Lancaster of Queen's, who secured the Clarendon job for Hawksmoor. The final design of the Queen's College buildings may have been completed by the builder William Townesend, but certainly Hawksmoor designed the screen to the street twenty years later, in 1733.

Clarke's role in the development of the Oxford stripped-down masculine baroque style is curious: he promoted it at Queen's College and practised it at Worcester College, where

The Peckwater Quadrangle, Christ Church, Oxford, built 1706-13 to the designs of Henry Aldrich. The first eighteenth-century Palladian palace-fronted composition, it anticipates the later Campbell designs for Grosvenor Square and John Wood's Queen Square, Bath.

he designed the library block in 1720 after simplifying an initial design by Hawksmoor, and again at Magdalen, where he designed the New Building in 1733. But he was also in touch with Oxford's extraordinarily early, almost premature, Palladian phase. In 1706 Henry Aldrich, Dean of Christ Church, designed Peckwater Quad at his college. Conceived as three matching palace fronts, embellished with giant Ionic pilasters and columns beneath the five-bay central pediments rising from a rusticated ground floor, this quad anticipated the pioneering urban Palladian palace schemes in Grosvenor Square, London (Colen Campbell, p21), and Queen Square, Bath (John Wood the Elder, p32), by some twenty years. Clarke was a close friend of Aldrich, and when the latter died in 1710 Clarke inherited his sketches for a library for the fourth side of the quadrangle and altered them, and in 1717 work began on a library based on Michelangelo's side palaces at the Capitol, Rome.

But it was not only for pioneering Palladianism and baroque that Oxford was remarkable: it also pioneered the Gothic revival. In 1716 All Souls decided to expand. Clarke was a power in the College so Hawksmoor was awarded the job of designing the new North Quad. But rather than working in his usual manner, Hawksmoor developed a fanciful, almost picturesque rococo style intended to be in sympathy with the existing medieval Gothic buildings. The inspiration for the twin towers on the east side was, perhaps, Beverley Minster, Humberside, which Hawksmoor knew, but also discernible are elements from Blenheim and St Anne's, Limehouse, of 1714-30. Inside all is classical with, for example, a Venetian window being contrived behind Gothic tracery.

Cambridge also had its influential amateur. Sir James Burrough designed, in a spirited provincial Palladian style, not only the Fellows' Building (1738-42) at Peterhouse and the new front of the Principal Court (1754-6), but also the chapel at Clare College

The entrance to All Souls College, Oxford, built 1716-35 to the designs of Nicholas Hawksmoor: an important early work in eighteenth-century Gothic.

The Radcliffe Library, Oxford, 1737-49, by James Gibbs; a classical composition of a very personal kind in which more interior space is given to architectural display than to the storing or reading of books. It was England's last major eighteenth-century baroque building.

(1763). Burrough was involved in the introduction of James Gibbs to Cambridge, by asking him in 1721 to improve on Burrough's own plans for the Senate House. No doubt Gibbs improved them out of recognition and in so doing produced one of his most ambivalent designs, showing himself to be neither Palladian nor baroque but, as in his church of St Martin-in-the-Fields (p105), something fresh and original in between. Two years later Gibbs designed the Fellows' Building (1723-9) at King's College which, with its keystoned windows and extraordinary frontispiece made up of a two-storey pedimented porch beneath a Diocletian window – all topped with a massive pediment – is much more overtly baroque. Eight years afterwards, in 1737, he appeared in Oxford to design the last major eighteenth-century baroque building in England: the Radcliffe Camera, an overblown round temple to the arts occupying the centre of a square envisaged by Hawksmoor. In its detail, the rotunda makes reference to the preceding fashions of the eighteenth century: a rustic basement with alternate bays pedimented in Palladian style below pairs of giant columns, and attic windows placed as a mezzanine – above the ground floor and *below* the *piano nobile* windows – with a shape and profile which is purely baroque.

The Greek revival first appeared at Cambridge, in full force and very early, with William Wilkins' Downing College, built between 1807 and 1821. This building, with Wilkins' slightly earlier Haileybury College, Hertfordshire, of 1806-9 (built as an educational institute by the East India Company) had a great influence on the design of early nineteenth-century institutes of learning, such as Tite's Mill Hill School. Interestingly, the only Oxford building to reflect the full-blooded archaeological spirit of the early nineteenth century is the somewhat belated Clarendon Press (1826-30) by Daniel Robertson and Edward Blore, but here the inspiration is Roman rather than Greek with the entrance elevation embellished with a magnificent Corinthian triumphal arch. By this time, in Cambridge (if not at his ornate neo-Greek University College, London, of 1827-8) Wilkins had rejected Greek and was extending colleges in the neo-Perpendicular and neo-Tudor manner, as Hakewill had done earlier at Rugby (p239). He gave Trinity College the Tudor Gothic New Court (1821-5), Corpus Christi the neo-Perpendicular New Court, Chapel and other buildings (1823-7); and King's College was given neo-Perpendicular additions including a fine entrance screen (1824).

The universities of Edinburgh and Dublin contain excellent buildings but were not influential like Oxford and Cambridge, nor in the forefront of architectural development, although Edinburgh does contain the only major late eighteenth-century neo-classical university building. In 1789 Robert Adam designed a quadrangle for the university which was mostly executed after his death, with certain alterations, by W.H. Playfair (1817-26) and a dome was added by Rowand Anderson in 1887. The east front, including the entrance to the street, is more or less as Adam intended and is, indeed, one of his noblest and most heroic works. The block is embellished with a giant six-columned articulated portico in which each column is a monolith twenty-two feet high.

Trinity College, Dublin, is the most magnificent ensemble of eighteenth-century university buildings in the British Isles – from Thomas Burgh's superb library of 1712-32 to Chambers' works of the 1770s – but nearly all are imitative of London models or fashion. The main, west front, begun 1752 – grander than any eighteenth-century Oxford or Cambridge college front – is modelled on Colen Campbell's third design for Wanstead House[7] with a few baroque additions such as giant swags over the Venetian windows in the end pavilions. Long thought to be the work of two English architects, Henry Keene and John Sanderson, the building is now attributed to the English amateur architect, Theodore Jacobsen. Running back behind the entry block are magnificent ashlar ranges forming an elongated, gigantic quadrangle with pedimented terminal blocks beyond which, in

Government and Institutional Buildings / 167

The west front of Trinity College, Dublin, begun 1752 to the designs of Theodore Jacobsen and derived from Colen Campbell's third design for Wanstead House.

the north, is the pedimented dining hall designed by Richard Castle in 1741 and gutted by fire in 1984 (now being restored). Of the interiors, the most important is Sir William Chambers' neo-classical apse-ended chapel (1775–1800). Important individual buildings within the college include the Printing House, attributed to either Richard Castle or E.L. Pearce, which is an extraordinarily advanced design for its date of 1734, having a small but perfect Roman Doric temple front, and the Provost's Lodge of 1759, which is an almost direct copy of the house Lord Burlington designed in 1723 for General Wade in London (p8), which in turn was derived from an original Palladio drawing in Burlington's ownership. Interestingly, the same source inspired – though not so directly – Stephen Wright while designing his University Library, Cambridge, in 1754. The Dublin essay, attributed to John Smyth or Henry Keene, contains a magnificent interior with a typical Irish feature – common in country houses – of an architecturally embellished first-floor staircase lobby (p59).

Museums

Museum buildings were largely a late eighteenth-century creation which found expression in, and indeed expressed, the then-fashionable neo-classical ideal of the temple of the arts in which art was married to technology. Throughout Europe, in the very early years of the nineteenth century, Greek temple-inspired museum buildings were designed which reflected, 'the historicist and didactic premises of neo-classical thought [and show] a reverence for the creative achievements of antiquity, and a wish to display those achievements for the education of mankind'.[8]

In England, these aspirations were first expressed, in a very personal way, by Sir John Soane's Dulwich Picture Gallery of 1811–14, and were summed up in Sir Robert Smirke's British Museum, designed in its entirety in 1823 as a massive Greek-detailed quadrangle

The Provost's Lodge, Trinity College, Dublin, begun 1759 to designs, perhaps by Henry Keene or John Smyth, based directly on the engraving published in 1725 of Lord Burlington's London house for General Wade. In the magnificent staircase hall (*right*) the decoration is rich Palladian and very architectural.

Above: The former Royal Academy picture gallery in Somerset House, Westminster, London, begun 1776 to the design of Sir William Chambers. This is an early example of top-lit gallery design.

Below: The Pantheon Room of 1802, perhaps by John Hope, attached to Ince Blundell Hall, Merseyside. Intended as a sculpture gallery, the room is a pioneering example of an architect designing an 'antique' space in an attempt to create the right atmosphere for the display of antique objects.

round a large open court. The former building, which incorporated Soane's idea of top-lighting into museum design (as did his own house in Lincoln's Inn Fields, p44, which is too personal and idiosyncratic to be included in a general discussion of museum design) was the first entirely independent museum/gallery to be built in Britain specifically for the display of fine art objects as opposed to curios. (The old Ashmolean Museum, Oxford, 1678-83, by Thomas Wood, was for the display of natural curiosities housed in cabinets, and was not designed to create special lighting or display effects.) Galleries to house painting and sculpture collections had evolved as appendages to other buildings, such as Chambers' top-lit Exhibition Room of 1776 at Somerset House, and notably in country houses, such as Lancelot Brown's Picture Gallery of 1761-4 at Corsham Court, Wiltshire; Adam's top-lit Sculpture Gallery (c1767) at Newby Hall, North Yorkshire; C.H. Tatham's influential Sculpture Gallery and Museum at Castle Howard, North Yorkshire (1800-1); the Pantheon-inspired rotunda at Ince Blundell Hall, Merseyside (1802); and John Nash's Picture Gallery at Attingham Hall, Shropshire (1807), which has a modest but revolutionary cast-iron roof with top-lighting, anticipating Soane's Dulwich Picture Gallery.[9] The British Museum, which is related both in its scale and its architecture to the near-contemporary Glyptothek in Munich (1816) by Von Klenze, and Schinkel's Altes Museum in Berlin (1825), was followed in England by the Greek Doric temple-fronted Yorkshire Museum, York (1827-30), by Wilkins, and the Rotunda Museum – domed and circular in plan as its name suggests – at Scarborough, North Yorkshire (1828-9), by R.H. Sharp.

Dulwich Picture Gallery, London, begun 1811 to the designs of Sir John Soane. The first free-standing purpose-built picture gallery in the British Isles, it continues the top-lit gallery tradition established in the late eighteenth century.

Notes

1 Quoted in Sir John Summerson's *Georgian London*, page 118 of 1969 edition.
2 Quoted in John Harris's *Sir William Chambers*, page 97 of 1970 edition.
3 R. Chambers, *Traditions of Scotland*, vol I, 1825.
4 Maurice Craig, *The Architecture of Ireland*, page 267 of 1982 edition.
5 J. Mordaunt Crook, *The Greek Revival*, page 126 of 1972 edition.
6 *An essay towards a description of Bath*, John Wood, 1742, with editions of 1749 and 1765.

7 Published in Colen Campbell's *Vitruvius Britannicus*, vol III, 1725.
8 J. Mordaunt Crook, op. cit., pages 107-8.
9 Earlier top-lit galleries had been designed in 1787 by Soane for Fonthill Abbey, Wiltshire (demolished 1807), in 1788 by George Dance the Younger at the Shakespeare Gallery, Pall Mall (demolished 1868), and in c1797-8 by John Nash for the picture gallery at Corsham Court. The latter had a cast-iron roof which quickly failed, and was demolished in 1844.

PLACES OF PUBLIC RESORT

The architecture of entertainment had no particular or individual forms in the eighteenth century. Inns, hotels, coffee houses, clubs and assembly rooms were cast in the domestic mould, looking like terrace houses, town mansions or modest country houses, while theatre designers, with a very few exceptions, were denied the opportunity to create buildings worthy of the art. This remained the case in the early nineteenth century, except that there was a growing tendency towards monumentality: a yearning encouraged and generally satisfied by the Greek revival, which made it possible for the owners and designers of these institutions – especially clubs – to create buildings of presence, while at the same time alluding to the institutions of the ancients.

Theatres

Of all building types, theatres have been the major victims of changes of fashion and the ravages of fire since the end of the 1820s. To describe the development of the British theatre by reference to existing buildings is impossible. A mere handful of curious and modest theatres survive, which at best are but faint shadows of more important and long-destroyed theatres, such as the Drury Lane Theatre, designed by Henry Holland in 1791 and burnt down in 1809. Only five survive in any substance. There is the peculiar and miniature Theatre Royal in Richmond, North Yorkshire (1788); the Theatre Royal, Bristol, designed in 1764-6 by James Paty with a plan and section as supplied by 'Mr Saunders, carpenter Drury Lane Playhouse,'[1] which has been somewhat altered internally; Robert Adam's Theatre and Market Hall, Bury St Edmunds, Suffolk (now the town hall), which he formed in 1775 from an older building; William Wilkins' Theatre Royal in the same town (1819), which retains its modest Greek revival exterior and the original auditorium with Greek detail and circular form; and the Theatre Royal, Drury Lane, Covent Garden (1810-12), by Benjamin Dean Wyatt which, though largely rebuilt and remodelled, retains its remarkable foyers and exterior.

Elevations retained when the theatre behind has been put to a new use survive in

The interior of the Theatre Royal, Richmond, North Yorkshire. Built in 1788, it is the only surviving small-scale eighteenth-century theatre interior in the British Isles.

The galleries in the Theatre Royal, Bury St Edmunds, Suffolk, built in 1819 to the designs of William Wilkins.

surprising numbers, but are generally of social or nostalgic rather than architectural interest. The façades of modest theatres similar to that at Richmond survive in Totnes, Devon (1707); in Kendal, Cumbria (the New Playhouse of 1758 and the Shakespeare of 1784); in Lancaster (the Grand, 1782); in Brecon, Powys (the Royal Theatre, 1784); in Penzance, Cornwall (1787); and in Wisbech, Cambridgeshire (1793).

More ambitious are the façades of the theatre in Stamford, Lincolnshire (1768); the theatre and assembly rooms, Truro (1772), where the stone façade boasts medallions of Shakespeare and Garrick; the Theatre Royal, Margate (1787); the theatre off the Pantiles, Tunbridge Wells, Kent (1801-2, and soon converted into a corn exchange), which has Greek Doric embellishment; the former Theatre Royal, Castle Street, Dundee (1807), by Samuel Bell; and the Theatre Royal, Bath, which, designed in 1804 by George Dance the Younger, is a fine neo-classical composition.

Meagre as they are, however, these remains do reveal one important aspect of British theatre design in the eighteenth and early nineteenth centuries: its modesty. Unlike France or Italy, the theatre in Britain was not subsidized from public funds. It was a commercial enterprise and each company was a private business – which had to pay for itself. Consequently theatre managers were more concerned with getting the maximum number of seats in the auditorium than with creating memorable architecture either internally or externally. This necessarily pecuniary approach meant that a fully developed theatre architecture did not blossom in Britain before the later nineteenth century. Eighteenth-century theatres, being only modest affairs, were often constructed behind a terrace (where building land would have been cheaper to lease) rather than being freestanding public buildings; and their exteriors, if embellished at all, were only done out in the fashionable motifs of the day, and could as easily have been town halls (such as the Adam theatre in Bury St Edmunds), chapels (such as the theatre in Stamford), or even terrace houses (such as the theatre in Totnes and the New Playhouse, Kendal, Cumbria, 1758).

The great London theatres, like Holland's Drury Lane Theatre, his Covent Garden Theatre interior (1792, destroyed by fire in 1808) and Sir Robert Smirke's magnificent Greek revival Covent Garden Theatre of 1809 (destroyed by fire in 1855), were exceptions. They shared some of the grandeur of the French and Italian theatres of the day, of which Victor Louis' immensely influential Grand Théâtre at Bordeaux, completed in 1780, is a magnificent example. Here Louis not only gave the auditorium heroic scale by embellishing it with a giant order of Corinthian columns through which the boxes protruded, but he also envisaged the monumental, free-standing building not just as a theatre but also as an entertainment centre, suitable, with its ancillary and concert rooms, for balls and fashionable parades. Henry Holland's Drury Lane Theatre imitated Bordeaux in that there were ancillary rooms and the street façade was to have contained a coffee house, shops and taverns, but all was on a much more modest scale. Nevertheless, it virtually bankrupted the owner/manager Thomas Sheridan, who had still not completed the theatre, or paid for it, when it was burnt down in 1809. It was replaced by the existing Theatre Royal, Drury Lane, designed by Benjamin Dean Wyatt and built 1810-12, which is even more Bordeaux-like: the foyer, arranged around a magnificent rotunda, is clearly designed to accommodate glittering social display. Samuel Beazley increased the theatre's monumental urban quality in 1831, when he added a magnificent Ionic colonnade to the long side elevation. He also added an entrance portico, an odd affair with piers rather than columns which does not begin to compete with Nash's Haymarket Theatre (1820-21). Here, as part of the Regent Street improvement (p34), Nash built a giant Corinthian portico on axis with the distant St James's Square. This was the country's first real example of a theatre both conceived and placed monumentally, in order to work as part of a large-scale urban design.

More typical of theatres in London and the provincial cities is the Theatre Royal, Bristol (1764). Externally the theatre had virtually no presence in the street (the original front was replaced in the nineteenth century and again recently), and internally comfort was surrendered unconditionally to the need to maximize the theatre's capacity. As in all eighteenth-century English theatres, the pit and higher galleries were packed with benches running from side to side, with no aisle, which filled up on the basis of first come first served. The level of lighting remained constant throughout the performance, as it did until gas lighting replaced candles or oil lamps in the early nineteenth century. The atmosphere of discomfort and compression can best be felt at the Theatre Royal in Richmond, where the remains of pit benches are still to be seen.

Inns, assembly rooms and hotels

Eighteenth-century inns, assembly rooms and hotels all have their roots, arguably, in the monasteries of the Middle Ages. Indeed, right into the early nineteenth century many coaching inns were ordered on monastic principles, with the dormitory and common eating room (buttery) arranged round a cloister-like central courtyard which was en-

The courtyard of the Saracen's Head, Daventry, Northamptonshire. Dated 1769, the inn combines highly fashionable architectural details with the traditional inn plan of a courtyard and ranges of stabling.

tered through a gatehouse (or rather an arch in the main façade of the inn). The Saracen's Head, Daventry, of 1769, for example, still has a courtyard, and many others, including the George and Dragon, Yarm, Cleveland (c1760), the Talbot Hotel, Ripley, Surrey (c1740), the Bear Hotel (c1720) and the Greyhound (c1740), both in Wincanton, Somerset, have large arches in their elevations, leading to yards, stabling and various quarters.

Some inns, particularly those in high streets, may be grandiose, frequently displaying all the characteristics of pompous town houses or even mansions; good examples are the Cock Hotel, Stony Stratford, Buckinghamshire (c1742); the Swan Inn, Tewkesbury, Gloucestershire (c1780); the Rose and Crown Inn, Wisbech, Cambridgeshire (c1760); the Talbot, Towcester, Northamptonshire (c1710 and later); and the former King's Arms Inn (now Dower House), Newbury, Berkshire (c1750). But there were others which, despite all their domestic allusions, could be nothing but inns. Somehow their designers could not help over-scaling the details, out-scaling the neighbours, and adding all manner of architectural elements, motifs and symbols that proclaimed the building as a place of public gathering and entertainments.

The Old Bell Chambers, Chepstow, Gwent, a tall and austere domestic-looking

The Red Lion Inn, Blandford Forum, Dorset, *c*1734 by the Bastard brothers. The centre arch led to a courtyard and stabling.

brick building of *c*1725–30, has on one side of the door a (later) single-storey bay, announcing the presence of the tap room; the Golden Lion, Fourcrosses, Powys, of *c*1760–70 draws attention to its purpose with a glut of cheery Gothic-glazed Venetian windows enlivening its façade; the Red Lion, Blandford, Dorset (*c*1734), sports giant pilasters and a pediment containing a rampant lion; the Greyhound, of the same date in the same town, is nine bays wide and of Bavarian baroque exuberance; the George, Stamford, Lincolnshire (1724), towers above its neighbours and bears a coat-of-arms; the King's Head Hotel, Richmond, North Yorkshire (*c*1720), is too large (eight bays wide) for a merchant's town house and in the wrong position (in the market place) for a local aristocrat's residence – it has to be an inn; the same applies to the George, Buckden, Cambridgeshire; the Dolphin in Southampton possesses a pair of full-height bows that proclaim its use as a place of public resort furnished with well-lit public rooms (as does the smaller Black Bear, Wareham, Dorset, of *c*1800) and the old Neptune Inn, in Whitefriar Gate, Hull (1794), is a striking, large-scale neo-classical composition that shames the neighbouring domestic terraces. Also in this category are those familiar country town inns which have plain elevations notable only for their prodigious length and usually with a single-storey colonnaded porch thrusting out over the pavement, as for

The Black Bear, South Street, Wareham, Dorset, an excellent example of a small early nineteenth-century inn.

example at the White Hart, Spalding, Lincolnshire (c1714, with a later Tuscan porch); the Rose and Crown, Tonbridge, Kent (c1730-40); the Swan Hotel, Harleston, Norfolk (1725-30); the Wynnstay Hotel, Oswestry, Shropshire (c1760-80); the Royal Oak, Sevenoaks, Kent, with a fine Greek Doric portico of c1820; and, of roughly the same date, the Grosvenor Hotel, Stockbridge, Hampshire, which has a massive first-floor bow bursting out of its centre and supported on columns.

Inns built not by local entrepreneurs but by aristocratic landlords strike a more sophisticated pose, as in Robert Adam's remodelling in 1776 of the Red Lion, Pontefract, West Yorkshire, for Sir Rowland Wynn, and Henry Holland's remodelling (1790) of the George Inn, Woburn, Bedfordshire, for the Duke of Bedford.

By the late eighteenth century, however, the function of the inn – or at least some inns – was undergoing a radical change, for from this building type emerged something altogether more suitable for the refined tastes of the later eighteenth and early nineteenth centuries: the hotel. Hotels as we know them, with restaurants, entertainment rooms, ballrooms and the like, are really the result of a cross-breeding of the inn with the country house, undertaken to flatter the conceits and attract the custom of the richer travelling public in late Georgian Britain, who traditionally had lodged for short periods at inns, and for longer periods in domestic-style houses let out as rooms. The Grand Parade in Bath, for example, built in c1740 by John Wood the Elder, seems to have been designed especially with lodgers in mind, for the landings were extended into little bays, increasing the floor area so that furniture and packing cases could more easily be carried up and down.

It was during the 1770s that the new building type began to emerge. The first sign was the addition to traditional inns of extra rooms for entertainment, rooms to act as assembly rooms and thus to attract the cream of local society. In 1767 the Old Ship Hotel, Brighton, East Sussex acquired an ornate Adamesque assembly room (to the designs of Robert Golden), to be followed by the Lion, Shrewsbury, Shropshire (c1780, an excellent example), the Royal Clarence, Exeter, Devon in 1770, the George, Grantham, Lincolnshire, in c1790, and the Royal Hotel, Southend, Essex, in the early nineteenth century.

Hotels proper began to appear in the 1790s, although the type had been pioneered as early as 1749, when Llandrindod Hall, in the developing spa town of Llandrindod Wells, Powys, was made into a 100-bed hotel in the modern sense, with suites of rooms for balls, concerts and billiards and shops for the sale of luxuries. It closed in 1787 (but the building survives), just before the hotel building boom – which lasted into the early decades of the nineteenth century – got under way. Good early examples are the Swan Hotel, Bedford (1792), by Henry Holland, which has first-floor bows on the side elevation and, like the contemporary George Hotel, Lichfield, Staffordshire, was built complete with assembly/ballrooms; the hotel (now County Rooms) in Hotel Street, Leicester (1792-1800), by John Johnson, which has a very handsome front elevation with three huge first-floor tripartite windows and niches, and the White Hart, Salisbury, Wiltshire, with its early nineteenth-century Ionic portico. The Warwick Arms Hotel, Warwick (c1790), has an ashlar façade and five-bay elevation with tripartite windows in blank arches, which is architecturally ambitious enough to justify the name of hotel – but by the last decade of the eighteenth century the line between smart inns and new hotels was becoming both impossible and unnecessary to define. Other examples of this ambiguous transitional type – the country town inn with architectural and social pretensions – are the Salutation Hotel, Perth (c1800), with Adamesque tripartite windows under Diocletian windows; the Beaufort Arms Hotel, Monmouth, which has a fine front elevation of c1815-25 with two-storey Greek Ionic pilasters embracing the centre three bays and supporting an entablature and an attic; the Angel Hotel, Abergavenny, Gwent, of similar date with a one-bay pediment and Doric porch with columns set *in antis*; the Swan Hotel, Hay-on-Wye, Powys, of c1810-20, with a three-bay central pediment; and the Lion Hotel, Builth Wells, Powys, of c1820, which has a five-bay three-storey façade with end and centre bays breaking forward, glazed with tripartite windows except for those in the centre bay, which are normal width.

As the century progressed so the scale of hotels grew, swelled by the growth of seaside resorts and spas, by the stage-coach boom of the early years of the century, which made travelling easier and more popular, and by the travel and trade generated by the canals. For example there are imposing canal-side hotels at Stourport, Hereford and Worcester (the Tontine of 1788); at Robertstown, Co. Kildare, of c1790; at Shannon Harbour, Banagher, Co. Offaly – now standing ruined amongst abandoned warehouses – at Tullamore, Co. Offaly, and at Goole, Humberside, where the Lowther Hotel dates from c1825.

Plate from Isaac Ware's 1738 edition of Palladio's *Quattro Libri* showing the elevation and part plan of his reconstruction of an Egyptian hall. This design had a great influence on eighteenth-century architects.

But not all provincial hotels were the product of the transport boom. The Stamford Hotel, Stamford, Lincolnshire (c1810–29), by J.L. Bond is a building of truly noble metropolitan scale, with giant Corinthian engaged columns rising from a rusticated ground floor and supporting a generous entablature. Here the scale reflects the fact that the hotel was built by the Tory Sir Gerrard Noel to woo support for his campaign against the Whig influence of the Cecils at Burghley. Other good examples of the monumental early nineteenth-century hotel are the hotel in David Stephenson's New Quay and Market Place, North Shields, Tyne and Wear (1806–17), which was included as part of the large-scale urban design; Thomas Cooper's Bedford Hotel, Brighton, East Sussex (1829), which has a monumental two-storey colonnaded Greek revival entrance hall; and the Regent Hotel, Leamington Spa, Warwickshire, by Charles Smith (1819).

Assembly rooms

Assembly rooms serving small towns were often combined not only with inns and hotels, but also with theatres (Waterford, Co. Waterford, c1780), markets (Newtownards, Co. Down, 1765), town halls (Huntingdon, 1745; Richmond, North Yorkshire, 1756; and Macclesfield, Cheshire, 1823), and libraries (Wareham, Dorset, c1799, now the Royal Dorset Yacht Club). In populous provincial towns, however, they might have an independent existence. In these cases architectural forms varied tremendously, the most architecturally ambitious being in York. Designed in 1731 by Lord Burlington, this was an archaeological essay on the reconstruction of an Egyptian hall as illustrated by Palladio in 1570. Significantly, the same design was also to be used in the City of London's Mansion House of 1737 (p151) and, in various forms, in churches (p61) and country houses (p61). The main façade at York was altered in 1828, but the interior survives as a room 112 feet long and 40 feet wide (nearly a 3:1 proportion), lit by an attic clerestory, and provided with a narrow aisle formed by a colonnade of giant Corinthian columns that runs round all four sides of the room. North of the Great Assembly Room is a smaller, much plainer Lesser Assembly Room reached through the screen of columns, and a cube and a round room. South of the Great Room were the offices and kitchen.

Less architecturally ambitious (York, after all, is the earliest neo-classical/archaeologically based interior in Europe) though larger in scale, are the New Assembly Rooms, Bath, designed in 1769 by John Wood the Younger. Containing ballroom, tea room and an octagonal card room, the building has a finely proportioned Palladian façade with pedimented windows at first-floor level and square attics above. The interior, which was damaged by bombing in 1941, contains restrained neo-classical plasterwork and ceilings and, in the ballroom, a giant coffered niche serving as a musicians' gallery.

Perhaps the most satisfying of all surviving assembly rooms is the Rotunda in Parnell Square, Dublin. This building – or rather group of buildings – is a remarkable survival, and almost complete. The governors of the Lying-in Hospital, begun in 1751 to the design of Richard Castle, sought to create an income for the hospital by building assembly rooms on an adjacent site. This took the form, initially, of an 80-foot-diameter rotunda with a flat ceiling, completed in 1764 to the design of John Ensor. A card room (now destroyed) linked the rotunda to the hospital. In 1784 additional accommodation was built, to the designs of Richard Johnston, which took the form of an L-shaped building with a ballroom in one arm, embellished with a shallow groin-vaulted ceiling supported on four pairs of columns, and in the other an elongated oval tea room. The main external elevation of these additions – to Cavendish Row – was treated with a splendid disregard for the

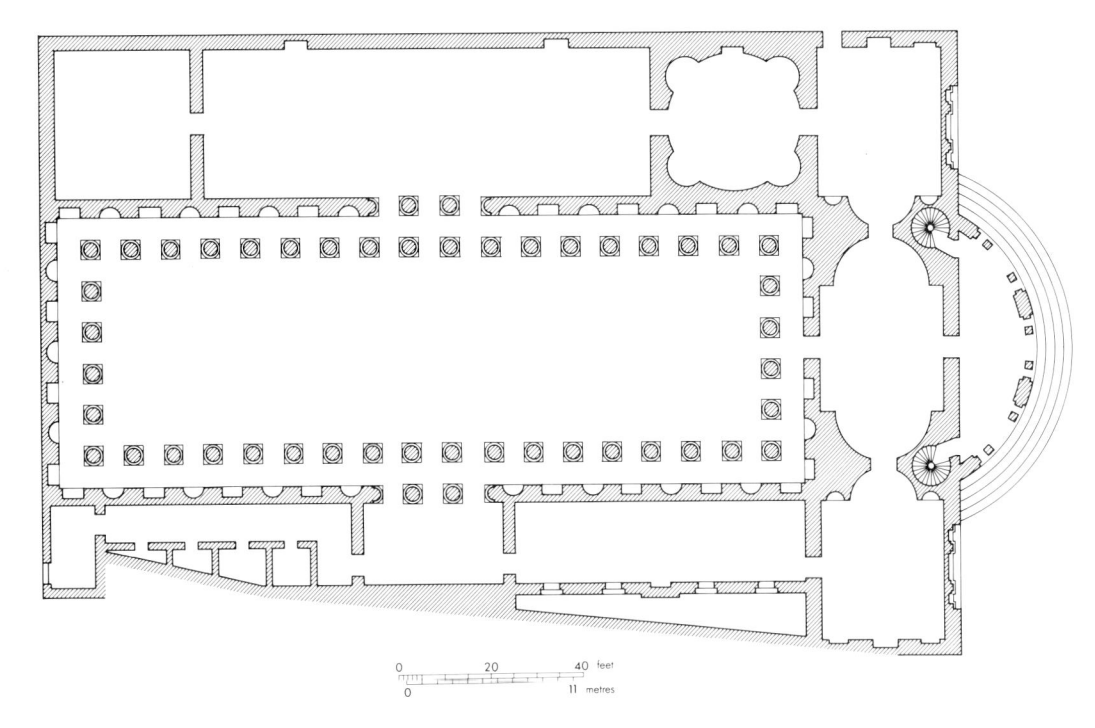

Above: The plan of the Assembly Rooms, York, as it was before later alterations.

Left: The interior of the Assembly Rooms, York designed in 1731 by Lord Burlington and inspired by Palladio's Egyptian hall.

Below: The Rotunda Assembly Rooms, Dublin. The most evocative of eighteenth-century assembly rooms, they were built in 1764 to the designs of John Ensor and extended from 1784 by James Gandon, who heightened the 80ft diameter drum and added the entrance pavilion.

problem of relating interior to exterior: the architect merely applied an imposing elevation derived from the published design of Adam's Kenwood House, in which the ground floor is windowless and what appears to be the main entrance, placed beneath the central pediment, leads into a closet off the tea room. At about the same time, James Gandon provided a proper main entrance leading directly into the Rotunda, which takes the form of a square neo-classical pavilion, each of its elevations being a play upon the theme of a triumphal arch. Gandon also, in c1785, raised the external wall of Ensor's rotunda and decorated it with Coade stone panels and a bucranium frieze.

A rotunda was also the form chosen for another remarkable building of public resort – the Montpellier Pump Room, Cheltenham, Gloucestershire. This is an exquisite building designed in 1817 by G.A. Underwood and enlarged by J.B. Papworth in 1825. Externally there is a single-storey colonnade reminiscent of the one that flanks part of the Dublin Rotunda, and the interior is dominated by a domed room lit by an oculus in the manner of the Pantheon in Rome. Other notable pump rooms – which must be regarded as specialized assembly rooms – are the Pittville Pump Room, Cheltenham, 1825–30, by John Forbes, and Thomas Baldwin's Pump Room,

Bath. The Pittville Pump Room has an exterior colonnade formed by Doric columns based on Stuart and Revett's engravings of the Temple on the Ilissus, and an excellent interior with a pendentive ceiling supporting a dome. The Pump Room, Bath, begun in 1791, is in a monumental and slightly dull late Palladian manner: only the Ionic colonnade linking the main building to the pavilion is especially memorable. The interior, perhaps completed by Palmer, has a huge rectangular room with a clear span of 60 by 46 feet, whose walls are embellished with giant engaged Corinthian columns rising directly from the floor, as in an Egyptian hall.

More typical of provincial assembly rooms are those in Stamford, Lincolnshire (1727); in Newcastle upon Tyne, designed in 1774 by William Newcombe and embellished with pediment and engaged columns; in Chichester, West Sussex, by James Wyatt (1781-3), which contains a large and austere room within a simple brick shell; in Edinburgh's New Town, designed by mason David Henderson in 1784 with a portico added in 1818; in Clifton, Bristol (1806), by Greenway and Kay, which is temple-fronted; and the Wellington Room, Liverpool (1815), by E. Aikin, which is of wonderfully severe Greek design.

In Scotland in the early nineteenth century assembly rooms took Greek revival form, with good examples in the County Assembly Rooms, Aberdeen (c1820-22), by A. Simpson and the Exchange Coffee Room, Castle Street, Dundee (1828-30), by George Smith. The latter's monumental façade has Greek Ionic columns over a Greek Doric order, while the interior contains a coffee room, reading room and library, as well as the assembly room.

Clubs and reading rooms

The development of the club – both as a building type and as a social institution – belongs to the period after 1830. In the eighteenth century various politically orientated clubs were indeed housed in purpose-built structures, but these were modelled closely on grand domestic prototypes, assembly rooms or institutional buildings. Boodle's, St James's Street, London, designed by John Crunden in 1775, echoes Robert Adam's Royal Society of Arts building in the Adelphi, with the notable later addition of a ground-floor bow similar to those on the drinking rooms of contemporary inns. Henry Holland, architect to the 'Grand Whiggery', designed (as would be expected) the Whig Brooks's Club, St James's Street, in 1776 in an unaffected and severe Graeco-Palladian manner. In 1787 James Wyatt designed the Tory White's Club (refronted in 1852) in the same street.

The pioneers of the building form that was developed by later nineteenth-century clubs are Decimus Burton's Athenaeum and John Nash's United Services Club (now the Institute of Directors), which face each other across Waterloo Place, St James's. The Athenaeum was begun in 1827, the USC a year earlier, and both are arranged around magnificent staircase halls, with a dining room on the ground floor and spacious reading rooms and drawing room above. Externally, the USC was remodelled in 1842, but the Athenaeum is boisterously Greek – with a frieze copied from the Parthenon– as is the slightly earlier (1822) Union Club by Smirke which, with its Greek Ionic portico, survives as part of Canada House, Trafalgar Square. But the Greek revival was not to be the style of the London club: by 1829 Charles Barry, at his influential Travellers' Club, Pall Mall, had introduced the Italianate into club architecture.

The West End type club was well established in provincial towns and cities by the early nineteenth century (but the membership was naturally rather different). In Liverpool the Lyceum, designed in 1800 by Thomas Harrison, is an extremely early and fine example of the Greek revival. It has a giant Greek Ionic pedimented portico set *in antis* for its front elevation in Bold Street, and giant engaged columns on the side elevation, and inside are a ground-floor reading room and a domed library. A perhaps more typical example of a provincial club is the Athenaeum, King Street, Stirling (1814-16), by W. Stirling. This is a determinedly provincial building which sprouts a tower and spire that, in Scotland, remained a desirable embellishment for any sort of institutional or semi-public building – for example Hutcheson's Hospital, Glasgow (1802-5), by David Hamilton, which has a tower and spire still inspired by Gibbs.

Another Athenaeum, of 1822, in Union Street, Aberdeen, reveals how the club overlapped with an institution unique to the early nineteenth century, for this Athenaeum is not a club as such but a reading room. Literary and Philosophical Institutes, subscription reading rooms and libraries grew up in the wake of the growth of the educated middle classes, in the atmosphere of sobriety that characterized English society after 1815. The garb these buildings took was almost exclusively Greek. Representative examples are the Mechanics' Institute, Wakefield (1820), the Literary and Philosophical Institutes in Bristol (1821-3) by C.R. Cockerell and Newcastle (1822) by John Green, and Barry's powerful

178 / *Georgian Buildings*

Above left: The Greek revival garden front of the Athenaeum, Pall Mall, London, 1827-30 by Decimus Burton. Beyond it is the Italianate façade of the Travellers', 1829-39 by Sir Charles Barry. Both were pioneering buildings in the development of club architecture.

Above right: The Bold Street frontage of the Lyceum Club, Liverpool, 1800-2 by Thomas Harrison. A very important transitional building, it has bold Greek details, anticipating the Greek vogue of the following decade, set in a façade of late eighteenth-century neo-classical form.

Left: The entrance hall of the Royal Institution of Fine Arts (now City Art Gallery), Manchester, designed 1824-35 by Sir Charles Barry in a sophisticated Greek revival manner. Greek revival was the customary style for reading rooms, literary and philosophical institutes and libraries, institutions which first appeared in the early nineteenth century.

Institution of Fine Arts (now City Art Gallery), Manchester, of 1824–35, which is influenced by Schinkel's Schauspielhaus, Berlin, and has a magnificent double-height entrance hall.

Reading rooms and mechanics' institutes were designed by Thomas Harrison in Manchester in 1802 (the Portico Library) and Chester in 1804 (the News Room), the same year in which Thomas Johnson designed Leeds Library.

Note

1 Quoted in Richard and Helen Leacroft's *Theatre and Playhouse*, 1984, page 102.

Plan of Boodle's Club, St James's, at ground level. Although similar in many ways to a large-scale town house, the plan form that characterizes the nineteenth-century gentlemen's club is beginning to emerge. A, morning room; B, bar, with coffee room above.

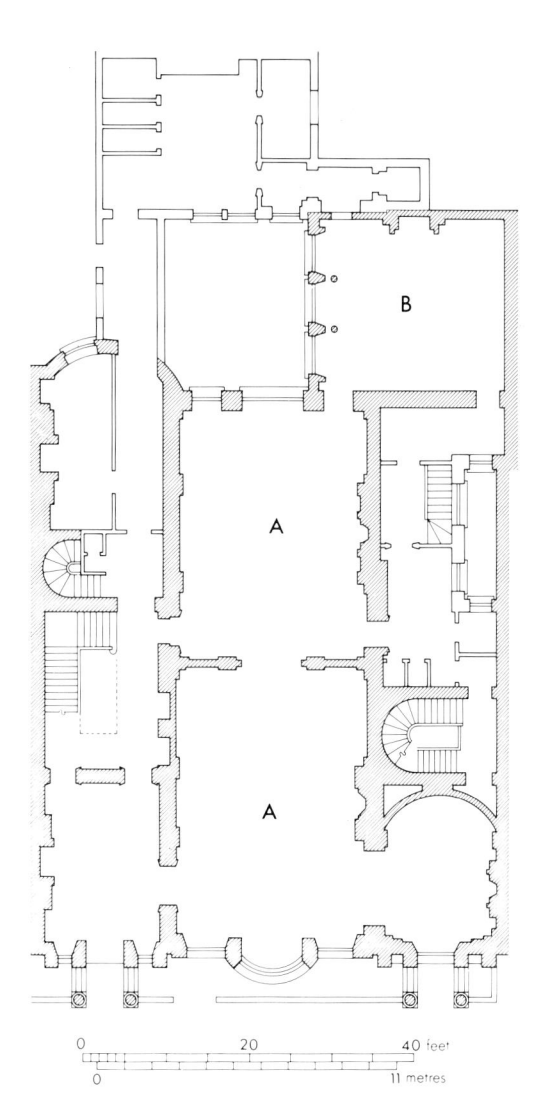

Boodle's Club, St James's Street, Westminster, 1775, by John Crunden.

GAZETTEER GREAT BRITAIN

See separate sections for London (p260) and Ireland (p284).

Abbotsford, Borders
3m W of Melrose
By William Atkinson, 1816–23. Early and influential Scottish baronial-style house. Picturesque skyline. South-west wing by William Burn, 1853.

Aberdeen, Grampian
St Andrew's Cathedral, King Street, by Archibald Simpson 1816, Gothic.
St Nicholas's Church West, nave rebuilt 1752–5 to design of James Gibbs. Simple ashlar exterior; inside, nave arcade formed by square piers supporting arches.
South Church, King Street, by John Smith 1830, Gothic.
North Church, also in King Street and by Smith 1830, but Greek revival with Ionic portico.
County Assembly Rooms, by Simpson *c*1820, in Greek revival manner.
Athenaeum Reading Rooms, Union Street, 1822.
Robert Gordon Hospital, 1730–32 by William Adam.
Old Aberdeen Town House, High Street, George Jaffray, 1788, in simple Palladian manner.
In **King Street,** uniform, granite-faced 3-storey houses of *c*1825 with arcaded ground floor.

Aberfeldy, Tayside
Bridge over River Tay, 1733 by General Wade; ramped parapet supporting obelisks.

Abergavenny, Gwent
Angel Hotel, Cross Street, early C19; 5 bays, 3 storeys, with centre bay breaking forward and pedimented; porch formed by columns set *in antis*. Also in **Cross Street, 13,** with full-width pediment containing pointed, Gothic-glazed window. **39,** with Regency pedimented door.
1–19 (odd) **Nevill Street** form excellent, varied group: No. 7, *c*1725, with pedimented door, segmental windows; 11, *c*1730 but refronted *c*1800.
In **Frogmore Street,** many modest C18 and early-C19 3-storey façades above shops, most rendered, some with cyma recta block cornices, such as **59, 60, 61,** and **13** with similar cornice in brick; **171-8,** *c*1830, form impressive 6-bay, 3-storey group with 2-bay pediment, arch leading to yard. This paired floor plan form also found at **67,** and at **7 Cross Street.**
Tan House, Mill Street, *c*1760, 3 by 1-bay, 3-storey brick box.
14-24 Monk Street, 2-storey group dating from *c*1790–1830.
2 Lower Monk Street, *c*1820, Doric porch. **4,** of similar date, with pedimented doorcase, coved eaves cornice.

Abingdon, Oxfordshire
Town Hall, 1678–80 by Christopher Kempster, with giant pilasters and open arcade, represents a type imitated in C18.
Gaol, 1805–11 by Sir Jeffry Wyatville; radial plan with octagonal centre.
Brick Alley Almshouses, beside churchyard, 1718–20 by Samuel Westbrooke, with giant arches containing balustraded 1st-floor galleries.
Tomkins' Almshouses, Conduit Road, *c*1733. 2 single-storey ranges.
Stratton House, Bath Street, dated 1722, by Benjamin Tomkins. Segmental windows, Doric pilastered doorcase topped by window flanked by pilasters.
Twickenham House, East St Helen's, *c*1760, with 3-bay pediment, Ionic columned porch. Inside, Chinese Chippendale staircase.
57 East St Helen's, dated 1732. Chequer brick, 5 bays with middle bay framed by pilaster strips.

Acton Hall, Gloucestershire
11m W of Nailsworth
3-storey brick house of *c*1760 with 5-bay front in conventional late-Palladian manner, centre 3 bays breaking forward and with pediment.

Adlestrop, Gloucestershire
4m W of Chipping Norton
Adlestrop Park, rebuilding of monastic ruins, 1750–59, by Sanderson Miller in his characteristic rococo Gothic manner.

Adlington Hall, Cheshire
4m E of Wilmslow
House C15–18 with main entrance in west range of *c*1750: magnificent portico, dated 1757. Perhaps by Charles Legh.

Airthrey Castle, Central Region
3m N of Stirling
Robert Adam, 1790. D-shaped mansion in Adam's symmetrical castle style.

Alcester, Warwickshire
7m W of Stratford-upon-Avon
St Nicholas's Church. Body by Edward and Thomas Woodward, 1729–30. Gothic exterior, classical interior, windows remodelled *c*1870.

Aldenham, Hertfordshire
2m NE of Bushey
Hilfield, Hilfield Lane, originally known as **Sly's Castle,** *c*1795 by Sir Jeffry Wyatville. Castellated; gatehouse contains portcullis.
North of Edge Grove, **Wall Hall,** *c*1802, castellated and turreted.

Aldingbourne House, West Sussex
4m E of Chichester
Villa of *c*1800, 2 curved bays on west front, south

front with central curved bay window and 2-storey iron veranda of c1814.

Alkrington Hall, Lancashire
2m s of Heysham
Designed by Giacomo Leoni, 1735. 7 bays and 3 storeys, 3-bay frontispiece framed by Ionic pilasters on rusticated ground floor. Plain entrance hall on axis of dining room flanked by pair of stairs of different sizes. Oak-panelled saloon on 1st floor with dado decorated as rusticated masonry.

Allerton
See Liverpool.

Allerton Mauleverer, West Yorkshire
7m E of Harrogate
St Martin's Church. Rebuilt c1745 in Norman or 'Saxon' style. Early evocation of this style. Perhaps by John Vardy.

Alnwick, Northumberland
Lion Bridge 1773 by Adam brothers.
In town, **Northumberland Hall,** Market Place, 1826 in Greek revival manner.
In Hulme Park, north-west of town, **Brizlee Tower,** 1777-83, again Gothic by Adam.
South of Alnwick, **Swansfield House,** 5 bays, by John Dobson 1823.

Alscot House, Warwickshire
3m s of Stratford-upon-Avon
Batty Langley-style rococo Gothic design of 1750-64 built by John Phillips.

Althorp, Northamptonshire
5m NW of Northampton
C16 in origin but largely remodelled during C18. Entrance hall, 1733 by Roger Morris, double-height with coffered ceiling. 1787-91 Henry Holland remodelled exterior and part of the interior – Blue Sitting Room, c1790. Other rooms contain features designed c1760 by James Stuart for Spencer House, London. **Stable** by Roger Morris c1732, with centre inspired by Inigo Jones's St Paul's, Covent Garden.

The stables at Althorp, Northamptonshire, c1732 by Roger Morris, with pediment inspired by Inigo Jones's St Paul's, Covent Garden.

Alton, Hampshire
Midland Bank, High Street, c1740. 5 bays with 3-bay pediment.
6 High Street, 6 bays, 3 storeys with pair of Venetian windows, c1730-40.

Alton Towers, Staffordshire
6m N of Uttoxeter
Garden of C19 house spectacular, with building of 1818-22 by John Buonarotti Papworth, including **bridge, Grecian** and **Gothic temples,** domed **conservatory, pagoda,** and **prospect tower** of c1824 by Robert Abraham. Also a **Choragic Monument** and a **Stonehenge.**

Amersham, Buckinghamshire
Baptist Church, off High Street, with pyramid roof and lantern, 1783.
Griffin Hotel, High Street, early C18.
Badminton House, Church Street, c1725.
Rectory, Church Street, 1732-5, centre embellished with blank giant arch and pediment.
Elmodesham House, High Street, early C18.
Piers Place, High Street, c1735.

Amesbury Abbey, Wiltshire
In Amesbury
Webb's house of c1660 rebuilt along lines of original, 1834-40, by Thomas Hopper.
Chinese Temple, 1772, by Sir William Chambers.

Amisfield Mains, Lothian
1m NE of Haddington
Garden temple and **icehouse,** c1750-60, perhaps by Isaac Ware. **Stable,** 1785 by John Henderson.

Ampthill, Bedfordshire
White Hart, Dunstable Street, early C18.
Avenue House, Church Street, finest house in town, built 1780 with simple 5-bay red brick façade, enlarged 1792-5 by Henry Holland.
37 Church Street, early C18, centre projection incorporating porch.
Beside church, **Dynevor House,** dated 1725; chequer-patterned brick façade. Doorway with fluted pilasters. Opposite, **Brandreth House** with door peculiar to this part of Bedfordshire (see Clophill). Flanking columns bend forward without capitals to become brackets supporting hood.
Ampthill Park, built 1694, perhaps to designs of Wren or William Wynne; redecorated and enlarged by Sir William Chambers 1769-71.

Anfield
See Liverpool.

Antony House, Cornwall
4m W of Plymouth
1720-24, probably to design of James Gibbs. Very plain exterior. Forecourt closely resembles design in Gibbs's *Book of Architecture* of 1728.

Apley Park, Shropshire
3m N of Bridgnorth
Symmetrical castellated Gothic house of 1811 by John Webb. Good Gothic interior.

Appleby, Cumbria
White House, Boroughgate, dated 1756. 3-storey, 3-bay corner house, all windows with Gothic ogee tops. Opposite, **Red House,** 1717.

Arbury Hall, Warwickshire
3m SW of Nuneaton
Outstanding rococo Gothic composition of c1750, produced by 'committee of taste' which included Sanderson Miller, Henry Keene, William Hiorne (cf Strawberry Hill; see Twickenham under London, Richmond upon Thames). Particularly

impressive is saloon's vaulted plaster ceiling by William Hanwell.

Ardrossan, Strathclyde
w *edge of Saltcoats*
Laid out in regular manner by Peter Nicholson, 1806, for Earl of Eglinton. 2-storey houses survive in Princes Street and Montgomerie Street.

Ardwick
See Manchester.

Arlington Court, Devon
6m NE of Barnstaple
1820, by Thomas Lee in good austere Greek revival manner.

Arncliffe Hall
See Ingleby Arncliffe.

Arniston, Lothian
3m s of Dalkeith
By William Adam 1726. Provincial Palladian with touches of baroque; double-height entrance hall with lavish rococo plasterwork by Joseph Enzer. West wing 1753 by John Adam.

Arundel, West Sussex
Castle, medieval but some additions of 1791–1815 by Robert Abraham survive rebuilding of *c*1890, notably library of 1801 with wooden sexpartite vaulting.
  In the park, **Hiorne's Tower,** *c*1790 by Francis Hiorne; triangular plan, Gothic detailing.
  Norfolk Arms, High Street, excellent large coaching inn, *c*1760–80, with centrally placed tall arch topped by wide arched window. **Nos.17, 19,** low, 2 storeys, eaves cornices, 19 with excellent pedimented door on consoles, *c*1720–40. **28,** *c*1780, Doric pedimented door with unusual incised triglyphs. **30, 32, 34,** 5-bay group of *c*1725–30 with Venetian windows to end 1st-floor bays; all with later shops, *c*1800–20, No.30 especially good. **37, 39, 41,** group with shallow 1st-floor canted bays of *c*1760–80. **57,** of *c*1820 with arcaded ground floor. **61,** large 5-bay, 2-storey house of *c*1760 with eaves cornice and pedimented Doric door. **63,** early C18. **65,** C18 with shop-front. **Arundel House,** *c*1740–50, with brick dentil cornice – an Arundel speciality; see 13, 37–41 High Street, 33 Tarrant Street.
  42–54 (even) **Tarrant Street,** good late-C18 group, 46–8 and 50 with paired doorcases.
  Arne Street, formed with irregular groups of late-C18 cottages.
  5–25 (odd) **Surrey Street,** regular 2-storey terrace dated 1821, with shared pedimented doors, 5 with good, bold contemporary shop. In Maltravers Street, series of good terrace houses. **3 (Worcester Lodge)** with blue headers and red brick dressing, brick dentil cornice, pedimented door, *c*1780; **10,** *c*1714. **13 (Duff House),** *c*1770–80 with pretty Doric door. **16,** *c*1740–60 with pair of full-height clapboard-clad bays flanking stone-pedimented door. **14,** similar composition but smaller and simpler. **15,** large house of *c*1740 with later porch. **17, 19, 21,** group of *c*1800. **25, 27, 29,** *c*1725–35, 2 storeys, modest, like almshouses, mullioned windows. **26 (Old Market House),** *c*1820 with pretty neo-classical porch. **45, 47, 49,** large, 3-storey rendered houses of *c*1830, **51** with 1-bay central pediment, pedimented door as at No.3. **52,** with pair of 2-storey canted bays flanking rudimentary pierced porch of *c*1830; lower ranges, one with excellent tripartite window set beneath arch decorated with blank fanlight and bat's-wing stucco moulding. **57–61** (odd), excellent 3-storey group of *c*1790, formed by 2 pairs, raised pavement.

Ascot Place, Berkshire
4m SW of Windsor
*c*1760, 2 storeys with 7-bay entrance front, pediment over 3 centre bays; some details C20.
  In grounds, near lake, **grotto,** apparently C18.

Ashbourne, Derbyshire
  Spalden Almshouses, beside church, 1723, 2-storey building round 3 sides of a courtyard and still with very conservative detail such as low 2-light mullioned windows.
  Cooper's Almshouses, Derby Road, 1800, simple 2-storey brick terrace with emphasized centre.
  Clergymen's Widows' Almshouses, 16–22 Church Street, 3-storey quadrangular composition dated 1768.
  Green Man and Black's Head Hotel, St John's Street, *c*1750–60.
  The Mansion, Church Street, 5-bay, 3-storey front of 1764, perhaps by Joseph Pickford, with projecting centre containing 3-storey composition of Tuscan porch and Venetian window topped by lunette. Interior includes domed octagonal music room of 1764–5 with rococo plasterwork. Entrance made 2-storey in 1784 when furnished with wrought-iron stair balustrade.
  Grey House, 61 Church Street, *c*1760; stone with pair of full-height canted bays flanking 1-bay pedimented centre embellished (like The Mansion and 42-4 St John's Street) with Doric porch topped by Venetian window and lunette.
  Hulland House, 40 Church Street, late C18.
  24–6 Church Street, *c*1725 with giant Ionic pilasters (façade now roughcast); **28 Church Street,** similar date with shell-hood.
  Dove House, Dovehouse Green, early-C18.
  42–4 St John's Street (now **Boots**) with centrepiece formed by 1st-floor Venetian topped by Diocletian window (porch lost?).
  37 St John's Street with upstairs room painted with pastoral scenes *c*1830 by one of local Bassano family.
  Lloyds Bank, Compton Street, *c*1775, ashlar with elements identical to 44 Friar Gate, Derby (qv), attributed to Pickford.

Ashdown House, East Sussex
3m SE of East Grinstead
By Benjamin Latrobe, 1794. Ashlar villa showing early use of Greek revival details. Porch has 4 Ionic columns with capitals modelled on those of Erechtheion. Staircase with lotus-leaf capitals to columns on landing.

Ashman's Hall, Suffolk
2m W of Beccles
House of *c*1810 in Wyatt manner. 9-bay east front with domed bow, quadrant office wing, Ionic colonnade on entrance front.

Ashridge Park, Hertfordshire
3m N of Berkhamsted
Begun by James Wyatt, 1808–17; completed and extended by Sir Jeffry Wyatville. Huge scale, asymmetrical plan, Gothic style. Spectacular interiors, especially staircase and chapel.

Aske Hall, North Yorkshire
2m N of Richmond
Large Gothic **garden temple** of *c*1740–45, possibly by Daniel Garrett.

Aston Hall, Shropshire
3m SE of Oswestry
By James Wyatt, 1789–93. 7-bay, 2-storey front framed by arched niches and blank ovals topped by garlands. Inside, restrained decoration, imperial staircase beneath dome.

Atcham, Shropshire
3m SE of Shrewsbury
Severn Bridge, 1769–71 by John Gwynn. **Tern Bridge,** 1774 by Robert Mylne.

Attingham Hall, Shropshire
3m SE of Shrewsbury
By George Steuart, 1783–5. 11-bay entrance front decorated with pediment supported on attenuated columns. Principal rooms on ground floor decorated in style of Wyatt; best is circular boudoir retaining highly coloured wall painting. Staircase and important top-lit picture gallery by John Nash, 1807–10, with coved cast-iron roof. (National Trust)

Audley End, Essex
1m N of Saffron Walden
Temple of Victory, 1772, **Palladian Bridge** and **teahouse** of 1782–3, all by Robert Adam, who remodelled interior of house 1763–5.

Avington, Hampshire
4m NE of Winchester
St Mary's Church, 1768–71. Brick embattled north tower. Door with Gibbs surround.

Aynho, Northamptonshire
5m SW of Brackley
St Michael's Church, 1723–5, possibly by local mason Edward Wing, provincial baroque.

Ayot St Lawrence, Hertfordshire
4m NW of Welwyn Garden City
New St Lawrence's Church, designed 1778 by Nicholas Revett, is one of the first buildings in England to display Greek revival motifs. Designed as an eye-catcher; columns of entrance front are based on those of Temple of Apollo at Delos.

Babraham Hall, Cambridgeshire
6m SE of Cambridge
1829–32 by Philip Hardwick; early example of Jacobean revival.

New St Lawrence's Church, Ayot St Lawrence, Hertfordshire, designed 1778 by Nicholas Revett and one of the first buildings in England to display Greek revival details.

Badger Hall, Shropshire
5m NE of Bridgnorth
James Wyatt's house of *c*1780 destroyed, but his **Pigeon House** survives, modelled on Tower of the Winds, Athens.

Badminton House, Avon
11m N of Bath
Completed 1691, perhaps to design of John Webb, but exterior and interior altered and embellished by William Kent, *c*1740. Staircase *c*1760.
 Worcester Lodge, in grounds, splendid decorated Palladian garden building by Kent, 1746. Especially good is dining room on first floor with seasons moulded in plaster. Also in grounds, **Ragged Castle, Castle Barn, Root House, Thatched Cottage,** 1748–56 by Thomas Wright; and **St Michael's Church,** designed by Charles Evans, completed 1785 as abbreviated version of St Martin-in-the-Fields with neo-classical details.

Baggrave Hall, Leicestershire
7m NE of Leicester
House of *c*1750 containing in drawing room mid-C18 Jacobean revival plasterwork.

Balbirnie House, Fife
1m N of Glenrothes
By Richard Crighton, 1815–19, Greek revival manner; Doric entrance portico. Inside, neo-antique gallery with series of saucer domes and Diocletian windows.

Baldersby (formerly Newby) Park, North Yorkshire
5m N of Ripon
Villa designed by Colen Campbell and built by William Etty, 1718–26. Therefore one of the earliest, and possibly the first, C18 Palladian villas. 2 storeys with pediment on giant columns. Interior damaged by fire 1900.

Baldock, Hertfordshire
 9 High Street, early Georgian, 5 bays, façade embellished with an order of giant rubbed red brick Corinthian pilasters with carved stone capitals and entablature.
 21 High Street, late C18, 7 bays with centre 3 projecting slightly and carrying a pediment into which rises the arched centre window.
 10–14A High Street all early Georgian, 14A the grandest, dated 1728.
 Simpson's Brewery, High Street with surviving large **Brewer's House** (No.23) looks *c*1750.
 43 Hitchin Street, 5 bays with lower wings, dated 1735.

Banbury, Oxfordshire
 St Mary's Church, 1792–7 by S. P. Cockerell. Square nave with shallow dome carried on Ionic columns, showing residual influence of Wren's St Stephen's, Walbrook, while treatment of both interior and exterior reflects Piranesian obsessions with scale. Cylindrical tower and semicircular porch by C. R. Cockerell, 1818, inspired by Archer's St Paul's, Deptford (see London); chancel 1873.
 Castle House, off Cornhill, *c*1750. 7 bays with hood on carved brackets over door.
 40 South Bar Street, dated 1784, 8 bays, Venetian window over arch with Coade stone-embellished door; **53** with Doric porch; **Linden House,** 1734 with giant pilasters and Gibbs door.

Barlaston Hall, Staffordshire
5m s of Stoke-on-Trent
Villa, 1756-8, almost certainly by Sir Robert Taylor. One of earliest and most important of the small compact country houses built during 'villa boom' of mid-C18.

Barnard Castle, Co. Durham
Market Cross, Market Place. Octagon of 1747 surrounded by Tuscan colonnade with pent roof, above which rises courtroom of 1814 with alternating Venetian windows and niches.

19, 21, 31-3 Thorngate are C18 **weavers' houses** of 3 storeys with long row of windows divided by stone mullions on top floor to light weavers' workshops. No.33 dated 1722. **8 Thorngate,** elegant late-C18 house of dressed stone.

36 The Bank, dated 1742, with rusticated quoins and segmental pediment.

Barnsley Park, Gloucestershire
4m NE of Cirencester
Dated 1720-21 and designed, perhaps by John Price, in vigorous West Country baroque manner. South elevation is 7 bays wide with 5-bay recessed centre and closely spaced Corinthian pilasters topped with attic; a composition which relates to Vanbrugh's King's Weston, near Bristol, of 1712. Interior contains large hall with good baroque/rococo plaster of c1731. Dining room c1780, by Anthony Keck.

Barnstaple, Devon
Guildhall, High Street, 1826 by Thomas Lee, faced with Ionic pilasters and pediment.

92 High Street, early C18 with good cornice; **97,** c1714 with giant angle pilasters.

Derby Lace Works, Vicarage Street, 1796-1821.

Trafalgar Lawn, Newport Road, development presumably c1805, includes 4-bay villa with Tuscan ground-floor colonnade in centre.

Barrington Park, Gloucestershire
10m w of Witney
Palladian, 1734, attributed to Henry Joynes.

Basildon Park, Berkshire
7m NW of Reading
House designed in a late-Palladian style by John Carr, 1776.

Entrance lodges, c1776, based on Tower of the Winds at Athens. (National Trust)

Bath, Avon
St Swithin's Church, London Street, Walcot, by John Palmer. Body 2 storeys with Ionic pilasters between windows, 1777-80; tower and sharply tapering spire, c1790. Inside, 6 giant Ionic columns, supporting entablature and flat ceiling, rise from shallow plinths.

Octagon Chapel, behind Milsom Street, opened 1767. Plan by Timothy Lightoler.

Lady Huntingdon's Chapel, Walcot Street, opened 1765. Round-headed windows with Gothic tracery; inside, Gothic gallery of 1783. Attached to chapel, **Minister's House,** 3 bays with canted bay furnished with ogee-topped Gothic windows and battlemented parapet.

General Infirmary (now **Royal Mineral Water Hospital**), 11-bay Palladian composition with 3-bay pediment; begun 1738 to design of John Wood the Elder.

King Edward's School, Broad Street. 2 storeys with 3-bay pediment, by Thomas Jelly 1752-4.

Pulteney Bridge, Robert Adam, 1764-74, loosely derived from designs by Palladio. Now altered.

New Assembly Rooms, John Wood the Younger, 1769-71, restored after bombing. Large-scale Palladian composition. (National Trust)

Old Gaol (now flats), Grove Street, 1772 by Thomas Warr Atwood in somewhat old-fashioned Palladian style which had become a Bath peculiarity by late C18.

Guildhall, High Street, 1776 by Thomas Baldwin. Externally in the Bath Palladian tradition though with some contemporary Adamesque details, but inside contains some fine, austere and fashionable neo-classical elements, especially cast-iron stair balustrade. Building extended in C19.

Great Pump Room, Abbey Churchyard, 1791-2 by Thomas Baldwin, completed 1793-6 by John Palmer.

Theatre Royal, Beauford Square, with entrance front of 1804 by George Dance the Younger; ashlar with fine neo-classical detail.

Among earliest houses of the period in Bath are **General Wade's House** in Abbey Churchyard, c1720, with rudimentary use of Palladian giant order, **5 Trim Street** of c1725 with use of pilasters to emphasize centre bay of elevation, and 3-storey, 5-bay **Rosewell House,** Kingsmead Square of 1736 by John Strahan with its rich baroque livery.

North side of **Queen Square,** 1729 by Wood the Elder, marks beginning of uniform Palladian development of Bath. 7 houses united in a 23-bay symmetrical compositon dressed with giant pilasters and columns and embellished with 5-bay central pediment and 3-bay end pavilions. At northern end of west side, 3 houses of c1730 by Wood united in single pedimented composition.

Beauford Square, c1732 by John Strahan, created with 2-storey uniform terraces embellished with segmental doorhoods, and full Doric entablature at parapet level.

Fountain House, Lansdown Road, c1735-40. Lively Palladian composition with central 1-bay pediment above Venetian window.

Old Orchard Street. Representative Palladian (c1740) uniform terrace. 3 storeys, pedimented 1st-floor windows, architraves to 2nd-floor windows, block cornice.

Pierrepont Street, c1740; **North** and **South Parades** and **Duke Street,** c1739-44. Of similar design and mostly erected under supervision of Wood the Elder. Also **North Parade Buildings,** c1750 by Thomas Jelly.

41 Gay Street. A more unusual design by Wood the Elder, 1740. Corner formed by 3-storey semicircular bay embellished with a variety of tripartite windows with Gibbs surrounds.

Bladud Buildings, London Road. By Jelly and Atwood, 1755, in manner of Wood.

The Circus, designed by Wood the Elder with Wood the Younger, 1754-66. Highly original design inspired by Colosseum, Rome, each storey embellished with an independent order of columns.

Royal Crescent, begun to design of Wood the Younger in 1767 and embellished with giant Ionic engaged columns rising from an ashlar ground floor, completes development sequence from Queen Square (1729-36) through **Gay Street** (c1735-55), The Circus (1754-66) and **Brock Street** (c1763-7) to the Crescent.

Good examples of loosely uniform late-Palladian streets are **Alfred Street,** c1772; **Bennett Street** and **Russell Street,** both begun 1773; and, slightly more inventive, **St James Parade** of 1768 by Jelly, where houses have large 1st-floor Venetian windows; **Walcot Parade,** London Street of c1770, stepped terrace on raised pavement; **The Paragon,** long, curving uniform terrace begun 1768 by Atwood.

Somersetshire Buildings, Milsom Street. Thomas Baldwin, 1781-3; neo-Palladian design with neo-classical details.

Cross Bath and **Bath Street Colonnade,** 1787 and 1791 respectively and built by Baldwin, are good examples of late-C18 spa architecture.

Great Pulteney Street, begun 1789 by Thomas Baldwin. Very regular, in the Bath Palladian tradition, 1100ft long and 100ft wide. Blocks of building given subtle emphasis with pilastered centres and end pavilions. **Argyle Street** and **Laura Place,** both by Baldwin, 1789, in same development and architectural style.

Lansdown Crescent, 1789-93 by John Palmer, a long, curving composition high above the town.

Somerset Place, a shallow crescent of c1790 by John Eveleigh, has its centre embellished with a giant baroque segmental pediment which embraces the 2 centre houses. His slightly earlier **Camden Crescent,** begun 1788, is more conventionally Palladian with central pediment and giant order. Of same type, though with pilasters only to pedimented centre, is **Norfolk Crescent,** c1790-1810, probably by Palmer.

Grosvenor Place, London Road, 1791 by Eveleigh, with centre embellished with giant columns sporting eccentric decoration, and **St James's Square,** 1791-4 by Palmer, are versions of urban tradition established by Wood 50 years before. Pattern continued into the early C19, but with more pronounced neo-classical and then Greek revival flourishes. For example: **Cavendish Crescent,** c1814-30; **Cavendish Place,** 1808-16, which has excellent ramped string courses and cornice; and **Sion Place,** all by John Pinch.

Pinch also built, in Bathwick, **New Sydney Place,** 1808, particularly handsome 4-storey terrace with ramped string course and cornice.

Also in Bathwick, hexagonal **Sydney Gardens,** by Charles Harcourt Masters, who built, in 1796, terminating feature at end of Great Pulteney Street, still thoroughly Palladian **Sydney Hotel** (now **Holbourne Museum**). Masters also responsible for design of **Widcombe Crescent,** 1805, which has interesting feature of paired, arched entrance doors within larger relieving arch with tripartite windows above; and of **Widcombe Terrace,** also 1805.

Buildings of most individual importance in Bath after 1800 are, first, J. M. Gandy's **Doric House,** Sion Hill, c1810, an advanced Greek revival composition; and second, **Beckford Tower,** Lansdown, designed c1825 by H. E. Goodridge, with Greek revival detail including top stage derived from the Choragic Monument of Lysicrates. Also by Goodridge, Italianate villas, especially asymmetrical **Montebello,** 1828, on Bathwick Hill; and **The Corridor,** off High Street, 1825, with bold neo-classical façade, Doric columns at ground level flanking shops.

Prior Park, Combe Down, just south of Bath. Built 1735-48 by Richard Jones to designs of Wood the Elder, who borrowed openly from Campbell's unbuilt 1715 design for Wanstead. East wing built to design by Jones; west wing rebuilt 1844; interior of house rebuilt after fire in 1836. In grounds, **Palladian Bridge,** 1755-6, probably to designs of Wood the Elder.

Widcombe Manor, Widcombe, built c1727 in flamboyant provincial Palladian style, not far from out-and-out baroque. 2-storey, 5-bay entrance with centre 3 bays breaking forward and topped by pediment. Frontispiece emphasized by paired, squat Ionic pilasters beneath pediment.

Beaumaris, Anglesey (Gwynedd)
On coast 4m NE of Menai Bridge
Gaol of 1828-9 by Hansom & Welch. Excellent, sinister structure with massive stone piers, sombre tripartite entrance door and rock-faced wall above.

On the Green, a **terrace** of 6 houses of 1824 by John Hall.

Beaumont Lodge, Berkshire
In Old Windsor
C17 house 'improved' by Henry Emlyn in 1789 using his 'British Order', composed of paired columns (analogy with oak tree) joined by Order of the Garter symbol with capitals composed of oak leaves, acorns and feathers.

Beckley, East Sussex
5m NW of Rye
Church House, dated 1744 on hopper head but looks c1720. 5-bay front framed by pair of giant Doric pilasters, centre 1st-floor window arched.

House next to church, c1720. Wood cornice, hipped roof.

Bedford, Bedfordshire
Town Hall (formerly **Sir William Harpur's School**), 1756; ashlar, 5 bays, 2 storeys, centre 2-bay pediment with 2 broad windows flanking niche. All windows have 2-light mullions.

Swan Hotel, 1794, by Henry Holland in austere neo-classical style.

Beech Court, Avon
6m SW of Bristol
C15 with early-C18 stone entrance front in local baroque manner: pilasters at corners of façade and emphasizing centre bay.

Belchamp Hall, Essex
3m W of Sudbury
House of c1720, still in C17 Wren tradition. Alterations dated 1790.

Belcombe Court
See Bradford-on-Avon.

Belle Isle, Cumbria
On island in Lake Windermere, 1m SW of Windermere town
Important early archaeologically inspired house, designed c1775 by John Plaw. Circular in plan with attached portico based on the Pantheon, Rome.

186 / Georgian Buildings

Belleville (Balavil) House, Highland
2m NE of Kingussie
Neo-classical essay on Palladian tower house, designed 1790 by Robert Adam.

Belmont Park, Kent
4m S of Faversham
Fine example of neo-classical house as developed by the Wyatt brothers. This one by Samuel Wyatt, 1787-92. Shallow bows, Coade stone plaques set in mathematical tiles. Fine drawing room and library with grained walls.

Belper, Derbyshire
Textile and spinning industrial town founded by Jedediah Strutt and Richard Arkwright in 1776. Most mills demolished 1956-64 except **North Mill** of 1803-4, with 'fireproof' iron structure.
    Mill workers' housing in **Long Row**, and **North** and **South Rows**, c1790. In **William, George** and **Joseph Streets 'cluster housing'** comprised of 4 houses built back to back, c1795.
    St Peter's Church, by Matthew Habershon 1824, neo-Perpendicular.

Belsay Hall, Northumberland
7m SW of Morpeth
By Sir Charles Monck for himself (with later help from John Dobson), 1806-17, in the most stunning, austere and powerful Greek revival style. Stone façades virtually blank, adorned only with widely spaced pilasters, full Doric entablature, Greek Doric portico set *in antis*. Windows merely holes in façade, without mouldings. Inside, 2-storey colonnaded hall; excellent Greek decoration.
    Belsay village, c1820-50, 2-storey terraces with open ground-floor arcades.

Belvoir Castle, Leicestershire
6m SW of Grantham
House of 1650 remodelled 1801-c1830 by James Wyatt, Benjamin Dean Wyatt and Matthew Cotes Wyatt. Externally, wonderfully romantic asymmetrical castle; interior classical.

Benham Park, Berkshire
2m NW of Newbury
Large, austere Graeco-Palladian house designed by Henry Holland and Lancelot Brown 1774. Altered in 1870.

Beningborough Hall, North Yorkshire
7m NW of York
Begun c1712, completed 1716. Probably designed by William Thornton, perhaps with advice from Thomas Archer. Entrance front articulated by rusticated pilaster strips and topped by heavy cornice with console brackets. (National Trust)

Berkeley Castle, Gloucestershire
11m W of Nailsworth
In grounds of castle, C18 and early-C19 castellated **kennel, lodge** and **deer house.**
    In town, early-C19 **Town Hall;** C18 **Berkeley Arms Hotel,** 7 bays with carriage arch; in grounds of C18 vicarage, picturesque thatched **hut.**

Berkley, Somerset
2m E of Frome
Church of St Mary the Virgin, 1751, containing delicate rococo plasterwork in dome. Perhaps designed by Thomas Prowse.

The Town House, Berwick upon Tweed, c1750-55, designed by Samuel and John Worrall under the influence of Vanbrugh and James Gibbs.

Berrington Hall, Hereford and Worcester
3m N of Leominster
Graeco-Palladian house designed by Henry Holland and perhaps Lancelot Brown, built 1778-81. One of the best of Holland's works. Stone, with giant tetrastyle Ionic portico. Main rooms on ground floor with rich and well-preserved interiors. (National Trust)

Berwick upon Tweed, Northumberland
    Town House, c1750-55, built by Joseph Dodds to designs supplied by Samuel and John Worrall of Spitalfields, east London, who were obviously influenced by work of Vanbrugh and James Gibbs.
    Barracks, 1717-19 and 1725 in Vanbrugh-inspired utilitarian baroque Office of Works style, possibly by Andrews Jelfe of the Ordnance Department, or Dugal Campbell.
    Garrison Hospital, Ravensdowne, early C18.
    Custom House, 18 Quay Walls, good austere neo-classical house of c1785.
    Former **Governor's House,** Palace Green, c1725, centre flanked with giant pilasters.
    Grammar School, Palace Street East, 1754.
    King's Arms Hotel, Hide Hill, mid-C18, 6 bays, 3 storeys; flanked by **house** with 4 Venetian windows.
    Union Chain Bridge, early suspension bridge, 1820 by Samuel Brown.
    Lions House, Windmill Hill, c1820, tall, free-standing.
    Various plain mid-to-late C18 **houses** in **Marygate,** 32-6 **West Street, Hide Hill** and **Quay Walls** – Nos.4-5 with pedimented doors, 21 with 4 Venetian windows. In Ravensdowne, good groups of early-C19 **houses,** especially Nos.2-16; also **Wellington Terrace** of 1820-25.

Betws-y-Coed, Gwynedd
13m S of Conway/Conwy
Waterloo Bridge, dated 1815, by Thomas Telford, with decorated cast-iron spandrels.

Beverley, Humberside
The Hall, Lairgate (now **council offices**), large, early C18, with later-C18 stone frontispiece.
Ann Routh's Hospital, 28 Keldgate, 1748 by James Moyser, with arcaded, pedimented façade looking c1800. Similar striking arcaded front to former **Tymperon Almshouses,** Walkergate, apparently of c1732.
Sessions House, North Bar Without, 1804–14 by Charles Watson, with large Ionic portico.
Guildhall, Register Square, has courtroom of c1765 with rococo ceiling, contemporary joinery.
Beverley Arms Hotel, North Bar Within, 1744 by William Middleton.
Many C18 **houses,** especially in **Ladygate, Saturday Market** and **55–63 North Bar Within,** c1740.
Girls' High School, Norwood, 1765, probably by Thomas Atkinson, with magnificent 5-bay, 3-storey façade crowned by full-width pediment. Inside, excellent rococo decoration.
Good late-C18 **shop** at junction of North Bar and Hengate; another in Market Place.

Bewdley, Hereford and Worcester
St Ann's Church. Body provincial baroque of 1745–8 by Edward and Thomas Woodward, tower 1695.
Bridge by Thomas Telford, 1745–9.
Manor House, High Street, c1720 but in late-C17 manner.
19 Load Street, large 9-bay, 4-storey house with 3-bay pediment of c1740–50. Also in Load Street, composition of 3-bay, 3-storey **houses** with 2-bay pediment flanked by pair of Venetian windows.

Biddick Hall, Co. Durham
3m NE of Chester-le-Street
Red brick, 5-bay, 2-storey house of c1723 which displays strong influence of Vanbrugh (who was working 3 miles away at Lumley in 1721). Centre bay framed by pair of giant Ionic pilasters supporting 1-bay pediment. Inside, good early-C18 wrought-iron and stone cantilevered staircase. Some neo-Georgian alterations of c1955.

Biddlesden, Buckinghamshire
5m NW of Buckingham
St Margaret's Church, 1730, with Gibbs windows.

Billinge, Merseyside
3m N of St Helens
St Aidan's Church, 1718. Mixture of individually rendered classicism and Gothic survival. Church extended 1908.

Bilston, West Midlands
SE edge of Wolverhampton
St Mary's Church, Oxford Street, 1829–30 by Francis Goodwin. Gothic, polygonal apse.

Binley
See Coventry.

Birchington, Kent
4m W of Margate
Quex Park. Large, rendered, somewhat dreary mansion of 1813. In park, two **towers.** One, round, castellated and of brick, was for firing cannon from. Other contained a peal of bells: known as Waterloo Tower and completed in 1819, it is topped by cast-iron battlements and an astonishing slender openwork spire and flying buttresses, inspired by tower of Faversham Church (qv), and made entirely of cast iron.

Birmingham, West Midlands
Cathedral of St Philip, Thomas Archer, built 1709–15; tower 1725.
St Paul's Church, St Paul's Square, 1777–9 by Roger Eykyns, still firmly in Gibbs tradition of St Martin-in-the-Fields but minus portico. Tower, in spirit of Gibbs, dates from 1823.
Holy Trinity, Camp Hill, Bardesley, 1820–23 by Francis Goodwin in neo-Perpendicular style.
Midland Bank, Waterloo Street, 1830 by Rickman & Hutchinson.
1 Jennens Row, red brick, good wooden doorcase, c1760.
St Paul's Square, c1790, not uniform but all of brick, generally of 3 storeys, 3 bays, most with pedimented doorcases. Good examples **1, 12–14, 34.**
St Martin's Place, terrace of red brick cottages with casement windows, c1800.
5 and **7 St Peter's Place,** c1790.

Bishop Auckland, Co. Durham
Bishop's Palace, medieval origin but much mid-to-late C18 work including Bishop Trevor's Gothic Gatehouse of 1760 by Sir Thomas Robinson. Screen wall and inner gateway by James Wyatt, 1796, Gothic with buttresses and corner tower. Inside, best C18 rooms are those by Wyatt arranged as formal processional way from chapel. Staircase hall of 1794 with spacious but plain imperial staircase, top landing supported over hall on Gothic piers of clustered shafts and foliage capitals. Drawing Room and Bedroom c1775–80 in neo-classical fashion and possibly by John Carr.
In park, curious Gothic **deer house** of 1767.
Bishop Auckland Castle, Gothicization by James Wyatt, c1795, of medieval castle.

Bisley, Gloucestershire
3m E of Stroud
Several ashlar houses in local baroque tradition, including **Jayne's Court,** c1720–30; **The Mansion,** c1725–40 (extended c1800); and **Rectory Farm,** dated 1743 on internal roof timber.

Blackburn, Lancashire
St Mary's Cathedral, St Peter's Street, 1820–26 by John Palmer in Commissioners' Gothic manner.

Blairquhan, Strathclyde
5m SE of Maybole
Tudor Gothic, inspired by Wilkins' Dalmeny (qv). Interior classical except for 2-storey Gothic saloon, 1820–24 by William Burn.

Blairuachder, Tayside
7m NW of Pitlochry
Farm of 1797 by George Steuart, symmetrical and classical with much blank arcading.

Blaise Castle House, Avon
NW edge of Bristol
House of c1795 by William Paty and John Nash, extended in late C19.

Blaise Hamlet, Avon
1m beyond NW edge of Bristol
Picturesquely grouped almshouses, in form of *cottages ornés*, by John Nash, 1811. (National Trust)

188 / Georgian Buildings

Blandford Forum, Dorset
Church of St Peter and St Paul, 1735–9 by John and William Bastard in style dependent on post-1711 London baroque churches.
Town Hall, Market Place, 1734, also by Bastards but notable for Palladian, not baroque design.
Red Lion Inn and **Greyhound Inn,** both built by the Bastards c1734 in the Market Place following fire of 1731. Both in provincial baroque style typical of the Bastards.
Also in Market Place, **3-house** composition with crowning pediment in style similar to Red Lion, c1734, also by John Bastard, as is **1 West Street** with 1-bay pediment.
Couper House, Church Lane, c1734 by the Bastards, again with central pediment supported by pilasters.
6–8 Salisbury Street, cottages with mathematical-tile cladding.

Blenheim, Oxfordshire
1m s of Woodstock
Palace by Vanbrugh 1705–16, completed by Hawksmoor 1722–3.
Chapel completed by Hawksmoor 1726–31.
Woodstock Gate, Hawksmoor 1727.
Column of Victory, Roger Morris 1730.
Bladon Bridge, Vanbrugh c1710–16.
Temple of Flora and Diana, Sir William Chambers 1766–75.

Blundeston House, Suffolk
3m N of Lowestoft
Sir John Soane, 1785–6. Compact 2-storey house with tripartite ground-floor windows.

Bognor Regis, West Sussex
The Dome, 1787, late-Palladian in style but with solecisms that suggest design by local builder.
Early-C19 semi-detached **houses** in **Waterloo Place**; and **Sudley Lodge,** High Street, Italianate villa of 1827, by John Shaw.

Bolton, Greater Manchester
Holy Trinity Church, Trinity Street, 1823–5 by Philip Hardwick in neo-Perpendicular Gothic.

Bonsall, Derbyshire
1m s of Matlock
A C18 and C19 centre of framework knitting. Just east of cross in **Market Place** is one of the few remaining **frame workshops** with large ranges of windows on each floor and external stairs. In **The Dale** another, dated 1737 over ground-floor door, with external stair to 1st floor which is lit by range of mullioned windows.

Boreham House, Essex
4m NE of Chelmsford
Dated 1728, probably built by Edward Shepherd to designs of Henry Flitcroft. Austere Palladian exterior. Wings altered by Thomas Hopper, 1812; Tuscan porch c1840.

Boston, Lincolnshire
Assembly Rooms, Market Place, 1826, with canted 1st-floor bay on Tuscan columns. Also **Theatre,** 1777, gutted.
Exchange Buildings, Market Place, 1772. 15-bay uniform terrace with 3-bay pediment.
Almshouses, Spain Lane, c1750, pedimented.
Fydell House, 1726, façade embellished with giant pilasters.

Part of an extraordinary uniform terrace of c1740–60 at 124–36 High Street, Boston, Lincolnshire. The façade articulated by pilaster strips makes a powerful urban composition.

20 High Street, fine house of c1760. **124–36,** extraordinary uniform terrace of c1740–60 with façade articulated by pilaster strips, forming recessed bays for windows and doors.
In Pump Square, late-C18 3-storey houses of various designs, best **No.2,** 2 bays, all windows tripartite, elongated pedimented door.
On the river, good irregular group of brick **warehouses** of c1820–30, presenting hipped gables to river.

Bourne, Lincolnshire
Sessions House, 1821 by Bryan Browning. Curious Greek revival composition with deeply recessed centre topped by pediment.

Bourne Park, Kent
4m SE of Canterbury
Early C18, 13 by 4 bays, 5 bay pediment breaking forward. Inside, excellent staircase looks c1720.

Bourn Hall, Cambridge
8m W of Cambridge
Earlier house remodelled by John Adey Repton, 1817; early example of Elizabethan revival.

Bourton-on-the-Water, Gloucestershire
10m SW of Chipping Norton
St Lawrence's Church, tower 1784 by William Marshall, stocky, framed by angle pilasters.

Bowden House, Wiltshire
3m S of Chippenham
1796 by James Wyatt. 2 storeys with bold 2-storey bay to garden façade, ringed with free-standing Ionic columns and flanked by tripartite windows within relieving arches.

Bowood House, Wiltshire
2m SW of Calne
House by Henry Keene and Robert Adam demolished 1955. Adam's south 'Diocletian wing' remains.
Many structures survive in grounds, including **cascade** of 1775, **grotto,** and Adam's bold neoclassical **mausoleum** of 1761–4.

Boyles Court, Essex
sw *edge of Brentwood*
Designed by Thomas Leverton, 1776. Austere, urban, late-Palladian exterior.

Bradbourne, Kent
4m w of Maidstone
Large 2-storey house with 3 very different brick fronts disposed in most peculiar way. Mainly completed *c*1714, though incorporating earlier house; further alterations *c*1770, *c*1774. Entrance (north) front is most modest of the façades, but sets theme with wonderfully wrought, brightly coloured red brick in two tones. West front higher because of extra length of ground-floor windows, with 3-bay pedimented centre. South front has 1-storey, 9-bay centre block with large 3-bay bow of *c*1775, flanked by 3-bay, 3-storey wings embellished with fine brickwork and framed by giant pilasters. Brickwork and some of design mannerisms invite comparison with nearby Finchcocks and Matfield Manor House, which may well have been by the same hand. Inside, collection of details from various dates: good staircase of *c*1714; 2-storey panelled entrance hall with coved ceiling; room on south front with Adamesque detail, *c*1775.

Bradford-on-Avon, Wiltshire
Baptist Chapel, St Margaret's Street, 1798. Pointed windows with Y-tracery, doorway with Tuscan columns and pediment. In same street, **Congregational Church,** also 1798, flat 5-bay front with pedimented gable, minister's house attached; **Liberal Club,** early C18.
Swan Hotel, Church Street, late Georgian, 3 bays with central Venetian window and 1-bay pediment above. In same street, **Church House,** large-scale, 3 wide bays with large, arched, rusticated door surround, Venetian window above and pediment above that. **Druce's Hill House,** *c*1720, in West Country baroque manner – as is one elevation of contemporary **Westbury House,** by the bridge: both feature 1-bay, 3-storey frontispieces embellished with tiers of pilasters of various orders. Another front of Westbury decorated with angle pilaster strips, doorway with block pilasters. Also in Church Street, **29,** of 1731, with tall arched door, Venetian window occupying all of tall 1st floor, 3 attic windows to 2nd floor, all crowned by 3-bay pediment.
In **Barton Orchard,** terrace of 3-storey C18 **weavers' houses,** 10–14 with later 4th storey.
26-32 Tory, late-Georgian terrace *c*1800–10, urban in composition with projecting centre and end houses with shallow canted bays.
9 Kingston Road, *c*1760, 3-bay pediment.
Group of good C18 houses of mixed dates in Woolley Street, especially **No.15** with Adamish doorcase and Venetian window; **17,** *c*1760, with Doric doorcase and pedimented window over; **19,** early C18, with Gibbs door.
Silver Street House, Silver Street, *c*1725, 7 bays with 3 pedimented windows on 1st floor.
In Market Street, **Pypett Buildings,** uniform group of 4 late-C18 3-storey houses stepping up the hill and linked by ramped-up cill course. Each has pedimented door.
Belcombe Court, just outside town, by John Wood the Elder, 1734, described by him as having 'the best tetrastyle frontispiece on square pillars [in fact Ionic pilasters] yet executed in or about Bath'.

On west front, slightly projecting pedimented wings; east front with another large pediment. Inside, octagonal study has coved ceiling with garlands and putti.
In grounds, domed **rotunda,** imposing **grotto.**
West of the town, **Wellclose House,** Turleigh Road, with heavy, powerful provincial Palladian 5-bay façade of *c*1730 with full-width crowning pediment.

Bradwell-on-Sea, Essex
8m NE of Burnham-on-Crouch
Bradwell Lodge, with wing by John Johnson, 1781–6, built as addition to Tudor house. Very fine neo-classical composition. Robert Adam and Angelica Kauffmann may have been concerned with interior.

Braintree, Essex
Horns Hotel, High Street, late-C18 with 2 bay windows and central archway.
37-9 Bank Street, 7 bays, with 3-bay pediment, octagonal glazing, *c*1760; **2 Brocking End,** excellent house of *c*1720.

Brandsby, North Yorkshire
13m N of York
All Saints' Church, 1767 by Thomas Atkinson. Body topped with central bell-cote supported internally by 4 Doric columns.

Brasted Place, Kent
4m w of Sevenoaks
Compact villa of 1784 by Robert Adam. Ashlar box dressed with Ionic pilasters.

Braxted Park, Essex
2m E of Witham
C17, rebuilt 1753–6 by Sir Robert Taylor. North front rebuilt 1804–6 by John Johnson.

Brecon, Powys
Royal Theatre, Danygaer Road, 1784.
Church House, Lion Street, early C18, 4 bays with quoins, egg-and-dart cornice, carved consoles. In same street, **4,** *c*1740, keystones to windows, Gibbs surround to door.

Bredgar, Kent
2m w of Sittingbourne
Downings, Silver Street, *c*1725, with centre Venetian window.
Swanton Street Farm, astonishing display of virtuoso brickwork within a remarkably ambitious baroque composition of 1719.

Brent Eleigh, Suffolk
6m NE of Sudbury
Brent Eleigh Hall, early C18 with *c*1815 pediment to garden front. Altered internally by Lutyens, *c*1930.
Almshouses, dated 1731 with mullioned windows and canopied paired porches.

Bretton Hall, West Yorkshire
5m NW of Barnsley
Provincial Palladian, *c*1730, designed by James Moyser. Simple rectangular block dressed with Palladian features. Remodelled *c*1815 by Sir Jeffry Wyatville: vestibule painted with Roman ruin composition.
In grounds, **conservatory** of 1827 built by W. & D. Bailey.

Brewood, Staffordshire
7m N of Wolverhampton
Speedwell Castle, in Market Place, *c*1750. Urban rococo Gothic composition with pair of 5-faceted bays, each 3 storeys high with variety of Gothic windows and details.

Bridge of Dun, Tayside
4m E of Tayside
1785 by Alexander Stevens with rococo Gothic embellishment.

Bridgnorth, Shropshire
St Mary Magdalene's Church, 1792-4 by Thomas Telford. Inspired by French neo-classicism and Greek revival. Chancel by Blomfield 1876.

Bridgwater, Somerset
Castle Street, 1723-5, speculation by Duke of Chandos. 3 storeys, mostly with architraves to windows. Good door surrounds, especially one with Doric pilasters set at right angles to façade.

The Lions, West Quay, rich baroque composition of *c*1730 with 1-bay frontispiece and good interiors.

Brighton, East Sussex
St Peter's Church, Victoria Gardens, 1824-8 by Sir Charles Barry, still Regency Gothic.

St Andrew's Church, Waterloo Road, 1827-8 by Barry; early example of Quattrocento revival.

Royal Pavilion, Old Steine, 1815-21 by John Nash. Exotic onion-domed 'Hindoo'-Gothic-detailed palace for Prince Regent. Some wonderful interiors quite match exterior in eclectic extravagance.

Town Hall, Market Place, 1830-32 by Thomas Cooper; massive ungainly Grecian pile.

Old Ship Hotel, West Street, with assembly room of 1767 by Robert Golden.

Marlborough House, Old Steine, strong composition attributed to Robert Adam, *c*1775, with pair of pedimented end pavilions containing large Venetian windows. Also in Old Steine, **44, 45, 46,** well preserved 3-storey group of *c*1795 with full-height canted bays, pedimented doors, black mathematical tile cladding. Other good groups are **6-12** of *c*1790 with pedimented doors, and **27, 28, 29** with pedimented doors and bays.

In **Pavilion Parade,** the northern extension of the east arm of the Old Steine terraces, some well preserved houses of *c*1790, especially **3-11** with segmental- and triangular-pedimented doors, 3 and 4 with cobble-built façades painted black with white-painted brick arches, window jambs and quoins.

68, 70, 71 Grand Parade, *c*1810-20 with 2-bay bow façades.

Bedford Square, *c*1810, irregular; **27-31** with bows and pilasters.

Regency Square, begun 1818; houses with bows.

Royal Crescent, facing the sea, 1798-1807; 3 storeys, faced with black mathematical tiles and with pedimented doorcases.

In Old Town, the **Lanes** – notably Union Street, Meeting House Lane, Brighton Place, Market Street – of townscape value but with few individually remarkable buildings.

In **Prince Albert Street**, a small quadrant with 2-storey bow windows; **10,** late-C18 brick house wrapped around a corner with handsome Doric segmental-pedimented doorcase; **15,** 5-bay, 3-storey free-standing house of *c*1760-70, red brick, keystones, quoins, later Tuscan porch.

7 Ship Street, *c*1780, pair of 2-storey canted bays – with their own cornices – flanking segmental-pedimented doorcase with neo-classical detailing. **16-17,** good brick pair of *c*1820. **61-2,** *c*1780, with Doric pedimented door, Gothic-glazed fanlight. **68,** *c*1780, with glazed header façade and pedimented door. **69,** 1780-90, façade of knapped flint with red brick window arches and jambs and corner quoins. **70,** *c*1790, with cobble-built façade and brick arches, jambs and quoins.

6 Bartholomews, excellent late-C18 shopfront.

Much of Regency Brighton designed by Charles Busby, from 1823, and still being built as late as *c*1850. Developments include **Kemp Town**, on which he worked with Amon Wilds: grander elements **Sussex Square,** *c*1823; **Lewes Crescent,** *c*1825, stucco, loosely uniform composition; and adjoining **Arundel Terrace**.

Busby also worked at Hove, creating monumental, palace-fronted **Brunswick Terrace,** and **Brunswick Square,** *c*1824-30.

A. H. Wilds (son of Amon Wilds) built **Oriental Place** and **Terrace,** 1825, **Sillwood Place,** 1827, conceived as uniform developments, and embellished with Wilds' characteristic ammonite capitals. Also, for himself, **Western Pavilion,** Western Terrace, *c*1827, with dome and 'Hindoo' details; and **Hanover Crescent,** *c*1827; **Park Crescent,** 1829.

Bristol, Avon
St Nicholas's Church, High Street, 1762-8 by James Bridges. Only shell and tower survive of this Gothic revival church.

St Michael's Church, St Michael's Hill. Nave 1774 by William Paty with interior a combination of Doric classicism and Gothic.

St Paul's Church, Portland Square, 1789-95 by Daniel Hague. Exterior, especially tower, very much in spirit of early-C18 picturesque Gothic.

Western Pavilion, Western Terrace, Brighton, *c*1827, by A. H. Wilds, clearly inspired by Nash's nearby Royal Pavilion.

Christ Church, Broad Street, 1786-90 by William Paty. Interior closely based on St Martin-in-the-Fields prototype.
St Thomas's Church, 1793 by James Allen. Interesting for its Roman barrel vault.
St George's Church, Brandon Hill, by Robert Smirke, 1821-3 in Greek revival style.
Holy Trinity Church, Hotwell Road, by C. R. Cockerell, 1829-30. Neo-classical.
Redland Chapel, Redland Green, 1740-43 by John Strahan and William Halfpenny; pedimented west front with paired Ionic pilasters and, inside, arcaded west end.
Old Council House, Corn Street, 1822-7 by Smirke, Grecian.
Royal Infirmary, Marlborough Hill: east wing 1786, centre 1788-92, west wing 1814.
Exchange, Corn Street, John Wood the Elder, 1740-45. 11-bay, 3-storey ashlar Palladian composition with 3-bay pediment and engaged Corinthian columns on a rusticated ground floor.
Exchange Market, High Street, 1744-5 by Samuel Glascodine, is part of same composition as above by Wood, who must have controlled overall design; plain, utilitarian, handsome.
Literary and Philosophical Institute, Park Street, 1821-3 by C. R. Cockerell. Grecian with tall, curved portico (gutted).
Theatre Royal, King Street, 1764-6 by James Paty. Auditorium, though much embellished in C19, survives largely intact. **Coopers' Hall,** King Street (now part of Theatre Royal), William Halfpenny, 1743; handsome provincial Palladian composition.
Commercial Rooms, Corn Street, 1810 by Charles Busby, with Soane-like interior.
Orchard Street, 1717-25. Terrace of 3-bay, 3-storey houses with baroque detail.
Dowry Square: 6-9 on north side *c*1727, baroque; 10-11 of 1746.
66, 68, 70 Prince Street, *c*1725-30, Probably by John Strahan. Ashlar, provincial baroque style. Nos. 66 and 68 identical; 70 of 3 bays with giant Ionic pilasters embracing centre bay and supporting segmental pediment.
12 St James's Barton, *c*1728, also has pair of giant pilasters framing centre bay and supporting segmental pediment.
The Royal Fort, Woodland Road, 1761 by James Bridges. 3-storey Palladian composition with good rococo interior.
Albemarle Row: No.5 dated 1762, by James Fear, carpenter; others of same date but still in baroque style reminiscent of Dowry Square. Of similar date and style are **Dowry Parade,** 1764 by Benjamin Probert and Robert Comfort, **King Square** and south side of **Brunswick Square,** *c*1770.
Berkeley Square, *c*1790-1800 in thin late-Palladian style, as are **Berkeley Crescent** and **Portland Square,** 1790-95.
South-east side of **Great George Street** *c*1790, No.7 especially good.
Upper and **Lower Arcades,** 1824-5, by James Foster.
Redland Court, Redland (2m NW of city centre), *c*1735 by John Strahan. 5-bay, 2-storey composition with 3-bay pediment.
Arno's Court, Arno Vale (1½m SE of city centre), Gothic, *c*1760, probably by James Bridges and Thomas Paty.

Clifton
Clifton Suspension Bridge, 1829-64, by I. K. Brunel. One of the earliest – and certainly the most dramatic – suspension bridges.
Assembly Room, The Mall, 1806-11 by F. H. Greenway and Joseph Kay; Grecian.
Clifton Wood House, Clifton Wood Road, 1721.
In Clifton Green, near bridge, **observatory,** 1729; also **Nos.10, 11, 12,** dated 1786.
In grounds of **Goldney House,** of *c*1720, altered *c*1860, good collection of garden buildings: **orangery,** *c*1730; **grotto,** with arcaded room, 1739; circular Gothic **garden house,** 1758.
On Clifton Hill, **Bishop's House,** dated 1711.
Clifton Hill House, 1746-50 by Isaac Ware. Austere, tall 5-bay façade, 3-bay pediment. Inside, excellent staircase, some good stucco ceilings.
Prospect House, *c*1765 by Thomas Paty.
Boyce's Buildings, by Thomas Paty 1763, uniform block in restrained baroque style with pedimented centre, Gibbs surrounds to windows; earliest uniform, planned terrace in Clifton (now partly demolished).
Upper Berkeley Place, late C18, red brick.
Windsor Terrace, 1790-*c*1810, with giant Corinthian pilasters on rusticated ground floor.
Saville Place, 1790-1810.
Cornwallis Crescent, 1791-1830.
Bellevue, 1792-1815, stone-faced terrace.
York Place, *c*1795.
Prince's Buildings *c*1796, convex crescent comprising pairs of houses with 1-storey links (now altered).
The Paragon, 1809-14, convex crescent with 1st-floor veranda.
Royal York Crescent, 1791-1818, massive at over 130 bays long; perched over vaulted, raised pavement.
Harley Place, *c*1820-30, with 1st-floor verandas.

Brizlincote Hall, Derbyshire
3m NW of Swadlincote
5-bay, 2-storey house, *c*1705-15, crowned by huge segmental pediment on all fronts.

Broadlands, Hampshire
1m S of Romsey
Earlier house altered 1788-92 by Henry Holland, who added Ionic portico and redecorated interior.

Broadway, Hereford and Worcester
5m SE of Evesham
Tower in neo-Norman style by James Wyatt, 1794.

Brocket Hall, Hertfordshire
1m W of Welwyn Garden City
James Paine, 1760-75. Large, tall house. Interior mixture of Adam style (library) and Paine's more personal neo-classical/rococo alternative (drawing room).
Bridge in park, by Paine 1772-4, as are **entrance screen** and **lodge,** *c*1770.

Brockhampton Park, Hereford and Worcester
2m E of Bromyard
Palladian red brick pile of little imagination with coarse details, *c*1750 by Thomas F. Pritchard; virtually identical to his Hatton Grange, Shropshire of 1764-8.

Brocklesby, Lincolnshire
10m W of Grimsby
Mausoleum for Lord Yarborough by James Wyatt, 1787–92. Very rich neo-classical interior.

Brogyntyn, Shropshire
1m NW of Oswestry
Francis Smith, 1735. Portico added 1814 by Benjamin Gummow.

Brompton, Kent
N edge of Gillingham
On the hill above Chatham Dockyard (see Chatham) are important and substantial remains of C18 fortifications and, between these and docks, remains of C18 naval community. Fortification composed of: **Fort Amhurst,** constructed 1755–8 under supervision of engineer Hugh Debbieg, and greatly altered and extended 1779–82; the **Great Lines,** 1755–8; the **Lower Lines,** 1779–82; the **Horn Work** of *c*1785; and **Brompton Barracks,** built 1804–6 with an officers' block added 1807.

C18 domestic buildings survive in grid of streets including **Mansion Row** which contains 3-storey red brick terrace (2–6, 6A, 7–12, 12A, 14–15) of *c*1750 but looking earlier; **Prospect Row** (2–20) which is less uniform with a variety of columned doorcases; 4–20 (even numbers) **Medway Road;** and in **Garden Street** 2, 4, 6 (early-C18 and early-C19 group) and 22, 24. In **High Street**, 6–12 are early-C18 with C19 shop-fronts.

Brookmans Park, Hertfordshire
2m NW of Potters Bar
Folly arch, large mock-medieval entrance to long-lost house called Gobions. Erected *c*1730, perhaps to design of James Gibbs; early example of medieval revival.

Brough Hall, North Yorkshire
4m SE of Richmond
C17 house much extended and altered *c*1730 and 1772–5 by Thomas Atkinson.

Bruern Abbey, Oxfordshire
5m SW of Chipping Norton
House of *c*1720 on site of Cistercian abbey. Good example of provincial baroque; south front of 7 bays with 3 central bays projecting under pediment supported on banded angle pilasters without capitals. Interior of house dates from after fire of 1780. North front rebuilt 1972 in imitation of south.

Bruton, Somerset
4m N of Wincanton
St Mary's Church, 1743 by Nathaniel Ireson. Fine chancel with delicate plasterwork.

Buckland House, Oxfordshire
4m NE of Faringdon
John Wood the Younger, 1755–7. Late Palladian, with very deep rustic basement. 3-bay pediment and pair of pavilions containing chapel and library. Inside, light rococo plasterwork. Enlarged 1910.

Builth Wells, Powys
Lion Hotel, Broad Street, handsome 5-bay, 3-storey building of *c*1820; all windows except those of centre bay tripartite. Also in Broad Street, **Lamb Hotel,** *c*1760–80. **4–10** (even), good early-C19 group, including remains of Ionic shop-front to No.8.

12 West Street, delightful 2-storey stuccoed Regency house with pair of full-height curved bays flanking trellis porch. **24, 26, 28,** good, varied C18 and early-C19 group, including **Hafod,** ungainly composition of *c*1790 with pair of 2-storey canted bays flanking pedimented door, 1st-floor Venetian window beneath pediment.

Bunny Hall, Nottinghamshire
7m S of Nottingham
Sir Thomas Parkyns, *c*1723. Crowned with massive segmental pediment.

Buntingsdale, Shropshire
1m S of Market Drayton
Francis Smith, completed 1721 in vigorous brick baroque manner. Enlarged 1857.

Burford, Oxfordshire
Wesleyan Chapel, High Street, built as grand baroque town mansion *c*1715, before being turned into chapel in 1849 when interior was gutted and urns removed from parapet. Façade fully rusticated and window divided by 6 giant fluted pilasters; cornice topped by balustraded parapet; pedimented door with Gibbs surround. Perhaps by Francis Smith.

Bull Hotel, with provincial baroque brick 4-bay, 3-storey front of *c*1715, framed by giant Tuscan stone pilasters. (Damaged by fire 1981.)

Girls' School, corner of Lawrence Lane and High Street. Originally 2 houses with façades remodelled *c*1730–50.

Castle's Almshouses, Church Lane, founded 1726 and simply a plain terrace of 4 dwellings.

Brewery, Witney Street, *c*1750.

Warwick House, High Street, front of *c*1730 on C17 house. Also in High Street, **Ridgeway,** *c*1750 with keystoned sash windows and carriageway.

Great House, Witney Street, built 1700 but with extension and some good interiors of *c*1750 including 1st-floor room painted with arabesques.

Burley-on-the-Hill, Leicestershire
1m NE of Oakham
Model farm, including offices and barn by James Playfair, 1788.

Burn Hall, Co. Durham
3m SW of Durham
Neo-classical **cowshed** of 1783 by Sir John Soane.

Burnley, Lancashire
Townley Hall, medieval house much altered in C18, with especially sumptuous double-height hall decorated with plasterwork in manner of Gibbs.

Burntisland, Fife
Church, C16 with extraordinary 2-stage C18 tower octagon and spire.

Burton Constable Hall, Humberside
8m NE of Kingston upon Hull
Late-C16 house with mid-C18 alterations. Interior: Timothy Lightoler created entrance hall, 1760; Long Gallery probably 1760 (but could be 20 years earlier); staircase hall also 1760; Ballroom 1778 by James Wyatt. Most notable work is Lightoler's, which is Jacobean revival.

Burton upon Trent, Staffordshire
St Modwen's Church, 1719–26 by William and Richard Smith, completed by Francis Smith. West tower with balustrade and urns. Inside,

Tuscan colonnade. Organ case, splended neo-classical design of *c*1771 by James Wyatt (according to J. M. Robinson).

22 Bridge Street with pedimented doorcase; opposite, **Trent House** with Ionic porch set *in antis*.

5 Horninglow has Tuscan doorcase of *c*1780; **167,** *c*1760, 5 bays, fine doorcase, centre window emphasized by 1-bay pediment; **180,** *c*1740-50; **181,** *c*1790, neo-classical columned doorcase flanked by tripartite windows, embellished 1st-floor window.

6-12 High Street have doors with broken pediments; **102,** early-C19 shop-front; **146,** *c*1760, 5 bays, 1-bay pediment, 1st-floor Venetian window, 2nd-floor Diocletian.

9 and **10 Lichfield Street,** early-C19 pair with tripartite ground-floor windows.

Bury St Edmunds, Suffolk

Market Hall and **Theatre,** Market Cross, reconstruction of 1774-80 by Robert Adam; free-standing, cruciform plan, Palladian in composition with neo-classical detail. Ground-floor rusticated arcade originally open. Theatre became town hall chamber after 1819.

In this year, **Theatre Royal,** Westgate Street, built to designs of William Wilkins the Younger. Modest stucco exterior but excellent, and unique, Greek-detailed interior with boxes and gallery supported on cast-iron columns. (National Trust)

Athenaeum, Angel Hill, early-C18 assembly room reconstructed 1789, perhaps by Francis Sandys, and altered again in 1804, when given stucco, Greek-detailed exterior. Inside, splendid ballroom with shallow barrel-vaulted ceiling, Adamesque decoration, *c*1790.

Provost's House, formerly **Clopton Asylum,** in Abbey grounds, *c*1730.

Old Gaol (called **The Fort**), 1803 by George Byfield. Only façade survives, powerful and menacing in manner of Dance's Newgate.

The Manor House, now **County Education Offices,** 5 Honey Hill, 1735 by amateur architect and Cambridge don Sir James Burrough. Archaic appearance.

82 Guildhall Street, plain 5-bay, 2-storey house of *c*1760, extended 1789 by Sir John Soane who added single-bay pedimented pavilions.

10 Crown Street, *c*1750 with bold Gibbs-surround door; **45,** pair of houses *c*1760 with shared pedimented porch.

4 Chequer Square, 5-bay, 3-storey house of *c*1810-20. Elegant example of its date.

35-6 Abbeygate Street, early-C19 shop-front.

Buscot Park, Oxfordshire

4m NW of Faringdon

*c*1770, 9 bays, 2 storeys, 3-bay pedimented centre, on north 2 generous symmetrical bows. Alterations and additions of *c*1939. (National Trust)

Butterton Grange, Staffordshire

3m SW of Newcastle-under-Lyme

By Sir John Soane, 1815; very striking and original 2-storey composition. 3-bay front divided by curious full-height canted pilasters. Centre bay deeply recessed between centre pilasters. Interior not by Soane.

Buxton, Derbyshire

St John the Baptist's Church, 1811 by John White. Tuscan portico, domed tower.

Devonshire Royal Hospital incorporates **stables** by John Carr, 1785-90.

Crescent containing **Assembly Room** with arcaded **Square** at rear, by Carr 1780-90. Ground floor arcaded, giant pilasters between windows.

29, 30, 31 Hall Bank, *c*1810.

Bywell Hall, Northumberland

3m W of Prudhoe

James Paine, *c*1760. Idiosyncratic design with 3 gable-like pediments to garden front, centre one supported on attached columns. Rusticated ground floor, asymmetrical wing behind.

Caerhayes Castle, Cornwall

7m SW of St Austell

By John Nash, *c*1808. Castellated, asymmetrical and rambling pile: large round tower, square tower and octagonal tower, Gothic traceried windows, battlements.

Caernarfon/Caernarvon, Gwynedd

Plas Bowman Inn, High Street, dated 1808, stone, 3 storeys. Also in High Street, **16,** 2 bays, 3 storeys, with round-headed windows set in arches and shop-front of *c*1820; **18,** dated 1768 on hopper, with pair of full-height canted bays.

7, 9, 11 Market Street, dated 1800 on hopper; tall 3-storey terrace houses.

32-7 Castle Square, uniform 3-storey brick terrace of *c*1800 with centre building (33), now **Castle Inn,** stuccoed and crowned by 3-bay pediment. One end of terrace demolished.

In **Eastgate Street,** 1-bay, handsomely decorated **house** with contemporary shop, *c*1830.

In **Wellington Terrace,** Regency stucco **villas,** one with porch with columns *in antis*.

Cairness House, Grampian

4m SE of Fraserburgh

James Playfair, 1791-7. Austere neo-classical manner influenced by Boullée and Ledoux. Clean, geometrical forms: especially striking are hemicycle of offices dressed with primitive Doric columns in massive arches, and Egyptian Billiard Room. Portico by Soane, *c*1800.

Cambridge, Cambridgeshire

Senate House, James Gibbs, improving initial design by amateur architect and Cambridge don Sir James Burrough, 1722-30.

Fellows' Buildings, King's College, by James Gibbs 1723-9. Very baroque in detail, especially giant pedimented porch. **Entrance screen** to College by William Wilkins the Younger, 1824-8, Gothic.

Westmoreland Building, Emmanuel College by John Lumley, 1719-22, in provincial mannerist/baroque style. Street front of **Emmanuel College,** 1769 by James Essex.

Peterhouse New Building, 1736-42 by Burrough, who worked in Gibbsian baroque/Palladian manner, and who also refronted Principal Court 1754-6.

Burrough designed **Clare College Chapel,** 1763, which was completed 1764-9 by Essex.

Sidney Sussex College Chapel and **Library,** 1776-87, both by Essex.

Downing College, by Wilkins, designed 1804, built 1807-21; influential early Greek revival design. Long 2-storey front with full-height hexastyle Greek Ionic portico.

Trinity College New Court, 1821-5 by Wilkins in Tudor Gothic style.
Corpus Christi College New Court, 1823-7 by Wilkins in neo-Perpendicular style.
St John's College New Court, by Rickman & Hutchinson 1825-31. Gothic, incorporating a 'Bridge of Sighs'. Other college bridges across Cam from 'Backs' of colleges include timber **Mathematical Bridge,** Queen's College, 1749 by William Etherbridge and James Essex, and **Trinity Bridge,** 1763-5 by Essex.
University Library, 1754 by 2nd-generation Palladian Stephen Wright, who was pupil of William Kent and inspired, in this design, by Burlington's house for General Wade, London.
Observatory, Madingley Road, by J. C. Mead 1822-3, with Greek Doric portico.
14 Kings Parade, c1730-40; **22,** corner house of c1750-60 with block cornice and good brick arches.
36 Trinity Street, good shop-front of c1825.
Rose Crescent, tightly curved paved court of c1820.
In Green Street, good white brick houses of c1820, especially **25, 26, 27.**
Fitzwilliam Street, 2- and 3-storey houses of 1821, white brick, round doors with imposts.
Maid's Causeway, 6 substantial houses, related to smaller houses in **Willow Walk, Short Street** and **Fair Street,** 1815-26 by Charles Humphrey.
16 Jesus Lane, excellent free-standing house of c1725, 3 storeys, 5 bays with 3-bay pedimented centre.
Kenmare House, 74 Trumpington Street, by James Essex, 1768. Yellow brick, 3 bays, 3 storeys, façade embellished with 4 Venetian windows. Also in Trumpington Street: **Fitzwilliam House,** 1727 with fine brickwork, pedimented doorcase; good panelled interiors. **Grove Lodge,** villa by William Custance, 1795, 3-bay pediment with Ionic screen.
Downing Terrace, Lensfield Road, c1815, 2-storey houses with façades embellished by giant blank arches.
2 Hills Road, villa of c1828 with doorway and internal fittings from Colen Campbell's Wanstead House.

Came House, Dorset
1m SE *of Dorchester*
By Francis Cartwright, c1754, in provincial Palladian style. Façade embellished with pilasters bearing Ionic capitals with inverted volutes.

Camperdown House, Tayside
1m NW *of Dundee*
1824 by William Burn, based upon Wilkins' Grange Park, Hampshire, of 1804-9. But here giant portico on east front is Ionic. Inside, state rooms are well separated from family rooms.

Cannon Hall, South Yorkshire
3m w *of Barnsley*
Alterations by John Carr, 1764-8. Staircase by Thornton, c1690. Now museum for Barnsley.

Canterbury, Kent
Methodist Church, St Peter's Street. William Jenkins, 1811.
County Gaol and Sessions House, Longport. Greek Doric style, 1806-10 by George Byfield.
Westgate House, St Dunstan's Street, large, plain red brick house dated 1760 on rainwater heads. Pedimented doorcase with Ionic half columns. Inside, overmantel in front room with painting in rococo border.
Barton Court, Longport, c1740, with centrepiece formed by rusticated Venetian window above rusticated door surround.
Hoystings, Old Dover Road. C18 Gothic with pointed windows and dormers in stepped gables.

Capel y Ffin, Powys
7m s *of Hay-on-Wye*
Chapel: simple rectangular hall, 25 by 13ft with rectangular windows, c1762. South porch of 1817.

Carlisle, Cumbria
Holy Trinity Church, Wigton Road, by Rickman & Hutchinson, 1828-30, in Gothic style.
Assize Courts, Court Square, 1810-12 by Sir Robert Smirke. Large-scale Gothic composition.
Town Hall, Market Place, 1717, 2 storeys with pedimented dormer over entrance.
Cumberland Infirmary, Newtown Road, by Robert Tattershall 1830-32. Greek revival, with giant Doric portico. Extended c1870.
In **English Street, bank** by Thomas Rickman, 1830; Gothic.
28 Abbey Street, late C18; fine Ionic doorcase. **38,** mid-C18; ashlar, tripartite window.
3 Castle Street, c1820; Grecian. **19,** ashlar, with pilasters to ground floor. **26-30,** also ashlar, with Ionic porches.
34 Fisher Street, c1820; Grecian. Unpretentious **façades** in Scotch Street, best one facing market, with pediments to 1st-floor windows, but now marred by poor reconstruction.

Carmarthen, Dyfed
Six Bells Inn (now row of houses), John Nash 1785. **Nolton House,** Orchard Street, 1785 by Nash.

Carstairs House, Strathclyde
10m SE *of Wishaw*
William Burn 1822, neo-Tudor, influenced by Wilkins' Dalmeny House.

Castle Bromwich, West Midlands
NE *edge of Birmingham*
Church of St Mary and St Margaret 1726, probably by Thomas White. Exterior highly wrought. Inside, Tuscan columns supporting arcade.

Castle Farm, Nottinghamshire
1m sw *of Worksop*
c1760, designed by the Duchess of Norfolk. Huge quadrangle with Gothic details, incorporating a tea pavilion.

Castle Goring, West Sussex
w *edge of Worthing*
By Biagio Rebecca, c1790. Entrance front castellated Gothic of flint and stone. Garden front Graeco-Palladian with Coade stone plaques. Inside, same split of styles.

Castle Hill, Devon
7m N *of Honiton*
Built 1689; from 1729 Roger Morris and Lords Burlington and Pembroke worked on a remodelling. Enlarged 1841, 1862; centre burnt 1934, reconstructed in plain Palladian style 1935-8.
Temple of 1772 and **menagerie** of 1775.

Castle Howard, North Yorkshire
4m W of Malton
By Vanbrugh, 1700–26, with assistance of Hawksmoor. West wing by Thomas Robinson, 1753–9. Sculpture gallery and museum, 1800–1 by Charles Heathcote Tatham.
Obelisk, 1714; **Pyramid Gate**, Vanbrugh 1719; **Temple of the Four Winds**, loosely based on Palladio's Villa Rotonda, Vanbrugh 1724; **Pyramid**, 1728; **Mausoleum**, Hawksmoor 1729, completed by 1742 under supervision of Daniel Garrett; **Exclamation Gate**, curious, massive rustic arch, Sir William Chambers c1770.

Catton Hall, Derbyshire
5m S of Burton upon Trent
Plain, large brick house of 1741 by William Smith using, perhaps, initial design by Gibbs. Interior extremely rich rococo.

Cawsand
See Kingsand.

Charlton Mackrell, Somerset
5m SE of Street
The Court, rectory of c1792. Plain front, but with entrance hall containing tripartite Gothic screen of slender wooden clustered Gothic shafts, in front of gracefully curving stair embellished with cast-iron Gothic-profiled balustrades (see Leighton Hall).

Charlton Park, Wiltshire
2m NE of Malmesbury
C17, altered 1772 by Matthew Brettingham the Younger, who provided spectacular neo-classical domed central hall and dining room.

Chatelherault, Strathclyde
2m SE of Hamilton
Dog kennel, 1731 by William Adam. Large-scale composition in provincial Palladian manner.

Chatham, Kent
Best-preserved of Britain's Royal Dockyards with several unique monuments to Georgian industrial building and technology.
Dock Admiral's house of 1703, **Dockyard gate** of 1717 in Vanbrugh Office of Works 'castle air' style. **Officers' terrace**, 1721–33, also Office of Works manner. Probably designed by dock carpenters, but perhaps approved and embellished by Vanbrugh as Comptroller of King's Works.
Clock storehouse, 1723; **Pay Clerk's Office**, c1730 with 2 good rusticated door surrounds.
Anchor Wharf, storehouses, 1774–85 and 1805; **Ropery**, completed 1792 – $\frac{1}{4}$ mile long and including early-C19 machinery.
Dock Chapel, 1808–11 by Edward Holl. **Sawmill**, 1814, designed by Marc Brunel.
(Brompton listed as a separate entry.)

Chelmsford, Essex
Shire Hall, 1789–91 by John Johnson. Portland stone in Palladian tradition with 3-bay pediment but with delicate and elegant neo-classical decoration.
Gaol, Springfield Road, Thomas Hopper 1822–8, Tuscan, extended 1848.
Bridge of 1787 by Johnson.
Mildmay Almshouses, Moulsham Street, 1758, red brick, 12 bays with 4-bay pediment.
26 High Street, c1725, with centre window framed by brick Ionic pilasters.

Cheltenham, Gloucestershire
St James's Church, Suffolk Square, begun 1825 to designs of Edward Jenkins, completed 1826–32 by J.B. Papworth; Regency Gothic.
St Paul's Church, St Paul's Road, 1827–31 by John Forbes. Handsome Greek 4-columned Ionic west portico; tall tower with cupola – details based on Ionic temple on the river Ilissus, Athens. Inside, gallery on cast-iron columns.
Holy Trinity Church, Portland Street, 1820–23 by George Underwood, with Gothic details.
North Place Chapel, 1816, Doric portico.
Municipal Offices, The Promenade, c1823. Magnificent long, monumental terrace, stucco, 4 storeys over basement. In centre, 4-columned Ionic portico standing on rusticated ground floor and breaking forward, with pediment set in 3rd floor which is treated as attic above.
Pittville Pump Room, 1825–30 by Forbes, ashlar front with colonnade of Ionic columns copied from Stuart and Revett's engravings of temple on Ilissus. Excellent domed interior.
Montpellier Pump Rooms and **Rotunda** (now **Lloyds Bank**), 1817 by G.A. Underwood, enlarged 1825 by Papworth. Externally, spacious 1-storey colonnade; internally, colonnaded room by Underwood, and Papworth's brilliant rotunda and domed room lit by central oculus.
Masonic Hall, Portland Street, 1820–23 by Underwood. Suitably mysterious-looking (architect was a Mason). Interior much as original.
Vittoria House, Vittoria Walk, the original spa, opened 1804. Exterior with bow in centre of each elevation, surrounded by colonnaded veranda.
In **Trafalgar Street** some interesting modest cottages of 1806 including **Rock Cottage**, *cottage orné* built of tufa, decorated with shells.
Royal Crescent, begun 1806, completed 1810, earliest important terrace in Cheltenham. Plain, astylar 3-storey stucco façade. Adjacent is **Crescent Terrace**, symmetrical stuccoed composition with pedimented central house.
Berkeley Place, c1810, ashlar, 4 storeys over basement with good iron verandas to 1st floor, fanlights.
In London Road, good pre-1820 terrace, **Oxford Buildings** and **Priory Buildings** and, set back from the road, excellent **Priory Parade** and **Oxford Parade** with good ironwork.
St Margaret's Terrace, North Place, c1820. Large ashlar houses, main façade embellished with pilasters and wrought-iron balcony.
Columbia Place, Winchcombe Street, c1820, stucco, continuous 1st-floor veranda.
Oriel Terrace, Oriel Road, 1824, with excellent cast-iron 1st-floor veranda. **Oriel Place**, c1815–20, pilasters with incised Greek motifs.
Dorset House, Pittville Town, good neo-Greek villa probably by John Forbes, c1825.
Lansdown Place, 1825–9 by Papworth. Tall houses, ashlar-faced, designed as pairs linked by recessed porches. Also by Papworth, the convex **Lansdown Crescent**, 1825–9. **Lansdown Terrace**, c1830, with 2-storey pedimented centre bays, probably by Papworth, as are **The Jearrads** (named after estate owners), a terrace of 'Italian' villas, each house with classical portico to 1st-floor room. **Suffolk Square**, c1825, once more by Papworth; and again by him, **Montpellier Parade**, villas of c1823.

196 / *Georgian Buildings*

Segrave Place, Pittville Central Drive, stucco 3-storey houses with horizontally channelled rustication to ground floor and continuous 1st-floor balcony with cast-iron anthemion decoration. Also in the Drive, **29-37,** good stucco terrace of 3-storey houses. Other terraces in the Drive, **45-53** and **59-67,** similar; all probably designed by Forbes, all *c*1825-30.

Chepstow, Gwent
Powis Almshouses, Bridge Street, dated 1716; L-shaped, 2 storeys, stone-pedimented doors connected by stone profiled string course, mullioned and transomed windows.

Old Bell Chambers, Bank Street, *c*1725-30; 4 storeys, 4 bays, segmental windows; canted ground-floor bays flank centre arch.

Five Alls Inn, Hocker Hill Street, late C18; immediately behind, tall, 3-storey, 3-bay house, *c*1760, with excellent brick and stone detailing, pedimented door. Also in Hocker Hill Street, **No.10,** early C18, bow windows to ground floor each side of door which has flat, unsupported hood; **1-2,** *c*1820, 3 storeys.

In **Bank Street,** 5-bay, 3-storey **house** of *c*1725; rendered, with stone cornice, segmental windows framed by simple stone surrounds with keystones; interior panelled, best room on 1st floor. Adjacent house on left 3 bays, 3 storeys; pedimented doorhood on consoles, 1st-floor window above with Gothic glazing, flanked by tripartite windows, other windows with Gothic glazing; behind, long 2-storey wing with tripartite windows. **No.13** especially good, *c*1830; 3 storeys, 1 bay, shallow bows to 1st and 2nd floor containing tripartite windows; roofed veranda to 1st floor, balcony to 2nd.

On one side of **Bridge Street,** good run of 3-storey Regency **houses,** almost all with bow windows to ground floor.

In **St Mary's Street,** good mix of C18 and early-C19 buildings, for example **9,** early C18 with segmental windows; **7** with early-c19 bow shopfront.

12 Middle Street, early C19, 3 storeys, 3 bays; all windows bipartite except 1st-floor centre which is arched with Gothic glazing; door with Gothic/Greek detailing.

Cheriton, Hampshire
2m s of New Alresford
Cheriton House, *c*1740, 5-bay, 3-storey composition with 1-bay open pediment in centre and asymmetrical wing. (See house in East Street, New Alresford.)

Chester, Cheshire
County Court, Prison, Armoury, Barracks within castle, in neo-classical manner by Thomas Harrison and built 1788-1822. Especially impressive are Greek Doric entrance of 1810-22 and semicircular **Shire Hall** with coffered semi-dome, 1791-1801.

Bluecoat School, Upper Northgate Street, 1717; quad with central pedimented block.

News Room, Northgate Street, 1808 by Harrison, who also designed **Northgate,** 1808; **Grosvenor Bridge,** 1827-33 (built by Jesse Hartley and George Rennie); **St Martin's Lodge,** Castle Esplanade, *c*1820 (for himself); and **Watergate House,** Watergate Street, 1820.

Abbey Square, 2 sides of uniform terrace houses of *c*1760-80.

25 Castle Street, pedimented composition of *c*1730, also **23** with good door.

51 Watergate Street, gabled and colonnaded as C18 version of C16/17 pavement house characteristic of Chester.

28 Eastgate Street, *c*1828, Greek, with pair of austere Greek Doric columns to entrance.

71 Foregate Street, *c*1750 with Gibbs door.

Forest House, Love Street, *c*1785.

6 St John's Street, *c*1750, with Corinthian angle pilasters and pedimented door.

In Vicar's Lane, former **rectory** (now **Grosvenor Club**), *c*1750, Gibbs door with pediment; also **The Groves,** *c*1750, containing room with lavish rococo plasterwork.

15 Lower Bridge Street, 1715 with Tuscan porch.

Stanley Place, short street of *c*1780.

Chesterfield, Derbyshire
87 High Pavement, *c*1765, 7-bay, 3-storey brick house with pair of 3-storey bays flanking central door.

42 St Mary's Gate, fine 5-bay early-C18 house.
On south side of Market Place, several distinguished C18 houses survive as façades only.

Chettle House, Dorset
6m NE of Blandford
Probably designed by Thomas Archer, *c*1715-25. 7 bays and quadrant-cornered end bays. Giant brick pilasters have eccentric capitals with inverted volutes. Magnificent entrance staircase hall with chamfered corners. End bays heightened *c*1900.

Chevening Park, Kent
2m NW of Sevenoaks
Important mid-C17 house possibly by Inigo Jones, with interesting C18 alterations and additions, including service pavilions, *c*1717-20, possibly by Thomas Fort and still in manner of Wren, and magnificent circular flying staircase of *c*1721 by Nicholas Dubois. Chimneypieces in Tapestry Room and Saloon copies of chimneypieces by Vanbrugh at Hampton Court and so probably by Fort, who was employed by the Office of Works.

Chicheley Hall, Buckinghamshire
2m NW of Newport Pagnell
Francis Smith, 1719-21, apparently influenced by Thomas Archer, and fine example of his style of baroque. Ramped-up parapet, decorative rather than classically correct use of giant pilasters. Michelangeloesque door on west front. Interior Palladian in style, possibly by Flitcroft.

Chichester, West Sussex
St John's Church, St John's Street, by James Elmes, 1812, neo-Greek but with octagonal plan.

Market House, North Street, by John Nash 1800-8; Greek Doric manner. Top storey of 1900.

Council House, designed by Roger Morris, 1731-3, Palladian with central entablature and attic flanked by recessed lower half-pediments; open arcade to street.

Assembly Rooms, James Wyatt 1781-3. Very plain.

5 East Pallant, *c*1760. Tripartite door with pediment over opening.

5 West Pallant, *c*1770. **10,** *c*1820, Greek Doric porch with columns *in antis*. **12,** tall, gaunt early-C18 house.

1 North Pallant, pedimented, and **5,** both c1760. **Pallant House** – the finest house in town – built c1712.

40 North Street, c1780, 3 storeys with delicate Doric porch. **43,** 2-storey early-C18 house with mid-C18 1st-floor cantilevered bay embellished with ogee windows and Gothic glazing; Ionic doorcase beneath. Also in this street, **Greyfriars (council offices);** plain mid-C18 façade; inside, elaborate staircase with iron balustrade.

37-8 South Street, c1800 with ground-floor bows. **44,** c1820 with central 1st-floor bow; adjacent, former **theatre** of 1792. **47,** c1770, with delicate door.

45-6 East Street, unusually early example – c1730 – of semi-detached houses.

In Westgate, **Marriott House,** c1725 with pedimented centre; also **15, 27-39.**

In **St Martin's Square,** good irregular group of Georgian buildings.

Friarsgate, Priory Road, large, mid-C18.

Chicksands Priory, Bedfordshire
5m SW of Biggleswade
Medieval remains Gothicized by Isaac Ware, c1750, and again after 1813 by James Wyatt.

Chillington Hall, Staffordshire
6m NW of Wolverhampton
Sir John Soane altered earlier house in 1785-9, adding 4-column giant Ionic portico. South front of 1724, by Francis Smith, in good baroque style. Interior contains interesting features including concealed mahogany water closet in Red Bedroom designed by Soane, and saloon with 'medieval' chimneypiece of c1788 by Soane.

Chippenham, Cambridgeshire
4m N of Newmarket
One of earliest model villages, shown on a map of c1710. Uniform rows of terraced and semi-detached **cottages** linked by outbuildings, of uncertain date but clearly pre-1800; handsome **school,** c1712, with tall arched windows.

Chippenham, Wiltshire
In the Market Place, a few C18 remains, notably **Angel Hotel,** c1770, 7 bays with Tuscan porch; **The Old Palace,** late C18, with pedimented door topped by Venetian window and flanked by tripartite windows; **No.33,** with central arched window and pedimented doorway; **38** with late-C18 front, pair of canted bay windows.

18 St Mary's Street, c1715-20; **44-9,** c1780 with canted bay windows; **44-5,** formerly an inn, with central pediment above 1st-floor Venetian and 2nd-floor Diocletian window, flanked by canted bays; **53,** early C18 with pedimented door, arched centre 1st-floor window; **54,** mid-C18, 8 bays with Tuscan porch; **61,** early C18, with 1-bay pediment and pedimented door.

Ivy House, Bath Road, c1730, free-standing, in imposing provincial baroque manner, with end bays breaking forward and crowned by segmental gable-pediments.

Chipping Campden, Gloucestershire
7m E of Evesham
Lygon Arms, High Street, early C19 with arched carriageway.

Cotswold House Hotel, High Street, early C19. Also in High Street, **Clifton House,** dated 1717, façade embellished with 3 Ionic pilasters and modillion eaves cornice; **Seymour House,** c1720, with coved eaves cornice; **The Martins,** early C18, with fluted Ionic pilasters to façade and modillion eaves cornice; **Dovers House,** c1759-60; **Bedfont House,** 1740 by Thomas Woodward, with 5-bay, 3-storey façade embellished with fluted Corinthian pilasters supporting deep cornice, door with Corinthian pilasters and segmental pediment.

Chirk, Clwyd
5m N of Oswestry
Hand Hotel, c1780, with Tuscan porch over pavement.

Chislehampton, Oxfordshire
6m E of Abingdon
St Katharine's Church, modest country building of 1763 following C17 chapel tradition with a few baroque flourishes such as paired Doric pilasters inside on south wall between windows facing blank arcade on north wall. C18 fittings.

Chorley, Lancashire
St George's Church, St George's Street, 1822 by Rickman & Hutchinson, Gothic.

Chorlton-on-Medlock
See Manchester.

Chute Lodge, Wiltshire
11m NE of Amesbury
1760, probably by Sir Robert Taylor and very much in his villa style, with pedimented 3-bay projection on entrance front, canted bay to garden and stair in central top-lit oval compartment.

Cirencester, Gloucestershire
Cirencester Park. Provincial baroque house of 1714-18, probably by local mason. Grounds contain important garden buildings, notably **Alfred's Hall** which, designed in 1721 by Alexander Pope, can be called the first Gothic castellated garden folly. Extended in 1732 and made asymmetrical. Also in grounds: **Pope's Seat; Square House,** castellated tower of c1730-41.

Rebecca Powell School, Dollar Street, c1717 with fine Gibbs-surround window of c1730. Also in this street, **30,** 1725, ashlar in provincial baroque style.

Woolgatherers, 53 Coxwell Street, C17 and early C18 merchant's house.

Pedimented 5-bay Palladian **house** in **Thomas Street**; and a similar one in **Cecily Hill,** c1760.

Museum, in Park Street, also fine example of Palladian urban design; 7 bays with 3-bay pediment, c1765.

14-16 Castle Street (Lloyds Bank), c1780; Palladian composition, ashlar, with Venetian windows in blank arches.

3-5 Oyer Street, c1750.

Clandon Park, Surrey
E edge of Guildford
Designed by Giacomo Leoni, c1730-33. Brick; entrance front with 3-bay stone-clad frontispiece topped by pediment formed within attic. East front centre emphasized with 1-storey pilasters at 1st-floor level. Interior more conventionally Palladian. Disparity of style between inside and out may be due to alterations of 1876. (National Trust)

Clare House, Kent
3m W of Maidstone
Exquisite neo-classical villa designed in 1793 by Michael Searles. Much use made of curved bays.

Claremont, Surrey
SW edge of Esher
Ashlar-clad Graeco-Palladian house built 1771-4 to designs of Henry Holland and Lancelot Brown.
  In grounds, **Belvedere** in 'castle air' style by Sir John Vanbrugh, c1715. (National Trust)

Clarendon Park, Wiltshire
3m E of Salisbury
Architect unknown, said to have been built 1737 but belongs stylistically to earlier Vanbrugh-Hawksmoor era. Entrance front 9 bays with segmental pediment over 3-bay centre, with 1st-floor central window set in semicircular recess breaking into pediment. Interior largely remodelled in C19.

Claverton Manor, Avon
2m E of Bath
By Wyatville, c1820, in Palladian manner with pair of segmental bows on south front.

Claydon House, Buckinghamshire
5m S of Buckingham
Initially designed in austere Palladian manner by amateur architect Sir Thomas Robinson, c1750; exterior partly remodelled c1860. Interior fitted out c1765 by Luke Lightfoot in extreme rococo fashion, including rococo Chinese Room and rococo Gothic Room, c1765-70. Saloon with more Kentian decoration. North Hall double cube 50 by 25 by 25ft. (National Trust)

Clearwell Castle, Gloucestershire
5m SE of Monmouth
Castellated house by Roger Morris, built 1725-30, perhaps the earliest example of consciously mock-medieval, if not exactly Gothic, revival. Centre flanked by massive, squat square towers; all symmetrical. Inside, little survives.

Clifton
See Bristol.

Cliveden, Buckinghamshire
3m NE of Maidenhead
House of 1850 by Barry but **Gazebo** of c1740 and **Blenheim Pavilion** c1735 by Giacomo Leoni. (National Trust)

Clophill, Bedfordshire
3m E of Ampthill
Clophill House, High Street, C18. Opposite, **Ivy House,** c1750, with strange door-hood (see Ampthill, St Neots) whose columns, rather than being topped with capitals, break forward to support hood.

Clumber House, Nottinghamshire
3m SE of Worksop
House demolished 1938. In grounds, **bridge** and various **garden buildings** by Stephen Wright, c1775. (National Trust)

Clytha Park, Gwent
4m SE of Abergavenny
Powerful Greek revival mansion by Edward Haycock, c1830. Hexastyle Ionic portico based on Erechtheion. Side elevation has curved bow dressed with Greek Doric colonnade. Inside, stair hall with octagonal lantern and screen of Greek Doric columns.

  In park, **Clytha Castle,** Gothic folly of c1795 by John Nash.

Coggeshall, Essex
5m E of Braintree
10 Church Street, curiously over-scaled 2-storey house, c1715. Also in Church Street, late-C18 **house,** 5 bays, pedimented porch and belvedere.
  1 East Street, early C19, 3 bays, 2 storeys; early-C19 door surrounds and shop-fronts on other houses in street, such as **11, 13** and **15.**
  8 West Street, with rusticated, Doric-pilastered doorcase, c1740.

Colchester, Essex
  St Peter's Church, North Hill. Tower of 1758.
  The Hollytrees, High Street. Free-standing 5-bay brick house of 1718.
  63 West Stockwell Street, dated 1733 on hopper at rear. Gibbs door. At rear, extension on Tuscan columns. **59** and **60,** c1750, share 3-bay pediment containing Venetian window.
  60 North Hill, c1760, 1-bay pediment containing Venetian window and quatrefoil windows.
  Grey Friars House, High Street, 1755, with pair of canted bays flanking door and central pediment.
  54 Head Street, 1767, has door of classical composition but with Gothic motifs; **59 North Hill,** c1760, has similar doorcase.

Coleby Hall, Lincolnshire
7m S of Lincoln
Temple of Romulus and Remus by Sir William Chambers, 1762.

Coleorton Hall, Leicestershire
3m E of Ashby de la Zouch
George Dance the Younger, 1804-8, stripped Gothic. Inside, Gothic tribune, galleried, vaulted, on 12-sided plan. Additions of 1862.

Coleshill, Oxfordshire
3m SW of Faringdon
Strattenborough Castle Farm, remarkable castellated eye-catcher dated 1792. Really a farm with barns, but given elevation towards Coleshill House (demolished 1952) with 2 sham towers, big arrow-slits and cross windows.

Comarques, Essex
4m N of Clacton
Early-C18 brick house with 3-bay pediment containing Diocletian window above 1st-floor Venetian window. Windows contain octagonal glazing bars of pattern favoured by Sir Robert Taylor.

Combe Bank, Kent
3m W of Sevenoaks
Villa designed by Roger Morris 1725. Palladian tower house, closely based on Burlington's Tottenham Park, Wiltshire of 1721. Much altered in C19.

Combe Hay, Avon
3m S of Bath
Manor House, with 2 major fronts, set at right angles, which date from different periods. Earlier one, of c1730, in the manner of John Strahan and so in a provincial baroque style, with a round-headed niche set at ground level and topped by oval niche. Other façade elegant late-C18 neo-classical affair (perhaps by George Steuart): only unusual details are corners emphasized with un-moulded semicircular niches topped by oval niches.

Compton Verney, Warwickshire
7m E of Stratford-upon-Avon
West range baroque of 1714 with giant Tuscan pilasters. South and east front remodelled, in sympathetic style, by Robert Adam 1761-7. Roman hall with scenes by Zucchi.
Also **orangery** and **bridge; stable** by Gibbs.

Congleton, Cheshire
St Peter's Church. Unpretentious provincial style, 1742 with Gothic tower of 1786. Good C18 interior, especially pulpit.

Conington, Cambridgeshire
6m SE of Huntingdon
St Mary's Church, 1737, with crude Gibbs surrounds to windows.

Constable Burton Hall, North Yorkshire
6m S of Richmond
Built 1762-8 to design of John Carr at his best. Correct yet original essay in Palladian idiom, inspired by Villa Emo.

Conwy/Conway, Gwynedd
Suspension bridge by Thomas Telford, 1821-6, hung from towers of design inspired by Conway Castle.

Cookham, Berkshire
2m N of Maidenhead
Tarry Stone House, 5 bays, *c*1725. Doorway with segmental pediment and window above flanked by pilasters.

Copt Hall, Essex
2m W of Epping
John Sanderson rebuilt house 1753-8 under amateur direction of Sir Roger Newdigate and Thomas Prowse. Garden front and wing added in 1895. Now a dramatic shell.

Corsham, Wiltshire
5m SW of Chippenham
Town Hall, High Street, dated 1784, with arcaded ground floor (originally open), 3-bay pediment; altered 1882. Also in High Street, **Methuen Arms Hotel,** *c*1800, with porch of paired columns; **No.19,** early C18, 3 storeys, with segment-headed windows; **40,** late C18 but still with 2-light mullioned windows in gables; **76,** early C18 with open swan-neck pediment. At south end of High Street **The Grove,** built 1737, 5 bays, 2 storeys, centre emphasized by segmental-pedimented, columned door surround topped by pilasters, and triangular pediment to 1st-floor window.
The Priory, Priory Street, 1776. In same street, **No.2,** *c*1725-30, has 3-bay front with 2-storey frontispiece formed by segmental-pedimented, columned door topped by triangular pediment.
On east side of town, **Corsham Court,** Elizabethan house enlarged by Lancelot Brown 1761-4 and altered 1797-8 by John Nash and John Adey Repton, who designed a top-lit picture gallery/music room with a cast-iron roof. This, along with most of their work, was destroyed *c*1844. Some good C18 interiors survive, especially picture gallery by Brown.

Coton House, Warwickshire
3m N of Rugby
Samuel Wyatt, 1785; villa with most Wyattesque motifs - shallow bays, tripartite windows in arched recess.

Cottesbrooke Hall, Northamptonshire
8m N of Northampton
1702-13, probably by Francis Smith and based on Buckingham House, London. Interior mid-to-late C18, especially staircase with rococo papier-mâché decoration.

Cound Hall, Shropshire
6m SW of Shrewsbury
Vertical house of 1704 by John Prince, containing remarkable late-C18 flying staircase.

Courteenhall Hall, Northamptonshire
5m S of Northampton
Samuel Saxon, 1791-4. Pedimented façade, ground-floor windows set within segmental arches. Some excellent interiors in style of Chambers.

Coventry, Warwickshire
County Hall, Bayley Lane, *c*1760-84. Front toward lane is of brick with stone dressings, possibly by Samuel Eglington. Elevation to Cuckoo Lane 5 bays, ashlar, composed of rusticated base with blind arcade and 3-bay Doric pediment.
Kirby House, Little Park Street, *c*1735 in baroque style of Francis Smith with giant Ionic pilasters having Adamesque capitals of *c*1775.
7 Little Park Street, *c*1730, with giant Corinthian pilasters.
In Binley, **St Bartholomew's Church,** 1771, probably by Robert Adam.

Cowes, Isle of Wight
St Mary's Church, West Cowes. Spectacular, bold Greek revival tower by John Nash, 1816.
St Thomas of Canterbury's Church, Terminus Road. Roman Catholic church of 1796 designed by Thomas Gabb. Yellow stock brick with windows in giant arches (now containing ugly later tracery). Last giant bay contains domestic-scaled windows of rectory.
Former **Wesleyan Chapel,** 19 Birmingham Road, *c*1830, with Gothic detail.
29, 30, 33 High Street, *c*1800 **41,** with pair of full-height canted bays, *c*1800. **62** has remains of Regency shop-front with Gothic detailing. **60-63,** *c*1810 with façade of blue headers and windows with red brick arches and dressings - a Cowes speciality. **88,** with 3-bay pediment, *c*1790, and pedimented doorcase.
4-10 Bath Road, *c*1820, with full-height curved and canted bays, 6 with a tiny contemporary curved shop, form a group with **Bar Hill House** (entered from Bar Hill), which has full-height neo-classically detailed bay and delicate doorcase with Gothic details.
16 Shooter's Hill has excellent Greek-detailed façade and shop of *c*1830.
Westbourne House, Birmingham Road, large urban composition of *c*1750. To street 8 bays, 2 storeys with angle and centre pilasters, moulded string course and red dressings to windows, which contain flush box sashes - all look *c*1725 in style. River front 3 storeys with 8 windows divided by giant pilasters into groups of 2-1-2-1-2; moulded string course breaks forward over pilaster shafts. (Partly demolished December 1984.)
Claremont House, Market Hill, *c*1800; canted bay, pedimented door. In same street, **15-18,** good group of mid-to-late C18 cottages. Off Market Hill, **1-5 Ward Cottages,** *c*1780 with unusual bulgy pilasters to doors. Rubble-built façades - as also at **Glebe Cottage,** Newport Road.

2 Castle Road, excellent clapboard cottage, *c*1780-1800, with keystones to architraved window surrounds. **8-10,** good 2-storey, 2-bay cottages with segmental windows to ground floor, string course, flush box sashes and dressings to windows, look *c*1725 but must be *c*1750. Similar examples are **5-7 Union Road** and **4-6, 24-6 Sun Hill.** Also in Sun Hill, **18 (Ivy House),** *c*1800, large, detached, with full-height, asymmetrically placed curved bay, tripartite pedimented door.

21 Union Road (Union House) and **23,** pair of *c*1800 clad in mathematical tiles, both with delicately detailed pedimented doors, 21 with pair of full-height canted bays.

Cranborne Lodge, Dorset
9m N of Wimborne Minster
In local late baroque tradition (see Encombe House), designed *c*1740. North front has massive triple keystones to 1st-floor windows. South front has giant Ionic pilasters.

Cranbrook, Kent
12m S of Maidstone
Providence Chapel, off Stone Street, 1828. Front has faceted bow faced with timber grooved to look like ashlar and supported on Tuscan piers. Interior with galleries on 3 sides.

Union Mill, also off Stone Street, 72ft clapboarded smock-mill on tall brick base. Dated 1814 and in full working order.

School House, Waterloo Road, 1727-9, recessed centre with Tuscan loggia. Architect was a John Fieldhouse.

In High Street, **Webster House,** *c*1725 with good Doric door surround, C19 bay windows. Opposite is **Shepherds,** *c*1720-25 with giant angle pilaster strips. Nearby, **High House,** *c*1730. 3 doors down is a good **clapboard house** with pedimented hooded door and canted bays with tripartite windows.

Hill House, St David's Bridge, long, low tile-hung house with early-C18 Corinthian doorcase.

Cranbury Park, Hampshire
3m N of Eastleigh
George Dance the Younger added ballroom and hall, *c*1780, to existing house. Exterior of these additions now altered, but ballroom interior survives and is one of Dance's most important works, introducing motif of pendentive ceiling on apses. Additions of 1830s by J. B. Papworth include tent room in Empire style.

Creech Grange, Dorset
3m S of Wareham
Dates from mid-C16. South front of 1738-41 by Francis Cartwright in modest Palladian manner.

Crichel House, Dorset
7m E of Blandford Forum
Exterior dated 1743; in an interesting example of C18 good manners, enlargement works of 1765 are in same Palladian style as original. East front bold composition with pediment above 1st-floor Venetian window linked by rusticated aprons to pedimented tripartite door. Inside, *c*1745 rooms in Kentian style, later part in early Wyatt style, probably by Biagio Rebecca, *c*1775.

Cricket Court, Somerset
2m S of Ilminster
Highly eccentric house of 1811 by Stephen Pitt for himself, including such unusual features as staircase which folds to prevent flood waters from the bathroom engulfing Pitt in his bed; hidden lens to spy on guests; and recess in roof to store his coffin. Awkward exterior, curious off-centre Tuscan portico on entrance front. Inside, some exquisite details including galleried landing with dome, circular domed library.

Criggion, Powys
7m NE of Welshpool/Trallwng
St Michael and All Angels' Church. Little brick church of 1774 with stone quoins and dressings. Nave has lancet windows, presumably C19. Inside, C18 box pews and pulpit and sounding board.

Croft Castle, Hereford and Worcester
5m NW of Leominster
Late C14 castle Gothicized 1765 by T. F. Pritchard: east front and staircase hall especially good.

Cromford, Derbyshire
2m S of Matlock
Early-C18 mining village developed by Richard Arkwright after 1771 when he chose it as the location for his textile factories.

St Mary's Church, Mill Road, built by Arkwright to designs of Thomas Gardner, 1792. Gothicized 1858.

In **Mill Road,** Arkwright's cotton-spinning **mill,** *c*1772-7. 3 storeys, originally 5. Mullioned windows, but none along road at ground level owing to fear of industrial espionage. Timber construction with no attempt at fire-proofing. In same complex, contemporary **offices.**

Cromford Canal by William Jessop and Benjamin Outram, 1793. At Cromford Wharf, early canal **warehouses.** Opposite, mill with manager's house **(The Shrubbery)** and **Rock House** where Arkwright first lived. **Masson Mill,** 1783, by Arkwright. Much enlarged in C20 but centre still the original 6-storey mill embellished with tiers of Venetian and Diocletian windows.

In **North Street, workers' housing** of 1771-6 by Arkwright. Stone-built, 3 storeys with range of mullioned windows at 2nd-floor level to light framework-knitting rooms.

At **Scarthin Nick, Greyhound Inn** of 1778 – like minor town hall with pedimented centre.

Willersley Castle, built by Arkwright 1789 to designs of William Thomas. Classical in plan and form, but romanticized by battlements and semi-circular turrets. Interior by Gardner after fire of 1791.

High Peak Canal Junction, canal aqueduct over River Derwent, 1792 by Jessop.

Cronkhill, Shropshire
4m SW of Shrewsbury
John Nash, 1802. First picturesque Italianate villa, asymmetrical; round tower with conical roof and deep, projecting eaves. (National Trust)

Croome d'Abitot, Hereford and Worcester
4m W of Pershore
St Mary Magdalene's Church: 1761-3 exterior is a serious early attempt at antiquarian Gothic, probably by Lancelot Brown. Interior, with elegant Gothic plasterwork, by Robert Adam.

Croome Court, 1751, in valley below church, by Lancelot Brown with advice of Sanderson Miller (see Hagley). Palladian with corner towers.

Interior completed after 1760 by R. Adam.
Garden Temple, *c*1760; **Orangery, Rotunda, Owl's Nest,** all *c*1760-65, by R. Adam.

Crowcombe Court, Somerset
6m SE of Watchet
Nathaniel Ireson, 1734. Provincial baroque. East front pedimented, south front with dramatic curved wings embracing stable court. Light rococo interior decoration. Damaged by fire 1963.

Croxdale Hall, Co. Durham
4m S of Durham
7-bay front, rubble with ashlar dressing, 3 ranges round courtyard, *c*1760 but probably older core. Inside, chapel contains the most elaborate Gothic revival decoration in north of England, similar to Wyatt's work of 1793 at Bishop Auckland (qv).

Cuerden Hall, Lancashire
2m N of Leyland
Remodelling of earlier house by Lewis William Wyatt, 1815. Classical but of picturesque composition: corner towers, central clerestory over staircase.

Culverthorpe Hall, Lincolnshire
4m S of Sleaford
Late-C17 house largely remodelled in C18, probably by Robert Morris, including east and west wings, each furnished with Venetian windows and lunettes, of *c*1734. South front of main house altered at same time. Inside, tripartite hall with 2 screens of paired fluted Corinthian columns.

Culzean Castle, Strathclyde
4m W of Maybole
Robert Adam, 1777-92. Large additions to medieval castle are symmetrically planned with classical detail but castellated and with towers – one of Adam's first works in the 'castle air' style of Vanbrugh. Service buildings irregular to make asymmetrical picturesque composition.
  Nearby, **model farm.** (National Trust for Scotland).

Dalmahoy House, Lothian
5m S of Queensferry
William Adam, 1725-8. Austere 3-storey double pile, 7 bays with 3-bay recessed centre.

Dalmeny House, Lothian
2m E of Queensferry
William Wilkins, 1814-17. Large, influential Tudor Gothic mansion.

Dalquharran Castle, Strathclyde
10m S of Maybole
Robert Adam, 1790 in particularly bold version of his castle style. Now a ruin.

Darlington, Co. Durham
  The Golden Cock, 12 Tubwell Row, *c*1780, with central bay window.
  Bennet House, Horsemarket, large mid-C18 double-pile house with rusticated quoins, Gibbs surround to door. Also in Horsemarket, **12A,** early C18. On south side of market place, **10,** late C18 with full-height bow and tripartite windows; **11** of 7 bays.
  13 High Row, with hopper dated 1733; **17-18** with 3-bay pediment.
  West Lodge, West Crescent, C18 with front of *c*1805 by James Backhouse.

Dartmoor Prison, Devon
N edge of Princetown
1805-9 by D.A. Alexander to house French prisoners of war. Much altered.

Davenport House, Shropshire
2m NE of Bridgnorth
Francis Smith, 1726. Main house connected to service blocks by curved brick walls. Inside, entrance hall with imitation ashlar decoration, door with Gibbs surround and wood-block rustication on wall of staircase hall. 1st-floor saloon has inlaid floor.

Daventry, Northamptonshire
  Holy Cross Church, 1752-8 by David Hiorne in tradition of Gibbs's St Martin-in-the-Fields.
  United Reformed Church in court off Sheaf Street, dated 1722.
  Moot Hall, Market Square, ashlar, ground floor arcaded, dated 1769. Side elevation *c*1804.
  Saracen's Head, Brook Street, has plain rendered front with hopper dated 1769, but superb rear elevation with finely detailed Ionic Venetian window to ground floor (now made into door). At right angles to this, splendid 3-bay brick elevation with pair of Venetian windows set in blank arches. This wing continued by long, 2-storey brick range containing stabling for inn, forming elongated court with parallel wing. Both wings ruinous in 1984.
  47-9 Sheaf Street, *c*1730, handsome brick terrace.
  5 Market Square, *c*1720, astonishingly bold coved hood to door.
  High Street contained most imposing of town's C18 houses, but these now reduced to mere façades with new shops and offices behind. However, front of **17** still notable, 7 bays, 3-bay pediment, Gibbs door surround; and **29,** *c*1730.

Daylesford House, Gloucestershire
3m E of Stow-on-the-Wold
S. P. Cockerell, 1788-93. Neo-classical mansion with French details but eclectic touches. Top of dome derived from Muslim architecture. Circular boudoir with lotus capitals and cloud-painted ceiling; morning room has fireplace, 1792, with 'Hindoo' embellishments and Indian figures as caryatids. Cockerell worked for the East India Company, and the house was for Warren Hastings.

Deal, Kent
  St George's Church, High Street, completed 1716 to design of Samuel Simons, advised by John James.
  Town Hall, High Street, dated 1803. Yellow brick with rudimentary Venetian window in centre of 1st floor; ground floor treated as loggia.

Debden, Essex
3m S of Saffron Walden
St Mary the Virgin and All Saints' Church. Medieval church with 1792 chapel by antiquary John Carter. This is octagonal and constructed of white brick with paper-thin tracery detailing and plaster ribbed vault.

Dedham, Essex
6m NE of Colchester
Former **Grammar School** and its neighbours (beside church), good early-C18 group. One dated 1732. Door with segmental pediment, giant angle pilasters.

Sherman's, *c*1730; façade framed by giant pilasters with central pedimented niche above pedimented door.

Denton Hall, North Yorkshire
1m NE of Ilkley
By John Carr, 1770-81. 9-bay entrance front. Full-height bay on side elevation. Inside, magnificent stair rising into domed gallery.

Derby, Derbyshire
All Saints' Cathedral Church. All but C16 tower by James Gibbs, 1723-5. Gibbs block surrounds to nave windows; interior developed from St Martin-in-the-Fields.
Gaol, Vernon Street, by Francis Goodwin, 1823-7. Greek Doric; altered 1880.
Friar Gate contains a number of extremely good large mid-C18 houses. **27,** *c*1765, centre emphasized with Doric-columned door topped by pedimented 1st-floor window with eared architrave. **41,** 1768, has most complex and satisfactory elevational design, thought to be by Joseph Pickford. Brick, 5 bays, 3 storeys. Surface of façade in 3 planes: bays 2 and 4 break forward, centre bay recessed, beneath giant arch, farther back than bays 1 and 5. Over 3 centre bays, large open pediment with 3 blocked-ball finials. Door tripartite, pedimented, with Adamesque details. **43,** *c*1770, centre bay breaking forward and with pedimented doorcase. **44,** 5 bays, 3 storeys, 3-bay centre with Venetian windows flanking pedimented door, 3 1st-floor windows set in large blank arches; *c*1770 by Joseph Pickford, and identical to Lloyds Bank in Ashbourne (qv) except that this is of brick, not ashlar. **45,** 1st-floor windows with triangular pediments. **65,** *c*1810, 8 bays with Ionic porch and mathematical tiles. **99,** *c*1750-60, with centre bay breaking forward and with Doric pedimented door; eared architraves to all windows.

Devizes, Wiltshire
Town Hall, 1806-8 by Thomas Baldwin, ashlar. Front elevation Palladian, rear neo-classical with centrally placed 3-bay full-height curved bow dressed with Greek Ionic columns. Inside, assembly room with Adamesque details.
New Hall, formerly **Cheese Hall,** Wine Street, 1750 by a certain Lawrence. Provincial Palladian composition with the solecism of centrally placed engaged column beneath pediment.
Black Swan Hotel, Market Place, dated 1737 on hopper head. 3 storeys, 7 bays divided into groups by 4 giant pilaster strips. Arch leads to rear. Also in Market Place, **Bear Hotel** consists of 2 buildings: one C17 refronted with stucco in early C19; other *c*1790-1800, elegant neo-classically detailed 2-storey house with pair of canted bays.
Long Street contains town's best sequence of Georgian houses, several of ambitious size. **8,** dated 1737. **9,** with tripartite opening. **10,** *c*1750. **11,** with neo-classical porch of *c*1790. **26,** with 3 storeys of paired bipartite windows flanking centre bay. **39 (The Rectory),** *c*1740.
16 Market Place, early C18 with shell-hooded door. **23 (Parnella House),** *c*1740-45; vigorous provincial design. 3-storey elevation enlivened by pair of 2-storey canted bays framing central 1-bay frontispiece; 1st-floor windows in bays wraparound Venetians. Ground floor rusticated, embellished with Tuscan colonnade. 1st-floor centre bay has rusticated niche containing statue of Aesculapius, for this was built as doctor's house. **17,** in modest Wren manner though probably *c*1710-20: brick, quoins, white wooden eaves cornice, hipped roof. Of similar type but more stately is **Brownston House,** 17-20 New Park Street, dated 1720, all strictly symmetrical. Door has segmental pediment. On other side of the road, **cloth factory** dated 1785 on lead hoppers.
Sandcliffe House, Northgate Street, early C18, stone-built with giant pilasters. In same street, **Northgate House** (formerly **Judge's Lodgings**), *c*1750.
29-30 St John Street, dated 1749 on hopper.
Greystone House, High Street, 1731, ashlar.
In **Lansdowne Grove** and **Lansdowne Terrace,** some excellent early-C19 **villas** and 3-storey **terraces.** Especially good are **1-4 Lansdowne Grove,** with anthemion-pattern cast-iron balconies and decorated iron door surrounds.

Devonport
See Plymouth.

Didsbury
See Manchester.

Ditchley Park, Oxfordshire
4m NW of Woodstock
Designed by James Gibbs 1720-31, built by Francis Smith. Strong sense of baroque movement in façade. Door with block surrounds; windows with architraves, keystones, brackets to cills; much quoining. William Kent decorated entrance hall, *c*1730, Henry Flitcroft drawing room.

Doddington Hall, Cheshire
7m S of Crewe
Samuel Wyatt, 1777-98. Earliest use of what became Wyatt's trademark: tripartite window in arched recess. Main rooms on 1st floor. Bow in centre of garden front. Elevations decorated with Coade stone plaques showing signs of the Zodiac.

Dodington Park, Avon
10m NE of Bristol
James Wyatt, 1793-1813. Noble Corinthian portico echoed inside by paired Corinthian columns in hall, leading to imperial staircase. House made asymmetrical by office and kitchen wing.
Lodges circular with dome, showing Wyatt influenced by French neo-classicism, *c*1802.
St Mary's Church, by Wyatt, 1800-5, forms part of outworks of house. Greek cross with central dome and four barrel-vaulted arms.

Dollar, Central Region
6m NE of Alloa
Dollar Academy, 1818-20 by William Playfair. Large, symmetrical classical pile with hexastyle giant Tuscan portico.

Doncaster, South Yorkshire
Christ Church, Thorne Road, by William Hurst, 1827-9; Gothic.
Mansion House, by James Paine 1745-8; top storey added 1801. Ashlar façade painted; ground floor rusticated; 1st floor with Corinthian columns and Venetian window. Doorway recessed, with blocked Ionic columns. Good staircase and magnificent rococo Banqueting Room.
19-20 South Parade, early C19; 1st-floor bows supported on elevated ground-floor colonnade.
At racecourse, a **grandstand** by John Carr, 1776, enlarged 1810-20; round-headed windows,

bows at ends. Also **Noblemen's Stand** of cast-iron construction, 1826.

Donhead Hall, Wiltshire
3m NE of Shaftesbury
Built 1724, house has remarkable similarities with Thomas Archer's slightly earlier Chettle House (qv), only 8 miles distant. Donhead is 2-storey, stone-built and, like Chettle, has unusual feature of projecting entrance hall (now dining room) expressed externally as bay with flat end and quadrant sides.

Donington Hall, Leicestershire
6m SW of Long Eaton
Designed by William Wilkins the Elder, 1790-93, in restrained Gothic manner. Ashlar with large-scale Gothic-arched entrance porch. Interior mostly classical in detail.

Donnington Grove, Berkshire
1m N of Newbury
Castellated Gothic house by John Chute, c1762. Particularly fine staircase with Gothic colonnade around top landing under lantern.

Dorchester, Dorset
Shire Hall, High West Street, 1795-7 by Thomas Hardwick. Austere, Portland stone, centre 3 bays on ground floor formed as rusticated entrance arcade. 1 courtroom original.

Portal survives from **County Gaol,** off North Square, 1789-95 by William Blackburn.

In High Street, **Bridge Hotel,** with late-C18 ashlar front; **23,** dated 1735 on hopper, with 1st-floor central pedimented tripartite feature.

Antelope Hotel, South Street, 1815, with shallow segmental bows. Also in South Street, good group of C18 brick **houses** including a contemporary shop-front. **Barclay's Bank,** South Street, c1785, faced with vitrified headers.

South Lodge, South Walks, c1760, later stucco on façade, but good contemporary interior including Chinese Chippendale staircase.

Wollaston House, Durngate Street, 1786.

Doune Park, Central Region
5m NW of Bridge of Allan
Home Farm, 1807-9, perhaps by William Stirling. Symmetrical, with classical detail and tower topped by spire.

Dover, Kent
Unitarian Chapel, Adrian Street, 1819 by Thomas Read, irregular brick octagon.

On **Western Heights,** massive network of **fortifications,** built 1793-1814 but still based on principles of Vauban. Notable features surviving are **The Citadel,** centre of scheme of fortifications; and **Drop Redoubt,** completed 1808, consisting of series of huge underground chambers. **Grand Shaft,** designed by Sir Thomas Hyde Page and completed 1802, brick shaft containing 2 interlocked spiral staircases.

5 Castlehill, c1760, best C18 house in town: centre 2 bays breaking forward under pediment; pedimented doorcase; bow on rear elevation.

Downton Castle, Hereford and Worcester
5m W of Ludlow
Richard Payne Knight, pioneer of the picturesque movement, designed house for himself. Begun 1772, asymmetrical, castellated and towered but with classical windows (existing Gothic ones are C19 alteration) and classical interior. Especially good is polychromatic Pantheon Dining Room, on which Nash may have advised.

Dreghorn, Strathclyde
2m E of Irvine
Octagonal **church** of 1780.

The Drum, Lothian
SE edge of Edinburgh
Designed by William Adam 1726-30 in strongly baroque-flavoured provincial Palladian manner. 2 storeys over basement with pedimented central feature containing pedimented door flanked by narrow windows and topped by large 1st-floor Venetian window. Very rich rococo interior.

Drummore House, Lothian
2m E of Musselburgh
Built c1760, with wide 3-bay front. Design corresponds to plate in George Jameson's *Thirty-three Designs,* 1765. Inside, fine rococo plasterwork with richly carved pediments inscribed with lines from James Thomson's poem *The Seasons.*

Drumtochty Castle, Grampian
5m N of Laurencekirk
By James Gillespie Graham, c1815. Castellated with tower inspired by Warwick Castle.

Duddingston, Lothian
In E Edinburgh
Villa by Sir William Chambers 1762-7, in chaste neo-classical manner that anticipates villa designs of later C18. 5 bays, 2-storey entrance front with giant Corinthian portico rising from ground, as in a Greek temple. Inside, ingenious stair but otherwise sparse detailing. Asymmetrically placed **stables** of c1762, where Chambers used Doric columns without bases, an early example.

Duff House, Grampian
SE edge of Banff
William Adam, 1735-9. Palladian block embellished with giant Corinthian pilasters.

Duffield, Derbyshire
2m S of Belper
Baptist Chapel, 1830. Adjacent, **Potterell's Almshouses,** 1810.

In Town Street, good collection of Georgian houses, especially **Gervase House** (No.48), c1785, with tripartite windows and Adam flourishes; **The Ferns** (No.56), 1-bay pediment on 3-bay front.

The Park, Tamworth Street, late Georgian; **Tamworth House,** c1714.

Dumfries House, Strathclyde
12m E of Ayr
Main front by John and Robert Adam, 1754-9. Very standard example of provincial Palladian style.

Dundas Castle, Lothian
1m SW of Queensferry
William Burn, 1818. One façade castellated, the other ecclesiastical Gothic.

Dundee, Tayside
St Andrew's Church, 1772 to designs of Samuel Bell, perhaps with James Craig. Simple rectangular plan. Inside, half-octagonal gallery.

St Ninian's Church, Methven Street, by David Neave 1829-30. Tower still inspired by 100-year-old designs of Gibbs.

Glassite Chapel, King Street, 1777, octagonal with round-headed windows.

7-21 Castle Street, pedimented façade of Samuel Bell's former **Theatre Royal**, 1807-9, with bust of Shakespeare in round niche on pediment.

Exchange Coffee Room, corner of Castle Street and Exchange Street, 1828-30 by George Smith. Fine Greek revival design. Inside, on 1st floor, coffee room, reading room, assembly room and library; fine staircase.

28 High Street, plain-fronted 4-storey house of 1785 with wall-head gable facing street.

Castle Hill House, 1 High Street, late-C18 house in provincial style.

7-19 King Street, 1815-19, probably by local architect David Neave in handsome neo-classical manner.

Nethergate House, 158 Nethergate, perhaps by Samuel Bell, built 1790. Fine door surround with engaged Ionic columns. On each side elevation, single-storey pavilion.

Morgan Tower, 135-9 Nethergate, Samuel Bell 1794, block of tenements with extraordinary feature of curved bay which, by rising 1 extra storey above 4-storey flanking elevation, takes form of a tower; impression reinforced by bay being separately roofed with Saracenic-looking ogee roof complete with Muslim crescent moon on weathervane; tower lit by tiers of curved rudimentary Venetian windows.

Milns Buildings, 136-40 Nethergate, c1790. Attributed to Samuel Bell, but if so hard to reconcile with nearby Nethergate House, for these buildings form archaic group, with large-scale Gibbs surrounds to doors, flat lintels containing massive fan-shaped keystones.

Reform Street, conceived by William Burn 1824, built by George Angus 1833. Fine austere neo-classical street with ground floor designed as uniform shops.

South Tay Street, laid out 1792. South side contains fine classical terrace built 1819-29 to designs of David Neave, in manner of Edinburgh New Town but with more decorative flourishes.

2-32 Springfield, suburban development of 1828. Beautifully detailed 2-storey terrace houses grouped in pairs descending hill. Balustraded parapets, shared Greek Doric porches.

Union Street, designed 1828 by David Neave with, like Reform Street, apartments above shops.

Dunstable, Bedfordshire
Chew Grammar School, 1719, pedimented front; adjacent, **Cart Almshouses** of c1723, in High Street South; both red brick.

Priory House, High Street South, c1730, stuccoed, arched windows on 1st floor.

Old Sugar Loaf Inn, High Street North, dated 1717.

Dunstall Priory, Kent
4m N of Sevenoaks
By Robert Lugar, 1806. Early example of asymmetrical Italianate villa. Inspired by Nash's Cronkhill (qv).

Durham, Co. Durham
St Cuthbert's Roman Catholic Church, Court Lane, by Ignatius Bonomi, 1827, Gothic.

Castle (now part of **University**) contains some interesting early Gothic revival work by Sanderson Miller, especially in Bishop's Dining Room (now Senior Common Room) and excellent windows in Norman Gallery, all 1752-3. **Gatehouse** romanticized c1790 in Wyatt manner. Gothic **Conduit House** of 1751.

Crown Court (formerly **Assize Court**) and **Gaol** by George Moneypenny, completed 1811 by Bonomi.

Bishop Cosin's Hall, Palace Green, c1725. Asymmetrically placed door with segmental pediment and deep tympanum full of carving, supported on Ionic pilasters.

5 North Bailey, c1740; shell hood added to door 1910. **22,** unusual doorcase of c1800 on older house: fluted balusters instead of pilasters. **44,** c1715-20, roughly dressed stone façade, swan-neck pedimented door; **46,** c1730-40.

1 South Bailey, 1730, 7-bay, 3-storey dressed stone façade, pilastered stone doorcase. **3 (Haughton House)** best Georgian house in town, built c1730; has bold Vanbrughian quality, with entire stone façade treated as banded rustication. Doorcase has flat cornice on massive carved brackets. **6,** early C18; early-C19 round-headed door with slender Greek Ionic columns.

Arts Centre, Castle Chare, double-pile house, front range dated 1741, back range probably slightly earlier. Rear wing has Venetian, tripartite and round windows set one above the other in rear elevation. Inside this wing, in ground-floor room, remarkable Palladian-rococo plasterwork, c1745.

47-9 Old Elvet, early-C18 terrace. **15** and **19,** dated 1764, have Chinese Chippendale stair balustrades.

Dursley, Gloucestershire
6m W of Nailsworth
Town Hall/Market House, 1738. Open arcade, niche with statue of Queen Anne.

Long Street contains numerous C18 houses including **Old Bell Hotel** (No.56), grandest C18 house in town, c1730. Ashlar, balustraded parapet. Shell-hood doorcase on detached Roman Doric columns. 1st-floor window above enriched with Ionic pilasters, window above that with Corinthian ones.

In Woodmancote, row of fine C18 houses, especially **Hill House.**

Earsham Hall, Norfolk
1m S of Bungay
Music room added to house by Sir John Soane in 1784. Shallow-coffered vaulted ceiling with pair of coffered apses.

Eastbourne, East Sussex
Compton Place, Jacobean house remodelled 1726 by Colen Campbell; exterior remodelled again in 1800. Campbell's work includes State Bedroom, c1728, with much stucco decoration including relief bust of Campbell himself.

Eastbury, Dorset
5m NE of Blandford Forum
Vanbrugh's great house destroyed; service wing of 1718-38 survives. 3-bay, 3-storey centre with round-headed windows on 1st floor. Strong, bold composition typical of Vanbrugh's stripped classical style.

East Dereham, Norfolk
Old Assembly Room, Market Place, 4 bays, pedimented, 1765. Also in Market Place, **Hill House,** c1745, with 3-bay pediment and rusticated pilasters. Similar pilasters on 3-storey **terrace** of same date in **Quebec Street.**

East Lulworth, Dorset
5m SW of Wareham
St Mary's Roman Catholic Church, 1786 by John Tasker. First Catholic Church to be built in England since Reformation. George III gave permission for its construction on condition that it did not look ecclesiastical, so it looks like large garden temple. Quatrefoil plan, central dome painted like sky, fine neo-classical interior.

Eastnor Castle, Hereford and Worcester
2m SE of Ledbury
1811-20 by Sir Robert Smirke; baronial, with forbidding symmetrical castellated and towered exterior, round-arched windows.

East Stratton, Hampshire
8m NE of Winchester
Model village of picturesquely thatched cottages by George Dance the Younger, 1806.
Stratton Park. Only Doric portico survives of Dance's important Greek revival house of 1803.

Eaton Mascott Hall, Shropshire
6m S of Shrewsbury
Provincial Palladian, 1734. Venetian windows flanking door; Diocletian window in 1-bay open pediment which rises above rest of centre.

Eaton Socon, Cambridgeshire
5m N of Sandy
White Horse Inn, *c*1750.
Tithe Farm, 2-storey octagonal house of 1797 by Robert Salmon.

Ebberston Hall, North Yorkshire
9m SW of Scarborough
Summer house designed by Colen Campbell 1718. 1 storey over semi-basement.

Ecton Hall, Northamptonshire
4m NE of Northampton
Early Gothic revival. Ashlar battlemented front dated 1756, attributed to Sanderson Miller.

Edge Hill, Warwickshire
6m NW of Banbury
Edgehill Tower, octagonal eye-catcher in form of ruined castle, based on Guy's Tower at Warwick. Designed 1745, with adjacent **cottage,** 1743, by Sanderson Miller; with exception of Alfred's Hall (see Cirencester) earliest of asymmetrical picturesque Gothic-detailed compositions.

Edinburgh, Lothian
St Andrew's Church, George Street. Oval body designed 1785 by Major Fraser, with tower and Corinthian portico by William Sibbald 1786-7.
St Cuthbert's Church, Lothian Road. Tower and steeple of 1789 by Alexander Stevens, based closely on Gibbs.
St Mary's Church, Bellevue Crescent, 1826 by Thomas Brown in classical manner of Smirke.
Law Courts, Parliament Square, High Street. C16 refaced in classical manner from 1804 by Robert Reid. Adjoining is contemporary **Signet Library** (1812-16), by same architect and in same style, with magnificent interior of 1813-22 by William Stark.
Royal Exchange (now **City Chambers**), High Street, 1753-61 by John Adam in provincial Palladian style.
Register House, overlooking North Bridge, by Robert Adam 1774-92. 13 bays, 2 storeys; essay in neo-classically detailed Palladian design. Especially good is dome over library. Extended by Robert Reid, 1822-30.
University, Chambers Street. Plan and east front based on Robert Adam's design of *c*1789, one of his most austere, sublime compositions. Completed by William H. Playfair and Robert Reid after 1817; Sir Rowand Anderson added dome in 1887.
Assembly Rooms, George Street, 1784-7 by John Henderson; portico 1818.
St Cecilia's Hall, Niddry Street, 1761 by Robert Mylne.
Merchants' Hall, 3-4 Hunter Square, 1788 by John Baxter the Younger, altered 1894.
John Watson School (now **Gallery of Modern Art**), 1825-8 by William Burn in Grecian manner, with giant Doric portico.
Royal High School, Regent Road, Calton Hill, 1825-9 by Thomas Hamilton; perhaps the finest Greek revival composition in the British Isles. Also on Calton Hill, castellated picturesque **Observatory** of 1776 by James Craig, Greek revival **Observatory** of 1818 by Playfair, and **Dugald Stewart Monument** of *c*1830 by Playfair, based on Choragic Monument of Lysicrates, Athens.
Royal Institution (**Royal Scottish Academy**), The Mount, 1822-6, extended by W.H. Playfair 1832-5 in powerful neo-Greek manner with Doric colonnades and portico.
West side, and part of east side of **George Square,** *c*1765 by James Brown, represent Edinburgh's earliest attempt at (loosely) uniform urban planning and building.
Gayfield House, East London Road, 1765 by Charles and William Butter, free-standing pedimented Palladian composition.
James Craig's plan for the **New Town** dates from 1766. Of the austere, uniform ashlar-faced houses it envisaged, best examples now are in **Queen Street,** built 1769-92 with **No.1** by R. Adam, 1770-71, **George Street,** and **North Castle Street,** especially **34-36, 39-59.**
Craig proposed 2 squares: **Charlotte Square** was built to a design Robert Adam produced for the corporation in 1791. It remains a handsome monument to refined and austere neo-classical taste.
St Andrew's Square contains several individual houses of note, especially **Dundas House,** 1771 by Sir William Chambers but altered externally 1828 and internally 1858. **No.26,** a 6-bay house of coursed rubble walling dressed with delicate neo-classical details, *c*1770, attributed to Chambers; also **21, 22, 24, 35, 36** of pre-1790.
Thistle Court contains modest 2-storey houses, reputed to be earliest built in New Town.
In **Old Town, Smith's Close,** High Street, tenement built *c*1720 as speculation by James Smith; **14 High Street (Tweeddale Lodging)** reconstructed by John Adam, 1752; **119 High Street,** early C18.
Chessel's Court (240 Canongate), *c*1750.
102-18 Nicholson Street and **9-15 Buccleuch Street,** *c*1780, are characteristically Scottish, tall tenements.
Buccleuch Place, laid out by James Brown, *c*1779, grandest street in Edinburgh's south side. **1-6,** *c*1790 by Brown with rusticated ground floor and tall ashlar façade; **7-13,** 1786-7; **17-19,** *c*1785.

St Bernard's Crescent, Edinburgh, 1824, by James Milne, an unusually bold expression of the Greek revival in street architecture.

Moray Place, magnificent 16-faceted circus of 1822-30 by James Gillespie Graham; centrepiece of the Moray Estate. Detail in austere Adam manner, each quadrant having pedimented centre with 4 Tuscan columns rising from a rusticated, arcaded basement. On axis with Moray Place, oval **Ainslie Place** and **Randolph Crescent,** both begun in 1820s.

Northern New Town, planned by Reid and Sibbald 1801-2, contains as its centrepiece **Drummond Place,** apsidal-ended square begun 1806 and built through the years to c1820; linked by **Great King Street,** built 1812-c1820, to **Royal Circus,** 1820 by Playfair and consisting of uniform 3- and 4-storey ashlar houses with rusticated ground floor.

On edges of the estate, either side of Great King Street, **Abercromby Place** and **Royal Crescent.** Both shallow crescents: former built c1807-20 to designs by Reid, J. G. Graham and others; latter begun 1823 under control of Thomas Brown.

Behind Drummond Place, **Bellevue Crescent,** designed 1818 by Thomas Bonnar.

Other excellent streets in this development: **Fettes Row,** begun 1821; **Heriot Row,** begun 1802 by Reid; **London Street,** 1806 by Reid; **India Street,** begun 1819 under control of Bonnar. **Broughton Place,** begun 1807 to design of Hugh Cairncross, with pedimented palace-fronted north side.

Western New Town was planned in 1809 by Graham; building began generally c1825. **Atholl Crescent,** 1825 by Bonnar, and **Coates Crescent,** begun 1813 by Robert Brown, make an elliptical circus. **Melville Street,** main axis of the estate, comprises long, uniform terraces, designed 1814 by Brown. **William Street,** 1824-5, contains shops.

Raeburn Estate, just north-west of Moray Place, includes **St Bernard's Crescent,** 1824 by James Milne, with uniform 2-storey houses embellished with 1- and 2-storey Greek Doric columns.

East of Calton Hill, magnificent, monumental **Royal Terrace,** begun 1821 to designs of Playfair. Opposite, **Hillside Crescent,** designed 1823 by Playfair, with houses linked by Greek Doric ground-floor colonnade.

Leith
North Leith Church, Prince Regent Street, by William Burn 1814-16; Grecian version of St Martin-in-the-Fields.
Town Hall, Richard and Robert Dickinson, 1827-8.
Exchange Building, Constitution Street, 1809 by Thomas Brown, incorporating 1783 **Assembly Room.**
In **Bernard Street,** purpose-built **bank** of 1804; Wyattesque bowed front with giant order.
Custom House, Richard Reid, 1811.

Egham, Surrey
Church of St John the Baptist, 1817-20 by Henry Rhodes, a Board of Works architect who attempted unsuccessfully to follow Soane's revolutionary ideas on composition and detail.

Elgin, Grampian
St Giles' Church, on island site in High Street. By Archibald Simpson, 1827-8. Massive hexastyle Greek Doric portico; tower crowned by essay on Choragic Monument of Lysicrates, Athens.

Elton Hall, Cambridgeshire
4m NE of Oundle
Gothic additions by John Carter, c1790.

Elvills, Surrey
1m W of Egham
Unusual example of C18 Tudor Gothic style by Stiff Leadbetter, 1766.

Ely, Cambridgeshire
Shire Hall and **Gaol,** Lynn Road, Charles Humfrey 1821-2. White brick, simple design with imposing tetrastyle Greek Doric portico.
White Hart Inn, Market Place, late-C18 front.
The Chantry, Palace Green, c1715-20. Hooded door, steep 1-bay pediment. Adjacent, brick house of similar date but simpler design.
3-5 Downham Road, before 1750, pair of 2-storey brick cottages forming 6-bay group of extraordinary design, with large-scale early-C18 details such as Venetian windows (throughout ground floor) and blank oval windows with keystones over round-headed doors.
Hill House, Back Hill, late C18.
Needham's School, Back Hill, 'For the instruction, clothing and apprenticing of boys.' Dated 1740, front of archaic design with mullioned and transomed windows.

Emsworth, Hampshire
2m E of Havant
In **The Square,** 2-storey former **school** of c1760 with 1st-floor Venetian window.
3 High Street, c1800 with Greek Ionic doorcase.
In **West Street, house** of c1730 with 2-bay eaves pediment; adjacent, **Keppel Lodge,** large, with stucco façade of c1820 and C18 return elevation.
1-3 King Street, pair of c1810 with ground-floor bows; **5-5A,** pair of c1810 with arcaded ground floor, Greek Doric entrance doors in lower entrance wings; **7,** c1780; **8,** early C19, with Greek Doric porch; **11 (Ivy House),** c1730, handsome door with eared architrave surround. **19** is particularly interesting for its timber façade made with thin planks set flush, probably prefabricated by shipbuilders and said to have been erected in a day in c1795. Excellent details, especially pedimented doorway flanked by full-height canted

bays and topped by tall, round-arched central window which rises into steep eaves pediment. Opposite is early-C19 free-standing **Wharf House.**

1 Queen Street, *c*1780, with hooded porch. **9-15** (odd), *c*1800, 2-storey group with simple pedimented doors. **16 (Newnham House),** *c*1780, with rusticated, probably Coade stone, door surround, shallow ground-floor bows set in arches. **23,** *c*1780, with Venetian windows and bay.

In Tower Street, **Trentham Cottage** with side windows embellished with stucco fan pattern and good fan-lit, arched door; **Trentham House,** *c*1820, stucco with iron balcony; **Saxted Lodge,** early-to-mid C18.

In **Havant Road, house** of *c*1825 with pair of tight, full-height bows and trellis porch.

Encombe House, Dorset
5m W of Swanage
Long, low country house of *c*1735 in style evoking Vanbrugh's baroque style and his picturesque concern for siting of buildings in landscape. Perhaps designed by amateur architect John Pitt, who inherited estate in 1734.

Endsleigh, Devon
6m SE of Launceston
Elaborate *cottage orné* of 1810-11 by Sir Jeffry Wyatville.

Erddig, Clwyd
2m S of Wrexham
Built *c*1684 to designs of Thomas Webb; extended *c*1720; in *c*1770, James Wyatt clad west front with stone and added 3-bay pediment. House remarkable for its contents, which reflect full social spectrum of C18 and C19 country-house life; especially good are servants' rooms, kitchen with rusticated fireplace. Dining room of 1826 by Thomas Hopper in Wyatt's neo-classical manner. (National Trust)

Esher, Surrey
St George's Church of 1540 contains masterly theatrical Newcastle Pew by Vanbrugh, 1723-6. North aisle of 1812.

Friends' Meeting House, Claremont Lane, 1797.

48-50, 76-8, 80 Milbourne Lane, early-C19 weatherboarded houses.

Esher Place, C15 house of Bishop Waynflete which became ruinous and, after 1729, was transformed for Henry Pelham by William Kent; one of earliest examples of rococo-Gothic manner. Kent added pair of 3-bay, 3-storey ranges to sides of gatehouse, 'Wolsey's Tower', which he also remodelled by adding 1-storey porch with ogee-headed door with fret-patterned imposts (1733). Entrance hall contains arched niche in which classical motifs mix freely with Gothic.

Eshton Hall, North Yorkshire
4m NW of Skipton
George Webster, 1825-7; early example of Jacobean revival.

Eton, Berkshire
Eton College includes important examples of C18 purpose-built boarding houses for pupils, rather like barracks but slightly more architectural. **Godolphin House,** Common Lane, 1722. 6 bays, 3 storeys (4th added later). Also in Common Lane, **Angelo's,** boarding house built *c*1790, red brick, 6 bays, 3 storeys. Another, perhaps architecturally more accomplished, boarding house is **Jourdelay's,** set back from High Street; 7 bays, originally 3 storeys; door with attached Ionic columns, decorated frieze and pediment; *c*1720 with wing of 1764.

Buildings of interest in Eton not in College use include **Provost Godolphin Almshouses,** 1714, 2 storeys, hipped roof.

Euston Hall, Suffolk
3m SE of Thetford
Sadly depleted house of C17 and C18 with work by Matthew Brettingham the Elder. Fire in 1902, demolition of pair of wings in 1950. Inside, only original staircase survives.

In grounds, excellent, richly decorated Palladian **temple,** 1746, Kentian in decoration.

Everton
See Liverpool.

Evesham, Hereford and Worcester
King Charles II Inn, Vine Street, *c*1740, with carved modillion frieze.

Midland Bank, Bridge Street, *c*1780, 5 bays, pediments to 1st-floor windows.

8 Bridge Street, early C18, balustraded parapet with urns.

88 High Street, early C19, stuccoed, with fluted giant Ionic pilasters.

Exeter, Devon
St George's Meeting House, South Street, 1760. Curved parapet on front elevation, pedimented porch, excellent galleried interior.

Former **Sessions House,** in the Castle, 1773-5 by Philip Stowey and Jones, whose plans were altered by James Wyatt.

Royal Devon and Exeter Hospital, Southernhay, large building of 1743-58 with archaic details; segmental windows with exposed box sashes, straight rusticated quoins. Alterations of 1772 include big pediment to centre block.

Topsham Barracks, Barrack Road, 1804; utilitarian, with pedimented centre and cupola.

Prison, New North Road, 1790; entrance with vermiculated rustication.

Higher Market, Queen Street, 1835-8 by George Dymond and Charles Fowler, with Greek Doric portico *in antis*; now mostly reconstructed.

Beside the Castle, in Castle Street, **Bradninch House,** *c*1800, with porch; **Rougemont House,** *c*1810, with pair of fat ground-floor bows supporting iron veranda to 1st-floor windows.

In the Close, **Royal Clarence Hotel,** C18 building redecorated externally 1827, assembly room added *c*1770; **5** and **6** with 2-storey C18 façades; **20** and **21** with façades of *c*1800 and good interiors of *c*1720, especially staircase; **15 (Chancellerie)** of *c*1740, with steep pediment. At eastern end of the Close, delightful cast-iron pedestrian **bridge** dated 1814.

Off the **Cathedral Yard,** south-west of the Cathedral, pair of brick **houses** of *c*1740, making 6-bay, 3-storey composition with rusticated brick door surrounds, corner quoins, quoins over party wall; also handsome 4-bay, 3-storey **house** of *c*1780 with fully rusticated façade, arched ground-floor windows, delicate pedimented door.

Southernhay has long runs of mostly uniform brick 3-storey terraces of *c*1780 and 1805-25; houses generally with arched ground-floor windows and rustic block Coade stone door surrounds.

Barnfield Crescent, c1805, and small fragment of **terrace** in Dix's Fields, c1808, with arched ground-floor windows in blank arcades.
Southernhay House, particularly handsome with full-width ground-floor Doric colonnade.
In **Bartholomew Street East,** irregular **group** of Georgian houses around churchyard of All Hallows, **32** with good Ionic doorcase.
143 Fore Street, 1714.
71 Holloway Street, good 3-bay, 3-storey house of c1825 with arcaded ground floor supporting giant Doric pilasters rising between windows to support full entablature. **72,** 2-storey, pedimented house of c1830 with bold Greek details such as tapering ground- and 1st-floor windows.
Pennsylvania Park, 2- and 3-storey houses of c1825, with 1st-floor verandas.
Colleton Crescent, c1805, 4-storey houses with arched doors decorated with Coade stone blocks.

Exmouth, Devon
A-la-Ronde, picturesque 16-sided *cottage orné*, 60ft-high octagonal central hall decorated with shells and bird models made of feathers, built c1795 for the Misses Parminter.
Point-in-View, chapel, almshouse and schoolroom, 1811.

Exton Park, Leicestershire
4m NE of Oakham
Fort Henry, in grounds of ruined country house, extremely pretty, and large, Gothic lakeside summer house looking c1765 but later.

Eynsham, Oxfordshire
Swinford Bridge, handsome classical composition of c1770 attributed to Sir Robert Taylor.

Fairfield, Greater Manchester
1m SW of Droylsden
Moravian settlement established 1788 by Benjamin Latrobe whose son, architect Benjamin Latrobe, seems to have designed the cottages (information: Gillian Darley).

Fairlawne, Kent
4m N of Tonbridge
Probably a medieval courtyard house in origin. Inside, richly decorated Great Room by James Gibbs, with carved woodwork, pedimented and columned doorcases, and wall panels of small-scale low-relief carving.

Falkirk, Central Region
Town Steeple, David Hamilton 1814. Square tower with lower stages embellished with Greek Doric columns, and spire still in Gibbs tradition.

Fallowfield
See Manchester.

Falmouth, Cornwall
Synagogue, Vernon Place, 1816.
Custom House, with handsome Greek Doric colonnade, c1830.
Classical and Mathematical School, Killigrew Road, Greek Doric, 1824.
Royal Hotel, Market Street, c1810.
1-3 Bank Place, C18, as are some brick **houses** in Arwenack Street.
Marlborough House, Marlborough Avenue, 1805-15, with handsome curved Ionic colonnade.
Other early-C19 **houses** in Stratton Place; Albert Terrace; Florence Place; Florence Terrace; Tehidy Terrace.

Fareham, Hampshire
Red Lion, East Street, front of 1819; segmental portico and bow windows.
68 High Street (Country Club), with full-height bows and pedimented door, c1790; **69 (Wykeham House),** c1785, with brown mathematical tiles, semicircular porch; **70 (Kintyre Hotel),** 1756.
Bishopswood, West Street, *cottage orné* of c1810 with thatched roof, veranda, tree-trunk columns, Gothic windows; enlarged early C20.
To east of town, **Cams Hall,** Portsmouth Road, 1771 by Jacob Leroux; ashlar north façade, with centre 3 bays emphasized by Ionic columns and pediment. On brick south front, central bow rising above main part of façade.

Faringdon House, Oxfordshire
In Faringdon
Ashlar villa begun c1780. On garden front, 2-armed open stair rises to terrace resting on elliptical arches. Inside, fine staircase hall also has 2-armed stair, rising on sides of hall.

Farley Hall, Berkshire
4m SW of Wokingham
Built 1730 but still in brick classical tradition of Queen Anne. Magnificent entrance hall, roughly square, reaches whole height of house to open cupola surmounting roof.

Farnborough Hall, Warwickshire
6m N of Banbury
House of c1684 with north front of c1750. Excellent entrance hall with plaster panelled wall, oval niches containing busts of emperors. (National Trust)

Farnham, Surrey
Willmer House, West Street (now **museum**), dated 1718. Provincial baroque, fine brickwork, 5 bays with emphasized centre bay, pilasters at corners.
23-4 West Street, pair of houses of 1790, one 5-bay, other 3-bay, linked by blind bay recess. **28,** c1718, 5 bays, centre bay emphasized by pediment and pedimented door. **39,** c1770.
3 Downing Street, dated 1717; 5 bays with 1-bay pediment. **46-7,** c1810; shared front door with segmental fanlight.
Masonic Hall, 42 Castle Street, c1720, bold Vanbrughian detail on side elevation.

Faversham, Kent
St Mary of Charity's Church, medieval with nave of 1754-5 by George Dance the Elder, altered in C19 restoration. Tower, 1799 by Charles Beazley with steeple that is an elegant essay on Wren's St Dunstan-in-the-East.
5 East Street, remains of interesting early-C18 brick façade, with rusticated angle pilasters. In same street, **Cooksditch,** c1790; pavilions c1798.
In **Preston Street,** good collection of C18 houses. **No. 76** has typical provincial rudimentary Venetian windows; **St Mary's Vicarage,** rusticated round-headed doorway.

Finchcocks, Kent
8m E of Tunbridge Wells
Tall 3-storey, 7-bay brick house dated 1725 and designed in baroque manner of Archer, but no doubt the work of local builder developing his provincial style (see Bradbourne, c1714; Matfield, 1728). Main block has entrance front on which

centre 3 bays break forward with pediment rising from 2nd-floor cornice into 3rd-floor attic, which has an Archer detail of round attic windows above pediment (see Roehampton, under Wandsworth in London); blind 1st-floor niche over front door. 2-storey Tuscan pilasters frame façade. 2-storey, 4-bay wings set forward and linked to main block by baroque device of quadrant. Inside, low, half-panelled entrance hall, running whole depth of house, with good staircase.

Fochabers Newtown, Grampian
7m NW of Keith
Bellie Church, 1795-7 by John Baxter the Younger, steeple derived from Gibbs.
Town laid out by Baxter, 1775-90.

Folkingham, Lincolnshire
8m S of Sleaford
House of Correction, Bryan Browning 1824-5. Powerful classical façade showing influence of Ledoux.

Fonthill Abbey, Wiltshire
6m NE of Shaftesbury
Fragments of James Wyatt's extravagant Gothic pile of 1796-1812 for Beckford still survive – part of north wing including Lancaster Tower, sanctuary and oratory.

Forcett Park, North Yorkshire
7m W of Darlington
Probably *c*1725; altered by Burlington's protégé Daniel Garrett *c*1735. Garden front based on C17 Lindsey House, Lincoln's Inn, then thought to be by Inigo Jones (see Holborn, Camden in London). Triumphal arch **lodge,** perhaps by James Paine, *c*1775.

Foremark Hall, Derbyshire
4m N of Swadlincote
David Hiorne, 1759-61. Smaller version of Isaac Ware's late-Palladian Wrotham Park, 1754 (qv).

Forfar, Tayside
Town Hall, 1786 by James Playfair in his especially refined neo-classical style.

Fort George, Highland
7m W of Nairn
Begun after '45 rebellion; outline design *c*1746 by Board of Ordnance, which employed William Adam working under Colonel Skinner.
John and Robert Adam were also employed, and designed **Ravelin Gate,** *c*1753, in grand Vanbrughian style.

Fourcrosses, Powys
8m E of Llanfyllin
Golden Lion Inn, 3 storeys with fine array of Venetian windows. Gothic glazing, *c*1780.

Fox Hall, West Sussex
5m N of Chichester
Hunting lodge, 1730, by Roger Morris and, perhaps, Lord Burlington. On 1st floor, cube room with large-scale Kentian decoration.

Frampton Court, Gloucestershire
7m SW of Gloucester
1730, perhaps by John Strahan or William Halfpenny; somewhat baroque interpretation of Colen Campbell's Stourhead of *c*1721.
Splendid Gothic **orangery,** *c*1750, perhaps by William or John Halfpenny, with ogee-arched windows and octagonal glazing pattern.

Frenchay, Avon
N edge of Mangotsfield
Unitarian Church, *c*1720. Good C18 interiors.
Frenchay Manor, 1736, perhaps by John Wood the Elder. 3-bay portico, pedimented 1st-floor windows.
Frenchay House, 1772.

Frome, Somerset
On bridge approach, from Market Place, **Bluecoat School** and **Almshouses,** 1726. Centre with quoins, arched windows. On either side, wings with mullioned 2-light windows.
In **Willow Vale,** some good early-C18 houses including **Nos.14-16** with semicircular doorhoods.
13 Bridge Street, early C18, door with broken pediment containing urn.
Mendip House, Welshmill Road, *c*1800, with tripartite doorway.
Monmouth House, Cork Street, *c*1790, large, plain, set at right angles to street.
Iron Gates and **Court House,** King Street, form very good group, 1710-20.
Vicarage, Vicarage Street, early C18.
12 Gentle Street, with good mid-Georgian façade, Venetian windows each side of centre bay. Other houses with gables to street, looking C17 but with good pedimented Georgian doors and details.
Packhorse Inn, Christ Church Street West, early C18 with coupled door topped with pair of

The orangery at Frampton Court, Gloucestershire, *c*1750, perhaps by William or John Halfpenny, an early and delightful example of eighteenth-century Gothic revival.

curly broken pediments, each containing an urn. In same street, **West Lodge,** mid-C18 with curly open pediment to door, framed by Venetian windows.

Vicarage, Gould's Ground, late C18, centre emphasized with 2-storey bow and pediment.

In **Sun Street**, irregular group of C18 **houses,** one with simple pedimented door and mullioned windows.

Trinity area, developed mostly in late C17, contains a number of interesting early-C18 **cottages** and **weavers' houses. 11 Trinity Street,** *c*1720, 2 storeys, stone with stone mullioned windows. **23 Castle Street ('The Old Hospital'),** formal brick building of *c*1770.

Gainsborough, Lincolnshire
All Saints' Church, Gothic tower, body built 1736-48. Nave elevation resembles St Martin-in-the-Fields. Inside, Corinthian capitals support entablature running full length of nave.

Galby, Leicestershire
5m E of Leicester
St Peter's Church, 1741 by John Wing the Elder. Early effort at 'honest Gothic'; but tower has classical window and pinnacles in a bizarre chinoiserie style of Wing's own invention.

Garendon Hall, Leicestershire
2m W of Loughborough
House demolished 1964 but remarkable **garden buildings** survive, designed by amateur architect and scholar Ambrose Phillipps in spirit of archaeological reconstruction of originals in Rome. **Triumphal Arch** based on Arch of Titus; **Temple of Venus,** *c*1735, based on Temple of Vesta.

Gateley Hall, Norfolk
4m SE of Fakenham
1726, plain brick house with baroque shaped gable ends. Inside, rich mid-C18 rococo decoration.

Gaulby
See Galby.

Gaunt's House, Dorset
3m N of Wimborne Minster
Lodge, 1 mile south-west of house (now Dumpton School), is fine *cottage orné* of *c*1810.

Gayhurst, Buckinghamshire
2m NW of Newport Pagnell
Church, 1728, perhaps by Edward Wing; in provincial baroque style.

Gestingthorpe, Essex
4m SW of Sudbury
Over Hall, chiefly of 1735, 7-bay front with 3-bay, taller, pedimented centre. Splendid drawing room, *c*1740.

Gibside, Tyne and Wear
6m SW of Gateshead
The Hall, *c*1603-20; altered *c*1750 and *c*1805; now a ruin.

Chapel, 1760-66 by James Paine. Palladio-derived, centralized church with saucer dome and 4-columned Ionic portico.

In grounds, **column** by Paine, 1760. **New Laundry,** 1744; **stable,** 1748; and **Gothic Banqueting House,** 1751 by Daniel Garrett. (National Trust)

Gilling Castle, North Yorkshire
11m E of Thirsk
Remodelled to designs of William Wakefield, *c*1725, in provincial baroque manner.

Glasgow, Strathclyde
St Andrew's Cathedral, Clyde Street, 1816 by James Gillespie Graham. Neo-Perpendicular.

St Andrew's Church, St Andrew's Square, 1739-56 by merchant and builder Allan Dreghorn. Fine, early fully-fledged essay on Gibbs's St Martin-in-the-Fields, but steeple based on another Gibbs design published in his *Book of Architecture* of 1728. Interior with Corinthian columns rising on plinths and carrying blocks of entablature, supporting barrel-vaulted ceiling.

St Andrew's-by-the-Green Episcopalian Church, Turnbull Street. Built 1750-51 to designs of masons William Paull and Andrew Hunter; handsome baroque composition, now gutted.

St George's Church, Buchanan Street, 1807 by William Stark. Sombre Tuscan neo-classical west elevation with tower and spire.

St David's Church, Ingram Street, Ramshorn, 1824-6 by Rickman & Hutchinson. Pioneer example of revival of early Decorated Gothic style; T-plan with tall, narrow pinnacled tower.

Hutcheson's Hospital, Ingram Street, 1802-5 by David Hamilton; a particularly Scottish composition. Street elevation has neo-classical elements of Adam, but above all rise tower and spire still derived from designs of Gibbs.

Trades House, Glassford Street, designed by Robert Adam, 1791-4. Complex elevation displaying Adam's belief in 'movement' (see p83). Dome above centre. Single-bay end wings are later, as is interior of 1887.

Stirling's Library (formerly **Royal Exchange**), Royal Exchange Square, 1827-9 by David Hamilton. Impressive Grecian pile with imposing Corinthian portico, round colonnaded tower, fine Graeco-Roman interior with Corinthian arcade supporting barrel-vaulted, coffered ceiling.

Court House, Gaol and **Public Offices,** Glasgow Green, 1807-14 by William Stark; rebuilt 1910 in Grecian manner retaining original giant Doric portico.

Royal Bank of Scotland, Royal Exchange Square, 1827 by Archibald Elliot the Younger. Front has hexastyle Greek Ionic portico.

1-3 Argyle Street, *c*1760; architraves and keystones to windows, string courses between storeys, quoins at corners. Similar survivor on corner of Trongate and Candleriggs, also *c*1760.

Charlotte Street contains derelict remains of late-C18 speculative development undertaken by Adam brothers: one exquisitely detailed 5-bay, 2-storey ashlar **house** with centre 3 bays breaking forward and crowned by pediment with round window in tympanum. At other end of street, surviving C18 **tenement** of traditional design with tightly curved staircase tower at rear.

42 Miller Street, somewhat similar in design to Adam's Charlotte Street house, but embellishments in conventional late-Palladian style. Built *c*1775 to designs of a John Craig.

Block formed by **Garth, Hutcheson, Wilson** and **Glassford Streets** contains most interesting, almost completely late-C18 set of buildings. Especially interesting is uniform group forming Wilson

Street, designed by Robert Adam c1790, though now much altered and mutilated. In Garth Street, simpler 4- and 5-storey late-C18 houses.

St Andrew's Square, with St Andrew's Church in its centre, developed as uniform square of 3-storey ashlar houses, c1786 to designs of William Hamilton. Though now mutilated, much of original development survives. **Nos. 10-15** on north side form best group; 10/11 has 5 bays, 3 storeys with 5-bay pediment, but 13 and 15 have lost top storey. Nos. 10, 11, 12 have rear stair turrets. **No. 30** on east side is best surviving example. Other partly original houses are 32 on east side; 34-8; 40-44 on south side which contain tripartite glazing.

31-59 Virginia Street, and building in Virginia Court behind, built 1817 as tobacco merchant's offices and houses, form fine Greek revival urban group. Virginia Street frontage ashlar, 4 storeys over basement with restrained, severe Grecian decoration. Virginia Court, reached through arch, contains houses of similar date and design but a storey lower.

Crown Arcade, behind 31-5 Virginia Street, c1820, reconstructed later in C19 but survives as remarkable Graeco-Roman interior: arcaded ground floor supports Ionic gallery with Diocletian windows in wall above.

Argyle Arcade, 98-102 Argyle Street, 1827-8 by John Baird.

Carlton Place, begun 1802 by Peter Nicholson, monumental uniform terrace facing Clyde, was first attempt in Glasgow to organize a whole street as symmetrical composition. **Laurieston House,** 1804, has particularly fine interior.

Glastonbury, Somerset
Congregational Church, High Street, 1814; bowed front, Gothic tracery in windows, squat porch.

Town Hall, Magdalene Street, designed 1813 by J. B. Beard but still Palladian, begun 1818.

Pump Room, opened 1754; 3-bay front.

In High Street, **Madras School,** 1815, with Gothic detailing; **29,** early C18, good doorcase.

In Magdalene Street, **Somerset House,** C18, with giant Doric pilasters, Tuscan porch; **Priory House,** with Venetian doorway.

Glen Orchy, Strathclyde
25m E of Oban
Church, 1810-11 by James Elliot; octagonal plan, Gothic.

Gloucester, Gloucestershire
St John the Baptist's Church, Northgate Street, 1732-4 by Edward and Thomas Woodward in provincial baroque manner. Tower medieval.

Shire Hall, Westgate Street, 1814-16 by Sir Robert Smirke; Grecian with Ionic portico *in antis*. Also in Westgate Street, **St Bartholomew's Hospital,** designed by William Price, 1788, Gothic.

Royal Infirmary, off Southgate Street, by Stiff Leadbetter and Luke Singleton 1758-61, in austere brick style. Enlarged 1827 by Thomas Rickman.

Deanery, 1 Miller's Green, plain 5-bay brick house, c1730 with pedimented door of c1770; good panelled interior.

St Nicholas House, Westgate Street, has ambitious early-C18 brick façade with quoined projecting centre. In same street, **Duke of Norfolk House** has early-C18 stone façade with Corinthian pilasters, cornice and balustrade.

Northgate House, London Road, mid-C18.

13 Southgate Street, good façade of c1760, with Venetian window over Ionic pedimented door.

Ladybellegate House, Ladybellegate, early C18, plain exterior but inside, remarkably rich rococo plasterwork. In same street, **Bearland Lodge,** c1720, 4 bays, 2 storeys crowned by large pediment containing deep relief carving by John Ricketts; **Bearland House,** c1730, composed like small country house with pedimented centre flanked by lower wings.

Stuccoed early-C19 **houses** and **villas** around **Gloucester Spa,** developed 1812-25. **Beaufort Buildings,** with Ionic porticoes; **Brunswick Square,** pilasters with fret pattern and anthemia. Villas include **Ribston Hall,** c1828, portico with grouped Ionic columns; **Sherborne House,** c1825; **Somerset House** (now **Judge's Lodgings**) 1815 by Sir Robert Smirke.

Gloucester Dock on Gloucester-Berkeley Ship Canal, opened 1827; **North Warehouse** c1825, others mostly by Telford, post-1830.

Glynde, East Sussex
3m E of Lewes
St Mary's Church, modest building of 1763 by Sir Thomas Robinson, friend of Lord Burlington and amateur Palladian architect. Venetian east window, galleried west end, good interior.

Gobions
See Brookmans Park.

Godmersham Park, Kent
7m SW of Canterbury
Mansion of 1732. North front brick with ashlar dressing, centre 3 bays set back slightly and containing bull's-eye mezzanine windows. 2-storey wings, c1780, linked by short, straight corridors with rusticated doorways. Best interiors are in hall with strong architectural decoration; other major rooms c1935, when house was remodelled: saloon has chimneypieces from 15 Queen Square, Bath, and panelling from 29 Old Burlington Street (General Wade's house), London.

Golden Grove, Dyfed
SE edge of Pembroke
Sir Jeffry Wyatville, 1826-37. Neo-Elizabethan, similar to his Lilleshall Hall (qv).

Golspie, Highland
5m SW of Brora
Church, 1738. Simple exterior. Inside, long Communion table running length of nave.

Goodwood House, West Sussex
4m NE of Chichester
South wing probably by Sir William Chambers, c1760, now squashed between elements of James Wyatt's post-1787 house, which includes 2-storey hexastyle portico. If by Chambers, this is his earliest attempt at villa design.

Stables by Chambers, 1757-63. **Kennels** by Wyatt, 1787, as is **Dower House,** called **Molecombe,** c1790-1806.

Goole, Humberside
Lowther Hotel, c1825-7, and **houses** of c1830, in Aire Street.

Gordonstoun House, Grampian
3m W of Lossiemouth
Altered 1772-6 by John Baxter the Younger.

Gorhambury, Hertfordshire
2½m W of St Albans
Villa of *c*1777-84 by Sir Robert Taylor, with Corinthian portico of 6 columns spaced to form 2 groups of 3 with wide space in centre. House altered 1816-26 by William Atkinson, and 1847 by William Burn. Inside, chimneypiece based on design by Piranesi.

Gosford House, Lothian
5m NE of Tranent
Robert Adam, 1790-1800. Neo-classical palace, main block with three gigantic tripartite windows topped with huge semicircular fanlights. Shallow central dome. Remodelled and extended 1883-91, largely gutted 1940, south wing rehabilitated 1951.

Gosport, Hampshire
  Royal Naval Hospital, Haslar, begun 1746, opened 1754, completed 1762. Design supplied by Theodore Jacobsen in 1745; executant architect James Horne. 3 sides of huge square, with 3-bay pedimented centre, arcaded ground floor, flanking wings.

The Grange, Hampshire
3m NW of New Alresford
C17 red brick house, remodelled 1804-9 by William Wilkins to form most influential early example of Greek revival house. Greek Doric portico modelled on Theseion, Athens; centrepieces of side elevation composed of piers and modelled on Choragic Monument of Thrasyllus. Additions of *c*1823-5 by S. P. and C. R. Cockerell. Gutted 1972.

Grantham, Lincolnshire
  George Inn, *c*1790, with assembly room.

Gravesend, Kent
  St George's Church, 1731-3, by Charles Sloane. Modest brick box with Gibbs surround to door.
  At southern end of High Street, late-C18 timber-framed **terrace** clad in clapboard and embellished with wooden architraves and window pediments.
  Milton Park Estate, including Berkeley Crescent, laid out by A. H. Wilds, *c*1830.

Great Amwell, Hertfordshire
1m SE of Ware
Amwell Grove, by Robert Mylne for himself, 1794-7; later enlarged.

Great Baddow, Essex
SE edge of Chelmsford
Vicarage, *c*1725, Roman Doric porch.
  The Vineyard, built 1740, altered 1760, 1907.
  West of this, early-C18 **house,** 5 bays, 2 storeys, giant pilasters.

Great Barr Hall, Suffolk
3m NE of West Bromwich, West Midlands
Great Barr Hall, 1777, castellated Gothic with towers and ogee windows. Spectacular staircase hall in centre, with ribbed ceiling.

Great Packington, Warwickshire
7m NW of Coventry
St James's Church, 1790 by Joseph Bonomi and Earl of Aylesford, in powerful antiquarian mood influenced by Roman baths (particularly Diocletian's in Rome) and Piranesi. Symmetrical centralized cruciform plan with 4 towers, and lit by massive Diocletian windows. Inside, square central cross-vaulted nave with Greek Doric columns, based on those of Greek Doric Temple of Neptune at Paestum; walls and ceilings painted to imitate ashlar.
  Great Packington Old Hall, begun 1693, greatly altered by Matthew Brettingham the Elder who added wings and altered and extended main elevation; work completed by 1772. Interior interesting, like church, for archaeological taste of Earl: decorated with help of Bonomi 1782-1802. Most notable is Pompeian Gallery, inspired by Earl's Greek and Roman vases. External terraces added 1812 by Henry Hakewill, who also carried out some interior work, e.g. Billiard Room.

Great Torrington, Devon
  Palmer House, New Street, 1752. 5 bays, 2 end bays framed by giant Ionic columns.

Great Witley, Hereford and Worcester
5m SW of Stourport-on-Severn
St Michael's Chapel, 1735, beside ruins of C17-19 Witley Court. Church perhaps designed or decorated by James Gibbs. Plain exterior, ashlar-clad in C19. Interior, with ceiling paintings from Cannons, in former county of Middlesex, 1713-*c*1747, forms most Italian-rococo ecclesiastical space in Britain.

Great Yarmouth, Norfolk
  St George's Church, 1714-16 by John Price in fine baroque style with apsed east end and tower based on west towers of St Paul's Cathedral.
  Royal Naval (now **St Nicholas's**) **Hospital,** 1809-11 by William Pilkington or Edward Holl. 4 blocks of 29 bays with round-arched colonnades, approached through triumphal arch.
  South Quay rich in historic buildings. **1-2,** *c*1710, **5,** early C18, **20** (now **Custom House**), dated 1720, built for rich herring merchant. 5 bays, 3 storeys, framed by higher 1-bay 'wings'; **74-5,** *c*1720, faced with square-knapped flint with brick dressings; 2-storey porch with Corinthian pilasters over Tuscan, all topped with pediment.
  51 King Street, early C18, with rusticated door surround below arched central window.
  The Vicarage, Church Plain, 1718, altered 1781.

Greta Bridge, Co. Durham
3m SW of Barnard Castle
Bridge by John Carr, 1773.

Greystoke Castle, Cumbria
5m W of Penrith
C14-19 house has several unusual picturesque **outbuildings** and **farms** designed by 11th Duke of Norfolk, *c*1778, especially **Fort Putnam** with castellated farmyard, and **Bunker Hill,** also castellated and with pointed windows.

Grimsthorpe Castle, Lincolnshire
4m NW of Bourne
North front rebuilt for Duke of Ancaster by Vanbrugh, 1722-6. 2-storey, 7-bay centre with arcaded windows flanked by paired banded columns. Flanking, and breaking forward, are 3-storey towers with 1st-floor Venetian windows. Inside centre block, a double-cube entrance hall. Unbuilt north front, designed 1722, essay on Houghton with Palladian terminal towers.

Guildford, Surrey
Holy Trinity Church, 1763 by James Horne in modest provincial Palladian manner. Interior c1890.
Corn Exchange (Tunsgate), High Street, by Henry Garling 1818, with giant Tuscan portico. Altered 1935, including respacing of columns.
25-9 High Street, provincial baroque house of 3 storeys with giant corner pilasters.
Mount House, Mount Street, c1730.
Semaphore House, Pewley Hill, 1821, with octagonal cupola.
15 Friary Lane, small weatherboarded, tile-hung C18 building containing enormous tread-wheel 15ft in diameter, geared to crane on waterfront.
Parson's (Stoke) Hospital, Stoke Road, pedimented centre, octagonal cupola; dated 1796 looks 1720.
Castle House, 49 Quarry Street, c1740.

Gunton Park, Norfolk
4m NW of North Walsham
Entrance front by Matthew Brettingham the Elder, 1742; gutted. Wings by James Wyatt, c1770.
St Andrew's Chapel by Robert Adam, 1769, with giant portico, resembles garden temple.

Gwrych Castle, Clwyd
1m W of Abergele
c1814, designed for himself by L.B. Hesketh, with much professional advice. Highly picturesque asymmetrical castle.

Hackness Hall, North Yorkshire
4m W of Scarborough
By Peter Atkinson the Elder, 1797, Palladian. Interior damaged 1910.

Hackwood Park, Hampshire
2m SE of Basingstoke
House of 1680s rebuilt by Samuel and Lewis Wyatt, 1800-13. South front has Ionic centrepiece with good neo-classical interior, especially dining room. But library has interesting late-C17 revival ceiling. C17-style carving by E. Wyatt in entrance hall.

Haddington, Lothian
Town House/Assembly Rooms by William Adam, 1742, but largely rebuilt 1788. Steeple by James Gillespie Graham, 1831.

Haddo House, Grampian
8m NE of Huntly
William Adam, 1732-5, in Scottish Palladian style.

Hadleigh, Suffolk
White Lion, High Street, c1800; **40,** c1820, with Tuscan colonnade and bow window to front.
Pykenham Almshouses, George Street, 1807. In same street, **No. 28,** with C18 façade.
43 Benton Street, C18; Gothic doorcase has triple, ringed shafts. **84** has Gothic Venetian windows.
21 Bridge Street, early C18.

Hafod, Dyfed
2m N of Cardigan
Church (Eglwys Newydd) by James Wyatt, c1800-3; Gothic. Damaged 1932.

Hagley Hall, Hereford and Worcester
6m NE of Kidderminster
Palladian ashlar tower house designed by Sanderson Miller, 1754-60, with assistance of amateur architects John Chute and Thomas Prowse. Inside, much rococo plasterwork. In Tapestry Room, medallions by James Stuart.
In grounds: **Temple of Theseus,** 1758 by James Stuart, based on his measured drawings made in Athens, and first example of Greek Doric temple built since antiquity; **Castle Folly,** 1747-8 by Miller; **Palladian Bridge,** 1764 by Thomas Pitt.

Hailes House, Lothian
SW edge of Edinburgh
By Sir James Clerk, c1770.

Haileybury College, Hertfordshire
2m S of Ware
Built by William Wilkins 1806-9 as training school for East India Company. Impressive Greek revival composition: 42-bay, 1-storey stone façade with central hexastyle portico and 2 tetrastyle porticoes in middle of flanking elevations. Above all, mighty dome of 1876 by Blomfield.

Hale, Hampshire
7m SE of Salisbury
St Mary's Church, remodelled by Thomas Archer, 1717, who added transept containing especially good door; altered in C19.
Hale House, designed by Archer for himself, but largely rebuilt c1792 by Henry Holland.

Halifax, West Yorkshire
The **Square Chapel,** in the Square, 1772. Large, with some architectural pretensions; 1st-floor Venetian windows in centre of the 2 main elevations. Inside now gutted.
Holy Trinity Church, Harrison Road, 1795 by Thomas Johnson. Classical, with domed tower.
Zion Congregational Church, Wade Street, 1819. Greek Doric.
Piece Hall, the Square, perhaps design of Thomas Bradley, 1775: massive neo-classical market of Roman quality with giant central courtyard surrounded by 2 and 3 tiers of arcades.
Somerset House, George Street, erected 1766 to designs of John Carr, served as houses, shops and banking chamber. Originally 3-storey, 17-bay composition. Elevation has 3-bay centre with long 1st-floor windows rising into 2nd storey and set over ground-floor arcade.
Hopwood Hall, Hopwood Lane, early-C18.
Holly House, off Horton Street, has 2-storey centre section of 1755, with later columned porch, flanked by pair of wings of c1765.
In **Woolshops,** group of early-C18 2-storey **houses** in very provincial baroque style. Elevations, framed by 2-storey pilasters, contain carriageway linked to window above by narrow strips of rustication flanked by 2 scrolls.

Hall Place, Berkshire
3m NW of Maidenhead
Façade c1730-35, with giant angle pilasters. Inside, splendid drawing room with stucco ceiling and wall panels.
Lodge, c1760, Gothic, castellated.

Halstead, Essex
Former **House of Correction,** Bridge Street, 1782.
22-4 High Street, c1775, unusual composition in which 2 houses are linked by pediment above shared doors, topped with Venetian and large Diocletian windows.

In the Causeway, **Courtaulds factory,** impressive white-painted, clapboarded late-C18 mill.
Bluebridge House, 1 mile east of town, 1714; brick, 5 bays, 2 storeys.

Hamilton, Strathclyde
Church, William Adam 1732, Greek cross plan with circular centre.

Hammerwood House, East Sussex
3m E of East Grinstead
Early Greek revival house, built 1790–92 to designs of Benjamin Latrobe. Ashlar-clad. North front with austere, unmoulded tripartite windows. West front an asymmetrical wing with Greek Doric *porte-cochère*. South front flanked by 1-bay pavilions with tetrastyle pedimented porticoes of unfluted Doric columns inspired by Doric temple at Delos and, in their flat capitals, by that at Paestum. Both pavilions contain classical reliefs in Coade stone.

Hampden House, Buckinghamshire
3m E of Princes Risborough
Pre-C18 house given Gothic exterior *c*1751.

Hampton Lucy, Warwickshire
4m NE of Stratford-upon-Avon
St Peter's Church, by Rickman & Hutchinson 1822–6; the best of their Gothic churches.

Hanbury, Hereford and Worcester
4m E of Droitwich
St Mary's Church, rebuilt 1792–5 to design of Thomas Johnson who, for Gothic tower, reproduced his own design of 1779 for St Nicholas's Church, Warwick. Partly rebuilt by Street, 1860.

Hardenhuish, Wiltshire
1m NW of Chippenham
St Nicholas's Church, 1779 by John Wood the Younger; Palladian, Venetian windows in north and south nave walls, tower with octagonal top and stone dome.

Hardwick, Shropshire
1m W of Ellesmere
Striking house by Francis Smith, *c*1720, with huge 3-bay segmental pediment carried on Corinthian pilasters.

Hardwick Hall, Co. Durham
7m SE of Durham
Plain house of *c*1740 around earlier core.
Important grounds in Kentian *jardin anglais* style, 1748–60, with major garden buildings by James Paine. Most now demolished or ruinous, but surviving are **gatehouse,** built as Gothic sham ruin; **Buon Retiro,** Gothic retreat with double-height room painted with book spines to look like library; **Temple of Minerva,** 1754–7, consisting of domed octagonal drum surrounded by Ionic colonnade.

Harewood House, West Yorkshire
5m N of Leeds
Plan and north façade by John Carr, 1759; scheme taken over by Robert Adam, who extended house and decorated interiors, *c*1765. Greatly altered by Sir Charles Barry, *c*1840. Fine entrance hall of 1765–7 survives.
Stables by Chambers, 1755–6.
Model village near house, by John Carr, *c*1760.

Harleston, Norfolk
7m SW of Bungay
Swan Hotel, 9-bay, 3-storey early Georgian front.
Candlers' House, excellent design of *c*1720. 1st-floor window with mask keystone.

Harleyford Manor, Buckinghamshire
2m SW of Marlow
Designed by Sir Robert Taylor, 1755: earliest example of villa type that became fashionable *c*1755–70. Exterior articulated but austere with Palladian motifs. Inside, central top-lit stair, with circuit of differently shaped ground-floor rooms.

Hartwell House, Buckinghamshire
1m SW of Aylesbury
Jacobean house with fine, richly decorated hall of 1740 by James Gibbs. East front reconstructed 1759–61 by Henry Keene.
In grounds, Ionic **canal temple** of *c*1723.
In neighbouring village of Lower Hartwell, **St Mary's Church,** by Henry Keene, 1753–5. Gothic, now a shell.

Hastings, East Sussex
St Mary-in-the-Castle Church, *c*1826 by Joseph Kay, placed in centre of the uniform Pelham Crescent which he also designed (see below). Greek Ionic portico outside. Inside, D-shaped, auditorium-like nave.
East Hill House, All Saints Street, 4 storeys with 2 bow windows, 1762 and later.
Torfield House, High Street, 5 bays with tripartite windows and deep Tuscan porch, *c*1780. Also in High Street: **Old Hastings House,** *c*1750; **106** with ambitious front with 2 canted bay windows; **4, 6 (Wellington House)** and **105** all with good carved brackets supporting doorhoods; **91,** *c*1800, with 2 bows for upper windows each containing curved Venetian window.
Croft House, The Croft, 2 canted bays, *c*1785.
Pelham Crescent, by Kay, built 1824–8. Highly decorated, 4 storeys, stucco-faced. Each house 1 wide bay except ground floor with door beside tripartite window, tripartite bow with veranda on 1st floor, tripartite window with smaller, curved veranda on 2nd floor, and Diocletian window on 3rd floor.
St Leonards, westward development along coast, founded 1828 by James Burton, inspired by Regent's Park layout. Ionic terraces along sea front. **Assembly Rooms** (now **Masonic Hall**) by Burton in Greek Doric style; picturesque villas at **St Leonards Gardens.**

Hatchlands, Surrey
5m NW of Guildford
Pedimented west front *c*1758, probably by Thomas Ripley. Interior by Adam *c*1759–60, one of his first jobs after returning from Italy: library based on C17 dome of Villa Pamphili; dining-room ceiling strewn with classical motifs – the Adam style had not yet coalesced. Altered by Joseph Bonomi 1797. (National Trust)

Hatfield, Hertfordshire
2–4 Fore Street, 15-bay composition of *c*1750; **East India House,** *c*1730; **12,** late-C18 with Adamesque doorcase.
52 Great North Road, *c*1800, has Coade stone door surround to pattern of Bedford Square, Camden, London; **69,** of similar date, with Gothic porch.

Hatton Grange, Shropshire
10m N of Ludlow
By Thomas F. Pritchard *c*1764–8, Palladian: compare with his Brockhampton Park (qv).

Haverfordwest, Dyfed
Foley House, Goat Street, 1794 by John Nash.

Hawkhurst, Kent
9m N of Battle
Wetheringhope House, on The Moor, *c*1725, brick, 3 bays, 2 storeys with pedimented Tuscan door below pedimented 1st-floor window.
Half a mile west of All Saints' Church, Highgate, **Marlborough House School,** 1723, with canted bays: a very early use.

Hay-on-Wye, Powys
Swan Hotel, Church Street, *c*1812. Also in Church Street, **5** and **6** with good Regency doors with bracketed hoods, *c*1820; **7–8**, hooded doors with pilasters inscribed with Soane-type fret-pattern decoration, a motif shared by door of **10**.
On corner of Church Street and **Oxford Road**, 5-bay, 2-storey **house,** *c*1780, forms fine composition with gabled stable, to which it is linked by screen wall containing arch leading to yard. Adjacent, in Oxford Road, 3-storey **house** with Gothic trellis porch and, extraordinarily, windows that diminish in width as well as height in each successive storey.
10 High Town has excellent shop of *c*1820.
18–20 Castle Street has Regency reeded door surround with hood above.
Belmont House, Belmont Road, 3-bay, 2-storey house, *c*1820; Doric porch.
Tinto House, Broad Street, 4 bays, 2 storeys, pediment floating above eaves level. In same street, **24,** 2 storeys, Regency hooded door with Gothic detailing; hooded doors, characteristic of Hay, also survive at **3, 5, 11,** and on house in Chancery Lane. **Prospect House,** Broad Street, dated 1775. On corner of Broad Street and Chancery Lane, ambitious 5-bay, 3-storey **house** with porch. Despite late-C18 detailing, house may be of early-C18 origin.
In Bullring, **Pemberton House,** 5 bays, 2 storeys, with good doorcase containing Chinese Chippendale fretwork pattern on soffit of pediment, and pair of chimneystacks arranged to flank main elevation, *c*1780.
4–7 Bridge Street all have hooded doorcases; **5** also has diminutive attic windows beneath eaves.

Heath, West Yorkshire
1m E of Wakefield
Heath Hall, John Carr 1754–80. Fine 2-storey, 11-bay house with detached wings
Heath House, enlarged by James Paine 1744–5.

Heaton Hall
See Manchester.

Hellaby Hall, South Yorkshire
1¼m W of Maltby
*c*1715; 5-bay front capped with giant serpentine baroque pediment supported by huge scrolls.

Helmingham Hall, Suffolk
9m E of Stowmarket
Moated house of *c*1500, altered *c*1750 and *c*1800 by John Nash and John Adey Repton, who reconstructed south front in Tudor Gothic style.

Helston, Cornwall
St Michael's Church, 1756, plain, provincial, by Bland of Truro; tower by Thomas Edwards.

Hereford, Hereford and Worcester
Shire Hall, St Peter Street, 1815–17 by Sir Robert Smirke; powerful Greek revival, with austere Doric portico.
General Hospital, Nelson Street, 1781–3 by William Parker; enlarged several times.
St Giles's Hospital, St Owen Street, ancient foundation rebuilt 1770.
St Ethelbert's Hospital, Castle Street, 1805; 1 storey, Gothic detailing.
County Gaol, Commercial Road, built 1795–6 by John Nash; Largely demolished 1929 with exception of heavily rusticated **Governor's House.**
Bluecoat Girls' School, Blueschool Street, with C18 façade.
Kerry Almshouses, Commercial Street, 1821; low brick ranges with pointed windows.
City Arms Hotel, High Street, built *c*1790 as Duke of Norfolk's town house. In **St Owen Street,** numerous Georgian houses: **19–21,** early-C18 pair; **12,** *c*1800.
2 St Nicholas Street, 1745.
6–7 Bridge Street, *c*1800, with shared segmental-pedimented doorcase.
Harley Court, St John's Street, façade of 1739.
Bewell House, Bewell Street (now buried in supermarket development), 1724, brick, 5 bays.

Hertford, Hertfordshire
Shire Hall, 1767–9 by Robert and James Adam. Large yellow brick block with arcades (once open) along part of ground floor. Top-lit rotunda to upper floor.
Bailey Hall, Bell Lane, *c*1720, 5 bays, 3 storeys, façade framed by giant pilasters, which also emphasize projecting 3-bay centre.
4–6 West Street, dated 1719.
28 St Andrew's Street, dated 1726; façade framed by giant Ionic pilasters.

Heveningham Hall, Suffolk
3m SW of Halesworth
Designed 1779 by Sir Robert Taylor in late-Palladian manner. 25-bay, 3-storey front; 7-bay centre embellished with detached giant Corinthian columns on ground-floor arcade; 3-bay end pavilions with attached columns. Interior by James Wyatt, 1780–84; one of his most exciting works. Especially good hall with columnar screen, tunnel-vaulted ceiling, restrained neo-classical details; Etruscan Room in style of Athenian red-figure vase painting.
Orangery of 1781 by Wyatt.

High Wycombe, Buckinghamshire
Guildhall by Henry Keene, 1757. 3 wide bays with pedimented centre, open ground floor colonnade.
Market Hall, High Street, 1761, by Robert Adam in modest Palladian manner.
In **Bull Lane, house** with flat brick ogee window surrounds. Dated 1729; if so, one of earliest domestic Gothic revival structures.

Hilborough Hall, Norfolk
2m SW of Swaffham
House of 1779 shows influence of nearby Holkham (where builder of this was agent) in having balustrades beneath 1st-floor windows.

Holkham Hall, Norfolk
2m W of Wells-next-the-Sea
Designed by William Kent and Lord Burlington c1731, built 1734-61. One of the supreme examples of the English Palladian style. Plan of building, with wings, reminiscent of Palladio's Villa Mocenigo. Elevation, of buff-coloured brick (Vitruvius recommended bricks) displays full repertoire of Palladian details and proportions. Corner towers, inspired by Wilton and perhaps designs in Serlio, have Venetian windows. Fine portico on axis with saloon. Interior planning reveals movement away from still-lingering C17 formality as seen at Houghton. Most impressive is entrance: Marble Hall based on reconstruction of Roman basilica illustrated by Palladio, and on his Egyptian hall.

In grounds, **Arch** of c1740 by William Kent; tall, pedimented, with austere Palladian decoration. **Great Barn,** Palladian in form, c1790 by Samuel Wyatt.

Holyhead, Anglesey (Gwynedd)
Admiralty Pier, 1821, **Custom House** and **Harbour Office,** 1830 by John Rennie.

Holywell Hall, Lincolnshire
7m SW of Bourne
Old house with major extensions and remodelling of 1732-64. West front c1760, in provincial manner.

Garden buildings, c1732, more sophisticated, in current London Palladian fashion. **Stable** 7 bays with central archway, pediment, blank walls pierced only by semicircular lights, and side entrance topped by 3 ball finials – very Burlingtonian. **Fishing Temple** with pedimented Doric portico *in antis*; identical to menagerie published by James Gibbs in his 1728 *Book of Architecture*. **Orangery** with 5-bay loggia.

Honiley, Warwickshire
3m W of Kenilworth
St John the Baptist's Church, dated 1723, in provincial baroque manner. Interior has Corinthian pilasters in apse.

Honington Hall, Warwickshire
9m S of Stratford-upon-Avon
House c1680, but splendid rococo interior c1740, especially domed octagonal room decorated in style of Kent, designed by John Freeman.

Hopetoun House, Lothian
2m W of South Queensferry
Begun c1700 by Sir William Bruce. East front 1723-56 by William, and then John and Robert Adam who also designed interior rococo work.

Hopton, Derbyshire
2m W of Wirksworth
Hopton Hall, Elizabethan house embellished with over-sized segmental pedimented entrance, c1780.
Sir Philip Gell Almshouses, 1719-22; mullioned windows.
Sycamore Farm House, C18, with brick façade built for prestige in stone region (cf Longstone Hall).

Horbury, West Yorkshire
2m SW of Wakefield
St Peter and St Leonard's Church built to design, and at expense, of John Carr, 1791. Tower scaled in 4 diminishing stages topped by rotunda of columns and conical spire. Nave 30 by 60ft with shallow segmental tunnel-vaulted ceiling and full-width apses at each end. Interior domestic or theatrical rather than ecclesiastical.

Horsham, West Sussex
Town Hall, Market Square, 1812, with Gothic detailing; rebuilt internally 1888.
Unitarian Church, Worthing Road, 1721; plain.
Park House, North Street, front portion c1720, brick, 2 storeys, 9 bays with 3 centre bays emphasized by channelled stone pilaster strips and topped by pediment.
Springfield Road, North Parade, late C18.
63 London Road, villa of c1820; **Brunswick Terrace** of same date, stucco; **Old House,** late C18 with double bow front.
13-17 Causeway, late C18. Off Causeway, in Morth's Gardens, **Regency Cottage,** early-C19 with curious, slightly concave façade.

Horton, Dorset
8m W of Ringwood
Horton Tower, c1750, remarkable brick folly consisting of tall octagon flanked by lower round towers. Gothic windows.

Horton Hall, Northamptonshire
6m SE of Northampton
House demolished 1936, but some garden buildings survive, notably **menagerie,** a remarkable rococo/Palladian composition of c1745, possibly by Daniel Garrett or Thomas Wright.

Houghton Hall, Norfolk
12m NE of King's Lynn
Designed by Colen Campbell, 1721-35; full and highly influential expression of early phase of English Palladianism. Formal 1st floor, containing series of apartments either side of saloon and hall on main axis, set above rusticated ground floor. Stone hall, inspired by hall at Inigo Jones's Queen's House, is 40ft cube. Main elevation framed by towers that were given domes by James Gibbs.

Outside gates, model village of **New Houghton,** consisting of 2 rows of detached brick houses, c1724.

Houghton Lodge, Hampshire
7m N of Romsey
Cottage orné of 1800. Gothic windows, bow containing circular drawing room with sky-painted ceiling.

House of Gray, Tayside
6m W of Dundee
Remarkable provincial baroque house of c1716. Name of architect Alexander MacGill has been linked with house.

Hovingham Hall, North Yorkshire
8m W of Malton
Designed by owner, Sir Thomas Worsley, in eccentric Palladian manner, c1750. Entrance front embellished with 3-bay pedimented centre derived from Kent's pavilions at the Horse Guards, London, and from Burlington's 1723 design for London house for General Wade. Tunnel-vaulted archway leads to ground-floor riding school.

Hull
See Kingston upon Hull.

Hulme
See Manchester.

Huntingdon, Cambridgeshire
Town Hall, Market Hill, 1745. Pedimented 3-bay projection, Tuscan porch and cupola, 1817. Assembly Room on 2nd floor. Courts of Justice with original fittings.
Former **County Gaol,** St Peter's Road, 1828; 2 pavilions and octagonal watchtower by William Wilkins survive.
154-5 High Street, late-C18 former gaol, yellow brick with giant pilasters; underneath, condemned cell with vault on brick pillar. Also in High Street, **Old Bridge Hotel,** late C18; **110,** dated 1727, 3 bays, 3 storeys, with brick giant pilasters and round-arched centre window; **111,** 6 bays with 2-bay pediment and Venetian window; **Cowper House,** early-C18 front with steep 3-bay pediment; **Ferrar House,** early C18; **Whitwell House,** dated 1727; **Montagu House,** c1800.
Castle Hill House, opposite St Mary's Church, 1787, yellow brick, with pedimented doorcase.

Hylands, Essex
3m SW of Chelmsford
1819-25, by William Atkinson; typical composition of its date. Long, low house with giant Ionic portico.

Ickworth, Suffolk
3m S of Bury St Edmunds
Gigantic domed round house, with lower wings, begun c1795, probably by Francis Sandys with Marco Asprucci for the Earl Bishop of Derry, a connoisseur with a strange architectural bent; completed c1830 by John Field. Exterior decorated with panels, probably Coade stone, based on Flaxman's illustrations for Homer. Inside, library with chimneypiece by Canova. (National Trust)

Ince Blundell Hall, Merseyside
2m N of Crosby
Provincial baroque, tending to Palladian; reminiscent of some designs of Francis Smith, c1720. Adjoining is **Pantheon Room,** 1802, with splendid coffered dome, intended as sculpture gallery; probably executed by John Hope.

Ingleby Arncliffe, North Yorkshire
6m NE of Northallerton
Cleveland Tontine Inn, ¾ mile south of the town, c1805; stables of 1806 with Gothic details.
Arncliffe Hall, John Carr 1753-4. Ashlar, 3 storeys. Two main fronts, formal and correct Palladian. Inside, spectacular rococo plasterwork.

Inveraray, Strathclyde
19m SE of Oban
Church by Robert Mylne 1796; 2 naves, one for English, other for Gaelic services. Placed at key point in planned town laid out c1740. Mylne designed 2 rows of tenements, **Arkland** and **Relief Land,** 1774-6.
Town House by John Adam, 1755-7.
Inveraray Castle, 1745-60 by Roger Morris, in curious Palladian-Gothic manner. Symmetrical Palladian country house plan, but exterior with turrets and battlements.

Inverness, Highland
High Kirk, 1772. Large, T-plan with fine tower.

Ipswich, Suffolk
County Gaol, William Blackburn 1786-90.
Mrs Smith's Almshouses, Museum Street, 1760, with simple brick front.
Great White Horse Hotel, Tavern Street, 1815.
Good group of Georgian buildings in **Lower Brook Street, 12** and **14** with delicate doorcases, **27-35** an early-C19 terrace with Greek Doric doors.
In **Tower Churchyard,** fine 5-bay mid-C18 **house** with Gibbs doorway.
16 Northgate Street, early C19.

Ironbridge, Shropshire
4m S of Telford
Iron Bridge, first cast-iron engineered structure in world, 1777-9, to design of T.F. Pritchard, with modifications by Abraham Darby III.

Iver, Buckinghamshire
3m E of Slough
Iver Grove, Wood Lane, 1722. Fine late-baroque house, embellished with motifs typical of Vanbrugh's Office of Works.
Iver Lodge, early C19, tripartite windows within arches; central canted bay contains door.
Riching's Park, house of c1790, mostly demolished, but **bridge, icehouse** and remains of **cascade** survive.

Jedburgh, Borders
Fine small, 2-storey castellated **gaol,** with round tower, 1823 by Archibald Elliot.

Kedleston, Derbyshire
4m NW of Derby
House is remarkable display of Robert Adam's original and creative talents and of his ability to adapt an existing plan brilliantly. Rebuilding of early-C18 house for Nathaniel Curzon began in 1759 under Matthew Brettingham the Elder, who provided basic plan with wings linked by quadrants as in Palladio's Villa Mocenigo, and began to build on north-east wing. North-west wing built 1759-60 by James Paine, who also made designs for both principal fronts of main block. As early as 1759 Adam had been consulted by Curzon; in 1760 he was put in charge of all design work. He built north front as modification of Brettingham-Paine design, which was derived from Wanstead; but south front, completed 1765, is all Adam, at his best. Designed in archaeological spirit, based on Arch of Constantine in Rome, composition displays Adam's theories of the picturesque, with 'diversity of form' and 'advance and recess'. Inside, hall and saloon on main axis; hall lined with detached pink alabaster columns, reminiscent of basilica hall at Holkham. Saloon treated as rotunda. Each side of main axis rooms mostly for entertaining not formal apartments.
In grounds, **north lodge,** 1761 by Adam; as are **Gothic temple,** 1759-60; **bridge,** 1769-70; **bath house,** 1761; **boathouse,** c1770; **stables,** 1767-9. **Rectory,** 1771 by Samuel Wyatt.

Kelso, Borders
Church, 1773 by James Nisbet with John Laidlaw and Robert Purves. Octagonal.

Kendal, Cumbria
Former **Moot Hall,** Market Place, 1759; corner tower, Venetian window.

Assembly Rooms (now **Town Hall**), Highgate, 1825-7 by George Webster; altered 1859, 1893.

New Playhouse (now part of **Working Men's Institute**), Market Place, 1758, altered.

Shakespeare Theatre, off Highgate in yard behind Shakespeare Inn, 1784, closed 1834.

Abbot Hall (now **art gallery**), 1759 by John Carr. Approached through stable archway. Entrance front of 3 widely spaced bays flanked by lower projecting wings; Garden front with 2 canted bays.

Queen's Hotel, Kirkland, early C19.

Gasworks, Parkside Road, incorporates classical pedimented building dated 1825, inscribed *Ex fumo lucem*.

118 Highgate, 1757; **134-6**, early C19. **13** and **19** Stricklandgate, late C18; **95**, dated 1724.

Kenmore, Tayside
6m sw of Aberfeldy

Church, 1760, probably by William Baker; earliest example of sophisticated ecclesiastical Gothic revival in Scotland.

Kennington, Oxfordshire
sw edge of Oxford

St Swithin's Church, 'Norman' style, by Daniel Robertson, 1828.

Kentchurch Court, Hereford and Worcester
10m sw of Hereford

John Nash, *c*1795, Gothic.

Kilarrow, Strathclyde
Bowmore, Islay

Church, 1769 for Daniel Campbell. Circular plan.

Kimberley Hall, Norfolk
3m NW of Wymondham

Built 1712 by William Talman; altered into Palladian tower house *c*1755 by Thomas Prowse. Interior remodelled by John Sanderson *c*1770.

Kinfauns Castle, Tayside
2m E of Perth

1820-25 by Robert Smirke. Vast stone castle of cube-like classical clarity.

Kingsand and Cawsand, Cornwall
5m s of Saltash

Adjoining villages on estuary opposite Plymouth.

Pebble Tree House, Heavitree Road, Kingsand, looks *c*1850 externally but, like adjoining house, **The Whispers**, Market Street, has good fielded panelled rooms on ground floor. Both houses united by full Doric eaves cornice. Also in Market Street, **Charlestone House**, fine fielded panelled room on ground floor. All *c*1725-45.

Melrose, The Cleave, Kingsand, stucco façade, cyma recta block cornice, looks *c*1730-40.

Trenarren, Garrett Street, Cawsand, façade framed by angle pilaster strip linked by string courses between floors. Ground-floor room has fielded panelling, Chinese Chippendale frieze to fireplace, *c*1750. Farther south down street, excellent red brick **house**, front embellished with angle pilaster strips, string courses, dentil cornice; Regency reeded door.

On hill above Kingsand overlooking Plymouth, **fort** of *c*1780.

King's Lynn, Norfolk

New Assembly Rooms, behind Guildhall, 1766-8 by local carpenter William Tuck and bricklayer Thomas King. Plain, yellow brick.

Gaol, Saturday Market, 1784 by Tuck. Rusticated frontispiece, 1st-floor panel decorated with festoons of shackles.

15-16 Tuesday Market, *c*1720, long, low group; **18**, *c*1740.

81 High Street, former **Mayor's House**, *c*1740. Provincial Palladian composition with pediments to 1st-floor windows.

6 King Street, *c*1735, modest brick house with hopper and downpipe made into central feature (see Wisbech). Also in King Street, **23**, *c*1730; **Museum**, *c*1730-40, ashlar Palladian house, 1st-floor windows with alternating triangular and segmental pediments.

King's Norton, Leicestershire
6m SE of Leicester

St John the Baptist's Church, 1760-75 by John Wing the Younger. Important example of Gothic revival showing more structural boldness and archaeological correctness than usual in C18.

Kingsnympton Park, Devon
5m sw of South Molton

Villa of 1740 by Francis Cartwright, based on Roger Morris's Marble Hill House, Twickenham, Middlesex.

King's Stanley, Gloucestershire
3m w of Stroud

Cloth Mill, 1812-13, early 'fire-proof' building with iron frame within, brick and stone without.

Kingston Lisle, Oxfordshire
4m w of Wantage

Mid-C18 house remodelled in early C19 with coffered tunnel-vaulted entrance hall, and vaulted corridor with large caryatids on fluted Doric columns framing approach to staircase.

Kingston upon Hull, Humberside

Trinity House, 1753-9, pedimented 9-bay entrance front. Inside, courtroom, 1773 by Joseph Page, with strange mixture of lavish rococo and neo-classical plasterwork

Trinity Almshouses, Postern Gate, by Charles Mountain the Younger, 1828. Damaged 1941.

Assembly Rooms (now **New Theatre**), Kingston Square, by Richard Sharp and Charles Mountain, 1830. Grecian.

Former **Neptune Inn**, Whitefriars Gate, 1794-6 by George Pycock. Very good, large neo-classical composition. Adjacent is long brick **terrace** of 1829-30 by Charles Mountain, incorporating 5-bay pedimented centre.

Pease Warehouses, High Street, 1743-5. Tall, deep timber structures within brick shells. Now flats. Also in High Street: **Blaydes House** (No. 6), *c*1760 by Joseph Page, with rich interiors, especially staircase. **22-4**, *c*1751, with paired pedimented Ionic doorcase. **Wilberforce House** (25), C17 but with excellent enriched staircase of *c*1760 and rococo plasterwork, especially in drawing room. **Bayles House** (46), also with good staircase, *c*1751. **Maisters House** (160), very fine Palladian house of 1744 by Joseph Page, austere brick exterior with stone pedimented doorcase, inside rich rococo plasterwork. (National Trust)

In **Bishop Lane**, row of 3-storey houses of *c*1740.

The Pease Warehouses, High Street, Kingston upon Hull, Humberside, 1743-5: early examples of warehouse architecture.

9-12 King Street, 1771, also probably by Page. Palladian composition including pedimented feature with Venetian window over arch leading to curving Prince Street, which contains rebuilt C18 terrace.
Parliament Street, 1796-1800, loosely uniform terraces of 3-storey, 3-bay houses with pedimented doorcases; similar is north side of **Albion Street.**
On east side of **Prince's Dock,** good collection of buildings of c1825-30, including stucco giant Ionic arch.
Minerva Terrace, by the Humber, c1830.
Haworth Hall, at northern end of Beverley Road, c1760. Ashlar façade in refined late-Palladian manner of Chambers, rear elevation with central full-height canted bay. Excellent interior.

King's Weston, Avon
NW edge of Bristol
Influential baroque villa built 1712-14 to designs of Sir John Vanbrugh; altered internally 1763-8 by Robert Mylne. Important elements are external door with large pediment embracing tripartite composition (a device that became particularly popular in Ireland), arcaded chimneystacks, and generous staircase rising in entrance hall – a logical and traditional arrangement eschewed by contemporary Palladians.

Kinmount, Dumfries and Galloway
4m W of Annan
1812 by Sir Robert Smirke, in his abstracted, cubical Greek revival manner.

Kirkleatham, Cleveland
1m S of Redcar
St Cuthbert's Church, fine building of 1763, perhaps by John Carr, attached to older tower, partly of 1731, and baroque octagonal **Mausoleum** by James Gibbs, 1740, for Marwood Turner. Stepped pyramid roof based on Mausoleum of Halicarnassus.
Turner's Hospital, large almshouse founded 1676; rebuilt by James Gibbs 1741-7. Plan of chapel derived from that of Wren's St Anne and St Agnes in City of London: cruciform, vaulted.

Kirtlington Park, Oxfordshire
5m W of Bicester
Built 1742-7 by William Smith and John Sanderson. Porticoed central ashlar box flanked by lower wings, inspired by plan of Nostell Priory. Rich interior including rococo Monkey Room painted by J.F. Clermont, c1745.

Detail of a rococo ceiling adorned with painted monkeys by J.F. Clermont, c1745, at Kirtlington Park, Oxfordshire.

Kitley House, Devon
6m SE of Plymouth
Remodelled c1820-25 in Elizabethan style by George Stanley Repton.

Knowsley Hall, Merseyside
Between Liverpool and St Helens
House of various dates, but south end of east range notable for being embellished with 2-storey, all-timber veranda formed by 5 pairs of Doric columns supporting Ionic columns, c1735.

Knutsford, Cheshire
St John the Baptist's Church, 1741-4 by John Garlive. Solid, provincial brick church.
Sessions House and **House of Correction,** Toft Road, 1817-19 by George Moneypenny. Suitably grim neo-classical design.
In **Church Hill,** early-C18 **house** with Gibbs surround to door.
12 Princess Street, 3-bay C18 house.
(Tatton Park listed as a separate entry.)

Lacock Abbey, Wiltshire
3m S of Chippenham
Additions to existing house, c1754 by Sanderson Miller in 'monastic' Gothic style; especially good plasterwork in Great Hall. (National Trust)

Lambton Castle, Co. Durham
1m NE of Chester-le-Street
Joseph Bonomi, c1796. Asymmetrical castellated Gothic. Enlarged by Ignatius Bonomi, c1820-28.

Lampeter, Dyfed
14m NW of Llandovery
St David's College, 1822-7 by C.R. Cockerell. Tudor Gothic quadrangle with cast-iron Tudor windows.

Lanark, Strathclyde
Church, 1777, barn-like, almost square, with tower.

Lancaster, Lancashire
St John's Church, North Road, 1754-5. Tower by Thomas Harrison, 1784, based on Choragic Monument of Lysicrates, Athens.

Castle, reconstructed by Harrison, 1788-1802, and J.M. Gandy, 1802-23, including **Shire Hall**, with important Gothic revival interior: ribbed Gothic vault on faceted semicircular plan.

Old Town Hall (now **Museum**), Market Street, 1781-3 by Major Jarrat. Ashlar, 3 bays, Doric porch 2 columns deep. Tower designed by Harrison, and also based on Choragic Monument.

Custom House, St George's Quay, by Richard Gillow, 1764. Palladian, with Ionic portico.

Skerton Bridge, by Harrison, 1783-8.

Lune Aqueduct, over Caton Road, 1794-7 by John Rennie and Alexander Stevens.

Penny's Hospital, King Street, 1720. Almshouses forming 1-storey quadrangle; central chapel with serpentine gable. Windows mullioned.

Ring o' Bells Inn, King Street, baroque terrace house of c1720, ashlar, fine Doric door surround.

Music Room, off Market Street, built c1770 but in provincial baroque manner of c1735. Rich, pilastered exterior; inside, rococo plasterwork.

By Castle Park, **house** of c1740, 3 bays with full-width pediment.

5-7 Queen Street, c1750, with front doors beneath large shared swan-neck pediment. In **Queen Square**, mid-C18 **house** with 4-bay pediment, Diocletian window.

In **Church Street**, **house** of c1780 with central 3-storey semicircular bay in which is set curved, pedimented doorcase.

Langley Park, Buckinghamshire
2m E of Slough
Stiff Leadbetter, 1775-8, altered c1855. Inside, octagonal room expressed as canted bay.

Langley Park, Norfolk
8m SE of Norwich
Probably older house drastically altered by Matthew Brettingham the Elder, 1745, to form Palladian tower house. Inside, some fine plasterwork, c1750, including allegorical figures in library; ceiling paintings of monkeys by J.F. Clermont also c1750.

Lodges by Soane, 1784-90.

Langport, Somerset
4m SW of Somerton
Town Hall, Cheapside, dated 1733. 3 semicircular stone arches on ground floor; pyramid roof with lantern.

Lloyds Bank, Market Street, c1730.

Ensor House, Bow Street, c1725-35; Gibbs surrounds to all windows, elongated angle pilasters.

Herd's Hill House, 1826. Garden front with pair of tripartite windows on ground floor, linked by entablature supported on pair of Greek Doric pilasters. On 2nd floor, arcade of 10 Doric piers supporting pair of terminating pediments.

Langton(-by-Partney), Lincolnshire
8m E of Horncastle
Church of St Peter and St Paul, c1725. Red brick box. Inside, all original fittings with pews in collegiate pattern.

Lasborough Park, Gloucestershire
4m SW of Nailsworth
Castellated, by James Wyatt 1794; small version of his Slane, Co. Meath of 1785-6.

Launceston, Cornwall
Impressive group of mid-C18 brick houses around large, free-standing **Castle Hill House,** 4 Castle Street, c1760. **No. 9,** now **museum,** c1740-60; 11 similar. Also in Castle Street is **Eagle House,** remarkably ornate provincial composition of c1740: 5 bays, 2 storeys; entrance front with 3-bay pediment breaking forward and emphasized, like angles of main body of house, with quoins. Garden front with canted full-height bays.

5 Southgate Street, pedimented, c1760; later ground floor. In same street, **10,** c1730 with coved cornice; **2-4,** 3-storey, slate-hung houses of c1725 with cornice running above first floor as well as at eaves level – as at adjacent house, which is stone-faced with pedimented door, c1740; and also at **6 High Street.**

On south-east side of church, fine tall **house** of c1780, with pedimented door, mask keystones (looking like Coade stone) to all windows.

Lawers House, Tayside
13m SW of Aberfeldy
William Adam, 1724-6.

Laxton Hall, Northampton
6m NE of Corby
Neo-classical house of 1805-11 by J.A. Repton. Exquisite interiors by George Dance the Younger, 1812, especially double-height domed entrance hall, in which screen of 4 Ionic columns is supported on semicircular arch cut into horizontally rusticated wall; excellent example of French neo-classicism.

Leamington Spa, Warwickshire
Developed from 1815 as 'new town' by E. Wiles. P.F. Robinson drew up plan for enlarging development 1823-6.

Pump Room, 1813 by Charles Smith, pre-dating development; only Tuscan colonnade survives.

Architecture of development modelled on Brighton: tall stucco terraces with pilaster embellishments and Greek Doric porches, for example:

Regent Hotel, Euston Place, 1818.
The Parade, c1820-25.
Beauchamp Square, laid out 1825.
Clarendon Square, 1825.
In **Warwick Street**, 2 very long **terraces.**
Waterloo Place, 35 bays long, with Ionic porches.

In **Portland Street**, some Regency **villas.**

Leasingham Manor House, Lincolnshire
2m N of Sleaford
Modest C18 street front, but behind is ambitious provincial baroque front of 1740 identical to that at Barn Hill, Stamford (qv), with Gibbs surrounds to ground-floor windows, pediments to 1st.

Leeds, West Yorkshire
Holy Trinity Church, 1722-7, probably to design of local mason William Etty; but a design for a church in Leeds was published by William Halfpenny in his *Art of Sound Building* of 1725. One of few early-C18 Palladian – rather than baroque – churches. Designer perhaps inspired by Palladio's basilica: inside, giant Corinthian columns (on short plinths which were altered in 1887) support

straight entablature running length of nave. At east end, segmental apse contains Venetian window with Burlingtonian Palladian details. Nave windows embellished externally with pediments, giving air of palazzo rather than church elevation. Tower, of Wren/Gibbs type, added 1839.
Brunswick Methodist Church, Brunswick Street, James Simpson, 1824. Greek revival façade.
Former **Leeds Library,** Commercial Street, by Thomas Johnson, 1808. Greek revival.
Armley House, Gott's Park, *c*1781, remodelled by Robert Smirke *c*1818, with Ionic portico; first Greek revival mansion in West Yorkshire.
Roundhay Hall, by John Clark, 1826, with giant Ionic portico and good top-lit staircase.
Park Square, late C18, 2-storey, with 3-storey pedimented houses marking centres of ranges.
Temple Newsam House, on SE edge of town, 1630. South wing 1796 by Johnson, but remarkably in keeping with style of original house, especially windows. Inside, some good rococo work of 1736–58. Sphinx gate, 1768, copy of gate at Chiswick House.

Leicester, Leicestershire
United Baptist Church, Charles Street, 1830. Greek revival.
County Rooms, Hotel Street, designed by John Johnson, 1792–1800, as a hotel. 3 large tripartite windows on 1st floor with niches between. Windows light one large front room with tunnel vault.
Royal Infirmary, Infirmary Road, by Benjamin Wyatt, 1771. Enlarged 1888–1929.
Fielding Johnson Hospital, Regent Road, *c*1815–20, with giant Corinthian pilasters.
Gaol, Welford Road, 1825–8 by William Parsons. Castellated baronial manner; enlarged 1844–6.
In St Martin's East, **No. 5 (Church House),** *c*1725; **7 (Provost's House)** of similar date. **21 St Martin's,** *c*1720. **17 Friar Lane,** *c*1750, 5 bays, 3 storeys with rusticated giant pilasters grouping segmental windows into 2 pairs, central bay with Venetian window, Diocletian above, pediment over all. **25–7** also good Georgian.
Spa Place, Humberstone Gate, terrace of 1789, middle houses sharing semicircular porch.
9–15 Southgate Street, 1795 by Johnson.
Around **New Walk,** leafy promenade planted in 1785, some fine groups of Regency buildings, especially **Waterloo House** on corner of Hastings Street, stuccoed, with incised Greek pattern on pilasters; **King Street,** where terrace of *c*1825 is articulated with giant pilasters; and **The Crescent,** *c*1810, with pedimented centre.

Leigh Court, Avon
Outside Bristol, 1m NW of Clifton Bridge
Thomas Hopper, 1814; Greek revival mansion with excellent interior, especially domed entrance hall with ring of Ionic columns, which leads to magnificent stairs with bronze balustrade, Ionic colonnade and ceiling with glazed coffering.

Leighton Buzzard, Bedfordshire
Friends' Meeting House, North Street, 1789, with simple original interior.
By old church, **Manor Farm House,** early C18, with centre bay flanked by 2 sturdy giant pilasters, door with rusticated Doric pilasters.

Leighton Hall, Lancashire
2m N of Carnforth
Medieval in origin, but 1760 centre, Gothicized *c*1810 under direction of Richard Gillow. Especially good is entrance hall with tripartite Gothic screen and curving stair. Billiard room (now dining room) with oval skylight.

Leith
See Edinburgh.

Leominster, Hereford and Worcester
House at junction of Vicarage Street and Market Street, *c*1770, 3 bays, 3 storeys, centre door flanked by Venetian windows on ground and 1st floor and Diocletians on 2nd.

Letheringsett Hall, Norfolk
6m SW of Sheringham
Remarkable amateur creation in Greek revival manner, 1808 by W. Hardy. Exterior embellished with mighty Greek Doric colonnade supporting full entablature.

Letton Hall, Norfolk
9m E of Swaffham
By Sir John Soane, an early work of 1783–9. White brick, discreet exterior. Fine entrance hall; staircase top-lit.

Lewes, East Sussex
County Hall, High Street, by John Johnson 1808; ground floor with Tuscan loggia.
All best houses are in long High Street. **32 (Lewes House)** *c*1730, large, blue-grey brick, Doric pedimented porch. **33 (School Hill House),** same date and scale; **61,** *c*1780, with large pedimented Doric door surround. **82 (St Swithin's House; Lloyds Bank),** *c*1780, Ionic pilastered door with Diocletian window above. **93 (Westgate House),** *c*1780, 3 storeys, 2 bays formed by 3-storey bows containing tripartite windows, Doric pedimented doorcase with good fanlight; façade clad in red mathematical tiles. **166,** *c*1810 by Amon Wilds, with his characteristic ammonite capitals to giant pilasters which frame the façade. **169 (Barbican House,** now **museum),** *c*1725. **211,** *c*1720, façade entirely of fine red rubbed brick. **212,** *c*1725. **220–21,** group of *c*1730, but enlarged – sundial dated 1824.
Pelham House, St Andrew's Lane, partly late C18, well hidden behind high garden wall.
Bartholomew House, Castle Gate, 3-storey, 2-bay pair of *c*1810, clad in black mathematical tiles.

Lichfield, Staffordshire
George Hotel, Bird Street, late C18. 9-bay front, 5 centre bays emphasized with pilasters. Inside, segmental barrel-vaulted ballroom on 1st floor – rare example of pre-C19 inn incorporating rather than acquiring a ballroom.
Donegal House (Guildhall), Bore Street, *c*1720, 5-bay elevation framed by giant Doric pilasters.
In Cathedral Close, **Newton's College** by Joseph Potter, 1800; ashlar, 11 bays with 3-bay pediment. Also in Close, **Selwyn House,** *c*1760, free-standing, door in canted bay. **23A,** late C18; 5 bays, Gothic with ogee windows, battlements. Beside Deanery (*c*1700) on north side of Close, C18 **house** with canted bays; in its grounds, octagonal **gazebo.**

20 St John Street, early C18; **26,** early C18; **28 (St John's Hospital),** c1820; rendered façade, colonnade to ground floor. **Davidson House,** Upper St John Street, c1820; pedimented centre with 1st-floor Venetian window.

National Westminster Bank occupies early-C19 house on corner of Friary and Bird Street, with rusticated ground floor. **11 Bird Street,** C18, with domed room with shell mosaic; **17,** c1720.

In Beacon Street, **West Gate House,** c1750-60. **Erasmus Darwin's House,** c1775; Venetian windows on ground and 1st floors. **Beacon Lodge,** c1820.

3, 15-17 Market Street have early-C19 shopfronts.

Stowe House, Stowe Street, c1720-30; freestanding. In same street, **Stowe Hill Mansion,** late C18; front has central bow.

Lilleshall Hall, Shropshire
3m SW of Newport
By Sir Jeffry Wyatville, 1826-33. Neo-Tudor.

Linby, Nottinghamshire
N edge of Hucknall
Castle Mill, on east edge of village, housed James Watt's first steam engine for cotton-spinning, installed 1785. Building originally dressed with Gothic details, towers and castellations; only towers remain after modernization.

Lincoln, Lincolnshire
Lincoln Castle contains **Assize Courts,** by Sir Robert Smirke, 1823-30, Gothic; also **Gaol** (now **Lincolnshire Record Office**), 1787 by John Carr and William Lumby. C18 **chapel** of Gaol has tiers of individual stalls to isolate convicts but allow them to see preacher.

On Castle Hill, **Judge's Lodging,** c1810 by William Hayward. 2 storeys, 9 bays with centre 3 pedimented. Above doorway with Tuscan columns set *in antis*, window with flanking niches. Also on Hill, **6-7,** mirror-plan pair of c1725.

Assembly Rooms, 76 Bailgate, with quoined front of 1744 partly concealed behind work of 1914. Inside, best Georgian room in Lincoln, with Ionic pilasters and high, square windows.

Bishop's College Hospital, formerly **Infirmary,** Wordsworth Street, 1776 by John Carr; pedimented 3-bay centre, wings with Venetian windows.

Lawn Asylum, Union Road, 1819-20 by Richard Ingleman; giant Ionic portico.

Grandstand, Saxilby Road, 1826; altered but still with iron verandas on Doric columns.

Bluecoat School, now **Lincoln School of Art,** Christ's Hospital Terrace, 1784 by Lumby. Ground-floor windows unusual: square, set in stone-headed blank arcade. Venetian window lights a 'Great Room'. Good staircase.

In Eastgate, **Cathedral School** (No. 8), late C18, brick, with 2 canted bays rising full height of front. **20-27,** c1740; **Disney Place,** 1736 by Abraham Hayward, brick with stone trim.

Butter Market, Sincil Street, façade of 1737 only with arches, Venetian window and pediment.

Saracen's Head Hotel, Stonebow, late Georgian with good wrought-iron balcony.

Archdeaconry, Greenstone Place, c1760, with emphasized centre bay: tripartite Doric door surround below 1st-floor Ionic Venetian window topped with 2nd-floor Diocletian and open pediment. In Greenstone Terrace, **Greenstone Holme,** mid-C18, with Venetian window to centre bay; **No. 3,** with tripartite door.

4, 5, 5A Minster Yard, C18 rendered façade; **7, 8,** 7-bay pair; and **9,** all late Georgian.

'Number Houses', by Exchequer Gate, irregular C18 group. **18,** late C18 with 2-storey bow windows; **21-2,** early C18, with 2-storey porch with scrolled pediment; **23,** 4 bays with angle pilasters.

3-4 Christ's Hospital Terrace, early C19.

Linley Hall, Shropshire
8m E of Montgomery
1743-6 by Henry Joynes, who had been Clerk of Works at Blenheim 1705-15. Building combines something of strength and originality, especially baroque movement, of Vanbrugh with current Palladian motifs and compositional devices.

Linton, North Yorkshire
7m N of Skipton
Fountains Hospital, according to Kerry Downes 'most heroically detailed almshouses in England'. Ashlar; towering entrance block with lantern above niche based on Venetian window, connected by 2-bay wings to pedimented pavilions that break well forward. Perhaps design of William Wakefield, c1725.

Littledean, Gloucestershire
10m SW of Gloucester
House of Correction, now **Record Office,** designed 1787-91 by William Blackburn.

Little Gidding, Cambridgeshire
7m SE of Oundle
St John the Evangelist's Church, with west façade of 1714; provincial baroque.

Liverpool, Merseyside
St Peter's Roman Catholic Church, Seel Street, 1788, sanctuary 1843. In north transept, domestic-style doorway.

Holy Trinity Church, St Anne's Street, 1790-92, ashlar, classical.

St James's Church, St James's Place, Toxteth, 1774-5, built and perhaps designed by builder Cuthbert Bisbrowne in very provincial manner. Inside, 3 galleries supported on contemporary cast-iron columns – a very early use. Extended 1900.

Toxteth Chapel, Park Road, enlarged 1774.

Holy Trinity Church, Church Road, Wavertree, 1794 by John Hope. Alterations of 1911.

St Luke's Church, St Luke's Place, by John Foster, 1802 and c1810-20. Perpendicular Gothic. Now gutted.

St Andrew's Presbyterian Church, Rodney Street, Foster 1823-4. Imposing composition with twin-towered Grecian front derived from C. R. Cockerell's (demolished) Hanover Chapel, Regent Street, London. Now mutilated.

Exchange (now **Town Hall**) built 1749-54 to designs of John Wood the Elder. Ashlar, Palladian, with arcaded rusticated ground floor supporting pilasters. Damaged by fire 1795; rebuilt by Foster, who added dome in 1802. Portico added 1811. Rich Empire interiors.

Wellington Rooms, Mount Pleasant, 1815 by Edmund Aikin. Expressive, though largely blank, neo-classical façade. In centre, bow ringed with Corinthian columns.

A group of houses in Duke Street, Liverpool, built c1765 and one of the earliest and most striking terrace developments in the city.

Bluecoat School, 1716-17, large red brick quadrangular building with pediment in centre block and complex fenestration.

159-61, 169-75 Duke Street, two groups of houses of c1765, among earliest terrace developments in Liverpool. Gable-like pediment over entire width of each façade, raised front doors embellished with rusticated pilasters.

Lyceum Club, Bold Street, 1800-2 by Thomas Harrison. Austere early example of Greek revival. Bold Street façade has centre recessed with unfluted Ionic columns, side bays with large tripartite windows. Inside, good domed room.

University Extra-Mural Department (formerly **Royal Institution**), Colquitt Street, built c1799 as house, with offices and warehouse at back; later Greek Doric porch.

139 Dale Street, ambitious design of c1785 with 3-bay pediment and Venetian window.

Rodney Street, handsome brick terraces forming key part of fashionable suburb developed c1780. **62** of 1796, 5 bays with 3-bay pediment, good doorcase. **51-75** form single composition with 5-bay centre pediment, c1790. Other groups c1810-20.

In **Seymour Street, Russell Street** – eastern extensions of Rodney Street – ever decreasing number of increasingly decayed early-C19 houses.

Abercromby Square, laid out c1815, built c1825-35; 3 sides survive.

Blackburne Terrace, Blackburne Place, 1826.

Gambier Terrace, most imposing of Liverpool terrace developments, built 1830-37 (west half only); 34 bays, 4 storeys, centre block with ground-floor Doric colonnade.

Percy Street, with impressive ashlar groups of c1825-30.

Fragments of tall terraces of c1830 survive in Upper Parliament Street; for example **Montpelier Terrace.**

Liverpool suburbs

Allerton
Allerton Hall, Clarke's Gardens, Woolton Road. Enlarged in early C19, but retains good front of c1740 with giant Ionic portico.

Anfield
Newsham House, in Newsham Park, late C18.

Everton
St George's Church, Heyworth Street, by Thomas Rickman and John Cragg, 1813. Neo-Perpendicular outside, but extraordinary interior with galleries, tracery and ceiling all of iron.

Sefton Park
Greenbank, now within **University Halls of Residence,** pretty Gothic house of c1810. Side elevation with 2-storey iron veranda.

Woolton
Woolton Hall, 1704, enlarged and remodelled 1774-80 by Robert Adam. Adam front of 3 centre bays framed by 2-bay pedimented pavilions, a fashionable device of c1780. Inside, Octagon Room is best of Adam's work, with good ceiling.

Llandrindod Wells, Powys

Llandrindod Hall, C18, converted to hotel use 1749 (closed 1787) after saline and sulphur springs were discovered in 1730s. Functioned like large modern hotel with suite of rooms for balls and concerts, billiard rooms and shops.

Llanfyllin, Powys

Council House, 24 High Street, late C18. Inside, upper room containing mural paintings showing neo-classical mountainscapes, painted c1812 by Captain Augerau, French prisoner of war. Also in High Street, **Post Office,** late-C18 with Gothic windows, including 2 of Venetian form.

Manor House, Vine Square, dated 1737, brick, segmental windows, keystones and quoins.

Llanidloes, Powys
Trewythen Arms Hotal, Great Oak Street, *c*1770. Inside, elegant contemporary staircase.

Lochwinnoch, Strathclyde
5m SW of Johnstone
St John's Church, 1806; Gothic, octagonal plan.

London
See separate section, p260.

London Colney, Hertfordshire
2m SE of St Albans
St Peter's Church, George Smith 1825-6. Early example of Norman revival.

Longdon upon Tern, Shropshire
3m NW of Wellington
Tern Aqueduct, on Shropshire Union Canal, 1793-4 by Thomas Telford; earliest cast-iron aqueduct.

Longford Hall, Shropshire
1m SW of Newport
By Joseph Bonomi, 1789-94; good example of early Greek inspired villa with asymmetrical plan. 2 storeys with giant Tuscan 4-column portico. Entrance hall with Grecian frieze. Offices, kitchen, servants' hall in asymmetrical wing.

Longhirst House, Northumberland
3m NE of Morpeth
1824-8 by John Dobson; eccentric Greek revival house with entrance framed by pair of giant columns. Stone-clad entrance hall and vaulted 1st-floor landing evoke some of the arid academic atmosphere of late-C18 French neo-classicism.

Longleat, Wiltshire
4m W of Warminster
Elizabethan house remodelled internally 1806-11 by Sir Jeffry Wyatville, in neo-Elizabethan style.

Long Melford, Suffolk
2m N of Sudbury
In High Street, **Mansel Hall,** 5 bays with central Venetian window over door, *c*1760; **Hanwell House,** with fine display of 4 Gothic-glazed Venetian windows, *c*1780.

Longner Hall, Shropshire
2m SE of Shrewsbury
*c*1805 by John Nash. Asymmetrical Tudor Gothic; good staircase hall with plaster fan vault.

Longstone Hall, Derbyshire
2m NW of Bakewell
1747; plain brick front; example of brick being used for prestige in stone region.

Longton, Staffordshire
St John the Baptist Church, King Street, 1792-5. Pointed windows to nave; transept and chancel 1827. Adjacent is **Church School** of 1822.

Boundary Works, King Street, dated 1819; one of the best surviving early potteries. 17 bays; taller 5-bay centre with rusticated arch, 1st-floor Venetian window, 2nd-floor Diocletian, all topped by open pediment.

Louth, Lincolnshire
The Mansion, Westgate, *c*1720. Free-standing, red brick, centre bay crowned by bold semicircular pediment. Also in Westgate: **The Limes** and **Lindsey House,** both mid-C18; **Westgate House,** early C19. **Thornton House,** *c*1800, 3 bays, 3 storeys, with pair of 3-storey bays containing tripartite windows. Centre bay with tall blind arch.

5 Upgate, *c*1760, brick, 5 bays, 3 storeys, pair of ground-floor canted bays, 1st-floor central Venetian window. In same street, **Mansion House,** late C18, angle pilasters.

The Priory, Eastgate, picturesque Gothic villa of 1818 by Thomas Espin for himself.

In **Mercer Row,** good Regency **shop**.

Lower Hartwell
See Hartwell House.

Lowestoft, Suffolk
55 High Street, *c*1770, central Doric doorcase flanked by Venetian windows.

Lowther, Cumbria
4m S of Penrith
Model village designed by Adam brothers *c*1760, but never completed to plan which envisaged a circus (only half built) flanked by 2 squares with smaller squares off.

Ludlow, Shropshire
Butter Cross, 1743-4 by William Baker. Ashlar, 2 storeys, open ground-floor arcade, clock tower; in provincial Palladian tradition.

Guildhall, Mill Street, rebuilt by Thomas F. Pritchard 1774-6, with rococo/Gothic door.

Hosyers' Almshouses, by Pritchard 1758; shallow quadrangle, with central pediment.

27 Broad Street, 5-bay, 2-storey house with 1-bay pediment crowning central tripartite door, *c*1780. In same street, **39,** 3-bay, 3-storey house with all apertures formed as Venetian windows, *c*1765.

14 Castle Square (now council flats), red brick, segmental windows, dated 1728.

Lumley Castle, County Durham
1m W of Chester-le-Street
Licensed 1379; altered 1580; then again *c*1721 by Vanbrugh, who created some remarkable interiors, especially library, decorated with deeply rusticated piers and stone fireplace with terms. Dining room of *c*1730 with grained panelling.

Luscombe Castle, Devon
2m SW of Totnes
Asymmetrical picturesque castellated house, 1799-1804 by John Nash.

Lydiard Tregoze House, Wiltshire
5m W of Swindon
Medieval house remodelled 1743-9, perhaps by Roger Morris, to form Palladian tower house. Entrance hall with coved ceiling and Kentian decoration.

Lyme Park, Cheshire
2m W of New Mills
Elizabethan house altered by Giacomo Leoni, 1725-35, in Continental baroque manner. 15 bays with 3-storey principal front containing central frontispiece formed by Ionic portico standing on rusticated arcaded ground floor. Attic storey behind pediment only, 1814-17 by Lewis Wyatt, who also remodelled interiors on east front to create dining room in neo-Wren style. (National Trust)

Lyme Regis, Dorset
Three Cups Hotel, Middle Row, late Georgian; 3 bays with Greek Doric columns supporting a bow.
Belmont, Pound Street. Main façade of *c*1785, conceived as advertisement for Coade stone, with dazzling array of Coade items: house belonged to Eleanor Coade from 1784.
4 Monmouth Street, with mid-C18 stone façade.
On the **Cobb,** many good examples of simple marine vernacular buildings of *c*1800–30.

Lypiatt Park, Gloucestershire
3m E of Stroud
Enlarged 1809 by Sir Jeffry Wyatville in Tudor Gothic Style.

Lytham Hall, Lancashire
In Lytham St Anne's
By John Carr 1757–64, in his own brand of rich Palladian baroque.

Macclesfield, Cheshire
Town Hall and **Assembly Rooms,** by Francis Goodwin, 1823–4, in Greek revival manner.
Sunday School, Roe Street, 1813–14.
Regency Mill, Clowens Road, 18 bays, 4 storeys, pedimented centre, dated 1796.
Jordangate House, Jordangate, dated 1728, tall 5-bay house with baroque flourishes. Opposite, **Cumberland House,** *c*1750.
19 King Edward Street, dated 1753 yet still in provincial baroque manner of the 1720s.
60–62 Chestergate, 5-bay, 3-storey brick house of *c*1720. Door with swan-necked pediment.

Madeley, Shropshire
4m s of Oakengates
St Michael's Church, octagonal, neo-classical, by Thomas Telford 1794–6.

Maentwrog, Gwynedd
3m sw of Ffestiniog
Oakly Arms Hotel, *c*1820, with 3 canted bays.

Maidenhead, Berkshire
Bridge by Sir Robert Taylor, 1772–7.

Maidstone, Kent
Unitarian Chapel, Market Buildings, 1736. Bold pilaster strips frame elevation.
Town Hall, High Street, 1762–3, north and south front 5 bays. Ground floor ashlar with blank arcading; pediments to 1st-floor windows. Inside, charmingly painted council chamber with rococo plasterwork. Also in High Street, **Royal Insurance offices,** 1827 by John Whichcord Senior. Restrained, with engaged 2-storey fluted Ionic columns above arcaded ground floor.
Sessions House, County Road/Lower Boxley Road, 1824 by Sir Robert Smirke; ashlar, small, austere and very controlled composition; excellent example of Smirke's astylar cubical Greek manner.
Gaol, Lower Boxley Road, 1811–19 by D. A. Alexander. Rugged ragstone perimeter wall encloses round tower, originally governor's office and prison chapel arranged so that all prisoners could see chaplain but not each other.
Oakwood Hospital, St Andrew's Road, 1830 by Whichcord. Grandiloquent, with pedimented centre.
Bluecoat School, Knightrider Street, built 1720; only 4 bays survive.
11 Lower Stone Street, early C18. **28,** 1716. Big columned, pedimented doorcase. Façade topped by richly carved console cornice extending to more modest No. 26.
Grove House, Week Street, early C18.
Mote Park, off Mote Road, built 1793–1801 to designs of D. A. Alexander. South front has Ionic colonnade across 5 centre windows, with 2-storey segmental bay at each end topped by Diocletian window in blank arch. On north front, centre tripartite window, full-height bow at each end. In grounds, **pavilion** of 1801 by S. Nelson in advanced Greek revival manner.
Turkey Court and **Paper Mill,** south of Ashford Road. Brick house of 1736; projecting from south-east corner, contemporary brick-based building used as mill. In 1740 mill was taken over by James Whatman.

Maldon, Essex
Blue Boar Hotel, brick front of *c*1800 on C15 building.
In **Gate Street,** C18 **house,** 5 bays, bold shell decoration in arches of 2 ground-floor windows.
22 High Street (Stonecroft), early C18, centre emphasized by rusticated pilasters. Also in High Street: **No. 3,** 3 bays with doorway formed by rusticated frame surmounted by pediment; **40–42,** handsome 5-bay, 3-storey group with central Venetian window topped by Diocletian, modern Doric colonnade along ground-floor frontage; **52,** *c*1724, with superimposed angle pilasters, upper ones in form of terms; **54–6,** *c*1725.

Mamhead House, Devon
4m sw of Topsham
By Anthony Salvin, 1828–38; neo-Tudor to resemble earlier castle. Eclectic interior including fan-vaulted staircase.

Manchester (Greater Manchester)
County Court, Quay Street, built *c*1770 as private house; became court 1878. Austere, classical, Tuscan porch.
City Art Gallery, Mosley Street, built as **Royal Institution of Fine Arts,** by Sir Charles Barry, 1824–35, in splendid Greek revival manner with Ionic portico and a raised attic derived from Schinkel's Schauspielhaus, Berlin. Also in Mosley Street, **Portico Library** (now **Lloyds Bank**), by Thomas Harrison, 1802–6. Greek Ionic portico *in antis.*
Byrom Street has group of late-Georgian houses; in **Lower Byrom Street** a Georgian house with excellent doorcase.
Manchester Arms, Lower Millgate, 5-bay house, *c*1760, good doorway: Tuscan columns with leaf capitals, triglyph frieze, pediment.
St John Street has 2 fairly complete Georgian terraces.

Manchester suburbs

Ardwick
St Thomas's Church, Ardwick Green North. Built 1741, widened 1777, lengthened 1831, tower of 1836.

Chorlton-on-Medlock
New town laid out 1793–4. Original houses survive in Oxford Road, especially **88–100** and **323–9.** In Grosvenor Square, 3-bay house, now **Ear Hospital.**

Didsbury
Woodland, Crescent Road, *c*1800. Shallow porch with Adamesque columns which, with window above, are set in giant blank arch.

Fallowfield
Unitarian Chapel, Wilmslow Road, 1790, perhaps by John Carr.
Platt Hall, Platt Lane, *c*1764. Pedimented front and pediment to central window, Ionic porch, lower wings. Architect perhaps Timothy Lightoler. Inside, excellent staircase.

Heaton
Heaton Hall, perhaps finest early neo-classical house in the country; designed 1772 by James Wyatt, who incorporated earlier house. South side with apsed centre block linked by colonnades to canted bay wings. Superb interior, especially domed room above saloon, with Etruscan paintings by Biagio Rebecca.

Hulme
Remains of **Bridgewater Canal buildings** between Chester and Egerton Roads; **wharves, warehouses** and **canal offices** in Chester Road, *c*1800.

Mapleton, Derbyshire
1m NW of Ashbourne
St Mary's Church, curious little C18 stone building with octagonal dome and lantern.
Clergymen's Widows' Almshouses, 1727. Centre flanked by giant rusticated pilasters.

Marford, Clwyd
3m N of Wrexham
Estate village with Gothic cottages, 1806–16 by George Boscawen.

Margam Abbey, West Glamorgan
1m SE of Margam
Large and spectacular **orangery** by Anthony Keck 1787–9.

Margate, Kent
Town Hall, 1821 by Edward White.
Pier, 1810–15 by John Rennie.
Royal Sea Bathing Hospital, Canterbury Road, 1820, Grecian with monumental Doric portico. Behind is earlier building of 1792–6.
Theatre Royal, Hawley Square, 1787; burnt 1829; remodelled 1874.
Cecil Square, laid out 1769 as part of early development. Original buildings survive on north and west sides of square. **No. 1,** 2 storeys, has Venetian windows on ground floor. **Cecil Street,** running off the square, has late-C18 houses on both sides and leads to **Hawley Square,** completed *c*1790.
In Hawley Street, **India House,** 1767. Adjacent, **The Limes,** early C19, rendered.
Fort Hill and **Fort Crescent** are beginnings of residential terrace development along road; **villas** of *c*1820 in the crescent. In Grotto Hill, fantastic **grotto** with circular and square chambers, linked by serpentine passages, carved out of solid chalk, all covered with patterned shellwork; probably late C18.

Marlborough, Wiltshire
In High Street, **Ivy House Hotel,** *c*1760, pedimented door, 2 Venetian windows on 1st floor; **Wykeham House,** dated 1761; **Merlin Tea Rooms,** *c*1720, with centre bay emphasized by pilasters in 2 orders; **The Priory,** *c*1820, with Gothic windows; **127,** *c*1760, with canted bays containing Venetian windows. **10-11 The Parade,** *c*1760, with Venetian window and pediment to both end bays.

Marlow, Buckinghamshire
Marlow Place, baroque house of *c*1720, possibly by West Country baroque architect such as Cartwright, Ireson or Bastard. Front embellished with pilasters topped by two sorts of capitals. Those in centre portion of house have inverted Ionic volutes, while those dressing the wings have capitals decorated with unlikely motif of 3 leeks. Inside, double-height entrance hall.
Post Office, High Street, pedimented centre, Ionic doorway, *c*1730.
29-31 West Street, *c*1725, brick with rusticated brick quoins. In same street, **47,** vitreous and red brick, 3 bays wide with blank attic storey and 3-bay pediment; **Nos. 81-3** similar, *c*1725.
Remnantz, High Street, big, virtually free-standing house, *c*1725, with canted bays framing pedimented door.

Martock, Somerset
5m S of Somerton
Market House, *c*1750, free-standing, 4 bays by 1; well-detailed Venetian window occupying short side. Ground floor arcaded.

Matfield House, Kent
5m E of Tunbridge Wells
Dated 1728 on hopper, and interesting for resemblance, both in plan and elevation, to Finchcocks (qv); surely work of same man. Façade framed by giant Tuscan pilasters, set in from corners, carrying blocks of white entablature with triglyphs (like Finchcocks) with 3 round-headed windows in slightly projecting centre flanked by segmental windows (also like Finchcocks).
Stables to rear, look *c*1725, dated 1779.

Matlock Bath, Derbyshire
1m S of Matlock
South Parade, *c*1790, incorporating **Hodkinson's Hotel.**

Matlock Green, Derbyshire
½m N of Matlock
5 Knowleston Place, 1753 and 1772; **15,** *c*1820, with porch.
Huntbridge House, *c*1760.
The Cliff, early industrial group including house dated 1757.

Mawley Hall, Shropshire
7m W of Bewdley
Dated 1730, by Francis Smith. Exterior decorated with pilasters, much renewed, but inside contains exceptionally well-preserved and exotic baroque decoration. Entrance hall has elaborate plaster military trophy overmantel, and column capitals with inverted Ionic volutes. Staircase handrail serpentine and furnished with snake's head at bottom; strings carved with reliefs of musical instruments. Little Drawing Room with marquetry in South German fashion. Upstairs bedroom has capitals decorated with kissing putti.

Mavisbank, Lothian
3m SW of Dalkeith
Villa, dated 1723, ashlar, in provincial Palladian manner with baroque details, for Sir John Clerk

by William Adam. Pioneering design and house type for Scotland. Now a ruin.

Melksham, Wiltshire
14 High Street, early C19 with giant pilasters.
17 Bank Street, c1820 with 2 shallow bows.
In Spa Road, **The Limes,** mid-C18 with canted bay, pedimented door with carved brackets; **8-14,** c1830, large, 3-storey semi-detached houses with classical and Gothic detailing; **16-18,** c1830.

Mellerstain, Borders
6m NW of Kelso
William Adam 1725; Robert Adam from 1760. Classical but castellated. Interior is magnificent Robert Adam.

Melville Castle, Lothian
1m SW of Dalkeith
James Playfair, 1786-91. Castellated Gothic with 4 round corner towers, but classical windows.

Melrose, Borders
4m E of Galashiels
Dry Grange Bridge, c1780 by Alexander Stevens, with classical and Gothic detailing.

Menai Straits, Gwynedd
Offshore from Bangor
Suspension bridge, Thomas Telford 1819-26.

Mereworth, Kent
6m NE of Tonbridge
St Lawrence's Church, 1744-6, perhaps the most convincing, and certainly the most interesting attempt at design of full-blooded Palladian rather than Wren/Hawksmoor/Gibbs-derived English baroque church. Architect not known; may have been Roger Morris. Body of building, particularly deep-eaved Tuscan pediment at west end, inspired by Inigo Jones's St Paul's, Covent Garden; but tower derived from Gibbs's St Martin-in-the-Fields. However, most impressive is interior: nave formed by arcade of giant Tuscan columns rising from floor as in Palladian Egyptian hall, supporting coffered barrel vault lit by large east Diocletian window. Aisles, as in Egyptian hall, narrow with engaged colonnade along aisle walls. Columns marbled, ceiling painted in imitation of coffering – all has feeling of archaeological reconstruction. Church never had pews, so columns could rise from floor unobscured. They lack moulded bases, because their lower portions were originally panelled.

Mereworth Castle, begun 1722, most satisfactory of the 4 versions of Palladio's Villa Rotonda built in England during C18. Designed by Colen Campbell, who seems to have been inspired by James Smith's c1708 drawn interpretation of Palladio's symmetrical villa. Although imitative, it is highly original in detail and contains some very rich rococo interiors, especially saloon.

Villa flanked by **pavilions** and, in grounds, a now ruinous Corinthian **arch**.

Mersham le Hatch, Kent
3m SE of Ashford
Robert Adam, 1762-5, simple Palladian design. Inside, some good Adam rooms.

Messing Park, Essex
5m NE of Witham
House of c1710, greatly enlarged c1815 with curved bays, and porch topped by tripartite window.

Methven, Tayside
6m W of Perth
Mausoleum, 1793 by James Playfair, takes form of temple emerging from base of rough masonry, showing influence of Ledoux.

The front elevation of Mavisbank, Lothian. Dated 1723 and designed by William Adam, it is the first Palladio-inspired villa built in Scotland.

Micheldever, Hampshire
6m NW of New Alresford
St Mary's Church, octagonal brick nave added to medieval church by George Dance, 1808-10.

Midford Castle, Avon
2m S of Bath
Part folly, part castle; ashlar with ace-of-spades plan. Possibly by John Carter, *c*1775.

Milborne Port, Somerset
3m NE of Sherborne
Town/Market Hall of Abingdon type, pre-1750; with (originally) arcaded ground floor, giant Tuscan pilasters.

Mildenhall, Wiltshire
1m E of Marlborough
Former **school** of 1823-4, designed by Robert Abraham. Cruciform plan, octagonal centre carrying square lantern; Gothic detailing.

Milford, Derbyshire
1m S of Belper
Rare example of late-C18 **industrial housing** on Hopping Hill, *c*1793-4. 2-storey, stone-built terrace with full-width garrets.

Milgate House, Kent
2m E of Maidstone
Early C18, with front that is simple version of that at nearby Bradbourne (qv).

Milton Abbas, Dorset
6m SW of Blandford
Milton Abbey. Most of remains of medieval monastic buildings to abbey, apart from Abbot's Hall, demolished *c*1769 and rebuilt in mock-medieval manner by Sir William Chambers, 1771-6. He had revivalist associative Gothic style forced on him by client, with whom he quarrelled bitterly, leading to takeover by Lancelot Brown after Chambers had built south front and kitchen wing, and established layout of west wing. Brown mostly responsible for interiors, followed *c*1776 by James Wyatt. Abbey is externally plain, classically proportioned house with light Gothic trimming and perfunctory battlements.

Model village beyond gates of house, designed initially by Chambers, 1773; modified and carried out *c*1786 by Brown. One of earliest model villages to provide dwellings for several classes. Thatched, with a few Gothic details.

Milton House, Northamptonshire
3m S of Northampton
Henry Flitcroft rebuilt main front and remodelled interior 1750-55. Dining room, tea room, library and gallery by Sir William Chambers, 1770-77, showing, especially in gallery, his rarely exposed baroque taste, including angle pilasters he himself condemned in his treatise of 1759.

Milton House, Oxfordshire
3m S of Abingdon
Early C18 house with wings and rococo Gothic chapel and library, 1764-72 by Stephen Wright.

Mistley, Essex
8m NE of Colchester
St Mary's Church: only two towers survive, in slightly remodelled state, of Robert Adam's building of 1776. Body demolished *c*1870. Plan bore resemblance to church plan published by Roger Morris in his *Rural Architecture*, 1750.

In centre of town, remains of **spa development** begun *c*1768. Central square dominated by **Malting Office,** 9 bays with 3-bay pediment.

Moccas Court, Hereford and Worcester
9m W of Hereford
By Anthony Keck, 1775-81. Very urban in design. Porch added 1792. Inside, central flying staircase under dome, Adam-style decoration.

Mogerhanger Park, Bedfordshire
2m W of Sandy
1809-11 by Sir John Soane, now **Park Hospital** and much altered internally. 3-storey entrance front, flanked closely by 2-storey wings that come forward and are linked by screen wall to which is attached semicircular hexastyle porch with partly fluted Doric columns.

Monmouth, Gwent
Town Hall, 1724, based on C17 Abingdon type; 6 by 3 bays, long side dressed with giant pilasters and with pediment in centre. Ground floor treated as open arcade.

County Gaol, 1788-90 by William Blackburn.

Beaufort Arms Hotel, Agincourt Square, main façade *c*1800 with Greek-detailed pilasters. Also in square, **King's Head Hotel,** *c*1760, with Doric porch extending over pavement. Adjacent, **Monmouth House** (now part of hotel), with 4-bay arcaded ground floor.

Overmonnow House, Drybridge Street, *c*1765, with pedimented door, arched 1st-floor window.

18 Monnow Street, *c*1780, blank arcades to ground floor, architraves to all windows, 1st-floor windows also with pediments; good fanlight. **56-8 (Cornwall House),** *c*1800, 3-storey, 5-bay centre block flanked by 1-bay, 1-storey wings. **42-4,** dated 1724. **102,** *c*1820, 3 storeys, 3 bays; all windows tripartite, door an essay on Venetian composition.

Castlehill House, Castlehill, *c*1715-20; coved-hooded doorcase on carved brackets.

In Monk Street, **Chapel House,** 3 centre 1st-floor windows narrow and grouped, a characteristic compositional device of 1700-14; door *c*1790. **8-10,** *c*1820; Ionic screen embracing 3 central 1st-floor windows; ground-floor windows set in blank arcade. **12,** with Greek Doric pedimented doorcase. **14,** *c*1820, trellis porch. **16-18** with shared pedimented Doric porch. **20,** *c*1820, trellis porch; giant arch embracing both door and 1st-floor centre window; neo-classical plaque takes place of 2nd-floor centre window.

St James's House, St James's Street, *c*1745, centre bay emphasized with Doric porch, round-headed 1st-floor window, architrave surround to centre 2nd-floor window. Also in this street, **The Grange,** mid-C18. Nearby, perhaps best **house** in the street: 3 storeys, 7 bays with 2 end bays breaking forward; Corinthian-columned porch with entablature embracing side windows, and detailing of *c*1780; round-headed 1st-floor centre window; dentil cornice. **No. 7,** *c*1740, hooded door. **18,** *c*1780, centre bay emphasized by pedimented door and 1st-floor window, architrave to 2nd-floor window which is flanked by bipartite windows. **25,** 2 storeys with 3-storey, 2-bay extension of *c*1830-40 with curious details: Doric porch, terms supporting cornice to ground-floor windows, foliage-embellished labels under 1st-floor cills.

Off St James's Street, **The Hollies,** *c*1750, brick.

In **St Mary's Street,** 2- and 3-storey terrace houses of *c*1740–1820, most with simple pedimented and hooded doors, for example **28, 37, 39;** while **25,** *c*1810, has tiny canted ground-floor bay.

1–9 (odd) **Glendower Street,** 3-storey terrace, *c*1725–35; segmental arches to ground- and 1st-floor windows, 2nd-floor windows square; hooded doors. **4** has delicate pedimented door of *c*1796.

In **Priory Street,** neo-classical street composition of some sophistication, reflecting metropolitan splendour of Nash's Regent Street. Designer – perhaps George V. Maddox, who arcaded site to create Priory Street *c*1830 – has put stucco uniform elevation accented with pilasters and pediments on awkward convex street frontage. Adjoining this ambitious project, earlier, more modest attempt of *c*1810–20 to wrap a terrace around a convex curve: **7–11** form asymmetrical group incorporating 3-bay pedimented feature. **7** has delicately detailed pedimented door. **8** has remains of contemporary shop.

Montgomery, Powys
   Town Hall, 1748 by William Baker. Brick, 2 storeys, originally open ground-floor arcade; altered 1828.
   Former **Gaol,** Gaol Road, *c*1830; only walls of cell block and octagonal centre survive.
   China House, Bishop's Castle Street, *c*1725–30. Adjacent, **Penygrislau,** tight segmental-arched windows, pedimented door, *c*1730. Also in this street, **1–4,** late-C18, 3-storey brick terrace.
   7–9 Broad Street, with simple Regency door. **3,** with Regency bow shop-front. Opposite, Regency flat shop-front flanked by doors with complex geometric fanlights.
   In **Kerry Street, house** has pedimented Gibbs door surround.
   Rock House, The Square, early C18, segmental windows, slender porch of *c*1820.
   Colomendy, Arthur Street, *c*1760; good pedimented doorcase of *c*1810. Also in this street, former **Wynnstay Arms Inn,** *c*1790, with mullioned and transomed windows in rear and side elevations.

Montrose, Tayside
   Church, 1791. Immense, simple exterior; inside, 2 tiers of galleries to seat 3,000. Tower of 1832.

Moor Park, Hertfordshire
4m SE *of Rickmansworth*
Earlier house remodelled 1725–7 by Sir James Thornhill to create one of most impressive C18 baroque buildings in England. Entrance front embellished with giant Corinthian portico which rises from ground level; inside, double-height galleried entrance hall with false-perspective painted dome and wall paintings.
   Tea Pavilion (17 Moor Lane) and **Gateway,** 1763–5 by Robert Adam.

Moor Park, Powys
2m NE *of Crickhowell/Crucywel*
Villa of *c*1770, with extraordinary plan composed of 4 semicircular towers attached to octagonal core. 4 main rooms lie on diagonal of main axis, so each room has a bowed end. Spiral stairs rise in central hall.

Moreby Hall, North Yorkshire
6m S *of York*
Impressive neo-Tudor mansion by Anthony Salvin, 1828–33.

Moreton, Dorset
7m W *of Wareham*
St Nicholas's Church, by James Frampton 1776. Gothic, with pretty plaster ceiling and cusped window tracery. Aisles added 1841, west porch 1848.
   Moreton House, 1744; extended 1774–81, when 7-sided centre bay was added to entrance front.

Moreton-in-Marsh, Gloucestershire
7m NW *of Chipping Norton*
White Hart Hotel, High Street, dated 1782. Also in High Street, **The Steps,** *c*1750; ashlar, with Venetian windows in ground floor.
   Lloyds Bank, late C18.
   Greystones, Oxford Street, late C18.

Morpeth, Northumberland
   Town Hall, designed 1714 by Sir John Vanbrugh; striking composition with centre 3 bays pedimented, end bays supporting pedimented towers. Rebuilt *c*1875.

Morton Hall House, Lothian
SE *edge of Edinburgh*
Built 1769, probably to design of John Baxter the Younger, provincial Palladian with 3 centre bays breaking forward beneath crowning pediment. Inside, fine staircase hall and characteristically Scottish arrangement of top-floor library.

Mountsorrel, Leicestershire
4m SE *of Loughborough*
Market Cross, 1793 by William Thomas.
   Rectory, 1782, very handsome. 5 bays with central tripartite windows, 3-bay pediment, urn in tympanum.

Nantwich, Cheshire
   Unitarian Chapel, Pillory Street, 1726.
   Barony Hospital, Middlewich Road, incorporates **workhouse** of 1780.
   Crewe Almshouses, Beam Street, 1767.
   At rear of **Crown Hotel,** C18 **assembly room.**
   Liberal Club, Mill Street, 1736.
   The Rookery, C18 house with wings.
   20 High Street, late C18; Venetian window, lunette above.
   52 Welsh Road, *c*1720, with pedimented door.

Narford Hall, Norfolk
4m NW *of Swaffham*
*c*1700 with a room of *c*1750 painted with cavorting monkeys by J. F. Clermont.

New Alresford, Hampshire
   6 East Street, stucco terrace house, façade *c*1780, with chinoiserie doorcase in which pediment has concave raked mouldings. Also in East Street, **National Westminster Bank,** 5 bays, 2 storeys with open 1-bay pediment; very similar in design to local Cheriton House (qv), *c*1740.

Newark-on-Trent, Nottinghamshire
   Town Hall, Market Place, 1773–6 by John Carr. Ashlar, Palladian, 7 bays, rusticated ground floor with arched windows. Centre has 3-bay loggia, and another above it with Tuscan columns

and a pediment. Inside is a market on ground floor and apsed assembly room above.

Saracen's Head, Market Place, inn of 1721. Also in Market Place, **Clinton Arms,** early C18.

Appleton Gate has early-C18 brick **houses** with variety of doorcases. One has centre bay emphasized by 1-bay pediment.

Wilson Street, begun 1766, contains 16 identical houses with minimal external features.

Good C18 brick **houses** in **Castle Gate, Lombard Street** and **Balderton Gate** – especially **Municipal Offices.**

Just outside town to north, John Smeaton's **viaduct** of 1770, carrying Great North Road.

Newbury, Berkshire

Former **theatre** of 1802, off Oxford Street.

5 Wharf Road, early C18, parapet with central blank lunette; later doorcase.

Lower Raymonds Buildings, Newtown Road, classical almshouses, 1796; pediment in centre. Opposite are **Upper Raymonds Buildings,** 1826, Gothic.

In West Mills, **Hunt Almshouses,** 1817, plain.

St Nicholas's House, West Mills, early C18.

28 Bartholomew Street, early C18.

24 Northbrook Street, dated 1724. Composite pilasters on upper floors, Venetian window; ramped parapet. **26,** c1750, with pilasters framing 2 middle bays. **91-2,** c1725, with giant pilasters.

Dower House, London Road (formerly **King's Arms Inn**), 1750 by James Clarke in Vanbrughian manner.

2 Bath Road, 5 bays, angle pilasters, 3-bay pediment; dated 1720.

On north-west edge of town, **Speen Court,** original part c1750. Angle pilasters.

Newby Hall, North Yorkshire

3m SE of Ripon

House of 1705, 2-storey wings and interiors by Robert Adam, who worked here c1767-72. One wing is procession of 3 apartments, middle of which is a rotunda with sculpture gallery each side, c1767-70. Interiors among finest neo-classical examples of period in Europe: especially fine are hall, tapestry room, library and gallery.

Newcastle upon Tyne, Tyne and Wear

All Saints' Church, 1786-96 by David Stephenson; elliptical, neo-classically detailed. Tower, with steeple and somewhat out of sympathy with austerity of rest of church, an afterthought forced on architect by congregation.

St Thomas's Church, Barras Bridge, by John Dobson 1828-9; Early English interior.

St Ann's Chapel, City Road, William Newton 1764-8; austere, neo-classical composition.

Library, 1736, probably by Daniel Garrett, attached to south side of medieval St Nicholas's Cathedral; fine Palladian composition.

Assembly Rooms, Westgate, 1774 by William Newton; ashlar with pedimented front.

Moot Hall, Castle Garth, 1810 by John Stokoe; important early Greek revival building with Doric portico.

Literary and Philosophical Institute, Westgate Road, 1822 by John Green; Grecian. Also in this road, **53-7,** 2 provincial baroque houses of c1730: 53 of 4 storeys, windows linked with stone aprons; 55-7 of 7 bays, 2 storeys with end bays framed by 2-storey Doric pilasters.

In Broad Chare, **Trinity House:** neo-Tudor façade of 1841 conceals hall of 1721, school of 1733, and 2 ranges of plain almshouses, 1787 and 1791. Chapel with porch of 1800.

Clavering House, Clavering Place, 1784, 7 bays with pair of canted bays framing 1-bay centre containing Venetian window above pedimented door.

In 1825-40 William Grainger and John Dobson rebuilt city centre in noble neo-classical fashion inspired by Nash's work in London. Detailing of buildings became increasingly neo-Grecian.

Eldon Square, 1825, one side of which survives, uniform ashlar terrace with restrained but exquisite detailing.

Leazes Crescent and **Leazes Terrace,** 1824-34 by Thomas Oliver, are similarly restrained.

However, **Grey Street,** the most powerful of their creations, begun in mid-1830s and building until early 1840s, has strong neo-Greek accents.

In **Saville Row, Saville Place** and **Queen's Square,** red brick **houses** with pedimented doorcases, c1790; and, especially good, **Summer Hill Terrace,** c1810-20.

New Lanark, Strathclyde

1m SW of Lanark

Cotton-manufacturing village laid out on model industrial and social lines. Founded c1784 by Richard Arkwright and David Dale, sold as going concern to Dale's son-in-law Richard Owen 1799. Over next 25 years Owen applied increasingly progressive ideas to running of works and of village.

Main surviving **mill** buildings, from south-east (upstream) 1781; 1790; 1826. All stone, austere, 5 storeys, hipped slate roofs. In last, floors supported on cast-iron columns and beams probably cast in village foundry.

Behind mills, **Institute for the Formation of Character,** built 1812, with delicate balcony.

Nearby, on bank south-east of highest mill, **New Institution,** 1816. Slender quatrefoil columns, set internally, act as ducts for hot-air heating.

Main Street, running from Long Row (**workers' cottages**) to **New Buildings** (which housed church on top floor) and on to Caithness Row, contains mix of buildings, but all stone-built and of severe design.

In centre of village, in main street, side by side, **David Dale's** and **Robert Owen's houses.**

Newliston House, Lothian

3m S of Queensferry

Robert Adam, 1789-90; late Palladian. Wings c1845.

Newport, Isle of Wight

St Thomas of Canterbury's Roman Catholic Church, Pyle Street, 1791, with pedimented gable and handsome Doric porch of c1820. Also in this street, **Chapel** (now **Apollo Theatre**), c1825.

Guildhall, corner of High Street and Quay Street, handsome composition by John Nash, built 1814-16. Front formed by Ionic portico over open arcade continuing along side elevation to High Street, which also has 1st-floor Ionic loggia.

Old **Literary Institute** (now **Country Club**), St James's Square, 1811 by Nash, with pedimented, pilastered ashlar façade over open arcade.

At **Parkhurst Prison,** administrative offices, timber-framed, 1799.

Hospital (originally **workhouse**), Crocker Street, c1770. 2 out of 3 long ranges survive.

Bugle Hotel, High Street, handsome 6-bay façade, c1760. Also in High Street, **20,** c1740 with round-headed centre 1st-floor window and canted bay on side; **43** and **122,** c1800 with good bow windows; **97-8,** late-C18 brick house, end bays breaking forward slightly with pediments to ground-floor windows; **146-7,** c1800.

23 St James's Square, c1720-30. **18A St James's Street,** c1730-40, with handsome rusticated stone door surround, moulded stone cornice; **106,** c1815.

17 St Thomas's Square, early C18 with keystone-voussoir lintels, panelled entrance hall, Chinese Chippendale staircase of c1760.

15-17 Lugley Street, irregular C18 pair sharing door with huge round-arched fanlight; **16-18,** pair of c1760 clad with yellow mathematical tiles over brickwork; **29,** c1800; **33,** with 1st-floor bay clad with timber grooved to look like rustication.

15-16 Holyrood Street, early C19.

14, 124-5 Pyle Street, mid-C18 cottages. **30-31,** c1725-40; all windows with later-looking mullions, hooded door. **95** and adjacent **Catholic Presbytery,** early C18; presbytery with Chinese Chippendale staircase of c1760. **137 (Pyle House),** c1800, 5 bays.

12-13 Quay Street, 2-storey, 2-bay pair, c1740, crowned with deep modillion cornice; 13 with late-C18 Gothic door surround. **17,** c1780, with pedimented door. **18-21,** excellent early-C19 group; **38,** c1825, stucco; **39,** c1735. **40,** with keystoned segmental windows, crowning eaves cornice, Regency Greek Doric door with various decorative elements formalized: triglyphs rendered as tubes, guttae as little cylinders.

Seal House, 30 Sea Street, c1725; segmental windows, flush box sashes. In same street, **Dolphin House,** large, early C18.

In **Chapel Street** area, brick **cottages** with segmental windows, flush sashes, looking early C18 but in fact c1820; especially **1-7** (odd), **8-13, 41 Chapel Street, 16-17 Union Street, 3-21** (odd) **Trafalgar Road.**

Newsham House
See Liverpool.

Newton Abbot, Devon
2 Highweek Street, c1790-1800, with curved bays containing tripartite windows.

Newtown, Isle of Wight
5m sw of Cowes
Town Hall, largely C18 but possibly on earlier stone plinth. Free-standing. One short side has steps to 1st-floor entrance door; other has 4-columned wooden porch.

Newtown, Powys
   Lion Inn, off Market Street, c1820.
   In High Street, **shop-front** of c1820.
   Bow **shop-front** of similar date in Broad Street.
   In The Bank, pair of early-C19 2-storey **houses** with cast-iron trellis porches.
   The Crescent, centrepiece of early-C19 industrial/residential suburbs contains 3-storey stucco houses, uniform and plain.
   Crescent Street, mostly c1820, 2- and 3-storey brick and stucco houses, most with simple pedimented door surrounds. **1** has Gothic door. **13-16,** good group with arched entrance to yard; 13 with wooden Gothic porch, 15-16 with trellis porch.
   In Commercial Street, **Lewes House,** with excellently detailed wooden Gothic porch. **5, 6, 7,** c1820, form 4-storey, 6-bay building designed to house '24 looms and rooms for 6 families'.
   1-5 Union Street, pair of 3-storey cottages with large top-floor windows to light looms.
   5 Bryn Street, mill and house composed as one building, but with different fenestration.
   In **Severn Square,** various red brick **houses** of c1790-1820.

5 Bryn Street, Newtown, Powys: a mill and house of c1825, composed as one building and distinguished by different fenestration.

Nonsuch Park, Surrey
1m NE of Ewell
1802-6 by Sir Jeffry Wyatville. Neo-Tudor; early example of asymmetry.

Normanby Park, Humberside
3m N of Scunthorpe
House of 1825-30 by Sir Robert Smirke; excellent example of his personal Greek revival manner, where forms are cubical and decoration sparse.

Normanton, Leicestershire
5m E of Oakham
St Matthew's Church has tower by Thomas Cundy, 1826-9, inspired by Archer's St John's, Smith Square, London. Nave of 1911.

Norris Castle, Isle of Wight
In East Cowes
James Wyatt, 1799. Romantic 'Norman' castle. Large, round east tower with long range of castellated buildings attached to form asymmetrical group.
   Extensive neo-Norman **farm.**

Northallerton, North Yorkshire
   Court House and **House of Correction** (now **H.M. Prison**), Zetland Street, John Carr 1784-8.

Northampton, Northamptonshire
   Gaol, off George Row, 1791-4 by Robert Brettingham, enlarged 1846, mostly demolished 1930. One range (now **County Library**) survives in Angel Street.

General Infirmary, Billing Road, Samuel Saxon 1791-3. Wings of 1887, 1891.

32 Market Square, mid-C18, with Gothic window. Also in Market Square, **Drury Chambers,** early C18.

57 Sheep Street, c1765; 5 bays with pair of Doric doorcases, tripartite bow and, above, Venetian window.

54-64 Derngate, with matching doorcases.

7 Bridge Street, late C18 with 2 storeys of bow windows. Also in this street, former **Bluecoat School** and **Orange School,** dated 1811.

Northleach, Gloucestershire
10m NE of Cirencester
House of Correction (now **Museum**), 1787-91 by William Blackburn. Ashlar, with sombre centre block in suitably forbidding style.

North Shields, Tyne and Wear
St Cuthbert's Roman Catholic Church, Albion Road, 1821 by Robert Giles; Gothic.

New Quay and **Market Place,** begun c1770, building of 1806-17 by David Stephenson, including **Northumberland Arms Inn.**

Northwick Park, Avon
9m N of Bristol
West front 1686, east front remodelled by Lord Burlington 1732. Inside, hall with ceiling based on Jones's design at Queen's House, Greenwich.

Norton-by-Galby
See Galby.

Norton Place, Lincolnshire
8m W of Market Rasen
1776 by John Carr, and one of his best small designs. Pedimented front, entrance emphasized with Doric porch and Ionic Venetian window above. Side elevations have deep canted bays. Inside, oval top-lit stair with galleried landing.

Norwich, Norfolk
Methodist Church, Calvert Street, 1810; doorway with Tuscan columns *in antis.*

Friends' Meeting House, Upper Goat Lane (off Pottergate), 1826 by John Thomas Patience. Centre of front elevation with 2-storey Doric portico, rear with 5 giant pilasters.

Octagon Chapel, Colegate, 1754 by local architect Thomas Ivory.

Assembly Rooms, Theatre Street, 1754 by Ivory; 5 bays, 2 storeys with central 1-bay pediment over segmental doorcase.

Shire Hall, Castle Meadow, 1822-3 by William Wilkins the Younger; neo-Tudor. Refaced 1913.

County Gaol, beside castle keep (now **Norwich Museum**) 1824-8 by Wilkins; castellated.

Blackfriars Bridge, St George Street, Sir John Soane 1783; widened.

38-40 Bethel Street, c1750.

In **Colegate,** 2 C18 **houses** forming irregular group: one of c1730 adjoining L-plan house, dated 1743, with giant Ionic pilasters.

15-17 Cow Hill (Holkham House), by Matthew and Robert Brettingham, c1750; unusual design with centre framed by half pediments and lower wings.

79 King Street, with Venetian window.

44 Magdalen Street, c1740; front embellished with giant pilasters, attic storey above cornice, Venetian window above enriched doorcase.

64, 65 Pottergate, early C18.

In **St Giles Street,** long runs of C18 houses: **28** with tripartite door topped by Venetian window, then Diocletian window; **31-3** with shared columned doorcase; **48** dated 1792; **50-52** dated 1727 on hopper head; **68 (Churchman's House),** c1750, with pedimented façade, pedimented doorcase, 1st-floor window embellished with scroll, extremely richly decorated interior with rococo plasterwork.

29-35 Surrey Street, 1761, and **25** and **27,** c1770, all by Ivory. In same street, **Norwich Union Fire Office,** 1764 by Robert Mylne with additions of c1790 by Soane.

In outer Norwich, **St Andrew's Hospital,** Thorpe, by Francis Stone, 1811, with pedimented 7-bay centre and wings; **Brecondale Lodge,** Martineau Lane, c1795 by Wilkins the Younger; villa with dome.

Nostell Priory, West Yorkshire
5m SE of Wakefield
Designed c1735 by amateur Palladian architect Colonel Moyser, erected under supervision of James Paine; plan based on Palladio's Villa Mocenigo. Interior c1766 by Robert Adam, one of his most magnificent works. (National Trust)

Nottingham, Nottinghamshire
Shire Hall, High Pavement, 1770-72, designed by James Gandon and built by Joseph Pickford in extremely refined neo-classical style. Altered and extended 1876, 1880.

Howe House, 19 Castlegate, c1780-90, with immense tripartite central 1st-floor window topped by large fanlight. Below, pedimented tripartite doorway. **No. 31** in same street also has tripartite door topped by tripartite window.

Bromley House, Market Place, 1752, a sophisticated Palladian design with alternating pediments to 1st-floor windows.

18 Low Pavement, remarkable design of c1745-50: 3 storeys, 2 bays, with every opening a Venetian window, those on ground floor with portion of pediment over side lights; pedimented Ionic door pushed to one side. In same street, **24-6,** c1725. **20-22 (Willoughby House),** 1730.

27 St Mary's Gate, 1760; built as theatre.

Nuneham Courtenay, Oxfordshire
4m E of Abingdon
Nuneham Park, ashlar house, centre block 1756-64 by Stiff Leadbetter. Alterations 1781, by Lancelot Brown and perhaps Henry Holland.

All Saints' Church, 1764 by Earl of Harcourt and James Stuart. Important as early example of Greek/Roman temple church, with centralized plan and dome (derived from Chiswick House) and hexastyle Greek Ionic portico.

Model village beyond grounds of house, built during early 1760s, composed of 2 parallel rows of 1-storey cottages constructed in pairs.

Nunnykirk Hall, Northumberland
8m NW of Morpeth
1825 by John Dobson and perhaps the finest of his classical houses. Tripartite garden front; channelled rustication; Ionic colonnade; central hall double-height, galleried and domed.

Oakley Park, Shropshire
3m NW of Ludlow
Remodelled 1819-36 by C.R. Cockerell. Fine

Greek revival house with archaeologically inspired double-height saucer-domed entrance hall, decorated with colonnade and frieze based on Ionic remains at Bassae discovered shortly before.

Ockbrook, Derbyshire
5m E of Derby
Moravian settlement of 1750. Chapel, 1751, and adjoining house; all neat brick.

Odsey House, Cambridgeshire
4m SW of Royston
Built 1722-9 as racing lodge for Duke of Devonshire, perhaps designed by William Kent. Appearance strangely urban for country house.

Old Alresford, Hampshire
1m N of New Alresford
St Mary's Church, body of 1753, tower of 1769 with archaic details.
 Old Alresford House, dated 1752, austere, brick, pedimented, set behind wrought-iron screen.
 Old Alresford Place, early C18, interior alterations of *c*1817.

Old Wolverton, Buckinghamshire
1m NW of Wolverton
Holy Trinity Church, 1810-15 by Henry Hakewill; early essay in Romanesque revival.

Ormsby Hall, Lincolnshire
8m NE of Horncastle
James Paine, 1752-5, in his restless Palladian style. East front of 3 well-spaced bays, end bays with tripartite windows in blank arches, middle canted bay containing Doric entrance porch by John Carr, who also made additions to rear 1803. Entrance hall with garlands and Roman busts.

Osberton Hall, Nottinghamshire
2m NE of Worksop
Greek Doric portico of *c*1805-6 by William Wilkins the Younger; one of the earliest on a British country house. Altered in later C19.

Ossington, Nottinghamshire
7m N of Newark-on-Trent
Holy Rood Church, 1782 by John Carr. Tall, round-headed nave windows in recessed arches linked by impost band. South door with pedimented porch. West tower topped with little dome.

Oswestry, Shropshire
 George Hotel, Bailey Street, *c*1735.
 Queen's Hotel, Leg Street, early C19, stucco.
 Wynnstay Hotel, Church Street, *c*1775; brick, 6 bays, 3 storeys, Tuscan porch over pavement. Also in Church Street, **Bellan School House,** excellent and unusual 7-bay, 3-storey house of *c*1770-80; centre bay with pedimented tripartite door flanked by canted bays of only 2 storeys; 3rd storey set back, topped by 3-bay terminal pediments. **35 Church Street** (former **Grammar School**), *c*1780.
 16-22 Upper Brook Street, sophisticated composition of *c*1790-1800, with tripartite windows beneath arches containing bat's-wing panels, shared pedimented doors, centrally placed arch to rear yard. **26-8,** tall 3-storey early-C18 brick pair.
 6 Lower Brook Street, *c*1740-45; cantilevered doorhood on brackets, full Doric eaves cornice. **12,** dated 1741. Also in this street, good **house** of *c*1800, 3 bays with centre breaking forward, round 2nd-floor centre window.

 2 Albion Hill, dated 1746; segmental windows, keystones, cornice.
 In **Welsh Wall,** 2-storey Gothic cottage, *c*1820.

Otterden Place, Kent
6m SW of Faversham
Neo-Tudor alteration and extension to Elizabethan house, 1802 by William Pilkington.

Over Whitacre, Warwickshire
7m W of Nuneaton
St Leonard's Church, 1766, good provincial baroque. Spire of 1850.

Oxford, Oxfordshire
 St Clement's Church, Marston Road, 1827 by Daniel Robertson in thin 'Norman' style; altered internally by E.G. Bruton, 1874.
 Christ Church: Peckwater Quadrangle. Important as 1st Palladian palace-fronted composition of C18. Designed 1706 by Henry Aldrich, built 1706-13. Each of 3 sides embellished with giant order of pilasters and columns beneath central pediment. 4th side of square formed by **Peckwater Library,** sketched by Aldrich before his death in 1710; design revised and built 1717-38 by colleague George Clarke. Based on Michelangelo's side palaces on Capitol, Rome. Finally completed *c*1772.
 All Souls College: North Quad extended in picturesquely composed associational Gothic style by Hawksmoor, 1716-35. **New Buildings** are of decorative Gothic form externally to complement existing medieval buildings, but classical inside. Most striking feature is a pair of towers forming entrance.
 Queen's College: Hall and **Chapel** front begun 1714 to design by George Clarke, produced under influence of Hawksmoor with help of mason William Townesend, and displaying layered façade and other features found on slightly earlier Clarendon Building. Street screen of 1733-6 by Hawksmoor.
 University College: Radcliffe Quadrangle, 1716-19 by Clarke.
 Magdalen College: New Building of 1733 also by Clarke.
 Worcester College: Library and **entrance block** 1720 and again by Clarke, using and simplifying Hawksmoor design to produce austere stone building with pediment to street front flanked by 2 short wings. In these, **Hall** and **Chapel** remodelled by James Wyatt, 1784 and *c*1790 respectively. Quadrangle front of this block also pedimented with open arcaded ground floor. **North range** of quadrangle, begun 1753 to Clarke's designs, completed in simple neo-classical manner by Henry Keene *c*1775. **Provost's Lodgings,** 1773-6, also by Keene.
 Balliol College also has alterations by Wyatt, 1792-4 to former **Hall** and **Library,** Gothic. Classical west side to **Garden Quad** by George Basevi, 1826.
 Oriel College, west side of **St Mary's Quad** by Daniel Robertson *c*1825, Gothic.
 St Hilda's College, Cowley Place, incorporates interesting Adamesque terrace house of *c*1780.
 Radcliffe Library (Camera), by James Gibbs, built 1737-49; classical composition of a very personal kind: round in plan, mixing baroque elements with conventional Palladian motifs.

The Radcliffe Observatory, Woodstock Road, Oxford; begun 1772 by Henry Keene and completed 1794 to designs by James Wyatt, it is one of the most extraordinary neo-classical designs in the country.

Radcliffe Infirmary, Woodstock Road, 1766-70 by Stiff Leadbetter and completed by John Sanderson.

Radcliffe Observatory, Woodstock Road, was begun 1772 to a design by Henry Keene, but owing to public criticism of his design he was obliged in 1773 to work to scheme prepared by James Wyatt. Completed 1794, it forms one of most extraordinary neo-classical compositions in the country. On a 2-storey range of elegant apartments sits an octagonal tower derived from Tower of the Winds in Athens. Like original, it bears panels depicting the 8 winds, one on each facet, here made of Coade stone. Below, on the 12-faced 1st floor, are Coade stone panels showing signs of the Zodiac.

Clarendon Building designed by Nicholas Hawksmoor for Oxford University Press, and constructed 1711-15. Ashlar, with giant Doric portico to street, layered wall surface. Press also occupies later **Clarendon Press,** Walton Street, 1826-7 by Daniel Robertson, including handsome Graeco-Roman triumphal arch to street. North wings completed by Edward Blore, 1829-30.

The Markets, 1773-4 by John Gwynn, reconstructed by Thomas Wyatt 1839.

Osney Bridge, Botley Road, 1767 by Robert Taylor; **Magdalen Bridge,** 1772-90 by John Gwynn.

20 St Michael's Street, known as **Vanbrugh House,** is a full-blooded baroque composition of c1720, with centre bay flanked by pair of giant Doric pilasters supporting deeply-projecting cornice. In same street, **24,** also c1720 and baroque with front topped by 2 curved gables.

1 Holywell Street, c1780, a handsome neo-classical composition; **61-2** a good baroque pair. Set back is pedimented **Music Room** of 1742.

8 New College Lane, plain brick house of c1725.

In St Giles', **Judge's Lodging,** good early-C18 Palladian composition with central pediment; **41,** baroque house with 4 gables, central porch.

On south side of High Street, group (**116 etc**) of 3-storey flat-fronted timber-and-plaster façades, c1790-1820.

Beaumont Street, 1824-8. Roughly uniform 3-storey, 3-bay houses, ashlar with restrained decoration.

Of same date, **St John Street.**

At south-west end of Walton Street, some modest but prettily detailed red brick **terrace houses** of c1820; and more ambitious group at southern end of Banbury Road.

Packington Hall
See Great Packington.

Painshill Park, Surrey
2m s of Weybridge
House of c1778, perhaps by Richard Jupp. Plain exterior; inside, oval drawing room and oval staircase.

More important is picturesque **park,** begun 1740. Buildings include **Gothic Abbey; Gothic Temple** or **Tent** with pendant tracery in ogee opening, c1742-5; **Folly Tower,** c1770.

Painswick, Gloucestershire
3m N of Stroud
Just outside town, **Painswick House:** central block c1725 in provincial Palladian with strong touch of baroque, perhaps by John Strahan; wings by George Basevi, c1827-32, one containing double-height dining room with coffered ceiling and cast of Parthenon frieze.

In town, several good houses in strongly provincial Palladian manner. In New Street, **Beacon House** of 5 bays, with 3-bay centre breaking forward, pediments to 1st-floor windows, ground floor rusticated; very rich rococo interior, ceiling dated 1769. **The Old Vicarage,** end of St Mary Street, ashlar, Gibbs surrounds to windows, segmental door, c1725-35.

Papplewick Hall, Nottinghamshire
2m NE of Hucknall
3-storey stone house of c1775 with pedimented entrance front. Blind side elevations, as in urban house. Good Adam-style interior.

Papworth Hall, Cambridgeshire
10m W of Cambridge
Now **Papworth Hospital;** Greek revival stucco mansion of 1809 by George Byfield. Hexastyle Ionic portico on west front; semicircular Greek Doric portico on south; giant Ionic columns *in antis* on east front. Inside, colonnaded hall.

Parbold Hall, Lancashire
6m NW of Wigan
1730, 7 bays wide with broad ashlar centre in which doorway and upper windows are Venetian. Inside, hall decorated with wooden blocks mimicking rusticated stone.

Parkend, Gloucestershire
7m SE of Monmouth
St Paul's Church, Gothic octagon with 4 projecting arms; 1822 by Henry Poole.
Gothic **rectory** of same date.

Parwich Hall, Derbyshire
5m N of Ashbourne
1747, well-wrought brick façade.

Patshull, Staffordshire
7m w of Wolverhampton
St Mary's Church, 1742 by James Gibbs. Cellular nave with chancel, west tower with cupola. Inside, coved ceiling. Partly reconstructed 1874.
Patshull Hall, rebuilt by Gibbs 1750-54; completed by William Baker; altered by William Burn, 1855.

Paxton House, Borders
4m w of Berwick upon Tweed
Palladian house of c1760, with wings of 1812 by Robert Reid containing picture gallery and superb bow-ended library with fitted bookcases.

Pell Wall House, Shropshire
½m s of Market Drayton
1822-8, a characteristic design by Sir John Soane. 2-storey, 3-bay entrance front has full-height pilaster strips with incised decoration; square ground-floor windows in round arches, also with incised Greek decoration. Porch altered; so is interior, but vaulted drawing room survives.
In grounds, curious triangular **lodge.**

Penicuik, Lothian
1m sw of town, **Penicuik House,** 1761-9 by rather belated neo-Palladian Sir John Clerk (son of Burlington's friend Sir James Clerk) with John Baxter the Elder. Essay on Wanstead. Towers added to ends by David Bryce, 1857. Now a ruin.
Also by Clerk, nearby quadrangular **stables,** 1766, with 2 entrances, one marked by Gibbsian steeple, other with reproduction of domed Roman building discovered in Stirlingshire (Central Region) but demolished 1743.
In town, **St Mungo's Church,** 1771, again by Clerk; west front with Roman Doric portico.

Penrith, Cumbria
St Andrew's Church, 1720-22. Handsome nave elevation embellished with broad pilaster strips. Inside, 3 galleries on Tuscan columns, with elongated columns above.
George Hotel, Market Place, in part c1725.
Crown Hotel, King Street, has façade of 1794. In same street, **Mansion House,** imposing house of 1750; 5 bays, with lower wings with Venetian windows.
Hutton Hall, Friargate, c1750-60.
In **Angel Lane,** house dated 1763 has shared pedimented doorcase, ogee-headed windows and double Venetian window.

Pennsylvania Castle, Dorset
On Isle of Portland, 3m s of Weymouth
Asymmetrical Gothic castellated house, 1800 by James Wyatt.

Penrhyn Castle, Gwynedd
2m E of Bangor
Most powerful of neo-Norman castles, built 1825-44 to design of Thomas Hopper. Keep inspired by Rochester Castle; inside, great hall, exotic library and staircase.

Penzance, Cornwall
Remains of **theatre,** 1787, in Chapel Street.
Egyptian House, 6 Chapel Street, c1830. Remarkable monument to early-C19 Egyptian vogue. Richly painted and decorated.
Good groups of early-C19 **houses** in **Clarence Place, Clarence Street** and **Regent Square.**

Peper Harow, Surrey
2m w of Godalming
Villa, 1765-8 by Sir William Chambers, now much altered. Interior good and typical of Chambers' academic style, especially hall; central stair. Additions and alterations by John Yenn 1791, C.R. Cockerell 1843, and in 1913.
Also by Chambers, **offices** and **stables** where, curiously, Bargate stone is cut and laid to look like brick.

Pershore, Hereford and Worcester
6m w of Evesham
1-5 Broad Street, c1770, has centre block with central Venetian door flanked by Venetian windows on ground and 1st floor; 1-bay, 2-storey wings also with Venetian windows. In same street, **12** has bow shop-front c1800.
Perrott House, Bridge Street, 3 storeys, 3 bays and every one, including door, split into 3. Side bays have Venetian windows in bows on ground floor, canted tripartite bays on 1st floor, flat tripartite windows on 2nd. Adam-style interiors. All must date from c1770-75. Also in Bridge Street, **7,** c1815, with iron upper veranda.
In High Street, **Midland Bank,** c1725-30.

Perth, Tayside
St Paul's Church, 1800-7 by John Paterson. Gothic.
County Buildings, Tay Street, by Sir Robert Smirke, 1815. Greek revival with Doric portico.
Marshall Monument, George Street, 1822 by David Morison, Pantheon dome with Ionic portico. Designed as public library; remodelled 1854 as art gallery.
Murray Royal Asylum for the Insane, Kinnoull, by William Burn, 1827. Roman Doric portico, central octagon.
Gaol, Edinburgh Road, 1810-14 by Robert Reid, with 4 radial blocks; altered 1842.
Old Academy, Rose Terrace, 1803-7, by Reid in Adamesque manner with 1st-floor tripartite window under segmental head with fan glazing, framed by engaged coupled Doric columns. Inside, domed octagonal schoolroom on 1st floor.
Salutation Hotel, South Street, c1800; imposing tripartite window under giant lunette with fan glazing.
Several late-C18 streets of interest; **St John Street,** laid out 1796-1801; **Atholl Crescent** and **Atholl Place,** 1797-1805; and in **Marshall Place** 2 terraces laid out by Reid. Individual houses of interest include **Blackfriars House,** Atholl Place, c1790; and **Boatland House,** Isla Road, villa of c1820 with semicircular bow and oval stair.

Peterborough, Cambridgeshire
Bull Hotel, Westgate, c1730. Also in Westgate, **Royal Hotel,** mid-C18.
Angel Hotel, Bridge Street, mid-C18.
In **Priestgate,** good group of C18 houses.

Peterhead, Grampian
Town House, with steeple derived from Gibbs designs, by John Baxter the Younger, 1788.

Petersfield, Hampshire
Lloyds Bank, in The Square. Good provincial Palladian composition of c1750-60.
9 Dragon Street, good long shop-front of c1800.

236 / Georgian Buildings

Peterstone Court, Powys
3m SE of Brecon
1741, of a simple but sophisticated design rare in mid-Wales in the mid-C18. Front of 2 storeys (3rd added in C19), 5 bays, middle 3 of which break forward. Door with Gibbs surround.

Petworth, West Sussex
8m SE of Haslemere
Petworth House dates largely from c1690 but contains some important C18 interiors built after fire of 1714, including Grand Staircase. Square Dining Room 1794-5, but decorated in style of c1690 - even to creation of Grinling Gibbons-style carvings, by Jonathan Ritson. In same manner and of same date, Carved Room. (National Trust)
 Town Hall, 1793, built for Lord Egremont by his estate surveyor. Dour stone façade with 3-bay pediment, blind arcading on 1st floor.
 Daintrey House, East Street, c1745. 7 bays, 3 storeys with 3-bay pediment.
 Newlands, Pound Street, c1790.
 Avenings, Golden Square, c1770; pedimented centre and Doric porch.
 Stone House, High Street, c1770; 3 bays, 2 storeys with Ionic doorcase and fanlight.
 North House, North Street, plain late-C18.

Philipps House, Wiltshire
9m W of Salisbury
Neo-classical mansion of 1812-17 by Sir Jeffry Wyatville, with hexastyle Ionic portico. Inside, domed imperial staircase with brass balustrade.

Pickhill Hall, Clwyd
2m SE of Wrexham
Designed by Richard Trubshaw c1725 in spirited baroque manner rare in Wales. 3-storey, 7-bay brick façade, centre 3 bays framed by giant Corinthian pilasters which rise from ground. Corners of main elevation emphasized by rusticated pilaster strips. 1st- and 2nd-floor windows immediately above Ionic porch embellished with architraves and, on 1st floor, also scrolls. Balustraded parapet, rising into 1-bay pediment over centre. Side elevations perfectly plain. Interior reconstructed.

Piercefield Park, Gwent
2m N of Chepstow
By Sir John Soane, completed 1793; externally similar to Soane's Shotesham Park (qv). Now a ruin.

Plas Newydd, Anglesey (Gwynedd)
3m SW of Menai Bridge
By James Wyatt, 1795-7; completed by Joseph Potter. Gothic. (National Trust)

Plymouth, Devon
 St Aubyn's Church, St Aubyn's Street, Devonport, 1770-71, probably by Charles Rawlinson. Heavy, pedimented west front from which rises octagonal spire; interior with galleries and giant columns.
 Town Hall, Ker Street, Devonport, 1821-3 by John Foulston in Greek Doric manner.
 Custom House, Plymouth, 1810 by David Laing; austere neo-classical design.
 Library (now **Oddfellows' Hall**), Ker Street, by Foulston c1821; neo-Egyptian.
 Royal William Victualling Yard, Stonehouse, by Sir John Rennie 1826-32. Large-scale complex whose design evokes early-C18 Office of Works style of Vanbrugh.
 Royal Naval Hospital, 1756-69 by A. Rouchead; much enlarged.
 Gun Wharf, 1718-25 by Office of Works under Vanbrugh.
 Government House, 1795; 9 bays, corner pavilions with Venetian windows.
 In Plymouth: **12 Barbican,** mid-C18, 4 storeys with quoins; **Wyndham Square,** c1815; **Portland Square,** early C19; modest late-C18 and early-C19 terraces in **Durnford Street.**
 In Stoke Demerel, villas, notably **Albemarle Villas,** St Michael's Terrace, 1825-36 by Foulston.

Pollok House, Strathclyde
W edge of Rutherglen
Designed in provincial Palladian manner by William Adam, erected by John and Robert Adam 1752; wings later.

Ponsonby Hall, Cumbria
4m SE of Egremont
1780, based on James Paine's St Ives, Bingley, West Yorkshire, of c1759 (demolished 1859).

Pontcysyllte Aqueduct, Clwyd
4m E of Llangollen
By Thomas Telford, 1794-1805; magnificent piece of canal engineering. 19 cast-iron arches on stone piers carry Llangollen Canal in cast-iron trough over River Dee.

Pontefract, West Yorkshire
 Red Lion Hotel, Market Place, remodelled by Robert Adam 1776 for Sir Rowland Wynn.

Pontypridd, Mid-Glamorgan
Remarkable rubble-built **bridge** over River Taff, 1755-6 by William Edwards. Span of 140ft, the longest achieved in Britain at the time; 3 cylindrical holes in each of the haunches to reduce the load.

Poole, Dorset
 St James's Church, 1819-21 by Joseph Hannaford and John Kent; Gothic.
 Congregational Church, Stanner Street, 1777.
 Guildhall, Market Street, built 1761; very handsome composition. End pedimented; arcaded ground floor. 1st-floor council chamber reached by pair of external semicircular stairs.
 Custom House, c1790, similar in form to Guildhall. Reconstructed after fire, 1813.
 Beside this, **Harbour Office,** 1822, with open ground floor on Tuscan columns.
 Mansion House, Thames Street, c1790. Tall blank arcading frames both semi-basement and round-headed ground-floor windows. Projecting centre bay contains semicircular Doric porch with Venetian window, lunette above, topped by pediment. In dining room, marble chimneypiece with carving of two fillets of salt cod.
 Beside churchyard, **Poole House,** c1730, reconstructed 1965. 3 bays, embellished with chains carved in Portland stone; Gibbs surround to upper central window. Nearby, **rectory,** 1786.
 West End House, West Street, 1716; central windows emphasized with scrolls; Ionic doorcase; parapet decorated with urns and pineapples. Also in West Street, **Joliffe's House,** c1730.
 Sir Peter Thompson's House (**Poole College**), Market Street, the finest house in Poole,

built 1746-9 by Bastard brothers under direction of John Bastard. 5 bays, 3 storeys, H-plan with centre bay slightly recessed but extra-wide, stuccoed to imitate ashlar and furnished with tripartite hooded door. On 1st floor, Venetian window; Diocletian above. On rear elevation, matching 1st-floor Venetian aligns internally along 1st-floor gallery. Also in Market Street, **No. 20,** *c*1760.

Beech Hurst, High Street, dated 1798.

Port Eliot, Cornwall
4m w of Saltash
Medieval and C18 house remodelled by Sir John Soane, 1804-6. South and east front 2 storeys, in simple castellated style. Inside, good circular drawing room with fine ceiling and chimneypiece with incised fret-pattern decoration. Gothic porch and entrance hall by Henry Harrison, 1829.

Portland, Dorset
St George's Church, Reforne. Unusual stone cruciform building, 1754-66 by Thomas Gilbert. Wren-like tower.

Portsmouth, Hampshire
Royal Dockyard and other military buildings
St Ann's, Dockyard Church, built 1785-6 to designs probably by John Marquand, and possibly Thomas Telford. Plain brick church with wide rectangular nave. Venetian east window. Delicate plasterwork.

No. 18 Store, formerly ropery, long range – nearly 1,100ft - of 3-storey, plain brick warehousing; built 1770, largely reconstructed 1960. **Passageway** dated 1771 links it to No.19 Store. **Nos. 9, 10** and **11 Stores,** all of 1778. **No. 16 Store,** dated 1771, 3 storeys, 18 bays. **No. 15 Store** is similar. **No. 17 Store,** 1789, 14 bays. **Nos. 24** and **25 Stores,** each rectangular with internal courtyard, 1782-90.

Pay Office (now **Royal Naval Film Corporation**), built 1798 under direction of Sir Samuel Bentham, Inspector General of Naval Works; displays experimental use of cast-iron 'fire-proof' construction.

South Office Block, pedimented, 1786-8.

Staff Officers' Mess, built 1729-32 as **Royal Navy Academy.** Remodelled 1808, badly damaged 1941. 3 storeys, symmetrical wings form shallow open-fronted courtyard. Entrance embellished by pedimented Doric doorcase.

Admiralty House, residence of Commander in Chief, designed 1784-6 by Samuel Wyatt. On each side of main block slightly recessed 1-storey link blocks lead to 1-storey pedimented wings.

Short Row, 1787, terrace of 5 3-storey brick houses. **Long Row,** also a good terrace of larger 3-storey houses, built 1717; now stuccoed.

Of Dock defensive works various parts date from, or were remodelled in, C18, including **King's Bastion.**

Of city's C18 fortifications, best survival is **Landport Gate** of 1760, which has something of air of Vanbrugh's bold, personal classicism.

Of complete C18 fortifications **Cumberland Fort,** Eastney, is far the most impressive survival. Begun 1746 as irregular 5-cornered star; reconstructed 1786, and gradually adapted during late years of C18.

Civilian buildings
St George's Church, St George's Square, Portsea, built 1754, probably designed by Dockyard surveyor. Exterior modest. Plan of some sophistication: cross contained in square, like Wren's St Anne and St Agnes. Inside bomb-damaged, but Tuscan columns still surround central space.

In Old Portsmouth, **60-62 St Thomas's Street,** mid-C18. In same street, **7** and **9** typical of late-C18 Portsmouth style with shallow 1st-floor bow windows. **11** and **13** of same date.

Quebec House, on foreshore near Bath Square, weatherboarded. Built 1754, right at water's edge for enthusiasts of sea bathing.

In Portsea, **88A St George's Square,** excellent, modest house of *c*1790, with shallow 1st-floor bow window, Adamesque pedimented doorcase.

In Southsea, **Hampshire Terrace,** begun 1820, survives in part, as does **King's Terrace,** *c*1810.

Potterspury, Northamptonshire
2m NW of Stony Stratford
Pretty **Congregational Chapel** of 1780.

Wakefield Lodge, 1748-50, a late work by William Kent in curiously rugged, masculine, even Vanbrughian baroque style. Over-large cyclopean details, ground-floor windows in depressed arches with squat Diocletians above, bold block cornice to 1st floor. Inside, however, essay on Inigo Jones's spiral stair in Queen's House, Greenwich.

Powderham Castle, Devon
4m N of Dawlish
Medieval and C17 house remodelled 1710-27 by John Moyle; completed *c*1754 by James Garrett, who designed staircase; altered and enlarged 1794-6 by James Wyatt, who added music room with coffered dome; castellations added by Charles Fowler 1837-48.

Preston, Lancashire
St Peter's Church, St Peter's Square, 1822 in Commissioners' Gothic by Rickman & Hutchinson.

Unitarian Chapel, Church Street, 1717.

Former **Court House,** Stanley Street, 1825 by Thomas Rickman; austere, classical.

Winckley Square, large, on undulating site, with well-planted centre. Houses mostly late-C18, brick, 3 storeys, plain.

Preston on Stour, Warwickshire
3m s of Stratford-upon-Avon
St Mary's Church, remodelled for antiquary James West by Edward Woodward, 1753-4.

Prior Park
See Bath.

Pusey House, Oxfordshire
5m E of Faringdon
By John Sanderson, 1753. 3-storey front with 2-storey wings and quadrant walls with niches.

In garden, **Chinese bridge** and **temple.**

Quernmore Park Hall, Lancashire
2m E of Lancaster
Thomas Harrison, 1795-8. 5 by 5 bays, 3 storeys, ashlar-faced, porch of 2 pairs of unfluted Ionic pilasters. Wings, linked to main block, have tripartite windows with columns as mullions. Entrance hall rises through 2 storeys with coved ceilings and Doric pilasters supporting Ionic

colonnade, all with good Greek revival details that would be extremely advanced for 1795, but probably date from 1842 by Alexander Mills.

Raby Castle, Co. Durham
7m SW of Bishop Auckland
Park Farm by James Paine, c1755; castellated.

Radley, Oxfordshire
2m NE of Abingdon
Radley College, nucleus of which is **Radley Hall,** built 1721-7 by William Townesend, mason of Oxford. Door has rusticated surround into which flanking pilasters partly disappear – a nice baroque touch. Window above emphasized by scrolls.

Radway Grange, Warwickshire
7m NW of Banbury
Elizabethan manor house owned and Gothicized by Sanderson Miller, 1744; one of earliest examples of C18 Gothic revival.

Ragley Hall, Warwickshire
8m W of Stratford-upon-Avon
East front by Robert Hooke, 1679. Ionic portico by James Wyatt, c1780, fronting double-height great hall by James Gibbs, c1750, with walls decorated with paired Composite pilasters. Study and billiard room by Gibbs; dining room by Wyatt.

Ramsey, Isle of Man
Court House, George Steuart c1798.

Ramsgate, Kent
St George's Church, Church Hill, 1824-7 by Henry Hemsley. Perpendicular Gothic, with tower inspired by medieval Boston Stump, Lincolnshire.
Clock House, Harbour Street, c1815, handsome neo-classical composition by John Shaw.
In **High Street,** a stretch of early-C18 houses, especially **No. 124.**
Townley House Mansion, Chatham Street, c1790, 5-bay, 3-storey centre flanked by 2-storey wings set slightly back. Centre bay with 2-storey bow supported on Tuscan columns; 1 window in bow, niches with statues on either side.
Nelson Crescent, 1798-1801, continues into **The Paragon,** 1816. Behind this is **Liverpool Lawn** which, in best Georgian town-planning manner, contains humbler terraces of 1826-37.
Royal Crescent, 1826, 4 storeys, stuccoed, embellished with pilasters.
Albion Place, 1817, with good balconies.
Wellington Crescent, c1820, yellow brick with continuous Greek Doric colonnade carrying 1st-floor veranda. In centre, gap to admit a road called **The Plains of Waterloo.** This in turn leads to **La Belle Alliance Square,** where some early-C19 3-storey houses survive.

Ravenfield, South Yorkshire
3m NE of Rotherham
St James's Church, Gothic, by John Carr 1756.

Reading, Berkshire
25 and **52 Market Place,** both c1820 with giant pilasters.
In **Friar Street,** some early-C18 houses.
Vicarage, West Street, 1727. Adjacent **house** of similar date with canopied door.
In **Oxford Road,** various early-C19 **villas.**
19 Castle Street, c1720-25. **63 (Holybrook House),** c1750; large doorcase with blocked columns; rococo ceiling to music room, good stair.

Seven Bridges House, Bridge Street, by Sir John Soane, 1790.
8 Church Street, c1720; giant angle pilasters but only 2 bays wide.
Several good C18 houses in **London Street** especially **73-9.**

Redcar, Cleveland
St Peter's Church, Redcar Lane, 1828-9 by Ignatius Bonomi; Gothic.

Reigate, Surrey
Old Town Hall, High Street, 1728.
The Barons, Church Road, 1721 in typical builder's baroque manner. 5-bay brick front, centre bay breaking forward slightly. Side elevation treated as separate composition with ramps back and front up to pair of tall chimneys. Pedimented Ionic doorcase, c1750-60.
Browne's Lodge, 22 West Street, dated 1786; central pediment with swag, Coade stone plaque. In same street, **Old West House,** c1720.

Richmond, North Yorkshire
Town Hall, Market Place, 1756, possibly by Thomas Atkinson. Contains Assembly Rooms as well as Council Chamber. Also in Market Place, **King's Head Hotel;** red brick, large scale, probably c1720.
Theatre Royal, behind Market Place, 1788. Only surviving small-scale C18 theatre in country, now much restored. Extremely plain exterior. Contains small pit and row of boxes.
Bridge, 1789 by John Carr.
Just outside town, **Culloden Tower,** decorative octagonal folly probably designed by Daniel Garrett in 1746. Gothic windows; inside, rich Gothic Kentian decoration.

Ringwould House, Kent
By Sir John Soane, 1813. Simple 2-storey yellow brick house; entrance front with pilaster strips.

Ripley, Surrey
3m SE of Woking
Talbot Hotel, High Street, c1740. Impressive inn, with large coach arch topped by pediment. Range to left of arch presumably later C18. Also in High Street, **Clock House,** early C18.
Ripley Court, Ockham Road, c1730, baroque.

Ripon, North Yorkshire
Holy Trinity Church, Kirby Road, 1826-8 by Thomas Taylor. Gothic, altered 1874, 1884.
Town Hall, Market Place, 1798 by James Wyatt, 5 bays, 2 storeys, part of terrace. Standard Graeco-Palladian temple composition; 3-bay pediment supported on engaged Greek Ionic columns on rusticated ground floor.
Court House, Minster Road, late Georgian, off-centre Tuscan porch. In same road, **Deanery,** late C17 but much altered in C18.
In **Park Street,** Georgian house with gazebo formed by 2 towers linked by arcaded walk.
The Hall, Bedern Bank, c1725.

Risley, Derbyshire
1m W of Stapleford
Latin School, 1706, brick with stone dressings in late-C17 manner. Forming group with it are **Girls' School,** 1724; **English School** for boys, 1728; and **English Master's House,** 1771; all conforming in style with 1706 building – fine example of Georgian good manners.

Rochester, Kent

Watts' Charity, High Street. 1771 by mason Isaac Dent in associative Gothic manner. Also in High Street, **Gordon Hotel,** early C18; **No. 42,** dated 1778, distinguished by long, curving stucco ribbon over 1st-floor windows with Adamesque wreaths below; **Berkeley House,** late C18, stucco, 3-bay front flanked by lower projecting wings.

Minor Canon Row, inside cathedral precinct, 1736. 3-storey brick terrace of 7 houses, plain fronts with strange cornice doorhoods cantilevered out of façade, rear with hipped gables and some mullioned and transomed windows.

Star Hill, developed c1790, brick terraces.

12-20 St Margaret's Street, 1724.

The Gleanings, c1800, Grecian front, castellated to river.

Fort Clarence, belated anti-Napoleonic defence work of 1812, in admirable Vanbrughian manner with stylized stone machicolations over gateway.

Rokeby Hall, North Yorkshire
3m SE of Barnard Castle

Designed by owner, amateur Palladian architect Sir Thomas Robinson, 1725-50. Of 1st-generation Palladian country houses it is the one most dedicated to proportional permutations of cube; in part Burlingtonian tower house, but with many individual touches from Robinson. South front has single-storey porch framed by baseless Doric columns – if these are Robinson's work, they are probably earliest Greek-inspired Doric columns in the country. Inside, double-height saloon.

St Mary's Church, parish church ¾ mile from house, designed by Robinson and consecrated 1778, very similar to his church at Glynde, East Sussex (qv). Simple box with pediment gables at east and west ends.

Rosebery House, Lothian
7m SE of Penicuik

Steading of c1800. Gate with Gothic windows, and tower supporting spire.

Rosneath Castle, Strathclyde
3m W of Helensburgh, across Gare Loch

Steading of 1800 by Alexander Nasmith; designed to look like ecclesiastical ruin.

Rotherham, South Yorkshire

Charity School (**Feoffes**), The Crofts, 1776 by John Platt. 5 bays with open 3-bay pediment. **Moorgate Hall,** Moorgate Road, east front of 1768 by Platt. **Clifton House,** dated 1782, perhaps by John Carr.

In **Bridgegate,** good but dwindling collection of C18 terrace houses; **25-7** of c1760 with 1st-floor Venetian window, 2nd-floor Diocletian, beneath crowning pediment.

Rousham House, Oxfordshire
5m NE of Woodstock

Jacobean house altered by William Kent 1738-41, including exquisite parlour, with large-scale doorcase and pedimented overmantel.

At same time Kent remodelled garden, creating groves, temples and castellated **cowshed,** c1738.

Rugby School, Warwickshire
In Rugby

Tudor Gothic **quadrangle** of irregular design by Henry Hakewill, 1809-16.

Ryde, Isle of Wight

St Thomas's Church, St Thomas's Street, 1827-8, in a very thin, incorrect Gothic manner.

Town Hall, Lind Street, 1830 by James Sanderson. Recessed Ionic portico over ground-floor Tuscan colonnade.

Ryde School, off Queen's Road, country house composition of c1820.

Crown Hotel, High Street, c1830, with 2 tall, fat bays flanking Greek Doric porch.

In **Lind Street,** next to Town Hall, 4 buildings with uniform façade and Tuscan colonnade, c1830.

Brigstocke Terrace, east of St Thomas's Street, imposing, 28-bay-wide, tall stucco uniform terrace of c1830, by Sanderson.

Rye, East Sussex

Town Hall, Market Street, 1743 by Andrews Jelfe. Brick, 2 storeys, open arcade.

George Hotel, High Street, 1719 with Tuscan porch, c1820, embellished with cast-iron balustrade.

Elder House, Mermaid Street, c1740, elevated door with hood, façade with ovolo-edged clapboard. Adjacent is **Quakers' House,** c1720-30; double door with hood. **First House,** Mermaid Street, dated 1789, 3 tripartite windows.

Lamb House, West Street, c1720, brick, carved brackets supporting doorhood. (National Trust)

Old Custom House, 60 Church Square, 2 storeys, 4 bays, red mathematical tiles over older timber frame, carved brackets to hooded door. Also in square, brick **water cistern,** c1735.

Sacombe Park, Hertfordshire
3m N of Ware

Large yellow brick Greek revival house of 1802-8. 1-storey Greek Doric porch on west front; semi-circular bow in centre of east front; 11-bay south front with segmental bow at each end linked by colonnade of 6 giant Greek Doric columns.

Saffron Walden, Essex

Baptist Chapels of 1744 and 1792, both in Hill Street; another of 1820 in London Road.

Town Hall, Market Place, 1761-2; gable of 1879.

Saffron Hotel, 6-12 High Street, late C18, with pair of canted bays framing pedimented door. Also in High Street: **7,** with pair of canted bays flanking central pedimented door set in blank arch. **37,** early-C18 façade with steep 3-bay pediment. **65,** c1725. **67,** with early-C18 doorcase. **73** and neighbour embellished with elongated pilaster strips with incised Soane-style decorations.

In **London Road,** villas of c1820.

13-17 Myddelton Place, large, early-C18.

23-7 Gold Street, C18.

5 Hill Street, c1725, with good doorcase.

On the **Common,** several early-C19 villas, e.g. **The Grove,** 1804.

In **Lime Tree Walk,** Adamesque **house** with ground-floor Venetian window.

St Albans, Hertfordshire

Marlborough Almshouses, Hatfield Road, c1730. Quadrangular in plan, 2 storeys, 17-bay pedimented centre. Windows of centre have stone surrounds, all mullioned and transomed.

Former **Silk Mill,** Mill Lane, c1790; brick.

1-5 Holywell Hill, early-C18 group; 1 has giant angle pilasters and segmental-arched carriageway. **40,** perhaps by Sir Robert Taylor, 1783.

240 / *Georgian Buildings*

Old Rectory, Sumpter Yard, late C18, Venetian windows flanking doorcase.
16 St Peter's Street (**The Grange**), mid-C18. 5-bay west front with Ionic doorcase; south front has 2 canted bays with Venetian windows between. **107 St Peter's Hill** (**Ivy House**), built *c*1720 by Sir Edward Strong for himself. 4 bays, 3 storeys, lower 2 framed by giant Tuscan angle pilasters; later pedimented doorcase.
Romeland House, Romeland Hill, *c*1710-20. 3-bay pediment; Venetian window on 1st floor.
Bleak House, Catherine Street, early C18; 1st-floor window with eared architrave.

St Ives, Cambridgeshire
4m E of Huntingdon
Barnes House, north-west of parish church, late C18, 2 canted bays; Gothic hybrid door with quatrefoils in spandrels, Doric pilasters and pediment.
5 Crown Street, early C18.
In **Bridge Street,** pair of early-C18 houses with giant pilasters.
Bridge House, early C18.

St Julian's Underriver, Kent
2m SE of Sevenoaks
House built 1818-20 by J. B. Papworth; early example of Jacobean revival. Enlarged 1835 by Papworth, and 1951. Interior lost.

St Neots, Cambridgeshire
7m N of Sandy
Bull Inn, Market Place, late C18, 7 bays, with broad archway topped by Venetian window.
King's Head, South Street, with brackets to doorhead growing out of demi-columns (cf houses at Ampthill and Clophill).

St Peter Port, Guernsey
St James's Church, 1817-18 by John Wilson in Greek revival manner.
Market Hall, 1822 by Wilson.
Elizabeth College, 1826, also by Wilson; Tudor Gothic.

Salford, Greater Manchester
St Philip's Church, St Philip's Place, by Robert Smirke, 1822-4. Semicircular Ionic portico; circular domed tower.
Town Hall and **Assembly Room,** Bexley Square, 1825 by Richard Lane. Ashlar Greek Doric portico.
Buile Hill (now **Science Museum**), Eccles Old Road, Grecian villa of 1825-7 by Sir Charles Barry.

Salisbury, Wiltshire
Guildhall, Market Place, by Sir Robert Taylor and William Pilkington 1788; enlarged 1829 by Thomas Hopper, who added Tuscan portico.
General Infirmary, Fisherton Street, austere composition by John Wood the Younger, 1767-71.
White Hart Hotel, St John Street, late C18.
68 The Close, 1718, baroque, with giant Doric pilasters. Also in The Close, **Malmesbury House,** 1719, ashlar façade; inside, Gothic library of *c*1750 with delightful canted bay.
In **Exeter Street,** row of houses – especially **81-2** – with scrolled Kentian door surrounds and 1st-floor bay windows, *c*1750.
In **St Ann Street,** several good C18 houses, especially last house (now beside ring road), with central feature incorporating pedimented 1st-floor window, *c*1780.

Saltoun Hall, Lothian
4m SE of Tranent
1818 by William Burn. Castellated Gothic with central tower inspired by Taymouth Castle (qv); excellent vaulted Gothic interiors.

Saltram House, Devon
1m SW of Plympton
House of C16 and *c*1745, altered by Robert Adam 1768-9. Exterior very plain. Inside, hall and stair in rococo manner of *c*1750, saloon and dining room magnificent Adam designs. (National Trust)

Sandbeck Park, South Yorkshire
2m SW of Tickhill
By James Paine, 1763-8, and one of his most dramatic façades: garden front has deeply projecting Corinthian portico supported on heavily rusticated arches. Main rooms on 1st floor; saloon has neo-classical ceiling of 1775, showing Paine's move from rococo.
Farmhouse, striking pedimented composition with large-scale details.

Sandhurst, Berkshire
3m NW of Camberley
Royal Military Academy, 1807-12 by John Sanders. Long, austere façade with giant Greek Doric portico.

Sandridge Park, Devon
3m SE of Totnes
By John Nash, *c*1805. Italianate stuccoed villa with round and square towers.

Sandwich, Kent
Many picturesque minor C18 houses, such as brick cottages in **Delph Street** or, in same street, houses with yellow bricks and flints making patterns beneath 1st-floor windows.
50 and **52 King Street,** late-C18.
Old Custom House, 19 Upper Strand Street, C18 brick façade.

Sarsgrove House, Oxfordshire
3m SW of Chipping Norton
Cottage orné by G. S. Repton, *c*1825. Inside, Soane-style drawing room with elliptical arches and groin-vaulted ceiling.

Sawbridgeworth, Hertfordshire
White Lion Inn, corner of London Road and Bell Street. Façade framed by giant pilasters, *c*1735.
Red House, 11 Bell Street, *c*1720. In same street, **No. 9** and **The Elms** are C18.
28 Knight Street, *c*1730 façade framed by giant Tuscan pilasters. Doric door with rusticated pilasters topped by window framed with brick rustic blocks. **No. 40,** *c*1730.

Saxby, Leicestershire
4m E of Melton Mowbray
St Peter's Church, 1788 by George Richardson, classical but with spire.

Saxby, Lincolnshire
7m W of Market Rasen
St Helen's Church, *c*1775, ambitious design with Tuscan portico *in antis,* good interior.

Saxlingham Nethergate, Norfolk
8m SE of Wymondham
Rectory, 1784-7 by Sir John Soane. North and south fronts with curved full-height central bays rising extra storey above eaves.

Scampston Hall, Humberside
7m SE of Pickering
Additions of 1803 by Thomas Leverton. 9-bay south front with domed, pilastered bow; on west front bow ringed with detached Tuscan columns.
In park, **Palladian Bridge,** *c*1775 by Lancelot Brown.

Scarborough, North Yorkshire
Rotunda Museum, R. H. Sharp, 1828-9, designed as tall, domed rotunda.
9 Sandside, former **Custom House,** early C18; **32-5,** early C18 block.
Long Westgate, Castlegate, Paradise all contain good number of modest Georgian brick houses, showing this to be an area of C18 expansion. **127-9 Long Westgate,** *c*1760, have doors sharing one large pediment. Also with good double doors, **37-9 Eastborough.**
In **St Sepulchre Street,** late-C18 house, upper-floor windows decorated with fanlights.
14 St Nicholas Street, early C18, with Ionic angle pilasters; interior interesting as it has identical staircases each side of central passage in Palladian country house manner.

Scone Palace, Tayside
2m N of Perth
1803-12 by William Atkinson. Castellated; first Scottish house with entirely neo-Gothic interior.
Model village of *c*1780.

Seaton Delaval Hall, Northumberland
3m S of Blyth
Built 1717-29, one of Vanbrugh's most powerful country house designs. Centre gutted 1822.

Sefton Park
See Liverpool.

Seton Castle, Lothian
1m N of Tranent
1790-91 by Robert Adam. Symmetrical castle-style house with classical details mixed with medieval machicolations and cruciform windows.

Sevenoaks, Kent
Sevenoaks School and **Almshouse,** built 1724-32 to designs of Lord Burlington, but no doubt executed without his supervision. In centre is 4-storey school, with pyramidal roof, octagonal lantern and cornice. Wings, set back, are a storey lower (though right wing unfortunately now heightened). Doorways, round-headed, are in wings. Flanking centre block, and set nearer road, identical pair of almshouses, each 2 storeys with taller, pedimented and rusticated arch leading to rear courtyard.
Lady Boswell's School, London Road, 1818; C. R. Cockerell's 1st building. 3 bays under pediment, doorways in 1-storey extension.
Royal Oak Hotel, High Street. Particularly good primitive Greek Doric porch, *c*1820.
The Manor House, High Street, *c*1800, unusual giant pilasters with Portland stone slabs instead of capitals.
The Old Vicarage, High Street, Doric door surround with rusticated pilasters, *c*1720.
The Old House, High Street, *c*1700-14. Centre bay breaking forward and pedimented; oval windows either side of central 1st-floor window.
Vine House, High Street, late C18, red brick. Door embellished with mask keystone and vermiculated rustic blocks of Coade stone. Also in High Street, **88-90,** late C18 houses with canted bays, wooden rustication between windows.
Kippington House, Kippington Road, *c*1760.
In **Mill Lane,** 1½ miles north of town, 10 2-storey cottages with pedimented centre. Built *c*1765 for lace workers.

Sezincote House, Gloucestershire
9m W of Chipping Norton
Designed by S. P. Cockerell *c*1805 for his brother, an Indian nabob; remarkable essay in Mogul/ 'Hindoo' manner. Main block 2 storeys, 9 bays by 5, crowned with powerful *chujja* or cornice. Above this, onion-shaped copper dome. Block linked by picturesque 15-bay quadrant to octagonal pavilion. Inside, principal rooms on 1st floor are classical. Saloon with *trompe-l'oeil* trelliswork. Staircase carried on exposed, decorative cast-iron girders.
In grounds, Indian **garden buildings** by Thomas Daniell, and Moorish **farm** with pinnacles and various Mogul details, *c*1808 by Cockerell.

Shardeloes, Buckinghamshire
5m N of Beaconsfield
By Francis Smith, 1726-7, reconstructed in Palladian manner, 1758-66, by Stiff Leadbetter, and with giant Corinthian portico by Robert Adam, 1759-61. Inside, library by James Wyatt, *c*1775.

Sharpham, Devon
2m SE of Totnes
By Sir Robert Taylor, *c*1770; one of his best villas. Excellent top-lit curving stair.

Sheffield, South Yorkshire
Methodist Church, Carver Street, by Revd William Jenkins, 1804. Powerful classical design in brick.
Royal Infirmary, Infirmary Road, built 1793 to designs of John Rawsthorne. Entrance front flanked by 2 fat, full-height 3-bay bows. Centre 3 bays crowned by pediment.
14-26 Carver Lane, workshop of *c*1800 with long rows of windows on 2 storeys.
Globe Works, Penistone Road, Greek-detailed factory of *c*1820.
On **Canal Wharf,** collection of excellent late-Georgian warehouses, one spanning canal on arched bottom storey.

Sheffield Place, East Sussex
4m E of Haywards Heath
James Wyatt, 1776-7 and 1789-90; inside, staircase and landing with slender quatrefoil Gothic columns supporting dome with Gothic decoration.

Shipston on Stour, Warwickshire
10m NW of Chipping Norton
George Hotel, High Street, *c*1730-40. Also in High Street, **White Bear,** with 2-storey canted bays; façade of *c*1770.
The Bell Inn, Sheep Street, *c*1760. Also in Sheep Street, **Manor House,** *c*1725; **Stokes House,** dated 1715; **No. 17,** dated 1714 and originally with mullioned windows (one preserved).
In **Church Street,** some good Georgian houses, especially **38** and **40.**

Shobdon, Hereford and Worcester
7m NE of Kington
Church of St John the Evangelist, 1753, a rococo Gothic fantasy in wedding-cake white and pale blue. Ogee nave windows; chancel arch in which Gothic motifs are used in wilfully non-

Shotesham Park, Norfolk. An early (c1785) and idiosyncratic design by Sir John Soane using a screen of pilasters in a blatantly non-structural manner.

structural way; Gothic pews, pulpit and fireplace in chapel; west gallery of 1810. Perhaps designed by Richard Bentley.

Shotesham Park, Norfolk
6m s of Norwich
Restrained, subtly designed neo-classical house of c1785 by Sir John Soane. Façade notable for 'screen' of 6 giant Ionic pilasters stopping short of corners of house. They support entablature above which rises pedimented attic storey.

Shotover Park, Oxfordshire
5m E of Oxford
Tall house, the work of a provincial builder, perhaps William Townesend. Main structure built 1714-18. Inside, hall with lavish plasterwork including fluted pilasters carrying entablature. Saloon panelled in oak, with a marble fireplace by William Kent.
Grounds, a rare survival of formal layout, begun c1718 and completed c1730, include long **canal** in front of house, vista closed by Gothic-detailed **garden temple** with corner turrets derived from Hawksmoor's North Quad of All Souls, Oxford – which was built by William Townesend who could, perhaps, have designed this temple c1730, one of earliest Gothic garden buildings in the country. Alternative attribution, on stylistic grounds, is to James Gibbs. Octagonal **temple** and **obelisk** on axis with west front of house, c1730-35, perhaps by Kent.

Shrewsbury, Shropshire
St Julian's Church, Wyle Cop, rebuilt 1749-50 by T.F. Pritchard. Street elevation much altered in C19 but back elevation to churchyard survives, in belated provincial baroque manner. Inside, arcade of giant Tuscan columns.
St Chad's Church, built 1790-92 by George Steuart, one of the most extraordinary, and successful, of British neo-classical churches. Ashlar, with refined neo-classical external decoration. Fat, circular nave linked to entrance block supporting tower topped with cupola. Inside, serpentine gallery staircase and attenuated iron columns supporting nave ceiling.
St Alkmund's Church, St Alkmund's Place, designed 1794-5 by John Carline in thin Perpendicular Gothic manner. Tower medieval. Tracery in windows originally of cast iron made by Coalbrookdale foundry; it survives in east and west nave windows.
St George's Church, Drinkwater Street, Frankwell, by Edward Haycock 1829-32, Gothic.
English Bridge, 1769-74 by John Gwynn, altered 1926.
Welsh Bridge, 1793-5 by John Carline.
Old County Gaol, Sydney Court, c1715. Very domestic in appearance, but cells survive in the basement. Present **County Gaol,** Howard Street, 1787-93 by J.H. Haycock and Thomas Telford. Classical, with central octagonal chapel.
Foundling Hospital (now **Shrewsbury School**), over Frankland Bridge, by Pritchard 1759-63, remodelled 1878.
Millington's Hospital, Frankwell (beyond Welsh Bridge), 1785 by J.H. Haycock.
Royal Salop Infirmary, St Mary's Place, large Greek Doric edifice signed Edward Haycock, 1826; but he consulted Sir Robert Smirke.
Allat's School (now **Health Centre**), Murivance, c1799-1810 by J.H. Haycock; neo-classical.
Lion Hotel, Wyle Cop, brick c1740-50. At rear, Adamesque assembly room of c1780. Adjacent is **house** (now **County Library**), c1730.
Marshall, Benyon & Bage's Flour Mill (now **Allied Brewers**), at edge of town in Spring Gardens, Ditherington, 1796-7, with earliest multi-storey iron-framed interior, brick walls.
The Square contains one good group, includ-

ing **8-9 (Walley's House),** rainwater head dated 1733.
10-11 High Street, 1766 by T.F. Pritchard.
46-7 Mardol, *c*1720.
1 and **2 Old Council House Court,** *c*1750 but earlier in appearance. Back elevation 11 bays with serpentine shaped gable ends.
25-6 Castle Street, *c*1780-85, Adamesque.
Windsor House, Windsor Place, fine house of 1741, Ionic pilastered doorcase. Inside, panelling in both oak and wych elm, good staircase.

Belmont contains largest of town's terrace houses. **Liberal** (now **Granville**) **Club** displays C16 half-timbered façade to Belmont Bank, but perfectly regular façade of *c*1750, with 3-bay pediment, to Belmont. **Belmont House,** *c*1700; adjacent is **Judge's Lodging,** *c*1705. **No. 10** has pedimented tripartite doorway of *c*1750. Rear of **15** has pair of tall, full-height canted bays.
Clive House, off College Hill, *c*1750.
St John's Hill contains unusual terrace in which all doorways are tripartite, *c*1780.
6 Quarry Place, *c*1790.
St Mary's Place, opposite St Mary's Church, contains 4-bay **house** of *c*1740-60.
In **Town Walls, The Crescent,** *c*1790, in which doors and ground-floor windows are topped with semicircular Coade stone bat's-wing panels. At junction of Town Walls and Beeches Lane, **Bowdler's School,** dated 1724. Off Town Walls, **Swan Hill Court,** Swan Court, pedimented façade to large garden, 1764 by T.F. Pritchard. 1-bay wings. Inside, Gothic fireplaces.

Shugborough, Staffordshire
4m E of Stafford
Earlier house remodelled 1790-98 by Samuel Wyatt, who created several notable archaeological/neo-classical interiors, especially circular entrance hall with Greek Doric columns of 'Delian' form. Outside, giant Ionic colonnade flanked by characteristic domed bows.

More important are grounds and garden buildings, which form a neo-classical picturesque counterpart to such earlier landscape gardens as Stowe and Stourhead. Buildings include Greek **Doric Temple,** probably designed by James Stuart *c*1764; **Triumphal Arch,** 1764-7 by Stuart, based on Arch of Hadrian in Rome; **Lanthorn of Demosthenes,** Stuart 1764-70, based on Choragic Monument of Lysicrates in Athens. Other garden buildings include Stuart's strange primitive Doric **Shepherds' Monument** of *c*1758, his copy of Athenian **Tower of the Winds** of 1764, and **Chinese House** of 1747.

Sidmouth, Devon
Fortfield Terrace, begun *c*1790, part of ambitious large-scale development undertaken by architect Michael Novosielski.

Sledmere House, Humberside
7m NW of Great Driffield
Begun 1751; greatly altered and extended 1781-8, probably to designs of Sir Christopher Sykes for himself, in manner of Samuel Wyatt. South front with 3 huge 1st-floor tripartite windows set beneath arches. Inside, magnificent groin-vaulted library.
Castle Farm, designed *c*1780, perhaps by John Carr, with pair of octagonal castellated towers.

Sir John Soane's 'barn à la Paestum' of 1798 at 936 Warwick Road, Solihull, West Midlands.

Solihull, West Midlands
Malvern Hall, early C18, altered *c*1780 by Sir John Soane. Also by Soane, who supplied design in 1798, **936 Warwick Road** which is a 'barn à la Paestum' of red brick, with giant columns.

Somersby Hall, Lincolnshire
6m NE of Horncastle
1722, very much in castle style of Vanbrugh and particularly reminiscent of his now-destroyed Nunnery of *c*1720 at Greenwich. 4 towers at corners, north part castellated, south front spanned by broad pediment, Hall and stair ingeniously planned, with entry by mock screens passage. Plan of house survives, bearing name of Robert Alfray, who claims to be 'inv. et delin.'

Southampton, Hampshire
Dolphin Hotel, High Street, *c*1760, with pair of fat bays rising from 1st floor and framing arch to courtyard.

In **Bugle Street** some good, modest C18 houses including **45,** with 2 canted bays; **47,** *c*1750.

3-storey stucco early-C19 terrace houses, with 2-storey bows cantilevered out from 1st-floor level, in **Queen's Terrace, Oxford Street,** and **Bernard Street** where **113-19** and **123-33** are particularly good.

In **Portland Street,** stucco terrace of *c*1825-30, articulated and decorated in manner of Nash.

Southill Park, Bedfordshire
3m SW of Biggleswade
Begun 1795 to designs of Henry Holland; superb example of austere, correct Graeco-Palladian style. Chaste ashlar exterior with pedimented centre block and Ionic colonnades and loggias on south front. Inside, saloon in red-and-gold Greek/Egyptian Empire style. Painted parlour with Louis XVI Pompeian painted ornamentation.

South Molton, Devon
Town Hall, 1739-43, designed by a certain Cullen. Ground floor with open rusticated arcades.

Sowerby, West Yorkshire
W edge of Halifax
St Peter's Church, 1761-3 by mason John Wilson in provincial Palladian style derived from local model of Holy Trinity, Leeds.

Spalding, Lincolnshire
White Hart, Market Place, c1714, early-C19 porch.
34 London Road, c1755 with 1-bay pediment, hipped roof. Also in London Road, **Welland Hall** (now **Old High School**), c1760, with richly carved doorcase.
Westbourne Lodge, Cowbit Road, c1765 by William Sands the Younger, provincial Palladian composition with bow windows to ground floor. At No. 4 in same road, **Langton House,** perhaps also by Sands, c1760-70 with segmental bow and Doric porch; **No. 3** by Sands, with pair of canted bay windows and Ionic porch.
Wisteria Lodge, Church Street, dated 1792; in same street, **No. 4,** 1721, with semicircular porch.
4 and **9 High Street,** early C18; **12,** dated 1746, by Sands. Also in High Street: **Holland House,** best house in town, dated 1768 and again designed by Sands. Complex façade with central pedimented door flanked by side windows, above it Venetian window, then square window with pair of thin, round-headed side lights, and above all pediment. To either side, canted bays with balustraded parapets. **Cley Hall,** dated 1764, with 'Tower of the Winds' door of c1780. **Yew Lodge,** c1820.
The Limes, Double Street, early C18.
Harrington House, Broad Street, c1730.
4 miles to south-east, at Moulton Chapel, **St James's Chapel,** octagonal, 1722 by William Sands the Elder.

Stafford, Staffordshire
Shire Hall, Market Place, 1795-9 by John Harvey to plan supplied by Samuel Wyatt, with 3-bay pediment and engaged Doric columns. Spacious entrance hall with segmental vault.
Gaol, Gaol Road, 1793-4 by Thomas Cook, enlarged 1832. In same road, **St George's Hospital,** 1814-18.
General Hospital, Foregate Street, 1769-72 by Benjamin and William Wyatt.
Lloyds Bank, Market Square, c1795, built as bank for Stevenson, Salt & Co, and designed to harmonize with nearby Shire Hall.

Stamford, Lincolnshire
Town Hall, St Mary's Hill, domestic in character; 1777, by Lovell or William Legg.
Assembly Rooms, St George's Square, 1727. 3-bay ashlar façade framed by pilaster strips. Inside one grand room, coved ceiling, big chimney-piece.
Hopkin's Hospital, St Peter Street, light-hearted Gothic; c1770, perhaps by Legg.
Stamford and Rutland Hospital, Deeping Road, J.P. Gandy, 1826, in Tudor Gothic manner.
Library (formerly **Market**), High Street, 1804 by Legg, with small but powerful Tuscan portico.
The Theatre, St Mary's Street, 1768. 5-bay ashlar façade, large central door with open pediment, round-headed window above.
Stamford Hotel, St Mary's Street, 1810-19 by J.L. Bond. Large-scale neo-classical elevation with engaged giant Corinthian columns.
George Hotel, High Street St Martin's, front of 1724, rear elevation of 1787-8 with full-height canted bays.
3 All Saints' Place, c1730, a good representation of 'Stamford baroque' style (see below). Windows have moulded surrounds; door with Gibbs surround. Façade topped by cornice.
13 Barn Hill, 5 bays, 2 storeys, dated 1740 on hopper. One of best houses in town, and typical of 'Stamford baroque' style, supposedly developed by local architect George Portwood: quoins, moulded modillion cornice, pedimented dormers, Gibbs surrounds to ground-floor windows, pediments to 1st-floor ones. Identical with Leasingham Manor (qv).
1 St George's Square, delightful mid-C18 façade, 3 bays, 2 storeys, square 1st-floor windows with eared architraves and keystones. Above, panelled parapet flanked by large scrolls.
14-17 High Street, c1700-15, curious, almost Bavarian, baroque terrace composition. Adjacent, **18-19,** 1719-36, and a now-altered early-C19 Corinthian shop-front. **21,** 1732, with 5-bay return in Ironmonger Street, 2 bays to High Street framed by fluted Doric pilasters rising from 1st floor, windows with bold Gibbs surrounds and fanned keystones; 5 bays in Ironmonger Street divided 2-1-2 by 4 giant Doric pilasters.
22, 23, 24 St Mary's Street, c1740 by Portwood. **2 St Mary's Place,** c1730-40; 6 bays, 2-storeys; 5 bays form main composition between rusticated giant Doric pilasters. 1st-floor windows have Gibbs surrounds. **3,** curious 2-bay, 2-storey house of c1740-50, decorated by 2 tiers of pilasters divided by cornice at 1st-floor level: Tuscan on ground floor, Doric above.
35 High Street St Martin's, c1735, is perfect Stamford house in which all openings are treated with Gibbs surrounds, door also pedimented, and façade framed with quoins and topped with mutule cornice. **47-50,** c1730-40. **66-7,** c1735, handsome front: all ground-floor windows with Gibbs surrounds, both doors pedimented, 1st-floor windows with eared architraves and keystones.
Rutland Terrace, 1829-31, 34 bays, 3 storeys, giant pilasters with anthemion capitals.
Austin House, Austin Street, has handsome garden front of c1800 with pair of 3-storey curved bays with Venetian and tripartite windows.
Several good early-C19 shop-fronts survive, for example **7 High Street, 4 St Mary's Street, 9 Ironmonger Street.**

Stanmer House, East Sussex
1m beyond NE edge of Brighton
Built 1722-7 to designs of Huguenot architect Nicholas Dubois, provincial Palladian.

Stannington, South Yorkshire
1m beyond W edge of Sheffield
Underbank Unitarian Chapel, 1742, designed together with caretaker's house to make striking composition. Front of chapel has pair of deep round-headed windows.

Stapleford, Leicestershire
4m E of Melton Mowbray
St Mary Magdalen's Church, 1783, probably by George Richardson. Early attempt at antiquarian Gothic.

Stirling, Central Region
Athenaeum, King Street, by William Stirling 1814-16. Curved frontage with spire.
Court House and **Gaol,** 1806-11 by Richard Crichton.

The Grosvenor Hotel, Stockbridge, Hampshire. Built c1810-20, this is a fine example of the eighteenth- and early nineteenth-century preference for bays on buildings, such as inns and clubs, dedicated to pleasure and relaxation.

Golden Lion Hotel, King Street, long pedimented elevation of c1780.

Several good early-C19 residential developments: **Melville Terrace,** c1815-25; **Allan Park,** c1818-36, partly by Alexander Bowie.

Stobo Castle, Borders
5m SW of Peebles
Archibald and James Elliot, 1805-11. Symmetrical castellated house with classical interior.

Stobs Castle, Borders
4m S of Hawick
Robert Adam, 1793, in castle style.

Stockbridge, Hampshire
6m S of Andover
Town Hall, 1810, yellow brick, very plain.
Grosvenor Hotel, c1810-20, huge centre bay carried forward on Tuscan columns.
White Hart, also early C19.

Stockeld Park, North Yorkshire
5m SE of Harrogate
By James Paine, 1758-63; hovers between English baroque freedom and Palladian convention. Tall 3-bay centre with pediment, closely flanked by wings which come forward, each containing broad blank arch breaking into pediment.

Stocken Hall, Leicestershire
8m NE of Oakham
c1735, 7 bays, 2 storeys, 3-bay centre with giant pilasters. All windows with Gibbs surrounds. Large C19 addition.

Stockport, Greater Manchester
St Thomas's Church, Wellington Road South, in Grecian style by George Basevi, 1822-5. Ionic portico contains stairs leading to galleries.
Woodbank Park, Woodbank, classical 3-bay villa of 1812 by Thomas Harrison.

Stockton-on-Tees, Cleveland
Town Hall, 1736, extended south 1744, altered in late C19. 5-bay north front. Tower, 1744, topped by wooden bell-stage.

48 Bridge Road, former booking office of c1825 for Stockton and Darlington Railway – and so the earliest building of its type.

Finkle Street has some good C18 houses, especially **No. 8,** with canted bays; and **10.**

16 Church Road, c1735; Gibbs surrounds to 1st-floor windows. **72 Paradise Row,** in Church Road, consists of 2 3-bay, 2-storey mid-C18 houses, one of which has a staircase lit by Venetian window with chinoiserie decoration of c1765. **80 Paradise Row** has door surround in which Doric columns turn Gothic and become trefoil instead of circular in section, and with quatrefoil metopes in frieze, c1765.

32 Dovecote Street, c1750.

Stoke Doyle, Northamptonshire
1m SW of Oundle
St Rumbald's Church, 1722. South door sophisticated piece of baroque design with segmental pediment and bold horizontal rustication.

Stoke Edith, Hereford and Worcester
6m E of Hereford
St Mary's Church, 1740, contains pair of giant Ionic columns forming screen in sanctuary; perhaps designed by Henry Flitcroft.

Stoke Poges, Buckinghamshire
2m N of Slough
Stoke Park, remarkable house begun 1789 by Robert Nasmith and completed by James Wyatt c1793-7. Body of house surrounded by Greek Doric colonnade and topped by early-C19 dome.
Hospital, to north of church, built by Thomas Penn, 1765: dwellings for 3 men and 3 women, Master's house and chapel.

Stokesley, North Yorkshire
6m S of Middlesbrough
St Peter and St Paul's Church, medieval with nave of 1771.

In High Street, **Barclays Bank,** c1780; **Market Place** and **High Street** have many modest Georgian **houses,** including **Manor House.**

Handyside House, 60-62 West Green, *c*1770; ambitious if small-scale composition: 3-bay centre block with pedimented door, 1-bay link blocks leading to pavilions.

Stone, Staffordshire

St Michael's Church, 1753-8 by William Robinson and William Baker; very early Gothic revival. Notable for absence of rococo Gothic details. Y-tracery to windows. Altered internally 1887.

Crown Inn, new front by Henry Holland, 1779, neo-classical, with pair of 3-storey brick bays.

Stoneleigh Abbey, Warwickshire

1m E of Kenilworth

West range, 1714-26, by Francis Smith; 15-bay front articulated with giant Ionic pilasters and embellished with Michelangelesque details, especially window frames.

Stony Stratford, Buckinghamshire

St Giles's Church, nave 1776-7 by Francis Hiorne in Gothic manner with tall wooden piers formed by clustered shafts carrying plaster rib vaults.

Congregational Church, High Street, and **Baptist Church,** Horsefair Green, both 1823 and both with full-width pediments.

In High Street, numerous red brick buildings dating from period of rebuilding following fire in 1742. Most notable is **Cock Hotel,** *c*1742, with lunette window above entrance. Nearly adjacent, **92-6,** of similar date and size, with arch to rear quarters. Also in **High Street, 75,** with early-C19, Greek-detailed shop-front; and a house of *c*1714-20 with shell hood to door.

Storr's Hall, Cumbria

1m s of Windermere

Peculiar and self-conscious Greek revival house of 1808-11 by J.M. Gandy. 2-storey entrance front with 1-storey Greek Doric colonnade carrying entablature embellished with prominent antefixae. Top-lit staircase expresses itself externally as shallow dome on squat drum.

In grounds, lakeside octagonal **temple,** 1804.

Stourbridge, West Midlands

6m sw of Warley

St Thomas's Church, begun 1726, perhaps by local bricklayer called Parker. Interior modelled on Wren's St James's, Piccadilly. Apse 1890.

Stourhurst, Lower High Street, *c*1760, has pair of canted bays with wrap-round Venetian windows. Adjacent **house** of *c*1770, with Gothic details.

Stourhead, Wiltshire

5m NW of Gillingham

House designed by Colen Campbell and built by Nathaniel Ireson, begun *c*1720; first pure C18 version of Inigo Jones/Palladio-inspired villa. Façade of 5 widely spaced bays with rusticated base derived from Palladio's Villa Emo. Entrance hall is 30ft cube with coved ceiling. Centre of house gutted by fire 1902, reconstructed with some alterations. Wings, added 1792-1804 by Moulton and Atkinson, contain picture gallery and library which has a tunnel-vaulted ceiling. Portico, though envisaged by Campbell, not built until 1841.

Grounds, laid out after *c*1741, second only to Stowe as example of landscape gardening. Structures in grounds include the following. **Temple of Flora,** 1745-55 by Henry Flitcroft, has tetrastyle Tuscan portico. Adjacent, **Rocky Arch** and remains of **Grotto Boathouse. Grotto,** 1740, tripartite structure with serpentine entrance added *c*1776. **Temple of Hercules** or **Pantheon,** by Flitcroft 1754-6, with 4-columned portico and rotunda body, inspired by Pantheon in Rome. **Five Arch Bridge,** 1749. **Temple of the Sun** or of **Apollo,** 1767 by Flitcroft, is colonnaded rotunda based on building illustrated by Wood in his book on Baalbec, 1757. **Rustic Cottage,** *c*1780, with Gothic details added 1806. (National Trust)

Outside immediate grounds, 1½ miles west of house, **Convent in the Wood,** picturesquely irregular thatched stone cottage with turrets, *c*1765-70. ½ mile beyond it, **Alfred's Tower,** 160ft high, triangular plan, 1769-72.

Stourport-on-Severn, Hereford and Worcester

Built by James Brindley, 1766-71, to serve his Staffordshire and Worcestershire Canal.

Methodist Chapel, High Street, 1787 and 1812.

Tontine Inn, beside canal basin at Mart Lane, 1788, forms centre of long uniform terrace.

Of the original development, late Georgian **terraces** survive in **Lichfield Road, York Street** and **Bridge Street,** with particularly good terrace on north side of **New Street.** Most of 3 storeys with pretty pedimented doorcases.

Stout's Hill, Gloucestershire

5m sw of Stroud

Gothic house, 1743, perhaps designed by William Halfpenny, for it is an enlarged version of orangery at Frampton (qv).

Stow-on-the-Wold, Gloucestershire

8m w of Chipping Norton

In The Square, **St Edward's House,** baroque, *c*1720, 2 bays framed by pair of giant Corinthian pilasters, central 1st-floor niche.

Stowe, Buckinghamshire

3m NW of Buckingham

House late-C17 in core with 13-bay, 2-storey north entrance front, stuccoed, never painted, with giant Ionic portico, *c*1720, perhaps by Vanbrugh. Now flanked by quadrant Ionic colonnade terminating in pedimented entrance pavilions. Work of Giovanni Battista Borra inside colonnades dates them to 1770-72. South front designed by Robert Adam and executed by Borra 1774, consisting of porticoed centre connected by recessed, lower 7-bay buildings to higher 3-bay pavilions. Inside (entering from north) entrance hall with coved ceiling connected, via cross passage containing 2 flights of stairs, to oval neo-classical hall by Borra, embellished with pink scagliola engaged columns, coffered dome and deep frieze of neo-classical figures by Valdré. Off this hall, Dining Room, decorated in Pompeian manner and with Kentian woodwork. In rustic, exquisite Gothic Library by Soane, 1802-6; and remains of Egyptian vestibule.

Interesting as house is, it is garden that makes Stowe of international importance. Work began 1713, under Charles Bridgeman until *c*1725. Around 1730-35 William Kent began to turn Stowe into one of earliest and most appealing of natural landscaped gardens. This was achieved with the use of a large number of garden buildings designed by Kent and others, including the following. **Rotondo,** with Tuscan colonnade supporting saucer dome, designed by Vanbrugh 1719, altered by Borra c1763. **Boycott Pavilions,** designed c1726 by James Gibbs in rugged Vanbrughian manner and toned down a little by Borra c1770. In Kent's Elysian Fields, his **Temple of Ancient Virtue,** c1735, formed by cellular rotunda with Ionic columns; and his crescent-shaped **Temple of British Worthies,** 1733, in which busts are set in pedimented niches, with stepped pyramid at centre. **Gothic Temple,** designed by Gibbs c1741, curious mix of early English detail on Elizabethan triangular plan. **Temple of Concord,** early neo-classical design with portico and peristyle in manner of Roman temple, built c1748-62 probably to designs of Kent, Richard Grenville and Borra; peristyle now stripped of most columns. **Palladian Bridge,** c1738-42, attributed to Gibbs. Massive **Corinthian Arch** on axis with portico, nearly 1 mile away from south side of house, designed 1766 by Thomas Pitt.

Stratfield Saye House, Hampshire
7m S of Reading
C17 with C18 alterations and additions, mainly c1775, including some interesting antiquarian work, especially dining room with ceiling copied from Wood's book on Palmyra; also print room.

St Mary's Church, in grounds of house, built 1754-8, perhaps to designs of amateur architect Thomas Pitt, in advanced neo-classical manner with Greek cross plan and octagonal central dome.

Stratford-upon-Avon, Warwickshire
Holy Trinity Church, medieval, with Gothic spire of 1763 by William Hiorne.

Town Hall, Sheep Street, 1767 by Timothy Lightoler and/or Robert Newman, with open ground floor. Standard good late-Palladian design.

Market House, on corner of Henley Street and Wood Street, 1821, with domed octagonal turret.

16 Church Street, with Gothic details of 1768: windows, bays, small battlements.

Late-Georgian houses in **Payton Street** and **Guild Street.**

Stratton Park
See East Stratton.

Stroud, Gloucestershire
Council Offices, High Street, early C18; bolection-moulded window architraves with keystones.

28, 29 High Street, early C19; **44, 45,** 6-bay composition of c1750 with moulded eaves cornice.

19, 20 Nelson Street, excellent early C19 pair with shared central pediment and door. In same street, **Laurel Villa,** c1725, with mullioned and transomed windows and coved eaves cornice.

Styal, Cheshire
1m N of Wilmslow
Quarry Bank Silk Mill, built 1784 by Samuel Greg. Brick shell, interior partly of traditional timber-frame construction, and partly of 'fire-proof' jack-arch construction, where small masonry arches span from joists. (National Trust)

Styche Hall, Shropshire
2m NW of Market Drayton
House by Sir William Chambers, 1762, in his austere early style; canted bay added 1796.

Sudbury, Suffolk
Lloyds Bank, 30 Market Place, with tall 3-bay canted centre, c1770-80.

Gainsborough House, 46 Gainsborough Street, c1720.

Sunderland, Tyne and Wear
Holy Trinity Church, Church Street East, 1719, enlarged 1735 by addition of nearly circular apse lit by Venetian window. West tower with quoins. Interior has giant Ionic nave columns supporting entablature, and flat ceiling remodelled 1803 by Thomas Wilson.

In Queen Street East, **Phoenix Lodge,** country's oldest Freemasons' lodge, designed 1785 by John Bonner; central arch contains aedicule and Masonic symbols. Interior of hall a double cube, with original neo-classical fittings.

Exchange, 1812-14 by John Stokoe.

In **Church Street East,** remains of 2 grand early-C18 **houses; No. 10** has angle pilasters.

Early-C19 houses in **John Street, Foyle Street** and **Athenaeum Street.**

Sunnyside House, Lothian
In Liberton, SE edge of Edinburgh
Robert Adam, 1785. Now golf club.

Sutton Scarsdale, Derbyshire
4m SE of Chesterfield
By Francis Smith, 1724, stone, 9-bay east front with 3-bay pediment supported on fluted engaged columns which, with pilasters articulating façade, are set on ground level. Now a ruin.

Swaffham, Norfolk
Oakley House, Market Place, perfect little pedimented brick town mansion, c1740. Also in Market Place, **Headmaster's House,** dated 1736, adjoining **school** of same date.

Swerford House, Oxfordshire
4m NE of Chipping Norton
C18 house remodelled by J.M. Gandy, 1824, in Greek revival manner.

Swinfen Hall, Staffordshire
2m SE of Lichfield
Designed by Benjamin Wyatt 1759, but looks more like c1710. Giant Ionic pilasters, attic storey above cornice. Now part of a prison.

Swinstead Old Hall, Lincolnshire
9m N of Stamford
Belvedere, c1720, probably by Vanbrugh. 3 bays, 2 storeys, ends rising to 3 storeys to form square towers. Principal windows arched.

Swynnerton Hall, Staffordshire
3m W of Stone
c1725-9, probably by Francis Smith. 3-bay centre dressed with 4 Doric pilasters, north door derived from Castle Howard; altered 1811, 1949, 1974.

Sydney Lodge, Hampshire
4m SE of Southampton
Sir John Soane, 1789-98. South and east elevations with mathematical tiles, rest white brick. Inside, fine oval staircase, library with ceiling in form of depressed cross vault.

Tardebigge, Hereford and Worcester
2m SE of Bromsgrove
St Bartholomew's Church, 1777 by Francis Hiorne. Classical body with Adamish details, tower furnished with tall spire.

Tattingstone Wonder, Suffolk
5m S of Ipswich
Extraordinary folly-cum-farmhouse, *c*1790, with one elevation treated as church with tower.

Tatton Park, Cheshire
2m N of Knutsford
1785-91 by Samuel Wyatt; completed and modified by Lewis W. Wyatt 1807-25. Plain neo-classical mansion with giant Corinthian portico, tripartite windows under blank arches. Inside, dining room in rococo manner of *c*1740-50.

In grounds, buildings including version of Choragic Monument of Lysicrates, Athens, by William Cole *c*1820.

Taymouth Castle, Tayside
5m SW of Aberfeldy
1806-10 by Archibald and James Elliot. Early Scottish picturesque Gothic. Most impressive feature is gigantic Gothic stair hall. House enlarged 1818-28 by William Atkinson and 1838-9 by J.G. Graham.

Teigh, Leicestershire
4m N of Oakham
Holy Trinity Church, C13 tower but nave of 1782 by George Richardson; collegiate interior.

Temple Newsam
See Leeds.

Tenterden, Kent
Unitarian Chapel, East Cross, humble brick exterior, inside good woodwork of 1746.

Town Hall, High Street, dated 1790, plain with veranda reaching across pavement.

19-21 High Street, late C18 clad in red mathematical tiles, white wood quoins, shallow modillion cornice. **114, 116, 120, 121, 123, 124-30** all more or less entirely timber-framed, clapboard-clad, late C18. Also in High Street, **East Hill House,** *c*1780, front with red mathematical tiles. In middle of façade virtuoso display by builder: wide door with pediment decorated with little Gothic crockets, above this on 1st floor Venetian window with moulded frieze and rusticated arch, on 2nd floor round window. **Craythorne House,** *c*1790, 3 wide bays faced with wood blocks cut to look like rusticated ashlar. **West Well,** dated 1711 with rainwater head on east side dated 1718, centre windows closely grouped beneath pediment with tapering pilasters.

8-11 East Cross, tall late-C18 tile-hung terrace. Also in East Cross, **Yew Tree House** and **Miriam House,** almost a pair with mathematical tile cladding, late C18. **No. 27,** timber-framed and clad with timber marked to look like coursed ashlar. **29 (The White House),** *c*1770 with Ionic pedimented doorcase flanked by Venetian windows. **35 (School House),** red mathematical tiles, *c*1785.

Chestnut House, Smallhythe Road, early-C18 front. In same road, **The Cedars,** early C18, with full-height contemporary brick bow with battlements, showing influence of Vanbrugh's castle style.

Homewood, Ashford Road, dated 1766.

Terling Place, Essex
3m W of Witham
Graeco-Palladian box built 1772-8 to designs of John Johnson. Ionic portico to garden front. Long, curving wings added 1818-21 by Thomas Hopper, who also created entrance front, library and staircase and - especially good - magnificent Greek revival double-height saloon with Parthenon frieze by J. Henning.

Tetbury, Gloucestershire
4m NW of Malmesbury
St Mary's Church, medieval tower, but nave 1771-81 by Francis Hiorne is early example of relatively correct antiquarian Gothic. Inside, clustered columns with cast-iron shafts, plaster vaults.

Tewkesbury, Gloucestershire
Swan Hotel, High Street, imposing building with façade of *c*1780 incorporating 1st-floor Venetian window over large arch. In **Barton Street,** pair of houses, *c*1780, one with pair of Venetian windows, other with 4 tripartite windows.

Some good **houses** in **High Street** including **39-40,** with pairs of Venetian windows on 1st and 2nd floor over arch; and **150,** *c*1770-80, 3 storeys, 1 bay, all windows Venetian.

Thame, Oxfordshire
Spread Eagle, Corn Market, magnificent inn of *c*1740 with brick pilasters.

91 High Street, *c*1750, with decorated brick façade. Also in High Street, **Hampden House,** mid-C18 with central canted bay window on 1st floor flanked by pair of Venetian windows.

Moat House, 18 Upper High Street, mainly C18 with handsome Doric doorcase. Inside, magnificent carved wooden rococo fireplace of *c*1750.

Thame Park. Built on site of C12 Cistercian abbey, present house now has 2 wildly contrasting façades: west of C18 uniformity, south of sprawling late-medieval asymmetry. Georgian portion designed *c*1745, in restrained manner, by William Smith. Inside, hall lavishly decorated with rococo ceiling, walls festooned with swags of fruit and flowers, doors with pediments on carved brackets.

Thaxted, Essex
6m SE of Saffron Walden
Swan Hotel, late C18; 9 bays.

Clarence House, near church, dated 1715 on hopper; acutely-arched segmental windows. Segmental-pedimented Corinthian doorcase.

Theale, Berkshire
5m E of Reading
Holy Trinity Church, 1820-22 by E.W. Garbett; in pioneering Early English style inspired by Salisbury Cathedral. Tower by John Buckler, 1827.

Thirsk, North Yorkshire
Fleece Hotel, Market Place, with Gothic-detailed canted bay, dated 1791.

Some good C18 **houses** in **Kirkgate,** leading to **Thirsk Hall,** built 1730, enlarged and wings added 1771-3 by John Carr.

Thorndon Hall, Essex
2m SE of Brentwood
Large, designed 1764 by James Paine; giant 6-columned Corinthian portico over rusticated ground floor; quadrant colonnades connecting main block with pavilions. Gutted 1878, rebuilt.

Thornham Hall, Norfolk
4m NE of Hunstanton
Front with arched centre window topped by Diocletian; wings; all *c*1790.

Tissington Hall, Derbyshire
4m N of Ashbourne
Jacobean house with C18 embellishments, including mid-C18 Gothic fireplace in hall based on design in Batty Langley's *Ancient Architecture Restored*, 1741.

Tiverton, Devon
St George's Chapel, John James, 1714-33.

Tobermory, Strathclyde
On Isle of Mull
Custom House and **Inn** for the British Fisheries Society, 1789 by Robert Mylne.

Toddington Manor, Gloucestershire
9m NE of Cheltenham
Amateur, though accurately detailed, neo-Perpendicular mansion built 1820-35 to designs of owner, C. Hanbury-Tracy.

Tonbridge, Kent
Rose and Crown Hotel, East Street, c1730-40; long, low front, large porch.
Ferox Hall, High Street, c1750. Giant pilasters frame façade and mark centre bay. Porch on stone Doric columns. Inside, 2-storey staircase hall.

Torquay, Devon
Late-Regency resort created almost single-handed by J.T. Harvey for Sir Lawrence Palk, inspired by Brighton or Cheltenham.
Harvey's designs include **Higher Terrace,** c1811; **Park Place; Park Crescent, Vaughan Parade,** c1830; and **Beacon Terrace.**
Hesketh Crescent, the most ambitious development, designed by J.T. and W. Harvey, completed 1848.

Totnes, Devon
Theatre, 1707, 28 High Street, retaining shell of auditorium, but only stage survives inside. Masks of Comedy and Tragedy over 1st-floor windows. Adjacent **house,** contemporary, with giant pilasters. In **Back Lane** a delightful Gothic house with canted oriels, c1760-80.

Tottenham Park, Wiltshire
5m SE of Marlborough
Designed by Lord Burlington, 1721 onward; wings added c1730; house enlarged and remodelled by Thomas Cundy 1823-6. Much altered.

Towcester, Northamptonshire
Sponne House (formerly **Talbot Inn**), Watling Street, c1710 but with later-C18 additions including porch and pedimented Venetian window. Also in Watling Street, **157,** c1725; **Post Office,** with projecting pedimented centre, dated 1799.

Trafalgar House, Wiltshire
5m SE of Salisbury
Built 1733, originally called **Standlynch;** owner's sister was married to Roger Morris, who designed centre of present house in conventional Burlingtonian/Palladian style. Inside, fine double-height hall, a cube room; and stair with Jonesian ceiling. John Wood the Younger added wings in 1766. In about the same year Nicholas Revett added porch; early example of Greek revival with columns based on C4 BC columns of Temple of Apollo at Delos.

Tranent, Lothian
George Stiel's Hospital (now **St Joseph's School**), 1822 by William Burn. Greek Ionic.

Trawscoed Mansion, Dyfed
6m SE of Aberystwyth
C17-19 house with late-C18 wing, with Ionic portico on either side. Inside, magnificent library.

Trefecca, Powys
6m NE of Brecon
Trefecca College, c1751, Strawberry Hill Gothic in style, crudely executed but early.

Tregothnan, Cornwall
2m SE of Truro
Tudor Gothic mansion of 1816-18 by William Wilkins the Younger. Interior classical, except Gothic staircase. Extension of 1842 by Lewis Vulliamy.

Trelissick, Cornwall
3m S of Truro
Impressive neo-classical mansion of 1824 by Peter Frederick Robinson. North front with 1-storey tetrastyle Greek Doric colonnade. South front with giant Ionic portico based on Erechtheion.

Tremadog, Gwynedd
1m N of Porthmadog
Model coaching town laid out for, and named after, William Madocks, 1805-12.
Behind Market Square, off Church Street, **Church,** 1806, Gothic, with delicately detailed Gothic arch to churchyard.
In Church Street, **Peniel Chapel,** 1811.
Market Square with roughly uniform 2-storey houses of coursed rubble dominated by taller **Market Hall** with arcaded ground floor, Coade stone keystones.

Trowbridge, Wiltshire
Town Bridge, 1777 by local builder Esau Reynolds. Beside it, domed **lockup** of 1758.
Major examples of early-C18 West Country baroque in Fore Street, including **Midland Bank,** c1730, with centre emphasized with Tuscan columns to door, windows above embellished with Corinthian columns supporting segmental pediment; also **Lloyds Bank,** c1730, with 1st-floor window heads alternating between flat cornices and segmental pediments, with triangular pediment in centre – 'so grand it recalls Genoa,' said Pevsner.
In **The Parade,** 4 imposing C18 ashlar **merchants' houses.** One 5-bay house, c1730, has door embellished with Tuscan columns forming composition with Corinthian-columned window above. Another, **Parade House,** with 3-bay pediment. Next to this, late-C18 house with heavily rusticated ground floor.
Westcroft, British Row, fine house dated 1744; 3-bay pediment, central Venetian window.
Bellefield House, Hilperton Road, c1793.

Truro, Cornwall
St John's Church, 1827-8 by Philip Sambell, Grecian.
Assembly Room, Theatre, now offices, 1772, by Christpher Ebdon. 3 bays, 2 storeys with full-width pediment, ground floor arched and originally open.
Infirmary, 1799, Calenick Street.
In **Boscawen Street** and especially **Lemon Street,** both begun 1794, large groups of plain ashlar 3-storey houses making fine street vista.

250 / *Georgian Buildings*

Prince's House, 1737, and **Mansion House,** c1755, both in Prince's Street and both by Thomas Edwards.

Trehaverne House, Kenwyn Road, early C18.

The Parade, Malpas Road, early-C19 group.

In Strangeways Terrace, 4-bay early-C19 **houses** with recessed entrance blocks.

Tunbridge Wells, Kent

Holy Trinity Church, Church Road, 1827–9 by Decimus Burton in thin Gothic manner.

Behind The Pantiles on **Strawson's, Corn Exchange,** built as **theatre** 1801–2, Greek Doric. Adjacent, **Royal Sussex and Victoria Hotel,** stuccoed, with giant pilasters, c1820. **7 The Pantiles,** 2-bay, 3-storey clapboard building with late-C18 shop and 1st-floor bay, dated 1768. **39–41,** house of c1730. **48** clad with board to look like rusticated stone blocks. **58–60** also with wood rustication, as **62** with canted bay.

Mount Sion, begun late C18, tile-hung.

Calverley Park Estate, laid out 1828 by Decimus Burton. Italianate villas disposed in serpentine layout. **Calverley Park Crescent,** c1830, 17 houses with continuous ground-floor verandas.

Tweedmouth, Northumberland
Across estuary from Berwick upon Tweed

Bridge Hotel, handsome provincial-style classical building of c1760, with 3-bay pedimented centre supported on ground-floor Tuscan colonnade.

Twizell Castle, Northumberland
9m SW of Berwick upon Tweed

Fantastic Gothic castle on the Tweed by James Nisbet, c1770; now a ruin.

Twyford House, Hampshire
3m S of Winchester

Early C18; front with 3 narrow middle windows. Rear elevation has 3 2-storey late-C18 bays.

In garden, small **summer house** with round-headed rusticated door and narrow windows.

Tyninghame House, Lothian
4m W of Dunbar, across Tyne Mouth

Early and excellent baronial-style mansion, 1829–30 by William Burn

Tyringham House, Buckinghamshire
2m NW of Newport Pagnell

Designed by Sir John Soane, 1793–7. Rectangular in plan with shallow bows in centre of south-east and north-west fronts. On south-east, bow ringed by free-standing Ionic columns which originally led to vestibule containing 4 Greek Doric columns supporting shallow groin vaults. Ground floor remodelled in C20.

Lodge by Soane, 1793; neo-classical.

Ugbrooke Park, Devon
4m NE of Newton Abbot

By Robert Adam, 1763–8, castellated; part of asymmetrical composition incorporating older house.

Ullapool, Highland

Town founded 1788 by Commissioners for Annexed Estates and British Fisheries Society; mostly 2-storey harled terraces.

Underley Hall, Cumbria
10m SE of Kendal

George Webster, 1825–8, in Jacobean revival manner. Enlarged 1872.

Uttoxeter, Staffordshire

White Hart Hotel, Carter Street, C18, with porch spanning pavement.

In Church Street, **Manor House,** c1760, 3-bay pediment embellished with 3 urns, pedimented door; **Jervis House,** with pair of canted bays.

Ven House, Somerset
2m NE of Sherborne

Designed by Nathaniel Ireson c1730, incorporating west elevation of 1698–1700; applied pilasters, segmental pedimented door to garden front. Wings, conservatory, redecorations 1835 by Decimus Burton.

Virginia Water, Berkshire
2m SW of Egham

'Temple of Augustus': ruins composed by Sir Jeffry Wyatville, 1826–9, from antique fragments brought from Leptis Magna, North Africa.

The Vyne, Hampshire
4m N of Basingstoke

House extended by John Webb 1654–6, with spectacular staircase of c1760 by John Chute. (National Trust)

Wadworth Hall, South Yorkshire
3m NW of Tickhill

Designed c1750 by James Paine in powerful, romantic mood. 3 very wide bays, doorway with broken pediment, Venetian 1st-floor centre window. Garden front flanked by 2 pedimented, rusticated arches.

Wakefield, West Yorkshire

St John's Church, St John's Square, 1791–5 by Charles Watson. Neo-classical.

St James's Church, Thornes, 1829–31 by Samuel Sharp. Grecian.

Court House, Wood Street, by Charles Mountain, 1807–10; Greek Doric portico. Also in Wood Street, **Mechanics' Institute** (now **Public Buildings**), 1820; Grecian.

In **St John's Square** and **St John's North,** uniform brick terraces of c1800; in **South Parade,** 3-storey terraces of c1775–1800.

Kettlethorpe Hall, Barnsley Road/Standbridge Lane, dated 1727, in Franco-Prussian style. Ground floor has 7 serpentine-pedimented windows curving in a disparate row.

Wakefield Lodge
See Potterspury.

Wallingford, Oxfordshire

St Peter's Church, nave and tower 1760–69, with slender Gothic spire of 1776 by Sir Robert Taylor.

Friends' Meeting House, Castle Street, simple brick cottage of 1724.

Former **Lamb Hotel,** High Street, early C18.

Calleva House, High Street, c1725. Centre bay framed by 2-storey brick Doric pilasters which rise from ground-floor pedestals; corners of house defined in similar way.

West side of **St Leonard's Square,** c1800.

Wallington Hall, Northumberland
10m W of Morpeth

South and north fronts c1735–53 by Daniel Garrett; Palladian.

Rothley Castle, folly 3 miles away by Garrett.

Bridge at edge of grounds, 1755 by James Paine.

Walsall, West Midlands
St Matthew's Church, medieval, remodelled 1820-21 by Francis Goodwin. Altered 1877, 1951; but Goodwin's iron window tracery, iron Perpendicular arcade piers and playful Gothic ceiling survive.

St Mary's Roman Catholic Church, Vicarage Walk, 1825-37 by Joseph Ireland, Grecian.

Warbrook House, Hampshire
5m SW of Wokingham
Extraordinary house designed in 1724 by John James for his own occupation, reflecting his belief that architectural beauty may be achieved by the 'greatest plainness'. Façade embellished with implied giant order consisting of white pilaster strips rising to completely plain horizontal 'cornice'.

Wardour Castle, Wiltshire
5m NE of Shaftesbury
Designed by James Paine, 1770-76, in refined, inventive and highly original Palladian manner. 9-bay south front, 2 storeys over rusticated ground floor with 3-bay central pediment on 6 Corinthian columns. Entrance front astylar with central Venetian window. Main rooms on 1st floor, connected to ground floor by magnificent top-lit circular staircase. Rooms of *piano nobile* decorated in delicate rococo/neo-classical style. Now Cranborne Chase School.

Ware, Hertfordshire
27 Baldock Street, early C18.
High Street contains several good C18 houses, such as **No. 67** of *c*1750; but most notable feature is series of C18 brick and clapboard **gazebos** overlooking river in gardens of High Street houses.

Amwell House, Hertford Road, *c*1730, with projecting 2-storey wings of *c*1760.

Grotto, Scott's Road, built *c*1770, small in scale but complex, with passages and chambers lined with flint, shells, quartz, bits of glass; small 2-light Gothic windows; 1 room with central pillar like Gothic chapter house.

Wareham, Dorset
Almshouses, East Street, 1741, with bold brick rustication that makes them look earlier.

Centre of town rebuilt after fire in 1762: brick terraces with deep dressings to windows, usually of red brick. Especially good examples in North Street, e.g. **11-12**.

Red Lion Hotel, on corner of South and West Streets, white brick with red brick dressings; opposite, **house** of red brick with white dressings.

Black Bear, South Street, excellent inn of *c*1800, 3 storeys, full-height bows each side of columned porch surmounted by black bear. Opposite, **Manor House,** dated 1712, a fine baroque composition. Also good brick houses of *c*1762 in **South Street** and **West Street.** In South Street, excellent bow **shop-front** of *c*1810.

47-9 North Street, *c*1810, with shared pedimented doorcase with semicircular fanlight.

Warminster, Wiltshire
New Meeting House, Common Close, 1798; C19 additions.

St Boniface College, Church Street, at core a house of 1796 by Joseph Glascodine.

Bath Arms Hotel, Market Place, rebuilt 1744.

14 East Street, dated 1767, astylar Venetian windows on 1st floor, tripartites above.

24 High Street, pilastered pedimented doorway topped by pilastered Venetian window.

Portway House, Portway, *c*1740. Centre emphasized with 2 tiers of pilasters and pediment.

Craven House, Ash Walk, 2 canted bay windows, Gibbs door; **32 Silver Street** also with Gibbs door; pilastered Venetian window above, central pediment crowning 7-bay façade.

Byne House, Church Street, dated 1755, with central Venetian window.

Warrington, Cheshire
Holy Trinity Church, Sankey Street, *c*1760, in manner of Gibbs with block surrounds to windows. Inside, 3 galleries carried on plinths supporting Corinthian columns. Tower of 1862.

Town Hall (formerly **Bank Hall**), Sankey Street, by James Gibbs, 1750. 9 bays wide with 3-bay pediment supported by Composite columns on rusticated base. Entrance on 1st floor reached by grand staircase. Good interior with pair of matching stairs in early-Palladian style. Magnificent **stable,** with rusticated, pedimented centre.

Warrington Academy, Bridge Street, *c*1755.

8 and **11 Academy Street** built 1760 as tutors' houses for Academy.

3 Winwick Street, 5 bays, pedimented door; **31,** 5 bays with 3-bay pediment.

25-9 Stanley Street, good C18 group.

84-6 Bold Street, detached; 86 of *c*1780 with 3-bay pediment.

Warwick, Warwickshire
St Nicholas's Church, Banbury Road. Tower and spire by Thomas Johnson in fairly convincing Gothic manner; nave 1779-80 by Thomas Johnson and Job Collins, with ingenious pyramidal roof.

Shire Hall, Northgate Street, by Sanderson Miller, 1754-8; Palladian, ashlar, with 3-bay pediment supported by engaged Corinthian columns.

The Shire Hall (foreground) 1754-8 by Sanderson Miller, and the County Gaol, 1779-82 by Thomas Johnson, in Northgate Street, Warwick. The gaol is an advanced neo-classical design with a screen of engaged baseless Greek Doric columns set along its façade.

Inside, pair of octagonal courts with rococo plaster domes and Corinthian columns.

County Gaol, adjacent to Shire Hall, 1779-82 by Johnson in austere neo-classical manner; 3-bay pediment and full-height baseless Greek Doric engaged columns set as screen along façade.

Former **Court House,** Jury Street, 1725-8 by Francis Smith. Arched ground-floor windows, Doric pilasters between 1st-floor windows, wall surface decorated entirely with rustication.

Judge's Lodging, Northgate Street, by Henry Hakewill, 1814. Neo-classical front.

Gasworks, Wallace Street, 1822, 11-bay stuccoed façade flanked by octagon pavilions.

Abbotsford House, 10 Market Place, 1714, attributed to Smith; giant pilasters.

Warwick Arms Hotel, High Street, *c*1790, neo-classical.

Good Georgian houses in Northgate Street, especially **Nos. 2, 4, 6,** 2-storey terrace of *c*1725 divided by thick pilaster strips which mark extra-thick fire-proof party walls.

8 Castle Street, *c*1720.

10 Church Street, *c*1780; 5-bay, 2-storey ashlar house with open-pedimented centre containing large round-headed tripartite window. Paired pilasters between 1st-floor windows.

28 Jury Street, *c*1775, pedimented frontispiece.

In Wallace Street, **worsted mill** and **master's house,** 1796.

Wedderburn Castle, Borders
In Duns
Designed by Robert Adam, built 1771-5 by James Nisbet. 9 bays, 3 storeys with 4-storey octagonal tower. Castellated, but all windows classical with drip-mould surrounds.

Weedon, Northamptonshire
4m SE of Daventry
Royal Ordnance Depot, begun 1803 as centre of command and royal refuge in case of French invasion; site was chosen as farthest point from any coast.

Originally there were Royal Pavilion and Cavalry Barracks, both demolished.

Surviving are 8 **barracks and warehouse blocks** facing each other in 2 rows of 4 across spur of Grand Union Canal. All red brick, 2 storeys; centrally placed entrances framed by stone Doric pilasters and entablatures. Ground floors lit by round-headed windows set in blank arcades; originally for storage or stabling. 1st floors were barracks. 4 south blocks stand on slope and have 3-storey rear elevations with vaulted, stone-built ground floors, treated externally with vermiculated rustication.

Across canal west and east of the blocks, 2 elegant yellow brick **watergates,** both containing portcullis which could be lowered (one still works) to prevent entry by water into depot.

Beyond western watergate, 12 barrel-vaulted brick **powder magazines,** built in pairs and separated by brick buildings full of sand.

Wellingborough, Northamptonshire
Friends' Meeting House, St John's Street, 1819.

Hatton House, Broad Green, late C18.

Leighton House, High Street, early C19, doorcase and windows with alternating rustication.

61-2 Oxford Street, early C19 with shared door surround. **West End House,** Oxford Street, late C18 with good array of Venetian windows.

Wellington, Shropshire
All Saints' Church, George Steuart 1790; basilica plan. Neo-classical west façade with 3 tall arches containing lunettes and Tuscan pilasters. Square tower, like lower stage of St Martin-in-the-Fields, supporting shallow dome.

Wells-next-the-Sea, Norfolk
House in Standard Road, C18, with huge Venetian window in centre rising double-height into 2nd floor; below, pedimented porch.

Wentworth Castle, South Yorkshire
2m SW of Barnsley
Formerly **Stainworth Hall.** Core of house *c*1670; east wing of *c*1710-20 built to Franco-Prussian influenced baroque design of German engineer Johann Bodt. Interior of *c*1724 in Anglo-Palladian manner of James Gibbs. South front, Palladian, 1759-64 by Charles Ross.

In grounds, **Stainborough Castle,** *c*1740, Gothic; Ionic **rotunda,** 1739; Gothic **umbrello.**

Wentworth Woodhouse, South Yorkshire
3m W of Rawmarsh
Really 2 large houses built back to back, of different dates, with different façades, separate plans and different levels. West front *c*1725-35, baroque with extremely lavish details. East front by Henry Flitcroft, begun 1734, in a pure Palladian form inspired by Colen Campbell's Wanstead. Wings by John Carr, 1782-4. Inside, marble hall, 1750-75, inspired by hall at Houghton and Queen's House, Greenwich. Staircase *c*1760, perhaps by Robert Adam.

The marble hall at Wentworth Woodhouse, South Yorkshire, begun 1750 and inspired by the halls at Colen Campbell's Houghton, Norfolk, and Inigo Jones's Queen's House, Greenwich.

Keppel's Column, huge Tuscan column of 1778 by Carr.

Rockingham Mausoleum, 1788 by Carr; 2-storey square tower topped by colonnaded drum.

At Lady Rockingham's Farm, **barn** of 1742-4 by Flitcroft.

Werrington, Devon
St Mary's Church, c1740, like Gothic garden pavilion; very curious.

West Dean Park, West Sussex
5m N of Chichester
Built 1804 by James Wyatt, mildly asymmetrical composition in simple late-medieval Gothic style. Much altered in 1893 by George & Peto.

West Malling, Kent
5m W of Maidstone
Malling Abbey, founded in C11, became from 1740 to 1764 the toy of Frazer Honeywood, who built himself c1745 a house among, and out of, its ruins. It incorporated medieval windows which dictated Gothic character of whole building, but was also one of earliest manifestations of C18 Gothic revival.

In High Street, early-C18 **Street House;** C18 **Vicarage,** with Gothic blank arcading; **Arundel House,** mid-C18; and **Connaught House,** c1800, upper floor faced with wood blocks grooved to imitate masonry and with large Venetian window, and contemporary shop-front below.

In Swan Street, **Cade House,** c1800. Also **Went House,** c1720, finest house in town: excellent brickwork, including deep, dentilled brick cornice, panelled parapet; fine interior. Opposite the house, **cascade** under Gothic arch, constructed 1810.

Weston, Avon
NW edge of Bath
Portis College, 1825-7 by S.F. and D.F. Page. Neo-Grecian almshouses with central chapel.

Weston Park, Staffordshire
7m E of Oakengates
In grounds, **Temple of Diana** and **Roman Bridge,** 1765 by James Paine.

At Home Farm, massive **barn** with Palladian terminal towers, 1768, probably by James Paine.

West Wycombe, Buckinghamshire
W edge of High Wycombe
St Laurence's Church, built 1763 for Sir Francis Dashwood, looks more like a ballroom than a church. 'Nave' 60 by 40ft in plan, surrounded by 16 giant Corinthian columns supporting rich entablature. Ceiling flat, painted to imitate coffering. Never pewed, but originally furnished with seats covered in green cloth. Other church furnishings among oddest in Britain. Font decorated with snake writhing up column in pursuit of 4 doves. Tower surmounted by hollow gilt ball furnished with seats.

West Wycombe Park (National Trust), early C18 in origin, segmental windows. Remodelled under Dashwood's control 1750-80. House now long, irregular, each side treated individually. West side dominated by deep Ionic portico 6 unfluted columns wide, 2 deep, designed by Nicholas Revett supposedly 1770-71 and based on Temple of Bacchus at Teos, measured by Revett 1764-6. On east front asymmetrically placed deep Tuscan portico of 1754-6. North front 11 bays, 3 centre and 2 end bays emphasized by rustication and framed by Ionic columns. Most impressive is south front, c1760 and probably to designs of John Donovell. Remodelled in form of deep double colonnade with Tuscan columns on ground floor, Corinthian columns above rising through 2 storeys to eaves level; centre breaks forward into tetrastyle portico. Some excellent interiors: mahogany staircase with marquetry; Blue Drawing Room with coved ceiling; Tapestry Room with fine Pompeian ceiling.

In grounds, buildings include **Round Temple** with fan-shaped Tuscan portico; **Temple of the Four Winds** inspired by Tower of the Winds in Athens, probably designed by Revett c1770-75. Also by Revett, **Island Temple,** 1778-80, with 6 tall Ionic columns to curved east front; **Temple of Daphne,** open with unfluted Ionic columns; **Temple of St Crispin,** sham chapel of flint with tower. **Mausoleum,** hexagonal, open to sky, entered through triumphal arch; built 1763-4, probably to designs of John Bastard. Nearby are **caves,** formed by Dashwood 1750-52, with pretty entrance façade with Gothic aperture, pointed niches and crowning gables. **Stable,** 1767-8 by Robert Adam.

On edge of West Wycombe Park, **Dower House** (originally **Rectory**), designed 1763 by Nicholas Revett. Curious flint structure flanked by pair of 1-storey wings with gable pediments looking away from centre block; central door embellished with large-scale Greek Ionic portico.

Weymouth, Dorset
St Mary's Church, St Mary Street, 1815 by James Hamilton. Neo-classical, with 3-bay pediment.

Royal Dorset Yacht Club, built c1799 as library and assembly room.

Gloucester Row, on seafront, good terrace, c1790, with splendid wrought-iron balcony becoming covered loggia in centre. Hamilton architect of south part.

Several early-C19 **terraces,** often with shallow-curved bow windows. Examples are **Royal Terrace, Royal Crescent, Belvidere, Waterloo Place, Brunswick Terrace, Devonshire Buildings, Pulteney Buildings** and **St Alban Street.**

At north end of St Mary Street, large bow-ended, stuccoed **shops and houses,** c1810.

1 mile to west of town, **Belfield House,** Buxton Road, designed 1785 by John Crunden in Adam manner. 3-bay Ionic portico flanked by Venetian windows. Inside, octagonal room.

Whaddon Hall, Buckinghamshire
4m W of Bletchley
Greek revival house of c1820. Entrance front with screen of Ionic columns copied from Erechtheion; garden front with semicircular bow in centre.

Whitby, North Yorkshire
St Mary's Church, fine Norman church with magnificent box pews and galleries, mostly of 1759, and 3-decker pulpit of 1778.

St Ninian's Church, Baxtergate, 1776-8, brick front, pointed windows, pedimented gable.

Town Hall, between Church Street and Market Place, 1788 by Jonathan Pickernell, pedimented ends with Venetian windows, open ground floor.

Haggersgate House, Haggersgate, good provincial Palladian house of c1760; 5 bays, 3 storeys with 3-bay pediment, Gibbs window surrounds.

Council offices, Brunswick Street, c1795, pretty Doric door with open pediment and painted *trompe l'oeil* fanlight – a speciality of Whitby. In same street, **No. 10,** c1800. **1-3 Brunswick Terrace,** c1780-90, with pedimented Ionic doorcases reached by tall, elegant steps.

18-19 Grape Lane, 4-storey early-C18 house with rusticated ground floor, giant Ionic pilasters framing façade; some good panelled rooms; at rear single, gigantic arched window lights entire height of staircase. Similar fenestration on rear elevation of **9-11 Upgang Lane.**

St Hilda's Terrace, built after c1778, loosely uniform row of wide houses, most with pedimented doors. Good examples are **3** and **4,** one with Roman and other with Greek Ionic pilasters to doors.

12-14 Bagdale, c1780; Gibbs window surrounds.

Just outside town centre at Low Stakesby, **Airy Hill,** built 1790. Centre bay of north façade of main house Venetian, set against rusticated background. This front with 3-bay crowning pediment. To garden front, 3-bay open pediment above tripartite door.

Whitchurch, Hereford and Worcester
5m sw of Ross-on-Wye
Old Exchange, corner of High Street and St Mary Street, c1760; open arcade to ground floor.

17 Green End, c1720; façade topped by cornice; fine shell-hooded door on carved brackets.

Talbot House, Hereford Street, 3 wide bays, 3 storeys with 1-bay pediment.

Whitehaven, Cumbria
Laid out on regular grid c1680 by Sir John Lowther as part of his development of town as coal port.

St James's Church, 1752-3, closes vista down Queen Street; modest exterior but well-preserved interior of high quality.

Friends' Meeting House, Sandhills Lane, 1722.

Whitehaven Castle (now **hospital**), Robert Adam 1768-9 in his castle style.

Old **Custom House,** East Strand, c1790, attenuated pilasters framing façade.

Somerset House, Duke Street, c1760 with Gothic detail.

In **Scotch Street,** groups of mid-C18 3-storey **houses,** most with simple pedimented door surrounds, plain stone architraves around windows, rendered façades; **No. 14** c1750-60, 5 bays, centre emphasized by quoins and top balustrade.

Good mid-C18 houses in **Irish Street,** especially **7;** in Howgill Street where **7** and **10** have doors framed by Gibbs surrounds and pediments on consoles; and in Roper Street.

Queen Street also retains many C18 houses, notably **151,** 5 bays with Ionic door surround, c1730-40. Fine Venetian door c1750 in **Duke Street.**

Banack Mills, now **Dobson & Musgrave factory,** Catherine Street, c1817; cast-iron columns supporting masonry jack-arched floors.

Whittinghame House, Lothian
3m s of East Linton
By Sir Robert Smirke, 1817, in his stripped, cubic neo-Grecian manner; altered 1827 by William Burn.

Wicken, Northamptonshire
3m sw of Stony Stratford
St John the Evangelist's Church, by Thomas Prowse, started 1758, completed c1768; serious attempt at correct Gothic revival.

Widcombe Manor
See Bath.

Wigan, Greater Manchester
St John's Roman Catholic Church, Standishgate, 1819. Ashlar, octastyle Ionic colonnade along ground floor. Interior decoration by J.J. Scoles, 1834.

St Mary's Roman Catholic Church, Standishgate, 1818. Neo-Perpendicular façade, Gothic interior.

Wilbury House, Wiltshire
Begun c1708 to design of William Benson; earliest C18 attempt at neo-Jonesian/Palladian villa. Plan based on Palladio prototype, with elevation, though somewhat baroque, inspired by Webb's nearby Amesbury House (thought to be by Jones) and Wilton (hence name). Portico altered 1740; roof changed and wings added 1775.

Wilford Hall, Nottinghamshire
1m w of West Bridgford
Large, austere neo-classical house, 1781 by William Henderson (alias Anderson), Adamesque.

Willersley Castle
See Cromford.

Willey Hall, Shropshire
3m E of Much Wenlock
By Lewis Wyatt, 1812-15; one of most powerful of neo-classical houses. Outside, giant tetrastyle Corinthian portico; inside, galleried, 2-storey tunnel-vaulted hall with glazed lantern leads to oval stair. Library with apsed end.

Wilton, Wiltshire
3m w of Salisbury
Town Hall, 1738; 6 bays, with angle quoins, hooded door. Clock turret added 1889.

Some good C18 interiors in seminal mid-C17 **Wilton House,** including ceiling of c1735 by Andieu de Clermont. In grounds, **Palladian Bridge,** 1736-7 by Lord Pembroke and Roger Morris; **Triumphal Arch** and **Casino** by William Chambers, 1757-74. Wyatt added **lodge** to arch c1800.

Wimborne Minster, Dorset
In Cornmarket, former **Friendly Society** building of 1738 with now-blocked ground-floor arcade. Also 2 Georgian inns: **White Hart** and **George.**

30-31 West Street, c1735.

In West Borough several good C18 buildings of group rather than individual interest, including **Wimborne Conservative Club,** c1780. Opposite, **Tivoli Cinema,** good mid-C18 front with eared and scrolled surround to 1st-floor centre window; now much mutilated.

Dean's Court, in surprising isolation on edge of town centre. Dated 1725, brick, 2 storeys over rusticated basement with north front of 7 bays and east of 5, both with 3-bay centre breaking slightly forward. North front with Ionic pedimented door topped by window embellishment with architrave flanked by large, leafy scrolls.

Wimpole Hall, Cambridgeshire
8m sw of Cambridge
Begun *c*1640, transformed 1689–1711. Library wing added by James Gibbs 1719–21. 2-storey brick chapel added *c*1721 to design of Gibbs, painted 1724 by Sir James Thornhill in fine illusionary style. Staircase in late-C17 block also by Gibbs. South entrance front refaced 1742–5 by Henry Flitcroft, and embellished with usual Palladian motifs such as Venetian and Diocletian windows, pediments to *piano nobile* windows. Flitcroft also added 2-storey centre bay with arched central window to garden front and a wing to balance Gibbs Library block, and remodelled much of interior including Library and Long Gallery. Sir John Soane designed Ante-Library 1791–3, with bookcases linked by shallow arches adorned with plaster paterae; and, in main house, created Yellow Drawing Room, T-shaped, domed, apsed, ingeniously planned.

In grounds, some important buildings include sham **castle** designed by Sanderson Miller 1749–50, built 1772; **St Andrew's Church** designed by Flitcroft 1748–9, heavily Gothicized 1887.

Picturesque, thatched **Park Farm,** 1794 by Soane. (National Trust)

Wincanton, Somerset
Town severely damaged by fire in 1747; houses quickly reconstructed in handsome manner. Of pre-fire buildings, best are:

Greyhound Hotel, Market Place, *c*1740; round-headed archway framed by Doric pilasters; canted bay window above. Also in Market Place, **Bear Hotel,** dated 1720, with rusticated archway.

In High Street, **White Horse Hotel,** dated 1733 and rich in provincial baroque mannerisms, including tapering angle pilasters. Also on High Street, **Dolphin Hotel** with Gibbs surrounds to ground-floor windows.

Ireson House, Grant's Lane, built by Nathaniel Ireson, a provincial baroque architect, for himself *c*1726. Gibbs surrounds to some windows. Altered *c*1850.

Best examples of post-fire reconstruction are in **Market Place** and **High Street**.

Winchester, Hampshire
Former **Guildhall,** High Street, dated 1713.
In Jewry Street, at 11A, remains of **gaol** of 1805, by George Moneypenny.

St John's Hospital, High Street, by William Garbett, 1817, Gothic; altered 1831, 1833.

Southgate Hotel, Southgate Street, dated 1715 on downpipe; centre 1st-floor window with brick pilasters and segmental pediment over Doric doorcase. In same street: **Serle's House,** *c*1710–20; free-standing. Giant Doric pilasters with swelling capitals rise at corners of building and emphasize centre bay, which projects by means of 1-bay quadrant corners (like Archer's Chettle House, qv). Inside, round entrance hall; behind it, staircase starting single and returning double. **No. 12,** *c*1720, 1st-floor centre window round-arched with raised surround.

City Mill, Eastgate Street, 1744. Also in Eastgate Street, **No. 4,** C18 shop.

11 The Close, façade dated 1727, 1-bay projection containing doorway.

46 High Street, *c*1820 with 2-storey high-arched centre window embellished with Greek Ionic columns. **105,** round-headed central windows to 1st and 2nd floors, *c*1720.

Abbey House, in Abbey grounds, *c*1750–60.

Hyde Abbey House, Hyde Street, late-Georgian façade, at rear school room of 1795 by Sir John Soane.

23 St Peter's Street, central pedimented door in centre bay flanked by canted bays, *c*1760.

In **Kingsgate Street,** some good examples of Winchester speciality: **houses** with large cantilevered 1st-floor bays. Also at **28** and **86 High Street**.

108 Colebrook Street, end bays with blank elliptical arches with male and female keystones, *c*1780–90. In same street, **26,** one arch on giant pilasters, one arched window in it, stepped parapet – later-Georgian revival of Vanbrugh? **34,** 3-storey neo-classical villa, *c*1790.

26–7 St Swithin Street, early C18 with taller wings forming flanking lower composition.

12, 18 St Thomas's Street, *c*1720. **21,** early C18; middle 1st-floor windows round-arched.

Good late-C18 **shop-fronts** at **4 Chesil Street, 70 Kingsgate Street** and **57 High Street**.

Windsor, Berkshire
Royal Windsor
Windsor Castle, remodelled inside and out by Sir Jeffry Wyatville 1824–40, to create remarkable architectural expression of Romantic revival. Exterior picturesquely medieval. Interior in eclectic mix of styles: Gothic Waterloo Chamber; French rococo Grand Reception Room; late-classical Drawing Rooms.

Frogmore House, Home Park, early-C18, transformed by James Wyatt 1792: towards garden, 7-bay arcade with Tuscan columns; inside, rather 'home-made' looking Pompeian Room.

In Great Park: **Forest Lodge,** 9 bays, 2 storeys, with centre 3 bays of 3 storeys with giant pilasters to upper part. **Fort Belvedere,** triangular tower by Henry Flitcroft *c*1750, extended 1827–9 by Wyatville; inside, octagonal dining room.

Windsor town
Masonic Lodge (formerly **Free School**), Church Lane, 1725, in English baroque style.

In **High Street,** late-C18 **house** with 4 stucco reliefs of putti representing the seasons.

Park Street, a particularly complete Georgian street; notable are **23–4,** late C18 with pair of doorways with block pilasters.

Hadleigh House, Sheet Street, late C18, 5 bays, Adamesque doorway.

Pump House, on Thames below castle, in Vanbrugh's stripped, bold classical Office of Works manner, *c*1718.

Winterborne Dauntsey, Wiltshire
4m NE of Salisbury
The Grange, *c*1730, with south range and 1st-floor drawing room of *c*1800. House very urban in design; tall pilasters at angles of façade.

Wisbech, Cambridgeshire
Town Hall, North Brink, 1810 by Joseph Medworth; 3-bay pediment, rusticated arcade at ground level.

Angles Theatre, Alexandra Road, 1793; brick shell survives.

Rose and Crown Inn, Market Place, *c*1760; 7 bays, 3 storeys with 3-bay pediment.

9 Old Market, *c*1770, with 2-bay pediment; **28-9,** *c*1790, forming pair with shared pedimented door and Venetian window above. Also in Old Market, **house** dated 1723 on hopper which, with lead downpipe, is made central feature of elevation.
Peckover House, North Brink, 1727; plain front elevation with segmental-pedimented doorcase; rear with pedimented door topped by 1st-floor Venetian, 2nd-floor Diocletian window. (National Trust)
7, 8 South Brink, 8 bays, 4-bay pediment with doors in bays under each end, *c*1750.
Union Place, small, uniform brick crescent of *c*1808, all houses with pedimented wooden doorcases, as at **York Row,** 1797, and **The Crescent** of *c*1808 by Medworth.

Wiston Hall, Suffolk
6m sw of Colchester
Sir John Soane, 1791; simple 3-bay block.

Witney, Oxfordshire
Town Hall, Market Place, mid-C18; one room over open colonnade.
Blanket Hall, High Street, dated 1721; tall and narrow with full width pediment.
Fleece Hall, Church Green, C18, remodelled *c*1820, with pair of bay windows.
Angel Inn, Market Square, with central door flanked by bow windows. Also in Market Square: **4,** *c*1750; pedimented façade with 1st-floor Venetian window over tripartite door. **16,** *c*1725; pediments to both door and window above.
Old Rectory, High Street, 1723. Also in High Street: **No. 10,** *c*1790-1800 with angle pilasters. **103** has excellent door of *c*1810 with rectangular fanlight.
20 Church Green, with door-window relationship as at 4 Market Square. **22** of *c*1760. **St Mary's,** house of *c*1770.
On **Wood Green,** to north of town, some good C18 **houses,** especially **43, 45, 53.**

Wivenhoe, Essex
3m SE of Colchester
Maple House, on Quay, with trellis porch, 2-storey curved bay matching that of its neighbour, **Trinity House,** *c*1820.
Anchor House, Quay Street, also early C19.
Corner House, East Street, *c*1820.

Woburn, Bedfordshire
5m N of Leighton Buzzard
Market House, 1830 by Edward Blore. Gothic.
George Inn (now **Bedford Arms Hotel**), George Street, remodelled 1790 by Henry Holland.
High Street and **Bedford Street** lined with consistently good modest C18 houses. Particularly good **terrace** at corner of High Street and Park Street, with façades articulated with giant pilasters. Also in High Street, **Old Rectory,** *c*1760, brick with centre emphasized by pair of banded columns supporting pairs of columns above.
Woburn Abbey, 1 mile to east. House medieval in origin with much C17 work, but main (west) front 1747-61 by Henry Flitcroft in sound Palladian manner. 3-bay pedimented centre block with engaged Ionic columns on rusticated base containing arched openings. Pediments to 1st-floor windows. Façade terminated at each end by 3-storey pavilion containing 1st-floor Venetian windows topped by Diocletians. All ground floor rusticated. Inside main house, state bedroom, by Flitcroft, has ceiling with heavy octagonal coffering inspired by Wood's *Palmyra* book of 1753; state saloon, also by Flitcroft, has coved ceiling, fireplace with caryatids. South wing, and interiors including eating room and library, by Sir William Chambers 1767-72. 1788-1802 Henry Holland altered elevation to this wing and remodelled interiors. His finest room is library with screen of Corinthian columns.
Stables with columned entrance by Flitcroft.
Basin Bridge by Chambers, altered by Holland. **Conservatory** (now **Sculpture Gallery**), with Greek Ionic temple at east end, and spectacular **Chinese Dairy** of *c*1791, by Holland
Woburn Park Farm, low ranges with pediments and porticoes; 1795 by Robert Salmon.

Wollaton Hall, Nottinghamshire
Between Nottingham and Beeston
In grounds of Elizabethan house, **Camellia House,** early glazed cast-iron structure of 1823 by Jones & Clark of Birmingham and Sir Jeffry Wyatville.

Wolterton Hall, Norfolk
7m sw of Cromer
Built 1727-41, in conventional Palladian manner, to design of Thomas Ripley. Rusticated ground floor which, on south front, has (later) open arcade and balustraded walk. Main north and south fronts 7 bays with 3-bay pediments. East wing of 1828. Inside, staircase is superb example of early-Palladian architectural style of interior decoration, with internal windows like those on exterior, some even with glazing bars.

Wolverhampton, West Midlands
St John's Church, St John's Square, 1758-76 by William Baker, derived from Gibbs's St Martin-in-the-Fields, especially west tower. Block surrounds to side windows. Inside, gallery on squat pillars carrying upper colonnade.
St George's Church, Bilston Road, 1828 by James Morgan; classical.
St Peter and St Paul's Roman Catholic Church, North Street, 1827-8 by Joseph Ireland. T-plan, Grecian, Diocletian windows light tunnel-vaulted nave.
Old Grammar School, John Street, 1712-14 by Francis Smith; now two shops.
Giffard House, North Street, *c*1727, with spectacular staircase.
Old Fallings House (now **St Chad's College**), north of city centre, *c*1720; baroque.
Rock House, Old Hill, with Gibbs surround.
Park Hill, Park Drive, *c*1725 with frontispiece formed by the 3 orders rising one upon the other.

Wolverley, Hereford and Worcester
2m N of Kidderminster
Sebright School, *c*1829, probably by William Knight. Gothic-arched features dominate façade.
Wolverley House, 1749-52 by William and David Hiorne; east front with 3-storey tripartite composition topped by a pediment.

Wolverton, Buckinghamshire
Holy Trinity Church, 1810-15 by Henry Hakewill. Early example of Norman revival. Altered *c*1870.

Wood Hall, Humberside
8m NE of Kingston upon Hull
1820 by Charles Mountain, inspired by Nash's Cronkhill: asymmetrical plan, round tower; but details standard classical, not Italianate.

Woodhall Park, Hertfordshire
4m N of Hertford
Designed 1777 by Thomas Leverton. House with pedimented 1-storey wings extended in 1795 when Ionic portico added to entrance front. Excellent neo-antique interior. Especially good is staircase hall topped by dome and decorated with delicate plaster. Entrance hall decorated in Etruscan style. Print room of 1782.

Woodhouse, Shropshire
5m SW of Ellesmere
Designed by Robert Mylne, 1773-4; strikingly original portico formed by pair of Ionic columns set *in antis* with another pair in front of them to make a porch.

Woodnewton Hall, Northamptonshire
4m N of Oundle
Bizarre composition of *c*1730: 3-storey pedimented centre, and 2-storey outer bays with portions of pediment returning against higher block.

Woodstock, Oxfordshire
Town Hall, 1766 by Sir William Chambers in fine, refined mid-Palladian style. 3-bay pediment, arcaded ground floor.
Almshouse, built 1797, utilitarian.
Marlborough Arms, Oxford Road, main block *c*1730; addition of *c*1780 with Venetian windows.
Hope House, on corner of Hensington Road, *c*1720, reflects style of nearby Blenheim Palace (qv). On side wall, 3 tiers of blind recesses framed by bold stone architraves with keystones.
The Rectory, Rectory Lane, C17 house remodelled in early C18, with 2 short corner towers flanked by earlier gable. Garden front shows influence of Vanbrugh: big 2-storey feature topped with open pediment supported on deep scrolls. Below, round-arched 1st-floor window with huge keystone and large moulded imposts on moulded scrolls with guttae.

Woolley, Avon
2m N of Bath
All Saints' Church, 1761 by John Wood the Younger, with cupola and Gothic windows.

Woolton
See Liverpool.

Woolverstone Hall, Suffolk
3m S of Ipswich
Designed *c*1776 by John Johnson. Centre block has 3-bay pediment. Pair of wings with cast-iron Doric columns and decorations, 1823 by Thomas Hopper.

Wootton Wawen, Warwickshire
6m NW of Stratford-upon-Avon
Wootton Hall, 1687 with C18 alterations. Ground floor with alternating pediments to windows.
In grounds, **Roman Catholic chapel** of 1813; bold classical interior with giant pilasters to walls, and Greek Doric columns forming chancel.
Manor Farm, *c*1720, carved concave doorhood, windows still mullioned and transomed.

Worcester, Hereford and Worcester
St Nicholas's Church, The Cross, 1730-35, a fine provincial baroque design, attributed to Thomas White or Humphrey Hollins. West end baroque with segmental pediment and pilasters. Tower based on alternative Gibbs design for St Martin-in-the-Fields, published 1728.
St Swithun's Church, Church Street, 1734-6 by Edward and Thomas Woodward. Baroque; interestingly planned, combining eastern entrance with eastern altar. Interior has shallow-vaulted ceiling. Exterior of east end more Palladian, with Venetian window flanked by round-headed aisle windows, but with typical baroque freedom in spacing of flanking pilasters.
All Saints' Church, 1738-42. East end pedimented and with paired pilasters. Wren-like tower. Church built by Richard Squire, design attributed to White. Inside, Doric colonnade supports tunnel-vaulted nave.
St Martin's Church, Cornmarket, 1768-72 by Anthony Keck. Gibbs surrounds to windows, and inside, vaulting and column arrangement inspired by Gibbs's St Martin-in-the-Fields.
St Clement's Church, Henwick Road, 1822-3 by Thomas Lee and Thomas Ingleman. Early example of Normal revival. Altered 1879.
Countess of Huntingdon's Chapel, Bridport, off Deansway, 1804, enlarged 1815, with galleried interior. With minister's house, forms small court.
Guildhall, High Street, designed *c*1718 by White, built 1721-4 in rich, full-blown baroque style. 9-bay, 2-storey centre block, 3-bay centre framed by Composite pilasters and crowned by segmental pediment filled with sculpture. Lower 3-storey wings form quadrangle.
Royal Infirmary, Castle Street, by Keck 1767-70, altered 1849-55 and in C20.
Severn Bridge and approach designed by John Gwynn 1771-80.
College House, The Close, *c*1735. Gibbs surrounds to door.
Britannia House, Upper Tything, remarkably full-blooded baroque composition for *c*1725.
In **Edgar Street,** good collection of early-C18 3-storey brick houses, including **No. 3,** dated 1732; **6** looks *c*1735, with Gibbs door surround; **13,** with Venetian window occupying all 2nd floor.
In **College Precinct,** group of smaller C18 houses, **No. 7** with pedimented door of *c*1775 decorated with trelliswork.
In **Broad Street,** good C18 houses; **48** of *c*1730-40, with façade framed by quoins with common early-C18 Worcester touch: centrally placed strip of quoins in deep parapet. **61** is a prodigy: 1 bay, 4 storeys with Venetian window to each floor (except ground, a modern shop) set in relieving arches, containing Gothic glazing bars, and embellished with humorous keystones showing C18 faces peering to one side or other. Above top window, parapet curves into semicircular pediment.
In **High Street,** where it becomes The Cross, early-C18 house, with swags beneath windows.
In **Bridge Street,** 2 sides of good, generally uniform **terrace houses: 8, 9, 16, 17** still have Doric doorcases with open pediments; between 9 and 10, hopper head dated 1789.
Regency terraces in **Britannia Square, St George's Square, Lansdowne Crescent.**

Workington, Cumbria
St John's Church, Washington Street, 1822-3 by Thomas Hardwick. Tuscan portico inspired by Inigo Jones's St Paul's, Covent Garden. Tower added 1847.

Wormleybury House, Hertfordshire
3m N of Cheshunt
By Robert Mylne, 1767-9. Portico added 1781-2. Interior by Robert Adam and Angelica Kauffmann 1777-9, one of best works of period, especially entrance hall with columns and Doric aedicules; domed staircase; drawing room.

Worthing, West Sussex
St Paul's Church, Chapel Road, by John Biagio Rebecca 1812. Greek revival with tetrastyle Tuscan portico and cupola. Interior 1893.

Early-C19 terraces, mostly 3 storeys with full-height bows: **Bedford Row (8-11** with pedimented doorcases) and **Montague Place** (especially **10, 12, 13**), both 1802-5; **York Terrace** on seafront.

1-14 Ambrose Place, *c*1820, with 2-storey timber trellis balconies, 14 with a bowed front.

Liverpool Terrace, *c*1830 by Henry Cotton, presents sustained 4-storey elevation of bow fronts accented with plain ironwork; **10** with single-storey Tuscan colonnade over pavement.

The Steyne, 4-storey uniform terrace: 1-7 and 12-34 of 1807-13.

Park Crescent, 1829 by Amon Wilds, serpentine in plan, elevations packed with heavy classical detail. Crescent approached through triumphal arch embellished with 4 bearded busts under main arch, 8 caryatids under side arches.

Best individual houses are **Beach House,** east of The Steyne, stuccoed villa by Rebecca; and **The Hollies,** at junction of High Street and Little High Street, 1814.

Wrotham Park, Hertfordshire
1m S of Potters Bar
Designed 1754 by Isaac Ware; archetypal mid-Palladian house. Garden front with Ionic portico flanked by 1-storey bays with Venetian windows, and octagonal-domed corner pavilions linked by 3-bay wings. Colonnade on entrance front. Interior destroyed by fire 1883.

Wroxton, Oxfordshire
2m NW of Banbury
All Saints' Church has tower by Sanderson Miller, 1747.

Wycombe Abbey, Buckinghamshire
On Marlow Hill, High Wycombe
House remodelled 1803 by James Wyatt to form rambling Gothic mansion. Inside, Gothic hall.

Wymondham, Norfolk
Caius House, Middleton Street, dated 1746 on hopper; good provincial baroque attempt at small uniform terrace. 7 bays with pedimented 3-bay centre framed by giant Doric pilasters, matching pilasters at angles. Central Doric doorcase. Also in Middleton Street, house of *c*1745, tripartite door with Gibbs surround and pediment.

Stanfield Hall, 2½ miles east of Wymondham Abbey, 1792 by William Wilkins the Elder, in neo-Elizabethan manner. Altered 1830-35.

Wynnstay Park, Powys
10m E of Machynlleth
Round **tower** at Nant-y-Bellan by Wyatville, 1810, modelled on Tomb of Cecilia Metella on Appian Way outside Rome.

Lodge by C.R. Cockerell, 1827; with 3 rusticated arches on ground floor, recessed attic above.

Yarm, Cleveland
4m S of Stockton-on-Tees
In High Street, **Union Arms,** *c*1762; and **George and Dragon,** *c*1760 – both with large coach arches.

12-16 Market Place, uniform brick terrace, *c*1760 but still with segmental window arches and flush box sashes.

124 High Street, 4 Venetian windows, *c*1780.

Yarmouth, Isle of Wight
9m W of Newport
Town Hall, The Square, dated 1763. Ground floor arcaded and originally open.

Yester House, Lothian
5m SE of Haddington
Large, solid house built 1699-1728 by James Smith and Alexander MacGill, embellished *c*1729 by William Adam, 1789 by Robert Adam. Their work mostly confined to interiors; especially fine is saloon of 1789, with powerful coved ceiling.

York, North Yorkshire
Mansion House, St Helen's Square, built 1726-33, very important provincial design by William Etty. Composition derived from Jones/Webb Queen's Gallery, Somerset House, published in *Vitruvius Britannicus*, 1715. 5 bays, 3 storeys with 3-bay pediment, giant Ionic pilasters on arcaded, rusticated ground floor. 1st-floor windows pedimented. Inside, fine staircase; on 1st floor and running full width of front, double-height state room of 1732-3.

Assembly Rooms, Blake Street, designed 1731 by Lord Burlington; inspired by Palladio's design for Egyptian hall, in turn based on written description of Vitruvius. Result at York is basilica with ratio of 1:3 in plan, containing 18 columns along each long side and 6 on each short side, rising straight from floor to a rich entablature. Behind columns, narrow aisle; above entablature, pilastered attic storey. Beside this hall, Burlington built smaller hall and domed rotunda room. Main façade of building, originally based on Palladio's account of Roman baths, and with apsidal arcaded entrance, was rebuilt in Greek revival style by J.P. Pritchett, 1828.

Assize and **Crown Court,** beside castle, by John Carr 1773-7. Ashlar, 2-storey palace front with raised ground-floor terrace, central pediment. Inside, domed courtroom. Opposite, matching **Female Prison** (now **museum**), also by Carr 1780-83; end bays added by Peter Atkinson 1802.

Bootham Park Hospital (former **County Lunatic Asylum**), by Carr 1772-7, altered 1814.

Workhouse, Marygate, 1792 by Thomas Atkinson.

Yorkshire Museum, 1827-30 by William Wilkins the Younger. Greek Doric portico.

Bar Convent, Blossom Street, begun 1765 to designs of Thomas Atkinson. Chapel of 1765-9; excellent design with dome supported on 8 Ionic columns.

Judge's Lodging, 9 Lendal, remarkable composition of *c*1718. Brick, 3 wide bays, 3 storeys over basement; tripartite front door with Ionic columns and mask keystone set against swagged stone surround. Elevation articulated by 2-storey giant angle pilasters without capitals. Inside, giant Corinthian columns in entrance hall, vaulted 1st-floor passage, and staircase in which each baluster is an Ionic column. Also in Lendal, **14-18,** 3-storey terrace, *c*1720.

2, 3, 4, 4A Precentor's Court, early-C18 terrace, most windows mullioned and transomed.

17-19 Aldwark, *c*1720, brick; 17 has excellent pedimented door with Gibbs surround.

The Old Residence, 6 Minster Yard, *c*1735; centre emphasized by consoled door surround linked to 1st-floor centre window, which has a pediment supported on consoles.

62 Low Petergate, *c*1725; façade topped by full Doric entablature; later Doric porch and wings. Also in Low Petergate, **65** has good, though mutilated, late-C18 shop-front.

Cumberland Row, 3-9 New Street, uniform terrace of 1746.

47 Bootham, 1752 by Carr. Most unusually, detached cornices sitting above brick arches to ground and 1st-floor windows.

Peasholme House, St Saviour's Place, 1752 by Carr. Brick, 5 bays, 3 storeys with central Ionic pedimented doorcase, façade framed with quoins, deep eaves cornice, keystones to windows.

Castlegate House, 26 Castlegate, 1762 by Carr: 5-bay, 3-storey brick front with 1st-floor windows strikingly composed in blank arcade linked by imposts, a device that became common in 1820s. Pedimented Doric porch. Garden elevation 7 bays with pair of 3-storey canted bays framing 1-bay centre, dominated by 1st-floor Venetian window lighting staircase.

Fairfax House, 27 Castlegate, built *c*1755, roofed 1760, dated on timber (information from Francis Johnson), fitted out internally by Carr, *c*1762. Brick, 5 bays, 3 storeys, 3-bay pediment; ground-floor windows with Gibbs surrounds, stone pedimented doorcase and quoins to corners. Interior in rich provincial Palladian style, but with some spectacular light rococo plasterwork, particularly dining-room, saloon and drawing-room ceilings; staircase hall has Palladian compartment ceiling and rococo panels on wall. Staircase with rich wrought-iron balustrade.

20 St Andrewgate, *c*1780 by Thomas Atkinson for himself; imposing 3-storey, 5-bay composition in brick with all-embracing pediment. Windows plain except for 1st-floor centre with stone surround. Pedimented door set in blank arch.

In Micklegate, **Queen's Hotel** is part of 10-bay pair of houses, *c*1730. **52-4,** 1757, attributed to Carr; angle quoins, 3-bay centre with pediment, quoins and, unusually, full Doric entablature at eaves and cornice (cf 62 Low Petergate). Pedimented door in end bay. Good interior. **86,** *c*1725, 5 bays, 3 storeys; excellent staircase; abstracted baroque treatment to doors in hall, where classical elements are reduced to flat planes. **Micklegate House (88-90),** 1753 by John Carr. 7 bays, 3 storeys; 3-bay pedimented centre and end bays break forward. Corinthian doorcase. **118,** *c*1730.

16-22 St Saviourgate, uniform terrace of *c*1740-45, generally similar to Cumberland Row (see above) but with unusual elongated cyma reversa bracket eaves cornice. Doors enriched with delicate neo-classical ornament of *c*1800. **24,** 3-bay red brick house, dated 1763 on hopper, with elegant neo-classical Regency door surround. **26,** built *c*1725, with bolection-moulded door surround. **29-31,** 2 storeys, dated on hoppers 1735 and 1739 respectively.

37 Stonegate, especially good shop of *c*1810; **46,** bow-window shop-front, *c*1810.

3 Gillygate, large yellow brick house of *c*1797, elevation embellished with pair of Venetian windows topped by pair of Diocletian windows.

11-12 High Ousegate, 9-bay, 3-storey provincial baroque composition which looks *c*1710 but carries hopper dated 1758. Centre bay, framed by crudely formed giant Ionic pilasters, contains pedimented 1st-floor window and remains of rusticated ground-floor arch. **13-14** (originally one house), looks *c*1710-20 but hopper dated 1763. 5-bay, 3-storey composition, also with centre bay emphasized, this time by Corinthian pilasters and segmental pediment to 1st-floor window, with rusticated ground-floor arch.

2 Walmgate (formerly **Dorothy Wilson's Hospital**), 1812; centre 3 bays emphasized by ground-floor windows and door set in blank arcade, with 1st-floor centre bay arched and blank.

LONDON

The Greater London area is divided into boroughs and subdivided into districts. Boroughs and districts are listed alphabetically, as are churches, public buildings, and house or street names within them.

London Borough of Barnet

Cockfosters
Oak Hill College, off Chase Side, early-C18 core enlarged in early C19.

Edgware
Day Almshouses, Stonegrove, 1828; symmetrical, gabled, bargeboarded.

Finchley
56 Hendon Lane, fine house of *c*1735.
In **East End Road, Manor House,** dated 1723; large, with rusticated door surround.

Hendon
In **The Burroughs,** by Watford Way, cluster of C18 cottages, one with good early-C18 elevation.
Hendon Place, Manor Hall Avenue, is embellished with giant portico of 4 brick columns with intermittent rustication supporting rich Corinthian capitals, thought to have come from Cannons, Stanmore, built 1713-15 by John James and James Gibbs, demolished *c*1738; it seems to have arrived at Hendon between 1756 and 1759.

High Barnet
In **Wood Street, Garret's Almshouses,** 1731; very simple 1-storey cottages. In same street, **7, 20,** early C18; **51-3,** early-C19 villas.

Mill Hill
St Paul's Church, Ridgeway, 1829-36; Gothic.
Mill Hill School Ridgeway, 1825-7 by Sir William Tite, in Grecian manner; giant Ionic portico centrally placed on long, low block.
Also in Ridgeway, **Belmont,** C18, altered, with pretty early-C19 Gothic **hermitage** in garden.

Totteridge
St Andrew's Church, Totteridge village, 1790; windows with Gibbs surrounds, west pediment.
Manor House, just west of the church, *c*1750.
On **Totteridge Green, Old House,** C18. In **Totteridge Village,** near church, **Garden Hill,** *c*1725; **Southernhay,** *c*1800. To west of church, **Totteridge House,** late C18.

London Borough of Bexley

Bexley
In High Street, **Cray House,** C18; **High Street House,** 1761; **Styleman Almshouses,** dated 1755, 2-storey pedimented row of 12 cottages.

Blackfen
Lamorbey Park, Burnt Oak Lane, *c*1744-8, altered 1784, then 1812 from which, possibly, neo-Jacobean detailing dates; if so, very early example of this fashion.

Foots Cray
Frognal House, Frognal Avenue, front of 1719.
180-6 Rectory Lane, row of 4 tall brick terrace houses dated 1737 (on an inaccessible brick); moulded wooden cornice; one late-C18 shop-front; rear elevations clapboarded.

Sidcup
Manor House, on Green, *c*1790, pedimented.
Sidcup Place, south of Green, has core of *c*1745. Originally in curious form of square centre with diagonal arms projecting from 4 corners; only one of these now visible.

Welling
Danson Park, villa of 1760-65 by Sir Robert Taylor in highly articulated late-Palladian manner. Interior not completed till *c*1770, by Sir William Chambers. 3 storeys over rusticated basement. Cruciform plan, 3-bay pedimented centre breaking forward on entrance front. Canted bays in centre of other elevations.

London Borough of Bromley

Beckenham
Beckenham Place, Beckenham Place Park, mansion probably of *c*1760-70, with giant 4-column Ionic portico brought from John James's Wricklemarsh House, Blackheath, of 1721, demolished 1787.
Copers Cope House, Southend Road, *c*1725. Pedimented centre bay with pilasters.

Bromley
Bromley College, College Road, mostly C17, but quadrangle of 1794-1805 by Thomas Hardwick.
Quernmore School, London Lane, incorporates important house of *c*1778, probably by Thomas Leverton, exquisitely detailed.
Stockwell College, St Blaise Avenue, incorporates former **Bishop of Rochester's Palace,** 1775.

Bromley Common
Elmfield, Bromley Common, early C18.

Chislehurst
Camden Place, off Prince Imperial Road, begun *c*1716, façade with giant pilaster strips; south façade late C18; additions and alterations *c*1860. Interiors remodelled by George Dance the Younger *c*1785-8, 1807, but little remains except for some details: ceiling in breakfast room, possibly neo-Egyptian fireplace in flanking pavilion.
Chesil House, off St Paul's Cray Road, *c*1770; arched front windows; crowning pediment.
Coopers, Hawkwood Lane, late-C18 façade.

Hayes
Hayes Grove, Prestons Road, fine front of *c*1730 framed by pilaster strips; wings neo-Georgian, by Ernest Newton 1899.

Keston
Holwood House, 1823-6 by Decimus Burton. 15-bay garden front with central bow ringed with giant Ionic columns; in wings, Greek Doric loggias; interior altered.

Plaistow
Holy Trinity Convent, Plaistow Lane, early C18; late-C18 garden front with full-height bow.

Sundridge
Sundridge Park, *c*1796-9 by Humphry Repton and John Nash. House has half-hexagonal plan with colonnaded domed bow, containing staircase, in apex. Interior and stables perhaps by Samuel Wyatt.

London Borough of Camden

Bloomsbury
St George's Church, Bloomsbury Way, 1716-31 by Nicholas Hawksmoor. Monumental Corinthian portico; curious tower derived from Pliny's description of stepped-pyramid Mausoleum of Halicarnassus.

St Pancras Parish Church, Upper Woburn Place, 1819-22 by H.W. and W. Inwood in Greek revival manner, 2 caryatid porches based on the Erechtheion, Athens.

British Museum, Great Russell Street, 1823-46 by Sir Robert Smirke. Monumental Greek revival design important in development of museum building type.

University College, Gower Street, Corinthian-porticoed entrance block of 1827-9 by William Wilkins.

Argyle Square, laid out *c*1830, built 1840s; neighbouring streets – **Argyle Street, St Chad's Street** of *c*1825-30.

6-10 Bayley Street, *c*1780.

Bedford Place, complete street of 1800-1 built under control of James Burton. **1-13, 15-17, 23 Bedford Row,** 1718; **29, 30, 34,** *c*1760. **Bedford Square,** 1776-86; first uniform square to be built in London, by William Scott and Robert Grews, perhaps to designs of Thomas Leverton; intact.

11-26 Bernard Street, *c*1805.

18-27 Bloomsbury Square, 1800 by James Burton; **5, 6** *c*1740-50, perhaps by Henry Flitcroft; **17** is C17 pair reconstructed *c*1782 by John Nash, with grand stucco façade. In **Bloomsbury Street, 24-60** (even), good long run of houses of *c*1780-95; **1-5,** *c*1760-70.

Burton Street, houses of *c*1810, built under control of James Burton.

Cartwright Gardens, ambitious uniform crescent begun by Burton *c*1807.

9-15 Dombey Street, with **10 Harpur Street,** façades of *c*1760; **19-22,** mid-C18 façades but excellent interiors of *c*1708.

Doughty Street and **John Street** form one long street of mainly early-C19 brick terraces, e.g. **19-28** John Street, *c*1805, **1-19** Doughty Street, *c*1815; houses at southern end of John Street, **2-5, 7-9, 29, 30, 33-6,** *c*1760.

Endsleigh Place, *c*1824, with block on corner of **Endsleigh Gardens** and **Upper Woburn Place,** by Thomas Cubitt. These and east side of **Gordon Square,** 1824-30, best surviving examples of his work in this area.

Gower Street, remarkably long with continuous, well-preserved brick terraces of *c*1780-1800; no attempt at uniform composition or grouping.

37, 55 Gray's Inn Road, *c*1714; **75-81, 139-51,** 1815.

Great James Street, complete, magnificent survival of *c*1722, all with 3-storey façades, cantilevered hooded doors on carved brackets.

In **Great Ormond Street,** large houses of *c*1720: **10** and **12** with especially rich panelled interiors; **1-7, 14-16, 21-7, 41-9** and **59,** *c*1720-25. **41** with excellent carved door surround.

3-6 Great Russell Street, 1800-10; **66-71,** *c*1778 by Nash, with stucco façade and Greek Ionic door surrounds.

89-91 Guilford Place, *c*1800. **1-12, 105-10 Guilford Street,** *c*1815; **61-82, 89-92,** *c*1810, mostly by Burton, 70-72 dressed with screen of giant Tuscan columns to form decorative termination to Queen Square.

46-70 (even) **Huntley Street,** *c*1790.

87-101 (odd) **Judd Street,** *c*1805.

43, 45, 47, 54, 58 Lamb's Conduit Street, early-C18 houses; **29-37,** with return to Dombey Street, *c*1760; **49,** *c*1820; **51** with Greek Doric shop-front of *c*1820 and interior of *c*1720.

1-4 Lansdowne Place, *c*1800.

2-19 Leigh Street, *c*1810-20.

11, 25, 43-7 Mecklenburgh Square, 1812 by Joseph Kay. **1-8 Mecklenburgh Street,** *c*1812.

1-11, 12-29 Montague Street, remarkably complete and uniform, 1800 by James Burton.

17-21 Northington Street, *c*1750.

26, 43-5, 47 Old Gloucester Street, *c*1715-25.

6 Queen Square, *c*1725; **14, 15,** battered survivors of *c*1730; **7,** *c*1790.

1-17 Regent Square, *c*1810-20.

3-5, 9, 13, 10-18 Rugby Street, excellent houses of *c*1720-25.

In **Russell Square,** houses of *c*1800-10 by James Burton on south and north sides, much mutilated; **38-43,** better preserved group on west side.

Southampton Place complete with 2 sides of 3-storey houses, *c*1740-50, perhaps by Flitcroft.

West side of **Tavistock Square** survives; 1824 by Cubitt. **18-44 Tavistock Street,** *c*1810.

14-22 Theobald's Road, 1760.

Part of west side of **Torrington Square** survives; 1821-5 by James and Robert Sim.

Northern end of **Woburn Square,** 1829 by the Sims. In **Woburn Walk,** uniform shops, 1822 by Cubitt.

Camden Town
All Saints' Church, Camden Street, 1822 by W. and H.W. Inwood in neo-Greek manner. In **Camden High Street,** early-C19 terraces behind later shops, as at **14-46.**

148-56, 162-74 Camden Street, semi-detached groups of *c*1825.

Drummond Street, with **North Gower Street,** contains good groups of houses, of various scales, *c*1820-25.

140-84 Eversholt Street, *c*1825.

36-94 Fortess Road, uniform terrace of *c*1830.

In **Kentish Town Road,** many groups of early-C19 buildings, e.g. **325-43,** and good, tall terrace, **52-64;** adjoining, on corner of **Jeffrey's Street,** stuccoed, pedimented semi-detached villas and terrace. **3-9** Jeffrey's Street, linked villas.

Mornington Crescent, *c*1820-25, brick houses.

Fitzrovia
28-36, 68-72, 91-7 Charlotte Street survive from original development of *c*1790-1800.
16-20 Cleveland Street, with shop-fronts, *c*1810.
East and south sides of **Fitzroy Square,** 1790-94 by Robert Adam; other 2 sides a little later; generally intact. Also substantial complete terraces of *c*1800-10 running off square in **Fitzroy Street** and **Conway Street.**
27, 29, 33-41 Goodge Street, *c*1765. **4-13, 19-26 Goodge Place,** *c*1780-1800.
52-62 Grafton Way erected under control of Adam brothers, *c*1790, **58** with particularly good interior; **33-47** of same date; **65-71** of *c*1810.
46-52 Maple Street, *c*1810.
20, 23 Nassau Street, *c*1775.
26-9, 33, 73 Newman Street, mid- to late C18.
In **Percy Street,** remains of early example of uniform street design, laid out *c*1764; **29, 30** have excellent interiors.
16-23 Scala Street, *c*1795.
24, 30 Tottenham Street look *c*1730-40.
9-12, 54-68 Warren Street, *c*1790-1800.
131, 135 Whitfield Street, shop-fronts of *c*1800.

Hampstead
St John's Parish Church, Church Row, 1744-7 by John Sanderson.
St Mary's Roman Catholic Church, Holly Walk, charming design of 1816.
26-38 Belsize Grove, *c*1825.
In **Benham's Place,** cottages of 1813.
In **Cannon Place, Cannon Hall (14)** and **Cannon Lodge (12),** early-C18 mansions.
5-9A, 11, 12, 16-28 Church Row, *c*1720, **5** with clapboard canted bay front, **12** with brick giant pilasters; **10,** *c*1780.
11 East Heath Road, *c*1750.
1-5 Elm Row, tall terrace of *c*1725.
In **Flask Walk, Gardnor House,** early C18, altered later C18; **37-45, 53-65,** early C19.
3 and **12 Frognal,** *c*1720; **104, 106,** pair of *c*1760; **108,** *c*1750.
In **Hampstead High Street, Stanfield House,** *c*1730; **70-76,** early and late C18; **82, 83,** early C18. **1-2 Hampstead Square,** *c*1725; **Vine House,** *c*1715.
110, 119, 121 Heath Street, *c*1725.
2, 3, 4 Holly Bush Hill, late C18; **5,** 1797, weatherboarded.
3-5, 15, 23-4 Holly Mount, early C18.
Keats Grove has pretty cottages, *c*1815-20.
6 and **12 The Mount,** early C18; **9,** *c*1750. **4, 5, 7 The Mount Square,** mid-to-late C18.
1-7 Mount Vernon, *c*1800-10.
10-14 New End, early C18 uniform group.
33-5 Pond Street, *c*1720.
Spaniards Inn, Spaniards Road, *c*1720-30.
Off **Squires Mount, Chestnut Lodge,** *c*1725. (National Trust)
1-4 Upper Terrace, *c*1740; **1 Lower Terrace,** *c*1760, but **2, 3** *c*1800.
Vale Lodge, Vale of Health, late C18 villa.
In **Windmill Hill,** group of large houses of *c*1715-20, **Volta House, Bolton House, Windmill Hill House.**

Highgate
1-6 The Grove, late-C17 with C18 additions.
Grove Terrace, Highgate Road, long, varied terrace of houses, *c*1780-*c*1810.
46 Highgate Hill West, 1729; **47,** *c*1730, with 3-bay pediment; **54,** *c*1740.
17, 19, 21 High Street, 1733; **23,** *c*1714. **42,** *c*1745; **64,** with Ionic shop-front of *c*1820.
106-8, 110 Highgate Hill, *c*1725.
In **Holly Terrace,** group of late-C18 houses.
2, 4 Hornsey Lane, *c*1730; **8, 10,** *c*1735, façade with Venetian and Diocletian windows.
Kenwood House, 1767-9 by Robert Adam; white brick façade embellished with decorated pilasters and pediment; good interior, especially library. Garden façade stuccoed.
In **Little Green Street,** collection of modest late-C18 shop-fronts.
47-9 North Hill, *c*1725. **17-19 North Road,** late C17 with later details, especially 19 with huge segmental-pedimented doorcase; **47-9,** *c*1790; **111-17,** *c*1800.
1-6 Pond Square, cottages, *c*1720-1810.
9 South Grove, *c*1720; **10,** 1725; **14 (Moreton House),** *c*1714, recently reconstructed.
In **Southwood Lane, Woolaston Paunceford Almshouses,** 1722; **6-12** (even), *c*1750-60.

Holborn
St Giles-in-the-Fields, St Giles High Street, 1731-3 by Flitcroft; Burlingtonian Palladian essay on Gibbs's nearby St Martin-in-the-Fields.
Gray's Inn: 2 Field Court, *c*1780. **1-2 Gray's Inn Place** and **8 Warwick Court,** altered early-C18 buildings. **Verulam Buildings,** 1805-11, and **Raymond Buildings,** 1825, terraces of domestic appearance but purpose-built as chambers.
Lincoln's Inn: Stone Buildings, 1774-80 by Sir Robert Taylor, monumental Palladian. Rear elevation forms courtyard with Taylor's Six Clerks' and Enrolment Office, 1775-7. **60 Carey Street,** fine house of 1731-2.
Temple, the remaining Inn of Court, is in City (qv).
Ampton Street, with **Cubitt Street** and **Frederick Street,** developed *c*1825-30 by Cubitt; interesting for variety of decoration.
1-21 and **6-24 Calthorpe Street,** 2 facing terraces of *c*1825; in adjoining streets houses of similar date, especially **2-9 Wren Street.**
Ely Place, close of 1773-6 by Charles Cole and John Gorham.
5, 6 Hatton Garden, *c*1735; **29,** *c*1720.
83-9 Leather Lane, *c*1720.
1, 2 Lincoln's Inn Fields, *c*1750-60; **6, 8, 15-16, 25-7,** loosely uniform row, *c*1740; **12, 13, 14,** built by Soane in 1792, 1812, 1824 for own house and museum; **24,** *c*1775; **57, 58,** by Henry Joynes, *c*1730; **65,** by Thomas Leverton, 1772; on south side, façade and portico of George Dance the Younger's **Royal College of Surgeons,** 1806-13, columns fluted by Sir Charles Barry, 1835-7.
47-57 Mount Pleasant, dated 1720.

Regent's Park
Of John Nash's Regent's Park development, buildings along east side of the Park are in Camden; remainder in St Marylebone, Westminster (qv).
Terraces from north-east corner of Park clockwise, by Nash except where stated: **Gloucester Gate,** 1827; **St Katharine's Royal Hospital,** 1826-8 by Ambrose Poynter; **Cumberland Terrace,** 1826, with James Thomson; **Chester Terrace,** 1825; **Cambridge Terrace,** 1825; **St Andrew's Place,** 1823-6; **Park Square,** 1823 (east side only in Camden). On east side of terraces,

Park Village West and **Park Village East,** laid out by Nash as model suburb to Park development, and including some important early picturesque Italianate and neo-Tudor villas by Nash; **Albany Street,** with brick terraces of *c*1820–25.

St Pancras
St Pancras Parish Church is in Bloomsbury (see above).

City of London

All Hallows Church, London Wall, 1765–7 by George Dance the Younger. Austere brick exterior; exquisite, pioneering neo-classical interior.

St Botolph's Church, Aldersgate Street, 1788–91 by Nathaniel Wright. Plain stuccoed exterior.

St Botolph's Church, Aldgate, 1741–4 by George Dance the Elder. Brick exterior, handsome obelisk spire, Gibbs surrounds to windows, Venetian windows on 3 sides; interior of 1889.

St Botolph's Church, Bishopsgate, 1727–9 by James Gould and Dance the Elder. Brick with stone-fronted, somewhat provincially baroque west front; inside altered by Michael Meredith, 1821.

St Dunstan-in-the West Church, Fleet Street, 1829–33 by John Shaw the Elder; Gothic.

St Mary Woolnoth Church, Lombard Street, 1716–27 by Nicholas Hawksmoor in his extraordinary, original baroque manner. Rusticated, twin-towered entrance front; monumental if small interior – altered 1875.

St Michael's Church, Cornhill, 1670–72 by Christopher Wren, tower by Hawksmoor, 1715–22, in Gothic manner.

Bank of England, Threadneedle Street. Magnificent buildings by Sir Robert Taylor, 1766–74, and Sir John Soane, 1788–1833, rebuilt 1921–37; only part of Soane's screen wall, 1795, 1805 and 1823–6, and Taylor's Court Room survive.

Custom House, Lower Thames Street, 1813–17 by David Laing, centre rebuilt by Sir Robert Smirke, 1825; spare neo-classical detailing.

Guildhall, Guildhall Yard, medieval in origin; but front by Dance the Younger, 1788–9; surprising mix of classical, Gothic and 'Hindoo' motifs – very early example of Indian influence.

Mansion House, Mansion House Street, built 1739–42 to designs of Dance the Elder. Palladian with giant hexastyle Corinthian portico; inside, excellent sequence of rooms, richly decorated, culminating in Egyptian hall, now with tunnel-vaulted ceiling by Dance the Younger, 1795.

St Bartholomew's Hospital, West Smithfield, main quadrangle by James Gibbs, 1730–59, 3 detached, stone-faced, pedimented blocks with spare Palladian detailing; in north-west range, excellent staircase, Great Hall.

Temple: in **Essex Street 32, 35** are *c*1750. **8 King's Bench Walk,** 1782; **9–11,** 1814, adjacent to stone-faced building of 1814 by Smirke. (Other 2 Inns of Court are in Camden, qv.)

Trinity House, Tower Hill, 1792–4 by Samuel Wyatt. 5 bays, tripartite windows.

Apothecaries' Hall, Blackfriars Lane, has façade of *c*1775.

Fishmongers' Hall, William Street, 1831–5 by Henry Roberts, neo-Grecian, temple-fronted.

Goldsmiths' Hall, Foster Lane, 1829–35 by Philip Hardwick, with magnificent neo-baroque hall.

Skinners' Hall, Dowgate Hill, street façade with giant pilasters of *c*1801–3 by William Jupp.

Stationers' Hall, Stationers' Hall Court, east front by Robert Mylne, 1800–1, neo-classical.

Watermen's Hall, St Mary-at-Hill, by William Blackburn, 1778–80; neo-classical, domestic-scale front with coupled Ionic pilasters.

Print showing the interior of Goldsmiths' Hall, City of London, built 1829–35 to the designs of Philip Hardwick.

America Square, Crescent, Circus, linked group of Bath-inspired urban spaces built under control of Dance the Younger, 1767-70; now virtually eliminated except a few tall houses (mostly reconstructions) in Crescent.

In **Brabant Court,** off Philpot Lane, excellent early-C18 brick house; doorcase with Doric pilasters supporting segmental pediment.

Ball Court, off Cornhill, contains **Simpsons** (chophouse), largely early-C18 building with later shop-front.

4 College Hill, C18 with good doorcase; **19-20,** early C19; **21,** set in small court, has early-C18 Ionic doorcase, good staircase of 1724.

79-81 Carter Lane, c1720.

42-6 Chiswell Street, uniform brick terrace of c1790, perhaps by Dance the Younger. Opposite, large, early-C18 house with fine brick detailing, carved door. All these part of **Whitbread's Brewery,** which incorporates Porter Tun Room of c1770, perhaps by Dance, with spectacular timber roof of unusually wide span.

42 Crutched Friars, fine brick house of c1725.

Cutler Street warehouses, off Bishopsgate. Large, important complex of early warehouses; but recently much mutilated. Oldest building, **Old Bengal Warehouse,** 1769 by Richard Jupp, survives in New Street (see also below). **Western Courtyard** survives as elevations only, 1792-4 by Jupp and c1820 by S.P. Cockerell; brick, austere, 6 storeys. **Eastern Courtyard,** part of which survives as elevations only, 1796-7 by Richard Jupp and 1800 by Henry Holland, incorporates 3 terrace houses of 1796-1800.

12, 13 Devonshire Square, off Bishopsgate, remarkably imposing houses of c1740.

45 Eastcheap, Corinthian shop-front of c1820 below reconstructed façade in style of c1720.

In **Fleet Street, Hoare's Bank,** 1829-32 by Charles Parker; neo-classical composition.

Frederick's Place, cul-de-sac of brick houses (now somewhat altered) built 1776 as speculation by Adam brothers.

9 Idol Lane, house of c1740 with excellent staircase, fireplaces; refronted façade.

7A and **9 Laurence Pountney Lane,** late-C17 houses altered in C18; 9 has good C18 shop-front.

5-7 New Street, group of late-C18 houses.

14 New Bridge Street, 1802 by James Lewis, 3-bay front with pediment and giant pilasters.

2-3 Philpot Lane, large free-standing house of c1720; **7-8** c1725, altered externally but, inside, good panelled rooms and staircases.

27-8 Queen Street, imposing pair of tall, early-C18 houses; pedimented Ionic doorcases.

34-6 St Andrew's Hill, c1775.

1 Salisbury Square, reconstructed façade of good 5-bay early-C18 house with giant pilasters.

14, 15 Tooks Court, early C18, both with façades framed with giant Ionic brick pilasters.

41 Trinity Square, old offices of **Navy Sick and Hurt Board,** 1772, designed in manner of contemporary terrace house. Adjacent, lower building, **42,** with rear elevation of c1720; inside, excellent top-lit stair with Soane-type detailing, c1790.

In **Widegate Street, 20, 21, 22** (façades only) and **24-5,** c1722. (On fringe of Spitalfields; for neighbouring streets, see under Tower Hamlets.)

3-5 Wardrobe Place, c1714 with later doorcases.

London Borough of Croydon

Addington
Addington Palace (now **Royal School of Church Music**), 1773-9 by Robert Mylne.

Croydon
St James's Church, St James's Road, 1827-9 by Robert Wallace; Gothic
61-5 Church Street, c1725.
Coombe Hill House (now **Ruskin House**), Coombe Road, early C18 with giant angle pilasters.
In **High Street, Wrencote,** fine house of c1715-20; rubbed brick embellishments.
17-19 South End, early C18.

Norbury
Norbury Hall, Craignish Avenue, early C19; trellis veranda, columns with Moorish capitals.

Shirley
Coombe House, Coombe Road, c1765; pedimented front façade.

Upper Norwood
All Saints' Church, Beulah Hill, 1827-9 by James Savage; Gothic. Adjacent is **school,** probably also by Savage. **75-7 Beulah Hill,** c1780.
10 Grange Hill, early C19.
126 Church Road (**Westow Lodge**), early C19; unusual design with trellised bowed veranda.
Norwood Grove, on Gibson's Hill, early C19, stuccoed with centrally placed full-height bow.

London Borough of Ealing

Ealing
Pitzhanger Manor, Walpole Park, off Mattock Lane. House with addition of 1768 by George Dance the Younger, bought and enlarged by Sir John Soane for himself, 1800-2. Brick entrance front has 4 free-standing Ionic columns carrying Coade stone figures, inspired by Arch of Constantine, Rome. Inside, top-lit, tunnel-vaulted entrance vestibule; front parlour with saucer dome incised with Soane's characteristic abstracted classical decoration; back parlour with starfish vault.

Northfields
In **Little Ealing Lane, Rochester House,** plain, early C18.

Southall
On **Norwood Green, The Grange,** late-C18 attached pair making 6-bay composition with end bays breaking forward.

London Borough of Enfield

Edmonton
In **Angel Place,** numbered 183-93 (odd) Fore Street, good group of mid-C18 houses, 4 of which have good pedimented doorcases. **238 Fore Street,** c1720. **258-60,** excellent pair of c1725.

Enfield
In **Bull's Cross, Elsynge Cottage,** late C18; asymmetrical, with all ground-floor windows Venetian and all upper ones Diocletian.
9-23 Gentlemans Row, good group of early-C18 houses, 11 weatherboarded.
In **Lea Valley Road, flour mill,** large, clapboarded, c1820.

In **The Town, Eagle House,** *c*1750.
Flour mill, Lea Valley Road, large and clapboarded, *c*1820.

Southgate
Arnos Grove, Cannon Hill, 1719; painted hall of 1723; interior altered by Sir Robert Taylor *c*1765.
On **The Green, Essex House** and **Arnoside,** both *c*1725.
Grovelands House, early villa by John Nash, 1797. Front embellishment with giant Ionic order. Delicate interior, especially good Birdcage Room.

Winchmore Hill
St Paul's Church, Church Hill, 1828.
Friends' Meeting House, Church Hill, *c*1790.

London Borough of Greenwich

Blackheath Park
(Most of this group of buildings is in Blackheath section of Lewisham, qv.)
Blackheath Park, Pond Road, Foxes Dale, laid out 1806, built up *c*1820 with detached and semi-detached villas; **7-21** Blackheath Park are *c*1810-20.
Brooklands, Brooklands Park, early Italianate villa of 1826.
The Paragon, 1793-1807 by Michael Searles; 6 pairs and central house of 3 tall storeys, laid out on shallow crescent, linked by 1-storey Doric colonnade. (Adjacent Paragon House is in Lewisham.)

Charlton
Charlton House, The Village, mansion of *c*1607-12, but mentioned here for its remarkable proto-Palladian plan, including large, full-depth central hall.

Greenwich
St Alfege's Church, Greenwich High Road, 1711-18 by Nicholas Hawksmoor; steeple added 1730 to design of John James. Exterior powerful essay in English baroque design, especially magnificent east end with huge open pediment supported by pair of Doric columns set *in antis*. Interior reconstructed after wartime bombing.
St Michael's Church, Blackheath Park, 1828-9 by George Smith; Gothic.
Greenwich Palace (now **National Maritime Museum**) and **Royal Naval Hospital,** either side of Romney Road. Begun in C17, but completed and added to in C18 and early C19. Notable are north-west pavilion of King Charles block, 1712; south pavilion, 1769 by James Stuart; long west front of 1811-14 by John Yenn – all in sympathy with John Webb's original work of 1662-9. North pavilion of Queen Anne block (designed by Wren and Hawksmoor 1699-1700) added 1725-31; south pavilions 1735; stone façade added to main block 1725. Queen Mary block (Wren 1699) not completed until *c*1735-43, by Thomas Ripley, loosely following original design; chapel interior 1779-89 by James Stuart. Hall, designed by Wren 1698, has wall painting by James Thornhill, not completed until 1727.
Attached to Palace, **Dreadnought Hospital,** 1763-4 by James Stuart in very utilitarian style. Inigo Jones's **Queen's House,** 1616-19 and 1630-35, first English neo-Palladian villa, contains curved staircase and cube hall constantly copied in later Palladian buildings; to each side, blocks of 1807-16 by D.A. Alexander (who also designed Tuscan colonnades linking them to Queen's House), originally school for children of naval men.

The Paragon, Blackheath, 1793-1807 by Michael Searles: a superb urban composition with semi-detached houses linked by colonnades.

Local History Library (originally **Woodlands**), Mycenae Road, villa of 1774 by George Gibson the Younger; early-C19 bow windows.

Best Georgian houses are found in several small clusters of streets:

College Approach, Nelson Road, King William Walk, uniform streets of c1829–30 by Joseph Kay; with stucco façades and Greek details. **Market,** incorporated within these streets, 1831. **King William Walk** also contains some early-C18 houses: **11,** with later bow windows; and **12-14. 10-13 Nevada Street,** c1775, tall brick houses with upper canted bay windows; **Spread Eagle Yard,** handsome stucco building, c1830, probably built as inn.

In **Croom's Hill,** remarkable run of good C18 and early-C19 houses of different sizes, irregularly grouped. **6-12,** perfect terrace of 1721 (dated on hopper head); exquisite brickwork, pilastered doorcases. **14,** set back, early C18. **24** has door set in central bow under 1st-floor Venetian window. **26,** c1791, forms entry to Gloucester Circus (see below). **32,** early C18 with later wings. **42, 44-6,** 1818, with shared porch. **52 (The Grange)** basically C17 with C18 additions. **54-60,** terrace of c1770. At top of hill, where road merges into **Chesterfield Walk,** several large detached mansions, most now looking C19; for example, **Parkhall,** built 1716–24 by John James for himself, which despite unpromising rendered Victorian exterior retains good interior. **White House,** c1694, has full-height bow of c1745. **Macartney House,** in the Walk, also C17, with additions and some interior details of 1802 by Sir John Soane. By far the best of these large houses, **The Ranger's House,** also in the Walk, c1720–25, has tripartite stone frontispiece embellished with Ionic columns, Venetian windows; flanked by lower, yellow brick, bow-fronted wings, c1750 and 1783. Excellent interior.

Gloucester Circus, built c1790–1807 by Searles, in fact a crescent formed by semi-detached houses linked by narrow, set-back entrance blocks; simple architectural elements juggled to set up subtle and complex counter-rhythms, exquisitely detailed, though now much altered. At end of Circus, **Royal Hill: 30-36,** c1760; **38,** late C18; **42,** altered early C18; **50-52, 58-64,** c1740. Nearby, **King George Street,** with good, modest early-C19 houses; **Royal Place; Diamond Terrace; Maidenstone Hill** – **35** has wooden C18 façade with imitation rustication on ground floor. In same group of streets, **Westgrove** includes **Point House,** 5 bays with pedimented centre, curving triangular bow on top floor; magnificent, columned entrance hall, high-relief plasterwork on staircase walls. Adamesque plaster ceiling in wing. **No. 17** by Searles, with usual subtle, sophisticated detailing; **14,** early C18. **31 Blackheath Road,** c1776–80, also by Searles; **37-45, 72-4,** fragments of C19 terraces. **1-11, 13-15 Greenwich South Street,** altered terrace of c1705–15; **91, 221,** early C18; **199-213,** early-C19 pairs. Also in this street, **Queen Elizabeth's Almshouses,** rebuilt 1817, probably by Jesse Gibson; classical. In **Egerton Drive,** groups of good early-C19 villas with Ionic porches. **2 Burgos Grove,** C18.

34-8 Maze Hill, part of 1807 terrace. **47-9,** early-C18 pair, very well detailed with brick quoins, angle pilasters, 2 entrances within Doric porch. **111-15,** c1750. **Vanbrugh Castle,** built by Sir John Vanbrugh for himself from 1717, in symmetrical castle style – with classical openings – and added to c1723 to become asymmetrical; interior much altered with only a few minor details of Vanbrugh's time surviving.

25-6 Park Row large, early-C19 pair. To east, **Trinity Hospital,** founded 1613 with pretty, Gothic-detailed, rendered façade of c1812. Beyond hospital, **Ballast Quay,** with good collection of late-C18 and early-C19 buildings. **1-12 Park Vista,** terrace of c1810–20; **13 (The Manor House),** early-C18; **15,** later C18; **16-18 and Park Place,** 1791. **122-4 Old Woolwich Road,** c1810–15; **130-42 (Morden Place),** dated 1808.

Shooters Hill

Severndroog Castle, off Castlewood Drive, by William Jupp, 1784. Triangular in plan, 3 storeys with 3 4-storey castellated octagonal towers, pointed windows.

Woolwich

St Mary Magdalene's Church, St Mary's Street, 1727–39, perhaps by Matthew Spray. Stock brick elevation; inside, galleries and Ionic columns.

Royal Arsenal, Beresford Square, includes **Royal Brass Foundry,** 1716 by Office of Works, probably by Vanbrugh, cubical centre with hipped roof crowned by lantern; former **Smithy** and **Gun-Boring Factory,** Dial Square, 1717–20, very much in Vanbrugh's bold, articulated, stripped classical style; **Board Room** and **Saloon** (old **Board of Ordnance Building),** c1717–18, excellent Vanbrughian building with pedimented centre, abstracted triumphal arch motif, at north end bow window facing river – very early use of this feature – inside, some massive stone fireplaces. Later Arsenal buildings follow Vanbrugh's bold, bleak Office of Works style; for example **main entrance** from Beresford Square, 1829 (additions of 1897), **Guardroom,** 1788 by James Wyatt.

Royal Artillery Barracks, Artillery Place, east half 1775–82, west half completed 1808 to form frontage over 1,000ft long. Stock brick elevation typical of domestic houses of the period, divided into blocks with various accents.

Connaught Barracks, Woolwich New Road, c1780, enlarged 1806.

Royal Dockyard, Woolwich Church Street: **Mould Loft,** 1815; **Superintendent's house** and **office,** with hipped roof and central clocktower, looking c1710 but in fact 1778–84.

(Old) **Royal Military Academy,** Academy Road, 1805–8 by James Wyatt. Tudor-style castellated pile with onion domes, symmetrical.

The Rotunda, Green Hill, extraordinary round building with tented Chinese roof supported on tall central column, designed by Nash; first erected in St James's Park 1814, re-erected in Woolwich 1819–21.

London Borough of Hackney

Clapton

West and part of north side of **Clapton Square** retain terraces and linked semi-detached houses of c1820; also good terrace off Square in **Clapton Place. 43-7 Clapton Common,** c1800; **49-67,** excellent terrace of $c1760$ with pedimented doorcases. **162 Lower Clapton Road,** imposing stuccoed villa of $c1810$; on corner of **Linscott Road, Salvation Army Hall,** built $c1823$ as **London Orphan Asylum.**

Hackney
St John the Baptist's Church, Mare Street, 1792-7 by James Spiller, who added extraordinary stone steeple, 1812-13.
Old Town Hall, Mare Street (now a **bank**), Palladian, 1802.
195 Mare Street, $c1715$; **226** and adjoining houses form unusual group of $c1820$ with 1-storey bays.
71-83 Paragon Road, $c1825$, semi-detached houses linked by colonnaded porches.
In **Sutton Place,** uniform terrace of $c1820$ facing semi-detached linked houses of $c1825$.

Homerton
2-3 Homerton High Street (Brook House), C16 with early-Georgian façade (National Trust); **140-42,** good pair of $c1750-60$.

Shoreditch
St John the Baptist's Church, New North Road, 1825-9 by Francis Edwards.
St Leonard's Church, Shoreditch High Street, 1736-40 by George Dance the Elder.
Geffrye Museum, Kingsland Road, large, 2-storey brick quadrangle, built 1715 as almshouses.
Shoreditch Training College, Pitfield Street, in neo-Grecian manner, built 1825 by D.R. Roper as **Haberdashers' Almshouses.**
16 Charles Square, fine house of $c1725$.
In **Hackney Road,** numerous early-C19 terraces and cottages: especially good are **359-63,** with cast-iron trellis porches; and **337-53.**
124-6 Hoxton Street, $c1720$.
318-60 Kingsland Road, remains of gigantic shallow crescent of $c1810-20$.
118½ Shoreditch High Street, beside St Leonard's Church, $c1720$. **190,** $c1725$, with giant Tuscan brick pilasters.

Stoke Newington
131-57 Balls Pond Road, terrace dated 1812.
Clissold House, Clissold Park, villa of $c1800$ by Joseph Woods.
47-67 Green Lanes, row of semi-detached villas of $c1825$, with bold ramped parapets.
31, 32 Newington Green, $c1780-90$; **44-6,** $c1760$.
Sanford Terrace, 14 uniform houses dated 1788.
11 Stoke Newington Church Street, $c1720$; **81-7** (odd), uniform group of $c1734$, excellent carved pedimented doors, fine interior detail, especially 81; **89, 91,** 1792, both with porches; **109-11,** $c1720$; **130,** good early-C18 interior behind later façade; behind **139,** group of 3 houses, 1769; **171, 173,** $c1715$; **235, 239-41,** $c1721$.
187 Stoke Newington High Street, façade alone survives of large house of $c1715$; adjoining **189, 191** of similar date and size.

London Borough of Hammersmith and Fulham

Fulham
St John's Church, Walham Green, 1827-8 by J.H. Taylor, Gothic, brick-built, lancet windows.
Fulham Palace, east block 1814 by S.P. Cockerell.
In **Church Gate,** a few very early C18 houses.
87 Fulham High Street, substantial brick house of $c1740-50$, now obscured behind later building.
Hurlingham House, Hurlingham Park, $c1760$ with stuccoed river front of 1797.
71-97, 93-107, 113-19, 146-8, 190 New King's Road, $c1810-20$; **128, 134, 136** (façade only), all $c1730$; **237-47,** good group dated 1795.
In **North End Road, The Grange** and **380,** altered houses dated 1714 and 1723.
On **Parson's Green, Belfield House,** $c1720$.

Hammersmith
St Peter's Church, Black Lion Lane, 1827-8 by Edward Lapidge.
In **Hammersmith Broadway,** garden front of **Butterwick House,** early C18, perhaps by Thomas Archer, moved to present site $c1910$. **99-117 Hammersmith Road,** $c1820$. **Hammersmith Terrace,** overlooking river, 16 houses of $c1755-c1770$.
In **Lower Mall,** beside river, **6-9,** $c1730-1830$ with collection of pretty Regency 1st-floor verandas; **10 (Kent House),** $c1760$ and $c1780$, with pair of full-height canted bays; **Westcott Lodge,** $c1730$. In **Upper Mall, 12** and **14 (Sussex House),** $c1726$; **26 (Kelmscott House),** $c1785$; **36,** $c1780$; **Corinthian Sailing Club,** $c1760-70$, with 5-bay pedimented centre and tripartite pedimented door.
St Peter's Square, $c1825-30$; groups of stuccoed houses linked by low walls.

London Borough of Haringey

Tottenham
Holy Trinity Church, Tottenham Green, 1828-30 by James Savage; Gothic.
Bruce Castle, C16 with north façade of $c1730$, later-C18 west wing. **5-6, 11-16 Bruce Grove,** linked pairs, $c1825$.
399 High Road, semi-detached pair of $c1780$; **530-36,** twin-pedimented composition of $c1825$; **581,** $c1790$; **583-5,** $c1720-25$, with giant pilasters; **664-6,** dated 1817; **794-802** (even), group of fine, large brick houses of $c1730-40$; **796 (Percy House),** especially good with pedimented doorcase; **808-10,** unusually elegant, handsome pair of $c1725$ with flanking lower stable blocks; **818,** $c1735$ with Ionic pedimented door, as at 30 Elder Street, Spitalfields; **867, 869,** probably $c1710$, 867 with pretty, early-C19 door, fanlight set below original hooded door surround.
8-18 Lordship Lane, linked pairs dated 1826.
Mountford House, Tottenham Green East, large pair of $c1820$ with porches and 1-storey bowed wing.
32 White Hart Lane, $c1730$ with excellently detailed brick façade.

London Borough of Harrow

Harrow
Harrow School: major additions of 1818-20 by C.R. Cockerell, in Tudor style to form symmetrical composition with the Old Schools. Several of the C18 and C19 buildings in **High Street** in res-

idential use by school, including **The Moretons,** 1806-26; **The Flambards,** *c*1790; **The Park,** 1795-*c*1805.

Little Stanmore
St Lawrence's Church, Whitchurch Lane, 1714-16 by John James for 1st Duke of Chandos. Medieval tower, unassuming exterior. Extraordinarily lavish baroque interior: shallow barrel-vaulted nave leads to chancel framed, as in a theatre, by proscenium formed by Corinthian columns supporting depressed arch; architectural details on ceiling are *trompe-l'oeil*, framing allegorical and Biblical paintings by Louis Laguerre, who also painted magnificent east wall. More *trompe-l'oeil* grisaille painting on north and south walls. Box pews and ironwork, *c*1720.

Pinner
Pinner House, Church Lane, dated 1721; centre bay emphasized by pediment, framed by pilasters embellished with sunken panels containing crisscross decoration, and carrying cushion capitals.

Stanmore
Bentley Priory. Sir John Soane designed additions to the mid-C18 house, 1788-1801. Enlarged 1810-18 by Sir Robert Smirke; now much altered, and damaged by fire 1980. Soane tribune and entrance hall of 1798 survive as important examples of early phase of romantic Greek revival: pendentive ceiling, with Greek Doric columns.

In **Stanmore Village,** several good Georgian houses: **Rectory,** 1721; **Regent House,** Church Road, with early-C18 door; **Mill House** and **The Rookery** among others in Stanmore Hill.

London Borough of Havering

Havering-atte-Bower
Bower House, on the Green, 1729 by Henry Flitcroft – his first building. 5 bays with 3-bay pediment. Wings *c*1800. Inside, entrance hall with staircase painting by James Thornhill.

Round House, Broxhill Road, 1793, oval, 3 storeys. Interior plan somewhat awkward. Possibly designed by John Plaw, but executed by local builder.

Hornchurch
Hactons, Hacton Lane, *c*1770; porch with Venetian window above, porticoed flanking pavilions.

Langtons (now **council offices**), North Street, 1760; 7 bays, 2 storeys.

Manor House, Nelmes Way, C16; south front of *c*1720 with rustication and Venetian windows.

Pennant Almshouses, High Street, rebuilt C18.

Rainham
Rainham Hall, The Broadway, free-standing brick house, begun 1729; archaic design with façade framed by quoins, divided by string course, topped by deep cornice, and all windows segmental with keystones and box sashes. Segmental pedimented porch. Excellent panelled interior, especially marbled hall. (National Trust)

Romford
Hare Hall, Brentwood Road, 1769-70 by James Paine; 5-bay house with attached giant Ionic portico supporting 3-bay pediment over rusticated ground floor. Inside altered.

33 Market Square, early C18.

Upminster
Harwood Hall, Harwood Hall Lane, off Corbets Tey Road, 1782, with castellated front.

In **St Lawrence Road,** west of church, **parsonage,** 1765. Opposite, early-C19 house with cast-iron veranda. Nearby, set back from road, **smock mill** with sails and fan, 1802-3.

London Borough of Hillingdon

Uxbridge and Harefield
Market House, Market Square, 1789. Central lantern, open ground floor with Tuscan columns which was used as exchange. Upper floor used for storing grain and as charity school.

Harefield House, on the village green, early C19. **Lodge** to **Harefield Place,** Harefield Road, an early-C19 *cottage orné*.

West Drayton
On **The Green,** several good C18 houses: **The Old House** and **Southlands,** both *c*1725; **Elmscroft,** C18; **Avenue House,** partly C18.

London Borough of Hounslow

Brentford
St Laurence's Church, High Street, body plain brick box of 1764, interior of 1889.

Syon House, mainly mid-C16 with earlier origins, remodelled internally 1761-9 by Robert Adam to form one of his most impressive works. Dining room 1764; drawing room, extremely delicate, 1766; long gallery 1766; entrance hall 1761 in Adam's early grand Roman manner with domed, coffered apses. Entrance gate and screen *c*1773. In grounds domed **conservatory** of 1828-30 by Charles Fowler: an early and important example of large-scale use of structural ironwork. (See also Syon Lodge, in Isleworth, below.)

Chiswick
Chiswick House, quintessential and highly influential Palladian villa, built 1723-9 to design of Lord Burlington. Derived from Palladio's Villa Rotonda, Vicenza, house is square in plan with central dome, portico on one side. Exterior exquisitely detailed, with pedimented windows; garden front, with 3 Venetian windows set in arches, based on Palladio drawing in Burlington's possession. Interior, by William Kent, has large-scale architectural decoration, much of it similar in scale and detail to exterior work. **Garden** also embellished by Burlington, who began work on it *c*1717.

In **Chiswick Lane South (112-20),** **Mawson Row,** terrace of *c*1730. In **Chiswick Mall,** excellent collection of Georgian houses: **Woodroff House,** *c*1720; **Morton House** and **Strawberry House,** both *c*1730; **Eyneham House** and **Bedford House,** 1760, built as one with 4-bay pediment; **Swan House,** early-C19. **Chiswick Square,** off Burlington Lane, *c*1700, forms forecourt to **Boston House,** *c*1715.

In **Church Street,** more C18 houses: **Lamb House,** weatherboarded; cottages in **Page's Yard: Wisteria,** *c*1715; **Ferryhouse,** *c*1810.

Hogarth House, Hogarth Lane, *c*1710-20, with later 1st-floor canted bay window.

In **Strand-on-the-Green,** numerous more modest C18 and early-C19 houses: **52-5** and **64-8.**

Isleworth
In **Church Street, 59, 61,** C18. Off it, in **Mill Plat, Grosvenor House, Dundee House.**

Syon Lodge, London Road, free-standing late-C18 house with delicately detailed neo-classical façade of *c*1780. (See also Syon House, in Brentford, above.)

116-22 Twickenham Road, C18 terrace.

Osterley
Osterley Park, Elizabethan house, embellished and altered by Robert Adam. Portico of 1762 with moulded soffit like Adam's hall at Shardeloes. Garden front, altered before 1761, perhaps by Sir William Chambers, has generously spaced windows and fine Doric porch. Entrance hall 1767-8, with magnificent apsed ends; staircase, 1768; Etruscan Room, *c*1776; all by Adam.

Lodge by Adam, *c*1763. (National Trust)

London Borough of Islington

Barnsbury
Holy Trinity Church, Cloudesley Square, begun 1826 by Sir Charles Barry; Gothic.

18-28 Barnsbury Park, articulated 2-storey terrace, *c*1825. **Barnsbury Square,** with a few surviving villas, **7-11, 27, 28,** and adjoining **Mountfort Crescent,** *c*1820-30, as are **62-82 Thornhill Road.**

Cloudesley Square and adjacent streets – **Bewdley Street, Cloudesley Road, Place** and **Street, Stonefield Street, Barnsbury Road** and **Street, Batchelor Street** – all *c*1820-30, with plain brick façades, good ironwork.

44-78 Hemingford Road, *c*1825-35, linked villas, as in **Richmond Avenue** where **46-72** have doors flanked by sphinxes and obelisks.

Liverpool Road, remarkable for length and preservation of early-C19 terraces: **95-105, 111-99,** *c*1820; **295-307 (Park Terrace),** dated 1822; **329-45,** *c*1825.

In **Ripplevale Grove,** linked and detached villas of *c*1820-25; also in **Malvern Terrace.**

Canonbury
In **Canonbury Grove,** early-C19 developments in various unusual forms: **13-22** of *c*1810. **Canonbury Place** dated 1780 on hoppers, **No. 1** with Adamesque pilasters, all stuccoed – an early example – except **Canonbury House,** though this also of *c*1780. **Canonbury Square** begun *c*1800 by Jacob Leroux; plain brick terraces, remarkably complete, as are similar terraces in surrounding streets such as **Alwyne Villas (21-37** dated 1821), **Canonbury Road** and, in **Canonbury Lane, 3-13,** *c*1760-70. **Compton Terrace,** off Canonbury Road, begun by Leroux *c*1806; tall brick houses.

Gibson Square, with emphasized centre and end pavilions, *c*1830, as is **Theberton Street.**

Clerkenwell
St James's Church, Clerkenwell Green, 1788-92 by James Carr.

Former **Middlesex Sessions House** (now **Masonic Halls**), Clerkenwell Green, 1779-82 by Thomas Rogers in imposing late-Palladian manner.

28-32 Britton Street, *c*1715-25; **54** and **59,** *c*1725, with fine carved brackets to doorhoods; **55,** *c*1820, with contemporary shop-front.

In **Charterhouse Square, Master's Lodge,** and additions to adjacent C15 gate, 1718; **4, 5** early C18; **12, 13, 14,** fronts of *c*1810; **22,** *c*1780 with Coade stone door surround.

16 Clerkenwell Green, with good Greek Ionic shop-front; **32,** early C18; **37A,** reconstructed pedimented house of 1737.

11 Jerusalem Passage, *c*1720.

49-50 St John's Square, *c*1780; **51, 52,** *c*1825.

82, 84 St John Street, pair of *c*1780, **22,** *c*1720. (See Finsbury for rest of street.).

In **Sekforde Street,** largely complete curving brick terraces, *c*1825; similar terraces in **Woodbridge Street.**

35-45 Skinner Street, *c*1730.

Finsbury
St Barnabas' Church, King Square, 1822-6 by Thomas Hardwick.

St Luke's Church, Old Street, 1727-33 by Hawksmoor with John James; obelisk spire; now gutted.

St Mark's Church, Myddleton Square, 1826-8 by W. Chadwell Mylne; Gothic.

Wesley's Chapel, City Road, 1777.

Honourable Artillery Company HQ, City Road, main block 1735, wings added 1828.

47 City Road, *c*1777 for John Wesley; front reconstructed. **319-87,** long terrace, *c*1810, with gradually-stepped façade.

In **Helmet Row, St Luke's Vicarage,** fine, large house dated 1734.

Lloyd Baker Estate – notably **Lloyd Square, Lloyd Baker Street, Wharton Street** – developed from *c*1819 on, contains interesting variety of housing types; notably, pedimented semi-detached houses in Lloyd Baker Street.

New River Company Estate, developed south of Pentonville Road after *c*1820, contains many brick terraces of *c*1820-30 with stuccoed ground floor, 1st-floor windows set in blank arches – notably **Claremont Square,** *c*1821; **Myddleton Square,** 1827; **Amwell Street; Mylne Street; Chadwell Street; Spencer Street; Percy Street;** a good long terrace in **Pentonville Road, 27-75,** and **34-44; Northampton Square,** begun 1802, and **Wilmington Square,** begun 1818, both complete; **Percy Circus,** *c*1830, partly destroyed.

In **Owen's Row,** 4 tall houses of *c*1760-70.

347-63, 372-90 St John Street, *c*1825.

47-61 Swinton Street, *c*1785.

Highbury
Highbury Place, Highbury Fields, built 1774-80, under control of James Spiller, as group of terraces; some unusual detail. **Highbury Terrace,** long, elegant composition, with link blocks between sections, centre pedimented and dated 1789.

Holloway
St John the Evangelist's Church, Holloway Road, begun 1826 by Sir Charles Barry; Gothic.

St Mary Magdalene's Church, Holloway Road, 1812-14 by William Wickings.

Islington
St Mary's Church, Upper Street; only tower and spire survive of Launcelot Dowbiggin's church of 1751-4.

St Paul's Church, at corner of Balls Pond Road and Essex Road, 1826 by Barry; Gothic.

246-90 Annett's Crescent (Essex Road), c1825.

31-43 Camden Passage, dated 1766.

Charlton Place, dated 1790; south side curved, named **Charlton Crescent**, dated 1795.

Colebrooke Row, built c1714 to c1830; **56-7** are earliest, **41, 42, 44, 53** c1760; **60-65** c1770; **34-6** c1775; **1-28** c1820. Duncan Terrace forms west side of Row, containing **New Terrace (50-58)** dated 1791, **46-9** of similar date, and **1-45** c1800-30.

7-35, 22-8, 53-61 Cross Street, c1775-80; **33, 35** with doorcases inspired by the Adams' Adelphi.

28, 30, 75-83, 294-300 Essex Road, groups of houses of c1720.

10-40, 11-23 Halton Road, c1810-20.

In **High Street, 37, 38, 112**, c1720; **80, 84-96**, c1750-60.

23, 24 Islington Green, c1750.

149, 194 Upper Street and **3 Terret's Place**, c1720.

Vincent Terrace and adjoining streets, especially **Noel Road**, good uniform brick compositions of c1825-30.

Royal Borough of Kensington and Chelsea

Chelsea
St Luke's Church, Sydney Street, 1820-24 by James Savage; important: pioneered revival of Gothic structural principles with stone-built vault.

Duke of York's Headquarters, King's Road, 1801-3 by John Sanders; giant Tuscan portico.

Royal Hospital, Royal Hospital Road, late-C17 by Sir Christopher Wren; but Sir John Soane added **stables**, 1814 - remarkable brick composition with much use of concentric blank arcading.

Carlyle Square, laid out c1830.

Cheyne Row, begun c1708; **10, 16-26, 30-34** survive of original buildings. **16, 20-28 Upper Cheyne Row**, c1716; **28** has Venetian window of 1767. **2 Cheyne Walk** has front of 1879 but early-C18 interior; **3-6**, c1717-18, very fine; **15**, c1717; **16 (Queen's House)**, of same date with ornate façade incorporating brick pilasters, and later bay window; **19-26**, terrace of c1760; **46-8**, c1714; **91-4**, c1775; **92** has canted bays and variety of Venetian windows. (**3, 24** and **93** in care of National Trust)

211 King's Road (Argyll House), important design of 1723 by Giacomo Leoni; **213-17**, group of c1720.

23, 24 Lawrence Street, c1720, with shared pedimented doorcase.

53 Old Church Street, c1720; **131-41**, c1810-15; **141**, free-standing house of c1800.

Paultons Square, laid out c1830.

Royal Avenue, laid out 1692-4, lined with early-C19 houses; **26-48** on west side are earliest, c1820.

St Leonard's Terrace, rich group of mid-C18 and early-C19 houses; **14-18**, c1820; **19-25, 31, 32**, c1810; **26-30**, c1765.

2-16 St Luke's Street, modest terrace of c1810.

Former **St Mark's College**, between King's Road and Fulham Road, c1690, with gallery of c1820 containing plaster cast of Parthenon frieze.

Smith Street, 2 long terraces, c1790-1810.

In **Swan Walk**, informal group of C18 houses: **1**, c1720, altered; **2**, c1715; **3**, c1790; **4**, c1730, altered c1820.

In **Sydney Street**, plain, uniform early-C19 terraces survive at **72-86** (even); good contemporary shops at **119, 121, 123**.

Kensington (High Street area)
St Barnabas' Church, Addison Road, 1828 by Lewis Vulliamy; Gothic.

Kensington Palace, largely C17 by Sir Christopher Wren, but some remodelling of 1718-26, notably cupola room, initiated by William Benson and Sir Thomas Hewett, with decoration by William Kent.

Aubrey House, Aubrey Road, c1750.

Campden Hill Square, begun 1827.

Earl's Terrace, plain brick houses of c1800-10; adjacent, **Edwardes Square**, 1811-19 - both by L.L. Changier.

In **Holland Park Avenue**, some ambitious villas of c1830-40; **4, 24-8** stuccoed, with engaged giant Tuscan columns and pediment. **10, 12 Holland Street**, c1720; **13**, c1740; **18-26**, c1725.

3-9 Kensington Church Street, c1740; **11-17**, c1725. **27, 41, 42 Kensington Square**, early C19; **28-30, 32-4, 43, 44**, façades of c1720-30; **35**, façade of c1750. (**33** in care of National Trust)

In **Young Street**, Thackeray's house, c1820.

South Kensington, Knightsbridge and Brompton
Holy Trinity Church, Cottage Place, off Brompton Road, 1826-9 by James Donaldson; Gothic.

Alexander Square and adjoining streets - **Alexander Place, South Terrace** - 1827-30.

Beauchamp Place, c1800-10.

Brompton Square, c1820, horseshoe-shaped; complete.

Egerton Crescent, c1830 by George Basevi.

33, 34, 40 Hans Place, c1790.

Pelham Crescent, Pelham Place, c1830 by Basevi.

88-91, 95 Sloane Street, c1785, 91 and 95 with Coade stone door surrounds; **139**, c1780.

London Borough of Kingston-upon-Thames

Kingston (Old Town)
Bridge, leading from Clarence Street, 1828.

2 Church Street (Old Crown Inn), early-C18 façade over C17 timber framing.

17 High Street, mid-C18, with 2 canted bays, central Venetian window. **52 (Picton House)**, c1730; brick front; inside, on ground and 1st floor, very good ceilings of c1745.

In **Market Place, Druidshead**, early C18.

43-7 London Road, c1790; **105**, early C18.

3 Surbiton Road, c1720, with later-C18 front incorporating door with Gibbs surround, flanked by full-height canted bays.

In **Villiers Road, Old Mill House**, c1780.

Surbiton
73 Ewell Road, early-C19 *cottage orné*.

London Borough of Lambeth

Clapham
(Most of Clapham is in Lambeth; the rest in Wandsworth, qv)

Holy Trinity Church, Clapham Common North Side, 1776 by Kenton Couse; portico of 1812.

St Paul's Church, Rectory Grove, 1815 by Christopher Edmonds.

13-21 Clapham Common North Side, loosely uniform terrace of 1714-20 by John Hutt – 12 a refronted house of c1730 – then mixture of later-C18 houses: **29,** 1754; **30-32,** 1752; **80,** 1819; **113,** 1763 and 1810. Similar groups along **Clapham Common South Side: 30-38, 44, 53,** good examples of c1790-1820. **Crescent Grove,** off South Side, c1825 by Francis Childs; stuccoed. **21, 81-4 Clapham Common West Side,** c1800. **Clapham Park Estate,** laid out 1825 by Thomas Cubitt but not completed until c1860. In **Clapham Road,** several terraces of 1800-25, for example **15-41,** c1800; **145-89,** c1820; **209,** c1750; **355, 359-61,** late C18.

39, 41, 43 Old Town, excellent early-C18 group.

17 The Pavement, 1824, with shop-front.

8, 10 Rectory Grove, late C18; **52,** c1780, with Coade stone door surround.

In **Wandsworth Road,** early-C19 terraces, for example **101-7, 372, 376, 335-7,** all c1820.

Lambeth, Kennington and Vauxhall
St John's Church, Waterloo Road, 1823-4 by Francis Bedford; Greek Doric portico with tower set above in manner of Gibbs.

St Mark's Church, Clapham Road, 1822-4 by David R. Roper; Greek, with Doric portico *in antis.*

General Lying-in Hospital, York Road, 1828 by Henry Harrison.

The Old Vic, Waterloo Road, built 1816 by Rudolph Cabanel as **Royal Coburg Theatre;** only arcaded side wall of original building survives.

In **Harleyford Road,** stucco terraces of the 1820s: **43-59,** 1824, built as school.

28-34 Hercules Road, c1810-20.

139-43 Kennington Lane, c1790; **155-7,** terrace of c1776-80; **161,** with pedimented door of c1730; **231-45,** excellent terrace of c1791; **363,** unusual house, c1825, probably by J. M. Gandy. **Kennington Park Road,** lined with terraces of c1775-1820; especially good are **87-167** (excluding 123), 1790-1820; **114-36,** 1787-90 by Michael Searles, flanking entrance to **Cleaver Square,** laid out c1788 but not built until c1800-10. **140-62,** c1775. **Kennington Road,** long, rich in late-C18 groups and terraces: **114-26** (even), c1760-70; **121-43,** varied late-C18 group; **163-9,** c1790; **233-91,** long, uniform terrace of c1788-92; **309-41,** c1787; **317 (Marlborough House),** by Searles, pedimented; **324, 326,** pedimented pair of c1785; **346-56,** handsome, irregular group of c1790. Off Kennington Road, **Walnut Tree Walk: 9-11,** c1750; **57-63,** c1755-60, with Gothic-detailed doors – remarkably early example.

96-102 Lambeth Road, c1790; **148-60,** tall group of c1789-95, with doors framed by pairs of half Ionic pilasters – most odd; **214 (The Rectory),** 1828, incorporating block of 1778; off Lambeth Road, **4-8 Pratt Walk,** c1775; **9-12,** c1810.

South Lambeth, Stockwell and Brixton
St Matthew's Church, St Matthew's Road, 1822-4 by Charles Porden.

In **Brixton Road,** various terraces of 1800-20; **91-137** and **206-18** are good examples.

87 South Lambeth Road (incorporating **Beaufoy Vinegar Factory**), c1810; good early industrial group; **210-18,** c1800; **274,** c1798.

146-66 Stockwell Road, dated 1786.

Herne Hill, Tulse Hill and Norwood
St Luke's Church, Norwood High Street, 1823-5 by Francis Bedford.

137-79 Brixton Hill, c1820.

Brockwell Hall, Brockwell Park, 1811-16 by D. R. Roper.

Streatham
Park Hill (now **St Michael's Convent**), off Streatham Common North, begun c1830 by J. B. Papworth.

40-42, 44 Streatham Hill, early-C19 villas.

40-42, 60-78, 84-90 Sunnyhill Road, modest villas of c1820-25.

London Borough of Lewisham

Blackheath
(Part of this region is in Greenwich, qv)

2 Blackheath Hill (Montague House), c1760; **20-22,** late C18, with canted upper bay window and wings; **98-100,** c1760. In **Dartmouth Grove, Sherwood** and **Lydia House,** important pair of 1776, probably by Thomas Gayfere the Elder, with half-pediments over lower wings. **25 Dartmouth Row,** c1750, with canted bays; **28,** 1794; **30, 30A,** c1750, with 3-bay crowning pediment, baroque details – back room in 30 with good rococo plaster ceiling; **34, 36, 36A,** C18.

On **Eliot Hill, The Knoll,** 1798. In **Eliot Place,** terrace of 1792-1805 by speculative builder Alexander Doull: **4-5, 7-8** are earliest. **8, 9 Eliot Vale,** 1805. **3-5 The Meadway,** 1804.

1-4 Grote's Place, with **Grote's Buildings** and **Lloyd's Place,** informal, mostly late-C18 group.

In **Montpelier Row,** long run of terraces: **1-4,** 1806-7; **5,** c1800; **6-14,** c1797; **15-16,** 1798; **20,** c1803 by Michael Searles, with shaped pediment; **22-3,** semi-detached pair of c1798.

In **South Row, Colonnade House,** 1804, simple but skilful composition by Searles, incorporating wrap-around 1-storey Tuscan colonnade. Off the Row, **Paragon House,** 1794 by Searles, with arcaded ground floor, full-height garden bow. (For adjoining Paragon by Searles, see Greenwich, Blackheath section.)

25-7 Tranquil Vale (Vale House), 1798.

Deptford, New Cross and Lewisham
St Paul's Church, Deptford High Street, begun 1713 to designs of Thomas Archer, completed 1720; one of most ingenious and successful of London's early-C18 baroque churches. Square plan; steeple sits on round tower which rises direct from ground, embraced by semicircular Tuscan portico.

Royal Navy Victualling Yard, Pepys Estate (best approached from Grove Street). Buried in GLC estate begun 1963. Buildings, all by James Arrow, 1783-8, are **Gateway,** 1788; **Colonnade** (offices and housing); **Rum Warehouses** and **Stables,** with pediment.

Albury Street, a remarkable survival: laid out c1706 by Thomas Lucas, a local bricklayer; by 1717, 40 houses had been built. All originally 2 storeys, houses were of various widths – 3, 3½, 4 bays – but variety was concealed by strong rhythm of uniform façade design, articulated by pilaster strips between which window bays were recessed. Individual touch added by different, deeply carved, consoled doorcases. Internally, most houses were different, with fascinating variety of plan forms and types of staircase design. Unfortunately, only 4 houses (**34-40**) remain on south side, 17 on north side of which only 6 (**21-31**) are not derelict (1985).

In **Deptford High Street, 11** of c1820, with Ionic porch and bowed front; **108** and **127-9** C18.

Stone House, 281 Lewisham Way, 1771-3 by George Gibson; centrally planned villa.

6-8, 10-12 New Cross Road, semi-detached villas of c1825-30 with giant pilasters decorated with ammonite capitals (see Old Kent Road, in Southwark).

124 Tanner's Hill, mansion of 1789; altered.

Downham
St John's Chapel, Bromley Road, 1824.

Lee
Manor House (now **Public Library**), Old Road, 1771-2 by Richard Jupp. Full-height bow on garden front.

Merchant Taylors' Almshouses, Lee High Road, 1826 by William Jupp the Younger.

Sydenham
St Bartholomew's Church, Westwood Hill, 1827-32 by Lewis Vulliamy; Gothic.

In **Jew's Walk, Farnborough House,** c1820.

32-4 Sydenham Road, c1740-45, with Gibbs surround to front door; **122,** c1800.

In **Westwood Hill, The Old Cedars,** c1785.

London Borough of Merton

Merton
Almshouses, 180 Kingston Road, 1797; modest.

Dorset Hall, Kingston Road, late C18. Also in Kingston Road, **Long Lodge,** late C18.

Mitcham
St Peter and St Paul's Church, Church Road, 1819-21 by George Smith; Gothic.

Tate Almshouses, 1829 by John Buckler, on **Cricket Green.**

Former **Sunday Schools,** 1788 and 1812, in **Lower Green West.**

Burn Bullock Inn (formerly **King's Head**), London Road, with Tuscan porch. Also in London Road, **White Hart Inn,** 1747, with Doric porch.

On **Cricket Green, The White House,** C18, façade of 1826 with semicircular bow.

Vicarage, Church Road, c1820; **60-64,** c1750-60.

In **Commonside West, Park Place,** c1800.

Wandle House, Riverside Drive, c1795; handsome house with bow window facing river, attributed to Robert Mylne.

Morden
Morden Hall (now **council offices**), Morden Hall Road, rebuilt c1750; exterior altered c1840. In Morden Hall Road, **Morden Lodge,** villa of c1815.

Morden Park (also now **council offices**), west of London Road, mansion of 1770 with good details: pedimented Venetian door linked to pedimented 1st-floor windows by balustrade and scrolls, and 2-storey bow windows on rear elevation.

Wimbledon
Ashford House, High Street, 1720; altered.

In **Hanford Row** and **West Place,** good group of late-C18 and early-C19 cottages.

On **Wimbledon Common, Mill House** and **windmill,** 1817-18; altered 1893. On west side of common, **The Keir,** 1789, stuccoed and with Grecian porch; **Stamford House,** c1720; **West Side House,** c1765.

2 and **4 Woodhayes Road** are an C18 pair; **6,** a Gothic lodge dated 1763 on lead pump head.

London Borough of Newham

West Ham
At west end of **Romford Road, 28/30,** a small terrace house of c1730-40, with clapboard façade and handsome consoled doorcase. Just to the west, **No. 2,** pedimented 5-bay house, c1810.

Stratford
In **Three Mills Lane,** good group of C18 industrial buildings; **House Mill,** dated 1776, large, brick, containing water wheel; opposite, **Clock Mill** (now converted to offices), 1817.

London Borough of Redbridge

Ilford
St Mary's Church, High Road, 1829-31 by James Savage; yellow brick, Gothic. Tower 1866.

Valentines, Valentines Park, brick mansion, dated 1769 on hopper; altered 1811.

Wanstead
St Mary's Church, 1787-90 by Thomas Hardwick. Severe neo-classical elevation with tall porch of 2 pairs of Tuscan columns. Inside, still Gibbsian: tall Corinthian columns on high pedestals, carrying arches, coved ceiling. Gallery, box pews, superb pulpit with sounding board carried on 2 thin palm-tree columns, all c1790.

In **Eastern Avenue** (formerly **George Lane**), **Reydon Hall,** good baroque house of c1720-25, with façade framed by tall, thin stone Composite pilasters supporting blocks of entablature. Adjacent, **Elm Hall,** also early C18 but altered.

In **High Street, Wanstead Manor House,** c1720, 7 bays, segmental windows and shell-hooded door.

In **Nutter Lane, The Applegarth,** early C18.

Of Colen Campbell's famous Wanstead House, very little survives. House stood in **Wanstead Park** (now a golf course) just east of ornamental lake, **The Basin; stables** survive as club house; also **gate piers,** off Overton Drive; **Grecian temple;** façade of **grotto** near canal at east end of park.

Woodford
St Mary the Virgin's Church, High Road, tower of 1708, Gothic body of 1817 by Charles Bacon.

To east, at Woodford Bridge, **Claybury Hall,** by Jesse Gibson, 1790; on garden front 3-bay bow embellished with paired Tuscan columns.

In **Salway Close,** near Woodford Green, **Hurst House,** 1714, with giant Corinthian pilasters and segmental pedimented doorcase; good staircase; wrought-iron garden railings.

On west side of **Woodford Green, Highams,** 1768 by William Newton; stuccoed, with giant pilasters. On east side, **Harts,** c1800; Ionic colonnade set between slightly projecting end bays; pediment on garden front. In grounds, sham **ruined abbey.**

London Borough of Richmond-upon-Thames

Barnes
On **Barnes Green, The Grange,** *c*1720.
In **Church Road, Homestead House,** *c*1725; **Strawberry House,** of same date.
3-14, 28-31 Barnes Terrace, C18, most with iron verandas and balconies; **31,** *c*1720, with a fat bow.

East Sheen
In **Christchurch Road, Percy Lodge,** *c*1750-60; 3 bays, with Venetian windows to front façade, bow windows to garden.

Ham
On north side of **Ham Common, Orford Hall,** early C18 with later wings. On west side, at south end of **Ham Street, Endsleigh Lodge,** *c*1800, with elegantly ramped-up wings; **Gordon House,** mid-C18, with canted bays on 2 end elevations; **Cassel House,** *c*1815. Farther up Ham Street, **Beaufort House** and **Grey Court,** mid-to-late C18, the latter with pediment; **Manor House,** earlier C18, with 3-bay pediment. In **Ham Gate Avenue, Ormeley Lodge,** *c*1720; 5 bays, centre bay of red rubbed brick, giant angle pilasters, excellent Corinthian doorcase with carved frieze containing cherub heads; by Ham Gate (of Richmond Park), **Park Gate House,** 1768.

Hampton
Beveree, west of High Street, early C19.
9 Church Street, *c*1800, with wings.
Garrick's Villa, Hampton Court Road, earlier-C18 house modernized by Robert Adam *c*1775; new front pilastered, porticoed. In grounds, **orangery,** now converted into house; Garrick's octagonal, porticoed **Shakespeare Temple,** *c*1758 also **grotto.**
33-5 High Street, altered terrace of *c*1720; **62-8,** small, late-C18 terrace with central niche, one contemporary shop-front; **78** (**Ivy House**), of various dates, but façade mostly C18 and of unusual design with shaped gables; **80-84,** *c*1780; **90,** early C18, with 1st-floor bay on thin columns; **100** (**Grove House**), *c*1726.
30 Station Road, *c*1780, with canted bays; **46-54,** modest terrace of *c*1715.
1 Thames Street, 1772; **22-6, 54-6,** also C18.

Hampton Court
Hampton Court Palace, although largely C16 and C17, does contain some small, but important, C18 elements. Gateway in Clock Court, 1732 by William Kent; pioneering example of C18 Gothic. Some interiors, such as rooms in north side of Fountain Court, decorated by Office of Works 1716-18, probably to designs by Vanbrugh, are interesting examples of English baroque interior design. Particularly striking are gargantuan marble fire surrounds, that in Guards' Chamber with life-size terms in form of Yeomen of the Guard. In Cumberland Suite, ceiling of *c*1735 is early example of Jacobean revival.
On **Hampton Court Green, Keeper's House,** 1716, divided in 2 in 1734; **Old Court House,** probably built *c*1710-14 to designs of Sir Christopher Wren, but much altered, with later upper floor, canted bay window; **Paper House,** *c*1713; **Faraday House,** with central canted bay, and **Cardinal's House,** both early C18. On north side, **Hampton Court House,** 1757 with later additions – in grounds, **grotto,** pre-1769, designed to simulate starry firmament; **Prestbury House,** early C18; **The White House,** *c*1750; **Chetwynd House,** *c*1790. In **Hampton Court Road, Ivy House,** *c*1780; **Park House,** 1720.

Hampton Wick
St John the Baptist's Church, St John's Road, 1829-31 by Edward Lapidge; starved Gothic.
2-8, 9, 16 High Street, mostly early C18; **60,** *c*1740-50, weatherboarded with canted bays and, inside, chinoiserie staircase.
2 Lower Teddington Road, *c*1725; **8** (**Riverside**) of same date but altered; **20-20B** (**Walnut Tree House**), also early-C18.
400 Park Road, villa of *c*1800, with veranda.
In **Sandy Lane, Bushy House** and **Thatched House,** originally single C19 *cottage orné*.

Kew
St Anne's Church, Kew Green, built 1710-14 as chapel, enlarged 1768 by John Joshua Kirby, who lengthened nave and added north aisle. West façade 1-storey portico, 1805 by Robert Browne. Extended and altered in C19, including 1837 by Sir Jeffry Wyatville, 1850 by Benjamin Ferrey; and in C20.
Royal Botanic Gardens. Aroid House No. 1, designed *c*1825-30 by John Nash; moved here in 1836 from Buckingham Palace, where its companion survives *in situ*. Cast-iron glasshouse, Tuscan pilasters along side walls, Ionic columns *in antis* along front. **Orangery,** by Sir William Chambers, built 1757 although dated 1761. Stuccoed; rusticated walls with 1st and last bays pedimented. **Temple of Aeolus,** domed rotunda with Tuscan columns; **Temple of Arethusa,** with pediment; **Temple of Bellona** with portico and shallow dome; **ruined arch;** all 1758-63 by Chambers, who also designed 163ft-tall **Pagoda** in 1761. **Queen's Cottage,** *c*1772, with Print Room, painted floral arbour room.
On north side of **Kew Green, Herbarium,** mid-C18; 8-bay centre with giant pilasters. Around the Green, **17-25,** varied group of C18 brick terrace houses; **33,** early C18, set back; **Royal Cottage,** *c*1820; **55** (**Herbarium House**), *c*1720, with Corinthian doorcase; **61-73,** group of mid-to-late C18 houses with canted bays, iron balconies – 71 of *c*1780, with centre ground-floor windows set in blank arcade; **83,** early C18. On east side, over main road, **2-4** (**Bank House**) and **18-22** are C18; **Waterloo Place,** dated 1816. **352 Kew Road,** *c*1785 with Adamesque doorcase.

Mortlake
103-5, 115, 117, 119, 123 High Street, good houses of various C18 dates.
On **Thames Bank,** varied group of C18 houses: **Thames Cottage, Bank House, Leyden House.**

Petersham
St Peter's Church, dating from C13 to C17, but now notable for quality of C18 interior. Box pews, galleries, 2-decker pulpit, all C18.
In **Petersham Road, Gort House,** *c*1720; **Church House** and **Reston Lodge,** early C19. **Montrose House,** *c*1725, segmental windows, Roman Doric porch. **Rutland Lodge,** built 1666, altered and heightened *c*1720; exquisite example of its time. Gutted by fire 1967.

In **River Lane, Petersham Lodge,** *c*1740, repaired and decorated by Sir John Soane 1781, irregular, pediment with rococo decoration on river front; **Manor House,** early C18.

Sudbrook Park, Sudbrook Lane, *c*1717-20 by James Gibbs. Extraordinary composition: 9 bays, brick with stone dressing; entrance on garden front, marked by giant Corinthian portico partly recessed into body of house, leads into central cube room which runs whole depth of house, is decorated with giant pilasters. Coved ceiling. Other rooms arranged as symmetrical self-contained apartments on either side of cube.

Richmond

St Mary Magdalene's Church, Paradise Road, medieval tower with yellow and red brick body of 1750. Arched nave windows with pediment over middle bays on south side. Much altered, especially internally, in C19.

Observatory, Old Deer Park, 1768 to designs of Sir William Chambers. 5- by 3-bay block, looking like plain, well-mannered country seat with over-large cupola on top. Inside, pair of adjoining octagonal rooms – expressed externally as canted bays – one of which contains good Chinese Chippendale gallery.

Richmond Bridge, 1774-7 by Kenton Couse and James Paine. Widened and altered 1937, but still has steep incline and is one of most beautiful of surviving C18 bridges.

Core of town is **Richmond Green,** around which stand the best Georgian houses. **No. 4,** *c*1750; **8-9,** 8 bays with pedimented 4-bay centre; **10,** of *c*1720-25; **11,** of same date with exceptionally good doorcase; **12,** *c*1720, with good carved doorcase.

Beside the Green, **Maids of Honour Row,** built 1724. Each house has 3 storeys, 5 bays, Doric pilastered doorcase with metope frieze. **No. 4** especially interesting for its hall decorated with topographical landscapes painted *c*1745 by Antonio Jolli.

On south-west side of **The Square,** near the Green, **Oak House,** 3 bays with Tuscan porch, excellent plaster ceiling of 1760 to 1st-floor front room. **Old Friars,** dated 1687, has small recessed wing, *c*1735, probably used as private theatre or assembly room; front has unusual quadripartite Venetian window.

Ancaster House, beside Richmond Hill entrance to Richmond Park, yellow brick, 1772.

Church Terrace contains excellent group of houses of *c*1725 with finely carved cantilevered doorcases and wooden modillion cornice.

5 Hill Street, fine 5-bay house, *c*1725, with altered ground floor, but retaining staircase and some panelled rooms.

19-23 Kew Foot Road, *c*1720; doorcases have brackets decorated with cherubs.

Michel's Almshouses, Michel's Place, 1811.

Off the Green, in **Old Palace Lane, Asgill House,** 1760-65 by Sir Robert Taylor. River front 3 bays with broad canted bay flanked by low wings capped with half pediments. Inside, central top-lit staircase. Octagonal room on upper floor with wall paintings.

In **Ormond Road, Lissoy,** early C18 with fine carved brackets to doorcase. **Nos. 1-7** and **Ormonde House** also early C18; **Newark House,** *c*1740, has Gibbs surround to door.

39 Petersham Road, late C18; **43-7,** early C18; **Ivyhall Hotel,** *c*1775-80; **55-61,** *c*1720; **63,** *c*1760.

3 Parkshot, *c*1820, **4-6,** good houses of 1734.

3 The Terrace, Richmond Hill, ambitious 3-bay house probably by Sir Robert Taylor *c*1770, and similar to his Ely House, Dover Street, of 1772 (see Mayfair in Westminster section). 2-bay, rusticated ground floor; aedicule surrounds to 1st-floor windows; 2-bay pediment above. **116,** *c*1771, with Diocletian windows on top floor. **118-20** and **124-6,** *c*1770. **The Wick,** 1775 by Robert Mylne; austere Graeco-Palladian composition in brick, with fine interiors including oval drawing room. **Wick House,** built 1772 by Sir William Chambers; now with altered street elevation.

34 Sheen Road, 1771, with tripartite 1st-floor windows; **41,** with early-C19 full-height bow window; **43-5,** early-C18; **95,** late-C18, 5 bays, lower wings. **Waterloo Place,** terrace of modest early-C19 cottages.

Richmond Park

Ham Gate has plain brick lodge of 1742; **Richmond Gate** stuccoed lodges of 1798 by Lancelot Brown.

Thatched House Lodge, *c*1727, with canted bay.

White Lodge, designed 1727-30 by the Earl of Pembroke and Roger Morris: 5-bay ashlar Palladian villa, 2 storeys high towards entrance front, 2 storeys over basement towards garden front which has 4-column Doric portico with central Venetian window. Corridor and *porte-cochère* on entrance front added by James Wyatt, 1801. Quadrant wings begun *c*1755 by Thomas Wright.

Teddington

St Mary's Church, Ferry Road, Teddington, tiny brick nave of 1753-4 inspired by larger and earlier church at Twickenham (see below).

Bushy House, Bushy Park, *c*1665, remodelled in C18 – exterior probably of 1737.

In **High Street, Elmfield House,** C18.

Twickenham

St Mary's Church, Church Street, body 1714-15 by John James, with bold external detailing – giant Tuscan pilasters on pedimented north and south elevations – constructed in exquisitely rubbed and gauged brickwork. Interior altered.

In **Church Street,** several modest C18 buildings, e.g. **The Fox Inn,** no. 47.

In **Cross Deep, Crossdeep House,** *c*1700, with later C18 additions including door of *c*1720; in grounds of St Catherine's School, **Pope's Grotto,** *c*1718; **Ryan House,** 1807.

2, 3, 22-5 The Embankment, good houses of *c*1720-30.

Marble Hill House, designed 1724 by Roger Morris, perhaps with Earl of Pembroke; outstanding example of that brand of English Palladian architecture based on proportions commensurate with a cube (see Rokeby). Exterior pedimented and pilastered with main entrance in rusticated ground floor. Inside, 24ft cube hall with architectural decoration.

1-15, 26-30, 33 Montpelier Row, beside Marble Hill House, splendid group of large terraced houses, *c*1722. Brick, 3 storeys, some 5 bays but mostly 3 or 4 with some excellent carved doorcases.

The Octagon, Orleans Road, designed by James Gibbs, 1720, as extension to now-demolished Orleans House. Tall, yellow brick, with gauged red brick angle pilasters; inside, one magnificent room with good rococo decoration.

In **Riverside, Riverside House,** c1810 with bow window; **Ferry House,** late C18.

In **Sandycombe Road,** East Twickenham, **Sandycombe Lodge,** symmetrical cottage with lower wings, designed and construction supervised in 1812 by the painter J. M. W. Turner.

Sion Row, 1-12 Sion Road, dated 1721, terrace of 3-storey houses with continuous eaves cornice with Doric soffit.

Strawberry Hill. From c1751 onwards Horace Walpole, with many inspired designers including John Chute, Richard Bentley, Thomas Pitt, Robert Adam, James Wyatt and James Essex, created a fantastic asymmetrical, towered Gothic villa. Earliest part reflected some interest in creating authentic rather than wildly inventive rococo Gothic forms – but not at expense of 'modern refinements of luxury'. Best example of this Bentley's inspired staircase and hall of 1751-61. Then a phase of creating earnest Gothic by using medieval tomb or screen designs for unlikely objects such as bookcases. After this, more convincing antiquarian work begun by James Essex, who designed Beauclerk Tower 1776. Building had tremendous influence on late-C18 taste.

London Borough of Southwark

Bermondsey and Rotherhithe
St Mary's Church, St Marychurch Street, begun 1714; west tower and spire of 1747.

St James's Church, Thurland Road, 1827-9 by James Savage.

A corner of **Bermondsey Square,** c1825, survives.

10 Fair Street, former **rectory** to St John's, Horsley Down (church now demolished), 1730-35, possibly by Hawksmoor.

8-11 Grange Walk, early-C18 remodelling of earlier structures; **67,** early C18.

In **St Marychurch Street, Peter Hills School,** terrace house of c1715-20.

23 Paradise Street, generous villa of 1814.

265 Rotherhithe Street (**Nelson Dock**), mansion of c1750 with frontispiece, belvedere. In same street, opposite Angel Inn, **Grice's Granary,** warehouse of c1780.

Dulwich
Dulwich College Picture Gallery, 1811-14 by Sir John Soane; pioneering work of gallery design, incorporating mausoleum.

In **College Road, Bell House,** 1767.

On **Dulwich Common,** some stucco villas of c1820. In **Dulwich Village, 57,** c1820; **59,** c1740; **97-105,** mostly early-C18.

In **Village Way, Pond House,** c1750, with later-C19 addition.

Southwark and The Borough
Holy Trinity, Trinity Church Square, 1823-4 by Francis Bedford; interior reconstructed.

St George the Martyr's Church, Borough High Street, 1734-6 by John Price; interior altered.

Unitarian Chapel, Stamford Street, 1823 by Charles Parker; only Greek Doric portico survives.

Guy's Hospital, St Thomas Street, begun 1722, inner court completed c1725, east wing of quadrangle to street 1738-9 (now reconstructed), west wing 1774-80 by Richard Jupp, who also designed Palladian stone frontispiece for centre block of quadrangle, 1774.

Imperial War Museum, Lambeth Road, built as **Bethlehem Hospital** 1812-15 by James Lewis; portico, dome 1838-46, Sydney Smirke.

London Fire Brigade Training Centre, Southwark Bridge Road, formerly **workhouse,** designed 1777 by George Gwilt Senior.

49 Bankside, c1720; **51-52,** dated 1712.

73-8 Blackfriars Road, c1800; **85-6,** c1790.

38, 40 and **50/52 Borough High Street,** reconstructed early-C18 houses; **101,** c1720.

In **Hopton Street, Hopton Almshouses,** 1752.

146-8 Long Lane, reconstructed, c1720-5.

In **London Road,** some fragments of uniform terrace of c1820: **2-14;** and **123-31,** which join with **112-19 Borough Road,** of same date, to make a block of St George's Circus.

Fragments remain of **Nelson Square,** c1805, perhaps by S. P. Cockerell.

Roupell, Whittlesey and **Theed Streets,** small-scale developments of c1820-30.

St George's Circus, laid out by Robert Mylne, c1770 (see London Road, above). **63-81 St George's Road,** terrace of 1791-4.

In **St Thomas Street, Treasurer's Apartment** and adjoining house, very early C18: **2-14,** 1819; **11-15,** c1780-90.

63-91 and **95-123 Stamford Street,** long, imposing terraces of c1820-40.

5 Stoney Street, c1725.

Trinity Church Square, complete and uniform, c1824-32, with contemporary terraces in **Trinity Street** and **Falmouth Road.**

33, 37 Union Street, c1810; **57-63,** with late-C18 shop-fronts; **100-12,** terrace of c1820.

West Square, virtually intact development of 1791-4, with south side of c1800-10.

Walworth, Camberwell and Peckham
St George's Church, Wells Way, 1822-4 by Francis Bedford; like his St John's, Waterloo (see Lambeth).

St Peter's Church, Liverpool Grove, 1823-5 by Sir John Soane.

Grove Chapel, Camberwell Grove, 1819 by D. R. Roper.

In **Asylum Road, Licensed Victuallers' Benevolent Institution Almshouses,** 1827-31 by Henry Rose; exceptionally large composition.

Camberwell Grove is remarkable for long runs of late-C18 and early-C19 terraces, especially **35-45,** c1800; **38-48** (even), linked semi-detached houses; **184-96.** Incorporated in Grove, **The Crescent,** stucco, c1830. **220,** rebuilt *cottage orné* of c1820. In **Grove Lane,** parallel to Grove, **18-62** (even), long brick terrace of c1800; **49-55,** c1820. In **Camberwell New Road,** laid out 1818, rich variety of early-C19 housing types – terraces (**254-82**), linked terraces, semi-detached houses (**202-28**) and villas (**84-90**) – as also in roads off to south-west, including **96-110 Vassall Road, 11-27 Cowley Road** and **Foxley Road.** In **Camberwell Road,** many terraces survive from development of c1790-1820; notable are **56-84; 86,** which bears handsome Coade stone plaques; **88-92,** all c1790; **117-55.**

In **New** and **Old Kent Road,** terraces survive, rather battered: **154-70 New Kent Road,** *c*1790; **155 Old Kent Road,** villa built by Michael Searles for himself, 1795; **220-50,** incorporating remains of terrace of subtle design by Searles, 1784; **884,** stuccoed villa embellished with pilasters bearing ammonite capitals, *c*1825-30 (similar villas in New Cross Road; see Lewisham). Off Old Kent Road, one long surviving side of **Surrey Square,** 1795-8 by Searles.

30-34, 82-4 Peckham Road, *c*1790. Also in Peckham, **4-10 Queen's Road,** early-C18; **30-54,** *c*1800.

140-52 Walworth Road, remains of uniform pedimented terrace of *c*1795; **294-303** of *c*1800.

London Borough of Sutton

Beddington
Camden House, The Brandries, early C18, with later-C18 additions perhaps by Richard Jupp.
282 London Road, late C18.

Carshalton
Carshalton House, mansion of 1680s, altered *c*1710, with numerous later-C18 alterations and additions – for example Corinthian-columned porch, and, inside, exquisite, arcaded Blue Parlour of *c*1750. In grounds, **water tower,** *c*1720, in Vanbrugh's utilitarian Office of Works style. Perhaps designed by Henry Joynes. Inside, contemporary tiled bathroom.

In **Carshalton Park,** where early-C18 Carshalton Place stood until 1927, large **grotto,** at head of canal-shaped lake. Inside, vestibule with niches, octagonal room with coved ceiling.

In **Festival Walk, The Old Rectory,** early C18.

In **The Square,** 9-bay stuccoed building with 4-columned Tuscan portico; possibly derived from plans by Giacomo Leoni, *c*1725.

2-12 West Street, early C18. **25 West Street Lane,** C18, weatherboarded.

Cheam
Park Lane has fine collection of picturesquely grouped weatherboarded cottages of various sizes and dates, mostly C18. **3-5 Park Road,** *c*1775.

London Borough of Tower Hamlets

Bethnal Green
St Matthew's Church, St Matthew's Road, 1743-6 by George Dance the Elder. Interior modern.

St John's Church, Cambridge Heath Road, 1826-8 by Sir John Soane. Nave remodelled internally.

In **Old Ford Road, 1-4 The Terrace,** *c*1780 with Coade stone door decoration. Opposite, **15-23,** irregular group of *c*1720-30.

2-11 Paradise Row, off Cambridge Heath Road, modest C18 group – mostly late.

16-18 Victoria Park Square, large houses of *c*1714 with very good panelled interiors.

Bow
Tredegar Estate, off Bow Road, developed *c*1820-30, with variety of house types for different classes to form balanced residential unit; still largely intact. Centre is **Tredegar Square,** with tall, uniform brick terraces with pedimented centres except north side, which is stuccoed and articulated with columns and pilasters in manner of Nash's Regent's Park development. In **Coborn Road,** pedimented linked villas and small shops; in **Coborn Street** larger, semi-detached houses; in **Rhondda Grove** more villas, though of different design; and in **Harley Grove,** which also contains Grecian stucco **chapel** of *c*1825-30. **Aberavon Road,** with uniform terrace of 2-storey houses; more in **Morgan Street.** On **Mile End Road/ Bow Road** frontage of estate, terraces of uniform 3-storey houses: **415-45** Mile End Road, *c*1824; **3-23** Bow Road, a similar terrace dated 1822; and **69-95** Bow Road. (For other buildings in Mile End Road see Stepney, below.)

Limehouse
St Anne's Church, Newell Street, 1714-30 by Nicholas Hawksmoor.

In **Butcher Road,** former late-C18 **rectory.**

78-88, 92, 102 Narrow Street, group of early-C18 brick façades.

11-23 (odd) **Newell Street,** terrace of modest houses of *c*1760-80; 11 of *c*1810, with bow front; **2/4,** free-standing brick house, *c*1803.

Poplar
All Saints' Church, East India Dock Road, 1821-3 by Charles Hollis.

In **Newby Place, rectory** to All Saints', handsome free-standing house of *c*1821-3.

In **West India Dock,** one section survives of tall, austere brick **warehouses,** built 1799-1802 to design of George and George Gwilt.

Spitalfields
Christ Church, Fournier Street, 1714-29 by Hawksmoor; his most monumental design.

41 Artillery Lane, *c*1775; **56-8,** pair of houses of *c*1720, refronted *c*1757 when 56 was given magnificent shop-front.

65-7 and **73-5 Brick Lane,** largely of *c*1710, mostly refronted; **122-44** (even), *c*1795; **149,** *c*1715-20 with 2nd-floor weaver's window.

Elder Street, built 1722-7, largely complete: **5, 7,** 1725, 5 with leaded, mullioned weaver's window; **9-13,** large houses of 1726; **15-17,** 1727, 15 with fine Doric doorcase; **19-21,** of same date, with baroque keystones and pilaster strips; **23,** also 1727, with façade of *c*1830; **24-6,** 1722; **28-30,** 1724, 30 with excellent Ionic pedimented door; **32-6,** 1725 – last of these adjoining **23-7 Folgate Street,** of same date. Also in Folgate Street, **10, 16-18,** remnants of long, uniform terrace of 1724; **17,** *c*1718; **19-21,** *c*1724.

Fournier Street, built mostly 1725-9. **2,** designed by Hawksmoor as rectory to adjacent Christ Church, 1726; **4/6,** 1726 by Marmaduke Smith, with giant brick pilasters framing 5-bay elevation; **14,** 1726, with most unusual columned doorcase; **27,** dated 1725; **39,** 1743, next to large, pedimented **chapel** of same date; **33A,** free-standing house in court between Fournier Street and Princelet Street (see below), *c*1721, by Samuel Worrall for himself. Typical of more modest houses, **8, 10** and **29-35** (odd), by Worrall 1725-6; **1-3,** a pair of *c*1755.

24-6, 34 Hanbury Street, *c*1721; **36-8,** *c*1705-10.

5-7 Heneage Street, *c*1825-30.

Princelet Street, one of the earliest surviving streets, **14, 17, 19, 20,** typical original houses of *c*1718-20 by Worrall; **21-5,** *c*1705-10.

4-7 Puma Court, façades of *c*1820 but earlier interiors, 4 and 5 with shop-fronts of *c*1820.

37 Spital Square, *c*1741.

5 White's Row, *c*1730; doorcase exactly to pattern published by Gibbs in 1728.

Widegate Street, at west end of Artillery Row, is just inside the City of London, qv.

2 and **6 Wilkes Street,** *c*1725; **10, 14, 16,** *c*1723; **13, 15,** rebuildings of *c*1780; **17-25,** uniform terrace of 1723 by Marmaduke Smith, with rusticated, pilastered door surrounds like those at 10 Folgate Street and 9 and 13 Elder Street.

Stepney

300-34, 394-410, 495-516 Commercial Road, good examples of terraces of *c*1805-20 which originally lined this long thoroughfare; other houses in adjacent streets and squares, such as **Albert Gardens,** a large quadrangle off Commercial Road, *c*1820, complete; west side of **Arbour Square,** *c*1810; **Sidney Square,** mostly *c*1820; **175-91, 184-208 Jubilee Street,** *c*1810.

84 Mile End Road, uniform pair of *c*1725; **96-124,** irregular terrace of *c*1780-1820: 102, of *c*1800, particularly good with keystoned door; **107-13** *c*1720; **137-9** *c*1730.

21-3 Stepney Green, *c*1730; **29-35,** *c*1720; **37,** magnificent house of *c*1715-20; **61-3,** *c*1740.

York Square and adjacent streets – **Barnes Street, Flamborough Street** – uniform, small-scale early-C19 development.

Wapping

St John's Church, Scandrett Street, 1756 by Joel Johnson; tower only survives.

In **The Highway, Free Trade Wharf,** block of brick warehouses dated 1794.

Only surviving buildings of **London Docks** are range of 2-storey buildings in Pennington Street, *c*1804; **Skin Floor,** 1811-13; and **entrance lodges** – all by D.A. Alexander.

Raine Street School, Raine Street, *c*1719.

St John's School, Scandrett Street, *c*1760, with additions of *c*1830; reconstructed internally.

Wapping Pier Head, Wapping High Street, on river, pair of handsome brick terraces of 1811.

Whitechapel

St George-in-the-East Church, Cannon Street Road, 1714-29 by Nicholas Hawksmoor; gutted.

St George Lutheran Church, Alie Street, with fine brick pedimented façade of 1762-3.

St Paul's Church, The Highway, 1820-21 by John Walters.

London Hospital, Whitechapel Road, begun 1752 to design of Boulton Mainwaring and Joel Johnson; original building survives as core of existing hospital.

Royal Mint, Tower Hill, 1807-12 by James Johnson, completed by Sir Robert Smirke.

30-44 Alie Street, terrace of *c*1715.

In **Batty Street,** Coade stone door surround of *c*1800 to 100 Commercial Road.

194-224 Cable Street, *c*1790-1810, with good shop-front at 214.

26-54 Cannon Street Road, terrace of *c*1820; beside it, **rectory** to St George-in-the-East; **116-28** are mixed late-C18 group.

66 Leman Street, façade only of *c*1760.

57-8 Mansell Street, extraordinary richly detailed baroque pair of *c*1715-20.

15-21, 25-45, 51-3 New Road, uniform terraces of *c*1800, with Coade stone door embellishments.

23, 25, 30 Prescot Street, *c*1790-1800.

28-34 Whitechapel Road, late-C18 group incorporating **Whitechapel Bell Foundry,** which has good early-C19 shop-front at 34, and return frontage of *c*1730 at **2 Fieldgate Street,** with rusticated door surround. South of Whitechapel Road, behind London Hospital, group of good early-C19 terraces in **Philpot Street, Ashfield Street, Stepney Way** and **Mount Street.**

London Borough of Waltham Forest

Leytonstone

At north end of High Road, **Leytonstone House** (now part of **hospital**), *c*1800; 5-bay centre with Tuscan porch and flanked by lower wings.

Walthamstow

Around St Mary's Church (**Church Hill**), to north, **Monaux Almshouses,** *c*1760, 1-storey with central gable pediment; to west of churchyard, **Squires Almshouses,** 1795, and **St Mary's Infants' School,** 1828; to south-west, **Vestry House,** built as workhouse in 1730 and enlarged 1756.

In **Forest Road,** some good large houses. **Water House** (now **William Morris Gallery**), 1762, with 2 full-height curved bays flanking handsome porch. **Brookscroft,** with 3-bay pediment. **Thorpe Combe,** also with 3-bay pediment; mid-C18.

398 Hoe Street (**The Chestnuts**), mid-C18.

115 High Street (**Northcott House**) *c*1750.

In **Shernhall Street, Walthamstow House** (now part of **convent**), late C18.

In **Woodford New Road,** incorporated in **Forest School,** row of handsome C18 houses.

London Borough of Wandsworth

Battersea

St Mary's Church, Battersea Church Road, 1775-7 by Joseph Dixon, in provincial manner.

44 Vicarage Crescent, early C18.

Clapham

(Most of Clapham is in Lambeth, qv.)

In **Lavender Gardens, No. 2** (**The Shrubbery**), 1796.

Putney

Winchester House, Lower Richmond Road, *c*1730, with west wing of *c*1760.

Roehampton

Manresa House (originally **Bessborough House**), Danebury Avenue, by Sir William Chambers 1760-68; conceived as villa modelled on Stourhead. Interior one of best examples of Chambers' early style. Also in the Avenue, **Mount Clare,** large villa of 1770-73 by Sir Robert Taylor, with portico of *c*1780.

Downshire House, Roehampton Lane, *c*1770, 6 bays, 2 storeys. Off **Clarence Lane, Grove House** (now **Froebel Institute**), 1777 by James Wyatt.

Roehampton House (now **Queen Mary's Hospital**), Roehampton Lane, 1710-12 by Thomas Archer.

278 / Georgian Buildings

Tooting
Hill House, Church Lane, late-C18 villa.

Wandsworth
All Saints' Church, Wandsworth High Street, body of 1779-80, but altered.
St Anne's Church, St Ann's Hill, 1820-24 by Sir Robert Smirke.
Friends' Meeting House, Wandsworth High Street, 1778.
In **Dormay Street, Wentworth House,** early-C18.
14 Garratt Lane, façade of *c*1760.
22-4 Putney Bridge Road, pair of *c*1714.
In **Wandsworth Plain, 1-6 Church Row,** excellent loosely uniform terrace of 1723.

City of Westminster

Belgravia
St Peter's Church, Eaton Square, 1824-7 by Henry Hakewill; neo-Grecian with giant portico.
St George's Hospital, Hyde Park Corner, 1828-9 by William Wilkins in Grecian manner.
Belgrave Square, 1825-40 by George Basevi, with free-standing corner mansions by other architects. Around the Square are earlier developments: **Chapel Street,** 1775-1811; **Chester Street,** begun 1805; **Halkin Street,** begun 1807; **Wilton Street,** 1817; **Motcomb Street,** with early-C19 terraces, including stuccoed and pedimented **Pantechnicon (Sotheby's, Belgravia),** *c*1830 by Joseph Jopling; **Wilton Place, Wilton Crescent,** both 1827.
Eaton Place, Eaton Square, Belgrave Place, Chester Square, all developed 1825-53 by Thomas Cubitt in monumental classical manner reminiscent of Nash's Regent's Park development.
Ebury Street has long terraces of more modest early-C19 brick and stucco houses, and J.P. Gandy's **Pimlico Literary Institute,** 1830, with Doric portico set *in antis*. **Nos. 162-170** and **180-88** are early-C18. At west end, across Pimlico Green, **Bloomfield Terrace,** early-C19 semi-detached cottages.

Charing Cross and Strand
St Mary-le-Strand Church, 1714-17 by Gibbs at his most Italian baroque.
Somerset House, Strand, designed by Sir William Chambers, begun 1776; first attempt to create large-scale public building for various Government offices. Style remarkably academic, planning and detail masterly and much influenced by French neo-classicism. East portion of Somerset House is **King's College,** built in matching style by Sir Robert Smirke, 1829-35. In same style, **West Court,** 1856 by Sir James Pennethorne.
Of the Adam brothers' **Adelphi** development of 1768-72 very little survives. Remnants include some of substructure, visible in **Lower Robert Street,** off York Buildings; **7 Adam Street,** on axis with John Adam Street, pedimented, with pilasters embellished with characteristic Adam honeysuckle motif; **8** and **9,** with plain brick façades and good doorways; **10,** with curved façade and very deep area; **18,** more imposing with arched door, returning to adjoin 2 John Adam Street. **8 John Adam Street (Royal Society of Arts),** 1772-4, with Greek Ionic columns, pediment, giant Adam version of Venetian window on 1st floor; good interiors, especially lecture hall with James Barry's allegorical wall paintings of 1777-83. **1-3 Robert Street,** with giant pilasters.
In **Buckingham Street** early-C18 houses: **9, 17, 18; 10,** doorcase with rusticated pilasters, 1st-floor canted bay; **13-14,** 1791-2.
Craven Street, laid out 1728-30 by Henry Flitcroft; **11-15, 31-41** *c*1730; but **25-30** at south end *c*1800. Ground floors altered, but many good panelled interiors remain, especially 32, with unusual stair hall.

Covent Garden
Covent Garden Market, The Piazza, Covent Garden, *c*1828-30 by Charles Fowler. Magnificent classical design incorporating Tuscan colonnades and Greek-detailed central covered arcade.
Theatre Royal, Drury Lane, 1810-12 by B.D. Wyatt. Massive brick exterior; later backstage and auditorium, but Greek Doric vestibule, domed entrance hall, 1st-floor foyer by Wyatt. External colonnades and porch, 1831 by Samuel Beazley.
24, 33 Betterton Street, *c*1720.
In **Goodwin's Court,** collection of uniform late-C18 bowed shop-fronts.
27-9, 33-5 Great Queen Street, *c*1725.
5-10 Henrietta Street, early C18 with later stucco façades.
28-31 James Street, *c*1740, **29** with late-C18 bowed shop-front.
15 King Street, 1773, with Venetian and tripartite windows framed by giant depressed arch; **36,** 1750; **37,** *c*1775, perhaps by James Paine, with curious arched and pedimented façade; **43,** 1716-17, perhaps by Thomas Archer, baroque with decorative but squat Corinthian giant pilasters, much altered internally.
25, 27 Mercer Street, rare, very modest houses of *c*1720; now largely reconstructed.
27 Monmouth Street, with good early-C19 shop-front; **61,** *c*1715.
In **Neal Street,** C18 and early-C19 houses, especially **33, 35** and **78.**
In **New Row,** good collection of early- and late-C18 houses: **4-9, 13.**
8 Russell Street, 1759.
31 St Martin's Lane, *c*1725; 1st-floor arched centre window, façade embellished with various Palladian motifs.
17/19 Shelton Street, excellent early-C19 shop-front.
34-8 Tavistock Street, *c*1732; **15** of *c*1725.

Mayfair and Piccadilly
St George's, Hanover Square, 1720-25 by John James, with imposing hexastyle Corinthian portico but weak tower.
Grosvenor Chapel, South Audley Street, *c*1730 by Benjamin Timbrell. Yellow brick and white stone.
Apsley House, Hyde Park Corner, built 1771-8 by Robert Adam; cased in stone and portico added 1828-9 by Benjamin Dean Wyatt with Philip Wyatt; some Adam interiors survive.
Albany, off Piccadilly, built 1771-6 by Sir William Chambers as **Melbourne House;** converted and enlarged 1802-4 by Henry Holland.
5 Albemarle Street, *c*1765; **7,** 1732; **8,** *c*1780; **37, 47, 49,** early-C18 in origin but altered; **50,** *c*1720 with good interior; **20-21 (Royal Institution)** has façade of 1838 over 2 C18 houses.
16 Arlington Street, 1736 by Gibbs, much altered but with excellent rusticated arch to street;

21, 1738 by Leoni, altered 1769 by Chambers; **22** (**Wimborne House**), spectacular mansion designed by William Kent 1740, completed 1750 by Stephen Wright, street façade rebuilt 1983; canted bays to park, extremely rich interior.

Avery Row contains rare collection of modest, mostly early, C18 houses: **4, 5, 6,** c1720.

35 Berkeley Square, c1745-50, with good, austere brick façade. **44,** 1742-4 by William Kent, with staircase and saloon of splendour unmatched in London terrace houses; **45,** c1745, possibly by Isaac Ware, stone-faced Palladian composition – as is **46.** Interior of 45 decorated by Chambers 1763-7. **49-52,** similar to 35. In south-west corner, remains of Robert Adam's **Lansdowne House** (now **Lansdowne Club**), 1762-8; façade set back and reconstructed, but some interiors survive, including George Dance's sculpture gallery of c1790.

11-13 Bolton Street, c1740; **14-18,** c1805; **19, 20,** c1735.

23, 25, 27-9 Brook Street, c1720-22 by George Barnes; **39,** 1821 by Sir Jeffry Wyatville; **41-3,** c1720; **66-8,** 1725, with 53 Davies Street, very rich interiors; **72,** 1726 by Edward Shepherd, with remarkably ornate brick façade; **76,** c1726 by Colen Campbell for himself (top storey later). **3, 7, 8, 52 Upper Brook Street,** c1725; **33,** 1767-8 by Sir Robert Taylor, with top-lit oval stair, vaulted entrance passage; **35, 36,** pair of 1737; **38,** c1805.

27, 28 Bruton Street, c1725; street also retains some houses of c1740: **23-4, 29, 31.**

Burlington Arcade, 1818-19 by Samuel Ware.

7 Burlington Gardens (now **Bank of Scotland**), remarkable large house of 1721-3 by Leoni, with stone façade (originally brick) dressed with giant stone pilasters (altered 1785-9 by John Vardy the Younger and Joseph Bonomi). (For Burlington House, see Piccadilly, below.)

33-4 Clarges Street, c1780, with Coade stone door surrounds; **35, 36,** c1725; **45, 46,** c1720.

4, 5, 9, 16, 17 Clifford Street, c1720; **8,** 1719, with painted staircase; **18,** dated 1717 but built 1723, typical homespun design of its date, with no West End pretensions.

Charles Street has sustained groups of excellent, mostly large houses of c1740-55 – **8, 10, 16-18, 20-23, 25-27, 39-41** – which have lampholders; and **48** which, like **16,** has obelisks in front of door. **37** formed from 3 houses of c1740; interior includes rococo panelling.

Chesterfield Street, remarkable survival of c1745-50, both sides still intact.

9 Conduit Street, 1779 by James Wyatt, dressed with giant pilasters, early example of coming fashion for stucco; **11, 43** and **47,** early C18; **46,** c1780, with arcaded 1st floor.

In **Curzon Street, 15** (**Crewe House**), detached mansion, built 1730 by Edward Shepherd but extensively altered. **18-23,** c1750; **28, 29, 30,** 1771, with interior of 30 by Robert Adam.

66 Davies Street, at corner of Bourdon Street, early C18 with stucco façade of c1820; **Bourdon House,** 1721-3, free-standing in walled garden.

2-5 Derby Street, modest group of c1720.

37 Dover Street (**Ely House**), 1772-6 by Sir Robert Taylor, with very fine, unusually detailed stone façade; interior remodelled 1909.

Dunraven Street contains entrances to bow-backed houses, altered c1800, overlooking Park Lane – **20-23** and **130-33 Park Lane.**

3-6 Grafton Street, group of remarkably large

A well-preserved town house of c1745-50 in Chesterfield Street, Mayfair: a typical example of Colen Campbell-influenced astylar terrace houses.

houses of 1771-3 by Sir Robert Taylor, façades austere and Palladian, interiors generous and neo-classical. **21-3,** c1770, with curious fenestration incorporating asymmetrically placed Venetian windows.

61 Green Street, 1730 by Roger Morris for himself; remarkable attempt to render a Palladian villa in town; originally had 2-storey, 3-bay centre (1 storey added later) breaking forward from higher 2-bay flanking blocks.

In **Grosvenor Square,** only one recognizably C18 house: **9,** c1725, tucked in north-east corner. **38** has good interiors of 1776-7 by John Johnson, behind Victorian stucco front. **16 Grosvenor Street,** 5 bays, 1724 by Thomas Ripley; **34,** 1725-8, exterior stuccoed c1796; **45, 49-51, 60, 66, 68,** c1720-30. **7 Upper Grosvenor Street,** built 1729 but now much altered; **44** and **45,** built 1727-31; **48,** built 1727-9.

25-35 Half Moon Street, irregular C18 group.

24 Hanover Square, ornate brick façade of c1717.

Hertford Street contains numerous good late-C18 houses, including **10,** 1769-71 by Robert Adam; **18,** c1765, with top-lit curving stair.

Remnants of uniform mid-to-late-C18 terraces in **Hill Street,** especially **8, 9, 10,** c1780; **17-19,** c1760.

Lancashire Court contains some rare, modest C18 houses: **9** and **12-13,** both c1710-15, retaining original stairs and panelling.

49 Maddox Street, c1725.

118, 165-9 New Bond Street, late C18.

280 / *Georgian Buildings*

The interior of the garden rooms at 11 and 12 North Audley Street, Mayfair, Westminster, 1725-30: one of the most remarkable small-scale Palladian domestic interiors in the country.

11 and **12 North Audley Street** have somewhat disorganized early-C19 stucco fronts concealing one of most remarkable interiors in London, built 1725-30, possibly under control of Sir Edward Lovett Pearce, who had worked for first occupier in Dublin. Oval staircase, octagonal room, saloon formed by 15ft cube flanked by pair of 10ft cube rooms; all richly decorated, with massive Venetian window and coffered dome to large cube.
 31-2 Old Burlington Street, built 1718-23 by Colen Campbell; pioneering examples of astylar Palladian street architecture. Nearby (No. 29) stood General Wade's House, now demolished.
 58 Old Park Street, *c*1800; **66-78,** *c*1720.
 In **Piccadilly, Burlington House (Royal Academy)** retains some important work of 1717-19 by Colen Campbell, most notably lower 2 storeys of the main façade and some 1st-floor interiors, in particular saloon. **94,** 1756 by Matthew Brettingham the Elder, in grand Palladian manner; **106,** 1761, with some interiors of *c*1765 by Robert Adam.
 3, 7, 10 Queen Street, *c*1750.
 29-36 Sackville Street date from 1730s - 29 with 1st-floor ceiling of 1770 by Robert Adam, 36 of 1732 by Flitcroft.
 8-10 St George's Street, *c*1723; **13, 16, 17, 30, 32** have unusual, German-inspired baroque fronts of *c*1717; **15,** imposing English Palladian of *c*1720.
 1 Savile Row contains William Kent interior of *c*1731 behind later façade; **3, 11-14, 16, 17** survive from uniform terrace of *c*1733-5.
 9-10 South Audley Street, *c*1738; **11-15,** *c*1736; **71,** remarkable house of 1736 by Edward Shepherd, with columned porch on side, front elevation sporting nothing but Venetian windows of various designs; **72,** also 1736, mostly altered.
 South Molton Street, remnants of regular late-C18 street, especially **17, 63, 19-26.**
 6 Stratton Street, late C18 with bow front.

Paddington
St Mary's Church, Paddington Green, 1788-91 by John Plaw; exceptional neo-classical composition, Greek cross with square centre.
 Some houses of *c*1828-30 in **Church Street.**
 Connaught Square and adjacent streets, *c*1828-30.
 Orme Square, *c*1818, houses much altered.
 3-5 Porchester Terrace, 1823-4 by J.C. Loudon for himself, with circular domed conservatory.

St James's and Trafalgar Square
St Martin-in-the-Fields Church, Trafalgar Square, 1722-6 by James Gibbs. The most important church built in Britain in C18; Gibbs's combination of classical propriety (temple front, basilica plan) and ecclesiastical requirements (tower, spire) much admired and imitated during next 100 years.
 Buckingham Palace, earlier house remodelled by John Nash 1825-30. Of his work, 21-bay garden front survives, with centrally placed full-height bow dressed with giant Corinthian columns; also some interiors, notably Music Room in bow on 1st floor, with blue scagliola columns.
 Clarence House, 1825-7 by Nash, enlarged 1873.
 Lancaster House, 1825 by B.D. Wyatt. Monumental Bath stone exterior; inside, extraordinarily grand staircase.
 St James's Palace has State Kitchen and adjoining building, 1717-18, perhaps by Vanbrugh; Stable Yard, 2-storey arcaded building with terminal pavilion, 1716-17 by Hawksmoor.
 St Martin's School, St Martin's Place, *c*1830 by Nash.
 Theatre Royal, Haymarket, imposing porticoed front of 1821 by Nash.
 Carlton House Terrace, off The Mall, 1827-33; Nash in most monumental classical manner.
 In **Cleveland Row, Stornoway House,** 1794-6 by Samuel Wyatt, altered externally; **8-12,** *c*1714, much altered.
 Warwick House, Stable Yard, 1770-71 by Sir William Chambers, altered externally, but retaining good staircase and fireplaces.
 34 Haymarket, shop of *c*1780 (formerly **Fribourg & Treyer**); Adamesque interior.
 In **Pall Mall, Athenaeum Club,** 1827-30 by Decimus Burton in powerful Greek revival style; **United Services Club,** 1826-8 by Nash; **Travellers' Club,** 1829-32 by Sir Charles Barry; **Royal Opera Arcade,** 1816-18 by Nash.
 2-9, 42-5 St James's Place, early-C18 houses, with modest brick houses of *c*1730; on other side of street, **Blue Ball Yard** contains galleried stables of 1742.
 later-C18 houses - **13-15, 19, 28, 29** St James's Place - and side elevation of **Spencer House.** Built 1762-5 by John Vardy, this is in correct, if somewhat belated, Palladian style of Burlington. Main façade, to Green Park, stone-clad, pedimented, with engaged columns; some excellent interiors including very early neo-classical room, 1759 by James Stuart, and other interiors by Sir Robert Taylor, *c*1772, and Henry Holland, 1785-92.
 4 St James's Square, imposing 4-bay house of 1726-8, perhaps by Edward Shepherd; **5,** 1748-51 by Matthew Brettingham the Elder, faced with

stone 1854; **9** and **10** (with adjoining **7 Duke of York Street**), 1736 by Flitcroft in austere, astylar Palladian manner; **11,** refronted by Robert Adam, 1774-6; **13,** *c*1740, unusual façade pointed to look like header bond; **15,** 1764-6, by James Stuart, very early and important example of Greek motif applied to domestic design – capitals on stone façade exact replicas of those on Erechtheion, Athens; interior largely 1791-4 by Samuel Wyatt; **20,** 1771-4 by Robert Adam with façade of magnificent and grave grandeur (originally of 3 bays, extended to 6 in 1936), excellent interior; **32,** 1819-21 by S.P. and C.R. Cockerell, with façade dominated by 3 handsome Venetian windows; **33,** by Robert Adam, 1770-72, with extension along **Charles II Street** by Sir John Soane.

In **St James's Street, Boodle's Club (28),** 1775 by John Crunden, with bow of 1821 by J.B. Papworth, large Venetian window; **Brooks's Club (60),** 1776-8 by Henry Holland, with austere façade embellished with giant pilasters; **White's Club (37-8),** built 1787-8 by James Wyatt, refronted 1852; **Carlton Club** (originally **Arthur's**), 1826-7 by Thomas Hopper in Palladian style; at bottom of hill, **Berry Bros & Rudd (3),** wine merchants, early-C19 shop on early-C18 building (originally pair of houses); **Lock & Co (6),** hatters, have late-C18 shop. Between these shops, passage to **Pickering Place,** paved court with modest brick houses of *c*1730; on other side of street, **Blue Ball Yard** contains galleried stables of 1742.

Suffolk Place and **Suffolk Street,** 1820-23 by Nash, uniform stucco terraces.

In **Trafalgar Square, Canada House** (formerly **Union Club** and **Royal College of Physicians**), by Sir Robert Smirke, 1822-7, altered 1925.

27-31 (odd) **Whitcomb Street,** *c*1725.

St John's Wood

St John the Baptist's Church, east end of St John's Wood Road, 1813 by Thomas Hardwick.

In **Elm Tree Road,** villas of 1820s.

47-9 Grove End Road, semi-detached pair of *c*1820.

32-40 Lodge Road, *c*1825.

31-7, 38-54 St John's Wood Road, *c*1825.

St Marylebone

All Souls' Church, Langham Place, 1822-4 by John Nash.

Christ Church, Cosway Street, 1824-5 by Philip Hardwick.

Holy Trinity, Marylebone Road, 1826-7 by Sir John Soane.

St Mary's Church, Marylebone Road, 1813-17 by Thomas Hardwick.

St Mary's Church, Wyndham Place, 1823 by Sir Robert Smirke, with tower and porch set on long south side of rectangular nave.

St Peter's Church, Vere Street, built 1721-4 by James Gibbs as estate chapel, with interior vaulting arrangement anticipating his work at St Martin-in-the-Fields.

Baker Street developed *c*1789-1800; **100-124** and **107-15** survive; **107, 108, 109, 115** with Coade stone door surrounds.

Bryanston Square, 1811 by Joseph Parkinson, long, narrow, terminated by stuccoed houses.

3-5 Cavendish Square, *c*1725; **11-14,** *c*1770,

15 St James's Square, Westminster, London, built 1764-6 to the designs of James Stuart. It is one of the earliest examples of accurately formed Greek details being used in a domestic building. The capitals are exact replicas of those on the Erechtheion.

stone-faced with pediments and Corinthian columns; **17, 18** of *c*1750; **20** has C20 stone façade but fine interiors of *c*1720 including painted staircase. **14 Cavendish Place,** excellent house of *c*1750 with fine Venetian window.

In **Chandos Street, Chandos House,** 1771, one of the best of Robert Adam's surviving London works; also numerous other brick houses of 1770-80.

Crawford Street, developed *c*1790-1810; many brick terraces survive, though generally altered.

Dorset Square, virtually complete, main and most imposing element of area developed *c*1795-1825, which includes **Blandford Square, Balcombe Street,** and **Gloucester Place** north of Marylebone Road.

117-23 George Street, *c*1815.

Gloucester Place, south of Marylebone Road, remarkable for sustained runs of tall terrace houses of *c*1800-10, interesting for variety of decoration, but no attempt to organize blocks into uniform or united composition.

Great Cumberland Place contains, at southern end, crescent and terraces of 1789.

At north end of **Harley Street,** good run of well-preserved houses of *c*1790-1800, **92-150, 103-41,** many with Coade stone door surrounds; at other end, **2** has particularly interesting decorated façade of *c*1800.

In **Manchester Square,** numerous tall brick

houses of c1776-85, with houses of similar dates in surrounding streets: **Fitzhardinge Street, Duke Street, Spanish Place, Manchester Street.**

5-15, 16-22 Mansfield Street, excellent houses by Robert Adam, c1775-80, with generous fan-lit doors. Axially placed at north end, group of contemporary houses in **New Cavendish Street** (**61, 63**), with pair of arched doors and arched window all decorated with Coade stone surrounds.

Montagu Square, parallel to and contemporary with Bryanston Square. **Upper Montagu Street** has some good unspoilt houses of c1800-25, **7-37** and **42-62,** with shop-fronts at **53-7.**

Old Quebec Street, both sides of c1800.

Portland Place, developed by Adam brothers and designed by James Adam as long street of monumental terrace houses composed as uniform street blocks, usually with pedimented centres; early and influential example of large-scale, uniform urban speculative development. Many houses survive, though most altered.

20 Portman Square, large house designed by Robert Adam, 1776; uniform façade with **21** (probably James Adam) makes single composition. 20 (**Home House**) has magnificent top-lit round staircase.

In **Queen Anne Street,** terraces of c1775-85.

Regent's Park development, by Nash, is partly in Camden (qv). Terraces in Westminster, reading clockwise around Park from Camden border at south-east corner, and by Nash unless stated, are: **Park Crescent,** 1812-22, at north end of Portland Place; **Park Square,** 1823-5 (west side); **Ulster Terrace,** 1824; **York Terrace East** and **West,** flanking **York Gate,** 1822; **Cornwall Terrace** and **Clarence Terrace,** both by Decimus Burton, 1821 and 1823; **Sussex Place,** 1822; **Hanover Terrace,** 1822-3; **Kent Terrace,** 1826. In the Park itself, surviving villas include **Grove House** (now **Nuffield Lodge**), 1822-4 by Decimus Burton; **St John's Lodge,** c1818 by J. Raffield, altered by Sir Charles Barry; and, best, **The Holme,** c1818 by Decimus Burton.

11-17, 22-34 Seymour Street, c1790-1810. Imposing house of c1775 on corner of Seymour Street and Portman Street.

Stratford Place, an enclave off Oxford Street, built 1774 to Adamesque designs of Richard Edwin.

29-47, 32-54 York Street, c1810-20.

Soho
Our Lady of the Assumption Roman Catholic Church, Warwick Street, 1778; deliberately domestic-looking façade; western half of interior preserves its C18 appearance.

St Anne's Church, Wardour Street; body by Wren destroyed by bombing, but extraordinary tower of 1801-3 by S.P. Cockerell survives.

23 Beak Street, c1825; **73-9,** 1718.

15, 16, 24, 52 Berwick Street, C18; **32,** c1730; **46-8,** c1755; **77-81,** group of c1736.

78 Brewer Street, c1800, excellent side elevation with blank Venetian and Diocletian windows; **80, 82** c1720.

46 Broadwick Street, c1730; **48-58** (even), uniform terrace of 1722-3.

4, 5, 6, 16, 17 Carlisle Street, mid-to-late C18 façades.

24, 45-7, 125-30 Carnaby Street, c1810-30.

2 D'Arblay Street, c1723; **23, 24,** c1725.

26-8 Dean Street, c1734; **67-8,** excellent pair of 1732; **76,** 4-bay house of 1732-5, with rusticated window surrounds, off-centre round-headed 1st-floor window, painted staircase; **86,** c1735; **88** retains rococo-detailed shop-front of 1791; **90,** c1760.

5 Frith Street, good house of c1731 with consoled door; **6-7,** much altered but originally c1718, with façade articulated by giant pilaster strips, doorcases grouped in centre; **15,** 1733, with early-C19 Gothic shop-front; **16, 17, 18,** altered group of c1735; **26,** c1735; **37, 38,** 1781; **39-41,** c1743; **44-9,** c1804; **58,** excellent house of c1800; **59,** of same date, with tripartite window to each floor; **60,** c1690 with good late-C18 doorcase.

2-8 Ganton Street, uniform terrace of c1825, forming group with similar **33-7 Marshall Street** and **1-10, 13-15 Newburgh Street.**

3 Gerrard Street dated 1734; **4, 5, 6, 16, 17,** c1730-34 but all more or less altered; **9,** probably 1759, larger than usual house, was inn in C18; **10, 11,** c1736; **30,** 1778; **36, 37, 38, 39,** uniform group of 1737, only ground floors remain at 37 and 38, and 36 is refronted. **2 Gerrard Place,** good 3-bay house of c1735.

11 Golden Square, 1778, with reconstructed façade; **21,** c1800-10; **23, 24,** c1720-25.

23 Great Pulteney Street, façade of c1790; **35-40,** c1720, much altered internally.

1 Greek Street, splendid, large corner house with austere Palladian façade of 1744-6, astonishingly rich rococo interior of c1754, staircase hall especially fine; **3,** c1744; **18,** c1800; **21,** c1800, with remains of contemporary Ionic shop-front; **27, 28,** altered pair of c1720; **48,** 1741-2, façade altered, but excellent panelled interior and good robust stair; **50,** 1736, with pilastered Doric door surround, round-headed 1st-floor centre window; **58,** c1720-25.

2 Kingly Street, c1800; **7-8,** c1720.

41 Lexington Street, c1780-1800; **44, 46,** c1720, refronted c1780; **45-53** (odd), c1720.

2-4, 7-8, 14-27 Lisle Street, substantial remains of uniform terrace of 1791, 18 pedimented; **34-6** of same date, with excellent bowed shop-fronts.

8, 9, 10 Little Newport Street, mid-C18; **11,** c1720, refronted c1800; **13-15,** irregular group of c1790-1810.

14 Manette Street, parish workhouse of 1770 by James Paine; much altered.

1-7 (odd) **Meard Street,** uniform group of 1732 with C19 stucco ground floors, uniform door surrounds with carved consoles (as at 48-58 Broadwick Street) and good, little-altered, panelled interiors; **2-6** (even), of same date though 6 refronted; **9-21** (odd), 1722, even less altered, with excellent panelled interiors.

20 Newport Court, c1772; **25-7,** c1790, with shop-fronts. **9 Newport Place,** c1715-20.

13-21 (odd) **Old Compton Street,** c1730, altered c1786; **27-33** (odd), 1724-8 but much altered except 29; **37,** 1728.

2, 3, 4 Peter Street, modest houses of c1800.

7 Poland Street, 1730, refronted; **15,** c1760.

4, 22-6 (even) **Rupert Street,** c1720-25.

21-2 Romilly Street, c1738; **24, 26,** c1780; **28-32,** altered group of c1734.

25 St Anne's Court, c1735.

2 Soho Square, c1735; **26,** 1758 for Sir William Robinson of Newby Hall, with large 1st-floor

Venetian window set in arch, good interior; **36,** façade of *c*1800; **37,** *c*1766, with Greek Doric shop-front of *c*1825; **38,** *c*1735, with later Corinthian shop-front.
7-9 Wardour Street, 1726; **27-31,** 1729, incorporating handsome arch to Rupert Court; **74,** *c*1830; **130-32,** *c*1730; **157-9,** *c*1800.

Westminster Abbey and Victoria
St John's Church, Smith Square, 1714-28 by Thomas Archer; London's boldest example of European baroque; idiosyncratic detailing; interior new.
Westminster Abbey has west towers and gable added 1734-45 to designs of Hawksmoor; Gothic, with some classical details
Westminster School, beside Abbey, incorporates some Georgian buildings, including exquisite **17 Dean's Yard,** *c*1820; **Dormitory,** 1722-30 by Lord Burlington.
7 Abingdon Street, *c*1750, pedimented, Palladian, perhaps by John Vardy.
Barton Street, completely of 1722, brick houses with segmental windows and variety of doorcases, forming group with **16-18 Great College Street** of *c*1720, **Cowley Street** almost entirely of *c*1720, **Lord North Street** completely of *c*1720 with curious absence of doorcases, leading to **Smith Square** which retains 2 groups of original houses of *c*1725 on north side.
13-18 Buckingham Gate, mix of C18 houses.
11 Great George Street, pedimented brick house of *c*1750-60.
36-8, 40 Great Smith Street, *c*1720.
43 Parliament Street, *c*1753 with Chinese Chippendale staircase.
5-13 Queen Anne's Gate, uniform terrace of 1772-4 with slightly archaic decoration; **14-24** of same date but highly fashionable, with central top-lit stairs, bowed rear elevations to St James's Park. Similar are **30-34 Old Queen Street.**
Vauxhall Bridge Road, laid out 1816, contains some original houses – **183-201** – as do some of adjacent streets developed at the same time: **Tachbrook Street, Churton Street, Denbigh Street.**
3-4, 84-5, 86 Vincent Square, early C19.

Whitehall
Admiralty, 1723-6 by Thomas Ripley, with tall Ionic portico squeezed awkwardly into small court; inside, some excellent rooms. Adjoining, **Admiralty House,** 1786-8 by S.P. Cockerell. **Screen** concealing Admiralty from Whitehall, 1759-61 by Robert Adam.
Dover House includes rear portion by James Paine, 1755-8, presenting handsome Venetian window to Horse Guards Parade; and Whitehall portion of 1787 by Henry Holland, with magnificent French-inspired portico set against ashlar rusticated screen wall, behind which is round, domed, columned entrance hall.
Horse Guards, Whitehall, designed *c*1745-8 by William Kent, built after his death by John Vardy *c*1750-60. Elevations to Park in textbook decorated Palladian manner, with various self-contained elements on different planes connected to form symmetrical composition displaying elevational movement described by Palladians as 'concatenation'. Whitehall elevation in form of courtyard with screen wall and gate. Inside, some fine rooms – for example Commander's Room with plaster ceiling in manner of Inigo Jones.
Paymaster General's Office, Whitehall, 1732-3 by John Lane; 5 bays with 3-bay pediment.
Treasury, facing Horse Guards Parade, 1733-6 by William Kent; handsome pedimented building in decorated Palladian manner, with much rustication and vermiculation, and details inspired by Burlington's house for General Wade. It was meant to have terminating towers.
Remaining government buildings of note in and around Whitehall are domestic in origin:
10-12 Downing Street, façades of 1766 by Kenton Couse; some excellent interiors to No. 10 including drawing room and fireplaces in manner of Kent, dining room of *c*1825 by Sir John Soane, who also designed dining room in No. 11. No. 10 extended in style of 1766 by Raymond Erith, 1960-66, who also altered interiors of 10-12.
Gwydyr House, Whitehall, 1772 perhaps by John Marquand.
Richmond Terrace, 1822-5 by Henry Harrison, with uniform façade and central pediment.

IRELAND

Compiled in association with the Irish Architectural Archive.

Abbey Leix, Co. Laois
Late-C18 house with some interiors by James Wyatt.

Aghold, Co. Wicklow
Anglican Church, T-plan, 1716.

All Hallows
See Drumcondra.

Altidore Castle, Kilpedder, Co. Wicklow
3m SW of Greystones
House of *c*1730, castellated *c*1790; but symmetrical with classical details and interior.

Annesbrook, Duleek, Co. Meath
5m SW of Drogheda
Late-C18 house embellished with Greek Ionic portico, *c*1820; asymmetrical wing of same date. Inside, Gothic ballroom.

Anneville, Mullingar, Co. Westmeath
*c*1740, probably by Richard Castle, with full-height half-octagonal bay in centre of entrance front. Inside, stair balusters in manner of Inigo Jones's Queen's House.

Antrim, Co. Antrim
Court House, 1726, with open ground-floor arcade.

Ardress House, Co. Armagh
6m N of Armagh
House of *c*1665, remodelled *c*1770 by George Ensor. Wings topped by urns inspired by Gandon's Custom House, Dublin. Adamesque plasterwork inside by Michael Stapleton. (National Trust)

Ardronan
See Dromiskin Glebe.

Armagh, Co. Armagh
Former **Armagh Palace,** built 1770 to design of Thomas Cooley; 3rd storey added 1786 by Francis Johnston.
In grounds, detached **chapel** by Cooley and Johnston, 1781-4, in form of Ionic temple; magnificent interior with coffered barrel vault.
Court House by Johnston, 1809.
Library by Cooley, 1771, pedimented, exquisitely detailed; extended *c*1820. Beside it, **Infirmary** by George Ensor, 1774.
Dobbin House, Scotch Street, by Johnston *c*1810. Severe astylar façade; tripartite door framed by 4 engaged Doric columns and with shallow fanlight.
In **Vicar's Hill**, C18 terrace.

Athy, Co. Kildare
Bridge, 1796, inscribed by 'Sir James Delehunty, Knight of the Trowel, Contractor'.

Avondale, Rathdrum, Co. Wicklow
House of 1779 perhaps by James Wyatt, though built by Samuel Hayes.

Ballina, Co. Mayo
Roman Catholic Cathedral, 1829, probably by Dominick Madden; Gothic.

Ballinasloe, Co. Galway
Market town at the end of a branch of the Grand Canal containing good groups of C18 houses. Nearby, **Garbally Court,** extensive neo-classical house of 1819 attributed to Joseph M. Gandy.

Ballingarrane, Clonmel, Co. Tipperary
House of 1797, probably by Richard Morrison. Inside, some Adamesque detailing.

Ballinlough Castle, Clonmellon, Co. Westmeath
7m SW of Kells
Reconstructed *c*1730. Entrance raised *c*1780 to form tower, castellated to match new Gothic wing, both perhaps by Thomas Wogan Browne. Inside wing, delicate Gothic and neo-classical detailing.

Ballycastle, Co. Antrim
Church, in The Diamond, *c*1755, with tripartite composition of window flanked by blind half-windows in west tower; octagonal spire.

Ballyfin, Mountrath, Co. Laois
5m NW of Port Laoise
One of Ireland's most important Greek revival houses, 1821-6 by Dominick Madden, then by Sir Richard and W.V. Morrison. Front with giant Ionic portico; on side, full-height bow embellished with giant columns; magnificent interior.

Ballyhaise House, Ballyhaise, Co. Cavan
5m NE of Cavan
*c*1733 by Richard Castle; important for it introduces motif of centrally placed bow in garden front, expressing curved (here oval) saloon on axis with entrance hall; wings *c*1800.

Ballyheigue Castle, near Tralee, Co. Kerry
House of *c*1760, turned into romantic castellated pile by Sir Richard and W.V. Morrison *c*1809. Now a ruin.

Ballymore, near Sheephaven, Co. Donegal
St John's Church, 1752, perhaps by Michael Priestley. Arched nave windows with Gibbs surrounds; large Venetian window at east end.

Ballynahown Court, Ballynahown, Co. Westmeath
6m SE of Athlone
1746; pedimented tripartite door.

Ballynatray, Glendine, Co. Waterford
By Grice Smyth, 1795. Colonnaded entrance front; inside, good early-C19 plasterwork including soffit to cornice in billiard room decorated with plaster cues and billiard balls.

Ballysallagh, Johnswell, Co. Kilkenny
5m NE of Kilkenny
*c*1740; pedimented entrance front; at back, full-height bay carrying staircase.

Banagher, Co. Offaly
7m NW of Birr
In main street, C18 **house** with pedimented Gibbs door surround set on a bow.
3 miles to north-east, **Shannon Harbour**, abandoned early-C19 canal port with warehouses and hotel.

Bantry, Co. Cork
Bantry House, large, rambling, 1740-1840.
New Street, long, curving, with many 3-storey C18 houses.

Baronscourt, Newtownstewart, Co. Tyrone
Begun c1780 by George Steuart; remodelled 1791-2 by Sir John Soane, with rich neo-classical interiors; more alterations in early C19 by W. V. Morrison and Robert Woodgate. Interior includes magnificent rotunda lit by oculus in coffered ceiling supported by Ionic columns.

Beau Parc, Co. Meath
5m NW of Navan
c1775, perhaps by Nathaniel Clements. Frontispiece with pedimented door topped by 1st-floor Venetian and 2nd-floor Diocletian windows. Quadrant walls link to wings of c1778.

Belfast, Co. Antrim
St George's Anglican Church, High Street, by John Bowden, 1816, with elegantly detailed Corinthian portico of 1788 from Ballyscullion House, Co. Londonderry, by Francis Sands and Michael Shanahan.
Presbyterian Church, Rosemary Street, by Roger Mulholland, 1783. Oval plan; front altered c1823.
Belfast Bank Head Office, originally **Market House,** 1764; converted to **Assembly Rooms,** 1776, with addition of upper storey to design of Sir Robert Taylor; exterior altered 1825; interior altered 1895.
Clifton House, Donegall Street, 1774 by Robert Joy, built as **Poor House.** Magnificent composition looking like country house with octagonal tower and stone spire.
Academical Institute, College Square, 1809-14. Long, low building, a much simplified version of designs provided by Sir John Soane.
Few pre-1830 houses survive in Belfast, but **7 and 8 Chichester Street,** 1804, are much in manner of contemporary Dublin architecture.

Bellamont Forest, Cootehill, Co. Cavan
By Sir Edward Lovett Pearce, c1730. Ireland's first fully-formed Palladian villa; exquisite design, with excellent detail. On 1st floor, columnar lobby; seemingly first use of feature that was to become very common in Ireland.

Belline, Piltown, Co. Kilkenny
4m E of Carrick-on-Suir
Late-C18 house; full-height canted bay in centre of entrance front; inside, octagonal hall.

Bellinter, Navan, Co. Meath
By Richard Castle, c1750. Centre block with tripartite door topped by Venetian window motif whose centre is blank niche. Large wings extended by walls with gateways. Excellent plasterwork in hall; top-lit 1st-floor lobby.

Belvedere, Lough Ennell, Co. Westmeath
By Richard Castle, c1740; important for early use of bows: full-height on 2 side elevations. Staircase in right-angled bay in centre of rear elevation. Inside, good rococo ceiling. In grounds, fantastic Gothic mock castle.

Belview, Co. Meath
12m W of Kells
c1765, perhaps by Nathaniel Clements. Wings linked to main block by quadrants; staircase in bow projection.

Bessborough, Piltown, Co. Kilkenny
By Francis Bindon, c1744. 9-bay pedimented front with pedimented door topped by niche. Burnt 1922, rebuilt by H. S. Goodhart Rendel.

Bonnetstown Hall, Kilkenny, Co. Kilkenny
Excellent house of 1737. Gibbs surrounds to ground-floor windows; Venetian door embellished with rustic blocks inspired by Pearce's 10 Henrietta Street, Dublin, of c1730. Garden front with 2 double-height central windows over central door and perron. Inside, good plasterwork.

Borris House, Borris, Co. Carlow
7m S of Muine Bheag
By Sir Richard and W. V. Morrison, c1820; typical of their symmetrical castellated manner. Interior largely classical, but fine Gothic staircase.

Boyle, Co. Roscommon
King's House, town mansion of c1720-30, attributed to office of Sir Edward Lovett Pearce. Handsome 11-bay façade with 3-bay pediment and Venetian windows on side elevation. Extraordinary construction: all storeys brick vaulted against fire. Interior features destroyed.

Bracklyn Castle, Killucan, Co. Westmeath
8m E of Mullingar
Late-C18 house with gate built as picturesque ruin.

Brianstown, Cloondara, Co. Longford
4m W of Longford
House of 1731 with Gibbs surrounds to windows, Venetian door. (House now only one storey high.)

Bridestown, Co. Cork
10m N of Cork
Late-Georgian house behind early office range which terminates in pair of extraordinary octagonal towers with elliptical windows at 1st-floor level and topped by pyramidal roofs (one survives).

Browne's Hill, Carlow, Co. Carlow
House of 1763 by a Mr Peters. Inside, curved entrance hall with curved pedimented door, octagon bedroom, rococo plaster in drawing room.

Buncrana Castle, Buncrana, Co. Donegal
Important house of 1718: 7-bay centre, door with swan-necked pediment; panelled interior.

Buttevant, Co. Cork
6m N of Mallow
Church, 1826; good, typical of Gothic 'First Fruits' churches.

Cahir, Co. Tipperary
'Swiss Cottage', *cottage orné* of c1814, perhaps by John Nash, with thatched roof and elaborate Gothic veranda.
Gothic **Protestant Church** of 1817 perhaps by Nash.

Caledon, Co. Tyrone
7m W of Armagh
House built 1779 to design of Thomas Cooley, enlarged and altered by John Nash 1808-10. Cooley's house follows Lucan House (qv) in plan. Full-height curved bow in centre of garden elevation expresses oval drawing room which is flanked by dining room and boudoir, latter with slightly vaulted ceiling decorated in delicate, richly coloured 'Harlequin' style. Nash added flanking domed, single-storey pavilion linked by colonnade, remodelled drawing room to make perhaps the best Regency room in Ireland, with friezes of classical figures, marbling, cut paper work.

Callan, Co. Kilkenny
Church, Green Street, *c*1830. Exterior dominated by giant Greek Ionic columns set *in antis*, tower in form of aedicule topped by obelisk.

Carlow, Co. Carlow
Roman Catholic Cathedral, *c*1828 by Thomas Cobden, Gothic.
St Mary's Church, *c*1755-80.
Court House, W. V. Morrison 1830; one of the finest in Ireland, with giant octastyle Greek Ionic portico set on podium reached by flight of steps and flanked by long, virtually windowless, half-octagonal bays housing courtrooms.

Carrick-on-Shannon, Co. Leitrim
Court House, *c*1825 by William Farrell. Inside, good stair leading to 1st-floor jury room.

Carrigglas Manor, Co. Longford
3m NE of Longford
Farmyard-stable complex of *c*1795 by James Gandon; some sophisticated French-inspired neo-classical details combined with a splendid rustic classicism suited to rural function of buildings.

Carton, Maynooth, Co. Kildare
C17-early C18 house remodelled *c*1740-51 by Richard Castle, altered again *c*1815 by Sir Richard Morrison; result very interesting. Exterior and complex wing plan typical of *c*1740. Inside, double-height saloon with sumptuous baroque plasterwork of *c*1740 by Francini brothers; Chinese room of 1759 with Chinese wallpaper and Chinese Chippendale giltwood overmantel; dining room of *c*1815 with screens at both ends, barrel-vaulted ceiling.
In grounds, **bridge** by Thomas Ivory, 1763; ornamental dairy, *c*1770; shell house.

Cashel, Co. Tipperary
Church of Ireland Cathedral, 1763-83.
Cashel Palace, 1730-32 by Sir Edward Lovett Pearce. Fine, large-scale urban Palladian design: on ground floor 2 end bays occupied by Venetian windows; inside, columned entrance hall.

Castle Blunden, Kilkenny, Co. Kilkenny
7-bay house of 1750-60, Gibbs windows, tripartite Doric porch, central 1st-floor niche.

Castle Browne (or Clongowes Wood), Clane, Co. Kildare
3-storey, symmetrical Gothic revival castle of 1788 by Thomas Wogan Browne. Inside, some Adamesque classical plasterwork.

Castle Coole, Enniskillen, Co. Fermanagh
Plan of house by Richard Johnston, dated 1789; type is that of Lucan House (qv), with centrally placed garden bow on axis with entrance hall. Plan adopted by James Wyatt, who built house 1790-98 and created one of the most perfect C18 houses in British Isles. Large (frontage including wings 275ft); details beautifully designed and exquisitely executed. Entrance front centre emphasized by pedimented Ionic frontispiece; garden front bow faced with giant Ionic columns. Wings terminate in pavilions. Inside, magnificent, austere entrance hall with Doric screen and full Doric entablature, oval saloon, characteristic Irish 1st-floor lobby lit by glass domes and topped by colonnaded gallery, perhaps derived from interiors of Parthenon, and Temple of Neptune at Paestum. (National Trust)

Castlecor, Ballymahon, Co. Longford
11m S of Longford
Extraordinary house of *c*1760-80, perhaps inspired by Stupingi hunting palace of Dukes of Savoy, near Turin. Large central octagon with 4 short wings projecting from 4 of the sides (plus C19 and C20 additions). Inside octagon, single lofty vaulted chamber with central 4-faced fireplace.

Castlegar, Ahascragh, Co. Galway
6m NW of Ballinasloe
Villa of *c*1803 by Sir Richard Morrison. Central bow on main front expressing oval saloon; centrally placed, top-lit stair.

Castle Howard, Avoca, Co. Wicklow
4m NW of Arklow
By Sir Richard Morrison, 1811. Asymmetrical castle in which monastic and military Gothic are combined. Fine interior with Gothic plasterwork, circular staircase with brass balusters.

Castle Hyde, Co. Cork
3m W of Fermoy
House of *c*1780 with magnificent oval staircase of *c*1810 by Abraham Hargrave. Wrought-iron bridge from top floor leads over chasm to high-level garden.

Castle Martyr, Castlemartyr, Co. Cork
Remarkable house that grew throughout C18 (dates of building *c*1720, 1764-81, *c*1800), finally achieving entrance front 17 bays long with giant pediment in 5-bay recessed centre. Inside, magnificent double-cube saloon with rococo plasterwork on ceiling in manner of Robert West.

Castletown, Celbridge, Co. Kildare
12m W of Dublin
The most important country house in Ireland, for it introduced sophisticated Continental neo-Palladian design and inspired a revolution in Irish architecture. Begun *c*1719-22 to designs of the Florentine Alessandro Galilei, who created façade and probably arcaded, curved wings, and perhaps general plan. Galilei returned to Italy 1719; project taken over *c*1726 by Pearce, who designed main interiors and probably details of plan - certainly plan resembles that of Pratt's Coleshill of *c*1650 (demolished), a source Pearce used elsewhere, as at Woodlands (qv) a few miles away. Double-height entrance hall has screen against inner side, carrying 1st-floor corridor. Staircase compartment at side (by Pearce but with stairs of 1759) was model for one of most common Irish country house arrangements. Reception rooms redecorated by Sir William Chambers *c*1760. On 1st

floor, late-C18 Print Room, and magnificent Pompeian Long Gallery.

East lodge based on Gothic design published by Batty Langley in 1741.

2¼ miles to west is **Conolly Folly,** 1740, attributed to Richard Castle: 140ft high eyecatcher with tall obelisk on arched lower storeys.

Castletown Cox, Piltown, Co. Kilkenny
Magnificent house of 1767-71 by the Sardinian Davis Ducart; details of Continental baroque extravagance, while composition of main block seems derived from William Wynde's *c*1702 Buckingham House, London, which had influenced country house design in early C18. Extensive wings terminating in domed pavilions; inside, magnificent rococo plasterwork.

Castle Upton, Templepatrick, Co. Antrim
7m N of Belfast
Late-C16 plantation house remodelled in castle style by Robert Adam from 1783; altered 1837.

Extensive and castellated **stables,** also by Adam.

In nearby churchyard, **Castle Upton Mausoleum,** Adam 1783; delightful little neo-classical composition with elevation derived from triumphal arch.

Castle Ward, Strangford, Co. Down
7m NE of Downpatrick
1760-73; notable for having entrance elevation in textbook Palladian manner, designed to please the man of the house, and garden elevation to his wife's taste in Strawberry Hill Gothic. Interior similarly divided: classical entrance hall and dining room, Gothic saloon and drawing room – this with spectacular Gothic ceiling with huge, udder-like pendentives.

In grounds, **temple,** mid-C18, modelled on Palladio's Il Rendentore church, Venice; early-C18 **canal lake.** (National Trust)

Castlewellan, Co. Down
4m NW of Newcastle
Town laid out in mid-C18, with 2 handsome, well-planted squares.

Court House, 1764, church-like.

Cavan, Co. Cavan
Protestant Parish Church, 1810 by John Bowden.

Court House, *c*1800 by Bowden; pedimented.

In **Farnham Street,** groups of good late-C18 and early-C19 houses.

Celbridge, Co. Kildare
12m W of Dublin
Former **Celbridge School,** *c*1728, probably by Thomas Burgh. (See also Castletown.)

Charleville, Co. Cork
In town centre, **market,** *c*1740, with arcaded ground floor and pedimented front elevation.

Charleville, Enniskerry, Co. Wicklow
2m W of Bray
House built 1797 to designs of Whitmore Davis, inspired by Lucan House (qv). Chaste interior of *c*1820.

The interior of Charleville Forest, Co. Offaly. Built 1797 to the designs of Francis Johnston, it is perhaps the first deliberately formed asymmetrical house in Ireland.

288 / Georgian Buildings

Charleville Forest (or **Castle**), **Tullamore, Co. Offaly**
Designed c1795-1800 by Francis Johnston; perhaps the first deliberately formed asymmetrical house in Ireland. Picturesque skyline with off-centre tower; excellent interior detail such as plaster groin vaulting in hall, fan-vaulted 1st-floor saloon with Gothic bookcases.

Clandeboye, Co. Down
2m SW of Bangor
Plain C18 house altered in early C19 by Sir Richard Morrison and Robert Woodgate to form 2-storey building with pedimented entrance front. Greatly extended in late C19.

Clermont, Co. Wicklow
House of 1730, perhaps by Francis Bindon and very like contemporary Furness (qv). Inside, rich plasterwork ceiling. Later wings.

Clogher, Co. Tyrone
16m SW of Dungannon
St Macartan's Church of Ireland Cathedral, 1744, perhaps by James Martin; altered 1818. Body with pedimented west end, Gibbs surrounds to window, square tower with pinnacles; interior with west gallery on Greek Ionic arcade of 1818.

Clongowes Wood
See Castle Browne.

Clontarf
See Marino.

Colganstown, Newcastle, Co. Dublin
10m W of Dublin
House of c1765, attributed to Nathaniel Clements and similar to Newberry Hall (qv). Simple, powerful design with centrally placed tripartite door topped by 1st-floor Diocletian window. From main block run extensive wings which, in true Palladian manner, relate villa to barn, stables and farm buildings.

Coolbanagher, Co. Laois
   Church, 1785 by James Gandon; now much altered with C19 ceiling, but his characteristic neo-classical wall treatment survives.
   Outside, **Portarlington Mausoleum,** also by Gandon; pedimented.

Coollattin (or **Malton**), **Shillelagh, Co. Wicklow**
16m W of Arklow
House of 1801-4 designed by the ageing John Carr of York - its main interest. Very conservative.

Coopershill, Riverstown, Co. Sligo
10m S of Sligo
Begun c1755, perhaps to design of Francis Bindon; not completed till 1744. 7-bay front, centre emphasized by Venetian door, 1st-floor Venetian, 2nd-floor tripartite windows.

Corboy, Co. Longford
5m E of Longford
Presbyterian Church, 1750, 1-storey with round-headed windows.

Cork, Co. Cork
   St Mary's, Shandon, Pro-Cathedral (known as **North Chapel**), 1808, remodelled c1827 by George Richard Pain.
   St Ann's, Shandon, Protestant Church, 1722, perhaps by John Coltsman, with tall, ambitious tower in 3 storeys (heightened 1749), each of which carries its own corner urns, all topped with small dome.
   St Peter's Protestant Church, North Main Street, 1783-8.
   St Finbarre's South, Roman Catholic Church (known as **South Chapel**), 1766 with original galleries, south transept of 1809.
   Custom House, good, early C18. Now part of **Crawford School of Art.**
   Skiddy's Almshouses, 1718-19, with arcaded ground floor; L-shaped plan.
   Corn Market, c1750, perhaps by Coltsman, survives in part.
   Male Prison, 1818-23 by James and George Richard Pain; one of best Greek revival buildings in Ireland. Massive Doric portico based on Stuart and Revett's drawings of Temple of Apollo at Delos.

The Male Prison, Cork, 1818-23, by James and George Richard Pain. It is one of the best Greek revival buildings in Ireland with a grimness well suited to its function. The central octagon and radial wings have now been demolished.

Mercy Hospital (formerly **Mayoralty House**), Prospect Row, 1765–73 by Davis Ducart; inside, good rococo plaster and mahogany stair. **Parliament Bridge**, 1806.

C18 domestic architecture of Cork has more varied character than that of Dublin: steep roofs; slate hanging; bow fronts and segmental windows, both unknown in Dublin; and many shared porches, something of a Cork speciality.

In town centre, many good early-C19 developments, for example **Commercial Buildings,** South Mall, 1811 by Thomas Deane.

Cratloe, Co. Clare
6m NW of Limerick
Church, dated 1781 and 1806, T-plan, barn-like, with round-headed sash windows and Gothic reredos. Inside, 3 bow-fronted galleries.

Crossdrum, Oldcastle, Co. Meath
12m W of Kells
Early-C19, 2-storey house; fine, large, round-arched tripartite door with large fanlight and elaborate glazing, attributed to C.R. Cockerell.

Crossmolina, Co. Mayo
Typical Gothic 'First Fruits' church, *c*1810.

Curraghmore, Portlaw, Co. Waterford
4m SE of Carrick-on-Suir
Medieval tower remodelled in C18 and mid-C19. Deep forecourt, *c*1755 by John Roberts, terminating with pedimented niches and containing powerful pedimented Palladian archways. Inside, barrel-vaulted hall, *c*1750; room with coved ceiling, baroque plasterwork, probably by Francini brothers; staircase of *c*1780; principal rooms by James Wyatt.

Damer House
See Roscrea.

Dartrey, Rockcorry, Co. Monaghan
House (formerly **Dawson Grove**) demolished but very important domed mausoleum of *c*1770 by James Wyatt remains. Also good early C18 octagon stable block by Richard Castle or E. L. Pearce. Now derelict.

Davidstown House, Castledermot, Co. Kildare
6m NE of Carlow
House of *c*1765, with pedimented tripartite door.

Derry, Co. Londonderry
Court House, Bishop Street, 1813–17 by John Bowden in Greek revival manner with tetrastyle Ionic portico. Inside court still open on one side. **Old Foyle College,** Strand Road, 1814 by John Bowden, with severe neo-classical detailing. **Bishop's Palace** (now **Masons' Hall**), Bishop's Street, mid-C18, wings *c*1760–70, repaired *c*1810. **Irish Society House,** by Cathedral churchyard, *c*1768; good interior. **Old Custom House, 33 Ship Quay Street,** 8 bays with fine pedimented stone doorcase; inside, some panelling, staircase dated 1741. In same street, **6,** *c*1760, 4 bays with segmental-pedimented doorcase; inside, good detailing, especially staircase. **8,** *c*1770, bold tripartite door with fanlight in Dublin manner.

In **Magazine Street,** good row of late-Georgian houses: **18, 19, 20** especially good.

Derrymore House, Bessbrook, Co. Armagh
1-storey *cottage orné*, *c*1790–800, with Palladian plan, thatched roof and Gothic details.

Dollardstown, Slane, Co. Meath
7m W of Drogheda
House remodelled *c*1735 by Richard Castle; now gutted. Front with typical Castle composition of niche topped by blank oculus above pedimented door. Rear and side elevations notable for display of different types of Venetian window.

Doneraile Court, Doneraile, Co. Cork
6m NE of Mallow
C17 house with ashlar front of *c*1730 by one of the Rothery family. Side elevation has full-height bows of *c*1805. Inside, oval staircase with Adamesque ceiling by Abraham Hargrave, *c*1810..

In grounds, early-C18 **canal lake.**

Downhill Castle, Co. Londonderry
5m NW of Coleraine
Classical and battlemented **Castle** of *c*1776–85 now a ruin.

In grounds, **Mussenden Temple,** delightful round, domed, colonnaded structure of 1780 by Michael Shanahan, who also designed **Mausoleum,** begun *c*1779 and based on Mausoleum of the Julii at St-Rémy, Provence. (National Trust)

Downpatrick, Co. Down
St Patrick's Protestant Cathedral has Gothic interior of 1798–1818, perhaps by Charles Lilly. **Presbyterian Church,** 1729, T-plan. **Southwell School** and **Almshouses,** built 1733 probably to design of Sir Edward Lovett Pearce. In centre, 1-bay pedimented block, supporting stone tower, flanked by lower ranges of cottages which terminate in school rooms. Beyond these, quadrants leading to houses for teachers.

Some good late-C18 terrace housing, notably in **English, Irish** and **Saul Streets.**

Dowth Hall, Slane, Co. Meath
8m W of Drogheda
1760, Palladian elevation; but inside some spectacular plasterwork possibly by Robert West: drawing room has rococo decoration on walls and ceiling, dining room ceiling with birds and clouds.

Drewstown, Athboy, Co. Meath
7m S of Kells
House of *c*1745, perhaps by Francis Bindon. 7-bay entrance front, curved bay on one side elevation. Inside, 2-storey hall with staircase rising behind bridge/gallery; a most dramatic device.

Drogheda, Co. Louth
St Peter's Church, *c*1753. Pointed windows containing Y-tracery; inside, excellent rococo plasterwork and galleries. Upper part of tower added *c*1790 to design of Francis Johnston. **Mayoralty House,** *c*1760 by Hugh Darley. Palladian, with centre pediment over 1st-floor Venetian window; arcaded ground floor.

Also C18, **Tholsel,** beside the bridge, perhaps George Darley; **Police Station,** Singleton Street, possibly designed by Francis Bindon.

Dromana, Cappoquin, Co. Waterford
10m W of Dungarvan
Mid-to-late Georgian house. Pedimented door with Gibbs surround.

Gateway to estate, *c*1826; Only Irish example

of Regency 'Hindoo'-Gothic architecture, with onion dome and ogee windows.

Dromard, Rathkeale, Co. Limerick
c1750 with full-height canted bay placed centrally on entrance front. 1-storey curved bays on side elevations. Also known as **Mount Brown**.

Dromiskin Glebe, Dromiskin, Co. Louth
5m s *of Dundalk*
1766; Venetian door with rusticated pilaster strips. Now known as **Ardronan**.

Dromoland Castle, Newmarket-on-Fergus, Co. Clare
Large, asymmetrical baronial-style castle of 1826 by James and George Richard Pain. Inside, much Gothic-detailed plasterwork.

Drumcondra House, Drumcondra, Co. Dublin
East front 1720, in English provincial baroque manner with full-height Corinthian pilasters. South front 1727-30 by Sir Edward Lovett Pearce; round-headed door topped by 3 closely spaced 1st-floor windows beneath pediment with arched tympanum, giving composition appearance of Venetian window. Now **All Hallows College**.

In grounds, early-C18 **temple front** by Alessandro Galilei or Pearce.

Dublin
St Mary's Pro-Cathedral, Marlborough Street, begun c1816 to designs of, perhaps, John Sweetman. Powerful Greek revival composition with huge hexastyle Greek Doric portico, cruciform plan, domed interior inspired by late-C18 French neo-classicism.

St Werburgh's Church, beside Castle, c1715. Front, probably by Alessandro Galilei, derived from Vignola's Gesù church, Rome; only lower portion now survives.

St Catherine's Church, Thomas Street, begun 1769 to designs of John Smyth. Standard aisled and galleried basilica plan, but magnificent north elevation of 5 bays with 3-bay pediment supported on giant Doric engaged columns, pedimented centre door. Tower unfinished.

St George's Church, Hardwicke Place, 1802-13 by Francis Johnston. Portico, tower and spire derived from Gibbs's St Martin-in-the-Fields, but with Grecian details.

St Stephen's Church, Upper Mount Street, 1824-5 by John Bowden. Neo-Grecian with Ionic portico, handsome tower topped by small dome.

Former **Black Church** (now **Chapel of Ease to St Mary's**), St Mary Street, c1830 by John Semple in his characteristic rectilinear Gothic with extraordinary interior formed by one gigantic parabolic arch.

Dublin Castle. South-east range of **Upper Castle Yard** c1760, rebuilt in replica following fire in 1941. North side in manner of c1700 but in fact of c1740. In centre of north side, set between 2 exquisite pedimented baroque gates, is building based on 1724 designs of Colen Campbell for Lord Pembroke's house in Whitehall. Dublin version, built c1760, has pedimented 1st-floor loggia of original, but also tall octagonal tower topped by dome probably designed by Joseph Jarrett. To north-east of Upper Castle Yard, good range of brick **buildings**, c1735. In **Lower Castle Yard**, former Chapel Royal with rich Gothic revival interior of 1807-14 by Francis Johnston.

Parliament House (now **Bank of Ireland**), College Green, is the most important public building erected in Ireland in first half of C18. Designed 1729 by Sir Edward Lovett Pearce, combining authority and classical propriety of English Palladian school with movement and drama of baroque – particularly in planning. To the Green, imposing giant Ionic portico flanked by Ionic colonnades forming quadrangle. James Gandon extended building 1782, creating another portico on Foster Place. Inside, domed central space, rebuilt after fire in 1792. Best of Pearce's interior is former House of Lords' Chamber; pioneering neo-classical design with coffered barrel-vaulted ceiling and Diocletian window.

Royal Exchange (now **City Hall**), begun 1769 to competition-winning design of Thomas Cooley. Ambitious building with neo-classical pretensions: in form, square temple with giant Corinthian portico and containing large, round, domed central space.

Trinity College, the largest C18 college complex in British Isles. **West front**, to College Green, begun 1752 (formerly attributed to Henry Keene and John Sanderson, but now to Theodore Jacobsen) essay on Campbell's third design for Wanstead House, with pedimented centre and rusticated base – but a few baroque embellishments such as swags above Venetian windows on higher terminating pavilions. Behind façade, massive stone quadrangle terminated by pair of porticoed buildings of 1775 by Sir William Chambers, one of which contains Chambers' magnificent **Chapel** of 1787-1800. Beyond quad, **Dining Hall**, c1741 and 1760 by Richard Castle and Hugh Darley (damaged by fire 1984); magnificent 27-bay **Library**, 1712-32 by Thomas Burgh; **Printing House**, 1734 by Castle or Pearce, extraordinary little Doric-porticoed, temple-like building. To south of main College axis, **Provost's House**, begun 1759, perhaps by Henry Keene or John Smyth. Very accurate essay on Burlington's London house of 1723 for General Wade, in turn based closely on Palladio drawing in Burlington's possession. Magnificent interior: lavish plasterwork, rusticated entrance hall, wrought-iron stair, 1st-floor lobby.

Former **Bluecoat School**, Blackhall Place, grandest of C18 schools, 1773-80 by Thomas Ivory in form of neo-classically detailed pedimented Palladian country house. 7-bay centre block, linked by quadrant wings to 3-storey pavilion, and topped by octagonal drum and faceted cupola.

Rotunda Lying-in Hospital, Parnell Street, c1751 by Richard Castle, looks much like his earlier Leinster House: form is of Palladian country house with rusticated ground floor, central pediment on Doric engaged columns, 1st-floor Venetian windows. In centre, tall, square tower carrying arcaded drum supporting cupola and obelisk. Inside, vaulted corridors to all floors; over entrance hall, 2-storey chapel with magnificent rococo plasterwork. Single-storey Doric quadrant arcades link Hospital to adjacent **Rotunda Assembly Rooms**, built by Hospital 1764 to provide income, to design of John Ensor. 80ft-diameter drum with clear-span flat ceiling. Originally card room was attached; now demolished. From 1784 additional buildings added, including elevation to Cavendish Row by Richard Johnston, under Gandon's supervision, based on Adam's published design of elevation of Kenwood House.

The Custom House, Dublin, begun 1781 to the designs of James Gandon, one of the most important neo-classical public buildings in the British Isles.

Façade completely independent from planning behind it: for example, if main door could be used it would lead into irregular cupboard behind niche in corner of tea room. Behind another part of this handsome screen, ballroom: 8 paired columns with palmette capitals supporting system of shallow groined vaults. In *c*1785 Gandon raised Ensor's rotunda and decorated it with Coade stone frieze and panels, and built entrance pavilion with each of 3 sides different essay on theme of triumphal arch.

St Patrick's Hospital, built 1746-8 with money left by Jonathan Swift, to designs of George Semple; handsome 2-storey building with fully rusticated façade, central pediment.

Dr Steeven's Hospital, built 1721-3 to designs of Thomas Burgh, façade with pedimented centre and end bays breaking forward slightly. Splendid open arcaded court behind.

Custom House, on Liffey, shares with Four Courts (see below) title of most imposing C18 neo-classical building in British Isles. Begun 1781 to designs of Gandon. Pedimented centre block terminated by tripartite compositions with recessed bays containing giant Doric columns set *in antis*; and details inspired by Chambers' Casino at Marino (qv), and repeated in end pavilions linked to main block by 7-bay Palladian ranges with open arcaded ground floor. Centre topped by colonnaded tower of baroque complexity. Interiors reconstructed.

Four Courts, built 1786-1802 to Gandon's designs, more completely neo-classical than Custom House, referring less to Palladian precedents or to work of Gandon's mentors. Giant Corinthian portico dominates centre block, linked to flanking blocks by arcaded screens incorporating centrally placed triumphal arches. Above all is huge, powerful neo-classical colonnaded rotunda topped by saucer dome, under which is circular hall from which radiate 4 court rooms. To west, range built 1776-84 to designs of Thomas Cooley; interior reconstructed.

King's Inns, block of legal buildings at northern end of Henrietta Street, begun 1800 to designs of Gandon. Elevations to Henrietta Street rise behind handsome screen wall. Northern elevation, towards a green, has pair of pediments linked by column screen and is topped by colonnaded tower with cupola, executed 1816 by Francis Johnston to Gandon's design. Library 1827 by Frederick Darley. Extended sympathetically in mid-C19.

General Post Office, O'Connell Street, retains magnificent giant Greek Ionic portico of 1814 by Johnston. (Gutted 1916, since rebuilt.)

Kilmainham Gaol (now **museum**), Kilmainham, *c*1796 by Sir John Traill, with suitably daunting details such as entrance gate decorated by chained serpents set in masonry frame.

Royal College of Surgeons, St Stephen's Green, 1806 by Edward Park and William Murray, has respectable façade embellished by pediment, sturdy colonnade of attached Doric columns on rusticated ground floor. Fine entrance hall, staircase and boardroom.

Dunsink Observatory, Castleknock, 1782 by Graham Myers; 2 storeys with central domed drum.

Viceregal Lodge (now **Arus an Uachtarain**), Phoenix Park, house of 1751 by Nathaniel Clements; extended several times after acquisition by government 1782, by Michael Stapleton, Robert Woodgate, Francis Johnston. Result is long, low stuccoed building with Regency air, pedimented portico of 4 giant Ionic columns. Inside, in centre of garden front, 1751 drawing room survives with elaborate rococo plasterwork; flanking room of same date has plasterwork illustrating theme from Aesop's Fables.

Charlemont House, Parnell Square, *c*1763-75 to designs of Sir William Chambers; important example of refined neo-classicism that had great influence on late-C18 Irish architecture. Notable is way Chambers links set-back centre block to neighbouring humbler terraces by quadrant walls.

Leinster House, Molesworth Field, Merrion Square, 1745-7 by Castle. Very much country house in town: 2 formal Palladian ashlar elevations, one pedimented, bow on north front; plan derived from Coleshill via Castletown. Fine interiors by Castle, Chambers and James Wyatt.

Tyrone House, Marlborough Street, *c*1740 by

Castle; altered externally 1835. Inside, some excellent rococo plasterwork, mahogany staircase similar to that at Russborough (qv).

Powerscourt House, South William Street, 1771 by Robert Mack. Powerful ashlar composition with provincial, archaic character unusual in urbane late-C18 Dublin. Tall centre block loaded with pediments, quoins, various baroque details, linked by 2 short quadrants to pedimented gates. Inside, some decoration – hall, staircase – in ageing Dublin rococo manner by James McCullagh, while reception rooms are in advanced Adamesque style by Michael Stapleton.

Belvedere House, Great Denmark Street, 1786 to designs by Stapleton, who set behind reticent brick façade a magnificent interior in rococo-inspired version of Adam style.

Ely House, Ely Place, 1771, equally reticent externally, looking like its brick neighbours though larger at 7 bays. Again, very rich interior, perhaps by Stapleton, particularly staircase with iron balustrade decorated with animals representing labours of Hercules.

Aldborough House, beside Royal Canal in Portland Row, completed 1798. Free-standing pedimented mansion with set-back central block linked by quadrant walls to street.

Newcomen's Bank, Castle Street, *c*1780 by Thomas Ivory, building of terrace house proportions – though doubled in size in late C19 – with exquisitely detailed neo-classical ashlar façade.

Despite much recent demolition Dublin remains one of the most extensive, certainly most evocative, Georgian cities in British Isles. The following streets include major buildings or groups.

Long runs of terraces of *c*1790 in **Baggot Street.**

D'Olier Street (now much mutilated), laid out *c*1799 by Wide Street Commissioners, lined with uniform terraces all with matching shop-fronts framed by Ionic pilasters; these survive in part at **10** and at **16,** which retains mezzanine gallery in shop with anthemion balustrade.

In **Dominick Street,** a few tall mid-C18 houses survive; **20** particularly important, containing spectacular rococo plasterwork of 1758 by Robert West.

Fitzwilliam Square, 1820–25, small, one of best preserved of Georgian squares. **Fitzwilliam Streets, Upper** and **Lower,** with **Fitzwilliam Place,** long rows of late-C18 to early-C19 terraces.

In **Fownes Street,** houses of *c*1730, most façades now rendered but retaining round-headed doors decorated by rustic blocks; a typical early-C18 Irish device. Threatened by demolition (July 1985).

Gardiner Street retains ever-decreasing number of tall brick terrace houses of *c*1787–1810, most doors embellished with large fanlights.

Harcourt Street, long runs of loosely uniform late-C18 4-storey terraces, now mostly reconstructed.

Henrietta Street, most memorable Georgian street in Dublin, short, completely lined with tall, gaunt, brick-fronted terrace houses, most with palatial interiors; built *c*1725–50. **Nos. 5–7** by banker and amateur architect Nathaniel Clements for himself. **9** by Sir Edward Lovett Pearce *c*1729, based on Lord Burlington's design for 30 Old Burlington Street, London: rusticated ground floor, pedimented door with block columns, round-headed 1st-floor centre window embellished with

An elevation in Henrietta Street, Dublin. Built *c*1725–30 the façade, with its simplicity and its subtle proportions, is typical of early eighteenth-century Irish urban design.

Ionic pilasters and keystone; magnificent interior including columned entrance stair hall with Palladian compartment ceiling. **10,** also by Pearce, *c*1730, introduced Venetian door into Irish architecture; this feature lost in C19 exterior alteration, but rich interior survives. **13** also with rich, generously planned interior.

Herbert Place, on Grand Canal, *c*1795; one of best uniform canal-side terraces.

Hume Street, with uniform houses of 1770–75 (many reconstructed *c*1968), leads into **Ely Place** of same date.

Merrion Square, most imposing of Dublin's urban spaces, begun 1762, possibly under control of George Ensor. 3 sides of loosely uniform 4-storey terrace houses, most of 3 bays, tripartite doors topped by huge, intricately glazed fanlights (3rd side largely occupied by garden of Leinster House). A few houses have pedimented doors; others, for example **35,** Venetian doors.

Mountjoy Square, later at *c*1792–1818 and more battered, contains good terraces (some recently rebuilt as replicas) with delicately detailed round-headed tripartite doors.

Molesworth Street contains a few early-C18 houses, all with altered façades.

Mount Street is in 2 parts: Upper with 2 long terraces of *c*1820; Lower (now mostly office blocks) with a few fragments of *c*1765–70, such as **No. 64** with pedimented tripartite porch.

North Great George's Street contains good houses of *c*1785 onwards, especially **39** and **47** with Venetian doors, **38** with tripartite door, **49–50** with pedimented tripartite doors.

Parnell Square, north side laid out *c*1755, by John Ensor; east side *c*1760; west side, which retains runs of tall terrace houses, mostly with tripartite pedimented doors, *c*1769–75.

St Stephen's Green, large square of organic rather than formal development: **85** with ashlar

Palladian façade, c1745 by Richard Castle, inside, excellent plasterwork by Francini brothers; **80** and **81,** pair of houses (80 of c1730 by Castle) joined and refaced to look like one; **119-20,** 5 bays, centre occupied by typical Castle motif of blank arch topped by oculus.

Dunboyne Castle, Dunboyne, Co. Meath
10m NW of Dublin
Front c1910 pastiche of Sir William Chambers' Charlemont House, Dublin. Inside, mid-C18 good rococo plasterwork.

Dundalk, Co. Louth
   Court House, c1820 by Edward Park and John Bowden in commanding Greek revival manner with giant Greek Doric portico set against blank wall.

Dundrum, Co. Tipperary
7m NW of Cashel
House of c1740 in manner of Sir Edward Lovett Pearce. Pedimented door topped by round-headed 1st-floor window. Inside, large hall with Palladian compartment ceiling. House heightened in C19.

Dungannon, Co. Tyrone
   Court House, 1830 by John Hargrave.
   12-16 Northland Row, c1760-65, extremely imposing terrace mostly of 4-bay houses, doors with Gibbs surrounds and flat cornice tops.
   Gortmerron House, Anne Street, sophisticated design of c1780 with tripartite pedimented door surmounted by 1st-floor Venetian, 2nd-floor Diocletian window.

Dunkathel, Glanmire, Co. Cork
3m NE of Cork
House of c1785 linked to office wing by screen wall with rusticated niches, all in manner of Davis Ducart but almost certainly by Abraham Hargrave. Inside, good stone imperial staircase, early-C19 decoration on hall walls and ceiling. Also known as **Dunkettle.**

Dunlavin, Co. Wicklow
12m NW of Athy
Court/Market House at centre of Market Square, 1743, perhaps by Richard Castle. Building attempts to find Palladian form for traditional use: cruciform plan, colonnades in returns, topped with cylindrical tower and fluted dome; all in stone.

Dunmurry, Co. Antrim
   Presbyterian Church, 1779, 1-storey, oblong with entrance front having 3 tall, round-headed windows divided by 2 pedimented doors, all with Gibbs surrounds.

Dysart, Delvin, Co. Westmeath
12m NE of Mullingar
House by George Pentland, dated 1757. Entrance front has pedimented door flanked by half-windows, Venetian composition on 1st floor incorporating central niche with Diocletian window in tympanum of crowning pediment. On sides, full-height curved bays.

Emo Park, Portarlington, Co. Laois
Massive and important country house begun 1791 to designs of James Gandon. Work ceased 1798, not completed until 1834-6 by Lewis Vulliamy, rotunda and dome not added until 1860. Entrance front Gandon's, with particularly bold neoclassical detailing.

Emsworth, Malahide, Co. Dublin
Exquisite villa of c1795 by James Gandon, with single-storey wings breaking slightly forward.

Enniskillen, Co. Fermanagh
   Court House, East Bridge Street, c1785, remodelled 1821 by William Farrell.
   Former **Infantry Barracks,** Queen Street, 1790; 3 storeys, handsome plain stucco façade around court, pedimented centre.
   In **Eden Street,** 2 small houses dated 1731.
   (See also Florence Court.)

Erindale, Carlow, Co. Carlow
2-storey Gothic house of c1800 with ingenious plan composed of a number of curved bows. Large fanlight over front door and side lights.

Fermoy, Co. Cork
Town laid out 1791 by John Anderson. **Protestant Church,** 1802 by Abraham Hargrave, neoclassical. In town centre, **Fermoy House,** c1790.

Florence Court, Enniskillen, Co. Fermanagh
Mid-C18 house, with wings of c1770 perhaps by Davis Ducart; rich, baroque-flavoured composition. Pedimented door flanked by demi-windows; Venetian window on 1st floor flanked by pedimented niches; another pedimented niche in centre of 2nd floor. Most windows have rusticated surrounds. In centre of rear elevation, canted bay with rusticated windows. Inside, rococo plaster of c1755 (some reconstructed after C20 fire). In hall, architectural decoration, complete with rusticated, pedimented chimneypiece. (National Trust)

Fort Shannon, Co. Limerick
13m NW of Newcastle West
Early-C19 1-storey villa composed of series of bows. Originally thatched.

Fota Island, Carrigtwohill, Co. Cork
Meandering C18 mansion, enlarged c1820 by Sir Richard Morrison, who provided some excellent archaeologically-inspired Regency interiors, notably hall, which is divided in 3 by screens of paired Greek Ionic columns.

Furness, Naas, Co. Kildare
House of c1735, perhaps by George Ensor; similar in design to Clermont (qv). Frontispiece formed by columned door with pedimented 1st-floor window and Diocletian above. 1-storey link connecting centre with quadrant leading to kitchen and stables.

Galtrim House, Summerhill, Co. Meath
7m s of Navan
House of c1802-5 by Francis Johnston, with 1-storey wings. Neo-Grecian details reminiscent of some of Gandon's work: entrance hall with shallow apse on one side, saloon with semicircular bay breaking into garden front.

Garbally Court
See Ballinasloe.

Gaulstown, Castlepollard, Co. Westmeath
Early-C18 house with Palladian geometrical plan formed by oblong hall running full depth of house and flanked by two smaller rooms, one of which contains staircase. Central oblong breaks forward, is pedimented and contains Venetian door topped by Diocletian window.

Glananea, Killucan, Co. Westmeath
8m E of Mullingar
Late-C18 house by Samuel Woolley with tripartite pedimented door. Inside, good plasterwork.

Glasterrymore
See Gloster.

Glengarriff Lodge, Glengarriff, Co. Cork
Asymmetrical 2-storey *cottage orné* of *c*1820 with traceried windows, thatched roof, 2-storey Gothic veranda.

Glin Castle, Glin, Co. Limerick
13m N of Abbeyfeale
Pretty stucco Gothic house of *c*1780–89. Symmetrical castellated centre block with full-height canted bays, central Venetian window, neo-classical interior plasterwork; flanked by longer, lower, asymmetrically placed battlemented wing. Whole house castellated in *c*1820–30. In grounds, several Gothic **folly lodges.**

Gloster, Brosna, Co. Offaly
6m NW of Roscrea
Large early-C18 house displaying many features characteristic of Sir Edward Lovett Pearce, but provincial in composition. Inside, double-height entrance hall with excellent architectural decoration of *c*1730, including pedimented doors, niches with large keystones and linked by imposts. On 1st floor, upper hall has shallow-arched, coffered ceiling. Also known as **Glasterrymore.**

Gormanston Castle, Gormanston, Co. Meath
3m NW of Balbriggan
Early-C19 symmetrical castle. Interior classical; excellent caryatid fireplace in dining room.

Gosford Castle, Markethill, Co. Armagh
9m NW of Bessbrook
1819–20 by Thomas Hopper; first large-scale, fully-fledged Norman revival castle in British Isles. Towers picturesquely grouped; Norman mouldings and details abound; inside, dining room with white plaster Norman decoration, library with Norman bookcases.

Gracehill, Co. Antrim
Well-preserved Moravian settlement founded in 1746 with separate houses for different sexes grouped around a square. **Church**, 1765, on the square, with plain exterior and doors for each sex; rich interior.

Graiguenamanagh, Co. Kilkenny
10m N of New Ross
Bridge, 1764, attributed to George Semple. Quoined arches, niches on breakwater.

Grange, Co. Louth
9m E of Dundalk
Roman Catholic Church, 1762. T-plan, arms very long; eaves very low. Inside, 3 galleries. Tower early C19.

Grey Abbey, Newtownards, Co. Down
1762, in conventional Palladian manner; but in centre of garden elevation, canted bay, *c*1785, with ground-floor ogee Gothic windows. Inside, octagonal Gothic room.

Hazlewood, Sligo, Co. Sligo
House of 1731 by Richard Castle, frontispiece derived from Pearce's Drumcondra (qv). Inside, fine Palladian plasterwork.

Headfort, Kells, Co. Meath
Large, severe house, built 1760–70 to designs of George Semple. Interior mostly by Robert Adam, 1771–*c*1776; his only country house interior surviving in Ireland. 'Eating parlour', double cube with coved ceiling, especially good.

Hillsborough, Co. Down
4m S of Lisburn
Remarkable little town, one side of main square formed by magnificent mid-C18 gates to forecourt of **Hillsborough House**, which is rambling late-C18 affair, altered in C19. Other sides formed largely by 3-storey, 3- and 4-bay houses of *c*1800 with semicircular-arched doors.
Church is most important building in town: *c*1760, perhaps by Sanderson Miller, it initiated Gothic revival in Ireland.
Hillsborough Fort, also *c*1760, Miller again probably involved in design. Symmetrical, castellated, with square towers.

Kilcarty, Kilmessan, Co. Meath
6m E of Trim
Designed *c*1770–80 by Thomas Ivory; supreme example of farmhouse raised to status of villa by skilful disposition of elements, sparing use of architectural decoration. Simple centre flanked by 1-storey wings from which extend quadrant walls linking to gable ends of farm ranges.

Kildoagh, Ballyconnell, Co. Cavan
5m W of Belturbet
Roman Catholic Church, dated 1796; long, low, narrow 1-storey building with 2 Gothic doors on entrance side. Inside, galleries at ends.

Kilkenny, Co. Kilkenny
Court House, *c*1790–95; pedimented Doric centrepiece, tripartite windows; plan seems derived from Gandon's now-lost Waterford Court.
Tholsel, 1761, probably by William Colles. 2 storeys, 5-bay Tuscan arcade over pavement, tall pitched roof supporting octagonal lantern.
Beside St Canice's churchyard, **Bishop's Palace**, 1735–6; door with Gibbs surround.
On east bank of Nore, opposite Castle, **Kilkenny College**, *c*1780; front door with large Dublin-type fanlight. South of Castle, **Switsir's Asylum**, set of 5 almshouses of 1803. Castle itself is largely reconstruction of 1826 by William Robertson.
Green's Bridge, 1764 by George Smith. Arches embellished with voussoir blocks, aedicules above breakwater, block cornice; design taken straight from Palladio's *Quattro Libri* III, plate vii.

Kilruddery, Co. Wicklow
Tudor revival mansion of *c*1820 (now partly demolished) by Sir Richard Morrison, set in most important early-C18 formal **garden** in Ireland, which includes 2 canals, a miniature amphitheatre and many statues.

Kilshannig, Rathcormack, Co. Cork
*c*1765 by Davis Ducart; remarkable combination of Continental baroque in details, such as mezzanine on entrance front, and of English baroque in plan, which seems simplified form of Vanbrugh's Castle Howard, North Yorkshire. Inside, fine rococo plaster by Francini brothers; hall with corner quadrant vault; off hall, curved stone stair modelled on Inigo Jones's tulip stair at Queen's House, Greenwich.

King's House
See Boyle.

Knockbreda
See Newtownbreda.

Ledwithstown, Ballymahon, Co. Longford
12m s of Longford
Perfect small Palladian house, probably by Richard Castle, looking *c*1735-40 but dated 1746 on hopper. Interesting miniature Palladian plan with long entrance hall leading into saloon which extends across almost two-thirds of back elevation. Cross-axis contains 2 staircases of different sizes.

Leixlip Castle, Leixlip, Co. Kildare
8m w of Dublin
Medieval castle partly rebuilt in C18. Good interiors of *c*1735 and *c*1755-60, especially staircase. Rococo Gothic glazing.

Lifford, Co. Donegal
1m w of Strabane
Court House, dated 1745, by Michael Priestley. Gibbs surrounds to windows and door. Gutted but now being restored.

Limerick, Co. Limerick
  Town Hall, Patrick Street, built 1805 as **Mercantile Buildings.**
  Custom House, 1765-9 by Davis Ducart. Frontispiece of fluted pilasters rising from rusticated arcaded ground floor and supporting full entablature. Interesting Continental baroque details: panelled piers, architraves to upper windows breaking upwards.
  Court House, by the Castle, 1810 by Nicholas and William Hannan; Roman Doric. Reconstructed 1957.
  St John's Square contains group of 10 houses of *c*1751 with stone oculi, niches, other Richard Castle details; probably erected under supervision of Francis Bindon.

Lisdonagh, Headford, Co. Galway
14m N of Galway
*c*1790; full-height bow in centre of entrance elevation expresses oval entrance hall. Hall walls painted with Ionic order and figures in grisaille.

Lodge Park, Straffan, Co. Kildare
7m N of Naas
Prime example of stretching frontage of essentially modest house by use of wings and pavilions. Design of *c*1775, perhaps by Nathaniel Clements. 5-bay centre block, with tripartite pedimented door, linked by quadrant wings to 3-bay pavilions, these linked to slightly lower 3-bay pavilions by straight wall.

Londonderry
See Derry.

Longfield, Goold's Cross, Co. Tipperary
6m NW of Cashel
1770; epitome of bay-fronted house. Entrance front has central full-height curved bay expressing oval entrance hall; rear elevation curved bow within which staircase rises; on side elevations full-height canted bays.

Lota, Glanmire, Co. Cork
3m NE of Cork
Fine house of *c*1765 by Davis Ducart. 9-bay centre block with wings leading to pavilions. Porch has curious French baroque detail: banded columns, concave curved entablature. Inside, wonderful staircase hall where stairs rise to half-landing by passing beneath coffered barrel vault supported on 2 pairs of Doric columns; these, with side passages, form a kind of triumphal arch which also supports 1st-floor gallery.

Loughcrew, Oldcastle, Co. Meath
12 w of Kells
Large, neo-classical house of 1821-9 by C.R. Cockerell, burnt 1965, but gate lodges survive sporting Delian Doric porticoes.

Lough Cutra Castle, Gort, Co. Galway
1811, by John Nash, sited dramatically on the shore of Lough Cutra. Fine asymmetrical composition with octagonal and round towers. Inside, much original decoration. **Lismore Lodge** also by Nash.

Loughgall, Co. Armagh
6m w of Portadown
Court House, *c*1750, 2 storeys over 5-bay arcade.

Lucan House, Lucan, Co. Dublin
7m w of Dublin
Exquisite and striking Palladian villa of *c*1775 by Agmondisham Vesey for himself, but in consultation with Sir William Chambers, James Wyatt and, over interior decoration, Michael Stapleton. 7-bay entrance front dominated by 3-bay frontispiece a storey taller than flanking bays, pedimented, with engaged columns rising from rusticated ground floor. Plan influential: Lucan is first of series of late-C18 Irish country houses organized around entrance hall, usually with columnar screen, on axis with round or oval saloon expressed as bow in centre of rear elevation; a form pioneered by Richard Castle at Ballyhaise (qv). Interior neo-classical, probably by Stapleton.

Luttrellstown Castle, Clonsilla, Co. Dublin
7m w of Dublin
Ancient castle remodelled in early C19, almost certainly by Sir Richard Morrison, in symmetrical romantic castle style. Some good interiors of same date: octagonal entrance hall with plaster Gothic vaulting and saloon ceiling in hybrid Gothic classical style. But most of the main interiors are of the 1960s.

Lyons, Hazlehatch, Co. Kildare
1797, by a Mr Grace. 9-bay entrance façade with full-height curved bows on either side. Porch formed *c*1805 with antique columns. Inside, archaeologically-inspired entrance hall with frieze of ox skulls and tripods based on that of Temple of Fortuna Virilis, Rome. Magnificent wall paintings by Gaspare Gabrielli decorate walls of dining room and music room.

Malahide Castle, Malahide, Co. Dublin
Medieval castle, one range rebuilt *c*1770; Gothic elevation; splendid rococo plasterwork.

Malton
See Coollattin.

Mantua House, Castlerea, Co. Roscommon
1747, attributed to Richard Castle. Tripartite central feature of door flanked by Doric columns, with niche and demi-windows topped by pediment on 1st floor, niche on 2nd floor. Now a ruin.

Marino, Clontarf, Co. Dublin
NE *edge of Dublin*
Casino, in form of Roman Doric temple, built 1758–76 to design of Sir William Chambers; very important influence on development of late-C18 Irish architecture, for it introduced vocabulary of French neo-classicism into Ireland in a most persuasive way. Interior exquisitely designed and detailed, with superb plasterwork.

Marlay, Rathfarnham, Co. Dublin
Late-C18 house with neo-classical frontispiece inspired by Gandon's Custom House, Dublin.

Midleton, Co. Cork
In main street, mid-C18 **Market House,** 5 bays with arcaded ground floor, arched 1st-floor windows, lantern.

Millmount, Maddockstown, Co. Kilkenny
3m SE *of Kilkenny*
Delightful villa of *c*1765 by William Colles for himself. Cruciform plan, 2 arms ending in curved bays, 3rd with Venetian entrance door.

Milltown, Shinrone, Co. Offaly
Mid-C18 house with centre bay breaking forward, pedimented and gable-ended side elevations.

Mitchelstown, Co. Cork
Kingston Square, large and complete, consisting of 2-storey C18 houses with one side (in fact a quadrangle) formed by **Kingston College,** a set of almshouses built 1771–5 by John Morrison for decayed gentlefolk.

Moira, Co. Down
5m NE *of Lurgan*
Church, 1723; simple classical body, splendid Doric segmental-pedimented west door.

Monasterevin, Co. Kildare
7m W *of Kildare*
Moore Abbey. Main block 1767; very plain but has pointed windows with Gothic glazing, hood moulds to ground and 1st floors. Inside, Gothic plasterwork in drawing and dining rooms.

Canal town with good groups of **warehouses, merchants' houses,** *c*1800. Also tall, gaunt 7-bay, 3-storey pedimented former **Charter School** of *c*1740 (now a **warehouse**).

Monkstown, Co. Dublin
Church of Ireland Church, *c*1830 by John Semple in his personal, stripped-down Gothic manner.

Mountainstown, Navan, Co. Meath
House of *c*1740–50 with entrance elevation embellished with giant Ionic pilasters. Handsome Venetian door with Ionic columns, half-urns over side lights.

Mount Henry, Portarlington, Co. Laois
Small house, *c*1800 by Sir Richard Morrison. Single-storey pedimented Ionic portico set between two shallow curved bows with only a single window in each storey. Inside, hall lined with Ionic columns and stone staircase with brass balusters.

Mount Ievers Court, Sixmilebridge, Co. Clare
12m SE *of Ennis*
Perfect example of tall Irish house, begun *c*1736 to designs of John Rothery – but looks *c*1700. Both fronts well composed, 3 storeys, 7 bays, but one stone and other brick. Elevations seem derived from Inigo Jones's Chevening, as published in *Vitruvius Britannicus,* Volume 1 of 1715. Inside, some good panelled rooms, primitive painted overmantel showing house and layout in original form. On top floor, a long gallery.

Mount Juliet, Thomastown, Co. Kilkenny
10m SE *of Kilkenny*
Large pile of *c*1770–80. 13-bay entrance front with full-height shallow bows at each end. Inside, good Adamesque plasterwork.

Mount Kennedy, Co. Wicklow
Excellent villa of 1782–4 by Thomas Cooley, based on a James Wyatt plan of *c*1772. 7-bay, 2-storey entrance front with pedimented tripartite door topped by huge Diocletian window. Plan of Lucan House type with saloon on axis with entrance hall and expressed as bow on garden elevation. Octagonal upper hall lit by circular domed lantern. Plasterwork by Michael Stapleton.

Mount Shannon, Castleconnell, Co. Limerick
2-storey C18 house with giant Greek Ionic portico of *c*1815 by Lewis Wyatt. Now a ruin.

Mount Stewart, Newtownards, Co. Down
Large, low house, enlarged 1825–8 by W.V. Morrison, incorporating at one end house of 1803 designed by George Dance the Younger which has excellent neo-classical interior. Centre of front dominated by giant 4-columned Ionic portico behind which is vast top-lit entrance hall.

In grounds, one of most architecturally interesting garden buildings in Ireland: **Temple of the Winds,** built 1780 to designs by James Stuart, based on Tower of the Winds in Athens. (National Trust)

Multyfarnham, Co. Westmeath
7m N *of Mullingar*
Wilson's Hospital School, interesting and extensive Palladian composition of *c*1760 by John Pentland.

Nenagh, Co. Tipperary
3-storey octagonal centre block of early-C19 radial **Prison** used as Governor's house. Handsome neo-classical details.

Newberry Hall, Carbury, Co. Kildare
4m E *of Edenderry*
Simple but powerfully designed 2-storey house of *c*1765, perhaps by Nathaniel Clements. As at Colganstown (qv), main elevation is dominated by tripartite door topped by huge Diocletian window. On garden elevation, curved central bow. Curved walls link centre block to 2-storey pavilions each with full-height canted bay.

Newbridge House, Donabate, Co. Dublin
3m NE *of Swords*
1737, probably by Richard Castle. 2 storeys; tripartite door. Wing of 1765 with rococo ceiling in saloon.

New Hall, Ennis, Co. Clare
*c*1766, probably to designs of Francis Bindon. On entrance front, full-height canted bay with pedimented doorcase; on side elevation, full-height curved bays. Octagonal entrance hall contains extraordinary cupboard designed to look like organ. Fine plasterwork in drawing room.

Newtownards, Co. Down
  Market Hall/Assembly Room in main square; excellent design of 1765 by Ferdinando Stratford. Lofty pedimented central feature, with 1st-floor Venetian window over handsome arched door, flanked by lower 5-bay blocks.

Newtownbreda/Knockbreda, Co. Antrim
3m s of Belfast
Church by Richard Castle, 1737. Cruciform plan with semicircular transept, west tower with spire, pedimented west door with Gibbs surround.

Newry, Co. Down
  Roman Catholic Cathedral, begun 1825 to designs of Thomas Duff; Gothic.
  Bank of Ireland occupies building of 1826 attributed to Francis Johnston.
  1 Trevor Hill, *c*1770, with centre bay emphasized by Venetian door topped by 1st-floor Venetian and 2nd-floor semicircular-arched window.
  In **Upper Water Street,** C18 houses.
  Leading north from town, **Newry Canal,** begun 1729 under direction of Sir Edward Lovett Pearce and Richard Castle.

Oldcastle, Co. Meath
12m w of Kells
Gilson School, 1821-2 by C. R. Cockerell. Domestic: 5-bay centre, 3-bay pediment, wings.

Oldtown, Naas, Co. Kildare
Ireland's first neo-Palladian house with wings, designed *c*1709 by Thomas Burgh for himself. Only one wing now survives.

Palace Anne, Ballineen, Co. Cork
9m w of Bandon
Only one wing now remains of this very important house built 1714. Brick with stone dressings, round-headed windows and curvilinear 'Dutch gable' adorned with pilasters and topped by triangular pediment.

Portaferry, Co. Down
  Court House, 1752.
  Portaferry House, 1790-1814 by Charles Lilly and William Farrell; good Regency interior.

Portarlington, Co. Laois
Laid out 1667, built up mostly during C18. Notable for the number of early houses presenting almost blank elevations to street, with main fronts to River Barrow.
  In town centre, **Market House,** *c*1800; arcaded, very simple but handsome.
  In main street, one 2-storey **terrace house** has, like Newberry Hall (qv), Diocletian window set over tripartite door, *c*1750-60.

Port Hall, Lifford, Co. Donegal
House designed 1746 by Michael Priestley, sited on River Foyle. Both main elevations pedimented, front door with fanlight and rusticated Gibbs surround. River elevation flanked by wings which form a deep court and were originally used as offices and warehouses.

Port Laoise, Co. Laois
  St Peter's Church, obelisk tower of *c*1790 attributed to James Gandon.
  Court House, 1812 by Richard Morrison, inspired in detail by Gandon's Custom House, Dublin.
  Radial **Prison,** *c*1830, probably by James and George Pain.

Powerscourt, Enniskerry, Co. Wicklow
3m w of Bray
Large, splendid and magnificently situated house created from older building *c*1731-40 by Richard Castle. Entrance elevation of 9-bay centre block pedimented, flanked by long articulated wings terminating in pedimented arches and obelisks. Garden front was fully rusticated in late C18 with full-height, curved, tower-like corner bays. Centre block gutted by fire 1974, destroying Egyptian Hall, one of best Palladian interiors in Ireland, and based on Palladio's own design, with arcade of giant columns, lofty clerestory.

Randalstown, Co. Antrim
  Presbyterian Church, *c*1790; elliptical plan.

Riverstown House, Riverstown, Co. Cork
4m NE of Cork
House of 1720, remodelled *c*1730. Unexceptional rambling exterior; but inside, magnificent dining room of 1734 by Francini brothers, their first work in Ireland: allegorical plaster ceiling, panels of large classical figures on walls, swags.

Robertstown, Co. Kildare
7m NW of Naas
Canal village with large late-C18 **hotel** (former **Grand Canal Hotel**), **canal bridge, canal installations.**

Rochfort
See Tudenham.

Rokeby Hall, Dunleer, Co. Louth
Built 1785-94 to Thomas Cooley's designs, but carried out by Francis Johnston. Plan related to that of Lucan House (qv).

Roscrea, Co. Tipperary
In Castle courtyard, **Damer House,** begun 1725 but not completed till *c*1750. Tall 9-bay elevation with swan-necked pediment, architraves to windows. Inside, excellent enriched staircase.

Rosmead, Delvin, Co. Westmeath
12m NE of Mullingar
C18 house a ruin, but elegant gate of *c*1770 survives – brought here from Glananea, Co. Westmeath; design inspired by Robert Adam's gate at Syon House, London, and executed by Samuel Woolley.

Roundwood, Mountrath, Co. Laois
7m w of Port Laoise
*c*1750; modest provincial Palladian elevation – but inside, magnificent double-height entrance hall with stair rising to half-landing, returning in 2 arms to form gallery sweeping into upper space of entrance hall. Geometrical stair balustrade, almost Chinese Chippendale.

Russborough, Blessington, Co. Wicklow
6m SE of Naas
Huge and beautiful house designed by Richard Castle, built 1741-*c*1750; best-preserved of Ireland's large country houses. Centre block comparable in design with Pearce's earlier Bellamont Forest (qv), extended by quadrant colonnades and pavilion to form 700ft frontage. Inside, excellent plasterwork, probably by Francini brothers, especially in staircase hall. Mahogany stair of most intricate and pompous design, 2 Doric column balusters per tread. Saloon hung with crimson velvet, with mahogany doorcases and dado.

Scregg, Knockcroghery, Co. Roscommon
5m SE *of Roscommon*
House of c1760; tripartite door with Venetian and Diocletian window above.

Seafield, Donabate, Co. Dublin
3m NE *of Swords*
Provincial Palladian villa, c1735-40, with magnificent porticoed entrance front, perhaps inspired by Pearce's Bellamont Forest (qv), but irregular and gable-ended side and rear elevations. Inside, splendid double-height hall running from front to back, with superimposed pilasters. Hall, and partial recession of portico into body of house to form loggia, reminiscent of Gibbs's Sudbrook, Richmond-upon-Thames, London, of c1717.

Seaford, Co. Down
Severe exterior of 1816-19, magnificent Greek revival interior, especially columnar hall and library with contemporary decoration.

Shannonbridge, Co. Offaly-Co. Roscommon
8m SW *of Ballinasloe*
Extensive **fortification** built 1804 to guard road and bridge: ramparts, redoubt, barracks.

Shannon Harbour
See Banagher.

Shelton Abbey, Arklow, Co. Wicklow
Vast Gothic pile of c1819, in Sir Richard Morrison's abbey style. Picturesque pinnacled roof line but largely symmetrical layout; inside, some good Gothic decoration, especially drawing room with plaster Gothic pendentives. Dining room and library classical.

Slane, Co. Meath
8m W *of Drogheda*
Slane Castle, begun 1785 to designs of James Wyatt; one of earliest symmetrical Gothic revival castles in Ireland. Completed by Francis Johnston. Plan of Lucan House type, but usual garden bow continues above eaves to form fat, round castellated tower. Interior largely neo-classical, with spectacular exception of huge circular ballroom in bow/tower, one of the finest Gothic revival rooms in Ireland. Gothic detailing by Thomas Hopper, c1820.
On the Boyne, **flour mill,** 1763-76, probably designed by Hugh Darley; pedimented centre, windows of diminishing size with Gibbs surrounds.

Stackallan House, Navan, Co. Meath
c1716; 7 by 9 bays, 3 storeys; 3-bay pediment.

Stillorgan House, Stillorgan, Co. Dublin
W *edge of Dun Laoghaire*
House demolished c1860, but in grounds **grotto** by Sir Edward Lovett Pearce, with 7 domed chambers. Also by Pearce, **obelisk** with rock base, inspired by Bernini. Both c1732.

Summer Grove, Mountmellick, Co. Laois
Well-preserved house of c1755 with pedimented frontispiece on entrance front, and pedimented door topped by Venetian and Diocletian windows. Ingenious entrance hall with stair screened by 3-bay arcade: in each arch a door, 2 leading to stair, one to cupboard. Good rococo ceiling in drawing room. Section of house interesting: rear has one more floor than front, allowing for tall entertainment rooms at front, but adequate number of small rear bedrooms for children and servants.

Swiss Cottage
See Cahir.

Timogue, Co. Laois
  Church, 1736; small, rustic, perfect and unaltered with 3-decker pulpit.

Townley Hall, Drogheda, Co. Louth
Magnificent, austere neo-classical house of 1794 by Francis Johnston. Square plan, with single storey Greek Doric porch. Inside, breathtaking central domed rotunda encircled by cantilevered staircase.

Trabolgan, Co. Cork
Across Cork Harbour from Cobh
Long, low C18 house; across drive, powerful stone Doric triumphal arch; very impressive.

Tralee, Co. Kerry
  Court House, early C19, by W. V. Morrison. Ionic portico, semicircular courts flanking central hall.
  In **Day Place,** groups of good C18 houses.

Trim, Co. Meath
  Gaol, c1827 by John Hargrave. Entrance block with channelled rustication of French neo-classical type, excellently daunting.

Tuam, Co. Galway
  Roman Catholic Cathedral, by Dominick Madden, 1827, in English carpenter's Gothic style.

Tudenham, Mullingar, Co. Westmeath
House (formerly **Rochfort**), of c1742, probably by Richard Castle. 7-bay entrance front, 1st-floor pilastered niche. Now a ruin.

Tullamore, Co. Offaly
Good example of Irish C18 planned town: centre is large square lined with modest 2-storey houses.
  St Catherine's Protestant Church by Francis Johnston, 1818.
  Market House, 7 bays, pedimented, arcaded ground floor, octagonal domed clock tower.
  Early-C19 **canal buildings,** including **hotel.**

Tyrrelspass, Co. Westmeath
10m S *of Mullingar*
Estate village formed in C18 around semicircular green. Houses in 2-storey pavilion form, some pedimented.

Vernon Mount, Douglas, Co. Cork
2m SE *of Cork*
Remarkable 2-storey villa of c1785: oval in shape with curved end bays; on entrance front, wide tripartite door with massive elliptical fanlight. Inside, drawing room with domed octagonal ceiling; oval landing at head of stairs with domed rotunda of marbled columns, overdoors with grisaille painting.

Wardstown, Co. Donegal
5m W *of Ballyshannon*
1740; symmetrical with tower-like bays; reminiscent of Vanbrugh. Now a ruin.

Waterford, Co. Waterford
  Church of Ireland Cathedral, 1773-9 by John Roberts; essay in manner of Gibbs's St Martin-in-the-Fields. Splendid Doric portico. Nave formed by Corinthian columns standing on high pedestals, supporting blocks of entablature from which springs vaulted ceiling of c1815.

Roman Catholic Cathedral, 1792 and also by Roberts with nave of Corinthian columns. Façade C19.

St Patrick's Roman Catholic Church, 1764; rectangular plan, baluster-fronted galleries curving around 3 sides, supported on thin Doric columns. At west end, another gallery; east end embellished with open-pedimented Doric entablature and pilasters.

St Olaf's Church of Ireland Church, 1734; now disused and gutted.

Assembly Rooms (now **Town Hall**), by Roberts, incorporating 'Play House'.

Around Church of Ireland Cathedral, groups of good C18 **houses** including, to south, former **Bishop's Palace,** c1741 by Richard Castle.

Chamber of Commerce, Gladstone Street, late-C18 mansion; oval, domed, cantilevered staircase.

Westport, Co. Mayo

Perhaps the most elaborate of Irish C18 planned towns: laid out c1780, with canalized river as main feature, flanked by tree-lined malls. In centre, octagonal space with a central column.

On edge of town, **Westport House,** c1731 by Richard Castle, with additional block of 1778, probably by Thomas Ivory. Wyatt employed 1781 to complete interior, including dining room. Barrel-vaulted entrance hall by Castle.

Wexford, Co. Wexford

St Iberius' Church, rebuilt c1775 by John Roberts as galleried rectangle, apse containing altar in middle of one of long sides, screened by arcade of giant Corinthian columns.

Woodlands, Santry, Co. Dublin

4m N of Dublin

Extraordinary villa of c1730-35, probably by Sir Edward Lovett Pearce. Front based on side elevation of Pratt's Coleshill, Oxfordshire. Plan simple: entrance passage with groin-vaulted ceiling leads to stairs at rear, and is flanked by pairs of rooms.

Woodstock, Inistioge, Co. Kilkenny

8m NW of New Ross

House of c1745 by Francis Bindon; tripartite pedimented door with niche and oculus. Now a ruin.

Yeomanstown, Naas, Co. Kildare

Early C18 double-gable-ended house, 5-bay entrance front, with pediment and wooden cornice.

Youghal, Co. Cork

Clock Gate, South Main Street, built 1771 by William Meade; extraordinary 5-storey, 2-bay structure straddling street on massive rusticated arch. Each storey recedes slightly, separated by string course. On top, domed octagonal lantern. Originally used as gaol.

BIBLIOGRAPHY

There are several books that I would like to acknowledge specially. Paramount are Nikolaus Pevsner's *Buildings of England* series – now being joined by volumes on Wales and Scotland – without which the writing of this book would have been a *great* deal more difficult. Howard Colvin's *Biographical Dictionary of British Architects 1600–1840* has provided an always reliable source of information about architects and buildings and been a welcome means of discovering and checking dates. Maurice Craig's books on Irish architecture, notably his *Architecture of Ireland* and *Classic Irish Houses of the Middle Size* have been invaluable, as has Mark Bence-Jones's *Burke's Guide to Country Houses: Ireland*.

Adam, Robert and James, *The Works in Architecture*, London 1773.
Beard, Geoffrey, *The Work of Robert Adam*, London 1978.
Bell, Colin and Rose, *City Fathers: the Early History of Town Planning in Britain*, London 1969 and 1972.
Berkeley, George, *Alciphron; or the Minute Philosopher*, 1732.
Bolton, A. T., *The Architecture of Robert Adam*, 2 vols, London 1922.
Boyle, Richard, Earl of Burlington, *Fabbriche Antiche*, 1730.
Bracegirdle, B., *The Archaeology of the Industrial Revolution*, London 1973.
Brett, C. E. B., *Buildings of Belfast 1700–1914*, London 1967.
Burke's Guide to Country Houses, Vol I, *Ireland* by Bence-Jones, Mark; Vol II, *Herefordshire, Shropshire, Warwickshire and Worcestershire* by Reid, Peter; Vol III, *East Anglia* by Kenworthy-Browne, John; Reid, Peter; Sayer, Michael; and Watkin, David.
Campbell, Colen, *Vitruvius Britannicus*, 3 vols (1715–25) reissued 1731; continued by Badeslade, T. and Rocque, J., 1 vol 1739; and Woolfe, John and Gandon, James, 2 vols 1767–71.
Campbell, R., *The London Tradesman*, London 1747.
Chambers, Sir William, *Treatise on Civil Architecture*, 1759, third edition with new introduction 1791.
Clifton-Taylor, Alec, *The Pattern of English Building*, London 1972.
Clifton-Taylor, Alec, *Six English Towns*, 1978; *Six More English Towns*, 1981; *Another Six English Towns*, London 1984.
Craig, Maurice, *Dublin 1660–1860*, London 1952.
Craig, Maurice, *Classic Irish Houses of the Middle Size*, London 1976.
Craig, Maurice, *The Architecture of Ireland from the Earliest Times to 1880*, London 1982.
Craig, Maurice and Fitzgerald, Desmond, the Knight of Glin, *Ireland Observed*, Cork 1970.
Crook, J. Mordaunt, *The Greek Revival*, London 1972.
Cruickshank, Dan and Wyld, Peter, *London: the Art of Georgian Building*, London 1975.
Colvin, Howard, *A Biographical Dictionary of British Architects 1600–1840*, London 1978.
Colvin, Howard and Harris, John, eds *The Country Seat*, London 1970.
Colvin, Howard, ed. *The History of the King's Works*, 6 vols, 1963–80.
Colvin, Howard and Craig, Maurice, *The Architectural Drawings of Sir John Vanbrugh and Sir Edward Lovett Pearce*, Oxford 1964.
Cooper, Anthony Ashley, 3rd Earl of Shaftesbury, *Characteristicks of Men and Manners*, 1714.
Darley, Gillian, *Villages of Vision*, London 1975.

de Breffny, Brian, *Churches and Abbeys of Ireland*, 1976.
Downes, Kerry, *English Baroque Architecture*, London 1966.
Downes, Kerry, *Nicholas Hawksmoor*, London 1959.
Dunbar, John G., *The Historic Architecture of Scotland*, London 1968.
Eastlake, C. L., *A History of the Gothic Revival*, London 1872, Leicester 1970.
Elmes, J., *Metropolitan Improvements*, London 1829.
Fowler, John and Cornforth, John, *English Decoration in the Eighteenth Century*, London 1974.
Friedman, Terry, *James Gibbs*, New Haven and London 1984.
George, M. Dorothy, *London Life in the Eighteenth Century*, 1925. Revised edition London 1976.
Genius of Architecture series: Watkin, David, *Athenian Stuart, Pioneer of the Greek Revival*, 1982; Harris, John, *William Talman, Maverick Architect*, 1982; Binney, Marcus, *Sir Robert Taylor: From Rococo to Neo-Classicism*, 1984.
Gibbs, James, *A Book of Architecture*, London 1728.
Girouard, Mark, *Life in the English Country House*, New Haven & London 1978.
Guinness, Desmond and Ryan, W., *Irish Houses and Castles*, London 1971, 1980.
Guinness, Desmond, *The Irish House*, 1975.
Guinness, Desmond, *Georgian Dublin*, London 1979.
Gwynn, John, *London & Westminster Improved*, London 1766.
Halfpenny, William, *The Art of Sound Building*, 1725.
Hall, Ivan and Elisabeth, *Georgian Hull*, Hull 1978.
Harris, John, *Sir William Chambers*, London 1970.
Harris, John, *The Palladians*, London 1981.
Hay, George, *The Architecture of Scottish Post-Reformation Churches*, Oxford 1957.
Hilling, John B., *Snowdonia and Northern Wales*, 1980.
Hilling, John B., *Historic Architecture of Wales*, 1976.
Hobhouse, H., *Thomas Cubitt, Master Builder*, London 1971.
Hogarth, William, *The Analysis of Beauty*, London 1753.
Hutcheson, Francis, *Inquiry into the Origins of our ideas of Beauty and Virtue*, London 1726.
Ison, Walter, *The Georgian Buildings of Bath 1700–1830*, 1948; Bath 1980.
Ison, Walter, *The Georgian Buildings of Bristol*, 1952.
Jones, Barbara, *Follies and Grottoes*, London 1953 (revised edition 1974).
Kent, William, *Designs of Inigo Jones*, London 1727.
Knight, Richard Payne, *An Analytical Inquiry into the Principles of Taste*, 1805.
Langley, Batty, *Ancient Architecture restored and improved...*, 1741, reissued 1747 as *Gothick Architecture improved...*
Langley, Batty, *Treasury of Design*, London 1745.
Laugier, Abbé, *Essai sur l'Architecture*, 1753.
Leacroft, Richard and Helen, *Theatre and Playhouse: an Illustrated Survey of Theatre-Building from Ancient Greece to the Present Day*, London 1984.
Leoni, Giacomo, *The Architecture of A. Palladio*, London 1715, 1721.
Lindstrum, D., *West Yorkshire, Architects and Architecture*, London 1978.
Liscombe, R., *William Wilkins 1778–1845*, Cambridge 1980.
Macaulay, James, *The Gothic Revival 1745–1845*, Glasgow 1975.
Malton, T., *A Picturesque tour through the Cities of London and Westminster*, London 1792–1801.
McKean, Charles and Walker, David, *Edinburgh: an illustrated guide*, Edinburgh 1982.

McKean, Charles and Walker, David, *Dundee*, Edinburgh 1984.
McParland, Edward, *James Gandon*, London 1985.
Morris, Robert, *Essay in Defence of Ancient Architecture*, London 1728.
Morris, Robert, *Lectures on Architecture*, London 1734.
Nicholson, Peter, *The New and Improved Practical Builder*, London 1823.
Olsen, Donald J., *Town Planning in London*, New Haven & London 1964.
Palladio, Andrea, *The Four Books of Architecture*, 1520. Edition of 1738 published in London by Isaac Ware.
Pevsner, Nikolaus, *The Buildings of England*, 47 volumes. Written by Nikolaus Pevsner with volumes or revised volumes contributed by a variety of authors. *The Buildings of Wales* series has started with a volume on Powys by Richard Haslam; *The Buildings of Scotland* series has volumes on Lothian by Colin McWilliam, and Edinburgh by Colin McWilliam, John Gifford and David Walker; and *The Buildings of Ireland* series has started with a volume on North-West Ulster by Alistair Rowan.
Pevsner, Nikolaus, *A History of Building Types*, London 1976.
Plaw, J., *Sketches for Country Houses, Villas and Rural Dwellings*, London 1800.
Port, M. H., *600 New Churches – a study of the Church Building Commission 1818-56*, 1961.
Price, Sir Uvedale, *Essay on the Picturesque*, 1794, expanded into 3 vols 1810.
Riou, Stephen, *The Grecian Orders*, 1768.
Robinson, John Martin, *The Wyatts: An Architectural Dynasty*, Oxford 1979.
Robinson, John Martin, *Georgian Model Farms*, Oxford 1983.
The Royal Commission on Historical Monuments: Volumes and pamphlets on cities and towns, from 1910.
Rutter, J., *Delineations of Fonthill and its Abbey*, London 1823.
Serlio, Sebastiano, *The Five Books of Architecture* 1537- 1547, English edition of 1611 republished 1982, New York.
Soane, John, *Lectures on Architecture*, edited by Arthur T. Bolton, London 1929.
Stroud, Dorothy, *The Architecture of Sir John Soane*, London 1961.
Stroud, Dorothy, *Henry Holland*, London 1966.
Stroud, Dorothy, *George Dance, Architect*, London 1971.
Stuart, James and Revett, Nicholas, *Antiquities of Athens*, 1762. Vols I-V published between 1762 and 1816 by various editors.
Summerson, John, *Georgian London*, London 1945, revised edition 1969.
Summerson, John, *The Life and Work of John Nash, Architect*, London 1980.
Survey of London, 41 Vols, published from 1900 by the LCC and then the GLC, London.
Ware, Isaac, *A Complete Body of Architecture*, London 1756.
Watkin, David, *The Life and Work of C. R. Cockerell*, London 1974.
Watkin, David, *The Buildings of Britain – Regency*, London 1982.
Watkin, David, *The English Vision: The Picturesque in Architecture, Landscape and Garden Design*, London 1982.
Whiffen, Marcus, *Stuart and Georgian Churches outside London*, London 1947.
Vitruvius Pollio, Marcus, *The Architecture of M. Vitruvius Pollio*, translated by W. Newton, London 1791.
Wood, John, *The Origin of Building*, 1741.
Wood, John, *An Essay towards a Description of Bath*, 1742, 1749 and 1765.
Wood, R., *Ruins of Palmyra*, 1753.
Wood, R., *Ruins of Baalbec*, 1757.
Wittkower, Rudolf, *Architectural Principles in the Age of Humanism*, 1949. Revised edition, London 1973.
Wittkower, Rudolf, *Palladio and English Palladianism* (Collected Essays), London 1983.
Youngson, A. J., *The Making of Classical Edinburgh*, Edinburgh 1966.

ACKNOWLEDGMENTS

I would like to thank the following people and organizations for their help in the compilation of this book: Desmond Guinness and Alastair Service for commenting on and correcting the text; William Garner of the Irish Architectural Archive, and members of the Irish Georgian Society for their help with photographs, advice on the text and additions to the Irish gazetteer; Desmond Fitzgerald for his corrections and additions to the Irish gazetteer; John Martin Robinson for reading and correcting the chapter on Buildings in the Country; Colin Amery, Neil Burton and Gavin Stamp for useful additions to the British gazetteer; Gillian Darley for tips on decorative details; Iain Mackintosh for advice on eighteenth-century theatre design; the late Robin Wright for his early comments on the text; Shirly Hind of the Architectural Press; Francesca Barran of the National Trust and Roger White, Secretary of the Georgian Group, for their help with photographs; Richard Hewlings for advice on Cornish architecture; Elizabeth Kershaw, Carol Bucknell, Amicia de Moubray and Penny Wright for help with research and typing the manuscript; Ralph Hancock for his valuable help in organizing and checking the gazetteer text; Barbara Mellor for her tireless good humour, careful editing of the manuscript and sound advice; and Victoria Cruickshank for her astonishing patience and encouragement.

The author and publishers would like to thank the following for supplying illustrations:

The plans and drawings on pages 24, 46 top and bottom, 47, 48 top and bottom, 49 top and bottom, 58 bottom right, 60 top and bottom, 63, 72 right, 80 bottom, 84 top, 86 bottom, 88 bottom, 92 bottom, 117, 137, 176 top and 179 top are by David Jenkins.

Architectural Press: 26, 69, 82, 132 bottom, 140 top and bottom, 141, 168 top, 178 bottom, 190 (photo Sam Lambert), 206 (photo Sam Lambert).
Martin Charles: 18 bottom, 138, 169.
Country Life Publications: 1, 18 top, 54, 65 bottom left and right, 93, 168 bottom, 181, 209, 219 right, 252, 287.
Hugh Doran: 58 bottom left, 75 bottom, 86 centre, 88 top, 89.
Georgian Theatre Royal, Richmond: 170
Keith Gibson: 108 left.
GLC Historic Buildings Division: 280
Irish Architectural Archive: 39 bottom right, 40, 50, 163.
Irish National Parks and Monuments: 152 bottom, 291.
Ironbridge Gorge Museum Trust: 136.
Tim Mercer: 135, 156.
National Trust: 171 (photo Nicolette Hallett).
RIBA Prints and Drawings Collection: 21, 52 top and bottom, 53.
Royal Commission on Ancient and Historical Monuments: endpapers, 39 top right, 43, 44 top, 62, 65 top, 67, 68 top, 72 left, 74, 75 top, 84 bottom, 86 top, 92 top, 99 right, 110 bottom, 113 top and bottom, 116 left and right, 118 top and bottom, 119 top left and right, bottom, 124, 125, 160, 176 centre, 183, 242, 243.
Royal Commission on the Ancient and Historical Monuments of Scotland: 73, 79 (photo Professor A. Rowan), 227.
Other photographs are by the author.

GLOSSARY

Abacus: flat slab forming top member of a column capital.

Acroterion: plinth supporting an ornament placed on the apex and ends of a pediment.

Aedicule: pedimented, columned or pilastered frame to a niche or window.

Aisle: secondary space running parallel to the nave, choir or transept of a church.

Antae: pilasters, or piers, with capitals different from the order they accompany.

Antis, in: a portico or colonnade framed by antae; also a portico or colonnade set on the same plane as framing antae or pilasters is called *in antis*.

Anthemion: Greek decoration in form of stylized honeysuckle flower.

Antefixae: ornamental projections set at intervals above a classical cornice.

Apse: semicircular or elliptical extension to a room or to the east end of a church.

Arcade: arches supported by piers or columns. BLIND ARCADE is applied as decoration to a wall surface.

Architrave: the lowest member of the classical entablature whose characteristic moulded profile is used to embellish door and window surrounds.

Ashlar: masonry fashioned in blocks with square corners and straight edges and laid with a flat face.

Astylar: of elevation, designed without columns, pilasters or piers.

Atrium: an inner court in Roman architecture, open to the sky, or top-lit and surrounded by colonnades or galleries.

Attic: the storey above the main entablature of the façade, usually with square windows.

Basilica: a Roman public hall described by Vitruvius and reconstructed by Palladio, with nave, aisle, apsed end and clerestory.

Bay: part of an elevation as defined by any recurring vertical feature such as columns, arches, windows.

Bay window: window of one or more storeys projecting from an elevation. When semicircular or elliptical in plan called a BOW WINDOW, when half-hexagonal or half-octagonal, called a CANTED BAY WINDOW.

Block cornice: cornice with top member supported on blocks of cyma recta or reversa profile.

Bond: for structural, economic and aesthetic reasons bricks are laid in many different ways. FLEMISH BOND, almost universal during the eighteenth century, has stretchers (bricks laid with the long side showing) and headers (bricks laid with the short ends showing) alternating on the same course. ENGLISH BOND, common pre-c1660 and post-1830, has alternate courses of headers and stretchers.

Bow window: see bay window.

Bucranium: ox skull used as decoration in classical frieze.

Bull's-eye window: small, oval or round window, often in tympanum of pediment. Also known as *œil de bœuf*.

Canted bay: see bay window.

Capital: the decorative cap of a column or pilaster.

Caryatid: female figure taking the place of column in supporting an entablature.

Cavetto: concave moulding of quarter-round profile.

Chancel: east end of church set apart for use of clergy.

Cill course: see sill course.

Coffering: sunken panels decorating soffits of an arch or ceiling.

Colonnade: row of columns supporting an entablature or arcade.

Colonnette: an attenuated column, usually of cast iron.

Column: in classical architecture a shaft with embellished capital and base and with a height and diameter proportionately related (see the Orders); ENGAGED COLUMNS: columns attached to a wall or slightly sunk into a wall, also called ATTACHED COLUMNS.

Composite: see the Orders.

Concatenation: Palladian theory of staccato elevational composition where the various elements in a long façade are designed as self-contained features, with major elements set on slightly different planes and linked by relatively minor elements, and reaching a crescendo in the centre of the composition.

Console: S-shaped scroll (usually decorated) set horizontally or vertically, supporting a cornice or entablature or set within an entablature; also called a BRACKET.

Corinthian: see the Orders.

Cornice: the top member of an entablature.

Corona: the central element of a cornice, with a flat vertical face and a soffit shaped to form a drip.

Cyma recta. composite moulding with a concave quarter-moulding set over, and of equal size with, a convex quarter-moulding.

Cyma reversa: the opposite form to the cyma recta, also called an OGEE moulding.

Dado: the lower part of an interior wall from which can rise an order of pilasters or engaged columns reaching to the ceiling cornice. DADO RAIL is a moulding set along the top edge of the dado.

Dentil: a course of small square blocks incorporated amongst the lower mouldings of an enriched cornice.

Diocletian window: semicircular window with tripartite glazing, so called because of its use in the Baths of Diocletian, Rome. Also known as a THERMAE window, or LUNETTE.

Distyle: see portico.

Doric: see the Orders.

Double pile: refers to the plan of a house which has two parallel ranges of rooms separated by a spine corridor. The form seems to have come into general use in country house design in the mid-seventeenth century, but has an earlier origin in vernacular design.

Enfilade: a set of rooms arranged within a house so that all the doors are on axis and, when open, a vista is obtained. A baroque country house planning device.

Entablature: the collective name for cornice, frieze and architrave.

Fillet: a small moulding (usually right-angular) used to separate larger curved mouldings.

Frieze: the central element in an entablature decorated differently according to the Order which it accompanies. PULVINATED FRIEZE has a convex profile.

Gibbs surround: the decoration of a door or window comprising alternating large and small blocks of stone (as quoining); or of large equally sized blocks set intermittently between runs of architrave.

Guttae: small half-cylindrical projections – perhaps representing pegs – set on the Doric architrave immediately below, and related to, the triglyph in the frieze.

Hexastyle: see portico.

Hipped roof: see roofs.

Hopper head: decorated, usually lead, rainwater head set at parapet/eaves level on top of a down pipe. Often embellished with date of building or initials of builder.

Impost: horizontal mouldings or block from which an arch springs.

In antis: see antis.

Intercolumniation: the interval of spacing between columns.

Ionic: see the Orders.

Jack arch: shallow, segmental vault (usually brick)

springing from joists spanning the main structural beams; part of early fire-proof construction.

Keystone: central stone in an arch.

Loggia: open, colonnaded or arcaded gallery along one side of a building. Also a free-standing structure with colonnades or arcades on one, two or three sides only.

Lunette: see Diocletian window.

Machicolations: a corbelled-out battlemented parapet of medieval military origin.

Mansard: see roofs.

Metopes: spaces between the triglyphs in a Doric frieze, embellished with rosettes or sculptures.

Modillions: small consoles set beneath the soffit of the corona of the Corinthian or Composite order.

Mullions: vertical bars in a mullion and transomed casement window. TRANSOM is the horizontal bar.

Mutule: the projecting square block, above the triglyph and under the soffit of the corona of a Doric cornice.

Nave: the main axis of a basilica church flanked by aisles.

Newel: central post of a winding staircase, or the post where the stairs join the landing. See stairs.

Oculus: circular opening, see bull's-eye window.

Œil de bœuf: see bull's-eye window.

Ogee: see cyma reversa.

Orders: six distinctly different orders of Greek and Roman derivation were used during the eighteenth and early nineteenth centuries: Greek Doric, Roman Doric, Tuscan or Tuscan Doric (a Roman invention), Ionic, Corinthian and Composite (a Roman invention combining Ionic and Corinthian elements). Each order had its own proper decoration (to entablature as well as to column capital), proportions (ratio of column diameter to column height), intercolumniation; and, if properly used, its proper symbolic value (simple and bold Doric or Tuscan for functional or masculine buildings, Corinthian for buildings of pleasure etc).

Ovolo: a convex quadrant moulding.

Patera: round or oval classical ornament, usually carved as an open flower.

Pedestal: a vertical block, embellished with appropriate skirting and dado rail carrying a column or statue.

Pediment: in origin, the formalized gable end of a pitched-roof temple. In the eighteenth and early nineteenth centuries often used purely decoratively and not expressing or reflecting the roof structure. This cosmetic use led to the development of various decorative pediment forms: the BROKEN PEDIMENT in which the apex is omitted; the OPEN PEDIMENT in which the centre of the bottom, horizontal cornice is omitted; the SEGMENTAL in which the triangular top is replaced with a curved top; and the SWAN-NECKED, like a broken pediment but the raking sides are serpentine.

Pendentive ceiling: the ceiling form resulting from the placing of a saucer dome over a right-angular room.

Perron: external, usually double-curved, stair leading to a door.

Piano nobile: the principal floor, derived from Italian Renaissance practice; usually the first floor, which has the advantage of being raised above street noise and dirt but not too distant a trek up the stairs.

Pier: a square-section support, usually for an arch.

Pilaster: a flat alternative to a column furnished with the same capital and set in shallow relief against a wall.

Pilaster strip: vertical element in an articulated wall surface without formal capital or base.

Plinth: projecting course at the base of a pedestal from which internal wall skirting is derived.

Podium: a continuous base or plinth supporting columns, from which the internal dado is derived.

Portico: a porch formed by columns and supporting either a flat entablature or a pediment. Can be of various widths: TETRASTYLE (four columns), HEXASTYLE (six), OCTASTYLE (eight), DECOSTYLE (ten), or DODECASTYLE (twelve). If it has only two columns between pilasters or antae it is called DISTYLE *in antis*.

Propylaeum: a columnar entrance to an enclosure.

Pulvinated: see frieze.

Quatrefoil: in Gothic architecture, a formalized four-lobed leaf-shaped tracery design; trefoils are three-lobed.

Quoin: dressed stone or rubbed brick at the angle of a building, usually raised and sometimes alternately long and short or (more baroque) rusticated and of even size.

Reeding: a series of small convex – often semicircular – mouldings set close and running parallel.

Roofs: a DOUBLE-PITCH roof is formed by two straight planes set at an angle and meeting at a point or ridge. All sides of a HIPPED ROOF slope from the ridge to the eaves. A GABLED MANSARD or GAMBREL is a pitched roof with each slope faceted to form a two-planed surface. The lower of these facets, nearer the eaves, is usually set at a steeper, more upright angle, than the facet joined to the ridge. MANSARD is the same basic form but with the gable ends replaced by roofs so that faceted roofs slope in from all sides of the building.

Rustication: the bold expression of joints in a masonry wall to give the impression of strength. The joints can be V-section chamfering or square-section channelling. BANDED RUSTICATION is when only the horizontal joints are emphasized. VERMICULATED RUSTICATION is when each block is textured to look rock-faced or like stylized worm-casts.

Scotia: a concave composite moulding formed by curves of two different centres.

Sill course: a string course set at the level of window sills.

Soffit: underside of an arch, lintel or large-scale moulding.

Stairs: a DOG-LEG has parallel flights rising alternately in opposite directions without an open well. These flights can be connected either by landings or winders (stairs curving around a newel) or a combination of both. A NEWEL STAIR rises around a central post or newel, which supports one end of the treads while the other is supported by the walls of the staircase compartment. WELL STAIR is of any form, and rises around an open well. FLYING STAIR cantilevers from the stairwell wall and does not have newels. GEOMETRIC STAIR is a flying stair that rises within a curve. An IMPERIAL STAIR rises in one flight to a half-landing and then continues in two flights rising each side of the single flight to the first floor (or occasionally vice versa).

String course: horizontal stone or brick course projecting from a wall.

Stucco: a fine plaster used to cover brick walls. The object was to protect the face from weather and to give the impression that the building was constructed of stone.

Swag: ornament suspended as a festoon.

Thermae: see Diocletian window.

Torus: large-scale semicircular convex moulding.

Tower of the Winds capitals: distinctive capitals decorated with palm fronds and acanthus leaves, found in the Tower of the Winds, Athens.

Tracery: in Gothic architecture, intersecting ribs, curved or of complex geometric profile, set within a window, or in blank arches set against a wall.

Transept: transverse passage, perhaps corresponding to width of nave and aisle, in a cruciform church.

Transom: see mullions.

Trefoil: see quatrefoil.

Triglyph: a plate, decorated with two V-section vertical grooves, set within the Doric frieze between metopes. Supposedly it represented stylized beam ends.

Tuscan: see the Orders.

Tympanum: the area between the lintel and the arch above it, or the triangular space within a pediment.

Vault: BARREL or TUNNEL vault is a continuous semicircular arch in section. GROIN or CROSS vaults have curved triangular surface produced by the intersection at right angles of two barrel or tunnel vaults. The curved lines caused by the intersection are called GROINS.

Venetian windows: also called SERLIAN or PALLADIAN windows. A tripartite opening with the centre window arched and rising above the side windows, which are half or a third the width of the centre window.

Voussoirs: wedge-shaped stones that form an arch.

Weatherboarding: also called CLAPBOARDING. Overlapping planks of wood of tapering section, used to clad a building.

INDEX *of buildings and places*

Page numbers in italic refer to illustrations.

Abbey Kirk, Paisley 123
Abbey Leix, Co. Laois 284
Abbey Square, Chester 32, 196
Abbot Hall, Kendal 218
Abbotsford, Borders 81, 180
Abbotsford House, Warwick 36, 252
Aberdeen 120, 150, 163, 177, 180
Aberfeldy, Tayside 140, 180
Abergavenny, Gwent 174, 180
Abingdon, Oxfordshire 132, 147, 148, 159, 180
Acton Hall, Gloucestershire 180
Adam Street, Strand 23, 278
Addington, Croydon 264
Addington Palace, Addington 264
Adelphi, Strand 23, 43, 146, 177, 278
Adlestrop, Gloucestershire 180
Adlestrop Park, Adlestrop 180
Adlington Hall, Cheshire 180
Admiralty, Whitehall 65, 143-4, 283
Aghold, Co. Wicklow 284
Airthrey Castle, Central Region 180
Airy Hill, Whitby 254
A-la-Ronde, Exmouth 96, 208
Albion Mill, London 135
Albany, Piccadilly 278
Albury Street, Deptford 30, 32, 45, *46*, 271-2
Alcester, Warwickshire 123, 180
Aldborough House, Dublin 40, 292
Aldenham, Hertfordshire 180
Aldingbourne House, West Sussex 180-81
Alfred's Hall, Cirencester Park 14, 16, 97, 197
Alfred's Tower, Stourhead 246
Alkrington Hall, Lancashire 66, 181
Allerton, Liverpool 223
Allerton Mauleverer, West Yorkshire 123, 181
All Hallows' Church, London Wall 112, 263
All Hallows College, Co. Dublin 290
All Saints' Cathedral Church, Derby 107, 108, 202
All Saints' Church, Brandsby 189
All Saints' Church, Gainsborough 109, 110, 210
All Saints' Church, Newcastle upon Tyne 118, 230
All Saints' Church, Nuneham Courtenay 116, *116*, 232
All Saints' Church, Woolley 125, 257
All Saints' Church, Worcester 109, 257
All Saints' Church, Wroxton 124, 258
All Souls' Church, Langham Place, 120, 281
All Souls College, Oxford 126, 165, *165*, 233, 242
Almshouses, Boston 162, 188
Almshouses, Brent Eleigh 162, 189
Almshouses, Wareham 162, 251
Alnwick, Northumberland 181
Alscot House, Warwickshire 77, 181
Althorp, Northamptonshire 6, 181, *181*
Alton, Hampshire 181
Alton Towers, Staffordshire 100, 181
Amersham, Buckinghamshire 181
Amesbury Abbey, Wiltshire 53, 98, 181, 254
Amisfield Mains, Lothian 181
Ampleforth, Bedfordshire 181, 198, 240
Ampthill Park, Ampthill 181
Amwell Grove, Great Amwell 212
Anfield, Liverpool 223
Angel Hotel, Abergavenny 174, 180
Angles Theatre, Wisbech 171, 255
Annesbrook, Co. Meath 284
Anneville, Co. Westmeath 61, 89
Antony House, Cornwall 181
Antrim 152, 284
Apothecaries' Hall, Blackfriars Lane 263

Apley Park, Shropshire 181
Appleby, Cumbria 181
Apsley House, Hyde Park Corner 278
Arbury Hall, Warwickshire 14, 77, 181-2
Arch, Holkham Hall 98, 216
Arch of Constantine, Rome 82, 217
Arch of Hadrian, Rome 99, 243
Arch of Titus, Rome 99, 243
Ardress House, Co. Armagh 284
Ardronan, Co. Louth 290
Ardrossan, Strathclyde 28, 182
Ardwick, Manchester 225
Argyle Arcade, Glasgow 130
Argyle Street, Glasgow 130, 210
Argyll House, King's Road 38, 270
Arlington Court, Devon 92, 182
Arlington Street, Mayfair 38, 278
Armagh 160, 284
Armagh Palace, Armagh 284
Arncliffe Hall, North Yorkshire 182, 217
Arniston, Lothian 56, 182
Arnos Grove, Southgate 265
Aroid House, Royal Botanic Gardens, Kew 273
Artillery Lane, Spitalfields 129, *129*, 276
Arundel, West Sussex 182
Ascot Place, Berkshire 182
Asgill.House, Richmond 73, 274
Ashbourne, Derbyshire 38, 162, 182, 202
Ashdown House, East Sussex 91, 182
Ashman's Hall, Suffolk 182
Ashmolean Museum, Oxford 169
Ashridge Park, Hertfordshire 81, 182
Aske Hall, North Yorkshire 98, 183
Assembly/ballroom, Lichfield 174, 221
Assembly Room, Bedford 174
Assembly Room, Brighton 174, 190
Assembly Room, Clifton 177, 191
Assembly Room, Deal 150
Assembly Room, Devizes 148, 202
Assembly Room, Exeter 174, 267
Assembly Room, Grantham 174, 212
Assembly Room, Huntingdon 150, 175, 217
Assembly Room, Newark-on-Trent 148, 230
Assembly Room, Newtownards 175, 297
Assembly Room, Salford 150, 240
Assembly Room, Shrewsbury 174, 242
Assembly Room, Southend 174
Assembly Room, Wareham 175
Assembly Rooms, Chichester 177, 196
Assembly Rooms, Chichester 177, 196
Assembly Rooms, Edinburgh 177, 205
Assembly Rooms, Macclesfield 150, 151, 175, 225
Assembly Rooms, Newcastle upon Tyne 177, 230
Assembly Rooms, Richmond 150, 175
Assembly Rooms, Stamford 177, 244
Assembly Rooms, Truro 171, 249
Assembly Rooms, Waterford 175, 299
Assembly Rooms, York 19, 152, 157, 258
Assize Courts, Carlisle 150, 194
Assize Courts, Lincoln 151, 222
Aston Hall, Shropshire 183
Atcham, Shropshire 183
Athenaeum, Pall Mall 177, *178*, 280
Athenaeum, Stirling 177, 244
Athenaeum Reading Rooms, Aberdeen 177, 180
Athy, Co. Kildare 284
Attingham Hall, Shropshire 85, 169
Audley End, Essex 98, 183
Avery Row, Mayfair 279
Avington, Hampshire 111, 183
Avondale, Co. Wicklow 284
Aynho, Northamptonshire 104, 111, 183
Ayot St Lawrence, Hertfordshire 15, 116, 183, *183*

Babraham Hall, Cambridgeshire 96, 183
Badger Hall, Shropshire 100, 183

Badminton House, Avon 65, 97, 101, 109, 183
Baggrave Hall, Leicestershire 78, 183
Balbirnie House, Fife 183
Baldersby Park, North Yorkshire 12, 54, 55, 99, 183
Baldock, Hertfordshire 183
Ballina, Co. Mayo 284
Ballinasloe, Co. Galway 284
Ballingarane, Co. Tipperary 284
Ballinlough Castle, Co. Westmeath 284
Ballycastle, Co. Antrim 106, 284
Ballyfin, Co. Laois 94, 284
Ballyhaise House, Co. Cavan 57, 60, *60*, 71, 75, 86, 284, 295
Ballyheigue Castle, Co. Kerry 81, 284
Ballymore, Co. Donegal 284
Ballynahown Court, Co. Westmeath 284
Ballynatray, Co. Waterford 284
Ballysallagh, Co. Kilkenny 284
Ballyscullion House, Co. Londonderry 285
Banagher, Co. Offaly 174, 285
Banbury, Oxfordshire 119, *119*, 183
Bank of England, City of London 15, 19n, 85, *127*, 128, 129, 263
Banqueting House, Whitehall 7
Bantry, Co. Cork 285
Barlaston Hall, Staffordshire 73, 184
Barn, Wentworth Woodhouse 101, 253
Barn, Weston Park 101, 253
'Barn à la Paestum', Solihull 101, 243, *243*
Barnard Castle, Co. Durham 152, 184
Barnes, Richmond-upon-Thames 273
Barnet, London 260
Barnsbury, Islington 269
Barnsley Park, Gloucestershire 54, 184
Barnstaple, Devon 184
Baronscourt, Co. Tyrone 89, 285
Barracks, Berwick upon Tweed 155, 186
Barracks, Chester 150, 196
Barracks and warehouses, Weedon 139, 252
Barrington Park, Gloucestershire 184
Barton Street, Victoria 283
Basildon Park, Berkshire 85, 100, 184
Basilica, Vicenza 131
Bassae, Greece 95, 233
Bath, Avon 20, *26*, 27, *27*, 30, 31, 32-3, *32*, 34, 35, 36, 37, 43, 94, 98, 112, 130, *140*, 141, 150, 157, 158, 160, 161, 163, 165, 171, 174, 175, 184-5
Baths of Diocletian, Rome 119, 212
Battersea, Wandsworth 277
Bear Hotel, Wincanton 172, 255
Beaufort Arms Hotel, Monmouth 174, 228
Beaumaris, Anglesey 158, 185
Beaumont Lodge, Berkshire 90, 185
Beau Parc, Co. Meath 285
Beckenham, Bromley 260
Beckenham Place, Beckenham 260
Beckley, East Sussex 185
Bedford 162, 174, 185
Bedford Estate, Bloomsbury 22, 23, 32
Bedford Hotel, Brighton 175, 190
Bedford Place, Bloomsbury 32, 261
Bedford Square, Bloomsbury 22, *22*, 23, 29, *48*, 50n, 214, 261
Beech Court, Avon 185
Belchamp Hall, Essex 185
Belcombe Court, Bradford-on-Avon 189
Belfast 118, 162, 285
Belfield House, Weymouth 253
Belgrave Square, Belgravia 278
Belgravia, Westminster 278
Bellamont Forest, Co. Cavan *58*, 59, 61, 62, 75, 87, 285, 297, 298
Belle Isle, Cumbria 84, *84*, 185
Belleville House, Highland 186
Bellie Church, Fochabers Newton 109, 209
Belline, Co. Kilkenny 61, 285

Bellinter, Co. Meath 59, 61, 285
Belmont, Lyme Regis 29, 225
Belmont, Shrewsbury *42*, 243
Belmont Park, Kent 85, 186
Belper, Derbyshire 136, 186
Belsay Hall, Northumberland 92, *92*, 94, 103, 186
Belsay village, Belsay Hall 103, 186
Belvedere, Claremont 97, 198
Belvedere House, Dublin 40, 292
Belview, Co. Meath 285
Belvoir Castle, Leicestershire 91, 186
Benham Place, Berkshire 85, 186
Beningborough Hall, North Yorkshire 186
Bentley Priory, Stanmore 85, *86*, 268
Berkeley Square, Mayfair 38, 279
Berkley, Somerset 186
Bermondsey, Southwark 122, 275
Berrington Hall, Hereford and Worcester 70, 85, 186
Berwick upon Tweed, Northumberland 150, *150*, 155, 186, *186*
Bessborough, Co. Kilkenny 57, 62, 285
Bethnal Green, Tower Hamlets 120, 276
Betws-y-Coed, Gwynedd 142, 186
Beverley, Humberside 31, 153, 187
Beverley Minster, Beverley 165
Bewdley, Hereford and Worcester 187
Bexley, London 260
Biddick Hall, Co. Durham 187
Biddlesden, Buckinghamshire 109, 187
Billinge, Merseyside 187
Bilston, West Midlands 187
Binley, Coventry 117, 199
Birchington, Kent 187
Birmingham 109, 187
Bishop Auckland, Co. Durham 187
Bishop of Rochester's Palace 260
Bishop's College Hospital, Lincoln 160, 222
Bishop's Palace, Bishop Auckland 187, 201
Bishop's Palace, Kilkenny 294
Bishop's Palace, Waterford 299
Bisley, Gloucestershire 12, 187
Black Bear, Wareham 173, *173*, 251
Blackburn, Lancashire 187
Black Church, Dublin 122, 290
Blackfen, Bexley 260
Blackheath, Lewisham 271
Blackheath Park, Greenwich 265
Blairquhan, Strathclyde 187
Blairuachdar, Tayside 101, 162, 187
Blaise Castle House, Avon 187
Blaise Hamlet, Avon 103, 187
Blandford Forum, Dorset 27, 31, 35, *35*, 36, 111, *111*, 149, *149*, 173, *173*, 188
Blenheim, Oxfordshire 12, 53, 54, 61, 64, 71, 89, 156, 164, 165, 188, 222
Bloomsbury, Camden 261
Bloomsbury Square, Bloomsbury 20, 261
Bloomsbury Way, Bloomsbury 106
Bluecoat School, Dublin 163, 290
Bluecoat School, Liverpool 162, 223
Bluecoat School and Almshouses, Frome 161, 209
Blundeston House, Suffolk 188
Blyth Hall, Nottinghamshire 69
Board of Ordnance Building (Board Room and Saloon), Woolwich 61, 71, 155, 266
Bognor Regis, West Sussex 188
Bolton, Greater Manchester 188
Bonnetstown Hall, Co. Kilkenny 285
Bonsall, Derbyshire 134, 188
Boodle's Club, St James's Street 177, *178*, 281
Bootham Park Hospital, York 160, 258
Boreham House, Essex, 65, 188
Borough, The, Southwark 275
Borris House, Co. Carlow 285
Boston, Lincolnshire 32, 37, 51, 123, 162, 188, *188*, 238
Bourne, Lincolnshire 188
Bourne Park, Kent 188
Bourn Hall, Cambridgeshire 16, 96, 188
Bourton-on-the-Water, Gloucestershire 188
Bow, Tower Hamlets 276
Bowden House, Wiltshire 85, 87, 188
Bower House, Havering-atte-Bower 268
Bowood House, Wiltshire 188
Boycott Pavilions, Stowe 97, 102, 247
Boyle, Co. Roscommon 285
Boyles Court, Essex 51, 189
Bracklyn Castle, Co. Westmeath 285
Bradbourne, Kent 189, 208

Bradford-on-Avon, Wiltshire 36, 134, 189
Bradwell Lodge, Bradwell-on-Sea 189
Bradwell-on-Sea, Essex 189
Braintree, Essex 189
Brandsby, North Yorkshire 189
Brasted Place, Kent 85, 189
Braxted Park, Kent 189
Brecon, Powys 171, 189
Bredgar, Kent 189
Brent Eleigh, Suffolk 162, 189
Brentford, Hounslow 83, 94, 268
Bretton Hall, West Yorkshire 100, 189
Brewer Street, Soho 282
Brewood, Staffordshire 43, 190
Brianstown, Co. Longford 285
Bridestown, Co. Cork 285
Bridge, Aberfeldy 140, 180
Bridge, Athy 284
Bridge of Dun, 190
Bridge, Maidenhead 140, 225
Bridge, Pontypridd 141, 236
Bridge, Swinford 140
Bridge, Wallington Hall 140, 250
Named bridges listed under their names
Bridgnorth, Shropshire 190
Bridgwater, Somerset 190
Brighton, East Sussex 19n, 34, 90, 174, 175, 190, *190*, 220
Bristol 12, 36, 109, 126, 130, 133, 170, 172, 177, 190-91
British Museum, Bloomsbury 167, 169, 261
Brixton, Lambeth 271
Brizlee Tower, Alnwick 181
Brizlincote Hall, Derbyshire 191
Broadlands, Hampshire 191
Broad Street, Ludlow 40, *42*, 224
Broad Street, Worcester 40, 257
Broadway, Hereford and Worcester 191
Broadwick Street, Soho *47*, 282
Brocket Hall, Hertfordshire 74, 191
Brockhampton Park, Hereford and Worcester 70, 191
Brocklesby, Lincolnshire 192
Brock Street, Bath 27
Brogyntyn, Shropshire 192
Bromley, London 260-61
Bromley College, Bromley 260
Bromley Common, Bromley 260
Brompton, Kent 192
Brompton, Royal Borough of Kensington and Chelsea 270
Brookmans Park, Hertfordshire 97, 192
Brooks's Club, St James's Street 177, 281
Brook Street, Mayfair *47*, 279
Brough Hall, North Yorkshire 192
Browne's Hill, Co. Carlow 285
Bruce Castle, Tottenham 267
Bruern Abbey, Oxfordshire 192
Brunswick Terrace, Hove 30, 190
Bruton, Somerset 192
Buckland House, Oxfordshire 192
Buckden, Cambridgeshire 173
Buckingham House/Palace, St James's 51, 76, 280, 287
Buckland House, Oxfordshire 69
Builth Wells, Powys *42*, 174, 192
Buncrana Castle, Co. Donegal 285
Bunny Hall, Nottinghamshire 192
Buntingsdale, Shropshire 54, 192
Burford, Oxfordshire 192
Burley House, Burley-on-the-Hill 54
Burley-on-the-Hill, Leicestershire 54, 192
Burlington Arcade, Piccadilly 130, 279
Burlington Gardens, Mayfair 8, 279
Burlington House, Piccadilly 8, 280
Burn Hall, Co. Durham 101, 192
Burnley, Lancashire 192
Burntisland, Fife 192
Burroughs, The, Hendon 260
Burton Constable, Humberside 78, 192
Burton Hall, North Yorkshire 73
Burton upon Trent, Staffordshire 192
Bury St Edmunds, Suffolk 132, *132*, 158, 162, 170, *171*, 193
Buscot Park, Oxfordshire 193
Butter Cross, Ludlow 132, 224
Butterton Grange, Staffordshire 91, 193
Butterwick House, Hammersmith 267
Buttevant, Co. Cork 285
Buxton, Derbyshire 33, 193
Bywell Hall, Northumberland 74, 86, 193

Caerhayes Castle, Cornwall 81, 193
Caernarfon/Caernarvon, Gwynedd 33, 193
Cahir, Co. Tipperary 97, 285

Cairness House, Grampian 91, 92, 193
Caius House, Wymondham 35, 258
Caledon, Co. Tyrone 86, 286
Callan, Co. Kilkenny 286
Calverley Park Estate, Tunbridge Wells 30, 250
Camberwell, Southwark 32, 275-6
Camberwell Grove, New Road and Road 275
Cambridge 16, 32, 40, 164, 165-6, 167, 193-4
Camden, London 261-3
Camden Place, Chislehurst 260
Camden Town, Camden 261
Came House, Dorset 194
Camellia House, Wollaton Hall 100, 256
Camperdown House, Tayside 94, 194
Cams Hall, Fareham 208
Canada House, Trafalgar Square 155, 177, 281
Cannon Hall, South Yorkshire 194
Cannons, formerly in Middlesex 212
Canonbury, Islington 269
Canonbury Grove development, Canonbury 269
Canterbury, Kent 194
Capel y Ffin, Powys 194
Carlisle, Cumbria 150, 161, 194
Carlow 286
Carlton Club, St James's Street 280
Carlton House, St James's 15, 72, 100
Carlton House Terrace, St James's 34, 280
Carlton Place, Glasgow 30, 211
Carmarthen, Dyfed 194
Carrick-on-Shannon, Co. Leitrim 286
Carrigglas Manor, Co. Longford 101, 286
Carshalton, Sutton 276
Carshalton House, Carshalton 276
Carstairs House, Strathclyde 96, 194
Cart Almshouses, Dunstable 161, 204
Carton, Co. Kildare 286
Cashel, Co. Tipperary 57, 106, 286
Cashel Palace, Cashel 57, 66, 286
Casino, Marino 98, *98*, 291, 296
Castle, Wimpole Hall 97, 255
Castle Barn, Badminton 101, 183
Castle Blunden, Co. Kilkenny 62, 286
Castle Bromwich, West Midlands 110, 194
Castle Browne, Co. Kildare 79, 286
Castle Coole, Co. Fermanagh 75, 87, *88*, 89
Castlecor, Co. Longford 75, 286
Castle Farm, Nottinghamshire 101, 194
Castle Farm, Sledmere House 101, 243
Castlegar, Co. Galway 89, 286
Castlegate House, York 43, 259
Castle Goring, West Sussex 90, 194
Castle Hill, Devon 194
Castle Howard, Co. Wicklow 81, 286
Castle Howard, North Yorkshire 12, 61, 71, 76, 97, 102, 103n, 169, 195, 294
Castle Hyde, Co. Cork 286
Castle Martyr, Co. Cork 286
Castle Mill, Linby 139, 222
Castle Square, Caernarfon 33, 193
Castletown, Co. Kildare 56-7, *56*, 59, 76, 81, 86, 87, 286-7
Castletown Cox, Co. Kilkenny 51, 57, 76, 287
Castle Upton, Co. Antrim 79, 287
Castle Ward, Co. Down 57, 77, *77*, 94, 287
Castlewellan, Co. Down 152, 287
Cathedral, Ballina 284
Cathedral, Cashel 106, 286
Cathedral, Waterford 109, 111, 298
Other cathedrals listed under saint's or other name
Catton Hall, Derbyshire 71, 195
Cavan 287
Cavendish-Harley Estate, St Marylebone 20, 21
Cavendish Square, St Marylebone 22, 281
Cawsand, Cornwall 218
Celbridge, Co. Kildare 287
Chandos House, Chandos Place 281
Charing Cross, London 278
Charlemont House, Dublin 40, 291, 293
Charles Street, Mayfair 279
Charleston, Fife 28
Charleville, Co. Cork 132, 287
Charleville, Co. Wicklow 86, 287
Charleville Forest, Co. Offaly 81, *287*, 288

306 / Index of buildings and places

Charlotte Square, Edinburgh 25, 26, 205
Charlotte Street, Glasgow 37, 210
Charlton, Greenwich 265
Charlton House, Charlton 265
Charterhouse Square, Clerkenwell 269
Château de Tourney, France 60
Chatelherault, Strathclyde 97, 195
Chatham, Kent 135, *135*, 155, *156*, 195
Chatsworth, Derbyshire 54, 60
Cheam, Sutton 276
Cheese Hall, Devizes 132, 202
Chelmsford, Essex 150, 195
Chelsea, Royal Borough of Kensington and Chelsea 270
Cheltenham, Gloucestershire 33, 176, 195-6
Chepstow, Gwent 172-3, 196
Cheriton, Hampshire 196
Cheriton House, Cheriton 196
Chester 32, 179, 196
Chester Castle, Chester 150, 196
Chesterfield, Derbyshire 42, 196
Chesterfield Street, Mayfair 279, *279*
Chesterfield Walk, Greenwich 266
Chestnut Lodge, Hampstead 262
Chettle House, Dorset 262
Chevening Park, Kent 57, 196, 296
Chew Grammar School, Dunstable 161, 204
Cheyne Row and Walk, Chelsea 270
Chicheley Hall, Buckinghamshire 66, 196
Chichester, W. Sussex 114, 149, *149*, 196
Chillington Hall, Staffordshire 85, 197
Chinese Dairy, Woburn Abbey 98, 256
Chinese House, Shugborough 98, 243
Chinese pavilion, Stowe 98
Chinese pavilion, Wrest Park 98
Chinese Temple, Amesbury Abbey 98, 181
Chippenham, Cambridgeshire 101, 197
Chippenham, Wiltshire 51, 197
Chipping Campden, Gloucestershire 12, 197
Chirk, Clwyd 197
Chislehampton, Oxfordshire 112, 197
Chislehurst, Bromley 260
Chiswell Street, City of London 137, 264
Chiswick, Hounslow 268
Chiswick Mall, Chiswick 268
Choragic Monument of Lysicrates, Athens 99-100, 185, 199, 205, 220, 243, 248
Choragic Monument of Thrasyllus 91, 212
Chorley, Lancashire 197
Chorlton-on-Medlock, Manchester 225
Christ Church, Bristol 109, 191
Christ Church, Newgate Street 105, 110-11
Christ Church, Oxford 165, *165*, 233
Christ Church, Spitalfields *104*, 107, 110, *110*, 126n, 276
Church, Ballycastle 106, 284
Church, Dreghorn 118, 203
Church, Coolbanagher 117, 288
Church, Crossmolina 122, 289
Church, Gayhurst 104, 210
Church, Glen Orchy 119, 211
Church, Hamilton 118, 214
Church, Hillsborough 125, 294
Church, Kelso 118, 217
Church, Kenmore 125, 218
Church, Kilarrow 118, 218
Church, Newtownbreda 115, 297
Church, Tyringham House 122
Other churches listed under saint's or other name
Church Row, Wandsworth 278
Church Terrace, Richmond 274
Chute Lodge, Wiltshire 73, 197
Circus, City of London 264
Circus, The, Bath 27, 32, *48*, 184
Circus Gardens and Place, Edinburgh 30
Cirencester, Gloucestershire 12, 14, 16, 97, 197
Cirencester Park, Cirencester 12, 14, 16, 97, 197
City of London 263-4
Clandeboye, Co. Down 288
Clandon Park, Surrey 60, 66, 67, 197
Clapham, Lambeth 270-71; Wandsworth 277
Clapham Park Estate, Clapham 270
Clapton, Hackney 266
Clare College, Cambridge 165, 193
Clare House, Kent 198
Claremont, Surrey 70, 85, 97, 198
Clarence House, St James's 280

Clarendon Building, Oxford 164, 234
Clarendon House, London 160
Clarendon Park, Wiltshire 66, 198
Clarendon Press, Oxford 166, 234
Classical and Mathematical School, Falmouth 163, 208
Clavering House, Newcastle upon Tyne 42, 230
Claverton Manor, Avon 198
Claybury Hall, Woodford 272
Claydon House, Buckinghamshire 63-4, *64*, 66, 71, 198
Clearwell Castle, Gloucestershire 78, 198
Clement's Lane, City of Lodnon 129
Clergymen's Widows' Almshouses, Ashbourne 162, 182
Clerkenwell, Islington 152, 269
Clermont, Co. Wicklow 288
Clifton, Bristol 142, 177, 191
Cliveden, Buckinghamshire 198
Clogher, Co. Tyrone 288
Clock Gate, Youghal 157, 299
Clongowes Wood, Co. Kildare 286
Clontarf, Co. Dublin 296
Clophill, Bedfordshire 181, 198, 240
Clopton Asylum, Bury St Edmunds 162, 193
Close, The, Salisbury 31, 240
Cloth Mill, King's Stanley 136, 218
Clumber House, Nottinghamshire 198
Clytha Park, Gwent 81, 95, 198
Coal Exchange, City of London 130
Cockfosters, Barnet 260
Cock Hotel, Stony Stratford 172, 246
Coggeshall, Essex 198
Colchester, Essex 35, *36*, 37, 42, 43, 198
Colebrook Street, Winchester 29, 255
Coleby Hall, Lincolnshire 198
Coleorton Hall, Leicestershire 198
Coleshill, Oxfordshire 198, 286, 299
Coleshill House, Coleshill 53, 57, 59, 71, 198
Colganstown, Co. Dublin 38, 74, 75, 288, 296
Colonnade House, Blackheath 271
Comarques, Essex 198
Combe Bank, Kent 38, 61, 69, 71, 198
Combe Hay, Avon 62, 198
Commercial Road, Stepney 277
Compton Place, Eastbourne 204
Compton Verney, Warwickshire 84, 199
Conduit Street, Mayfair 43, 279
Congleton, Cheshire 199
Conington, Cambridgeshire 109, 199
Conolly Folly, Castletown 287
Conservatory, Bretton Hall 100, 189
Conservatory, Carlton House 100
Conservatory, Syon House 100, 268
Constable Burton Hall, North Yorkshire 199
Convent in the Wood, Stourhead 246
Conwy/Conway, Gwynedd 199
Coolbanagher, Co. Laois 117, 155, 288
Coolattin, Co. Wicklow 288
Cooper's Hall, Bristol 133
Coopershill, Co. Sligo 288
Copt Hall, Essex 199
Corboy, Co. Longford 288
Corinthian Arch, Stowe 98, 246
Cork 35, 76, 111, 158, 161, 288, *288*
Corn Exchange, City of London 130
Corn Exchange, Guildford 133, 213
Corn Exchange, Paris 131
Corpus Christi College, Cambridge 166, 194
'Corridor, The', Bath 130
Corsham, Wiltshire 199
Corsham Court, Corsham 169, 169n, 199
Coton House, Warwickshire 85, 199
Cottage, Edge Hill 97, 205
Cottesbroke Hall, Northamptonshire 199
Council House, Chichester 149, *149*, 196
Cound Hall, Shropshire 199
County Assembly Rooms, Aberdeen 177, 180
County Buildings, Perth 151, 235
County Court, Chester 150, 196
County Fire Office, Regent Street 129
County Gaol, Dorchester 159, 203
County Gaol, Huntingdon 156, 159, 217
County Gaol, Montgomery 159, 229
County Gaol, Norwich 158, 232
County Gaol, Warwick 157, *251*, 252
County Rooms, Leicester 174, 221
County and Shire Hall, Maidstone 151
Couper House, Blandford Forum 31, 168
Courteenhall Hall, Northamptonshire 199

Court House, Armagh 153, 284
Court House, Carlow 153, 286
Court House, Castlewellan 152, 287
Court House, Derry 153, 289
Court House, Dundalk 153, 293
Court House, Dunlavin 152, *152*, 293
Court House, Glasgow 151, *151*, 153, 210
Court House, Kilkenny 153, 294
Court House, Loughgall 152, 295
Court House, Northampton 153
Court House, Port Laoise 153, 297
Court House, Wakefield 153, 250
Court House, Warwick 152, 252
Court House, Waterford 153
Courtroom, Barnard Castle 152, 184
Courtroom, Dorchester 150, 203
Courtroom, Huntingdon 150, 217
Courtroom, Warwick 150, 252
Covent Garden, Westminster 278
Covent Garden Market, Covent Garden 132, 133, *133*, 278
Covent Garden Theatre, Covent Garden 151, 171
Coventry, Warwickshire 199
Cowes, Isle of Wight 120, 199-200
Cowley Street, Victoria 283
Cowley Road, Camberwell 32, 275
Cowshed, Burn Hall 101, 192
Cranborne Lodge, Dorset 200
Cranbrook, Kent 200
Cranbury Park, Hampshire 85, 200
Cratloe, Co. Clare 289
Creech Grange, Dorset 200
Crescent, Buxton 33, 193
Crescent, City of London 264
Crescent, Shrewsbury 29, 243
Crewe House, Curzon Street 279
Crichel House, Dorset 200
Cricket Court, Somerset 200
Criggion, Powys 200
Croft Castle, Hereford and Worcester 200
Cromford, Derbyshire 135, 139, 200
Cronkhill, Shropshire 16, 90, 200, 257
Croome Court, Croome d'Abitot 70-71, 200-201
Croome d'Abitot, Hereford and Worcester 125, 126, 200-201
Croom's Hill, Greenwich 266
Crossdrum, Co. Meath 289
Crossmolina, Co. Mayo 122, 289
Crowcombe, Court, Somerset 12, 201
Crown Arcade, Glasgow 130, 211
Croxdale Hall, Co. Durham 201
Croydon, London 264
Cuerdon Hall, Lancashire 16, 201
Culloden Tower, Richmond 238
Culverthorpe Hall, Lincolnshire 201
Culzean Castle, Strathclyde 78, *79*, 201
Cumberland Fort, Eastney 237
Cumberland Infirmary, Carlisle 161, 194
Cumberland Terrace, Regent's Park 30, 35, 262
Curraghmore, Co. Waterford 289
Custom House, City of London 19, 263
Custom House, Dublin 87, 284, 291, *291*
Cutler Street warehouses, City of London 127, 139, *139*, 264

Dairy, Hamels Park 101
Dalmahoy House, Lothian 56, 201
Dalmeny House, Lothian 90, 95, 96, 201
Damer House, Roscrea 297
Dalquharran Castle, Strathclyde 79, 201
Danson Park, Welling 73, 260
Darlington, Co. Durham 201
Dartmoor Prison, Devon 159
Dartrey, Co. Monaghan 289
Davenport House, Shropshire 64, 201
Daventry, Northamptonshire 108, *172*, 201
Davidstown House, Co. Kildare 289
Daylesford House, Gloucestershire 85, 90, 201
Deal, Kent 150, 201
Dean's Court, Wimborne Minster 254
Dean Street, Soho 129, 282
Debden, Essex 201
Dedham, Essex 36, 62, 201-2
Deepdene House, Surrey 96
Delos, Greece 84, 91, 116, 150, 183, 214, 249
Delphi, Greece 94
Denton Hall, North Yorkshire 73, 202
Deptford, Lewisham 271-2
Derby 37, *37*, 107, 108, 110, 134, 136, 158, 182, 202

Index of buildings and places / 307

Derry 153, 289
Derrymore House, Co. Armagh 96, 289
Devizes, Wiltshire 42, 132, 148, 202
Devonport, Plymouth 16, 151, 236
Didsbury, Manchester 226
Ditchley Park, Oxfordshire 66
Dockyard Gate, Chatham 155, *156*, 195
Doddington Hall, Cheshire 85, 202
Dodington Park, Avon 91, 100, 202
Dog kennel, Chatelherault 97, 195
D'Olier Street, Dublin 25, 130, 292
Dollar, Central Region 202
Dollar Academy, Dollar 163, 202
Dollardstown, Co. Meath 289
Dolphin Hotel, Southampton 173, 243
Dominick Street, Dublin 40, *40*, 292
Doncaster, South Yorkshire 152, 202
Doneraile Court, Co. Cork 289
Donhead Hall, Wiltshire 203
Donington Hall, Leicestershire 203
Donnington Grove, Berkshire 77, 203
Dorchester, Dorset 150, 159, 203
Doric House, Bath 94-5, 185
Doric Temple, Shugborough 99, 243
Dormitory, Westminster School 163, 283
Dorset Square, St Marylebone 281
Doune Park, Central Region 101, 203
Dover, Kent 203
Dover Street, Mayfair 43, 274, 279
Dover House, Whitehall 283
Downham, Lewisham 272
Downham Road, Ely 35, *35*, 206
Downhill Castle, Co. Londonderry 94, 99, 289
Downing College, Cambridge 16, 166, 193
Downing Street, Westminster 283
Downing Terrace, Cambridge 32, 194
Downpatrick, Co. Down 161, 162, 289
Downton Castle, Hereford and Worcester 16, 78, *80*, 203
Dowth Hall, Co. Meath 289
Dreadnought Hospital, Greenwich 265
Dreghorn, Strathclyde 118, 203
Drewstown, Co. Meath 61, 289
Drogheda, Co. Louth 150, 289
Dromana, Co. Waterford 66, 289-90
Dromard, Co. Limerick 61, 290
Dromiskin Glebe, Co. Louth 290
Dromoland Castle, Co. Kildare 16, 290
Dr Steeven's Hospital, Dublin 160, 291
Druce's Hill House, Bradford-on-Avon 36, 189
Drum, The, Lothian 56, 203
Drumcondra House, Co. Dublin 59, 290, 294
Drummore House, Lothian 203
Drumtochty Castle, Grampian 81, 203
Drury Lane Theatre, Covent Garden 170, 171, 172; *see also* Theatre Royal
Dry Grange Bridge, Melrose 227
Dublin 23, 25, 35, 38, *39*, *40*, *41*, 46, 48, 50, 51, 59, 87, 89, 109, 115, 128, *128*, 130, 131, *131*, 143, 144, *144*, 153-5, 157, 160, 161, 163, 175-6, 285, 289, 290-92
Dublin Castle, Dublin 144-5, *144*, 290
Duddingston, Lothian 56, 73, *73*, 82, 91, 203
Duff House, Grampian 203
Duffield, Derbyshire 203
Dugald Stewart Monument, Edinburgh 100, 205
Duke Street, Liverpool 37, 223, *223*
Duke Street, Whitehaven 41
Dulwich, Southwark 275
Dulwich College 36
Dulwich College Picture Gallery *18*, 19n, 167, 169, *169*, 275
Dumfries House, Strathclyde 82, 203
Dunboyne Castle, Co. Meath 293
Dundalk, Co. Louth 153, 293
Dundalk Castle, Lothian 203
Dundas House, Edinburgh 51, 205
Dundee 109, 118, 130, 171, 177, 203-4
Dundrum, Co. Tipperary 293
Dungannon, Co. Tyrone 293
Dunkathel, Co. Cork 293
Dunlavin, Co. Wicklow 132, 293
Dunmurry, Co. Antrim 293
Dunsink Observatory, Dublin 291
Dunstable, Bedfordshire 161, 204
Dunstall Priory, Kent 90, 204
Durham 19, 36, 204
Durham Cathedral 95
Dursley, Gloucestershire 148, 204
Dysart, Co. Westmeath 59, 61, 293

Eaglesham, Strathclyde 28
Ealing, London 264-5
Earsham Hall, Norfolk 204
Eastbourne, East Sussex 204
Eastbury, Dorset 61, 155, 204
East Dereham, Norfolk 204
East Hill House, Tenterden 38, 248
East Lulworth, Dorset 117, 205
Eastney, Portsmouth 237
Eastnor Castle, Hereford and Worcester 95, 205
Easton Neston, Northamptonshire 12, 36, 64
East Sheen, Richmond-upon-Thames 273
East Stratton, Hampshire 102, 205
East Street, New Alresford *41*, 196, 229
Eaton Mascott Hall, Shropshire 205
Eaton Place and Square, Belgravia 278
Eaton Socon, Cambridgeshire 205
Ebberston Hall, North Yorkshire 97, 205
Ebury Street, Belgravia 278
Ecole de Chirurgie, Paris 150
Ecton Hall, Warwickshire 77, 205
Edge Hill, Warwickshire 14, 97, 205
Edgehill Tower, Edge Hill 97, 205
Edgware, Barnet 260
Edinburgh 25-7, 30, 34, 51, 108, 118, 119, 130, 147, 150, 154, 155, *155*, 163-4, *164*, 177, 205-6, *206*
Edinburgh University 166, 205
Egham, Surrey 12, 206
Egyptian Hall, Mansion House 107, 151-2, 175, 263
Egyptian hall, Palladio's original design *see* Palladio in Architects index
Egyptian Hall, Piccadilly 45
Egyptian House, Penzance 45, 235
Elder Street, Spitalfields *134*, 276, 277
Eldon Square, Newcastle upon Tyne 34, 230
Elgin, Grampian 120, 206
Elizabeth College, St Peter Port 164, 240
Eltham Lodge, Greenwich 53
Elton Hall, Cambridgeshire 206
Elvills, Surrey 206
Ely, Cambridgeshire 35, *35*, 161, 206
Ely House, Dover Street 43, 274, 279
Ely House, Dublin 40, 292
Emo Park, Co. Laois 89, 293
Emsworth, Co. Dublin 90, 293
Emsworth, Hampshire 206
Encombe House, Dorset 67, *67*, 74, 207
Endsleigh, Devon 96, 207
Enfield, London 264
Enniskillen, Co. Fermanagh 293
Erddig, Clwyd 207
Erechtheion, Athens 91, 95, 120, 182, 198, 249, 253, 261, 280
Erindale, Co. Carlow 293
Esher, Surrey 14, 207
Esher Place, Esher 207
Eshton Hall, North Yorkshire 207
Eton, Berkshire 207
Eton College, Eton 207
Euston Hall, Suffolk 97
Everton, Liverpool 122, 223
Evesham, Hereford and Worcester 207
Exchange, Bristol 130, 191
Exchange, Leningrad 131
Exchange, Liverpool 130-31, 222
Exchange Coffee Rooms, Dundee 177, 204
Exeter, Devon 29, 133, 174, 207-8
Exeter Change, Strand 130
Exmouth, Devon 96, 208
Exton Park, Leicestershire 208
Eynsham, Oxfordshire 208

Fairfax House, York 37, 259
Fairfield, Greater Manchester 208
Fairlawne, Kent 208
Fallowfield, Manchester 226
Falkirk, Central Region 29, 208
Falmouth, Cornwall 163, 208
Farm, Sezincote House 101, 241
Faringdon House, Oxfordshire 208
Farley Hall, Berkshire 208
Farnborough Hall, Warwickshire 208
Farnham, Surrey 36, 37, 208
Faversham, Kent 126, 208
Female Prison, York 19, 152, 157, *157*, 158, 258
Feoffes Charity School, Rotherham 162, 239
Fermoy, County Cork 293
Finchcocks, Kent 62, 189, 208, 226

Finchley, Barnet 260
Finsbury, Islington 269
Fishing lodge, Rockingham 100
Fish Market, Newcastle upon Tyne 133
Fishmongers' Hall, William Street 134, 263
Fitzrovia, Camden 262
Fitzroy Square, Fitzrovia 262
Fleet Street, City of London 106, 107, 111, 129, 264
Florence Court, Co. Fermanagh 66, 293
Flour mill, Slane 135, 298
Fochabers Newtown, Grampian 28, 109, 209
Folkingham, Lincolnshire 158, 209
Folly Arch, Gobions 97, 192
Folly lodges, Glin Castle 100, 294
Fonthill Abbey, Wiltshire 169n, 209
Foots Cray, Bexley 260
Forcett Park, North Yorkshire 51, 209
Foremark Hall, Derbyshire 72, 209
Forest Road, Walthamstow 277
Forfar, Tayside 209
Fort Clarence, Rochester 156, 209
Fort George, Highland 209
Fort Henry, Exton Park 208
Fort Shannon, Co. Limerick 293
Fota Island, Co. Cork 293
Fountains Hospital, Linton 162, 222
Four Courts, Dublin 147, 153, 291
Fourcrosses, Powys 173, 209
Fournier Street, Spitalfields *24*, 36, 276
Fox Hall, West Sussex 65
Frame workshops, Bonsall 134, 188
Frampton Court, Gloucestershire 70, 98, 109, *209*, 246
Free School, Windsor 162, 255
Free Trade Wharf, Wapping 277
Frenchay, Avon 209
Frenchay Manor, Frenchay 209
Friar Gate, Derby 37, *37*, 181, 202
Frith Street, Soho 282
Frogmore House, Windsor 255
Frome, Somerset 12, 159, 161, 210
Fulham, Hammersmith and Fulham 267
Fulham Palace, Fulham 267
Furness, Co. Kildare 293
Fydell House, Boston 51, 188

Gainsborough, Lincolnshire 109, 110, 210
Galby, Leicestershire 123, 210
Galerie d'Orléans, Paris 130
Galeries de Bois, Paris 130
Galloway House, Dumfries and Galloway 56
Galtrim House, Co. Meath 293
Gaol, Abingdon 159, 180
Gaol, Beaumaris 158, 185
Gaol, Berwick 150, 186
Gaol, Chester 150, 196
Gaol, Derby 158, 202
Gaol, Glasgow 151, 210
Gaol, King's Lynn 157, *158*, 218
Gaol, Leicester 158, 221
Gaol, Lincoln 159, 222
Gaol, Maidstone 159, 225
Gaol, Nottingham 159
Gaol, Perth 159, 235
Gaol, Youghal 157, 299
Garbally Court, Ballinasloe 284
Garden buildings, Rousham House 97, 239
Garden temple, Aske Hall 98, 183
Garendon Hall, Leicestershire 99, 210
Garrick's Villa, Hampton 273
Gately Hall, Norfolk 51, 71, 210
Gaulby *see* Galby
Gaulstown, Co. Westmeath 293
Gaunt's House, Dorset 96-7, 210
Gayhurst, Buckinghamshire 104, 210
Gay Street, Bath 27, 43, 184
Geffrye Museum, Shoreditch 162, 267
Genealogical Office, Dublin 144-5, *144*, 290
General Infirmary, Bath 160, 161, 184
General Infirmary, Northampton 160, 232
General Infirmary, Salisbury 159, 240
General Wade's House, Bath 37, 184
General Wade's House, Mayfair 8, *9*, 51, 145, 167, 194, 211, 216, 280, 290
George and Dragon Inn, Yarm 172, 238
George Hotel, Lichfield 174, 221
George Hotel, Stamford 173, 244
George Inn, Buckden 173
George Inn, Grantham 174, 212

308 / *Index of buildings and places*

George Inn, Woburn 174, 256
George Stiel's Hospital, Tranent 161, 249
George Street, Edinburgh 25, 26, 205
Gerrard Street, Soho 282
Gestingthorpe, Essex 210
Gesù church, Rome 290
Gibside, Tyne and Wear 210
Gilling Castle, North Yorkshire 66, 210
Glananea, Co. Westmeath 294, 297
Glasgow 30, 37, 55, 129, 130, 131, 133, *134*, 151, *151*, 153, 177, 210-11
Glassite Chapel, Dundee 118, 203
Glasterrymore, Co. Offaly 294
Glastonbury, Somerset 150, 211
Gleanings, The, Rochester 90, 239
Glengarriff Lodge, Co. Cork 97, 294
Glen Orchy, Strathclyde 119, 211
Glin Castle, Co. Limerick 100, 294
Gloster, Co. Offaly 66, 294
Gloucester 159, 211
Gloucester Circus, Greenwich 33, *33*, 266
Gloucester Place, St Marylebone 281
Glynde, East Sussex 111, 211
Gobions, Hertfordshire 97, 192
Godmersham Park, Kent 211
Golden Grove, Dyfed 211
Golden Lion Inn, Fourcrosses 173, 209
Goldsmiths' Hall, Foster Lane 134, 263
Golspie, Highland 211
Goodwin's Court, Covent Garden 129, 278
Goodwood House, West Sussex 211
Goole, Humberside 174, 211
Gordon Castle, Grampian 28
Gordonstoun House, Grampian 212
Gorhambury, Hertfordshire 212
Gormanston Castle, Co. Meath 79, 294
Gosford Castle, Co. Armagh 95, 294
Gosford House, Lothian 212
Gosport, Hampshire 159, 212
Gothic Temple, Stowe 97, *98*, 247
Gothic Temple, Painshill Park 97-8, 234
Gracehill, Co. Antrim 294
Grafton Street, Mayfair 43, 44, 279
Graiguenamanagh, Co. Kilkenny 294
Grand Canal Hotel, Robertstown 174, 297
Grand Parade, Bath 31, 174
Grand Théâtre, Bordeaux 171
Grand Theatre, Lancaster 171, 220
Grange, The, Hampshire 16, *91*, 93, 94
Grange, Co. Louth 294
Grange, The, Winterborne Dauntsey 255
Grantham, Lincolnshire 174, 212
Granville Club, Shrewsbury 37, 243
Gravesend, Kent 212
Gray's Inn, Holborn 154, 262
Great Amwell, Hertfordshire 212
Great Baddow, Essex 212
Great Barn, Holkham Hall 101, 216
Great Barr Hall, Suffolk 212
Great College Street, Westminster 283
Great James Street, Bloomsbury 261
Great North Road, Hatfield 29, 214
Great Packington, Warwickshire 119, 212
Great Packington Old Hall 212
Great Pulteney Street, Bath 22, 33, 34, 185
Great Pump Room, Bath 176-7, 184
Great Queen Street, Covent Garden 30, 278
Great Torrington, Devon 212
Great Witley, Hereford and Worcester 111, *112*, 212
Great Yarmouth, Norfolk 111, 160, 212
Greek Street, Soho 38, 282
Green Street, Mayfair 31, 38, *49*, 279
Green's Bridge, Kilkenny 141, 294
Greenwich, London 265-6
Greenwich Palace, Greenwich 143, 265
Greta Bridge, Co. Durham 212
Grey Abbey, Co. Down 294
Grey Friars House, Colchester 42, 198
Greyhound Hotel, Wincanton 172, 255
Greyhound Inn, Blandford Forum 173, 188
Greyhound Inn, Cromford 139, 200
Greystoke Castle, Cumbria 212
Grey Street, Newcastle upon Tyne 34, 230
Grimsthorpe Castle, Lincolnshire 69, 212
Grove House, Regent's Park 282
Grovelands House, Southgate 265
Grosvenor Chapel, South Audley Street 111, 278
Grosvenor Estate, Mayfair 20, 21, 25

Grosvenor Hotel, Stockbridge 174, *245*
Grosvenor Square, Bath 27
Grosvenor Square, Mayfair 21, 30, 31, 32, 165, 279
Guildford, Surrey 111, 133, 213
Guildhall, Bath 150, 184
Guildhall, City of London 150, 263
Guildhall, Ludlow *41*, 43, 224
Guildhall, Newport 148, 230
Guildhall, Poole 148, 236
Guildhall, Salisbury 148, 240
Guildhall, Worcester 148, 257
Gun-Boring Factory, Woolwich 155, 266
Gunton Park, Norfolk 117, 213
Guy's Hospital, Southwark 160, 161, 275
Gwrych Castle, Clwyd 213

Hackness Hall, North Yorkshire 213
Hackney, London 266-7
Hackwood Park, Hampshire 90, 213
Haddington, Lothian 213
Haddo House, Grampian 56, 213
Hadleigh, Suffolk 213
Hafod, Dyfed 213
Haggersgate House, Whitby 37, 254
Hagley Hall, Hereford and Worcester 14, 15, 70, 97, 99, *99*, 213
Hailes House, Lothian 213
Haileybury College, Hertfordshire 166, 213
Hale, Hampshire 213
Hale House, Hale 213
Halifax, West Yorkshire 128, 132-3, 213
Hall Place, Berkshire 213
Halstead, Essex 35, 213-14
Ham, Richmond-upon-Thames 273
Ham Common, Ham 273
Hamels Park, Hertfordshire 15, 9b, 101
Hamilton, Strathclyde 118, 214
Hammersmith and Fulham, London 267
Hammersmith, Hammersmith and Fulham 267
Hammerwood House, East Sussex 91, 214
Hampden House, Buckinghamshire 214
Hampstead, Camden 262
Hampton, Richmond-upon-Thames 99, 273
Hampton Court, Richmond-upon-Thames 273
Hampton Court Green 273
Hampton Court Palace 14, 196, 273
Hampton Lucy, Warwickshire 214
Hampton Wick, Richmond-upon-Thames 273
Hanbury, Hereford and Worcester 214
Hanover Square, Mayfair 106, 111
Hardenhuish, Wiltshire 115, 214
Hardwick, Shropshire 214
Hardwick Hall, Co. Durham 214
Hare Hall, Romford 268
Harewood House, West Yorkshire 83, 103, 214
Harewood village 102-3, 214
Haringey, London 267
Harleston, Norfolk 174, 214
Harleyford Manor, Buckinghamshire 72-3
Harrow, London 267-8
Harrow School, Harrow 164, 267-8
Hartwell House, Buckinghamshire 214
Haslar, Gosport 160, 161, 212
Hastings, East Sussex 34, 45, 214
Hatchlands, Surrey 82, 103n, 214
Hatfield, Hertfordshire 29, 214
Hatton Grange, Shropshire 70, 215
Haverfordwest, Dyfed 215
Havering, London 268
Havering-atte-Bower, Havering 268
Hawkhurst, Kent 215
Haworth Hall, Kingston upon Hull 219
Hayes, Bromley 260
Haymarket, St James's 129, 130, 280
Hayes, Bromley 260
Hay-on-Wye, Powys 174, 215
Hazlewood, Co. Sligo 294
Headfort, Co. Meath 294
Headley, Surrey 32
Head Street, Colchester 43, 198
Heath, West Yorkshire 215
Heath Hall, Heath 215
Heaton, Manchester 226
Heaton Hall, Heaton 69, 84, 226
Hellaby Hall, South Yorkshire 215
Helmingham Hall, Suffolk 215
Helston, Cornwall 215
Hendon, Finchley 260
Hendon Place, Hendon 260

Henrietta Street, Dublin 38, 39, *39*, 155, 285, 292, *292*
Herne Hill, Lambeth 271
Hereford 215
Hertford 215
Hertford Street, Mayfair 279
Heveningham Hall, Suffolk 8, 85, 215
High Barnet, Finchley 260
Highbury, Islington 269
Higher and Lower Market, Exeter 133, 207
Highgate, Camden 262
High Ousegate, York 36, 259
High Pavement, Chesterfield 42, 196
High Street, Bath 130
High Street, Boston 32, 37, 188, *188*
High Street, Halstead 35, 213
High Street, Huntingdon 38, 217
High Street, Kingston upon Hull 35, 218
High Street, Lewes 36, 221
High Street, Stamford 37, 129, 130, 244
High Street, Winchester 129, 255
High Street, Witney *41*, 256
High Street St Martin's, Stamford 35, 36, 244
Highweek Street, Newton Abbot 43, 231
High Wycombe, Buckinghamshire 14, 132, 148, 215
Hilborough Hall, Norfolk 69, 215
Hillingdon, London 268
Hillsborough, Co. Down 125, 294
Hillsborough House, Hillsborough 294
Hoare's Bank, Fleet Street 129, 264
Holborn, Camden 262
Holkham Hall, Norfolk 38, 63, 68-9, *68*, 69, 70, 83, 93, 101, 145, 215, 216, 217
Holloway, Islington 269
Holme, The, Regent's Park 282
Holwood House, Keston 261
Holy Cross Church, Daventry 108, 201
Holyhead, Anglesey 216
Holy Trinity Church, Guildford 11, 213
Holy Trinity Church, Leeds 12, 106, 112, 113, *113*, 220, 243
Holy Trinity Church, St Marylebone 120, 281
Holy Trinity Church, Teigh 126, 248
Holy Trinity Church, Theale 122, 248
Holy Trinity Church, Wolverton 123, 256
Holywell Hall, Lincolnshire 216
Holywell Hill, St Albans 37, 239
Home Farm, Doune Park 101, 203
Home House, Portman Square 44, 45, *49*, 282
Homerton, Hackney 267
Honiley, Warwickshire 105, 106, 216
Honington Hall, Warwickshire 216
Honourable Artillery Company HQ, Finsbury 269
Hope House, Woodstock 12, 257
Hopetoun House, Lothian 55, 216
Hopton, Derbyshire 13, 216
Hopton Almshouses, Southwark 162, 275
Hopton Hall, Hopton 216
Horbury, West Yorkshire 117, 216
Hornchurch, Havering 268
Horse Guards, Whitehall 8, 145, *145*, 146, 216, 286
Horsham, West Sussex 216
Horton, Dorset 216
Horton Hall, Northamptonshire 216
Horton Road Hospital, Gloucester 159
Hosyers' Almshouses, Ludlow 162, 224
Hotel, Shannon Harbour 174, 285
Hotel, Tullamore 174, 298
Hôtel-Dieu, Lyon 147
Hôtel des Invalides, Paris 143
Houghton Hall, Norfolk 45, 62-3, *62*, *63*, 64, 65, *65*, 66, 69, 83, 102, 212, 216, 252
Houghton Lodge, Hampshire 96, 216
Hounslow, London 268
House of Correction, Folkingham 158, 209
House of Correction, Knutsford 158, 219
House of Correction, Littledean 159, 222
House of Correction, Northleach 159, 232
House of Gray, Tayside 216
House of Lords chamber, Westminster 7
House Mill, Stratford 135, 272
Hove, Brighton 30, 190
Hovingham Hall, North Yorshire 51, 216
Hull *see* Kingston upon Hull
Hulme, Manchester 226
Hurlingham House, Fulham 267
Huntingdon, Cambridgeshire 38, 156, 159, 217

Hutcheson's Hospital, Glasgow 162, 177, 210
Huthwaite Hall, North Yorkshire 73
Hutton, Borders 142
Hyde Park Corner 278
Hylands, Essex 217

Ickworth, Suffolk 90, 217
Ilford, Redbridge 272
Il Redentore Church, Venice 287
Imperial War Museum, Southwark 275
Ince Blundell Hall, Merseyside *168*, 169, 217
Infirmary, Armagh 160, 284
Ingleby Arncliffe, North Yorkshire 217
Inveraray, Strathclyde 217
Inveraray Castle, Inveraray 217
Inverness, Highland 217
Ipswich, Suffolk 217
Iron Bridge, Ironbridge 141, *141*, 217
Iron bridge, Paddington 142
Ironbridge, Shropshire 29, 141, *141*, 217
Iron bridge, Stanford 142
Iron Bridge, Sunderland 142
Isleworth, Hounslow 269
Islington, London 269
Iver, Buckinghamshire 217
Ivy House, Chippenham 51, 197

Jedburgh, Borders 217
John Adam Street, Strand 23, 43, 278
John Watson School, Edinburgh 205

Kedleston, Derbyshire 15, 66, 74, 82–3, *82*, *83*, 89, 217
Kelso, Borders 118, 217
Kemp Town, Brighton 34, 190
Kendal, Cumbria 171, 217–18
Kenmore, Tayside 125, 218
Kennington, Lambeth 33, 271
Kennington, Oxfordshire 123, 218
Kennington Lane, Kennington 45, 271
Kennington Road, Kennington 33, 271
Kensington, Royal Borough of Kensington and Chelsea 270
Kensington Palace, Kensington 270
Kentchurch Court, Hereford and Worcester 218
Kentish Town Road, Camden 261
Kenwood House, Highgate 83, 176, 262, 290
Keppel Street, Bloomsbury 22
Keston, Bromley 261
Kew, Richmond-upon-Thames 15, 98, 99, 100, 273
Kilarrow, Strathclyde 118, 218
Kilcarty, Co. Meath 101, 294
Kildoagh, Co. Cavan 294
Kilkenny 141, 150, 153, 161, 294
Kilmainham Gaol, Dublin 157, 291
Kilruddery, Co. Wicklow 294
Kilshannig, Co. Cork 76, 295
Kimberley Hall, Norfolk 70, 218
Kimbolton, Cambridgeshire 56
Kimbolton Castle, Hampshire 76
Kinfauns Castle, Tayside 218
King Edward's School, Bath 163, 184
Kingsand, Cornwall 218
King's Arms Inn, Newbury 172, 230
King's College, Cambridge 166, 193
King's College, Somerset House 278
King's Court, Westminster 153
King's Head Hotel, Richmond 173, 238
King's House, Boyle 285
King's Inns, Dublin 39, 117, 154, 291
King's Lynn, Norfolk 38, 157, *158*, 218
King's Norton, Leicestershire 125, 126, 218
Kingsnympton Park, Devon 70, 218
King's Road, Chelsea 38, 270
King's Stanley, Gloucestershire 136, 218
Kingston, Kingston-upon-Thames 270
Kingston College, Mitchelstown 28, 162, *163*, 296
Kingston upon Hull 32, 35, 38, 133, 135, 173, 218–19, *219*
Kingston Lisle, Oxfordshire 218
Kingston-upon-Thames, London 270
King Street, Covent Garden 43, 278
King's Weston, Avon 61, 71, 219
Kinmount, Dumfries and Galloway 93, 219
Kirby Hall, North Yorkshire 71
Kirk *see* Church
Kirkleatham, Cleveland 162, 219
Kirtlington Park, Oxfordshire 70, *219*

Kitley House, Devon 219
Knightsbridge, Royal Borough of Kensington and Chelsea 270
Knockbreda, Co. Antrim 115, 297
Knowsley Hall, Merseyside 219
Knutsford, Cheshire 11, 158, 219

Lace workers' cottages, Sevenoaks 134, 241
Lacock Abbey, Wiltshire 219
Ladykirk House, Berwickshire 51
Lambeth, London 270–71
Lambton Castle, Co. Durham 81, 219
Lampeter, Dyfed 164, 219
Lanark, Strathclyde 220
Lancaster 35, 150, 162, 171, 220
Lancaster House, St James's 280
Landport Gate, Portsmouth 237
Langley Park, Buckinghamshire 220
Langley Park, Norfolk 70, 220
Langport, Somerset 148, 220
Langton(-by-Partney), Lincolnshire 220
Lansdown Crescent, Bath 33, 185
Lansdown Place, Cheltenham 33, 195
Lansdowne House, Berkeley Square 279
Lanthorn of Demosthenes, Shugborough 99, 243
Lasborough Park, Gloucestershire 79, 81, 220
Latin School, Risley 162, 238
Launceston, Cornwall 220
Law Court, Palace of Westminster 154
Law Courts, Edinburgh 154, 205
Lawers House, Tayside 56, 220
Lawrence Street, Chelsea 35, 270
Law Society Hall, Chancery Lane 155
Laxton Hall, Northamptonshire 92
Leamington Spa, Warwickshire 175, 220
Leasingham Manor House, Lincolnshire 220
Leazes Terrace, Newcastle upon Tyne 34, 230
Ledwithstown, Co. Longford 57, 295
Lee, Lewisham 272
Leeds 12, 106, 112, 113, *113*, 221
Leeds Library, Leeds 179, 221
Leicester 174, 221
Leigh Court, Avon 221
Leigh Kirk, Paisley 123
Leighton Buzzard, Bedfordshire 221
Leighton Hall, Lancashire 195, 221
Leinster House, Dublin 51, 59, 89, 160, 290, 291, 292
Leith, Edinburgh *108*, 150, 206
Leixlip Castle, Co. Kildare 295
Lemon Street, Truro 32
Lendal, York 31, 259
Leominster, Hereford and Worcester 40, 221
Leptis Magna, now in Libya 250
Letheringsett Hall, Norfolk 221
Letton Hall, Norfolk 221
Lewes, East Sussex 36, 221
Lewes Crescent, Brighton 34, 190
Lewisham, London 271–2
Leytonstone, Waltham Forest 277
Library, Stamford 133, 244
Lichfield, Staffordshire 175, 221
Lichfield House, St James's 43, 280
Lifford, Co. Donegal 295
Lilleshall Hall, Shropshire 96, 211, 222
Limehouse, Tower Hamlets 276
Limerick 35, 76, 295
Linby, Nottinghamshire 139, 222
Lincoln 151, 159, 160, 222
Lincoln's Inn, Holborn 128, 154, 262
Lincoln's Inn Fields, Holborn 16, 30, 37, 44–5, *44*, *51*, *154*, 169, 262
Lindsey House, Holborn 37, 51
Linton, North Yorkshire 162, 222
Lion Bridge, Alnwick 181
Lion Hotel, Builth Wells 174, 192
Lion Hotel, Shrewsbury 174, 242
Lisdonagh, Co. Galway 61
Lisle Street, Soho 282
Lismore Lodge, Lough Cutra 295
Literary and Philosophical Institute, Bristol 177, 191
Littledean, Gloucestershire 159, 222
Little Gidding, Cambridgeshire 222
Little Stanmore, Haringey 111, 268
Liverpool 33, 37, 122, 130–31, 162, 177, *178*, 222–3, *223*
Llandrindod Hall, Llandrindod Wells 174, 223
Llandrindod Wells, Powys 174, 223

Llanfyllin, Powys 223
Llanidloes, Powys 224
Lloyd Baker Estate, Finsbury 269
Lloyds Bank, Stafford 128, 244
Lochwinnoch, Strathclyde 119, 224
Lodge, Gaunt's House 96–7, 210
Lodge, Loughcrew 100, 295
Lodge, Tyringham House 100, 250
Lodge, Wynnstay Park 100, 258
Lodges, Basildon Park 100, 184
Lodges, Dodington Park 100, 202
Lodges, Richmond Park 274
Lodge Park, Co. Kildare 74
London 260–83
London Colney, Hertfordshire 123, 224
London Hospital, Whitechapel 159, 160, 161, 277
Londonderry *see* Derry
London Docks, Wapping *136*, 137–9, 277
Longdon upon Tern, Shropshire 224
Longfield, Co. Tipperary 71
Longford Hall, Shropshire 91, 224
Longhirst House, Northumberland 92, 93
Longleat, Wiltshire 78, 224
Long Melford, Suffolk 224
Longner Hall, Shropshire 81, 224
Long Nethergate, Scarborough 35, 241
Longstone Hall, Derbyshire 13, 216, 224
Longton, Staffordshire 224
Lord North Street, Victoria 283
Lord Pembroke's House, Whitehall 145, 290
Lota, Co. Cork 76, 295
Lothbury, City of London 30
Loughcrew, Co. Meath 100, 295
Lough Cutra Castle, Co. Galway 295
Loughgall, Co. Armagh 152, 295
Louth, Lincolnshire 224
Lower Hartwell, Buckinghamshire 214
Lower Mall, Hammersmith 267
Lowestoft, Suffolk 224
Low Pavement, Nottingham 40, 232
Lowther, Cumbria 102, 224
Lowther Hotel, Goole 174, 211
Lucan House, Co. Dublin 57, 86, *86*, 87, 89, 286, 287, 295, 297
Ludlow, Shropshire 40, *41*, *42*, 43, 132, 162, 224
Lumley Castle, Co. Durham 224
Luscombe Castle, Devon 81, 224
Luttrelstown Castle, Co. Dublin 79, 295
Lyceum Club, Liverpool 177, *178*, 223
Lydiard Tregoze, Wiltshire 70, 224
Lyme Park, Cheshire 67, 91, 94, 224
Lyme Regis, Dorset 29, 225
Lyons, Co. Kildare 295
Lypiatt Park, Gloucestershire 225
Lytham Hall, Lancashire 225

Macartney House, Chesterfield Walk 266
Macclesfield, Cheshire 225
Madeley, Shropshire 119, 255
Maentwrog, Gwynedd 225
Magdalen College Chapel, Oxford 81
Maidenhead, Berkshire 140, 225
Maids of Honour Row, Richmond 274
Maidstone, Kent 129, 134, 148, 151, 159, 225
Maison Carrée (Roman temple), Nîmes 99
Maison de Force, Ackerghem 158
Maisters House, Kingston upon Hull 38, 218
Malahide Castle, Co. Dublin 295
Maldon, Essex 225
Male Prison, Cork 158, 288, *288*
Malling Abbey, West Malling 253
Malt House, Chipping Campden 12
Malton, Co. Wicklow 288
Malvern Hall, Solihull 243
Mamhead House, Devon 225
Manchester 177, 178, *178*, 225
Manchester Square, St Marylebone 281–2
Manor House, Combe Hay 198
Manresa House, Roehampton 73, 277
Mansfield Street, St Marylebone 282
Mansion, The, Ashbourne 38, 182
Mansion House, City of London 61, 151, 175, 263
Mansion House, Doncaster 152, 202
Mansion House, York 8, 12, 152, *152*, 258
Mantua House, Co. Roscommon 62, 295
Mapleton, Derbyshire 226
Marble Hill House, Twickenham 63, 70, 71, 274
Marford, Clwyd 103, 226
Margam Abbey, West Glamorgan 226

Margate, Kent 161, 171, 226
Marino, Co. Dublin 98, *98*, 291, 296
Market, Charleville 132, 287
Market, Hungerford 133
Market, Stamford 133, 244
Market Cross, Barnard Castle 152, 184
Market Hall, Bury St Edmunds 132, *132*, 170, 193
Market Hall, High Wycombe 132, 215
Market Hall, Newtownards 175, 297
Market House, Dunlavin 132, 293
Market House, Dursley 148, 204
Market House, Martock 132, 226
Market House, Midleton 132, 296
Market House, Tullamore 132, 298
Market House, Uxbridge 132, 268
Market Place, Blandford Forum 35, *35*, 36, 188
Market Place, North Shields 133, 175, 232
Market Place, Yarm 31, 258
Marlay, Co. Dublin 296
Marlborough, Wiltshire 226
Marlborough Almshouses, St Albans 162, 239
Marlborough House, Kennington 271
Marlow, Buckinghamshire 51, 226
Marlow Place, Marlow 51, 226
Marshall, Benyon and Bage's Flour Mill, Ditherington 136, *136*, 138, 242
Martock, Somerset 132, 226
Marylebone, Westminster 281–2
Masson Mill, Cromford 139, 200
Matfield, Kent 189, 208
Matlock Bath, Derbyshire 226
Matlock Green, Derbyshire 226
Mausoleum of Halicarnassus 219, 261
Mausoleum of Julii, St Rémy 289
Mavisbank, Lothian 55, 226, *227*
Mawley Hall, Shropshire 64, 226
Mayfair, Westminster 278–9
Mayoralty House, Drogheda 150, 289
Meard Street, Soho 282
Mechanics' Institute, Wakefield 177, 250
Melksham, Wiltshire 227
Mellerstain, Borders 78, 227
Melrose, Borders 78, 227
Melville Castle, Lothian 79
Menai Straits, Gwynedd 142, 227
Merchants' Hall, Edinburgh 133, 205
Mereworth, Kent 107, 108, 110, *114*, 227
Mereworth Castle *54*, 55, 62, 71, 227
Merrion Square, Dublin 23, 25, *41*, *48*, *50*, 292
Mersham le Hatch, Kent 84, 227
Merton, London 272
Messing Park, Essex 227
Methodist Church, Sheffield 112, 241
Methven, Tayside 227
Micheldever, Hampshire 119, 228
Micklegate, York 37, 259
Middlesex Sessions House, Clerkenwell 152, 269
Midford Castle, Avon 78, 228
Midleton, Co. Cork 132, 296
Milborne Port, Somerset 228
Mildenhall, Wiltshire 164, 228
Milford, Derbyshire 228
Milgate House, Kent 228
Mill, Cromford 135, 200
Miller Street, Glasgow 37, 211
Mill Hill, Barnet 260
Mill Hill School, Mill Hill 163, 166, 260
Mill and house, Newtown 140, 231, *231*
Millman Street, Bloomsbury *46*
Millmount, Co. Kilkenny 75, 296
Milltown, Co. Offaly 51, 296
Milton Abbas, Dorset 102, 228
Milton Abbey, Milton Abbas 15, 78, 228
Milton House, Northamptonshire 228
Milton House, Oxfordshire 228
Mistley, Essex 103, 117, *117*, 228
Mitcham, Merton 272
Mitchelstown, Co. Cork 28, 162, *163*, 296
Moccas Court, Hereford and Worcester 51, 228
Mogerhanger Park, Bedfordshire 228
Moira, Co. Down 296
Monasterevin, Co. Kildare 229
Monkstown, Co. Dublin 296
Montague Street, Bloomsbury 32, 261
Monmouth, Gwent 38, 147–8, 174, 228
Montgomery, Powys 159, 229
Montpelier Row, Twickenham 274
Montpellier Pump Room, Cheltenham 176, 195

Montrose, Tayside 120, 229
Moore Abbey, Monasterevin 77–8, 229
Moor Park, Hertfordshire 54, 229
Moor Park, Powys 73, 229
Moot Hall, Newcastle upon Tyne 151, 230
Moray Place, Edinburgh 34, 206
Morden, Merton 272
Morden Hall and Park, Morden 272
Moreby Hall, North Yorkshire 229
Moreton, Dorset 229
Moreton-in-Marsh, Gloucestershire 229
Morpeth, Northumberland 148, 229
Mortlake, Richmond-upon-Thames 273
Morton Hall House, Lothian 229
Mote Park, Maidstone 225
Mountainstown, Co. Meath 296
Mount Clare, Roehampton 277
Mount Henry, Co. Laois 296
Mount Ievers Court, Co. Clare 57, 296
Mount Juliet, Co. Kilkenny 296
Mount Kennedy, Co. Wicklow 87, 296
Mountrath House, Mayfair 8
Mount Shannon, Co. Limerick 94, 296
Mountsorrel, Leicestershire 229
Mount Stewart, Co. Down 94, 296
Multyfarnham, Co. Westmeath 163, 296
Murray Royal Asylum for the Insane, Perth 161, 235
Museum, Cirencester 37, 197
Museum, Farnham 36, 209
Museum, King's Lynn 38, 218
Mussenden Temple, Downhill 99, 289

Nantwich, Cheshire 229
Nant-y-Bellan *see* Wynnstay Park
Narford Hall, Norfolk 70
Needham's School, Ely 161, 206
Nelson Street, Stroud 35, 247
Nenagh, Co. Tipperary 159, 296
Neptune Inn, Hull 173, 218
New Alresford, Hampshire *41*, 196, 229
New Assembly Rooms, Bath 175, 184
Newark-on-Trent, Nottinghamshire 148, 229–30
Newberry Hall, Co. Kildare 38, 75, *75*, 86, 87, 288, 296, 297
Newbridge House, Co. Dublin 296
Newbury, Berkshire 172, 230
Newby Hall, North Yorkshire 83, 169, 230, 282
Newcastle upon Tyne 34, 42, 118, 133, 151, 230
Newcomen's Bank, Dublin 128, 292
New Cross, Lewisham 271
New Exchange, Strand 130
Newgate Gaol, City of London 157, 158
Newgate Street, City of London 105–6, 111
Newhailes House, Lothian 55
New Hall, Co. Clare 61, *61*, 296
New Hall, Devizes 132, 202
New Houghton, Houghton Hall 102, 216
Newington Green, Stoke Newington 30, 267
New Lanark, Strathclyde 139–40, *140*, 230
Newliston House, Lothian 230
Newmarket, Suffolk 7
New Playhouse, Kendal 171, 218
Newport, Isle of Wight 230
New River Company Estate, Finsbury 269
Newry, Co. Down 297
Newsham House, Anfield 223
News Room, Chester 179, 196
New St Lawrence's Church, Ayot St Lawrence 116, 183, *183*
Newton Abbot, Devon 43, 231
New Town, Edinburgh 25–6, 30, 34, 177, 205, 206
Newtown, Isle of Wight 231
Newtown, Powys 134, 140, 231, *231*
Newtownards, Co. Down 132, 297
Newtownbreda, Co. Antrim 115, 297
New Quay, North Shields 133, 175, 232
Nonsuch Park, Surrey 81, 95, 231
Norbury, Croydon 264
Normanby Park, Humberside 93
Normanton, Leicestershire 231
Norris Castle, Isle of Wight 81, 95, 231
Northallerton, North Yorkshire 231
North Bar, Beverley 31, 187
North Audley Street, Mayfair 38, *49*, *280*
North Church, Aberdeen 120, 180

Northfields, Ealing 264
North Hill, Colchester 37, 198
Northleach, Gloucestershire 159, 232
North Leith Church, Leith *108*, 109
North Mill, Belper 136, 186
North Shields, Tyne and Wear 133, 175, 232
Northwick Park, Avon 64, 232
Norton-by-Galby, Leicestershire 210
Norton Place, Lincolnshire 73, 232
Norwich 112, 158, 232
Norwood, Lambeth 271; *see also* Upper Norwood 264
Nostell Priory, West Yorkshire 70, 83, 219, 232
Nottingham 40, 150, 153, 232
Nuneham Courtenay, Oxfordshire 15, 102, 116, *116*, 232
Nuneham Park, Nuneham Courtenay 232
Nunnery, Greenwich 243
Nunnykirk Hall, Northumberland 92, 232

Oakley Park, Shropshire 95, 232–3
Observatory, Richmond 274
Ockbrook, Derbyshire 233
Octagon, The, Twickenham 275
Octagon Chapel, Bath 112, 184
Octagon Chapel, Norwich 112, 232
Odsey House, Cambridgeshire 233
Officers' Terrace, Chatham 155, 195
Old Aberdeen Town House, Aberdeen 150, 180
Old Alresford, Hampshire 233
Old Bell Chambers, Chepstow 172–3, 196
Old Burlington Street, Mayfair 8, *9*, 30, 31, 38, 45, *49*, 280
Oldcastle, Co. Meath 297
Old Council House, Bristol 151, 191
Old County Gaol, Shrewsbury 156, 159, 242
Old Court House, Hampton Court 273
Old Gaol, Bury St Edmunds 158, 193
'Old Hospital, The', Frome 159, 210
Old Kent Road, Walworth/Peckham 276
Old Ship Hotel, Brighton 174, 190
Oldtown, Co. Kildare 56, 297
Old Town, Edinburgh 30, 205–6
Old Town Hall, Lancaster 150, 220
Old Wolverton, Buckinghamshire 233
Orangery, Frampton Court 98, *209*, 246
Orangery, Royal Botanic Gardens, Kew 100, 273
Orleans House, Twickenham 66
Ormsby Hall, Lincolnshire 74, 233
Ossington, Nottinghamshire 233
Osterley, Hounslow 269
Osterley Park, Osterley 82, 83, 269
Oswestry, Shropshire 34, 35, *174*, 233
Otterden Place, Kent 233
Over Hall, Gestingthorpe 210
Over Whitacre, Warwickshire 109, 123, 233
Oxford 12, 36, 104, 123, 126, 160, 161, 164–5, *165*, 166, *166*, 169, 233–4
Oxford Market, St Marylebone 22

Paddington, Westminster 280
Paestum 87, 91, 101, 119, 212, 214, 243, 286
Pagoda, Royal Botanic Gardens, Kew 98, 243
Painshill Park, Surrey 98, 234
Painswick, Gloucestershire 234
Painswick House, Painswick 234
Paisley, Strathclyde 123
Palace Anne, Co. Cork 297
Palace of Westminster 16, 154
Palazzo Barberini, Rome 60
Palazzo Caprini, Rome 8
Palazzo Iseppo Porto, Vicenza 8, *9*, 152
Palladian Bridge, Audley End 98, 183
Palladian Bridge, Hagley Hall 98, 213
Palladian Bridge, Prior Park 98, 185
Palladian Bridge, Scampston Hall 241
Palladian Bridge, Stowe 98, *99*, 103n, 247
Palladian Bridge, Wilton 98, 254
Palladian temple, Euston 97
Pall Mall, St James's 169n, 177, *179*, 280
Palmyra 15, 82, 84
Panopticon, Richmond, Virginia 159
Pantheon, Rome 78, 83, 84, 98, 128, 145, 169, 175, 185
Panton Hall, Lincolnshire 60, 71
Papplewick Hall, Nottinghamshire 234
Papworth Hall, Cambridgeshire 234

Index of buildings and places / 311

Paragon House, Blackheath 271
Paragon, The, Bath 22, 31, 185
Paragon, Blackheath Park 33, 265, *265*
Parbold Hall, Lancashire 64, 234
Park Crescent, Regent's Park 34, 282
Parkend, Gloucestershire 234
Park Farm, Raby Castle 101, 238
Park Farm, Wimpole Hall 101, 255
Parkhall, Chesterfield Walk 266
Parkhurst Prison, Newport 230
Park Village, Regent's Park 30, 263
Parliament House, Dublin 12, 128, 143, 144, *144*, 290
Parliament Street, Kingston upon Hull 32, 219
Parnell Square, Dublin 23, 292
Parnella House, Devizes 42, 202
Parthenon, Athens 87, 177, 248, 270
Parwich Hall, Derbyshire 13
Patshull, Staffordshire 106, 235
Patshull Hall, Patshull 235
Paxton House, Borders 235
Paymaster General's Office, Whitehall 144, 191, 283
Peacock's School, Rye 36
Pease Warehouses, Kingston upon Hull 135, 218, *219*
Peckham, Southwark 275
Peckover House, Wisbech 38, 256
Pelham Crescent, Hastings 45, 214
Pell Wall House, Shropshire 235
Penicuik, Lothian 235
Penicuik House, Penicuik 56, 235
Penitentiary, Millbank 159
Pennington Street Stacks, London Docks 137
Pennsylvania Castle, Dorset 81, 235
Penny's Hospital, Lancaster 162, 220
Penrhyn Castle, Gwynedd 95, *95*, 235
Penrith, Cumbria 235
Penzance, Cornwall 45, 171, 235
Peper Harow, Surrey 73, 235
Percy Street, Fitzrovia 46, 262
Perrot House, Pershore 42, 235
Pershore, Hereford and Worcester 42, 235
Perth, Tayside 119, 151, 159, 161, 174, 235
Peterborough, Cambridgeshire 235
Peterhead, Grampian 150, 235
Peterhouse College, Cambridge 165, 193
Petersfield, Hampshire 235
Petersham, Richmond-upon-Thames 273-4
Petersham Lodge, Petersham 274
Peterstone Court, Powys 236
Petworth, West Sussex 148, 236
Petworth House, Petworth 91, 94, 236
Philipps House, Wiltshire 236
Philips and Lee Mill, Salford 136
Piazza, Covent Garden 7, 20
Piazza d'Armée, Livorno 20
Piccadilly, Westminster 278-9
Pickhill Hall, Clwyd 236
Piece Hall, Halifax 132-3, 213
Piercefield Park, Gwent 70, 236
Pigeon house, Badger Hall 100, 183
Pinner, Haringey 268
Pittville Pump Room, Cheltenham 176-7, 195
Pitzhanger Manor, Ealing 90, 264
Place Royale, Paris 20
Place Vendôme, Paris 50
Plaistow, Bromley 261
Plas Newydd, Anglesey 236
Pliny the Younger's villa, Laurentium 8
Plymouth, Devon 159, 161, 236
Point House, Westgrove 266
Pollok House, Strathclyde 236
Pompeii 73
Ponsonby Hall, Cumbria 70, 236
Pontcysyllte Aqueduct, Clwyd 236
Pontefract, West Yorkshire 174, 236
Pontypridd, Mid Glamorgan 141, 236
Poole, Dorset 38, 148, 236-7
Pope's Grotto, Twickenham 16, 274
Poplar, Tower Hamlets 276
Portaferry , Co. Down 297
Portaferry House, Portaferry 297
Portarlington, Co. Laois 28, 38, 297
Portarlington Museum, Coolbanagher 288
Port Eliot, Cornwall 237
Porter Tun Room, Chiswell Street 136, 138, 264
Port Hall, Co. Donegal 297
Portico Library, Manchester 178, 225
Portis College, Weston 253

Portland, Dorset 111, 237
Portland Place, St Marylebone 34, 282
Port Laoise, Co. Laois 153, 297
Portman Square, St Marylebone 44, *49*, 282; *see also* Home House
Portsea, Portsmouth 237
Portsmouth, Hampshire 155, 159, 237
Portway House, Warminster 36, 251
Potterspury, Northamptonshire 67, 237
Powderham Castle, Devon 237
Powerscourt, Co. Wicklow 40, 61, 297
Powerscourt House, Dublin 40, 292
Presbyterian Church, Belfast 118, 285
Presbyterian Church, Holborn 122
Presbyterian Church, Randalstown 118, 297
Preston, Lancashire 237
Preston on Stour, Warwickshire 124, 237
Prince Street, Bristol 36, 191
Prince's Lodging, Newmarket 7
Princes Street, Edinburgh 25
Prior Park, Bath 70, 98, 185
Prison, Nenagh 159, 296
Prison, Port Laoise 159, 297
See also Gaol
Public Offices, Glasgow 151, 153, 210
Pulteney Bridge, Bath *140*, 141, 184
Purbrook, Hampshire 73
Pusey House, Oxfordshire 237
Putney, Wandsworth 277

Quarry Bank Silk Mill, Styal 135, 139, 247
Queen Anne's Gate, Victoria *48*, 283
Queensberry House, Mayfair 8, 37
Queen's Chapel, St James's Palace 111
Queen's College, Oxford 164, 233
Queen's Gallery, Somerset House 8, *9*, 37, 128, 129
Queen's House, Greenwich 7, 53, 64, 67, 76, 216, 232, 237, 252, 265, 284, 294
Queen Square, Bath 27, 30, *32*, 34, 165, 184, 211
Queen Street, Edinburgh 25, 205
Queen Street, Lancaster 35, 220
Quernmore Park Hall, Lancashire 237
Quernmore School, Bromley 260
Quex Park, Birchington 187

Raby Castle, Co. Durham 101, 238
Radcliffe Infirmary, Oxford 160, 161, 234
Radcliffe Library, Oxford *166*, 234
Radcliffe Observatory, Oxford 234, *234*
Radley, Oxfordshire 238
Radley College and Hall, Radley 238
Radway Grange, Warwickshire 238
Ragley Hall, Warwickshire 57, 63, 69
Rainham, Havering 268
Rainham Hall, Rainham 268
Ramsey, Isle of Man 238
Ramsgate, Kent 123, 238
Randalstown, Co. Antrim 118, 297
Ranger's House, Chesterfield Walk 266
Ravelin Gate, Fort George 156, 209
Ravenfield, South Yorkshire 238
Raynham Hall, Norfolk 53
Rectory, Saxlingham Nethergate 15, 87, 240
Reading, Berkshire 238
Redbridge, London 272
Redcar, Cleveland 238
Red Lion Hotel, Blandford Forum 173, *173*, 188
Red Lion Hotel, Pontefract 174, 236
Reform Street, Dundee 130, 204
Regent Hotel, Leamington Spa 175, 220
Regent Street, Mayfair/St Marylebone 20, 34, 45, 129, 130, 172
Regent's Park, Camden/St Marylebone 20, 30, 34, 46, 129
Register House, Edinburgh 147, 205
Reigate, Surrey 238
Rialto Bridge, Venice 141
Richmond, North Yorkshire 150, 170, *170*, 171, 172, 173, 238
Richmond, Richmond-upon-Thames 274
Richmond Bridge, Richmond 274
Richmond Garden, formerly in Surrey 14
Richmond Green, Richmond 274
Richmond Hill, Richmond 43, 274
Richmond House, Whitehall 71
Richmond Park, Richmond-upon-Thames 274
Richmond Terrace, Whitehall 283
Richmond-upon-Thames, London 273-5
Ringwould House, Kent 238

Ripley, Surrey 172, 238
Ripon, North Yorkshire 148, 238
Risley, Derbyshire 162, 238
Riverstown House, Co. Cork 297
Robert Gordon Hospital, Aberdeen 163, 180
Robertstown, Co. Kildare 297
Robert Street, Strand 23, 278
Rochester, Kent 90, 156, 239
Rochester Castle, Rochester 95, 235
Rochfort, Co. Westmeath 298
Rockingham, Co. Roscommon 100
Rodney Street, Liverpool 33
Roehampton, Wandsworth 73, 277
Roehampton House, 53, 209, 277
Rokeby Hall, Co. Louth 57, 87, 297
Rokeby Hall, N. Yorkshire 64, 69, 239
Romford, Havering 268
Ropery, Chatham 135, *135*, 195
Roscrea, Co. Tipperary 297
Rosebery House, Lothian 239
Rose and Crown Hotel, Tonbridge 174, 249
Rose and Crown Inn, Wisbech 172, 255
Rosmead, Co. Westmeath 297
Rosneath Castle, Strathclyde 239
Rotherham, South Yorkshire 162, 239
Rotherhithe, Southwark 275
Rothley Castle, Wallington Hall 250
Rotunda, Woolwich 266
Rotunda Assembly Rooms, Dublin 175-6, *176*, 290-91
Rotunda Lying-in Hospital, Dublin 160, 161, 175, 290
Rotunda Museum, Scarborough 169, 241
Round House, Havering-atte-Bower 84, *84*, 268
Roundwood, Co. Laois 297
Rousham House, Oxfordshire 65, *65*, 72, 97, 101, 239
Royal Arsenal, Woolwich 266
Royal Artillery Barracks, Woolwich 156, *157*, 266
Royal Bank of Scotland, Glasgow 129, 210
Royal Borough of Kensington and Chelsea, London 270
Royal Botanic Gardens, Kew 15, 273
Royal Brass Foundry, Woolwich 155, 266
Royal Circus, Edinburgh 30
Royal Clarence Hotel, Exeter 174, 207
Royal College of Physicians, Trafalgar Square 155, 280
Royal College of Surgeons, Dublin 155, 291
Royal College of Surgeons, Lincoln's Inn 16, 155, 262
Royal Crescent, Bath 20, 27, *27*, 32-3, 184-5
Royal Dockyard, Woolwich 266
Royal Exchange, City of London 130
Royal Exchange, Dublin *131*, 155, 290
Royal Exchange, Edinburgh 130, 147, 205
Royal Hospital, Chelsea 143, 270
Royal Hospital, Dublin 143
Royal Hotel, Southend 174
Royal Infirmary, Gloucester 159, 211
Royal Infirmary, Worcester 159, 257
Royal Institution, Edinburgh *155*, 205
Royal Institution, Mayfair 278
Royal Institution of Fine Arts, Manchester 177, *178*, 225
Royal Insurance Office, Maidstone 129, 225
Royal Military Academy, Sandhurst 156, 240
Royal Military Academy, Woolwich 266
Royal Mint, Tower Hill 147, 227
Royal Naval Hospital, Great Yarmouth 160, 212
Royal Naval Hospital, Haslar 160, 161, 212
Royal Naval Hospital, Stonehouse 161
Royal Navy Sick and Hurt Board Office, Trinity Square 147, 264
Royal Navy Victualling Yard, Deptford 271
Royal Oak Hotel, Sevenoaks 174, 241
Royal Opera Arcade, Pall Mall 130
Royal Pavilion, Brighton 19n, 90, 190
Royal Salop Infirmary, Shrewsbury 161, 242
Royal Sea Bathing Hospital, Margate 161, 226
Royal Society of Arts Building, Adelphi 177, 278

312 / Index of buildings and places

Royal Theatre, Brecon 171, 189
Rugby School, Warwickshire 164, 166, 239
Russborough, Co. Wicklow 59, 61, 66, 297
Rutland Lodge, Petersham 273
Ryde, Isle of Wight 239
Rye, East Sussex 36, 239

Sackville Street, Mayfair 31, 280
Sacombe Park, Hertfordshire 239
Saffron Walden, Essex 239
St Albans, Hertfordshire 37, 139, 162, 239-40
St Alfege's Church, Greenwich 265
St Alkmund's Church, Shrewsbury 124, 126, 242
St Andrewgate, York 259
St Andrew's Chapel, Gunton Park 117, 213
St Andrew's Church, Dundee 109, 203
St Andrew's Church, Edinburgh 118, 205
St Andrew's Church, Glasgow 108, *108*, 210
St Andrew's Church, Holborn 107
St Andrew's Square, Edinburgh 25, 26, 38, 51, 205
St Anne's Church, Dublin 105
St Anne's Church, Kew Green 273
St Anne's Church, Limehouse 165, 276
St Anne's Church, Wardour Street 282
St Anne and St Agnes's Church, City of London 162, 219, 237
St Bartholomew's Church, Binley 117, 199
St Bartholomew's Church, City of London 110
St Bartholomew's Church, Tardebigge 123, 247
St Bartholomew's Hospital, Smithfield 160, 263
St Bernard's Crescent, Edinburgh 34, 206, *206*
St Botolph's Church, Aldersgate Street 263
St Botolph's Church, Aldgate 263
St Botolph's Church, Bishopsgate 263
St Bride's Church, Fleet Street 106, 107, 111
St Catherine's Church, Dublin 115, *115*, 290
St Chad's Church, Shrewsbury 118, *118*, 205, 242
S. Chiara (church), Rome 105
St Clement's Church, Oxford 123, 233
St Clement's Church, Worcester 123, 257
St David's College, Lampeter 164, 219
St Dunstan-in-the-East Church, Cannon Street Road 126, 208, 277
St Dunstan-in-the-West Church, Fleet Street 263
St Edward's Church, Stow-on-the-Wold 36, 240
St George's Chapel, Edinburgh 118, 205
St George's Church, Bloomsbury Way 20, 106, 261
St George's Church, Dublin *108*, 109, 290
St George's Church, Edinburgh 119
St George's Church, Everton 122, 223
St George's Church, Great Yarmouth 111, 212
St George's Church, Hanover Square 106, 111, 278
St George's Church, Portland 111, 237
St George's Church, Ramsgate 123, 238
St George's Hospital, Hyde Park Corner 161, 278
St George's Street, Mayfair 38, 280
S. Giacomo degli Incurabili (church), Rome 105
St Giles-in-the-Fields Church, St Giles High Street 107-8, 262
St Giles's Church, Elgin 120, 206
S. Giorgio Maggiore, Venice 149
S. Giovanni in Laterano, Rome 105
St Ives, Cambridgeshire 240
St Ives, West Yorkshire 70, 236
St James Garlickhithe Church, City of London 110
St James's, Westminster 280
St James's Barton, Bristol 36, 191
St James's Church, Bermondsey 122, 275
St James's Church, Great Packington 119, 212
St James's Church, Piccadilly 20, 106, 110, 111

St James's Palace, St James's 280
St James's Square, St James's 20, 31, 43, *48*, 172, 280, *281*
St James's Street, 31, 130, 177, 280
St James Street, Monmouth 38, 228
St John the Baptist's Church, Egham 122, 206
St John the Baptist's Church, Hackney 122, 267
St John the Baptist's Church, Honiley 105, 106, 216
St John the Baptist's Church, King's Norton 125, 126, 218
St John the Baptist's Church, Knutsford 111, 219
St John the Evangelist's Church, Shobdon 16, 241
St John the Evangelist's Church, Wicken 125, 254
St John's Church, Bethnal Green 120, 121, 276
St John's Church, Horsleydown 104, 275
St John's Church, Lochwinnoch 119, 224
St John's Church, Montrose 120
St John's Church, Shobdon 124, *125*, 241
St John's Church, Smith Square 283
St John's Church, Waterloo Road 109, 120, 271, 275
St John's Church, Wigan 123, 254
St John's Church, Wolverhampton 108, 256
St John's Church, Workington 123, 258
St John's Lodge, Regent's Park 282
St John's Square, Limerick 35, 295
St John's Wood, Westminster 281
St Julian's Underriver, Kent 96, 240
St Katherine's Church, Chislehampton 112, 197
St Laurence's Church, West Wycombe 116, *116*, 253
St Lawrence Jewry Church, Gresham Street 110
St Lawrence's Church, Little Stanmore 111, 268
St Lawrence's Church, Mereworth 107, 108, 110, 114, *114*, 227
St Leonard's, Hastings 34, 214
St Leonard's Church, Over Whitacre 109, 123, 233
St Luke's Church, Chelsea 17, 122, 270
St Luke's Church, Old Street 104, 114
St Macarten's Cathedral, Clogher 288
St Margaret's Church, Biddlesden 109, 187
St Mark's College, Chelsea 270
St Martin-in-the-Fields Church, Trafalgar Square 105, *105*, 106, *106*, 107, 108, 109, *109*, 110, 113, 114, 118, 120, 150, 166, 183, 187, 201, 202, 206, 210, 227, 257, 280, 290, 298
St Martin's Church, Allerton Mauleverer 123, 181
St Martin's Church, Worcester 108, 257
St Martin's School, St James's 280
St Mary of Charity's Church, Faversham 126, 187, 208
St Mary Cornhill Church, City of London 123
St Marylebone, Westminster 281-2
St Mary-le-Bow Church, Bow 106
St Mary-le-Strand Church, Strand 105, 278
St Mary Magdalene's Church, Croome d'Abitot 125, 126, 200
St Mary Magdalen's Church, Stapleford 125, 244
St Mary's Cathedral, Blackburn 187
St Mary's Church, Avington 111, 183
St Mary's Church, Banbury 19, *119*, 183
St Mary's Church, Conington 109, 199
St Mary's Church, Cowes 120, 199
St Mary's Church, Cromford 139, 200
St Mary's Church, East Lulworth 117, 205
St Mary's Church, Glynde 111, 211
St Mary's Church, Lower Hartwell 14, 124, 214
St Mary's Church, Michelderver 119, 228
St Mary's Church, Mistley 117, *117*, 228
St Mary's Church, Paddington 119, 280
St Mary's Church, Patshull 106, 235
St Mary's Church, Preston on Stour 124, 237
St Mary's Church, Stratfield Saye House 116, 247
St Mary's Church, Tetbury *124*, 125, 248
St Mary's Church, Twickenham 111, 274

St Mary's Church, Walsall 123, 251
St Mary's Church, Wanstead 109, 272
St Mary's Church, Wigan 123, 254
St Mary's Pro-Cathedral, Dublin 123, 290
St Mary's, Shandon, Pro-Cathedral, Cork 111, 288
St Mary and St Margaret's Church, Castle Bromwich 110, 194
St Mary the Virgin's Church, Berkley 186
St Mary Woolnoth Church, Lombard Street 263
St Matthew's Church, Bethnal Green 276
St Matthew's Church, Brixton 120, 271
St Michael's Chapel, Great Witley 111, *112*, 212
St Michael's Church, Aynho 104, 111, 183
St Michael's Church, Badminton House 109, 183
St Michael's Church, Cornhill 263
St Michael's Church, Madeley 119, 225
St Michael's Prison, Rome 158
St Michael's Street, Oxford 12, 234
St Neot's, Cambridgeshire 198, 240
St Nicholas's Church, Alcester 123, 180
St Nicholas's Church, Hardenhuish 115, 214
St Nicholas's Church, Warwick 123, 214, 251
St Nicholas's Church, Worcester 109, *110*, 257
St Nicholas's Street, Scarborough 45, 241
St Pancras, Camden 263
St Pancras Parish Church, Bloomsbury 120, *121*, 123, 261
St Patrick's Church, Waterford 112, 299
St Patrick's Hospital, Dublin 160, 291
St Paul's Church, Birmingham 109, 187
St Paul's Cathedral, City of London 6, 104
St Paul's Church, Bristol 126, 190
St Paul's Church, Covent Garden 7, 114, 123, 227, 258
St Paul's Church, Deptford 30, 111, 114, 183, 271
St Paul's Church, Perth 235
St Paul's Church, Sheffield 106, 110
St Peter Port, Guernsey 164, 240
St Peter's Church, Galby 123, 210
St Peter's Church, London Colney 123, 224
St Peter's Church, Saxby 123, 240
St Peter's Church, Vere Street 22, 106, 281
St Peter's Church, Wallingford 124, 250
St Peter's Church, Walworth 120, 275
St Peter and St Leonard's Church, Horbury 117, 216
St Peter and St Paul's Church, Wolverhampton 123, 256
St Philippe-du-Roule (church), Paris 123
St Rumbald's Church, Stoke Doyle 111, 245
St Stephen's Church, Walbrook 119, 183
St Stephen's Green, Dublin 23, 35, 38, 292-3
St Swithun's Church, Kennington 123, 233
St Thomas's Church, Stockport 122, 245
St Thomas's Church, Stourbridge 110, 246
St Werburgh's Church, Dublin 290
Salford, Greater Manchester 136, 240
Salisbury, Wiltshire 31, 123, 159, 174, 240
Salisbury Cathedral, Salisbury 123
Saltoun Hall, Lothian 25
Saltram House, Devon 83, 240
Salutation Hotel, Perth 174, 235
Sandbeck Park, S. Yorkshire 74, *74*, 240
Sandhurst, Berkshire 156, 240
Sandridge Park, Devon 90, 240
Sandwich, Kent 240
Saracen's Head Inn, Daventry *172*, 201
Sarsgrove House, Oxfordshire 97, 240
Sawbridgeworth, Hertfordshire 240
Saxby, Leicestershire 123, 240
Saxby, Lincolnshire 240
Saxlingham Nethergate, Norfolk 240
Scampston Hall, Humberside 85, 241
Scarborough, North Yorkshire 35, 45, 169, 241
Schauspielhaus, Berlin 177, 225
School, Mildenhall 164, 228
Scone Place, Tayside 81, 241
Scone village, Scone Palace 102, 241
Scregg, Co. Roscommon 298

Seafield, Co. Dublin 59, 298
Seaford, Co. Down 298
Seaton Delaval Hall, Northumberland 12, 54, 241
Sebright School, Wolverley 164, 256
Sefton Park, Liverpool 223
Sessions House, Beverley 153, 187
Sessions House, Knutsford 158, 219
Seton Castle, Lothian 79, 241
Sevenoaks, Kent 134, 161, 174, 241
Sevenoaks School and Almshouse, Sevenoaks 161, 162, 241
Severndroog Castle, Greenwich 266
Sezincote House, Gloucestershire 17, *18*, 90, 101, 241
Shakespeare Gallery, Pall Mall 169n
Shakespeare Temple, Hampton 99, 273
Shakespeare Theatre, Kendal 171, 218
Shannonbridge, Co. Offaly/Co. Roscommon 298
Shannon Harbour, Banagher 285
Shardeloes, Buckinghamshire 73, 82, 241
Sharpham, Devon 73, 241
Shawfield, Glasgow 55
Sheffield 106, 110, 112, 160, 241
Sheffield Place, East Sussex 78, 241
Shelton Abbey, Co. Wicklow 79, 298
Shepherd's Monument, Shugborough 99, 243
Sherman's, Dedham 36, 62, 202
Shipston on Stour, Warwickshire 241
Shire Hall, Chelmsford 150, 196
Shire Hall, Chester 150, 196
Shire Hall, Dorchester 150, 203
Shire Hall, Gloucester 151, 211
Shire Hall, Hereford 151, 215
Shire Hall, Hertford 149, 215
Shire Hall, Lancaster 150, 220
Shire Hall, Nottingham 153, 232
Shire Hall, Stafford 128, 244
Shire Hall, Warwick 150, 153, 251, *251*
Shirley, Croydon 264
Shobdon, Hereford and Worcester 16, 124, *125*, 241
Shooters Hill, Greenwich 266
Shoreditch, Hackney 267
Shotesham Park, Norfolk 15, 70, 85, 236, 242, *242*
Shotover Park, Oxfordshire 242
Shrewsbury 37, *42*, 52, 118, *118*, 124, 126, 136, *136*, 156, 159, 161, 174, 242-3
Shugborough, Staffordshire 15, 91, 98, 99-100, 243
Sidcup, Bexley 260
Sidcup Place, Sidcup 260
Sidmouth, Devon 243
Signet Library, Edinburgh 154, 205
Silk Mill, Derby 134
Silk Mill, St Albans 139, 239
Sir Peter Thompson's House, Poole 38, 236-7
Sir William Harpur's School, Bedford 162, 185
Six Clerks' and Enrolment Office, Lincoln's Inn 154, *154*, 263
Skiddy's Almshouses, Cork 161, 288
Skin Floor, London Docks 137-8, *137*, *138*, 277
Skinner's Hall, Dowgate Hill 263
Slane, Co. Meath 135, 298
Slane Castle, Slane 87, 298
Sledmere House, Humberside 101, 243
Smith Square, Victoria 283
Smithy, Woolwich 155, 266
Soho, Westminster 282-3
Soho Square, Soho 282-3
Solihull, West Midlands 101, 243, *243*
Somersby Hall, Lincolnshire 78, 243
Somerset House, Halifax 128, 213
Somerset House, Strand 8, *9*, 37, 128, 129, 146-7, *146*, 154, *168*, 169, 278
Somersetshire Buildings, Bath 33, 34, 185
Southall, Ealing 264
Southampton 173, 243
Southampton Place, Bloomsbury 31, 261
South Audley Street, Mayfair 21, 40, 111, 280
South Bailey, Durham 36, 204
South Brink, Wisbech 35, 256
Southend, Essex 174
Southernhay, Exeter 29, 207
Southgate, Ealing 265
Southill Park, Bedfordshire 85, 243
South Kensington, Royal Borough of Kensington and Chelsea 270
South Lambeth, Lambeth 271

South Molton, Devon 243
Southsea, Portsmouth 237
South Street, Wareham 129, *129*, 251
Southwark, London 275-6
Sowerby, West Yorkshire 243
Spalden Almshouses, Ashbourne 162, 182
Spalding, Lincolnshire 174, 244
Speedwell Castle, Brewood 43, 190
Spencer House, St James's 51, 82, 280
Spitalfields, Tower Hamlets 276-7
Square, The, Richmond 274
Stackallan House, Co. Meath 298
Stafford 244
Stamford, Lincolnshire 12, 35, 36, 37, 129, 130, 133, 148, 161, 171, 173, 175, 220, 244
Stamford Hotel, Stamford 175, 244
Stamford and Rutland Hospital, Stamford 161, 244
Standard Road, Wells-next-the-Sea 38, 252
Stanfield Hall, Wymondham 81, 258
Stamford, Worcestershire 142
Stanmer House, East Sussex 244
Stanmore, Harrow 267-8
Stannington, South Yorkshire 244
Stapleford, Leicestershire 125, 244
Stationers' Hall, City of London 133, 263
Steading, Rosebery House 101, 239
Stepney, Tower Hamlets 277
Stillorgan House, Co. Dublin 298
Stirling, Central Region 177, 244-5
Stirling's Library, Glasgow 131, 210
Stobo Castle, Borders 245
Stobs Castle, Borders 79, 245
Stockbridge, Hampshire 174, 245, *245*
Stockeld Park, North Yorkshire 74, 245
Stocken Hall, Leicester 66, 245
Stock Exchange, City of London 131-2
Stockport, Greater Manchester 122, 245
Stockton-on-Tees, Cleveland 245
Stockwell, Lambeth 271
Stoke Doyle, Northamptonshire 111, 245
Stoke Edith, Hereford and Worcester 245
Stoke Newington, Hackney 267
Stoke Park, Avon 78
Stoke Poges, Buckinghamshire 245
Stokesley, North Yorkshire 245-6
Stone, Staffordshire 246
Stone Buildings, Lincoln's Inn 154, 262
Stonegate, York 130, 259
Stoneleigh Abbey, Warwickshire 54, 66, 246
Stony Stratford, Buckinghamshire 172, 246
Stornoway House, St James's 280
Storr's Hall, Cumbria 45, 92, 246
Stourbridge, West Midlands 110, 246
Stourhead, Wiltshire 12, 55, *55*, 62, 70, 71, 73, 99, 246, 277
Stourport-on-Severn, Hereford and Worcester 174, 246
Stout's Hill, Gloucestershire 77, 246
Stowe, Buckinghamshire 14, 64, 70, 71, 84, 97, 98, 99, *99*, 102, 103n, 246-7
Stow-on-the-Wold, Gloucestershire 36, 246
Strand, Westminster 278
Stratfield Saye House, Hampshire 116, 247
Stratford, Newham 272
Stratford-upon-Avon, Warwickshire 150, 247
Strattenborough Castle Farm, Coleshill 198
Stratton Park, East Stratton 16, 91, 93, 102, 205
Strawberry Hill, Twickenham 77, 81, 124, 275, 287
Streatham, Lambeth 271
Stroud, Gloucestershire 35, 247
Stupingi hunting palace, near Turin 286
Styal, Cheshire 135, 139, 247
Styche Hall, Shropshire 247
Sudbrook Park, Petersham 59, 64, 274, 298
Sudbury, Suffolk 247
Suffolk Place and Street, St James's 280
Summer Grove, Co. Laois 298
Summerhill, Co. Meath 38, 61
Summer house, Ebberston Hall 97, 205
Sunderland, Tyne and Wear 142, 247
Sundridge, Bromley 261
Sundridge Park, Sundridge 261
Sunnyside House, Lothian 247
Surbiton, Kingston-upon-Thames 270

Surrey Square, Walworth 33, 276
Suspension bridge, Clifton 142, 191
Suspension bridge, Conwy 142, 199
Suspension bridge, Hutton 142
Suspension bridge, Menai Straits 142, 227
Sussex Square, Brighton 34, 190
Sutton, London 276
Sutton Scarsdale, Derbyshire 54, 247
Swaffam, Norfolk 247
Swan Hill Court, Shrewsbury 52, 243
Swan Hotel, Bedford 174, 185
Swan Hotel, Hay-on-Wye 174, 215
Swan Inn, Harleston 174, 214
Swan Inn, Tewkesbury 712, 248
Swanton Street Farm, Bredgar 189
Swerford House, Oxfordshire 247
Swinfen Hall, Staffordshire 66, 67, 247
Swinford Bridge, Eynsham 140, 208
'Swiss Cottage', Cahir 97, 285
Switsir's Asylum, Kilkenny 161, 294
Swynnerton Hall, Staffordshire 247
Sycamore Farm House, Hopton 13, 216
Sydenham, Merton 272
Sydney Lodge, Hampshire 247
Syon House, Brentford 83, 94, 100, 268, 297
Syon Lodge, Isleworth 269

Talbot Hotel, Ripley 172, 238
Talbot Hill, Towcester 172, 249
Tardebigge, Hereford and Worcester 123, 247
Tattingstone Wonder, Suffolk 248
Tatton Park, Cheshire 94, 100, 248
Taymouth Castle, Tayside 81, 240, 248
Teddington, Richmond-upon-Thames 274
Teigh, Leicestershire 126, 248
Temple, City of London 263
Temple of Ancient Virtue, Stowe 97, 247
Temple of Apollo, Delos 84, 116, 158, 183, 249
Temple of Apollo Epicurus, Bassae 95
Temple of Augustus, Athens 150
'Temple of Augustus', Virginia Water 250
Temple of Bacchus, Teos 84, 253
Temple of Bellona, Royal Botanic Gardens, Kew 99, 273
Temple of British Worthies, Stowe 97, 247
Temple of Concord, Stowe 99, 247
Temple of the Four Winds, Castle Howard 97, 102, 195
Temple of Hercules, Stourhead 99, 246
Temple on Ilissus 116, 177, 195, 232
Temple Newsam House, Leeds 78, 221
Temple of Philip, Delos 150
Temple of Poseidon/Neptune, Paestum 87, 119, 212, 286
Temple of Theseus, Hagley Hall 99, *99*, 213
Temple of Venus, Garendon Hall 99, 210
Temple of Vesta, Rome 99, 210
Temple of Vesta, Tivoli 85, 99, 128
Temple of the Winds, Mount Stewart 100, 296
Tenterden, Kent 38, 248
Tern Aqueduct, Longdon upon Tern 224
Terrace, The, Richmond Hill 43, 274
Terling Place, Essex 248
Tetbury, Gloucestershire 124, 125, 248
Tewkesbury, Gloucestershire 172, 248
Thame, Oxfordshire 248
Thame Park, Thame 248
Thaxted, Essex 248
Theale, Berkshire 122, 248
Theatre, Bury St Edmunds *132*, 170, 193
Theatre, Penzance 171, 235
Theatre, Stamford 171, 244
Theatre, Truro 171, 249
Theatre, Tunbridge Wells 171, 250
Theatre Royal, Bath 171, 184
Theatre Royal, Bristol 170, 172, 191
Theatre Royal, Bury St Edmunds 170, 171, 193
Theatre Royal, Drury Lane 170, 172, 278
Theatre Royal, Dundee 171, 203
Theatre Royal, Haymarket 172, 280
Theatre Royal, Margate 171, 226
Theatre Royal, Richmond 170, *170*, 171, 172, 238
Theseion, Athens 91, 92, 151, 153, 212
Thirsk, North Yorkshire 248
Tholsel, Kilkenny 150, 294
Thorndon Hall, Essex 74, 248
Thornham Hall, Norfolk 248

Index of buildings and places

Timogue, Co. Laois 298
Tissington Hall, Derbyshire 77, 249
Tiverton, Devon 27, 249
Tomb of Cecilia Metella 100, 258
Tonbridge, Kent 174, 249
Tontine Inn, Stourport-on-Severn 174, 246
Tooks Court, City of London 37, 264
Tooting, Wandsworth 278
Tottenham, Haringey 267
Tottenham, Wiltshire 8, 69, 198, 249
Tottenham Park, Wiltshire 8, 69, 198, 249
Totteridge, Barnet 260
Towcester, Northamptonshire 172, 249
Tower Hamlets, London 276
Tower of the Winds, Athens 95, 100, 120, 183, 184, 205, 234, 243, 244, 253, 296
Tower of Wynnstay, Wynnstay Park 100, 258
Town Hall, Abingdon 132, 147, 180
Town Hall, Blandford Forum *149*, 188
Town Hall, Brighton 151, 190
Town Hall, Chichester 114, 196
Town Hall, Deal 150, 201
Town Hall, Devizes 148, 202
Town Hall, Devonport 151, 236
Town Hall, Dursley 148, 204
Town Hall, Glastonbury 150, 211
Town Hall, Huntingdon 150, 217
Town Hall, Langport 148, 220
Town Hall, Leith 150, 206
Town Hall, Macclesfield 150, 151, 225
Town Hall, Maidstone 148, 225
Town Hall, Monmouth 147-8, 228
Town Hall, Morpeth 148, 229
Town Hall, Newark-on-Trent 148, 229
Town Hall, Nottingham 150
Town Hall, Petworth 148, 236
Town Hall, Richmond 150, 238
Town Hall, Ripon 148, 238
Town Hall, Rye 148, 239
Town Hall, Salford 150, 240
Town Hall, Stamford 148, 244
Town Hall, Stratford-upon-Avon 150, 247
Town Hall, Warrington 70, 251
Town Hall, Whitby 148, 253
Town Hall, Woodstock 148, 257
Town House, Berwick upon Tweed 150, 186, *186*
Town House, Peterhead 150, 235
Townley Hall, Co. Louth 89, *89*, 92, 298
Trabolgan, Co. Cork 298
Trafalgar House, Wiltshire 64, 249
Trafalgar Square, Westminster 155, 177, 280
Tralee, Co. Kerry 298
Tranent, Lothian 161, 249
Travellers' Club, Pall Mall 177, *178*, 280
Trawscoed Mansion, Dyfed 249
Treasury, Whitehall 145, *145*, 283
Tredegar Estate, Bow 276
Trefecca, Powys 249
Trefecca College, Trefecca 249
Tregothnan, Cornwall 95-6, 249
Trelissick, Cornwall 249
Tremadog, Gwynedd 28, 249
Trades House, Glasgow 133, *134*, 210
Trim, Co. Meath 298
Trim Street, Bath 36, 184
Trinity College, Cambridge 166, 194
Trinity College, Dublin 166-7, *167*, 290
Trinity House, Tower Hill 133, 263
Trinity House, Kingston upon Hull 133, 218
Trinity Square, City of London 147, 264
Triumphal Arch, Garendon Hall 99, 210
Triumphal Arch, Shugborough 99, 243
Trowbridge, Wiltshire 36, 249
Trumpington Street, Cambridge 40, 194
Truro, Cornwall 32, 171, 249-50
Tuam, Co. Galway 298
Tudenham, Co. Westmeath 298
Tullamore, Co. Offaly 28, 132, 174, 298
Tulse Hill, Lambeth 271
Tunbridge Wells, Kent 30, 250
Turkey Court and Mill, Maidstone 134, 225
Turner's Hospital, Kirkleatham 162, 219
Tweedmouth, Northumberland 250
Twickenham, Richmond-upon-Thames 274-5
Twizell Castle, Northumberland 250
Twyford House, Hampshire 250
Tynghame House, Lothian 81, 250
Tyringham House, Buckinghamshire 15, 85, 93, 100, 122, 250

Tyrone House, Dublin 59, 291-2
Tyrrelspass, Co. Westmeath

Ugbrooke Park, Devon 78, 250
Ullapool, Highland 250
Underley Hall, Cumbria 96, 250
Union Club, Trafalgar Square 177, 280
United Services Club, Pall Mall 177, 280
University College, London 166, 261
University Library, Cambridge 167, 194
Upminster, Havering 268
Upper and Lower Arcades, Bristol 130, 191
Upper Brook Street, Mayfair 45, *48*, 279
Upper Brook Street, Oswestry 34, 233
Upper Norwood, Croydon 264
Uttoxeter, Staffordshire 250
Uxbridge, Hillingdon 132, 268

Vanbrugh Castle, Greenwich 15, 76, 78, 266
Vanbrugh House, Oxford 12, 36, 234
Vere Street, St Marylebone 106
Vauxhall, London 271
Vaux-le-Vicomte, France 60
Ven House, Somerset 250
Vernon Mount, Co. Cork 75, 89, 298
Verulam Buildings, Gray's Inn 154, 262
Victoria, Westminster 283
Viceregal Lodge, Dublin 291
Villa Emo, Fanzolo 246
Villa Mocenigo, Marocco 82, 216, 217, 232
Villa Pamphili, Rome 214
Villa Pisani, Bagnolo di Lonigo 100
Vill Pisani, Montagnana 59
Villa Pogliana (or Poiano), Polana Maggiore 53, 54
Villa Rotonda, Vicenza 55, 97, 116, 195, 227, 268
Villa Saraceno, Finale de Agugliaro 59
Villa Trissino 100
Virginia Street, Glasgow 129, 130, 211
Virginia Water, Berkshire 250
Vyne, The, Hampshire 250

Wadworth Hall, South Yorkshire 74, 250
Wakefield, West Yorkshire 153, 177, 250
Wakefield Lodge, Potterspury 67, 237
Wallingford, Oxfordshire 124, 250
Wallington Hall, Northumberland 140, 250
Walsall, West Midlands 123, 251
Waltham Forest, London 277
Walthamstow, Waltham Forest 277
Walworth, Southwark 120, 275
Wandsworth, London 277
Wanstead, Redbridge 272
Wanstead House, Wanstead 6, 52-3, *52*, 54, 56, 57, 66, 69, 70, 82, 83, 104, 166, 185, 194, 217, 235, 252, 272
Wapping, Tower Hamlets 277
Warbrook House, Hampshire 67, 74, 251
Wardour Castle, Wiltshire *endpapers*, 74, 75, 85, 251
Wardstown, Co. Donegal 61, 298
Ware, Hertfordshire 251
Wareham, Dorset 129, *129*, 162, 173, *173*, 175, 251
Warehouses, London Docks 138-9, 277
Warehouses, Weedon 139, 252
Warehouses, West India Docks 138-9
Warminster, Wiltshire 36, 251
Warrington, Cheshire 70, 251
Warwick 14, 27, 36, 123, 150, 152, 153, 157, 174, 251-2, *251*
Warwick Arms Hotel, Warwick 174, 252
Warwick Castle, Warwick 81, 97, 205
Warwick House, St James's 280
Waterford 109, 111, 112, 253, 298-9
Waterloo Bridge, Betws-y-Coed 142, 186
Waterloo Place, Pall Mall 177, 280
Watermens' Hall, St Mary-at-Hill 133, 263
Weavers' cottages, Newtown 134, 231
Wedderburn Castle, Borders 252
Weedon, Northamptonshire 139, 252
Welling, Bexley 260
Wellingborough, Northamptonshire 252
Wellington, Shropshire 252
Wellington Rooms, Liverpool 177, 222
Wells-next-the-Sea, Norfolk 38, 252
Wentworth Castle, South Yorkshire 252
Wentworth Woodhouse, South Yorkshire 64, 66, 70, 101, 252-3, *252*
Werrington, Devon 253

Wesleyan Chapel, Burford 37, 192
Westbury House, Bradford-on-Avon 36, 189
West Dean Park, West Sussex 253
West Drayton, Hillingdon 268
Western Pavilion, Brighton 190, *190*
West Ham, Newham 272
West India Dock 272
West India Dock, Isle of Dogs, Poplar 137, 138-9, 276
West Malling, Kent 253
West Mill, Belper 136
Westminster, London 278-85
Westminster Abbey, Westminster 123, 143, 283
Westmorland Street, Dublin 25, 130
Weston, Avon 253
Weston Park, Staffordshire 101, 253
Westport, Co. Mayo 28, 299
Westport House, Westport 28, 299
West Stockwell Street, Colchester 35, *36*, 198
West Street, Builth Wells *42*, 192
West Street, Farnham 36, 37, 208
West Wycombe, Buckinghamshire 116, *116*, 253
West Wycombe Park 83, 91, 100, 253
Wexford 299
Weymouth, Dorset 253
Whaddon Hall, Buckinghamshire 253
Whitbread's Brewery, Chiswell Street 137, 264
Whitby, North Yorkshire 37, 148, 253-4
Whitchurch, Hereford and Worcester 254
Whitechapel, Tower Hamlets 277
Whitechapel Bell Foundry 277
Whitehall, Westminster 283
Whitehall Palace, Whitehall 55
White Hart Hotel, Salisbury 174, 240
White Hart Inn, Spalding 174, 244
Whitehaven, Cumbria *41*, 254
White House, Washington, D.C. 86
White Lodge, Richmond Park 274
White's Club, St James's Street 177, 281
White's Row, Spitalfields 93, 277
Whittinghame House, Lothian 254
Wick, The, Richmond 274
Wick House, Richmond 274
Wicken, Northamptonshire 125, 254
Widcombe Manor, Bath 185
Wigan, Greater Manchester 123, 234
Wilbury House, Wiltshire *53*, 57, 70, 254
Wilford Hill, Nottinghamshire 254
Willersley Castle, Cromford 200
Willey Hall, Shropshire 93, 254
Wilson's Hospital School, Multyfarnham 163, 296
Wilton, Wiltshire 254
Wilton House, Wilton 53, 69, 70, 254
Wimbledon, Merton 272
Wimborne Minster, Dorset 254
Wimborne House, Arlington Street 279
Wimpole Hall, Cambridgeshire 66, 97, 101, 255
Wincanton, Somerset 27, 172, 255
Winchester, Hampshire 29, 129, 255
Winchmore Hill, Ealing 265
Windmill Hill, Hampstead 262
Windsor, Berkshire 162, 255
Windsor Castle, Windsor 255
Winterborne Dauntsey, Wiltshire 255
Wisbech, Cambridgeshire 35, 38, 171, 172, 255-6
Wiston Hall, Suffolk 256
Witney, Oxfordshire *41*, 256
Wivenhoe, Essex 256
Woburn, Bedfordshire 256
Woburn Abbey, Woburn 82, 98, 256
Woburn Park Farm, Woburn 101, 261
Woburn Walk, Bloomsbury 130, 261
Wollaton Hall, Nottinghamshire 100, 256
Wolsey's Tower, Esher Place 14, 207
Wolterton Hall, Norfolk 65-6, *65*, 71, 256
Wolverhampton, West Midlands 108, 123, 256
Wolverley, Hereford and Worcester 164, 256
Wolverton, Buckinghamshire 123, 256
Woodford, Redbridge 272
Wood Hall, Humberside 257
Woodhall Park, Hertfordshire 85, 257
Woodhouse, Shropshire 84, 257
Woodlands, Co. Dublin 59, 286, 299
Woodnewton Hall, Northamptonshire 257
Woodstock, Co. Kilkenny 299
Woodstock, Oxfordshire 12, 148, 257

Woolley, Avon 125, 257
Woolton, Liverpool 223
Woolton Hall, Woolton 223
Woolverstone Hall, Suffolk 257
Woolwich, Greenwich 266
Wootton Hall, Wootton Wawen 257
Wootton Wawen, Warwickshire 257
Worcester 40, 109, 110 123, 159, 257
Worcester College, Oxford 164-5, 233
Worcester Lodge, Badminton House 65, 97, 98, 183
Workers' housing, Belper 139, 186

Workers' housing, Cromford 139, 200
Workers' housing, New Lanark 139-40, *140*, 230
Workers' housing, Newtown 140, 231
Workington, Cumbria 258
Wormleybury House, Hertfordshire 258
Worthing, West Sussex 258
Wotton House, Buckinghamshire 51
Wrotham Park, Hertfordshire 72, 258
Wroxton, Oxfordshire 124, 258
Wycombe Abbey, Buckinghamshire 258
Wymondham, Norfolk 35, 81, 258

Wynnstay Hotel, Oswestry 174, 233
Wynnstay Park, Powys 100, 258

Yarm, Cleveland 31, 172, 258
Yeomanstown, Co. Kildare 299
Yester House, Lothian 258
York 8, 12, 19, 31, 36, 37, 43, 61, 130, 152, *152*, 157, *157*, 158, 160, *160*, 169, 258-9
Yorkshire Museum, York 169, 258
York Terrace, Regent's Park 30, 282
Youghal, Co. Cork 157, 299

INDEX of architects and designers

Page numbers in italic refer to illustrations.

Abraham, Robert 129, 164, 181, 182, 226
Adam, James 149, 215, 282; Shire Hall, Hertford 149, 215; Portland Place 282
Adam, John 23, 34, 37, 82, 118, 147, 210, 262, 264, 278; Arniston 182; Dumfries House 203; Hopetoun House 216; Inveraray 28; Lion Bridge 181; Lowther Village 102, 224; Pollok House 236; Portland Place 282; Ravelin Gate, Fort George 209; Royal Exchange, Edinburgh 130, 205
Adam, Robert 66, 70, 73, 74, 84, 85, 89, 101, 132, 144, 146, 156, 169, 171, 174, 176, 191, 227, 262, 290, 297; Adelphi 23, 278; Admiralty House 283; Airthrey Castle 180; Apsley House 278; Audley End 183; Belleville House 186; Bowood House 188; Bradwell Lodge 189; Brasted Place 189; Brizlee Tower, Hulme Park 181; castle movement 78-9; Castle Upton 287; Chandos House 281; Charlotte Square 25-6, 37; Charlotte Street 210; Compton Verney 199; Croome Court 201; Culzean Castle 78, *79*, 201; Dumfries House 203; Edinburgh University 166, 205; Frederick's Place 264; Garrick's Villa 273; Gosford House 211; Harewood House 214; Hatchlands 214; Hertford Street 279; Home House 44, *49*; Hopetoun House 216; Kedleston 15, *82, 83*, 82-3, 217; Kenwood House 262; Lansdowne House 279; Lion Bridge 181; Lowther Village 102, 224; Mansfield Street 282; Market Hall and Theatre, Bury St Edmund's *132*, 170, 193; Marlborough House 190; Mellerstain 227; Mersham le Hatch 227; Newby Hall 230; Newliston House 230; Nostell Priory 232; Osterley Park 269; Pollok House 236; Portland Place 34, 282; Portman Square 282; Pulteney Bridge, Bath *140*, 14, 184; Ravelin Gate, Fort George 209; Red Lion Hotel 236; Sackville Stret 280; St Andrew's Chapel, Gunton Park 213; St Bartholomew's Church 117; St James's Square *47*, 280, 281; St Mary Magdalene's Church, 125, 200; St Mary's Church, Mistley 117, *117*, 228; Saltram House 240; Seton Castle 241; Stobs Castle 245; Shire Hall, Hertford 149, 215; Strawberry Hill 77, 275; Sunnyside House 247; Syon House 94, 268; Trades House 133, *134*, 210; Ugbrooke Park 250; Wedderburn Castle 252; Wentworth Woodhouse 252; West Wycombe Park 253; Whitehaven Castle 254; Wilson Street 211; Woolton Hall 223; Wormleybury House 258; Yester House 258
Adam, William 8, 55-6, 82; Abbotsford 180; Arniston 182; Chatelherault 97, 195; Dalmahoy House 201; Drum, The 203; Fort George 156, 209; Haddo House 213; Hamilton Church 118, 214; Hopetoun House 216; Mellerstain 229; Pollok House 236; Robert Gordon Hospital 180; Robert Gordon College 163; Town House/Assembly Rooms, Haddington 213; Yester House 258

Aheron, John 13
Aikin, Edmund 177, 222
Aldrich, Henry 165, 233
Alexander, D. A. 159, 137-8, *137, 138*, 225, 227
Allen, James 191
Anderson, John 293
Anderson, Rowland 166
Anderson, William 254
Angus, George 130, 204
Archer, Thomas 30, 53, 105, 111, 114, 183, 203, 208, 231, 255; Beningborough Hall 186; Butterwick House 267; Cathedral of St Philip, Birmingham 187; Chettle House 71, 196; Finchcocks 208-9; Hale House 213; King Street 278; Roehampton House 277; St Mary's Church, Hale 213; St John's Church, Smith Square 283; St Paul's Church, Deptford 271
Arkwright, Richard 135, 139, 186, 200, 230
Arrow, James 271
Asprucci, Marco 90, 217
Atherton, William 81
Atkinson, Peter 258
Atkinson, Peter, the Elder 213
Atkinson, Thomas 37, 187, 189, 192, 238, 258, 259
Atkinson, William 81, 180, 212, 217, 241, 248
Atwood, Thomas Warr 31, 157, 184
Aylesford, Earl of 119, 212

Backhouse, James 201
Bacon, Charles 272
Bage, Charles 136
Bailey, W. & D. 100
Baird, John 130, 211
Baker, Henry Aaron 25, 130, 292
Baker, William: Butter Cross 132, 224; Kenmore 125, 218; Patshull Hall 235; St John's Church, Wolverhampton 256; St Michael's Church, Stone *246*; Town Hall, Montgomery 229; Westmorland Street 25, 130
Baldwin, Thomas 33, 34, 148, 150, 176, 177, 184, 185
Barbon, Nicholas 22
Barry, Sir Charles 198, 214, 262; Buile Hill *240*; Holy Trinity Church, Barnsbury 269; Royal Institution of Fine Arts 177-8, *181*, 225; St John's Lodge 282; St Peter's Church, Brighton 190
Basevi, George 122, 233, 234, 270, 278
Bastard, John and William: Couper House 188; Greyhound Inn 188; Market Place, Blandford Forum 35, *35*, 188; Market Place, Poole 38, 236 7; Red Lion 173, *173*, 188; St Peter and St Paul's Church 111, *111*, 188; Sir Peter Thompson's House 38, 236-7; Town Hall, Blandford Forum 149, *149*, 188; West Street 188; West Wycombe Park 253
Baxter, John, the Elder 56, 235
Baxter, John, the Younger 28, 109, 135, 150, 205, 209, 212, 227, 235
Baxter, Samuel 45
Baxter, William 108
Beard, J. B. 150, 211
Beazley, Charles 126, 208

Beazley, Samuel 278
Bedford, Francis 109, 120, 271, 275
Belanger, F. J. 131
Bell, Samuel 109, 171, 204
Benson, William 7, 53, 254, 270
Bentham, Sir Samuel 237
Bentley, Richard 77, 124, 242, 275
Bernini, Gianlorenzo 7
Bindon, Francis 61, 285, 288, 289, 293, 296, 299
Bindon, John 35, 295
Blackburn, William 133, 159, 203, 217, 222, 232, 263
Blore, Edward 166, 234, 256
Bodt, Johann 252
Bond, J. L. 174
Bonnar, Thomas 206
Bonner, John 247
Bonomi, Ignatius 204, 219, 238
Bonomi, Joseph 81, 91, 119, 212, 213, 214, 219, 224, 279
Borra, Giovanni Battista 84, 99, 246, 247
Borromini, Francesco 7
Boscawen, George 103, 228
Boullée, E.-L. 193
Boulton & Watt 137
Bowden, John 153, 285, 287, 289, 290, 293
Bowie, Alexander 245
Bradley, Thomas 132, 133, 213
Bramante, Donato 9
Brettingham, Matthew, the Elder 70, 82, *82, 83*, 207, 212, 213, 220, 280
Brettingham, Matthew, the Younger 195
Brettingham, Robert, the Elder 232
Brettingham, Robert the Younger 231
Bridgeman, Charles 246
Bridges, James 191
Brindley, James 246
Brown, Lancelot 72; Benham Park 85, 186; Berrington Hall 186; Claremont House 85, 198; Corsham Court, 169, 199; Croome Court 70, 200; Milton Abbas 102, 228; Milton Abbey 228; Nuneham Park 232; Richmond Gate 274; St Mary Magdalene's Church, Croome d'Abitot 125, 200; Scampston Hall 241
Brown, Robert 206
Brown, Samuel 142, 186
Brown, Thomas 109, 206
Browne, Robert 273
Browne, Thomas Wogan 79, 284, 286
Browning, Bryan 158, 188, 209
Bruce, Sir William 216
Brunel, Isambard Kingdom 142, 191
Brunel, Marc 195
Bryce, David 235
Buckler, John 248, 272
Buguiet, Pierre 159
Burdon, Rowland 142
Burgh, Thomas 105, 160, 166, 287, 290, 291, 297
Burlington, Richard Boyle 3rd Earl 7, 8, 10, 14, 56, 64, 66, 105, 114, 144, 211; Assembly Rooms, York 61, 107, 151, 174, *175, 176*, 258; Castle Hill 194; Chiswick House 55, 65, 98, 116, 268; Fox Hall 209, *209*; General Wade's House 8, *9*, 38, 51, 145, 167, 194, 283, 290, 292; Holkham Hall 68-9, *68, 69*, 216; Mountrath House 8; Northwick Park 232; Richmond House 71;

316 / Index of architects and designers

Burlington, Richard Boyle – *cont.*
Sevenoaks School 162, 241; Tottenham House 198, 249; Westminster School 163, 283
Burn, William 204, 235; Blairquhan, Strathclyde 187; Camperdown House 94, 194; Carstairs House 96, 194; Dundas Castle 203; Gorhambury 212; John Watson's Hospital School 163, 205; Murray Royal Asylum for the Insane 235; North Leith Church *108*, 109, 206; Saltoun Hall 240; Tranent Hospital 161; Tynghame House 81, 250
Burrough, Sir James 165–6, 193
Burton, Decimus: Athenaeum 177, *179*, 280; Calverley Park 30, 250; Clarence Terrace 282; Cornwall Terrace 282; Holwood House 261; Holy Trinity Church, Tunbridge Wells 250
Burton, James 20, 32, 34, 214, 261
Busby, Charles 30, 34, 190
Butter, Charles 205
Butter, William 205
Byfield, George 158, 193, 194, 234

Cabanel, Rudolph 271
Campbell, Colen 6–8, 12, 32, 53–5, 64, 66, 104, 162; Baldersby House 54–5, 59, 183; Burlington House 280; Brook Street *47*, 279; Compton Place 204; Ebberston Hall 97, 205; Grosvenor Square design 21, 30, 31, 32, 165; Houghton Hall 62–3, *63*, 65, 69, 216; Mereworth Castle *54*, 55, 62, 114, 227; Old Burlington Street *30*, 31, *15*, *49*; Shawfield 55; Stourhead 55, *55*, 62, 70, 246; *Vitruvius Britannicus* 6–7, 13; Wanstead House 6, *52*, 52–3, 54, 62–3, 69, 104, 166, 167, 194, 252, 272; Whitehall, Newhailes House 55, 145
Campbell, Dugald 186
Carline, John 126, 242
Carr, James 269
Carr, John 43; Abbot Hall 218; Arncliffe Hall 217; Assembly Rooms, Buxton 193; Assize Court, York 19, 152, 258; Basildon Park 85, 100, 184; Bishop's College Hospital 222; Bishop's Palace, Bishop Auckland 187; Bootham, York 259; Bootham Park Hospital 160, 258; Bridge, Richmond 238; Cannon Hall 194; Castle Farm 101, 243; Constable Burton Hall 73, 199; Coollattin 288; Court House and House of Correction, Northallerton 231; Crescent 33, 193; Denton Hall 202; Devonshire Royal Hospital 193; Doncaster racecourse 202–3; Fairfax House 259; Female Prison, York 19, 152, 157, *157*, 258; Harewood House 214; Harewood Village 103, 214; Heath Hall 215; Huthwaite Hall 73; Lincoln Castle Gaol 159, 222; Lytham Hall 225; Micklegate, York 37, 259; Moorgate Hall 239; Norton Place 232; Peasholme House 259; Rockingham Mausoleum 259; St Peter and St Leonard's Church 117, 216; Somerset House, Halifax 213; Thirsk Hall 248; Town Hall and Assembly Rooms, Newark 148, 227; Unitarian Chapel, Fallowfield 228; Wentworth Woodhouse 252, *252*
Carter, John 19, 123, 201, 206, 226
Cartwright, Francis 70, 194, 200, 218
Castell, Robert 8
Castle, Richard 59–62, 67, 89; Anneville 61, 89, 284; Ballyhaise 60, *60*, 86, 284; Bellinter 61–2, 285; Belvedere *60*, 61, 71, 285; Bessborough 57, 285; Bishop's Palace, Waterford 299; Carton, Maynooth 286; Connolly Folly 287; Court, Dunlavin 132, 152, *152*, 293; Dartrey 289; Dining Hall, Trinity College, Dublin 290; Dollardstown 289; Hazlewood 294; Ledwithstown 57, 295; Leinster House 51, 160, 291; Mantua House 195; Market House, Dunlavin, 132, 152, *152*, 293; Newbridge House 196; Newry Canal School 287; Newtownbreda 115, 297; Powerscourt 61, 297; Printing House, Trinity College, Dublin 167, 290; Rotunda Lying-in Hospital, Dublin 160, 290; Russborough 59, 66,

297; St Stephen's Green 35, 293; Trinity College, Dublin 167, 290; Tyrone House 59, 291–2
Chalgrin, J. F. T. 123, 146
Chambers, R. 147
Chambers, Sir William 11–12, 17, 43, 71, 72, 81, 89, 97, 99, 145, 199; Albany 278; Ampthill Park 181; Arlington Street 278; Berkeley Square 279; Casino, Marino 98, *98*, 291, 296; Castle Howard 195; Castletown 286; Chapel, Trinity College, Dublin 290; Charlemont House 40, 291, 293; Chinese buildings 97, 98; Danson Park 73, 260; Duddingston 56, 73, *73*, 82, 203; Dundas House 51, 205; Goodwood House 211; Harewood House 214; Lucan House 86, *86*, 87, 295; Manresa House 73, 277; Milton Abbas 102, *102*, 228; Milton Abbey 78, 226; Observatory, Richmond 274; Orangery, Kew Gardens 100, 273; Osterley Park 269; Peper Harow 235; St Andrew's Square 38, 205; Somerset House 8, *146*, 146–7, 154, *168*, 169, 278; Styche Hall 247; Temple of Romulus and Remus 198; Town Hall, Woodstock 148, 257; *Treatise on Civil Architecture* 11–12, 15, 17; Trinity College, Dublin 167, 290; Warwick House 280; Wilton House 254; Woburn Abbey 256
Changier, L. L. 270
Childs, Francis 271
Chute, John 77, 203, 213, 250, 275
Clark, John 221
Clarke, George 104, 233
Clarke, James 230
Clements, Nathaniel: Beau Parc 285; Belview 285; Colganstown 74, 288; Henrietta Street 292; Lodge Park 74, 295; Newberry Hall 75, *75*, 296; Vicerregal Lodge 291
Clerk, James 56
Clerk, Sir John 55, 56, 235
Clermont, Andieu de 254
Clermont, J. F. 70, 219, 220, 229
Cobden, Thomas 286
Cockerell, C. R. 16, 95, 120, 128; Gilson School 297; Grange, The *91*, 91–2, 212; Hanover Chapel 222; Harrow School 267; Holy Trinity Church, Bristol 191; Lady Boswell's School 241; Literary and Philosophical Institute 177, 191; Loughcrew 295; Nant-y-Belan 100, 259; Oakley Park 95, 232–3; Peper Harow 235; St David's College 164, 219; St James's Square 281; St Mary's Church, Banbury 183
Cockerell, S. P: Admiralty 282; Daylesford House 85, 90, 201; Fulham Palace 267; Grange, The *91*, 91–2, 212; Nelson Square 275; St Anne's Church, Wardour Street 282; St James's Square 281; St Mary's Church, Banbury 119, 183; Sezincote House 17, *18*, 101, 241; Western Courtyard, Cutler Street warehouses 264
Cole, Charles 262
Cole, William 100, 248
Colles, Alderman 150
Colles, William 75, 294, 296
Collingwood, J. 159
Collins, Job 123
Coltsman, John 288
Comfort, Robert 191
Cook, Thomas 244
Cooley, Thomas: Armagh Palace 284; Caledon 86, 286; Four Courts 147, 153, 291; Mount Kennedy 87, 296; Rokeby Hall 87, 297; Royal Exchange, Dublin 131, *131*, 290
Cooper, Thomas 151, 174, 190
Corbett, Edward W. 122
Cotton, Henry 258
Couse, Kenton 270, 274, 283
Cragg, John 122, 223
Craig, James 203, 205
Craig, John 37, 210
Crichton, Richard 183, 244
Crunden, John 177, 179, 253, 281
Cubitt, Thomas 261, 262, 271, 278
Cundy, Thomas 231, 249
Custance, William 194

da Volterra, Daniele 105

Dale, David 230
Dance, George, the Elder: Mansion House, City of London 61, 107, 151–2, 263; St Botolph's Church, Aldgate 263; St Leonard's Church, Shoreditch 267; St Matthew's Church, Bethnal Green 276; St Mary of Charity's Church, Faversham 208
Dance, George, the Younger 15, 28–9; All Hallows Church, London Wall 112, 263; America Square, Crescent, Circus 264; Camden Place 260; Coleorton Hall 198; Cranbury Park 85, 200; East Stratton 102, 205; Guildhall, City of London 150, 263; Laxton Hall 92, 220; Mansion House, City of London 152, 263; Newgate Gaol 157–8, 193; Pitzhanger Manor 264; Royal College of Surgeons, London 16, 155, 262; St Mary's, Micheldever 119, 228; Stratton Park 16, 205; Theatre Royal, Bath 171, 184; Whitbread's Porter Tun Room 136, 264
Daniell, Thomas 241
Darby, Abraham, III 141, 217
Darley, George 289, 290, 291
Darley, Hugh 150, 298
Davis, Whitmore 86, 287
Deane, Thomas 289
Debbieg, Hugh 192
Dent, Isaac 239
Dickinson, Richard 150, 206
Dickinson, Robert 150, 206
Dixon, Joseph 277
Dobson, John 34, 92, *92*, *93*, 103, 186, 224, 230, 232
Dodds, Joseph 186
Donaldson, James 270
Donovell, John 253
Doull, Alexander 271
Dowbiggin, Launcelot 269
Dreghorn, Allan 108, 210
Druce 36
Dubois, Nicholas 196, 244
Ducart, Davis 75–6; Castletown Cox 51, 57, 76, 287; Custom House, Limerick 295; Dunkathel 293; Florence House 293; Kilshannig 76, 294; Lota 76, 295; Mercy Hospital 289
Duff, Thomas 297
Dymond, George 207

Edwards, Francis 267
Edwards, Thomas 215, 250
Edwards, William 236
Edwin, Richard 282
Eglington, Samuel 199
Elliot, Archibald the Elder 81, 217
Elliot, Archibald, the Younger 129, 210, 245, 248
Elliot, James 81, 119, 211, 245, 248
Elliot, William 51
Elmes, James 196
Emlyn, Henry 90, 185
Ensor, George 284, 292, 293
Ensor, John 23, 25, 160, 290, 291
Espin, Thomas 224
Essex, James 40, 77, 193, 194, 275
Etherbridge, William 194
Etty, William: Baldersby Park 12, 183; Holy Trinity Church, Leeds 106, 112–13, *113*, 220–21; Mansion House, York 8, 12, 152, *152*, 258; Seaton Delaval Hall 12, 241
Evans, Charles 109, 183
Eveleigh, John 185
Eykyns, Roger 109, 187

Farrell, William 286, 293, 297
Fear, James 191
Ferrey, Benjamin 273
Field, John 217
Fieldhouse, John 200
Flitcroft, Henry 8; Bloomsbury Square 261; Boreham House 65, 188; Bower House 65, 268; Craven Street 278; Ditchley House 202; Duke of York Street 281; Milton House 226; Sackville Street 31, 280; St Andrew's Church, Wimpole Hall 255; St Giles-in-the-Fields Church 107–8, 262; St James's Square 31, 281; St Mary's Church, Stoke Edith 245; Southampton Place 31, 261; Stourhead, 98–9, 246; Wentworth Woodhouse 64, 70, 252, *252*, 253; Wimpole Hall 255; Woburn Abbey 256

Fontana Carlo 7, 105, 158
Forbes, John 176, 195
Fort, Thomas 197
Foster James 130, 131
Foster, John 222
Foulston, John 16, 151, 236
Fowler, Charles 100 132, *133*, 207, 237, 278
Frampton, James 227
Francini brothers 286, 289, 293, 297
Fraser, Major 205
Freeman, John 216

Gabb, Thomas 199
Gabriel, Jacques Ange 146
Galilei, Allesandro 7, 12; Castletown House *56*, 56-7, 286; Drumcondra House 290; St Werburgh's Church, Dublin 105, 290
Gandon, James 71, 294; Carrigglass Manor 101, 286; Coolbanagher Church 117, 288; Custom House 284, 291, 297; Emo Park 89, 293; Emsworth 90, 293; Four Courts 147, *152* 153-4, 291; King's Inns 39, 154-5, 291; Parliament House, Dublin 290; Rotunda Assembly Rooms 174, 290-91; Shire Hall, Nottingham 232
Gandy, J. M: Cowley Road 32; design for Commissioners' churches 122; Doric House 94-5, 185; Kennington Lane 45, 271; Lancaster Castle 220; Shire Hall, Lancaster 220; Storr's Hall 45, 92, 246; Swerford House 247
Gandy, J. P. 161, 244, 278
Garbett, E. W. 248
Garbett, William 255
Gardner, Thomas 200
Garling, Henry 133, 213
Garlive, John 219
Garrett, Daniel: Aske Hall 98, 183; Castle Howard 195; Culloden Tower 238; Forcett Park 51, 209; Gothic Banqueting House, Gibside 210; Gothic Towers, Gibside 210; Horton Hall 216; Library, Newcastle upon Tyne 230; Wallington Hall 250
Garrett, James 237
Gayfere, Thomas, the Elder 271
George & Peto 253
Gibbons, Grinling 90-91
Gibbs, James 13, *13*, 36, 113; All Saints' Cathedral Church, Derby 202; Antony House 181; Arlington Street 278; Bank Hall 70, 251; *Book of Architecture* 13, 107, *109*, 210, 216; Boycott Pavilions, Stowe, 14, 97, 102, 247; Cannons 260; Catton Hall 195; Cavendish-Harley Estate 21-2; Compton Verney 199; Ditchley House 65, 66, 202; Fairlawn, Kent 208; Fellows' Building, King's College, Cambridge 166, 193; Folly Arch, Brookmans Park 192; Hartwell House 214; Hendon Place 160, 260; Houghton Hall *62*, 216; influence 66, 107-10, 114, 118, 150, 186, 187, 191, 192, 202, 203, 209, 210, 216, 227, 251, 252, 256, 262, 271, 277, 298; Mausoleum, Kirkleatham 219; Octagon, Orleans Road 275; Orleans House 66; Radcliffe Library 166, *166*, 233; Ragley Hall 238; rococo Gothic designs 76; St Bartholomew's Hospital 160, 263; St Martin-in-the-Fields Church *105*, *106*, 106-10, 118, 150, 166, 187, 191, 202, 210, 229, 256, 262, 280, 298; St Mary-le-Strand Church 105, 278; St Mary's Church, Patshull 235; St Michael's Chapel, Great Witley 111, *112*, 212; St Nicholas's Church West, Aberdeen 180; St Peter's Church, Vere Street 281; Senate House, Cambridge 166, 193; Shotover Park 242; Sudbrook Park 59, 64, 274; Town Hall, Warrington 251; Turner's Hospital 162, 219; Wimpole Hall 66, 255
Gibson, George, the Younger 266
Gibson, Jesse 272
Gilbert, Thomas 111, 237
Giles, Robert 232
Gillow, Richard 220, 221
Glascodine, Joseph 251
Glascodine, Samuel 191
Golden, Robert 174
Gondoin, Jacques 146, 150
Goodridge, H. E. 130, 185

Goodwin, Francis 150, 151, 158, 187, 202, 225, 251
Gorham, John 262
Gould, James 263
Graham, James Gillespie 34, 81, 203, 206, 210, 213, 248
Grainger, Richard 34
Grainger, William 230
Green, John 177, 230
Greenway, F. H. 177, 191
Greg, Samuel 247
Grenville, Richard 99, 247
Grew, Robert 22, 23, 261
Gwilt, George 137, 138, 276
Gwilt, George, Senior 137, 138, 275, 276
Gwynn, John 183, 234, 257

Habershon, Matthew 186
Hague, Daniel 126, 190
Hakewill, Henry 123, 164, 166, 212, 233, 239, 256, 278
Halfpenny, John 98, 209
Halfpenny, William: *Chinese and Gothick Architecture Properly Ornamented* 98; Coopers' Hall 133, 191; Frampton Court 70, 98, 209; Holy Trinity Church, Leeds 106, 112-13, *113*, 220-1; Stout's Hill 77, 246
Hall, John 185
Hamilton, David 131, 162, 177, 208, 210
Hamilton, Nicholas 253
Hamilton, Thomas 163, 164, 205
Hamilton, William 211
Hannaford, Joseph 236
Hannan, Nicholas 295
Hannan, William 295
Hansom J. A., & Welch, Edward, 158, 185
Hanwell, William 182
Harcourt, Earl of 232
Hardwick, Philip 86, 134, 183, 188, 263
Hardwick, Thomas 109, 123, 150, 159, 203, 258, 260, 269, 272, 281
Hardy, W. 221
Hargrave, Abraham 293
Hargrave, John 293, 298
Harrison, Henry 237, 271, 283
Harrison, Thomas: Chester Castle 150, 196; Grosvenor Bridge 196; Lancaster Castle 220; Lyceum Club 177, *179*, 223, *223*; News Room, Chester 179, 196; Northgate, Chester 196; Portico Library 179, 225; Quernmore Park Hall 237-8; St John's Church, Lancaster 220; St Martin's Lodge 196; Shire Hall/Court, Lancaster 150, 220; Watergate House 196; Woodbank Park 245
Hartley, Jesse 196
Harvey, J. T. 249
Harvey, Jacob 249
Harvey, John 244
Harvey, W. 249
Hawksmoor, Nicholas 31, 105, 106, 107, 121, 155, 166; All Souls College, Oxford 126, 165, *165*, 233; Blenheim Palace 188; Christ Church, Spitalfields 107, 276; Clarendon Building 164, 234; Easton Neston 12, 36, 64; Mausoleum, Castle Howard 195; Queen Anne Block, Greenwich Palace 265; Queen's College, Oxford 233; St Anne's Church, Limehouse 276; St Alfege's Church, Greenwich 265; St George-in-the-East Church 277; St George's Church, Bloomsbury Way 20, 106, 261; St James's Palace 280; St Luke's Church, Old Street 104, *104*, 114, 269; St Mary at Cornhill Church, City of London 123; St Mary Woolnoth Church, City of London 263; St Michael's Church, Cornhill 263; Westminster Abbey 123, 283
Haycock, Edward 95, 161, 198, 242
Haycock, J. H. 159, 242
Hayward, Abraham 222
Hayward, William 222
Hemsley, Henry 238
Henderson, David 177, 205
Henderson, John 181
Henderson, William 254
Henning, J. 248
Hewett, Sir Thomas 7, 270
Hiorne, David 72, 108, 201, 209, 256
Hiorne, Francis 123, 124, *125*, 182, 246, 247, 248
Hiorne, William 181

Hoban, James 86
Hogarth, William 10
Holl, Edward 160, 195, 212
Holland, Henry 15, 84; Albany 278; Althorp 181, *181*; Benham Park 85, 186; Berrington Hall, 85, 186; Broadlands 191; Brooks's Club 177, 281; Carlton House 15; Claremont House 85, 198; Crown Inn, Stone 246; Dover House 283; Drury Lane Theatre 170; Eastern Courtyard, Cutler Street warehouses 264; George Inn, Woburn 174; Hale House 213; Nuneham Park 232; Southill Park 243; Spencer House 280; Swan Hotel, Bedford 174, 185; Woburn Abbey 98, 256
Hollins, Humphrey 109, 110, 257
Honeywood, Frazer 253
Hooke, Robert 57, 63, 69, 238
Hope, John *168*, 169, 217, 222
Hope, Thomas 96
Hopper, Thomas: Amesbury Abbey 181; Boreham House 188; Carlton Club 281; Chelmsford Gaol 195; Conservatory, Carlton House 100; Erdigg 207; Gosford Castle 95, 294; Guildhall, Salisbury 148, 240; Leigh Court 221; Penrhyn Castle 95, 235; Terling Place 248
Horne, James 111, 212, 213
Humfrey, Charles 206
Hunter, Andrew 210
Hurst, William 202
Hutcheson, Francis 10
Hutchinson, Henry 187, 194, 197, 210, 214, 237
Hutt, John 271
Hyde, Sir Richard 222

Ingleman, Richard 222
Ingleman, Thomas 123, 257
Inwood, H. W. and W. 120, 121, 123, 261
Ireland, Joseph 123, 251, 256
Ireson, Nathaniel 12, 192, 201, 246, 250, 256
Ivory, James 101
Ivory, Thomas 128, *128*, 163, 290, 292, 294, 299
Ivory, Thomas 112, 232

Jacobsen, Theodore 160, 166, 167, 212, 290
Jaffray, George 150, 180
James, John 67, 71, 201, 251; Cannons 260; Hendon Place 260; Parkhall 266; St George's Church, Hanover Square 106, 111, 278; St John's Church Horsleydown 104; St Lawrence's Church, Little Stanmore 268; St Luke's Church, Old Street 104, 114, 269; Warbrook House 67, 251
Jameson, George 203
Jarrat, Major 150, 220
Jarrett, Joseph 144
Jelfe, Andrews 148, 186, 239
Jelly, Thomas 163, 184, 185
Jenkins, Edward 195
Jenkins, Rev William 112, 194, 195, 241
Jessop, William 200
Johnson, James 147, 277
Johnson, Joel 159, 277
Johnson, John 174, 189, 195, 221, 248, 257, 279
Johnson, Thomas 123, 157, 178, 213, 214, 221, 251, *251*, 252
Johnston, Francis, Armagh Court House 153, 284; Armagh Palace 284; Bank of Ireland, Newry 297; Chapel, Armagh Court House 284; Chapel Royal, Dublin Castle 290; Charleville Forest 81, 288; Dobbin House 284; Galtrim House 293; General Post Office, Dublin 291; Kings Inns 155, 291; Library, Armagh 284; Rokeby Hall 57, 87, 297; St Catherine's Church, Tullamore 81; St George's Church, Hardwicke Place *108*, 109, 290; St Peter's Church, Drogheda 289; Slane Castle 87, 298; Townley Hall, Drogheda 89, *89*, 92, 298
Johnston, Richard 87, *88*, 286, 290
Jones, Inigo 8, 37, 38, 51, 52, 53, 67, 69, 71, 209, 246, 254, 283; Chevening Park 196, 296; Lothbury designs 30, 31; Piazza, Covent Garden 7, *9*, 20;

318 / *Index of architects and designers*

Jones, Inigo – *cont.*
Prince's Lodging 7; Queen's House, Greenwich 7, 53, 61, 64, 76, 216, 232, 237, 265, 284, 294; St Paul's Church, Covent Garden 114, 123, 181, 229, 258
Jones, Richard 185
Jones & Clark 256
Jopling, Joseph 278
Joy, Robert 162, 285
Joynes, Henry 37, 222, 262, 276
Jupp, Richard 160, 234, 264, 272, 275, 276
Jupp, William 263, 266
Jupp, William, the Younger 272

Kames, Henry Home, Lord 10, 11
Kauffmann, Angelica 189, 258
Kay, Joseph 45, 177, 191, 214, 266
Keck, Anthony 51, 108, 159, 184, 226, 228, 257
Keene, Henry 166; Arbury Hall 77, 181–2; Bowood House 188; Guildhall, High Wycombe 14, 132, 148, 215; Hartwell House 214; Provost's House, Trinity College, Dublin *166*, 167, 290; Radcliffe Observatory 234, *234*; St Mary's Church, Lower Hartwell 124, 214; Worcester College, Oxford 233
Kempster, Christopher 147
Kendall, Henry E. 123
Kent, John 236
Kent, William 8, 14, 65, 72, 76, 194; Arlington Street 38, 278–9; Badminton House 183; Berkeley Square 38, 279; Carlton House 72; Chiswick House 268; *Designs of Inigo Jones* 13, *145*; Ditchley House 65, 202; Esher Place 207; garden buildings 76, 97; Hampton Court Palace 273; Holkham Hall 68–9, *68*, *69*, 98, 216; Horse Guards 145, *145*, 146, 283; Houghton Hall 63, *65*; Kensington Palace 270; Odsey House 233; Rousham House 97, 101, 239; Savile Row 280; Shotover Park 242; Stowe 97, 99, 246–7; Treasury 145, *145*, 146, 283; Wakefield Lodge 67, 237; Wimborne House 278–9; Worcester Lodge, Badminton House 98, 183
King, Thomas 218
Kirby, John Joshua 273
Klenze, Leo von 169
Knight, Richard Payne 16, 78–9, 80, 203
Knight, William 164, 256

Laidlaw, John 118, 217
Laing, David 19, 236, 263
Lane, John 144, 283
Lane, Richard 240
Langley, Batty 14, 43, 77, 78, 124, 249, 287
Lapidge, Edward 267, 273
Latrobe, Benjamin 91, 159, 182, 208, 214
Laugier, Abbé 16, 17, 101
Le Roy, J. D. 15
Leadbetter, Stiff 160, 206, 211, 220, 232, 234, 241
Ledoux, C.-N. 100, 157, 158, 193
Lee, Thomas 92, 123, 182, 184, 257
Legg, William 133, 244
Leigh, Charles 180
Leoni, Giacomo 10, 52, 66–7, 76, 276; Alkrington Hall 181; Argyll House 38, 270; Burlington Gardens 279; Clandon Park 60, 66–7, 197; Cliveden 198; Lyme Park 67, 224; Queensberry House 8, 37
Leroux, Jacob 208, 269
Leverton, Thomas 22, 51, 85, 189, 241, 257, 260, 261, 262
Lewis, James 264, 275
Lewis, Thomas 22
Lightfoot, Luke 64, 198
Lightoler, Timothy 78, 112, 150, 184, 192, 228, 247
Lilly, Charles 289, 297
Lombe, Thomas and John 134, 135
Loudon, J. C. 280
Louis, Victor 130, 171
Lucas, Thomas 30
Lugar, Robert 90, 204
Lumby, William 159, 222

McCullagh, James 40, 292
MacGill, Alexander 258
Mack, Robert 40, 292
Mackenzie, Sir G. S. 100
Madden, Dominick 94, 284, 298
Maddocks, William 249
Maddox, George V. 229
Maderno 105
Mainwaring, Boulton 159, 277
Marquand, John 237, 283
Marshall, William 188
Martin, James 288
Masters, Charles Harcourt 185
May, Hugh 53
Mead, J. C. 194
Meade, William 299
Mézières, Lecamus de 131
Michelangelo 233
Middleton, William 187
Miller, Sanderson 14, 70, 77, 124; Adlestrop Park 180; All Saints Church, Wroxton 124, 258; Arbury Hall 77, 181; Croome Court 70, 200–201; Durham Castle 204; Ecton Hall 77, 205; Edgehill 14, 97, 205; Hagley Hall 14, 70, 97, 213; Hillsborough Church 125, 294; Lacock Abbey 77, 219; Radway Grange 77, 238; Shire Hall, Warwick, 14, 150, 153, *251*, 251–2; Wimpole Hall 97, 255
Mills, Alexander 238
Mills, Peter 37, 51
Milne, James 34, 206
Molesworth, John 7, 56
Monck, Sir Charles 92, 94, 103, 186
Moneypenny, George 158, 204, 219, 255
Morgan, James 256
Morison, David 235
Morris, Robert 8, 10, 11–12, 64, 71–2, 113, 201
Morris, Roger 9, 114; Althorp 64, 181; Castle Hill 194; Chichester Council House 114, 149, 196; Clearwell Castle 78, 198; Column of Victory, Blenheim 188; Combe Bank 38, 61, 69, 71, 198; Fox Hall 65, 204; Green Street 31, 38, *49*, 279; Inveraray Castle 70, 78, 217; Lydiart Tregoze 70, 224; Marble Hill House 63, 70, 218, 274; Palladian Bridge, Wilton House, 98, 254; St Lawrence's Church, Mereworth 114, *114*, 227; Trafalgar House 64, 249
Morrison, John 162, 163, 296
Morrison, Sir Richard: Ballyfin 94, 284; Ballyheigue Castle 81, 284; Borris House 285; Carton 286; Castlegar 81, 286; Castle Howard 81, 286; Clandeboye 288; Court House, Port Laoise 153, 297; Fota Island 293; Mount Henry 296; Shelton Abbey 79, 298
Morrison, William Vitruvius: Ballyfin 94, 284; Ballyheigue Castle 81, 284; Baronscourt 89, 285; Borris House 285; Carlow Court House 153, 286; Mount Stewart 296; Tralee Court House 298
Mountain, Charles 250, 257
Mountain, Charles, the Younger 218
Moyle, John 237
Moyser, Colonel 232
Moyser, James 187, 189
Mulholland, Roger 285
Murray, William 291
Myers, Graham 291
Mylne, Robert 15, 84–5, 131; Addington Palace 264; Amwell Grove 212; Canongate 205; Custom House and Inn, Tobermory 249; Inveraray 28, 217; King's Weston 219; Norwich Union Fire Office 232; Stationers' Hall 133, 263; Tern Bridge 183; Wandle House 272; Wick, The 274; Woodhouse 84–5, 257; Wormleybury House 258

Nash, John 120; All Souls' Church, Langham Place 120, 281; Almshouses, Blaise Hamlet 103, 162, 187; Aroid House, Royal Botanic Gardens 273; Bloomsbury Square 261; Buckingham Palace 280; Caerhayes Castle 81, 193; Caledon 87, 286; Carlton House Terrace 280; Clarence House 280; Clytha Castle, Gwent 81, 198; Corsham Court 199; County Gaol, Hereford 215; Cronkhill 16, 90, *90*, 200, 257; Cumberland Terrace 30, 33–4, 262; Foley House 215; Great Russell Street 261; Guildhall, Newport 148, 230; Haymarket Theatre 172; Kentchurch Court 218; Lough Cutra 295; Longner Hall 81, 224; Luscombe Castle 81, 224; Market House, Chichester 196; Nolton House 194; Pantheon Dining Room, Downton Castle 203; Picture Gallery, Attingham Hall 169, 183; Regent Street development 20, 34, 45, 129, 172; Regent's Park 262–3, 276, 282; Rockingham 100; Rotunda, Green Hill 266; Royal Opera Arcade 130; Royal Pavilion 90, 190; St Mary's Church, Cowes 120, 199; Sandridge Park 90, 240; Six Bells Inn, Carmarthen 194; Suffolk Place, Street 281; 'Swiss Cottage' 96, 97, 285; United Services Club 177, 280; York Terrace 30, 282
Nasmith, Alexander 239
Nasmith, Robert 245
Neave, David 203, 204
Newcombe, William 177
Newman, Robert 247
Newton, William 230, 272
Nicholson, Peter 28, 30, 182, 211
Nisbet, James 118, 217, 250, 252
Novosielski, Michael 243

Oliver, Thomas 34, 230
Outram, Benjamin 200
Owen, Robert 230

Page, D. F. 253
Page, Joseph 38, 133, 218, 219
Page, S. F. 253
Pain, George Richard 16, 158, 159, 288, 290, 297
Pain, James 16, 158, 159, 288, 290, 297
Paine, James 15, 43, 73–4, 81, 278; Bridge, Wallington 140, 250, Brocket Hall 74, 191; Bywell Hall 74, 86, 193; Chapel, Gibside 116, 210; Dover House 283; garden buildings, Hardwick Hall 214; Hare Hall 268; Heath House 215; Home Farm, Weston Park 101, 253; Kedleston Hall 74, 82, 217; Lodge, Forcett Park 209; Mansion House, Doncaster 152, 202; Nostell Priory 70, 232; Ormsby Hall 74, 233; Parish Workhouse, Manette Street 282; Park Farm 238; Richmond Bridge 274; St Ives 70, 236; Sandbeck Park 74, *74*, 240; Stockeld Park 74, 245; Thorndon Hall 248; villa design 43, 72, 73–4; Wadsworth Hall 73–4, 250; Wardour Castle 74, *75*, 85, 251; Weston Park 253
Paine, Tom 142
Palladio, Andrea 6, 7, 8, 10, *11*, 15, 39, 51, 53, 54, 69, 144, 184, 246, 254, 290; Basilica, Vicenza 131; Egyptian hall 107, 114, 151, 174, 227, 258, 297; farms 100; Il Redentore Church 287; Palazzo Iseppo Porto 8, *9*; Piazza d'Armée 20; *Quattro Libri* 8, 37, 66, *141*; Rialto Bridge 141; Villa Emo 73; Villa Mocenigo 82, 217, 232; Villa Pisani 59; Villa Pogliana 53, 54; Villa Rotonda 55, 97, 229, 268; Villa Trissino 216
Palmer, John 33, 177, 184, 185, 187
Papworth, J. B. 33, 96, 100, 176, 181, 195, 200, 240, 271
Park, Edward 153, 291, 293
Parker, Charles 129, 264, 275
Parker, William 215
Parkinson, Joseph 281
Parson, N. 158
Parsons, William 221
Paterson, John 119, 235
Patience, John Thomas 232
Paty, James 180, 191
Paty, Thomas 191
Paty, William 109, 187, 190, 191
Paull, William 210
Payne, Rev John 13
Peacock, James 19, 131
Pearce, Edward Lovett 12, 57–9, 66, 67, 144; Bellamont Forest *58*, 59, 62, 75, 285, 297, 298; Cashel Palace 57, 286; Castletown *56*, 57, 286; Dartrey 289; Drumcondra House 290; Dundrum 293; Gloster 294; Henrietta Street *39*, 39–40, 285, 292; King's House 285; Newry Canal 297; North Audley Street 38, 280, *280*; Parliament House, Dublin 128, *143* 144, 290; Printing House, Trinity College, Dublin 167, 290;

Index of architects and designers / 319

Seafield 59, 298; Southwell School and Almshouses 162, 289; Stillorgan House 298; Summerhill 38, 61; Woodlands 59, 299
Pembroke, Henry Herbert 9th Earl 63, 98, 194, 254, 274
Penson, Thomas 159
Pentland, George 61, 293
Pentland, John 163, 296
Phillips, Ambrose 99, 210
Phillips, John 77, 181
Pickernell, Jonathan 253
Pickford, Joseph 37, 182, 202, 232
Pilkington, William 148, 160, 212, 240
Pinch, John 185
Piranesi, Giambattista 74, 119, 157, 212
Pitt, John 67, 207
Pitt, Stephen 200
Pitt, Thomas 98, 213, 247, 275
Platt, John 106, 162, 239
Plaw, John 84, 101, 119, 185, 268
Playfair, James 79, 92, 101, 193, 209, 229
Playfair, W. H: Circus Gardens 30; Circus Place 30; Dollar Academy 163, 202; Dugald Stewart Monument 100, 205; Edinburgh University 166, 205; Hillside Crescent 206; Observatory, Calton Hill 205; Royal Circus 30, 206; Royal Institution, Edinburgh 155, 155; Royal Terrace 206; St Stephen's Church, Vincent Street 119
Poole, Henry 234
Pope, Alexander 16, 97, 197
Porden, Charles 120, 271
Portwood, George 244
Potter, Joseph 221, 236
Poynter, Ambrose 262
Pratt, Sir Roger 53, 57, 70–71, 160, 299
Price, John 32, 54, 111, 184, 212, 275
Price, William 211
Price, Sir Uvedale 16
Priestley, Michael 284, 295, 297
Prince, John 21, 199
Pritchard, T. F. 52, 70, 141, 162, 191, 200, 215, 217, 224, 242, 243
Pritchett, J. P. 258
Probert, Benjamin 191
Prowse, Thomas 70, 125, 186, 199, 213, 218, 254
Pugin, A. W. N. 16, 122
Purves, Robert 118, 217
Pycock, George 218

Raffield, J. 282
Rawlinson, Charles 236
Rawsthorne, John 160, 241
Read, Thomas 203
Rebecca, Biagio 90, 194, 200, 228, 258
Reid, Robert 26, 119, 154, 159, 205, 206, 235
Rennie, George 196
Rennie, Sir John 216, 220, 226, 236
Repton, G. S. 97, 219, 240
Repton, Humphry 17, 72, 81, 261
Repton, J. A. 16, 92, 96, 188, 199, 215, 220
Revett, Nicholas 15, 81, 84, 100, 176–7, 253, 288; *Antiquities of Athens* 14, 15, 100; church design 115–16; New St Lawrence's Church, Ayot St Lawrence 116, 183, *183*; Trafalgar House 84, 249; West Wycombe Park 84, *84*, 253
Reynolds, Esau 249
Rhodes, Henry 122, 206
Richardson, George 123, 240, 244, 248
Ricketts, John 211
Rickman, Thomas 122, 123, 194, 211, 223, 237
Rickman & Hutchinson 187, 194, 197, 210, 214, 237
Riou, Stephen 15
Ripley, Thomas 65–6, 71, 82, 143–4, 162, 214, 256, 265, 279, 283
Ritson, Jonathan 236
Roberts, Henry 134, 263
Roberts, John 109, 111, 289, 298, 299
Robertson, Daniel 123, 166, 218, 233, 234
Robertson, William 294
Robinson, P. F. 45, 220, 249
Robinson, Sir Thomas 64, 69, 111, 187, 198, 211, 239
Robinson, William 143, 146, 246
Rogers, Thomas 152, 269
Roper, D. R. 267, 271, 275
Rose, Henry 275

Ross, Charles 252
Rothery, John 57, 296
Rothery family 289
Rouchead, Alexander 161, 236

Salmon, Robert 101, 205, 256
Salvin, Anthony 225, 227
Sambell, Philip 249
Sampson, George 128
Sanders, John 156, 240, 270
Sanderson, James 239
Sanderson, John 66; Copt Hall 199; Kimberley Hall 218; Kirtlington Park 70, 219, *219*; Pusey House 237; Radcliffe Infirmary 160, 234; St John's Parish Church, Hampstead 262; Trinity College, Dublin 166, 290
Sands, Francis 285
Sands, William, the Elder 244
Sands, William, the Younger 244
Sandys, Francis 19, 90, 193, 217
Saunders, George 17
Savage, James 17, 122, 264, 267, 270, 272
Scamozzi, Vincenzo 69, 100
Schinkel, Karl Friedrich 169, 177, 225
Scoles, J. J. 254
Scott, William 22, 23, 261
Searles, Michael 33, 198, 271, 266, 276
Semple, George 17, 160, 291, 294
Semple, John 122, 290, 296
Serlio, Sebastiano 36, 53, 69, 216
Shanahan, Michael 99, 285, 289
Sharp, R. H. 169, 218, 241
Sharp, Samuel 250
Shaw, John 188, 238
Shaw, John, the Elder 263
Shepherd, Edward 21, 31, 38, 40, 279, 280
Sibbald, William 205, 206
Sim, James 261
Sim, Robert 261
Simmons, John 21, 30
Simons, Samuel 201
Simpson, Archibald 120, 177, 180, 206
Simpson, James 221
Singleton, Luke 159, 211
Skinner, Colonel 156, 209
Sloane, Charles 212
Smeaton, John 230
Smirke, Sir Robert 92–3, 95, 120, 151, 153; Assize Courts, Carlisle 150, *150*, 194; Assize Courts, Lincoln 222; British Museum 167, 169, 261; Council House, Bristol 151; County Buildings, Perth 151, 235; Covent Garden Theatre 171; Eastnor Castle 95, 205; Kinfauns Castle 81, 218; King's Bench Walk 263; Kinmount 93, 219; Normanby Park 93, 231; Royal College of Physicians 155, 281; Royal Mint 147, 277; Royal Salop Infirmary 161, 242; St Anne's Church, Wandsworth 278; St George's Church Bristol 191; St Mary's Church, Wyndham Place 281; St Philip's Church, Salford 240; Sessions House, Maidstone 225; Shire Hall, Gloucester 151, 211; Shire Hall, Hereford 151, 215; Union Club, London 177, 280; Whittinghame House 254
Smirke, Sydney 275
Smith, Charles 220
Smith, Francis 12; Abbotsford House 36, 252; Buntingdale 54, 192; Chicheley Hall 199; Court House, Warwick 152, 252; Davenport House 201; Ditchley House 202; Hardwick 214; Kirby House 199; Mawley Hall 64, 228, *229*; Old Grammar School, Wolverhampton 256; Shardeloes 241; Stoneleigh Abbey 54, 66, 246; Sutton Scarsdale 54, 247; Swynnerton Hall 247; Wesleyan Chapel, Burford 192
Smith, George 123, 177, 204, 224, 272
Smith, George 141, 294
Smith, James 55, 205, 258
Smith, John 120, 180
Smith, Marmaduke 36, 277
Smith, William 192
Smith, William 170, 195, 219, 248
Smith, William 120, 227
Smyth, Grice 284
Smyth, John 115, 167, 290
Soane, Sir John 15, 22, 29–30, 32, 33, 85–6, 91, 101, 120–2, 206; Bank of England 15, *127*, 128, 147, 263; 'Barn à la Paestum' 243; Baronscourt 89, 285;

Bentley Priory 85–6, 86, 268; Blundeston House 188; Butterton Grange 91, 193; cowshed, Burn Hall 192; Charles II Street 281; Chillington Hall 85, 197; Dairy, Hamels Park 15, 96, 101; Downing Street 283; Dulwich College Picture Gallery 167, 275; Earsham Hall, Norfolk 204; Guildhall Street 193; Holy Trinity Church, Marylebone 120, 281; Law Court, Palace of Westminster 16, 154; Letton Hall 221; Lincoln's Inn Fields 44, 44–5, 262; Macartney House 266; Malvern Hall 243; Mogerhanger Park 228; Norwich Union Fire Office 232; Park Farm 101, 255; Pell Wall House 235; Piercefield Park 236; Pitzhanger Manor 90, 264; Port Eliot 237; Ringwould House 238; St John's Church, Bethnal Green 120, 121, 276; St Peter's Church, Walworth 120, 275; Saxlingham Rectory 15, 87, 240; Shotesham Park 15, 85, 236, 242, *242*; Stables, Royal Hospital, Chelsea 270; Sydney Lodge 247; Tyringham House 15, 100, 250; Wimpole Hall 255; Wiston Hall 256
Soufflot, Germain 147
Spiller, James 122, 267, 269
Spray, Matthew 266
Squire, Richard 109, 257
Stapleton, Michael 40, 86, *86*, 284, 291, 292, 295, 296
Stark, William 151, 153, 159, 210
Stephenson, David 118, 133, 174, 230, 232
Steuart, George: All Saints' Church, Wellington 252; Attingham Hall 85, 183; Baronscourt 89, 285; Blairuachder 101, 187; Court House, Ramsey 238; Manor House 198; St Chad's Church, Shrewsbury 118, *118*, 242
Stevens, Alexander 190, 220 227
Stirling, William 101, 177, 203, 244
Stokoe, John 151, 230
Stone, Francis 232
Stone, Nicholas 37, 51
Strahan, John 70, 184, 191, 198, 209
Stratford, Ferdinando 132, 297
Stretton, S. and W. 150
Strutt, Jedediah 139, 186
Strutt, William 135–6
Stuart, James 99–100, 110, 115–16, 288; All Saints' Church, Nuneham Courtenay 116, *116*, 232; *Antiquities of Athens* 14, 15; garden buildings 99–100, 243; Lanthorn of Demosthenes, Shugborough 100, 243; Lichfield House, 15 St James's Square, 43, 281; Shugborough 99–100, 243; South Pavilion, Greenwich Palace 265; Spencer House 280; Temple of Theseus, Hagley 99, 213; Temple of the Winds, Mount Stewart 296
Sweetman, John 123, 290
Sykes, Sir Christopher 243

Talman, William 54, 60, 69, 71, 218
Tasker, John 205
Tatham, C. H. 169, 195
Tattershall, Robert 161, 194
Taylor, J. H. 267
Taylor, Sir Robert 28–9, 43, 44, 72, 148; Arnos Grove 265; Assembly Room, Belfast 285; Asgill House 73, 274; Bank of England 128, 263; Barlaston Hall 73, 184; Bridge, Maidenhead 227; Chute Lodge 73, 197; Danson Park 73, 260; Ely House 34, 279; Gorhambury 212; Grafton Street 43, 44, 279; Guildhall, Salisbury 148, 240; Harleyford Manor 72, *72*, 214; Heveningham Hall 8, 85, 215; Holywell Hill 37, 239; Osney Bridge 234; Purbrook 73; Reduced Annuity Office, Bank of England 148; St Peter's Church, Wallington 250; Sharpham 73, 241; Six Clerks' and Enrolment Office, Lincoln's Inn 154, *154*, 262; Spencer House 280; Stone Buildings, Lincoln's Inn, 154, 262; Swinford Bridge 208; Terrace, The Richmond Hill, 43, 274; Upper Brook Street 45, *47*, 279
Taylor, Thomas 238
Telford, Thomas: Bridge, Bewdley 187; bridge design 142; Conway Suspension

Index of architects and designers

Telford, Thomas – *cont.*
Bridge 142, 199; County Gaol, Shrewsbury 159, 242; Gloucester Dock 211; Menai Suspension Bridge 142, 227; Pontcysyllte Aqueduct 236; St Ann's Dockyard Church, Portsmouth 237; St Mary Magdalene's Church, Bridgenorth 190; St Michael's Church, Madeley 119, 225; Tern Aqueduct 224; Waterloo Bridge, Betws-y-Coed 142, 186
Thomas, William 200, 227
Thomon, Thomas de 131
Thomson, James 30, 33, 262
Thornhill, Sir James 227, 255, ?5
Thornton, William 186, 194
Thorpe, John 53
Timbrell, Benjamin 111, 278
Tite, Sir William 122, 166, 163, 260
Townesend, William 164, 233, 238, 242
Townsend, Sir Roger 53
Traill, Sir John 157, 291
Trubshaw, Richard 236
Tuck, William 157, 218
Turner, J. M. W. 275
Turner, John 160
Tusher, John 117

Underwood, G. A. 176, 19

Vanbrugh, Sir John 12, 21, 67, 74; Belvedere 97, 198; Blenheim 12, 53, 54, 61, 64, 71, 156, 188, 257; Board of Works 155–6; 'castle air' 12, 76, 155, 195, 198, 207, 248; Castle Howard 61, 71, 195, 198, 207, Eastbury 155, 204; Grimsthorpe Castle 212; Hampton Court 196; influence 57, 78, 158, *186*, 187, 222, 237, 243, 248, 257, 294, 298; King's Weston 184, 219; Lumley Castle 224; military buildings 155–6; Newcastle Pew, St George's Church, Esher 207; Nunnery, Greenwich 243; Office of Works Style 195, 217, 236, 255, 257, 276; Old Board of Ordnance 61, 71; Royal Brass Foundry 266; Seaton Delaval Hall 241; Stowe 246, 247; Town Hall, Morpeth 148, 227; Vanbrugh Castle 16, 76, 266
Vardy, John 51, 66, 82, 145, 280, 283
Vardy, John, the Younger 279
Vesey, Agmondisham 86, 87, 295
Vignola, Giacomo da 290
Villain, Philippe 158
Vitruvius 15, 68, 107, 151, 258
Vulliamy, Lewis 89, 155, 249, 272, 293

Wade, General George 180
Wakefield, William 66, 162, 210, 222
Wallace, Robert 264
Ware, Isaac 8, 23, 38, 66, 72, 100–1, 181, 191, 209, 258, 279
Ware, Samuel 130, 279
Watson, Charles 152–3, 187, 250
Webb, John 7, 52; Amesbury Abbey 53, 181; Badminton House 183; farmstead design 100, 101; Greenwich Palace 265; Queen's Gallery, Somerset House 8, *9*, 37, 258; Vyne, The 250; Wilton House 53
Webb, Thomas 207
Webster, George 96, 207, 218, 250
Welch *see* Hansom & Welch
West, Robert 40, 286, 289, 292, 296
Westbrooke, Samuel 180
Wheler, G. H. 233

Whichcord, John, Senior 129, 225
White, Edward 226
White, John 193
White, Thomas 110, 194, 257
Wickings, William 269
Wilds, A. H. 190, 212
Wilds, Amon 190, 221, 258
Wiles, E. 220
Wilkins, William, the Elder 81, 203, 258
Wilkins, William, the Younger 90, 91, 95–6; college design 166; County Gaol, Huntingdon 217; Corpus Christi College, Cambridge 166, 194; Dalmeny House 90, 187, 201; Downing College, Cambridge 166, 193; Grange, The *91*, 91–2, 212; Haileybury College 166, 213; King's College, Cambridge 166, 193; Osberton House 92, 233; St George's Hospital 161, 278; Theatre Royal, Bury St Edmunds 170, *171*, 193; Tregothnan 95–6, 249; Trinity College, Cambridge 166, 194; Yorkshire Museum 169, 258
Wills, Isaac 105
Wilson, John 114, 164, 240, 243
Wilson, Thomas 247
Winde, William 51, 76
Wing, Edward 104, 105, 111, 183, 210
Wing, John, the Elder 123, 210
Wing, John, the Younger 125, 218
Wood, John, the Elder 27, 32; Belcombe Court 189; Bristol 32, 184–5; Exchange, Bristol 130, 191; Exchange, Liverpool 130, 222; Frenchay Manor 209; Gay Street, Bath 43, 184; General Infirmary, Bath 160, 161, 184; Grand Parade, Bath 31, 184; Prior Park 70, 98, 185; Queen Square, Bath 27, 30, *32*, 35, 165, 184; Royal Crescent, Bath 20, 184
Wood, John, the Younger 32; All Saints', Woolley 125, 257; Buckland House 69, 192; Circus, Bath 32, 184; New Assembly Rooms, Bath 184; Royal Crescent, Bath 20, 27, *27*, 32, 184–5; St Nicholas' Church, Hardenhuish 115, 214; Salisbury General Infirmary 159, 240; Trafalgar House 249
Wood, Robert 15, 81, 256
Wood, Thomas 169
Woodgate, Robert 285, 288, 291
Woods, Joseph 267
Woodward, Edward and Thomas 123, 124, 180, 187, 197, 211, 237, 257
Worrall James 186
Worrall, Samuel 186, 276, 277
Worsley, Sir Thomas 51, 216
Wren, Sir Christopher 6, 10, 31, 55, 104, 109, 144, 196, 282; Ampthill Park 181; Christ Church, Newgate Street 110–11; Old Court House, Hampton Court 273; plans for City of London 20; Queen Mary Block, Greenwich Palace 265; Royal Hospital, London 143, 270; St Ann and St Agnes's Church, City of London 162, 219, 237; St Bride's Church, Fleet Street 111; St Dunstan-in-the-East Church, City of London 126, 208; St James's Church, Piccadilly 20, 106, 111, 246; St Michael's Church, Cornhill 263; St Stephen's Walbrook Church, City of London 183; Surveyor of Royal Works 155
Wright, Nathaniel 263
Wright, Stephen 38, 167, 194, 198, 279
Wright, Thomas 78, 99, 101, 183, 216, 274

Wyatt, Benjamin 66, 160, 221, 244, 247
Wyatt, Benjamin Dean 170, 172, 186, 278, 280
Wyatt, James 34, 71, 84, 85; Abbey Leix 284; Ashman's Hall 182; Ashridge Park 182; Assembly Rooms, Chichester 177, 196; Aston Hall 183; Badger Hall 100, 183; Belvoir Castle 91, 186; Bishop's Palace, Bishop Auckland 187, 201; Bowden House 85, 87, 188; Curraghmore 289; Castle Coole *165*, 87, *88*, 286; Chicksands Priory 197; Conduit Street 43–4, 279; Dodington Park 91, 100, 202; Eglwys Newydd, Hafod 213; Erddig 207; Frogmore House 255; Goodwood House 211; Grove House 277; Gunton Park 213; Heaton Park, 69, 84, 226; Heveningham Hall 85, 215; Lasborough Park 220; Leinster House 291; Library, Shardeloes 241; Lucan House *86*, 86–7 295; Mausoleum, Brocklesby 192; Milton Abbey 226; Mount Kennedy 87, 296; Norris Castle 81, 95, 231; organ case, St Modwen's Church, Burton-upon-Trent 193; Pennsylvania Castle 235; Pigeon House, Badger Hall 100, 183; Plas Newydd 236; Powderham Castle 237; Radcliffe Observatory 234, *234*; Ragley Hall 238; Royal Military Academy 266; Sheffield Park 78, 241; Slane Castle 79, 87, 220, 298; Strawberry Hill 275; Tower, Broadway 191; Town Hall, Ripon 148–9, 238; West Dean Park 253; Westport 299; White's Club 177, 281; Worcester College, Oxford 233; Wycombe Abbey 258
Wyatt, L. W: Cuerden Hall 16, 201; Hackwood Park 90–1, 213; Lyme Park 91, 94, 224; Mount Shannon 94, 296; Tatton Park 94, 248; Willey Hall 93–4, 254
Wyatt, Matthew Cotes 186
Wyatt, Philip 278
Wyatt, Samuel 84, 243; Admiralty House, Portsmouth 237; Albion Mill 135; Belmont Park 186; Coton House 199; Doddington Hall 85, 202; Great Barn, Holkham Hall 101, 216; Hackwood Park 90–1, 213; Rectory, Kedleston 217; St James's Square 281; Shugborough 243; Stornoway House 280; Sundridge Park 261; Tatton Park 94, 248; Trinity House 133, 263
Wyatt, Thomas 234
Wyatt, William 244
Wyatville, Sir Jeffry: Abingdon Gaol 159, 180; Ashridge Park 182; Bretton Hall 189; Brook Street 279; Claverton Manor 198; cottage orné, Endsleigh 207 Golden Grove 211; Hilfield 189; Lilleshall Hall 96, 211, 222; Longleat 78, 224; Lypiatt Park 225; Nonsuch Park 81, 95, 231; Phillips House 236; St Anne's Church, Kew Green 273; Temple of Augustus, Virginia Water 250; Windsor Castle 255; Wollaton Hall 256
Wynde, William 287
Wynn, Sir Rowland 174
Wynne, William 181

Yenn, John 235, 265

Zucchi, Antonio 199

5 10 20

Section from South to